RUSSIAN AND EAST EUROPEAN STUDIES

Charles Jelavich, *Tsarist Russia and Balkan Nationalism. Russian Influence in the Internal Affairs of Bulgaria and Serbia, 1879–1886*

RUSSIAN FAR EASTERN POLICY
1881-1904

RUSSIAN AND EAST EUROPEAN STUDIES

Russian Far Eastern Policy
1881-1904

WITH SPECIAL EMPHASIS ON THE CAUSES OF THE RUSSO-JAPANESE WAR

Andrew Malozemoff

UNIVERSITY OF CALIFORNIA PRESS

BERKELEY AND LOS ANGELES · 1958

University of California Press
Berkeley and Los Angeles
California

Cambridge University Press
London, England

FOREWORD

By THE MIDDLE of the 1930's the history seminar conducted on the Berkeley campus by the late Professor Robert J. Kerner had attracted a sizable group of dedicated young scholars bent on launching upon their own voyages of discovery into what was a *terra incognita* in our American historiography. Here the early ties between Russia and her "colonies" in Alaska and California were studied, the background for the diplomatic relations between Russia and China during the seventeenth century were explored, the fundamentals of Russian expansion into the Pacific area were examined, and various aspects of the history of the Slavic world were assessed.

One of the outstanding members of this seminar was Andrew Malozemoff, whose all-consuming passion was the history of Siberia and Russian policy in the Far East, a subject that he virtually ate, dreamed, and breathed. The present monograph is the result of his investigations. In his book, Andrew Malozemoff coolly and objectively analyzes the events that culminated in the conflict; he reassesses and reëvaluates the data and in so doing brings the events into sharp focus and into a new light.

Unfortunately, Andrew Malozemoff did not live to receive the recognition to which his book will entitle him. After his death in 1952, his mother, Dr. Elizabeth Malozemoff, took upon herself the task of seeing that his manuscript was published. The resultant monograph is now not only a befitting memorial to her son's scholarship as a historian, it is also a tribute to Robert J. Kerner as a teacher. I feel sure my colleagues throughout the United States will join me in welcoming the present volume.

OLEG A. MASLENIKOV

Berkeley, California
April 1, 1958

CONTENTS

Contents

I

THE RUSSIAN POSITION IN THE FAR EAST, 1860–1890

THE PROGRESS of Russian expansion to the Far East was very rapid. In about seventy years (1582–1648) the Russians advanced as far as some of the present northern, eastern, and southern boundaries of Russia.[1]

Plans for this movement to the east had been worked out by the Russian administration over a long period. It was well understood that river routes were best in the wilderness, and that these routes should be connected by portages guarded by *ostrogs*, or stockades. Furthermore, the value of the government fur trade, the development of which was the motivation behind the eastward expansion, was clearly realized. To coördinate the activities of the fur traders, the officials in the outposts, and the many private enterprises and to derive the greatest profit from them, the government set up an intricate and rather efficient administration. This administration had its roots in Moscow and branches reaching to the remotest points of the Russian possessions.

FAILURE OF THE ORIGINAL SETTLEMENT

In spite of the courage of individual Russians, and in spite of many government expeditions and a complex administration, the colonization of the region went on very slowly. Even in the period 1860–1890 the severe climate, the sparse population, transportation difficulties, lack of food bases, and the inadequacy of defense led many people to regard the vast land as economically insignificant. Its acquisition caused some disappointment and even severe criticism.[2]

The sparseness of population was both a result and a cause of the lack of efficient transportation, especially along the Amur River, which was to serve as the line of communication for the new territories. In the original settlement of 1857, Count Nikolai Nikolaevich Muraviev-Amurskii, Governor General of Eastern Siberia, ordered a specially conscripted regiment of transbaikal (east of Lake Baikal) cossacks to settle, with their wives and children, along the Amur River in villages twelve to eighteen miles from each other. From this chain of posts the cossacks were to guard the frontier, perform postal service duties, and expedite the shipment of supplies down the Amur to the main Russian

---

[1] For notes to chap. i see pp. 253–258.

post at Nikolaevsk near the mouth of the river.[3] The Ussuri region was settled in a similar manner. In 1859, recently conscripted peasants from the transbaikal region, the "infantry cossacks," were ordered to the Ussuri valley and moved there by slow stages. Their migration with families and cattle took more than a year and a half.[4]

Moreover, the original pioneers were soon reinforced by new groups of "cossacks," with the result that by 1861 the Amur line of communication had sixty villages, with a population of 11,850.[5] Even so, the settlers were too few for efficient colonization. The left bank of the Amur had been previously uninhabited except for the region around its confluence with the Zeya, where there were a few Chinese and Manchu villages.[6] The new settlers had to clear fields and trails and perform other exacting duties. Most of the men were required for postal and transport work, leaving less than half of them free to engage in agriculture. Thus, when the conscripted settlers were granted permission to return to the transbaikal region if they wished to do so, they were very joyful. Many risked the dangers of the long journey and the prospect of returning penniless to their original homes.[7]

The population was too sparse to warrant establishment of regular means of land transportation; for more than twenty years transportation by land was insignificant.[8] Along the main line of communication, the Amur River, the natural difficulties were then almost insurmountable at certain times of the year. In the middle of its course at Blagoveschensk, the Amur freezes by the end of October, and the ice breaks about the twentieth of April. Hence, in a normal year, the river is covered with ice for 173 days and is free for 192. For 17 to 27 days before it freezes over, the river is filled with ice floes, and for an equal period it is dangerous during the thaw.[9] Navigation was limited to an average of 140 days for such frail barges and river steamers as could operate in the shallow waters of the Amur above Blagoveschensk. Because there were few draft animals in the new settlement, the ice-covered Amur was used but rarely as a winter highway, although the light snowfall facilitated its use in this historic Russian manner.[10]

During the periods of the freeze-up and thaw, communications were usually discontinued entirely. As late as 1882 only telegraphic communications were maintained at these times along the vital lifeline to Russia.[11] Other impediments to transportation were the natural hazards of large rivers, such as shoals, snags, shifting and blind channels, and bars. Under these conditions transportation facilities on the Amur were slow to develop, and although the river offered a fairly safe and rapid descent, its ascent was a tedious, dangerous, and lengthy undertaking.[12] Until there was a much greater influx of population and an accompanying increase of transportation facilities, the Amur served less as a line of communication than as a line of limitation for Russian expansion.

In the early period of colonization, unforeseen difficulties prevented the realization of Muraviev-Amurskii's hope of making the Amur valley serve as a food base for Russian Far Eastern possessions.[13] His expectations were based upon accounts of the abundant rainfall and luxuriant vegetation along the Amur. The colonists soon found, however, that the heavy rainfall, especially in the summer months, was unfavorable to agriculture.[14] Cereals had a tendency to run to straw, yielding a poor grain, and sometimes the grain did not ripen completely. Along the coast of the Sea of Japan the fogs and the dampness of the soil during the short period of vegetation forced the settlers to abandon their fields.[15]

Vegetables and grains grew in abundance but "underwent some changes."[16] Bread made out of local grains had an unpleasant taste and when eaten produced a state of dizziness, or "intoxication," which gave rise to the name "intoxicating bread."[17] It was only after years of experiments and the research of the botanical expedition of 1889 that the phenomenon was explained by the discovery of a microscopic parasitical growth on the grain. Measures were then taken to eliminate it.[18]

The short time available for farming, the unfavorable climate, and the grain diseases brought misery to the settlers. Instead of supplying the Russian Far East with grain, the Amur valley actually had to import grain in large quantity from Europe and America via Nikolaevsk or Vladivostok, and from the transbaikal region.[19] In spite of the abundance of pastures, the cattle industry suffered from the same climatic disadvantages and showed little promise.[20] Until the end of the nineteenth century, beef cattle were imported into the Amur region from Korea, Manchuria, Mongolia, and the transbaikal region, for settlers as well as for Russian troops.[21]

When, after more than thirty years of Russian occupation, no remedies for the failure of agriculture in the Amur region had been found, the policy of attempting to establish a food base there was severely criticized by semiofficial organs. The findings of the expeditions sent by the Eastern Branch of the Imperial Geographical Society, edited by Professor S. I. Korzhinskii in 1892, condemned the Amur region as totally worthless for the settlement of surplus populations of Russia. The editor stated that "it is necessary to work out an entirely different system of economy and to cultivate other plants, more suitable to local climatic conditions."[22] In this he recommended a virtual abandonment of the idea of making a food base of the valley.

The failure of the Amur valley as a food base greatly lessened the strategical value of the river as a line of communication. The sale of Alaska and the rapid decrease of the fur trade on the coast of the Sea of Okhotsk[23] diminished the economic importance of the Primorsk (coastal) region for Russia, and military posts were abandoned on the coast and in Kamchatka.[24] The new line of communication did not supersede the overland mail route from Yakutsk to Okhotsk and Kamchatka, nor did it remove the main dependence of Kamchatka on supplies brought from Canada and California.[25] The inability of the new food base to achieve new economic foundations for the Russian northeastern coast was manifest.

The failure of the food base brought one more direct and disastrous consequence for this area. Expecting a profitable trade in food supplies produced on the Amur, the Russian government prohibited the previously unhindered trade between the indigenous population of the coast and the whalers and sealers of foreign nations who frequently bartered food products for native furs. This prohibition and the inability of the Russians to substitute other food products for that trade brought about a devastating famine in 1878, which resulted in the virtual extermination of the natives along the entire coast of the Sea of Okotsk, for two thousand versts (about 1,200 miles) from the region of Udsk to Anadyr.[26] A further decrease of the fur trade inevitably followed.

For similar reasons the entire defensive system of the new Russian possessions was weakened. Because of the shortage of food supplies, in August, 1865, only a naval contingent in the port of Nikolaevsk and 7 officers and 732 men of regular troops were left in the entire Amur and Ussuri regions. Most of them were at the post of Novgorodsk, near the junction of the Russian, Chinese, and Korean borders.[27] The battalion assigned to Sakhalin was scattered among twelve posts to enable the men to supplement their rations by hunting and truck farming. Nevertheless, the lack of provisions necessitated the virtual abandonment of many posts; Tikhmenevskii post, for example, which had 25 men in 1869, was reduced by 1872 to a ridiculously small garrison of 3 because of "the difficulties of getting supplies."[28] The post was on the west coast of the island of Sakhalin not far from the mouth of the Amur River and was therefore advantageously situated for obtaining reinforcements and supplies.

The peaceful character of the native population on the left bank of

the Amur and the almost total absence of a Chinese and Manchu population on the Chinese right bank (except for the district around Argun)
gave to the Russians a false sense of security in regard to their line of
communication. When, in 1868, bands of Chinese and Manchus in the
Ussuri region, locally known as Manzas, attacked Russian settlements
on the Ussuri and even on the island of Askold, fifteen miles from
Vladivostok, the defensive provisions failed, and the Manzas destroyed
several villages and created a panic among the settlers.[29] The raiders
were finally driven away after a year of "Manza war";[30] their incur-
sion had exposed the insecurity of the Russian frontier and of its lines
of communication. This incident was recalled when the question of
security came up again in 1881.[31]

Even the Russian naval forces in the Far East could not be depended
upon for protection. For twenty years after the last use of the navy
to implement national policy, in 1858, the naval forces of Russia in the
Far East declined in strength. The major function of Russian warships in this period consisted of patrolling the sealing waters of the
northern Pacific Ocean and of transporting supplies and small bodies
of troops from the mainland to the posts of Sakhalin.[32] Rather than
incur the trouble and expense of a rigorous patrol, Russia adopted a
policy of leasing whaling and sealing rights to foreign companies,
chiefly American. Thus, an American named Lindholm, from San
Francisco, was given whaling rights in the rich inland waters of the
Sea of Okhotsk, and he jealously tried to keep out all interlopers.[33] And
the American firm of Hutchison, Cole, Phillips and Company in 1871
was granted a twenty-year lease of sealing rights on the Commander
Islands for a purely nominal rental of 5,000 rubles a year.[34]

The deplorable condition of the Russian navy in the Far East could
hardly have been avoided under the existing conditions. The sparseness of population in the Russian Far East, the severity of the climate,
and the failure of the new food base compelled the navy to take an
inactive role. In 1854, Muraviev-Amurskii, by making Nikolaevsk on
the Amur the main Russian naval port instead of Petropavlovsk in
Kamchatka,[35] had exchanged a relatively ice-free port for one that was
icebound for six months and fogbound for several months more.[36] The
strategical mobility of the Russian fleet was curtailed for most of the
year. Even when the naval port was transferred to Vladivostok in 1872,
the situation was not greatly improved. Because of the failure of the
food base, Russian ships formed a habit of dropping into Japanese
ports for supplies of coal and food which were not to be had or were
too expensive in their own Far Eastern base.[37] The lack of docking

facilities in the Russian ports until 1886[38] made the Russian squadron dependent on the docks of Japanese ports or on those of the more remote ports of Hong Kong and Shanghai.[39] Undoubtedly, until such conditions were remedied, Russian naval forces in the Far East were of little importance.

One of the principal points in Muraviev-Amurskii's plan for the acquisition of the left bank of the Amur was the use of that river to improve trade relations between Russia and China. In his historic memorandum of 1849, in which he analyzed the reasons for the necessity of that acquisition, he wrote:

> I consider that the only way to uphold our trade with China is to change it from a local to an export trade, and by navigating the Amur River to deliver the products of our industries to all the northeastern provinces of China, [which are] more remote from the present place of economic activities of the English and therefore from their annihilating competition with us.[40]

In the years following Muraviev-Amurskii's final departure from the Far East in 1861, none of his plans came so near being a total failure as the one mentioned in the foregoing quotation. With the existing transportation across Siberia, and in the face of competition of European sea-borne goods, Russia in the early stage of her industrial development could not hope to find a market for her manufactured products in China proper. The plan became feasible only when supplemented by other plans for improving transportation facilities to the Far East by means of a railroad from Lake Baikal to the Amur.[41] The transportation axiom that freight costs by sea are many times cheaper than those by land and inland waterways must have been familiar enough to Muraviev-Amurskii to make him aware of the improbability of success. The new series of treaties between European powers and China in 1860–1869 and the opening of several northeastern Chinese ports put an end to his hopes that Russia might enjoy a noncompetitive trade in that area.[42]

One phase of Russo-Chinese trade—the tea trade—offered a great opportunity for the commercial development of the Amur River. From the amount of tea imported it is evident that consumption of tea by Russians was constantly increasing.[43] In 1872 the Amur River began to be used as a regular transportation route for the importation of tea into European Russia. Even though this route proved to be cheaper by one and a half rubles per pood than the traditional caravan route of Tientsin-Kalgan-Kiakhta, the distance to Irkutsk was so great and prompt delivery so uncertain that the new route soon lost its importance. In the beginning, some 150,000 poods were taken to Russia by the Amur, but within five years the volume decreased to less than 15,000.[44]

The decline of the Amur trade route was hastened by the ukase of 1862 which opened the frontiers of European Russia to the importation of tea.[45] An attempt was made to maintain the Kiakhta and Amur River trade route for tea by establishing a differential tariff. The tariff was 15 kopeks on each pound on the Asiatic frontier and 30 to 35 kopeks a pound on the European frontier. This artificial measure, however, did not check the decline.[46]

The greatest blow to the Amur and Kiakhta tea route came with the opening of the Suez Canal in 1869. Freight costs of tea sent to Russia then became seven or eight times cheaper by sea than by the overland route.[47] Russian merchants began to desert their established "factories" at Hankow and move south to Foochow in order to be closer to the direct route through the canal.[48]

The Russian export trade to northeastern China was of little value, whereas "local trade" through Kiakhta into Mongolia and indirectly to the hinterland of China was valued at more than 1,000,000 rubles a year.[49] Russian export to Tientsin, the main center of foreign trade in northeastern China, continued to diminish from the already petty figure of 39,600 rubles in 1873 to 29,800 and 25,000 rubles in the next two years.[50]

Except for those that went to China's Mongolian and Turkestan dependencies, Russian exports to China seem to have been of little value. Reliable statistics of this trade, however, are lacking for the period before 1880; most of the shipments of Russian goods to China were handled by non-Russian shipping companies, and there is a strong possibility that many Russian products came to China without being identified as Russian.[51] With the exception of a few Finnish sailing vessels, from 1860 to 1871 no Russian merchant vessel entered Chinese ports.[52] In those years the Navigation and Trading Company of Odessa tried to establish regular steamship navigation between the Black Sea ports and Hong Kong[53] but after a few trial voyages abandoned the attempt.[54] After this failure, ships visited Chinese ports only occasionally until 1879—one visited Tientsin, for example, in 1877. "To our regret," wrote K. A. Skal'kovskii, "in these three years [1877–1879] no ships arrived there under the Russian flag, except in 1877, when there came one sailing vessel of 82 tons."[55] In the same year, Tientsin was visited by 142 foreign vessels with an aggregate of 81,918 tons.[56]

Russian trade relations with Japan were even more insignificant. As late as 1879 the entire trade consisted of Japanese exports to the value of 49,177 yen, and imports to the value of 10,280 yen.[57] The actual trade relations, however, were probably greater, for Russian ships in Japanese ports purchased supplies which were not included in the export figures.

The economic decline and instability of the Russian ports in the Far East clearly reflect the unpromising condition of Russia's Far Eastern trade. Nikolaevsk on the Amur decreased in importance and in population.[58] However, judging from the number of ships that entered its harbor, it maintained its position as a port. The character of the cargoes (mainly provisions and government supplies), the predominantly European origin of the cargoes, the larger profits made by foreign merchants, and the tremendously high cost of living[59] again indicate the failure of the Amur valley to serve as a good food base and of the river as an efficient route of transportation for goods either to or from the transbaikal region.

Vladivostok, the main port of the Far East after 1872, experienced a similar decline.[60] Soon after the transfer of the naval base from Nikolaevsk to Vladivostok, the latter was declared a free port,[61] probably to reduce the expenses of the maintenance of its garrison. Until 1880 the port was visited mainly by foreign vessels and trade was predominantly in foreign hands;[62] provisions were expensive, and imports, which consisted chiefly of food, exceeded exports by a ratio of more than ten to one.[63] No goods except patterns and samples were sent to the port from Russia by way of the Amur.[64]

It is evident, therefore, that the possession of the left bank of the Amur and the Primorsk district and the opportunity of navigating the Amur River brought little, if any, economic benefit to Russia from 1860 to 1880. On the contrary, the possession of these territories, it has been estimated, caused a deficit to the state of more than 55,000,000 rubles before 1880,[65] although the total population had not yet reached 100,000. The profit from the development of these new territories went to foreign merchants and shipowners who supplied the new settlements. It went to Chinese merchants, whose business accounted for most of the exports of the Primorsk region,[66] and to Japanese, who by the provisions of the treaty of 1875 were given the right to fish in the waters of the southern half of Sakhalin.[67] This treaty almost entirely eliminated the Russian exports of fish to Japan.

However, the causes for the temporary failure to make the Russian Far East a valuable territory were neither fundamental nor irremediable. Even hostile contemporary critics recognized in the Russian Far East a country of opportunities and a land of the future.[68] By 1880, an important increase in gold production, envisaged by Muraviev-Amurskii as early as 1848,[69] began to change the outlook from one of disfavor to one of interest, at least.[70] As Muraviev-Amurskii realized, the basic requirement of the new territories was an increased population, which would remove the causes of the inefficient transportation, insufficient food production, and lack of security.[71]

ATTEMPTED REMEDIES AND THEIR SHORTCOMINGS

Muraviev-Amurskii foresaw and actually experimented with ways of settling the newly acquired territories. After his departure, military settlements, free colonists, and convict labor were tried. His efforts were premature, and aside from his introduction of the first colonists, his work in building up a permanent population in the Russian Far East was insignificant.[72]

The successors of Muraviev-Amurskii had a better opportunity to promote immigration to the Far East. The liberation of the serfs by Alexander II in March, 1861, left millions of domestic serfs without any attachment to the soil. Thus a large population was made available for settlement in the Far Eastern territories. On April 27, 1861, the first settlement law opened the Amur region to both Russian and foreign colonists.[73] Remaining in effect until 1882, this law allowed the settlers to occupy up to 100 dessiatines (i.e., 270 acres) of land for each head of a family on the payment of three rubles a dessiatine. As an additional and not inconsiderable inducement,[74] a ten-year exemption from conscription and a twenty-year exemption from taxes was granted. After the passage of this law, an eastward migration of peasants from European Russia began and grew in numbers with each decade. In the 1860's, 150,000 to 200,000 peasants crossed the Ural Mountains on their way to Siberia; only a relatively small number of them, however, reached eastern Siberia,[75] the majority having settled elsewhere on the way.

The earliest volunteer settlers were not very successful, because they came from dissimilar areas. Those of 1862 were from the provinces of Poltava, Tambov, Orel, and Voronezh. In the years that followed, settlers came from these or similar regions of temperate climate and rich "black soil." Hence conditions in the new region seemed strange to all of them and presented new problems.[76] Furthermore, most of these pioneer settlers were not experienced farmers but farm hands of limited resources and resourcefulness. Their failures and disappointments can therefore be easily understood.

Additional inducements were offered in 1866 when the Department

of the Tsar's Domains opened 470,000 dessiatines of choice land in
the Far Eastern regions and increased the period of exemption from
taxation to twenty-four years.[77] These provisions attracted a wave of
pacifist sectarians, like the Molokani and the Dukhobors, who from
1866 to 1869 settled in large numbers around Blagoveschensk.[78] Though
more successful than most of the other colonists, their antisocial character kept them from playing any significant role in the building of
the Amur valley as an efficient line of communication and as a food
base.[79]

The previously mentioned climatic and geographical hardships and
the character of the earlier volunteer settlers, together with floods,
hostile raids, and the absence of government help,[80] caused a decrease
in the flow of volunteer settlers into eastern Siberia in the decade following 1870.[81] By far the greatest factor in the failure of this type of
colonization was the lack of government interest in promoting it. Until
1881, settlers were given no financial assistance for their six-thousand-
mile trek or for the actual settlement in the Far East.[82] Furthermore,
the local administration favored a settlement by the unwilling "cossacks," who were granted large areas of land, and who, because of
their other duties, were least able to exploit them.[83] A system of pre-
emption allowed the earlier settlers to acquire and rapidly exhaust the
more promising localities, with the result that latecomers were faced
with the added difficulties of poor soil and unfavorable locations.[84]

Unable to attract many volunteer settlers, the government turned
to the use of convicts in settling some of the Russian Far Eastern
possessions, mainly the island of Sakhalin. Both free and convict labor
had been introduced into Sakhalin before 1869. In 1859 Muraviev-
Amurskii sent the first party of convicts to Sakhalin to exploit the
Due River coal mines, but since the coal mined there could not be
transported, the project was abandoned.[85] In 1868 an attempt was made
to establish an agricultural colony on the island, using both volunteer
settlers and convicts. Within three years the project failed and the
volunteer settlers were "completely ruined."[86]

By Imperial decree in April, 1869, Sakhalin became the place of exile
for the most hardened criminals. After an experimental party of 800
convicts was established there in that year, annual convoys of hundreds
of convicts, many of whom were followed by their families, were sent
across Siberia.[87] Beginning in 1879, when regular communications between European Russia and the Far East were established by sea,[88]
criminals were transported more frequently and in greater numbers.
In the next twenty-five years, more than 30,000 convicts were sent from

Russia and Siberia to the island, at a total expenditure of 30,000,000 rubles for deportation, settlement, and administration.[89] It is doubtful whether the value received from this colonization was worth the expenditure.[90]

The measures outlined above were intended to solve the immediate problem of underpopulation of the Russian Far Eastern possessions. Their failure became more apparent by 1879 when the first census was taken of the Oriental and native population in the Russian Far East.[91] This census and the subsequent registration of non-Russian immigrants show that the number of Chinese, Manchu, and Korean settlers was increasing in the same proportion as the Russian.

The Koreans began to infiltrate into the Ussuri region after 1862, although emigration of Koreans was punishable by death. In certain periods of famine, as in 1869, they crossed the Russian frontier by the thousands.[92] The Koreans readily accepted the Russian customs and language and were soon listed in the census as Russian-Korean citizens.[93] More than 500 of the Chinese and Manchus, who could not be assimilated, crossed the Russian border annually after 1870, increasing the original Manza population of the Ussuri and the Amur. In 1885 there were 10,353 registered Chinese in the Ussuri region and probably some 4,000 unregistered Chinese, as contrasted with 17,000 Russian settlers and 13,000 officials, soldiers, and other temporary residents. Adding Koreans and Manzas to the number of Chinese, the ratio of Orientals to Russian settlers was 1.43 to 1.[94]

Statistics concerning the economic significance of this infiltration of Orientals were even more humiliating to the administration. In 1885, in the Ussuri region, the amount of land per capita cultivated by the cossacks and settlers was 0.6 dessiatine and by the Chinese 1.1 dessiatines,[95] and yet the Chinese were at this time the chief exporters of Ussuri products and were the principal retail merchants for the Russian settlers, as well as for the natives and their own nationals.[96] Their lower standard of living and intensive type of agriculture soon enabled them to control the commerce of the region.

This condition of growing Oriental competition illustrates once more the administration's neglect of the problem from the beginning. Only when the situation became politically and strategically dangerous after 1881 were steps taken to restrict Oriental immigration, trade, and agriculture and thereby protect and promote these activities for the Russians. These restrictions had favorable results for the territory.[97]

Administrative neglect was evident in other activities. From 1883 to 1887 a large group of Russian and Chinese gold diggers (the correct term for independent surface operators), variously estimated at 7,000 to 12,000 men, established themselves on the Zheltuga River, a tributary of the Albazina, in the extreme northern part of Manchuria.[98] Called by its settlers "the Republic of the Zheltuga," and frequently referred to as "the California of the Amur,"[99] this colony defied both the Chinese and the Russian governments, which repeatedly ordered them to disperse. It was ruled according to democratic principles and rigid camp laws.[100] Situated near the Amur River, this "California of the Amur," with its gold rush fever, to a large extent disrupted the traffic on the Amur by drawing into its community provisions and men sent down the Amur on official business.[101] It also was a point of friction between the Chinese and the Russian governments.[102] The only administrative effort to restrict the community was the formation of a cordon of guards to confiscate "illegally obtained" gold as it came through the Russian frontier.[103] The extermination of this picturesque horde was left to the Chinese.[104]

In the Ussuri region and the lower reaches of the Amur, the Russian government failed to establish its authority among the natives—the Golds, the Orochons, and the Manzas. The Treaty of Aigun of 1858 and the Treaty of Peking of November, 1860, permitted the Chinese inhabitants of the left bank of the Amur and the right bank of the Ussuri to retain their local administration and justice.[105] Apparently the Chinese took advantage of these provisions; for in 1866 when I. P. Nadarov made a military-statistical survey of the native inhabitants in the northern Ussuri region, he found that although the region (except the coastal part) according to all available evidence had only nine Chinese inhabitants in 1860, the Chinese immigrants had established new centers of local administration and justice.[106] Nadarov discovered among the native Golds a prevalent conviction that the region was governed by the Chinese and not by the Russians.[107] He reported: "From the accounts of most of the natives I have come to the conclusion that the Golds and the Orochons to this day pay a *iasak* (tribute) to the Chinese *noions* (officials) every year, to the amount of two sables from each family."[108] Such was the Russian hold on the district closest to their new administration center at Khabarovsk.

In the first quarter of the century after the acquisition of the new Far Eastern territories the most important step taken by Russia to overcome her territorial and economic insignificance in the Far East was the formation of the "Volunteer Fleet" for the maintenance of regular communications between the Black Sea and the ports of the Far East. During the Anglo-Russian crisis at the conclusion of the

Russo-Turkish War in 1878, five fast German merchant vessels were bought by public subscription in Russia with the idea of turning them into commerce-raiding auxiliary cruisers.[109] When the imminent threat of war had passed and no adequate employment for these ships was found,[110] the directors of the Volunteer Fleet Company and its chairman, K. P. Pobedonostsev, evolved a plan to use this fleet for regular Far Eastern voyages.[111]

The plan was put into effect in 1879. Assisted by a subsidy of 36,000 rubles for each voyage and the guarantee of large government cargoes,[112] the ships of the Volunteer Fleet began their activity in the Far East under extremely favorable conditions. Russian merchants promised their coöperation in exporting their cargoes of tea on these ships.[113] The ships had ample cargoes both to and from the East. Besides government cargoes, they carried convict passengers to Sakhalin and replacements for the troops in the Far East. The ships sailed westward to their main home port, Odessa, loaded with tea and other products of the Orient.[114] Although the Volunteer Fleet was not a financial success, the losses of the enterprise were not great. The Russian government realized that the ships had done much to raise Russian prestige in the Far East and willingly took over the deficits of the company.[115]

Although the appearance of the vessels was hailed with delight by the Russians, especially in the Primorsk region,[116] and although the Russian Volunteer Fleet played an important part in the development of Russian trade in the Far East, it had two detrimental effects on the course of Russian Far Eastern history. In 1882, as an experiment, the Russian government sent a shipment of settlers to the Far East from Odessa on vessels of the Volunteer Fleet. About 250 families were transported at government cost. After this experiment the government adopted a policy of shipping settlers and assigned for this purpose an annual budget of 315,000 rubles.

This new and systematic policy of subsidizing immigrants to the Far East weakened the transit facilities for the settlers who used the land route across Siberia. At the same time, the charges to the prospective settlers using the sea route—90 rubles per adult and 45 rubles per child—were too high to attract many settlers. Thus the settlers were discouraged by both land and sea. From 1882 to 1891, when famine struck western Siberia and renewed the migration to the Far East, almost all who started out to eastern Siberia by the land route settled on the way. The number of colonists transported by sea never exceeded 2,000 a year, and for the entire seventeen years of the shipping program only 16,000 were so transported.[117]

The second detrimental effect of the Volunteer Fleet was the further weakening of the Amur River as the main line of communication between the settled regions of Siberia and the Pacific. The new policy tended to favor the Primorsk region over the Amur, which contained only 35 per cent of the total number of immigrants to the Russian Far East.[118] There was a continued decline of population in Nikolaevsk in the years following 1879, and a decline of freight shipments from the transbaikal region down the Amur.[119] With growing population on the Amur, transport facilities increased correspondingly, although their use was local for the most part.[120] The Amur River served the Amur region but was not the vital link to Siberia that was needed.

The most effective program adopted in these twenty years to aid the new Russian Far East resulted in the complete reversal of the policy of Muraviev-Amurskii. The Far East became in fact a Russian colony, separated from the mother country by a long sea voyage, instead of an integral part of the Russian Empire closely linked with its other component parts. However, certain conditions were emerging which would force a definite though gradual reversion to the original concept of Empire unity proposed by Muraviev-Amurskii.

Neglect of Foreign Policy

In the period 1860–1885 the major interests of Russia lay in the West, the Near East, and central Asia. There were other reasons why Russia lacked a definite foreign policy in the Far East. Because her position there was unsatisfactory, if not precarious, from the economic and strategic standpoint, she could not afford to adopt an aggressive policy. Even if Russian diplomacy had been able to win some advantages, neither Russian arms, nor commerce, nor population would have been able to utilize them. Therefore, with the exception of a few formal actions and the conclusion of some long-standing but not grave disputes, nothing of importance was accomplished in the Far East for a quarter of a century.

With the decline of Russian interest in the Far East, there was a corresponding decline in the caliber of Russian statesmen and diplomats sent there. Diplomatic service in the Far East was looked upon as exile,[121] and a minister accredited to a country where there was little diplomatic activity would contrive to obtain long leaves of absence, leaving in his post totally inexperienced secretaries as chargés d'affaires.[122] A general complaint arose concerning the incapacity and inactivity of the Russian consuls, who for the most part were foreign merchants chosen to represent Russian commercial interests in addition to their own.[123] The majority of the Russian governors general, whose "proconsular" powers enabled them to influence foreign policy,[124] were distinctly second-rate. Until the administration of Baron A. N. Korf in 1884, they were extraordinarily inactive. No governor general visited Kamchatka in the ten years preceding 1881,[125] and only one visited the island of Sakhalin in twenty-five years.[126]

The most outstanding example of the neglect of Russian foreign policy during these twenty-five years was the Russian attitude toward Korea. From 1860 on, Russia and Korea had been neighbors, but until 1884 there was no attempt to open Korea to Russian trade or to place existing trade on a legal basis by treaty.[127] Before statistics were kept of this trade, Russian troops in the Ussuri region had depended on imported Korean cattle for food supplies,[128] and Koreans, crossing the border without official permission, traded freely in the border settlements.[129] Lieutenant Colonel Vebel reported in 1889: "Korea values Russian trade more than Russia does Korean trade. Korea sends 10,000 head of cattle annually . . . the chief buyers are the army and the officials. This brings Korea about 500,000 rubles a year." Local Russian commanders from military posts on the border made whatever arrangements were necessary for conducting this unrestricted trade. They occasionally took the liberty of crossing the border without permission, to negotiate trade regulations with minor Korean officials.[130]

The importance of Korea as an additional food base was not ignored in the ministerial circles of Russia. In 1874 the Minister of Communications, K. N. Pos'iet, one of the veterans of Muraviev-Amurskii's enterprises of 1853–1858,[131] in a memorandum proposing the abolition of the exile system suggested that, "as the Primorsk and Amur regions suffer from a lack of grain, cattle and labor, it is necessary to have close relations with Korea, which has all of these."[132] In other words, the minister proposed Korea as a food base for the Amur and Ussuri valleys. The suggestion was not followed; nevertheless, the Russian Far Eastern possessions continued to use Korea as an auxiliary food base, and Koreans, on their own initiative, migrated to the Ussuri region and relieved some of the pressing need for labor.

Russia also showed a remarkable lack of interest in the political and geographical facts about its eastern neighbor in the period 1860–1884. Russian explorers and geographers avoided the country, and information concerning it was generally borrowed from foreign sources.[133] The publications of the Russian General Staff containing information on all territories adjacent to Russian Asiatic borders showed interest in Korea only after 1884,[134] and not until 1886 were agents of the General Staff sent to observe conditions there.[135]

This period of neglect ended as a result of the opening of Korea to foreign trade. The first treaty of commerce between Korea and Japan, in 1876, was followed, after a short delay, by similar treaties between Korea and the United States, England, and France.[136] On July 7, 1884, a Treaty of Friendship and Commerce was signed between Russia and Korea.[137] By this step Russian diplomacy seems to have followed the example of the other powers. The treaty made no appreciable difference in Russo-Korean trade relations or the Russian attitude toward Korea.

Besides making the customary arrangements for mutual trade, the treaty included a provision which allowed warships of either country the right to visit any port of the other signatory country, irrespective of whether that port was an open or a closed one.[138] This provision enabled Russian naval forces to take an active interest in the ports and harbors of Korea, which had been closed to vessels of other nations. Before the treaty was ratified and the Russians could take advantage of this provision, a crisis between England and Russia developed in the Far East, because the British claimed that Russia intended to seize one of these closed ports.[139]

A comparison of Russian policy toward Korea before and after 1884 shows that in all probability Russia's policy toward Korea during the Sino-Japanese disagreement over Korea's status in 1884–1885 was the same as Japan's. Both Russia and Japan genuinely wanted an independent Korea, although perhaps for different reasons.[140] In 1888–1889 Russian policy toward Korea became better defined. Although a new commercial treaty, signed in 1888,[141] opened a few more ports for Russian trade, Russian policy toward Korea remained nonaggressive and almost indifferent. A conference held in St. Petersburg on May 8, 1888, to determine a Russian policy on the Korean question, accepted the views of General Baron A. N. Korf, Governor General of the Amur province, and I. A. Zinoviev, chief of the Asiatic Department of the Ministry of Foreign Affairs. These views were:

The acquisition of Korea not only would give us no advantages but would be accompanied by a considerable number of disadvantageous consequences.

Being a very poor country, Korea cannot be for us a profitable commercial market, especially in view of the absence of industries in our own possessions on the Pacific ...

Situated on the flank of Manchuria, Korea, under certain conditions, could be transformed by us into an important strategic base, but the advantages of this base lose their significance because of the disadvantages and difficulties which are connected with its defense. Korea is too remote from the centers where we command sufficient armed forces...

Finally, the acquisition of Korea would disturb our relations not only with China but also with England, which also has certain designs in that country.[142]

The two statesmen mentioned above then analyzed the policy of Japan toward Korea in the previous few years. They claimed that Japan had changed her plans with respect to Korea after encountering an adamant Chinese government. She had been content with the provisions of the Tientsin Convention;[143] but recently she had again been anxiously trying to find a way to insure Korea against seizure by the Chinese. The memorandum asserts: "This direction of Japanese policy is completely in agreement with our views, and we ought to try to support the cabinet of Tokyo in this direction."[144]

The policy toward Korea expressed by the Ministry of Foreign Affairs conformed with the opinions of the local officials and the actual condition of Russo-Korean trade relations. In the opinion of the Russian agent of the General Staff, Lieutenant Colonel Vebel, who was in Korea in 1889, in regard to strategy, "we can ignore Korea entirely. In case of Manchurian operations she forms a secure flank. As an ally she can do no good; as an enemy she is powerless."[145] Economically, Russian trade with Korea remained insignificant. In 1886 the imports of Korea from its neighbors amounted to (in Mexican dollars):

Japan	2,508,000
China	455,000
Russia	14,000[146]

The figures for 1888–1889 show a proportional increase in trade with all nations.[147] In 1888 there were only four Russian merchants in Korea, all of them in Chemulpo, the oldest open port in Korea and the one farthest from the immediate sphere of possible Russian influence. At the same time, there were in Korea six English, eleven American, twenty-two German, and more than four thousand Japanese merchants.[148]

Russian policy toward Japan was equally passive. After the conclusion of the prolonged negotiations over Sakhalin which ended in the exchange of the southern half of Sakhalin for a group of the Kuril Islands that had been in the possession of Russia, an "era of good feeling" followed, during which there were no disputes.[149] It has been shown that Russo-Japanese trade was insignificant. Russia was not in a position to compete with Japan in markets of the Far East. These conditions probably influenced Russia to follow the initiative of the United States in yielding to Japanese insistence for revision of "unequal treaties" in 1882.[150]

It is apparent, from the situation described above and from Russia's policy toward Korea in 1888, that Russian policy toward Japan was one of sympathy and friendship. In the years 1888–1889 Russia and Japan drifted into a minor diplomatic crisis. In 1888, Japan, always eager for revision of her "unequal treaties," announced that on this matter she would deal separately with each nation. Willing, as on the previous occasion, to come to agreement with Japan, Russia took the initiative and signed a Treaty of Commerce and Navigation with Japan in the spring of 1889, revising the old Russo-Japanese treaties. By the new treaty, Russia was granted a most-favored-nation treatment in exchange for her abandonment of the rights of extraterritoriality. However, Russia was urged by the European powers not to ratify this treaty, because it weakened the position of other powers in Japan. Russia persuaded the Japanese government to postpone ratification for an indefinite time. News of the signing of the treaty had been circulated previously, and this postponement aroused public opinion in Japan against Russia. Incidents occurred which led to the murder of some Russian sailors, and mutual dissatisfaction with the diplomatic negotiations of 1888–1889 ended the "era of good feeling" between Russia and Japan.[151]

Russia's attitude toward Manchuria is further evidence of the neglect of diplomatic activity in the Far East for almost a quarter of a century. The first article of the treaties of Aigun and of Peking gave Russia the right of navigation and trade along the Sungari, the principal tributary of the Amur, flowing from Manchuria.[152] Several expeditions, either sent directly or encouraged by the Russian government, were dispatched to take advantage of these privileges; but in 1864, 1866, and 1869, they were impeded by Chinese officials in Manchuria, who forbade the members of the expeditions to disembark. When they landed in spite of these prohibitions, Chinese officials forbade the population to trade with them, under the threat of severe punishment.[153] Besides these semiofficial expeditions, five private expeditions attempted to establish trade relations on the Sungari; but all met with similar opposition.[154] For fifteen years after 1870 no attempt was made to enter the Sungari, and there is no evidence that Russian diplomacy tried to accomplish what local officials had failed to do.[155]

When the Supplementary Treaty of Peking, signed in March, 1862,[156] finally established reciprocal rights of Chinese and Russian subjects to free trade for one hundred li (35 miles) beyond their own border,[157] the Chinese merchants in Manchuria quickly took advantage of this provision. They enjoyed a lucrative trade in the Russian border settlements.[158] The Russians, however, were not able to take advantage of this arrangement in Manchuria, because they had few goods to trade. Furthermore, the Chinese, following a traditional policy of maintaining uninhabited strips of territory as buffers on their frontiers, left a stretch of wilderness along the frontier of the Amur. This strip, some two hundred miles wide, except in the triangle formed by Manchuria, Korea, and the Ussuri region, was inhabited only by bandits, semibarbarous hunters, and refugees from China and Russia.[159] This population was hardly conducive to the establishment of good trade relations.

Most of the foreign imports into Manchuria came through its single treaty port of Newchwang (Inkou), which had an active trade,[160] and which dominated the markets of all Manchuria.[161] Yet this port was hardly ever visited by Russian ships until after 1889.[162] In northern Manchuria, farthest removed from Inkou, Russian trade about 1885 was considered "insignificant."[163]

Under the existing conditions of inadequate economic bases and poor transportation, Russia had little opportunity to improve its trade relations with Manchuria by means of diplomacy. A more significant factor in the failure of Russian diplomacy to solve the problem of trade relations with Manchuria lay in Russo-Chinese relations of that period. China's anger at Russia's highhanded policy in the settlement of the Kuldja affair[164] in 1871–1881 continued in the subsequent years and created an unfriendly and hostile attitude on the part of Chinese officials toward Russian trade in Manchuria.

After a quarter of a century of haphazard measures of colonization, unstable means of communication, and passive diplomacy, Russia held a position inferior to that of China in the Far East. In the period 1881–1888 this became apparent and was afterward remedied by the construction of the Trans-Siberian Railway. That enterprise was to fill many pressing needs of the Far Eastern Russian possessions and to fulfill the requirements of an active foreign policy in the Far East.

II

THE SHIFT OF RUSSIAN INTEREST FROM THE NEAR EAST TO THE FAR EAST AND THE TRANS-SIBERIAN RAILROAD PROJECT

A RUSSO-CHINESE war over the Kuldja affair was narrowly averted by the diplomatic efforts of Marquis Tseng at St. Petersburg. Li Hung-chang's support of a peaceful settlement prevailed over widespread demands for war in the court circles of Peking.[1] However, the inevitable aftermath of the crisis strained Russo-Chinese relations for more than a decade after the signing of the Treaty of St. Petersburg on February 14, 1881.[2] A part of Admiral Lesovskii's squadron remained in the Far East after the futile demonstration in 1880.[3] Russian troop reinforcements sent to the Far East were kept there as part of the permanent garrison.[4] China increased her military force and thus gave Russia further occasion to be concerned about her intentions.

THE NEED FOR A TRANS-SIBERIAN RAILROAD AS A DEFENSE AGAINST CHINA

The attitude and policies adopted by the Chinese after 1881 helped to prolong the Russo-Chinese crisis. A noted authority on Chinese international relations wrote: "The treaty signed by Marquis Tseng resulted in making China arrogant; Russia's backward step had astonished the Chinese; they attributed to intimidation what was only self-interest and foresight, and they jumped from panic to the most outrageous boasting."[5] A more conservative estimate of the result of China's diplomatic victory in the Kuldja affair states: "China learned for the first time that diplomacy must be backed by weapons."[6] China did not delay in making use of this type of diplomacy. On the heels of the military reconquest of Chinese Turkestan by Marshal Tso Tsung-tang's army, she launched a gigantic political and diplomatic offensive aimed at restoring her dwindling or dormant prestige and influence in Tonkin, Annam, Burma, Tibet, Korea, and Manchuria.[7]

Minor successes in the initial steps of this offensive encouraged the Mandarin war party which had counseled war against Russia in 1879–1880. When China's military intervention successfully ended the Korean-Japanese clash in 1882,[8] these patriots looked upon the outcome

[1] For notes to chap. ii see pp. 258–264.

as "a great Chinese victory." Their country's increased influence in Korea and a corresponding decline of Japanese influence seemed to justify this opinion. Two thousand Chinese troops remained in Korea, and Koreans took Chinese instructors for their army.[9] The war party grew chauvinistic. In the Luchu dispute and in 1883 the mandarins tried to involve China in a war with Japan. In 1883 and 1884 they looked for war with France. Unfortunately for China and the peace of the Far East, they succeeded in their quest.[10] In the main, however, from 1882 to 1884 Li Hung-chang "turned all cries for war into cries for preparedness."[11]

For several years after 1881 no acute crisis or serious dispute arose in Russo-Chinese relations. In view of the Chinese attitude, however, there were minor incidents and problems which could have become serious. Faced by the soldiers of the zealous and arrogant Marshal Tso,[12] Russian troops remained to occupy Chinese Kuldja until March 1883,[13] and the boundaries of the ceded part of the Ili valley were not finally agreed upon until October, 1883. The violation of Chinese territory by Russian gold seekers, the presence of an undefined Russo-Chinese frontier adjacent to the southern Ussuri district,[14] the Russian right of navigation of the Sungari River,[15] and a host of minor abuses of border trade and diplomacy[16] could easily have provided a cause for war in the East, if either of the two nations had been seriously disposed to seek an issue.

Certainly, many Russians felt that war was imminent and inevitable.[17] Opinions differed greatly on the strength of the Chinese army. Some recognized authorities stated that the Chinese troops would prove to be a match for the Russians.[18] War was particularly feared in the Far East, where many frontier incidents proclaimed the new spirit of Chinese aggressiveness.[19] In spite of the fact that the offensive strength of the Chinese army under Marshal Tso in Chinese Turkestan comprised 180,000 men, of which 40,000 were armed with modern weapons,[20] the officers of the Russian General Staff agreed that the main and most dangerous thrust by China would be one launched from Manchuria at the Amur River valley.[21] Sparsely settled, weakly defended, and strategically unsound, at right angles to the Chinese lines of attack, the Russian line of communications, contiguous to the Chinese border for more than 1,000 miles, was considered absolutely indefensible. The only way for the Russians to defend the territory along the Amur was to launch an offensive in Manchuria.[22]

The menace to the Russian Far East was accentuated by the development of Chinese influence in Korea, and particularly in Manchuria.

For three centuries Manchuria was considered closed to Chinese immigration, and special passports were demanded from the Chinese who desired to enter that country.[23] Because of the unsettled conditions during the Tai-ping rebellion, many refugees from central China illegally penetrated the forbidden land during the 1860's, but most of them settled in southern Manchuria and had no effect on Russian possessions in the Far East.[24] In 1878 Russia repealed the earlier prohibition and gave great encouragement to the colonization movement by granting permission for the emigration of Chinese women to areas beyond the Great Wall of China. A colonization bureau was established in 1880.[25]

The work of this colonization bureau seems to have been directed toward northern Manchuria by means of volunteer, joint-enterprise, exile, and military settlements.[26] Two strategic areas received particular attention. The first was between Ninguta and Hunchun, opposite the Russian settlements in the southern Ussuri region, which received a great influx of settlers in 1881. This movement was directed by the brother of Li Hung-chang, who organized a military government for the district.[27] The second was north of Tsitsihar on the main route—Tsitsihar to Blagoveschensk by way of Megen and Aigun—and was sponsored by the governor of the Heilungkiang province.[28] Although Russian agents noted that the work of colonization was badly conducted and was not very successful,[29] a longer study brought realization of the seriousness of the situation. The incontrovertible fact was that in 1882–1890 there were thirty times more Chinese colonists in northern Manchuria than there were Russian colonists in the Amur and Primorsk regions.[30]

Besides promoting the colonization of Manchuria, the Chinese government greatly increased its military preparedness in that country. After 1881 the number of troops in Manchuria was continuously increased and they were rearmed with modern weapons. In 1885, when a general rearmament and reorganization of Manchurian troops took place, the Chinese forces in China's three Manchurian provinces, on a peacetime footing, amounted to 85,000 men; 50,000 of these, in recently organized formations, were trained and reasonably well armed.[31] Among other significant preparations was the formation of the North China Fleet, suggested and encouraged by Li Hung-chang after 1883.[32] As part of the naval preparation, the Chinese government established a fortified naval base at Lüshunkow, on the Liaotung Peninsula.[33] This harbor was fortified under the direction of French military engineers in the following year, and eventually it was named Port Arthur[34] for

Lieutenant William Arthur who was in command of the gunboat *Algerine.*

Although the development of Manchuria by the Chinese assumed menacing proportions for the Russian Far East, it does not necessarily follow that it was aimed against Russia or was intended as a menace. The principal aim of Chinese policy in this period was to establish a strong influence in Korea; a settlement in Manchuria would be helpful in the attainment of that goal. Chinese statesmen realized that Manchuria, on the flank of Korea, offered a strategic approach to that country.[35] In the evolution of Russian policy in the Far East the important factor was that Russian statesmen at least suspected—and many influential writers, officials, and officers in the Far East were absolutely certain—that China had adopted and was carrying out a program aimed against Russia.[36]

In 1885 Russia's and China's distrust of each other grew more acute. In that year, because of Korean intrigues[37] China was constantly trying to discover Russia's policy in Korea, and vice versa.[38] Relations on the border went from bad to worse. In a war with France over Tonkin, the southern Chinese squadron was destroyed and the French gained command of the sea.[39] However, the success won by the Chinese land forces at Langson increased Chinese confidence. A Russian analysis, perhaps slightly biased, states: "The Tonkin war had made them [the Chinese] so arrogant that on the Ili, the upper reaches of the Usa, the Enisei, and on the Ussuri River, there are daily misunderstandings."[40] The destruction of the "Zheltuga Republic" in the winter of 1885–86 is a characteristic example of the strong new Chinese activity. After an official ultimatum to the inhabitants of this "California of the Amur," the Chinese government collected troops at Aigun and in the depth of winter attacked the Zheltuga camp. The 5,000 remaining inhabitants were cut off from the Amur River, scattered, beaten, and massacred, and the camp was burned to the ground.[41] The Chinese pursued the refugees across the frozen Amur River into the Russian cossack settlements of Ignashina and Amazar, where they continued the bloody punishment.[42] At the same time, other detachments destroyed incipient mining camps in Manchuria on the Sapozha and Arakan rivers.[43]

China began to seek new footholds on the eastern coast of Korea in this period of activity. In 1885 the Chinese government asked Russia to return a part of the Primorsk region around Posieta Bay. This area would make an ideal outlet to the sea for the newly settled regions of Hunchun and Ninguta in northeastern Manchuria.[44] Having failed in its attempt to regain the Posieta Bay territory, the Chinese government tried to link Manchuria with the Sea of Japan by asking Korea to cede to China the Bay of Goshkevich and a strip of territory along the right bank of the Tumen River.[45] Finally, there was even a project to occupy Port Lazarev; but this matter was postponed.[46]

In many respects, China's activity in her adjoining vassal states reacted against the Russian position in the Far East. Certain minor points of friction were in time eliminated by the delineation of the frontier between Manchuria and southern Ussuri in 1886,[47] and by the destruction of the camp on the Zheltuga. The major problem, however, remained inherent in the geographical position of the Russo-Chinese border in the Far East; the problem could only be eliminated by revolutionary changes of transportation.

The basic weakness of Russian Far Eastern possessions—the sparse population along the lengthy frontier and the inadequate lines of communication—remained the key to the unsolved problem of defense. The population could not support the troops required for its defense. In 1886 the Russian land forces in the Far East, excluding the settled cossacks, numbered only 15,000 men, of whom 11,000 were stationed in the immediate neighborhood of Vladivostock.[48] Since Siberia had no troops to spare, the nearest base for reinforcements was European Russia, 4,000 miles away.[49] According to the calculations of the officers of the Amur military district, it would take eighteen months for troops from Russia, in route march, to reach the Primorsk region.[50] Russian naval forces in the Far East were not of primary importance against China, since by the creation of the northern Chinese squadron China had the largest fleet in Far Eastern waters.[51] After the failure of Admiral Lesovskii's cruise in 1880, the Chinese were not to be frightened by a naval demonstration.[52]

In the 1880's the Russian government took numerous steps to remedy its weak position, particularly in regard to the character of its population in the Far East. It has been shown how in 1882 the government adopted a policy of subsidizing the transportation of settlers from European Russia on the ships of the Volunteer Fleet. The policy of assisting colonists was furthered by both the central and the local governments. In 1881 a temporary law, which became permanent in 1889, established government aid for settlers migrating across Siberia.[53] In January, 1882, a local land law was approved by the Tsar, which contained some farsighted provisions and had beneficial results.[54] It provided that non-Russian subjects could not purchase land in the Far East without special permission from the governor general.[55] Each settler was granted fifteen dessiatines of land, for which he need not pay for three years. Settlers must offer proof to the officials on the Siberian frontier that they had sufficient resources to get them to their destination and ensure their support for the first year.[56] As a result of these measures, the character, success, and consequent popularity of the settlement were greatly improved. Whereas, before 1882 the average number of new settlers in each year was 601 persons, the annual average for the years 1882 to 1899 was 4,076.[57]

Another beneficial action of the government was the division of Russian possessions east of Lake Baikal into administrative units. Until 1884 the entire region was governed from Irkutsk, "and it must be admitted," wrote N. G. Matiunin, "it was administered very badly."[58] During this entire period most of the administrative measures were of a minor character, and no serious plans were undertaken to draw the Far Eastern possessions into closer ties with Russia.[59] In 1884 this region was divided into governor-generalships, those of Irkutsk and Priamur (Cis-Amur), which consisted of the transbaikal, Amur, and Primorsk *oblasts* (districts) and the island of Sakhalin. The administrative center was moved to Khabarovsk, which was closer to the Far Eastern boundaries.[60] From 1884 on, more attention was paid to the needs of the Russian Far East, particularly since the first governor general of the new administrative division was the talented and energetic General A. N. Korf.[61]

Under the new governor general, legislation in 1884 restricted Russian citizenship for Koreans and curtailed the time Koreans were permitted to reside in Russian territory.[62] Finally, the Russo-Korean treaty of 1888 prohibited all Korean immigration into Russian possessions.[63] More stringent rules were applied to Chinese immigration. In 1886 a joint conference of governors and other high officials met at Khabarovsk. It decided to expel all Chinese immigrants living more than fifty versts from the Chinese frontier. This action undermined the economic and political importance of the Chinese among the native Russian subjects.[64] Customs-free trade had been guaranteed to the Chinese within this fifty-verst strip by the Commercial Regulations of the Treaty of St. Petersburg of February, 1881,[65] and it was necessary to treat in a different manner the Chinese along the Amur River and in the more densely populated southern Ussuri. On May 29, 1888, the Council of State gave formal approval to Korf's suggestion to impose a poll tax on all Chinese subjects on Russian territory. By this measure the Chinese settlers—especially those who established permanent residences on Russian soil as merchants, farmers, tailors, carpenters, and so forth—were subjected to economic discrimination.[66] A large number of Chinese farmers were evacuated, but not without their revolting and destroying several isolated Russian communities near Nikolsk-Ussuriisk.[67]

The internal policy of Russia in the Far East, by adopting the principle of "Russia for the Russians," established one phase of a policy of defense against the Chinese menace. The measure that was expected to answer every need for defense was the building of a railroad to link the Russian Far East with European Russia; this became the subject of much discussion in 1886. Russian officials in the Far East began to mention the need for a trans-Siberian railroad to serve as a defense against China,[68] particularly Manchuria.[69] The levelheaded Baron A. N. Korf and Lieutenant General N. P. Ignatiev, the Governor General of Irkutsk, petitioned the Tsar for the construction of such a railroad. In view of the enormous amount of money needed for such an undertaking and the fact that Russia was then in the midst of one of her periodic financial crises, they suggested two railroad branches: one from Vladivostock to the Ussuri, and another from the upper Amur to the Ob River. These railroads, they stated, would permit all-steam transportation of goods and troops from European Russia to the Far East in one and a half to two months, instead of a corresponding number of years.[70] These popular, official, and governmental requests for a railroad to protect Russia's Far Eastern provinces against a possible or probable Chinese invasion were some of the most important causes of its construction, as may be seen by the statement of the commission which outlined the project of the Trans-Siberian Railway in 1887 that the purpose of the railroad was primarily strategic.[71]

The internal conditions of the Russian possessions in the Far East were one of the principal reasons for building the railroad. It was necessary to obtain the interest and the patronage of the Tsar if the road was to be built. The energetic work and the numerous petitions of Governor General Korf called the attention of Alexander III to the crying needs of the Priamur.[72] In the spring of 1886, Alexander III wrote:[73] "I have read many reports of the governors general of Siberia and I must confess with sorrow and shame that the government has heretofore done practically nothing to satisfy the needs of this rich but neglected region. But it is time, it has long been time." In the same year, Alexander issued the edict which was to launch the project of the Trans-Siberian Railway. He decreed: "Let a railroad be built across Siberia on the shortest way possible."[74] From then on, the con-struction of the railroad was a certainty.

RUSSIAN, BRITISH, AND CHINESE RELATIONS IN REGARD TO KOREA

It has been shown that Russia did not have an active policy toward Korea in the 1880's and yet active "intrigues" in Korea were attributed to Russia. The nature, origin, and intention of these "intrigues" played an important part in creating a distrust of Russia in the Far East and increasing Korea's political entanglements. These in turn led to the formulation of a basic Russian policy in Korea with regard to China.

The immediate background of the political conflicts in Korea ap-peared in the Sino-Japanese crisis of 1884–1885. On December 5 and 6, 1884, a palace revolution occurred in Seoul against the pro-Japanese party in Korea. Japan and China intervened, but before peace was restored the two nations almost came to violence.[75] The Sino-Japanese agreement at Tientsin on April 18, 1885, was merely a postponement of the clash of Chinese and Japanese interests in Korea. Since each of the two countries had pledged not to take any measures of direct inter-vention without notifying the other signatory, the extension of their interests went on by undercover diplomacy and unrestricted economic methods.[76] It became convenient for Korea to accuse Russia of intrigues and to gain the support of China, or to charge China with aggressive intentions and try to get the support of Russia. It also was convenient for China to draw the attention of Korea to alleged Russian designs on her territory in order to gain a more dominant influence there, to involve England in Korean affairs as a counterinfluence against Japan and Russia, or even to seek an agreement with Russia on the grounds that Korea was menaced by another power. Japan was able to use the fear of Russian expansion into Korea to seek an advantage there for herself; and finally, Germany through the person of G. P. Möllendorff, the German-born vice-president of the Korean Ministry of Foreign Affairs, might have been influenced by the Wilhelmstrasse "to lure the Russian bear to Far Eastern pastures."[77]

Indubitably Russia was a factor in affairs of the Far East, though her weakness there was recognized. But she was far more important to the other nations of the Far East as a political "bugbear" to be conjured up when necessary in Korean intrigue. The powers in the Far East promoted the idea of a Russian desire for an ice-free port on the Pacific as the specific aim of the alleged Russian aggression.[78]

The origin of the idea of an ice-free port is lost in obscurity. Some

writers claim that the Russians had desired such a port since the time
of Muraviev-Amurskii, although it is difficult to believe that the idea
was a policy when Russia in the Far East had neither a merchant nor
a naval fleet. Under such circumstances, the incident at Tsushima in
1861[79] cannot be accepted as proof of a Russian search for an ice-free
port. There are no indications that the Russian government was dissatisfied with the port of Vladivostok before 1885. The tremendous
expenditures for its fortification and development in 1877–1879 indicate that it was to serve as the main port of Russia in the Far East.[80]
Certainly, before 1885 Russia had neither the resources nor the naval
strength in the Far East which would require the acquisition of an
ice-free port in Korea.

In 1876, Japanese diplomats sought to gain the coöperation of Korea
and China in the opening of Korea to Japanese trade by warning them
of "the Russian danger," of the Japanese distrust of Russian activities on the Tumen River which indicated an advance to the south,
and of the certainty of the Russian occupation of Tsushima in the im-
pending Russo-Chinese war.[81] In 1878, Li Hung-chang, in order to
preserve the existing relations between Korea and China, initiated the
plan to open Korea to international trade and to fix Korea's status as
a vassal of China by the wording of treaties between the two countries.
To induce Korea to open up her ports and to become a vassal of China,
he warned her that unless she did so "she would be isolated in case of
a Russian attack."[82] Finally, in 1880, both Great Britain and the
United States warned Korea that Russia might seize the northeastern
part of her territory, including Port Lazarev.[83] The foremost person
to warn Korea of this threat was the American Commodore, R. W.
Shufeldt, who was then attempting to open Korea to American trade
by treaty.[84]

The spreading of this allegation of Russian intentions, and particularly of the theory of the ice-free port, was given great impetus in
1882 by the publication of a book on Korea that became extremely
popular and was widely read—*Corea, the Hermit Nation* by William
Elliott Griffis. The author might be considered an authority on Japan,
having resided there as a missionary and an educator for many years,
but he had spent little time in Korea. Yet, perhaps because of his pro-
lific writings, his authority was accepted by many, and the impression
of Russian aggressive intentions toward Korea, particularly in 1861
and 1881 when Russian warships allegedly demanded the opening of
trade relations in eastern Korean ports, acquired general currency.[85]

In 1885 the matter of the ice-free port was brought up once more in the Anglo-Russian negotiations which involved Port Hamilton. On March 30, 1885, local Russian authorities broke their pledge to refrain from further advances on the Afghan frontier until the joint Anglo-Russian commission should finish the delimitation of the new northern border of Afghanistan, and precipitated an acute crisis in Anglo-Russian relations.[86] Roused to a high pitch of excitement, England prepared for war.[87] Among other measures, she chose to follow a traditional strategic plan—to attack Russia with her fleet at some weak point in Russia's far-flung possessions. With Vladivostock as the objective, the British Admiralty decided to occupy two Korean islands at the southern extremity of the peninsula, which enclosed a safe anchorage known as Port Hamilton.[88] The occupation of these islands would advance the British fleet 1,200 miles farther from their nearest base at Hong Kong and would bring it within easy operating distance of Vladivostock,[89] which was only 850 miles from the port.

The initiative for this step came from London, and negotiations were started to obtain approval of this measure by China. In order to justify this "temporary" measure, a rumor was circulated that Russia had intended to seize these islands and that the British fleet was merely acting to forestall the aggressive Russian step.[90] Marquis Tseng, the Chinese Minister to London, fell in with the suggestion and stated that the Chinese preferred to see England rather than Russia occupy Port Hamilton. He "thought it would be agreeable with his government" and said that "China is very distrustful of Russia at the present moment and fears that if Port Hamilton is not taken by England, it will fall into Russian hands."[91]

On April 26, 1885, simultaneously with an announcement to China, Korea, and Japan, Admiral Sir William Dowell occupied Port Hamilton with a British squadron,[92] thereby launching a new phase in the history of the Russian search for an ice-free port. About the same time, apparently fearful of the extension of Chinese and Japanese influence in his kingdom, the King of Korea suggested that the Russian Tsar take Korea as a protectorate. The suggestion was entirely foreign to Russian immediate interests and was refused.[93] In this offer, communicated to the Russian Minister to Korea, or in one immediately following it, G. P. Möllendorff proposed a treaty with Korea by which Russia would guarantee the integrity of Korea and would receive, in return, Port Lazarev on the eastern coast.[94] The proposed treaty was not consummated, but it caused Möllendorff to be considered pro-Russian and brought the idea of the ice-free port once more into prominence.

By May 6, 1885, the Russian government was aware that the British planned to occupy Port Hamilton but not that they had actually done so.[95] On that day, Tseng notified Granville, the British Secretary for Foreign Affairs, that the Russian Minister at Peking had asked China for permission for Russia to occupy some other place, and that he thought the Japanese government might make a similar request.[96] The Russian proposal to occupy a port to the south of Port Hamilton would have split the already weak Russian squadron in the Far East and would have placed the Russians between the British advance base at Port Hamilton and their main base at Hong Kong. As there were only two satisfactory locations for ports on the east coast of Korea—Port Lazarev and Unkovskii Bay[97]—Port Lazarev again gained prominence.

Although the Anglo-Russian war crisis over central Asia had been dispelled by May 2, 1885,[98] the British squadron remained in occupation of Port Hamilton. The Japanese and Korean governments formally protested the occupation,[99] and the British government attempted to end the protests by offering to purchase or lease the islands from Korea.[100] This indication of a more prolonged occupation aroused the opposition of China also.[101]

Möllendorff delivered the first Korean protests against the occupation of Port Hamilton on May 19, while in Japan,[102] and he resumed his intrigue with Russian diplomats in the Far East. During this visit to Japan, he approached the Russian legation in Tokyo and suggested that Russia supply instructors for the Korean army. At the invitation of Möllendorff, Alexis de Speyer, a counselor of the Russian legation, went on an unauthorized mission to Seoul and tried to get the Korean government to adopt the plan. Apparently he acted rather aggressively[103] but failed in his mission, for Möllendorff was no longer influential in the governing circles of the Korean capital[104] and the Korean Foreign Office had already decided to invite American instructors, a choice quite satisfactory from the Russian point of view as expressed in May, 1888.[105]

The unofficial attempts to involve Russia in Korean affairs failed, but rumors and actual proof of such attempts helped to increase the distrust of Russia in the Far East. The situation was aggravated further by the appearance of suggestions in the Russian press for Russia to take retaliatory action against England and occupy a port in eastern Korea, preferably Port Lazarev.[106] There is no indication that the idea was accepted in official circles at that time. The later memorandum on Russian policy, in May, 1888, speaks of the search for an ice-free port in a disparaging tone as "our supposed intentions."[107] There is no doubt, however, that Russia used this proposal to put pressure on China and gain its support to force the withdrawal of the British from Port Hamilton.[108]

In all probability, Russia never even considered a permanent occupation of Port Lazarev. In 1885 the Russians did not even know whether Port Lazarev was or was not an ice-free port.[109] The most probable reason, however, for not seeking to occupy it was its geographical location. The port is a branch bay of the much larger and definitely ice-free bay of Gensan,[110] on which the treaty port of Gensan was situated.[111] The desire to possess Port Lazarev was comparable to "the desire to obtain a house whose yard and gates would remain in another's hands, who would permit us to leave our house under their surveillance."[112] Any serious effort to obtain Gensan was out of the question, for it would be in direct violation of international law and would incur the hostility of every nation in the Far East. Besides it was too great a task for Russian resources and interests in that part of the world.

By the end of 1885 the situation in Korea had reached a curious impasse. Mutual distrust and the cautious pursuit of individual national policies without actually intending to force any issue had placed England, China, Korea, and Russia in an atmosphere of intrigue. The key to the situation was the King of Korea, who secretly played a double game. Yuan Shih-kai, the Chinese supervisor and Li Hung-chang's agent at the Korean court, reported that the King had approached Carl Weber, the Russian Minister to Korea, and had "pleaded for protection from China and asked that five Russian ships be stationed in the port of Yuensan"; while "to Yuan he pleaded for the protection of China and requested that China station soldiers permanently in Korea."[113] In June, 1886, Yuan again reported that the King of Korea was asking for Russian help to achieve his country's complete independence from China with the help of Russian ships. Li Hung-chang's attempt to confirm this statement brought forth a denial from the Russian Foreign Office that any such communication had been received, and an indignant denial by Weber, who stated that if China should "press the matter there would be war."[114]

A solution of the Korean problem was first sought by Li Hung-chang in the attempt to gain international guarantees for the integrity of Korea, as well as to reaffirm the recognition of its vassal status. But the second part of the program was rejected by Japan,[115] and the United States, clinging to a policy of isolation, refused to accept the

responsibility for such guarantees.[116] A more practicable solution was
advanced by Great Britain and enlarged upon by Li Hung-chang. On
December 12, 1885, Salisbury telegraphed Sir Nicolas O'Conor, the
British chargé d'affairs at Peking, to inquire whether the Chinese
government was prepared to guarantee the "nonalienation" of Port
Hamilton if the British withdrew from the islands.[117] A definite offer
was made on April 14, 1886,[118] and this provided Li Hung-chang with
the necessary document with which to convince Russia of the authen-
ticity of the offer.

Li then turned to Russia and invited the Russian chargé d'affaires
at Peking, Lodyzhenskii, to Tientsin for a conference.[119] In three conversations—on September 12, 25, and 29—the policy of Russia toward
Korea was elucidated. Lodyzhenskii stated positively that Russia had
no territorial designs on Port Hamilton or on any other part of Korea.
In the third conversation, Li Hung-chang in turn assured Lodyzhenskii
that China likewise had no territorial ambitions in Korea. The two
statesmen then decided to embody their views in a secret agreement
concerning Korea. On September 31 Lodyzhenskii gave Li Hung-chang
his draft of the proposed agreement, which included three articles:
(1) Russia would accept Chinese suzerainty in Korea, and China would
recognize Korea's status in international relations as affirmed by its
treaties; (2) both nations would respect the territorial integrity of
Korea; and (3) the existing regime in Korea could be changed only by
an agreement between China and Russia.

Li Hung-chang objected to the third article of the agreement as
too binding, and such slight changes as Lodyzhenskii then proposed
Li considered equally unsatisfactory. Lodyzhenskii, on his part, refused to commit Russia to a guarantee of the vassal relationship of
Korea to China, a point insisted upon by the Peking government.[120]
The negotiations ended early in October with a verbal agreement by
the two statesmen that their respective countries would refrain from
making any demands on the territorial integrity of Korea.[121]

The verbal guarantee of October, 1886, gave Li Hung-chang sufficient basis for proceeding with his plan. On November 5, 1886, Sir
John Walsham, the British Minister to China, wrote to the British
Foreign Secretary that "the Chinese government felt themselves in
a position to assure Her Majesty's government, on the faith of the
Russian guarantee that the temporary occupation of Port Hamilton
could be relinquished without risk as regards the future."[122] On November 19 an official guarantee of the "nonalienation" of Port Hamilton
was given to Walsham by the Chinese government. After its accept-

ance, Port Hamilton was evacuated on February 27, 1887.[123] The relinquishment was particularly desirable because the British admirals
in the Far East had for more than a year been in agreement that
"it is not desirable to hold Port Hamilton, and that, until it is made
a first class fortress, it would be a source of weakness in war time to
the cruising power of the squadron in the China command."[124]

A similar argument in regard to the Korean ports was soon expressed
by the Russian Admiralty. In 1886–1887 a special committee of admirals met under the chairmanship of the General-Admiral Grand Duke
Alexander Mikhailovich and decided that Russian occupation of any
Korean port would lead to a weakening of Russia's defensive powers
in the Far East.[125] The possession of Port Hamilton or Port Lazarev
would no doubt be advantageous in the event of cruiser warfare, by
bringing the Russian cruisers closer to the shipping lanes of English
commerce in the Far East;[126] but the advantage to be gained from this
was problematical in the long run, and the strategic significance only
temporary.

The effects of the Port Hamilton incident were widely felt. The
success of China's threat to occupy a Korean port if the British did
not evacuate Port Hamilton established a dangerous precedent. In the
conference of May 8, 1888, the same idea was incorporated by the
Russians into a defensive scheme against the possibility of Chinese
aggression in Korea. The memorandum stated:

As a war with China over Korea appears in all respects an undesirable event,
from our view; in any case, there can either be a naval demonstration in the
Chinese waters or our occupation on the Korean coast of some point, preferably
close to our frontier. In such a case we must declare to the Chinese government
that we shall evacuate the occupied place as soon as the Chinese government, on
its part, will withdraw its troops from Korea.[127]

The threat to occupy an ice-free port then became an instrument of
national policy.

Furthermore, the incident reversed the naval policy of Russia in
the Far East and thus led indirectly to the building of the Trans-
Siberian Railway. The British occupation of Port Hamilton showed
how easily the Russian Far Eastern squadron could be blocked in the
Sea of Japan. In time of war, Russian warships would not be able to
use neutral ports; the Russian squadron would therefore be forced
into a defensive role for lack of coaling stations. Also, the fleet would
be useless against England, since it was not strong enough to defeat
the China squadron of the British; yet the fortifications of Vladivostok
and its garrison secured it against any *coup de main* that might be

attempted by the British fleet. In 1887 Russia adopted a new defensive policy for her Far Eastern possessions. This depended on land
forces rather than naval strength. The Far Eastern squadron was
reduced to a minimum.[128] Vladivostok declined in importance as a naval
base, and by 1888 it was reported to be almost deserted in comparison
with its state during the brief period of Russian naval supremacy
in the Far East in 1879–1880.[129]

As part of the new policy, the vessels of the Volunteer Fleet were
placed under the control of the Ministry of Naval Affairs and were
once more equipped to act as destroyers of commerce in time of war[130]
The Russian government then took direct control of the maintenance
of its communications from European Russia to the Far East. Only
when the Trans-Siberian Railway was in operation across the continent of Asia was the Volunteer Fleet returned to its civil status.[131]

There is a possibility that the rise of Japan was a factor in the
Russian decision to build a trans-Siberian railroad. The available
documents do not indicate this to be so, but the development of Japanese sea power at that time might have influenced Russia to change
her naval policy and to base the defense of the Far East on land forces
supported by a continental railroad.

In 1877, at the time of the Satsuma rebellion, the Japanese navy
was made up of a conglomeration of small vessels[132] fit for little else
except scouting or fighting among themselves, manned by 1,200 sailors
and 260 marines. Within six years from that date the Japanese
navy underwent a remarkable transformation. Modern second-class
warships, designed and built in England, formed the nucleus of an
efficient naval squadron.[133] Construction docks at home supplemented
the squadron with lighter craft, and work was hurried to complete
repair docks and establish naval bases in the Inland Sea of Japan.[134]

The six years from 1883 to 1889 witnessed an even more remarkable advance of naval power in Japan. A program of shipbuilding
was undertaken in Japan in 1883. It projected the construction of
more than twenty warships, including six large ones.[135] The ability
to fulfill the program in six years and to plan an even further increase of naval strength placed Japan well on the way to becoming
the leading naval power in the Far East. No other nation had shipyards in the Far East which could build even a second-class warship.

By the late 1880's, therefore, the Japanese navy had gained the
necessary numerical and technical strength to make the Russian naval
position in the Sea of Japan a defensive one. The Japanese fleet could
cut off Russian naval communications to the Far East at Tsushima

Strait.[136] The current theory of the importance of the torpedo boat gave added emphasis to this possibility. In the years following 1885 a school of naval strategists claimed that the era of the supremacy of heavy battleships was over. The small, swift torpedo boat was considered more than a match for the heavier ships, especially in such restricted areas as channels and coastal waters.[137] The Japanese seem to have adopted this theory, at least in part, for they bought or constructed a large number of such vessels.[138] It was not until the invention and widespread adoption of the torpedo-boat destroyer that the theory was weakened.[139] In any event, the proximity of Japan to Russian Far Eastern possessions and her actual, possible, or supposed supremacy in the Sea of Japan cannot be discounted as a factor which brought about the building of the Trans-Siberian Railway.

By 1889 the "era of good feeling" between Russia and Japan was at an end, and Japanese public opinion showed a distrust of Russia.[140] The two nations had as yet had no conflicts. The program of coöperation with Japan, outlined in the Memorandum of May 8, 1888, was put into operation. When a distorted report of an interview with Li Hung-chang alarmed D. E. Shevich, the Russian Minister to Japan, by its implied threats to the status of Korea, Shevich brought the news to Count Okuma Shigenobu. Shevich pointed out that any attempt by China to make a "Hong Kong or Gibraltar" out of Fusan, on the southern tip of Korea, would be a danger to Russia. Okuma reassured the Russian Minister that Japan was eager to maintain the status quo in Korea, and that he did not believe the report true, because China was bound by the Tientsin Convention to notify Japan of any such action. Moreover, Japan would have the right to take similar action toward Korea, and this would neutralize the advantages obtained by the Chinese. Count Okuma apparently promised to keep an eye on all actions of the Chinese government in Korea and to notify Russia, "if as according to the agreement, Japan should be notified."[141] Such relations with Japan were eminently satisfactory from the Russian point of view. They can be characterized by the words of Alexander III, who commented on the above dispatch: "this is very interesting, and not at all bad for us."[142]

Besides being needed for countering the menace of Chinese expansion into northern Manchuria, the railroad would be needed for transportation of men and supplies in the event of a Russo-Chinese conflict over Korea. In view of the continued Anglo-Russian tension, the hostility of England was to be expected should this contingency occur. Russia therefore could not depend primarily on her Far Eastern squadron for the defense of her Far Eastern possessions. A trans-Siberian railroad would to some extent answer the defensive requirements of Russia's Far East—it would bring economic benefits and also settlers who would build up the internal strength of the territory.

Until the railroad was built, Russia was forced to adopt a "cautious policy" toward the events in Korea and remain passively opposed to any attempts by China to change the status of Korea "as long as Russia's honor can be preserved."[143] The vague Russian goals in the territories of the Far East made the alleged plans of aggression in Korea, and especially the proposal for an ice-free port on the coast of Korea, unofficial and unrealizable aspirations. An early comment on this subject, possibly written by a high Russian official with a knowledge of contemporary documents, still remains valid:

> For a long time Russia was suspected of having designs on a Korean port, but these fears were exaggerated and could only refer to a remote contingency. Russia has been uniformly cautious, and has only absorbed countries neglected by owners or neighbors. Besides her maritime requirements always have been moderate. Vladivostock sufficed as a naval station in the Pacific, and it remained as the most southern part of Asiatic Russia for over thirty years.[144]

THE SHIFT OF RUSSIAN INTEREST FROM THE NEAR EAST TO THE FAR EAST

The shift of Russian interest from the Near East and central Asia to the Far East was gradual and was punctuated by hesitations and digressions. There is no published document that decreed or announced the change, or even advised it. The pronouncement of Alexander III in 1886 that "it has long been time" to pay attention to the needs of the Far Eastern territories stands as one of the first of a few milestones in the shift that occurred. But within the period 1886–1891 the shift was definitely accomplished, for by the latter date Russia had irrevocably committed herself to the building of the trans-Siberian railroad, and interests in the Near East and central Asia were relegated to a secondary position—at least for the time being.

In 1885 Russia was actively interested in affairs in Egypt, Turkey, Bulgaria, and central Asia; these were considered far more important than the growing complications in the Far East. This preference cannot be attributed to any accidental neglect of the Far East by the Foreign Office. Toward the end of the 1880's the Asiatic Department of the Foreign Office transacted most of the business involving the Balkans, Egypt, central Asia, the Far East, and even America, while the Chancellery specialized in direct relations with central and western European countries.[145] The neglect of the Far East was therefore neither a result of internal rivalry within the governing circles of Russia nor an administrative relegation of one area to a less influential department.

Instead, the neglect was in part due to practical considerations of foreign policy. In spite of the diplomatic check received by Russia at the Congress of Berlin, she still had opportunities to consolidate her influence in Bulgaria; whereas in central Asia her recent large territorial acquisitions demanded immediate consolidation by military and economic means, such as strategic railways. M. D. Skobelev's campaign of 1880–1881 in central Asia was immediately followed by the construction of the trans-Caspian railroad.[146] Furthermore, the paramount influence of Russia in most parts of Persia began to be challenged by English diplomacy in 1880, after the plans of an Anglo-Afghan bloc to resist Russia broke down during the second Afghan war, 1878–1879.[147]

The details of Anglo-Russian rivalry in central Asia are not directly pertinent to the history of the shift of Russian interest. It is sufficient to state that the rivalry took the form of bitter dispute, and the Russian Minister to Teheran, I. A. Zinoviev, won notable triumphs for his country in the struggle and was therefore made the head of the Asiatic Department.[148] In central Asia, after the passing of the acute war crisis in May, 1885, certain elements of friction remained. Seemingly irreconcilable differences of opinion in regard to the Russo-Afghan frontier threatened at various times to break down the negotiations and renew Anglo-Russian rivalry.[149] However, on July 22, 1887, the differences were composed, and a final protocol was signed at St. Petersburg which ended further misunderstandings.[150] Although boundary commissions continued their work for four more years, rectifying the frontier, by 1887 central Asian affairs were no longer matters of importance in Russian foreign policy.

In the Near East, Russian interests centered mainly on Bulgaria. Russian intrigues were successful in removing Prince Alexander of Battenberg from the Bulgarian throne in 1886, but they were unable to insure the election of a pro-Russian king of Bulgaria, mainly because Russia's erstwhile political allies in Europe—Germany and Austria—had made different alignments.[151] In February and March, 1887, England, Italy, and Austria joined in a Mediterranean pact, which, supplementary to the pact of December 12, announced their adherence to a policy of status quo in the Mediterranean in general, and particularly in the Balkans.[152] On June 18, 1887, the Reinsurance Treaty between Germany and Russia was signed, but during the negotiations Bismarck let Russia know of the secret Austro-German Alliance of 1879, which was still in effect. There was no doubt from then on that the Three Emperors' Alliance was at an end.[153]

The defeat of Russia in the Balkans became assured. On July 7, 1887, the Bulgarian Assembly elected Prince Ferdinand of Saxe-Coburg, a nominee of Austro-Hungarian interests, as king of Bulgaria. Russia went on with her own plans for a regency council in Bulgaria, which she hoped to control, although she was aware of the Anglo-Austrian-Italian coöperation and that no help could be expected from Germany.[154] Finally, in December, 1887, Russia gave up the unequal struggle. On December 17, 1887, N. K. de Giers, the Russian Minister of Foreign Affairs, speaking about Russian policy in Bulgaria, said to the British Ambassador: "We wash our hands of the whole concern."[155] In January, 1888, assurances were sent to all European courts that the status quo in Bulgaria was acceptable to Russia.[156]

By the end of 1887, therefore, the diplomatic situation in the Near East and central Asia was favorable for the shift of Russian interest to the Far East. Furthermore, by that time the critical events and the knowledge of the precarious Russian position in the Far East were drawing attention there. Other factors helped to contribute to this shift. The French reverses in the Tonkin war of 1884–1885, which had had a menacing result for Russian possessions in the Far East, led to the fall of the ministry of Jules Ferry and a reversal of certain French financial policies. This reversal "forced the French capitalists to seek less exotic markets."[157] French capital sought a profitable return on Russian ventures—foundries, mines, and even government bonds. The inflow of capital enabled Russia to recover rapidly from the financial crisis which had been chronic from the early 1860's to 1886. Bankers' commissions dropped from 5 per cent in 1884 to 2 per cent in 1887, with the result that I. A. Vyshnegradskii, the Russian Minister of Finance, was able to obtain the first large French loan—500,000,000 gold francs—in that year.[158] Financial means for the building of the trans-Siberian railroad were therefore also ready.

The industrial development in connection with the inflow of foreign capital and the resultant liberation of internal resources created an industrial and financial boom. In 1881 the government ceased granting railroad concessions to private companies and adopted a policy of building new lines and purchasing the existing private lines.[159] This policy liberated more private capital, which turned to the purchase of railroad bonds and helped to finance the construction of a trans-Siberian railroad by the state. The policy also freed private entrepreneurs for service in the state railroads. Toward the end of the 1880's numerous suggestions were put forward for the construction of a railroad across Siberia, continental in scale yet of a limited nature.[160]

Thus, by 1887, political and economic forces in the west favored a shift of Russian interests to the Far East, with the railroad as the first agency, while strategic and economic considerations in the East drew Russian interests toward the Pacific. On June 18, 1887, a conference of high officials[161] met at St. Petersburg to discuss the necessity of a trans-Siberian railroad. The conference unanimously acknowledged

that in the interest of state and especially in the interest of strategic considerations the more rapid communications between European Russia and the distant East become with the years more and more pressing, in spite of the fact that even in the future, due to the limited amount of Siberian freights, a profit can come only after some time.[162]

On the following day the Tsar approved the decisions of the committee and ordered the Minister of Communications to proceed with the survey for a trans-Siberian railroad.[163]

The actual construction was delayed from year to year. In 1888 I. A. Zinoviev turned Russian interests to the scene of his former triumphs in Persia and "delayed all sorts of affairs" not relevant to his own projects.[164] For two years the fate of the trans-Siberian project hung in the balance while plans for railroad penetration of Persia,[165] and even a railroad across Persia to the Persian Gulf, were seriously discussed.[166] Fortunately for the project of the trans-Siberian railroad, Russian commercial interests had natural advantages of easy communication with Persia and were thus able to compete favorably with England. Zinoviev eventually opposed the plans for a trans-Siberian railroad which would provide an easier access for British goods to central and northern Persia.[167] On November 8, 1890, an agreement was signed between the Shah of Persia and the Russian government whereby the Shah pledged that he would permit no railroads to be built in his country without Russia's approval.[168] For ten years the control of this "veto" of railroad construction in Persia made it impossible for the English to steal a march on the Russians in Persia while Russia was busily engaged in the construction of the Trans-Siberian railway.

On February 27 and March 5, 1891, the Council of Ministers arranged for the means and methods of constructing that railroad. The construction was to begin from the eastern and western terminals at the same time.[169] On March 31, 1891, the Tsarevich, Nicholas, on a tour of the Far East, took part in the ceremony of inaugurating the construction of the trans-Siberian railway[170] by personally emptying the first wheelbarrow full of ballast for the embankment of its eastern terminal—Vladivostok, "Ruler of the East."

III

THE RISE OF AGGRESSIVE IDEOLOGIES AND THE RUSSIAN FAR EASTERN POLICY DURING THE SINO-JAPANESE WAR

THE NINETEENTH century witnessed a growing fermentation of imperialistic views in Russia influenced by episodes of expansion both at home and abroad. The annexation of Georgia by Russia in 1801 strengthened the concept that a sort of "manifest destiny" dictated that the Caucasian territories separating Georgia from Russia also be incorporated into the Empire. The English conquest of Sind and subsequent temporary occupation of Afghanistan aroused at least a keen interest if not counteraction by the Russians in the trans-Caspian regions. In the Near East, international rivalries and claims on the Turkish Empire always kept Russian interests alive, especially in the Balkans.

New Men and Motives in Far Eastern Affairs

Tsars, responsible statesmen, and influential generals developed ideas of Russian economic and strategic needs; but it was the Slavophiles of the nineteenth century, representing a wide stratum of cultured society, who presented and propagated ideas of imperialistic expansion in the guise of a "holy mission." The Slavophiles varied in the scope and method of their exposition; among them were historians (K. Bestuzhev-Riumin, N. N. Strakhov), writers (A. S. Khomiakov, I. S. Aksakov), and even poets (A. V. Grigoriev). Consequently their ideas reached and influenced readers of various kinds. In general, the Slavophiles stressed the religious, racial, and cultural affinity between the Balkan peoples and the Russians, drawing upon ample historical evidence to show that the Balkan peoples would like to draw closer to Russia.[1]

After the partial liberation of the Balkan Slavs (of Serbia and Bulgaria), by the Russo-Turkish War of 1877–1878, and particularly after the anti-Russian trend of events in Bulgaria in 1886–1888, the Slavophile movement began to lay less emphasis upon Pan-Slavism. A new school of thought arose in the 1880's which stressed the idea that Russian culture was in direct contrast to the culture of Europe and must therefore develop along its own social and political lines.[2] From that position it was but one more step to claim that Russia, with a culture midway between the cultures of Europe and that of the Orient, had a

[1] For notes to chap. iii see pp. 264–273.

"historical mission" to spread western culture to the Orient. The extremists of this school of "Easterners" (*Vostochniki*) considered Russian culture more closely affiliated with that of the Orient than with that of Europe and felt that it was Russia's "historical mission" to merge with the Orient by incorporating it into the Russian Empire.[3]

Precedent and past historical experience helped to promote this imperialistic idea. Korea had sought Russian protection and even the establishment of a Russian protectorate in the 1880's. In the same period, General M. N. Prjevalskii, the most noted and respected Russian explorer of territories adjacent to Russia's Asiatic frontiers, popularized the concept that the inhabitants of Mongolia and Sinkiang were eager to become Russian subjects. In 1887 he wrote:

The nomad Mongols, the Dungans, that is, the Mussulman Chinese, and the inhabitants of Eastern [Chinese] Turkestan, especially the latter, are all more or less possessed with the idea of becoming subjects of the White Tsar, whose name, equally with that of the Dalai Lama, appears in the eyes of the Asiatic masses as surrounded with a halo of mystic might. These poor Asiatics look to the advance of the Russian power with the firm conviction that its advent is synonymous with the commencement of a happier era, a life of greater security for themselves.[4]

Logically and honestly, the learned explorer took cognizance of the fact that this attitude in Chinese Turkestan was due to the maladministration of the Chinese officials and the severity of their recent reconquest of Sinkiang in contrast to the relatively just rule of the Russians in Russian Turkestan, which had been annexed more than twenty years before.[5] Furthermore, he admitted that the Mongols, in making the choice of allegiance, would gravitate to Russia only because that choice would be "the lesser of two evils."[6] Nevertheless, Prjevalskii's views offered sound argument for an aggressive policy in Asia.

Legal support for a policy of aggression was supplied in the same period by Professor F. F. Martens, the foremost Russian authority on international law and an adviser to the Foreign Office. In two pamphlets, *Russia and China* and *Russia and England in Central Asia*, he attempted to justify Russian conquests in central Asia and to prepare a similar justification for an aggressive policy toward China by advocating the principle that "international rights cannot be taken into account when dealing with semibarbarous peoples."[7]

The concept of Russia as a cultural missionary (*Kulturträger*) in the Orient was clearly expressed by V. P. Vasil'ev, Russia's foremost and world-renowned Sinologue, in 1883 in a public lecture at the University of St. Petersburg. After exultingly approving Russian conquests in the Caucasus and the trans-Caspian region, Vasil'ev emphasized that in contrast to Europeans, Russians advanced in the East as "liberators" of peoples oppressed by "the tyranny of internecine strife and impotency"; and he concluded: "Would it not be rather a crime before humanity were we to renounce the sacred duties designated to us and refuse to aid the 'oppressed'?"[8]

The ideology of Russian expansion toward the East thus had many interpretations. A. Brückner, one of Russia's leading historians, defended a view that the uninterrupted advance of Russia in Asia was a benefit to world civilization,[9] and Vladimir Solov'ev, Russia's leading philosopher, in a strangely chauvinistic article written in 1890, maintained that Russia must advance in Asia in order to defend Europe against the "yellow power," and that inferior races must either submit to the superior ones or "disappear."[10] The gradations of the imperialistic concept as propounded by the Vostochniki and their followers are many, and their tenets are sometimes bewildering. Because of their popularity and ubiquity in Russian cultural and official circles, the Vostochniki represented a powerful ideological support of renewed Russian interest in the Far East.[11]

Probably the most influential early exponent of Russian expansion in Asia was Prince Esper Esperevich Ukhtomskii.[12] His noble descent and enormous wealth assured him a prominent position in high society. As a publisher and editor of the St. Petersburg *News* (*Peterburzhskie Vedomosti*) Ukhtomskii maintained a policy of printing liberal and at times radical views in curious juxtaposition with his own chauvinistic ideas.[13] In 1889 he traveled in Russian central Asia as a member of the Bureau of Foreign Concessions and returned aghast at the Russians' lack of interest in their Asiatic possessions and their opportunities.[14] He thereupon began to advocate Russian imperialism in the East.

In 1890–1891 Prince Ukhtomskii accompanied Tsarevich Nicholas on a voyage to the Far East in the capacity of tutor and lecturer on peoples and territories visited by the future monarch.[15] On his return he wrote an account of that voyage which was published in de luxe editions in England, France, Germany, and Russia,[16] possibly to propagandize the awakening of Russian interest in the Orient. Through the medium of his newspaper, pamphlets, and articles in European periodicals,[17] Ukhtomskii propagated the already familiar theme that because of their kinship with the Orient the Russians would succeed in subjugating the East "by the secret powers of emotional sympathy."[18] He expressed the quintessence of the ideology of the Vostochniki thus:

Asia—we have always belonged to it. We have lived its life and felt its interests. Through us the Orient has gradually arrived at consciousness of itself, at a superior

life. . . . We have nothing to conquer. All these peoples of various races feel themselves drawn to us, and are ours, by blood, by tradition, and by ideas. We simply
approach them more closely. This great and mysterious Orient is ready to become
ours.[19]

In June, 1904, when Russia was already suffering initial defeats at
the hands of Japan, proving the inadequacy of her preparations for a
grandiose imperialistic role in the Far East, Ukhtomskii broke out in
expressions of blatant and unabashed chauvinism. He forecast that
Russia would defeat Japan and compensate herself for the expenses
of the war by taking a large section of China. This would lead to a
Russo-Chinese war in which the Chinese would be conquered. The
English would then intervene, and Russia would have to drive the
English out of India.[20]

Ukhtomskii had many critics who lampooned him with derisive re-
marks. He was labeled a "superpatriot" and a "faddist," and contemporary critics sarcastically attacked his "yellow Russia" (*zheltoros-
siia*).[21] But despite his weakness for collecting Buddhist statues, his
vague and bewildering expositions, and his occasional glaring errors
in predictions, he was a practical statesman. He had traveled in and
read widely about the Orient. He remained a close friend of Nicholas II
and became an assistant to S. Iu. Witte, whom he greatly admired.[22]
He was a known proponent of the Russo-Chinese alliance which eventually materialized. In 1896 and again in 1900 he was entrusted with
special secret missions to the Far East. In 1896 he became the first
chairman of the Russo-Chinese Bank and a director of the Chinese
Eastern Railway, agencies which were then the spearheads of a practical Russian policy of expansion in the Far East.[23]

Until the beginning of the construction of the Trans-Siberian Railway, the Vostochniki were prominent only as theoreticians. The decision
to construct the railroad opened an enormous range of real opportunities to the Vostochniki, who found an influential and unexpected protagonist in S. Iu. Witte, the able Russian Minister of Finance.

Witte rose from humble origins to a position of enormous power.
He started as a clerk on the Odessa railroad at a salary of forty-five
rubles a month and eventually was appointed to posts in which he
disposed of almost half of the budget of the Russian government.[24] He
was a self-made man, struggling to the top by dint of his ambition,
perseverence, keenness, and ability to make and utilize friends. Good
fortune also played some part in his rise to power. He enjoyed the
patronage of Alexander III, although this came to him more as recognition of his services than as a mark of favoritism.[25] Witte had had a

limited education and was uncultured, but his keen interest in economic and cultural questions rapidly matured him and gained for him the friendship and admiration of Russia's leading businessmen and many statesmen.[26] The noted American engineer and financial expert John Hays Hammond, whose personal dealings with many prominent men in all parts of the world qualified him to make comparisons, ranked Witte with Cecil Rhodes as a "constructive business genius, empire builder, and statesman."[27] However, to many, particularly in court circles, Witte was a parvenu, a man of no background, who had dangerous "socialist" tendencies and disagreeable Jewish friends and relations.[28]

The tremendous influence exercised by Witte in Russian affairs was inherent partly in the office of Minister of Finance. I. A. Vyshnegradskii, his predecessor in the Ministry, had established the practice of estimating the revenue from various sources by the amount received in the preceding fiscal year.[29] The Russian Ministry of Finance could show a consistently large surplus of revenue over expenditures,[30] making no allowance for the increase of revenue concomitant with the general recovery of the nation after the famine of 1891, the impetus to heavy industry produced by the large railroad construction programs, and the influx of capital and credit. This surplus was left to the discretion of the Minister of Finance, who through the operations of the State Bank could invest large sums in loans, subsidies, or any other transaction.[31] Therefore, constitutionally, the Russian Minister of Finance possessed exceptional powers. Moreover, he was necessarily consulted on all military and political matters involving large financial expenditures.[32] He was also the supreme commander of a small army of frontier guards and a small fleet of coast guards for the protection of customs barriers. Witte took particular pleasure in being the honorary "chief" of his "army" and enjoyed wearing the uniform of a general.[33]

As Minister of Finance from 1892 to 1903 Witte greatly expanded the activities of his office, and at the end of that period the Ministry of Finance actually embraced several ministries. It controlled trade and commerce, communications by land and by sea, labor, industrial and agrarian credits, and, to some extent, education. The budget of the Ministry of Finance rose in that time from 122,000,000 rubles a year to 366,000,000 rubles, and the joint budget of the Ministry of Finance and the Ministry of Communications rose from 187,000,000 rubles to 822,000,000—which represented a rise from 20 per cent to 43 per cent of the total national budget.[34] Although the Comptroller General of the Empire accused Witte in 1903 of spending more than

100,000,000 rubles illegally without proper accounts, the Ministry of Finance at that time still had more than 380,000,000 rubles as unassigned funds to be used at its discretion.[35] This financial arrangement gave Witte a peculiarly strong position in the affairs of state and an unusual degree of financial independence for the support of his own policies and projects.

For a time Witte's personal influence paralleled the rise of his official influence. Nicholas II, in the first years of his reign, looked upon Witte as his "prime minister," accepting his father's advice to keep the old and trusted ministers.[36] Witte's opinion was the determining factor in the appointment of several ministers.[37] By utilizing his constitutional prerogatives and assisting enterprises by subsidies from the State Bank, Witte enlarged his circle of friends and subservient followers both in Russia and abroad.[38] Within a short time after his appointment as acting minister of finance, Witte was recognized in the international press as the "first statesman of Russia."

Witte's political and economic ideas for the promotion of the financial and industrial welfare of Russia followed a simple pattern. Possibly it was derived from the German national economist Friedrich List, whose work Witte edited in the 1880's and used in his lectures on national economy in 1900–1902.[39] The state, Witte believed, should take an active part in the promotion of those industries which are the bases of the economic strength of the country. By subsidizing enterprises, the state would attract foreign capital for other industrial enterprises, and their apparent financial success would in turn give the state a good opportunity to obtain foreign loans with which to finance the subsidies. The multifarious activities of the state in the national economic life would permit it to promote certain national economic interests deemed backward in comparison with those of Europe, and to derive great profit for itself by participating in some of the more lucrative enterprises.[40]

In his memoirs and public utterances, Witte did not even hint at the probability that unless the state enterprises became enormously successful there would be a day of reckoning, or that the "fictional" surplus of the budget was more than liquidated by the increase of national indebtedness.[41] He also seems to have ignored the thought that his stress on industrialization would cause a further impoverishment of the peasant and drag down the economy of the state.[42] By his wholehearted support of state railroad construction in Russia, Witte did bring about a rejuvenation of heavy industry which for almost a decade lent an aura of prosperity to Russian industry as a whole and gave him and his adherents grounds for boasting of their achievements.[43]

Witte showed no interest in the Far East before 1892.[44] In his early years he was a Slavophile; later he became a "Westerner" in that he exhibited a keen desire to see Russia catch up with the industrial progress of western Europe.[45] However, after his appointment to the position of acting minister of communications (February 27, 1892) and acting minister of finance (September 11, 1892)[46] his thoughts turned to the Far East and the benefits that could be derived by Russia from the national and international significance of the trans-Siberian railroad. At the time, this was an enormous undertaking for a backward industrial state. It fitted in with Witte's plan to encourage heavy industries. It promised to create an outlet for the grain of western Siberia and in many other ways strengthen the economic position of Russia.

But Witte saw far greater implications in the building of the railroad. In a report of November 18, 1892, on "Measures for the Construction of the Great Siberian Railroad" he described the basis for Russo-Chinese economic unity. He argued that the production of tea in India and Assam had undermined the Chinese tea trade, which in time would collapse in the face of this new competition. With the completion of the trans-Siberian railroad, rapid transit of Chinese tea to Europe would give China a new opportunity to export this product and at the same time permit Russia to compete with England in China in the sale of cotton, wool, and metal goods.[47] The railroad would also permit Russia to maintain a fleet in the Far East which "could be considerably strengthened, and which in case of political complications in Europe or in the Asiatic East would acquire an especially important significance in dominating all commercial movements in the waters of the Pacific."[48]

It has been suggested that Witte sponsored Russian interests in the Far East to avoid complications in the West and to secure a period of peace for Russia.[49] But it seems more likely that Witte, often called an "opportunist," first saw in the construction of the trans-Siberian railroad a possible means of achieving his economic policies. In the period 1892–1903 he also continued to show interest in railroad developments in central Asia, in plans to open an ice-free port at Murmansk with a railroad connection with St. Petersburg, in the building of the naval port at Libau, in the creation of a large navy, and in other projects in line with the promotion of Russian heavy industry.[50] Witte's interest in the Far East grew from relatively modest beginnings and even at its height fell far short of the plan of a "Russo-Chinese Empire" attributed to him by Alexander Ular, the contemporary critical anti-Russian journalist.[51]

Witte's own indecision concerning the proper course to follow in the Far East was revealed in his relations with the notorious and in many ways fantastic plan of Petr Alexandrovich Badmaev.[52] This Buriat (whose name was originally Zhamsaran Badmaev) came to St. Petersburg to work in his brother's Tibetan pharmacy, which had been established in 1853.[53] Sometime during a varied career as a student in the Department of Oriental Languages of St. Petersburg University, a translator of ancient Tibetan medical texts, a lecturer on Mongolia at the St. Petersburg University, and since 1875 an employee of the Asiatic Department of the Ministry of Foreign Affairs, Badmaev came in contact with high society.[54] He made the acquaintance of Prince Ukhtomskii, who introduced him to Witte. When Badmaev was converted to the Greek Orthodox faith he changed his name to Petr Alexandrovich, taking his patronymic from his godfather, Alexander III.[55]

In February, 1893, Badmaev submitted a memorandum to Witte in which he analyzed Russia's historic mission in the Far East,[56] with a request that it be transmitted to Alexander III. Badmaev suggested that, in addition to the trans-Siberian railroad, Russia should also construct a railroad to Lanchow-fu, the capital of the Chinese province of Kansu, and that there, in the "backyard" of China, Russia should secretly promote a general rebellion of Tibetans, Mongolians, and Mohammedan Chinese against the Manchu dynasty. Succeeding in their rebellion, Badmaev predicted, the leaders would ask the Russian Tsar to take them under his protection, and a large group of Asiatic peoples would be incorporated into the Russian Empire without bloodshed. To accomplish this plan, Badmaev urged that a trading company be established among the Russian Buriats who had commercial and religious connections with Mongolia and Tibet. He would employ several thousand Buriats for the purpose of propagating his idea under the cloak of genuine commercial enterprise and at the same time arming the dissident population of Mongolia and Kansu.[57]

A year before this, Witte had rejected a plan for the construction of a railroad through northeastern Mongolia and Manchuria to Vladivostok.[58] But he supported Badmaev's plan, and with an accompanying memorandum submitted it to Alexander III. According to Witte, Badmaev's plan "expressed serious views" and illustrated "a new point of view in practical matters of policy." Pointing out to the Tsar that the trans-Siberian railroad would have a tremendous importance in Russian relations with the Far East as well as with Europe, Witte warned that "European governments will attempt to arouse the aggressive intentions of China against us, to seize the weakly defended eastern sector of the trans-Siberian railroad with all the territory adjacent to it, including the Primorsk region with Vladivostok." He argued, however, that if the Badmaev plan resulted in the success forecast for it, "Russia from the shores of the Pacific Ocean and the peaks of the Himalayas would dominate not only Asiatic but also European affairs."[59]

Witte offered to put Badmaev's plan into action immediately and promised to find the necessary funds for it "without any official connection."[60] Alexander III doubted that such a plan would be successful, commenting that it was "so novel, so unusual, and fantastic."[61] But Badmaev persevered. He argued that with a 2,000,000-ruble loan at 4 per cent, and with a ten-year amortization, he could start enterprises which would in a short time permit him to finance the political features of his plan by the tremendous profits earned by his trading and cattle-dealing company.[62] Witte also expressed doubts about the success and ethics of the plan in August, 1893, but Badmaev finally gained the necessary Imperial approval.[63] Badmaev received credit for 2,000,000 rubles in November, 1893, and in 1896 he received an additional smaller subsidy.[64] He appeared in Peking in 1895 and 1897 with a suite of Mongolian attendants, as if on some undisclosed mission. However, events in the Far East had turned Russian policy into a far more practical course, and lacking further support, Badmaev and his plan were eliminated from Russian Far Eastern affairs.[65] P. A. Badmaev and Company in 1900 sold their headquarters near Chita to the Governor General of the Priamur *oblast,* to be used as a cattle quarantine station. This ended even the economic function of the project.[66]

To promote the progress of the trans-Siberian railroad Witte chose a powerful ally. In 1893, by a master stroke which greatly influenced his relations with the next ruler, Nicholas II, Witte persuaded Alexander III to appoint the Tsarevich president of the Control Committee of the Trans-Siberian Railway. The Tsar argued that the Tsarevich was too young and immature for such a post.[67] However, the Tsarevich became the president of a committee created by Witte for the express purpose of "avoiding all barbed wires in relations with other ministers"[68] in Witte's main enterprise, on which Witte was the authority and in which he was the "leading spirit."[69] Furthermore, Nicholas when he became Tsar retained the presidency, in accordance with his own wish,[70] and became directly affiliated with the Russian railroad penetration of Manchuria.

The character of Nicholas II and his role in determining the course of Russian policy is still obscure. Most of his private letters and annotations of official papers were too brief to reveal clearly his ideas on the affairs of state.[71] Writers who have analyzed his character, with an attempt to be scrupulously fair, generally have portrayed him as being continually torn between an urge to accept the views of his advisers and a desire to assert his own views.[72] This analysis may explain his unpredictable behavior in violation of Russia's international commitments, such as his sudden expression of friendship toward the German Emperor at the meeting at Björkö in 1905 and his unexplained, sporadic personal interference in Russian Far Eastern affairs.

Nicholas II lacked consistent determination and accepted the guidance of such dubious advisers as K. P. Pobedonostsev, E. E. Ukhtomskii, and his favorite uncle, the reactionary Grand Duke Sergei Alexandrovich,[73] as well as of the more modern and practical Witte. Maturing under the influence of a sycophantic court, and urged toward the assertion of his own will in the affairs of state, the young Tsar grew impatient with the intelligent opposition which hindered his will. Nicholas II not only had a mind of his own but could claim to be an authority on the Far East by reason of his personal observations and impressions during the voyage of 1890–1891. It can hardly be asserted that the saber blow he received in an attempt on his life by a Japanese fanatic while in Japan passed without impression.[74] Though the Russian government was satisfied with official apologies and the expressions of regret from the Japanese Imperial family for the unforeseen occurrence, the visit of the Tsarevich to Japan was hastily and impolitely concluded,[75] and in later years Nicholas II carried a visible scar and suffered severe headaches as mementoes of the occasion.[76]

The aggressive views of the early Vostochniki matured into a policy which received ministerial and imperial sanction under Nicholas II, without which it could not have attained fruition. Imperialism had become popular, and its aims seemed possible of attainment. An able observer of Russian affairs with understandable exaggeration and in a slightly humorous vein wrote in 1896: "There is not a graduate of the Corps de Pages, an Officer of the Guards, nor an employee of the Foreign Ministry, it is asserted, who is not firmly convinced that all Asia, including, of course, India, is part of Russia's birthright, and that the policy of the Tsardom should be shaped in accordance with these great expectations."[77]

THE EVOLUTION OF RUSSIAN POLICY DURING THE SINO-JAPANESE WAR

In the opening years of the decade 1890–1900 Russia was not in a position to adopt aggressive policies. The refusal of Germany to renew the Reinsurance Treaty in 1890 placed Russia in precarious isolation. The Franco-Russian Alliance, eventually concluded on January 4, 1894, was only gradually and laboriously evolved.[78] Until then, Russia of necessity moved cautiously in international affairs. Minor crises, such as the Anglo-Russian dispute over The Pamirs in 1892, were carefully averted.[79] Even in the matter of the Armenian massacres on the border of the Russian Empire, the aging and ailing Russian Minister of Foreign Affairs, N. K. de Giers, hesitated to intervene even by diplomacy for fear that England would interpret such an intervention as exertion of pressure by Russia.[80] In the Near East, therefore, Russia preferred to act in a concert of power[81] and to maintain the status quo.[82]

A cautious policy was even more imperative in the Far East, where Russia was handicapped both by her isolation in Europe and by the strategical weakness of her eastern possessions. Furthermore, Russian commercial interests in the Far East were lagging behind those of other European powers, and even the Russian Greek Orthodox Church was carrying on no missionary work in China. Consequently, in 1891 when an outbreak against foreigners occurred in China, aimed at missionaries and European commercial establishments in the interior, the appeal of France for joint action in September of that year did not even include Russia.[83] However, even on this occasion, which was of little concern to Russia, the Russian Minister to China acted in accord with other European ministers in signing the Protocol of September 9, 1891, which informed their governments of the situation in China and suggested remedial measures.[84]

On November 21, 1891, the French Minister of Foreign Affairs, Alexandre Ribot, met Giers in Paris and in a conversation elicited Russia's reaction to the protocol. Giers stated that Russia's policy toward China must be "prudent." He said that the missionaries should be persuaded to remain near the coast and that China should be informed that all Europe was in accord on the Chinese crisis; Giers felt, however, that joint action would be difficult to obtain.[85]

The French Minister of Foreign Affairs again appealed for joint action, on December 2, this time to Russia also.[86] In view of the gradual formation of the Franco-Russian Alliance, Giers found it difficult to refuse the French appeal. He played for time, stating that he had just returned to St. Petersburg and had had no time to study the matter.[87]

Germany and other nations refused to take action, on the grounds that China was strong enough to quell the disorders[88]—which China soon did. This dissolved the crisis and removed Giers from an embarrassing position.

Russia was satisfied with her inactive status in the Far East and continued to retain it. The 1891 project for the construction of the trans-Siberian railroad envisaged its completion in twelve years.[89] This meant that until 1903 Russia could not expect a great change in her position in the Far East. The secret Badmaev plan, which had been accepted, was intended to be a farsighted and gradual program. There was no need to hurry events.

But in June, 1894, the second Tonghak rebellion in Korea plunged the Far East into a new era of intensive international rivalry. The Tonghak (Eastern Learning) Society, after a number of changes in its program, aimed to drive out the influence of westerners in Korea; but this program manifested itself principally in riots against the reactionary Korean administration and in acts against feudal land-owners.[90] The rebellion of 1893 aroused only slight international interest, for although American, Japanese, Chinese, British, and German warships were assembled at Chemulpo (the port for the capital, Seoul), the Tonghaks were crushed before foreign troops could land.[91] But in March, 1894, equipped with arms from Japan and backed by Japanese *ronin* (hired gangsters and soldiers of fortune),[92] the Tonghaks quickly spread through the southern Korean provinces. In May they defeated government forces sent against them, and in June they once again threatened the capital.[93] British, French, Japanese, and Chinese warships again assembled at Chemulpo, and even Russia belatedly sent a gunboat.[94]

On June 2 the King of Korea made a formal request for Chinese intervention, and on June 7 the Tsungli Yamen (Chinese Ministry of Foreign Affairs) notified Komura, the Japanese chargé at Peking, that China would send troops to Korea "to restore the peace of our tributary state."[95] Japan then notified China that she also would send troops to Korea, adding that she had never recognized Korea as a tributary state of the Chinese Empire.[96] In accordance with the Tientsin Convention of 1885, both China and Japan then proceeded to send troops to Korea. China sent troops to southern Korea, the heart of the rebellion, but Japan sent her numerically superior forces to the vicinity of the capital. Before many units had landed, the Korean government had the rebellion in hand; nevertheless, both countries continued to send more troops.[97]

The Korean government asked both Japan and China to withdraw their troops from Korean territory. Japan, however, had set forth a new program on June 22 which indicated that Japanese troops would not withdraw until Korea reformed her administration.[98] According to Chinese official statements made to Count A. P. Cassini, the Russian Minister to Peking, the Japanese made several offers which would have given both China and Japan control of the Korean government, but China refused them, faithfully adhering to the Russo-Chinese understanding of October, 1886 (the Li-Lodyzhenskii Agreement).[99]

On June 22 Li Hung-chang appealed to Russia for mediation. In a personal conversation, which supposedly occurred by chance, Li informed Cassini that England had offered to mediate, but that he had declined the offer because he felt that, on the basis of the Russo-Chinese Agreement of 1886, Russia, as the third party involved, had the exclusive right to be the mediator. Cassini saw in this offer an excellent opportunity to increase Russian prestige in the Far East and "to prevent the inevitable, and for us highly undesirable, open conflict in Korea."[100]

Cassini's views were fully supported by Giers, who also wanted to forestall English mediation.[101] On June 23 the Russian Minister of Foreign Affairs instructed Khitrovo, the Minister to Tokyo, to advise the Japanese government to withdraw its troops from Korea simultaneously with China.[102] In a conversation with Mutsu Munemitsu, the Japanese Minister of Foreign Affairs, on June 25, Khitrovo expressed this Russian view. Mutsu, however, categorically reaffirmed that Japan would not evacuate Korea without some guarantee that new disorders would not break out as soon as Japanese troops were withdrawn. He asserted that Japan had no intention of establishing herself in Korea or of beginning a war with China.[103]

On the same day, the Korean government asked the ministers of the legations in Seoul to transmit to their governments an official request to induce a simultaneous withdrawal of Chinese and Japanese troops.[104] This offered Russia an opportunity to choose either an official mediation based on the Korean request or continue in the unofficial course initiated by Li Hung-chang. Russia took the unofficial course. For a month, in numerous representations in St. Petersburg, Tokyo, and Seoul, Russian diplomats tried to persuade Japan to withdraw simultaneously with China, but they encountered the same argument: the exigency of the situation demanded the continuance of Japanese occupation of Korea.[105] In this type of mediation the Russian representatives tried not to show favor toward either party but advised Japan and China to act simultaneously.[106] However, Mutsu attempted to postpone any decisive answer by suggesting on July 12 that reforms were already in progress in Korea. At the peak of the crisis in July he was either ill or feigning illness to avoid further embarrassing conversations with Khitrovo.[107]

During July the Chinese refused to negotiate until the Japanese withdrew their troops.[108] Li Hung-chang hoped for a stronger Russian expression of mediation. He suggested a joint Russo-Chinese-Japanese convention to consider reforms for Korea.[109] Although Li had been clearly told that Russia would not interfere in Korean affairs,[110] he persisted in trying to involve her in them. He tried to promote discord between Russia and Japan by informing the Japanese indirectly that it was Russia who had originated the mediation idea and who was insisting upon it.[111] He tried to spur Russia to activity by stating that Japan had asked England to mediate, and that England was forcing China to accept this mediation.[112] In an even more fantastic scheme, Li informed Cassini that the British Minister to China was urging that all Korea be given to Japan.[113] He took it for granted that a joint European mediation was forthcoming, and in London and St. Petersburg he suggested zones of withdrawal for Chinese and Japanese troops.[114] After assuring Russia on July 3 that her participation in a three-power—Russian, Japanese, and Chinese—solution of the Korean problem would be the just reward for her mediation, two days later, without informing Russia, he appealed to England, France, and the United States for their mediation.[115]

Li Hung-chang's diplomatic machinations were apparently too crude to succeed. The European powers were genuinely interested in ending or abating the Korean crisis and conferred with each other in a frank atmosphere. It did not take long, therefore, for the Russians to discover Li Hung-chang's double-dealing game.[116] Even after the Sino-Japanese War broke out, Giers wrote to Cassini:

We do not regret at all . . . that we refused the offer made to us by Li Hung-chang, through you, to intervene directly in the question of Korean reforms, and to take upon ourselves, so to speak, an authoritative mediation in favor of the existing status quo, i.e., as Li Hung-chang essentially understood it, in the interest of China. The Ministry of Foreign Affairs clearly acknowledged that [the matter of] reforms served only as a pretext for the conflict between the Chinese and the Japanese, and that in consequence of our unofficial mediation we could easily have involuntarily found ourselves avowed enemies of Japan under the banner of China and the sly Viceroy of Pechili.[117]

From the beginning of the Sino-Japanese crisis, the Russian government maintained its noncommital policy of giving persistent but friendly advice to both China and Japan.[118] The Russian chargé at Seoul was exasperated by this form of "inactivity" and dared to chide the Ministry of Foreign Affairs for it. He was politely reprimanded and, reminded that he was not in a position to see what was going on in the diplomatic world, was informed that the seeming "inactivity" actually represented a real effort by Russian diplomats to initiate some sort of collective action by European powers.[119]

Among Russian diplomats and statesmen concerned with the Far Eastern crisis there were divergent views about the policy being followed. The fear that England would take a leading part in mediation was shared by both Giers and Cassini.[120] But this fear was soon dispelled when England gave clear indication of her intention to organize collective mediation. The idea was broached to the Russian government at St. Petersburg by Sir Frank Lascelles, the British Ambassador, on July 9.[121] After being favorably received in Russia, the idea was introduced in the European capitals by the Earl of Kimberley. This "intervention commune" plan not only had the full approval of Russia[122] but also the support of France, Germany, and Italy.[123] However, it envisioned these powers as serving only in an advisory capacity.[124] Before the powers could agree on the principles of application of the plan, war broke out.

The Russian diplomats did not agree on which nation was mainly responsible for the outbreak of the war. Weber considered the Chinese principally to blame because of their intervention in Korea to confirm its status as a "tributary state."[125] However, he also considered that the reform program which the Japanese had been planning for at least two years was evidence that Japan did not want to come to an agreement with China.[126] Cassini was a noted Sinophile and collector of Chinese *objets d'art*. By his solicitous concern for the Chinese cause, he served Li Hung-chang's purpose by transmitting Li's baseless rumors. Khitrovo in Tokyo was unconcerned. He felt that Japan would be easily defeated and that the status quo would in that way be restored.[127] In St. Petersburg, Count D. A. Kapnist, Director of the Asiatic Department of the Ministry of Foreign Affairs, considered Japan the principal instigator of the war and suggested the "diplomatic expedient" of temporarily occupying a Korean port (Port Lazarev) to induce Japanese withdrawal.[128]

It is clear that the issues of Korean reforms and the Tonghak rebellion were only pretexts. In 1895 Witte and Badmaev officially placed on record the now widespread idea that Japan's purpose in going to war with China was to forestall the strong position Russia would acquire after completing the trans-Siberian railroad.[129] Premier Ito Hirobumi followed closely the plans for the railroad and acquired a collection of documents on its progress; he naturally was aware that it would be many years before Russia would become a power in the Far East.[130] It hardly seems probable that Japan would have risked the issue in 1894 with a small army and only the beginning of a fleet,[131] for there was plenty of time in which she could develop a sizable army and navy.

Another widely held view is that the Japanese statesmen were anxious to distract their people from home affairs and were anxious to avert civil disturbances by arousing wartime patriotism.[132] This view has been advanced by Japanese writers, and the turbulent nature of internal Japanese politics before the war, contrasted with the subsequent period of patriotic support for the government, give it weight.[133]

Historical accounts based on Chinese documents[134] point out that for years following the Tientsin Convention of 1885 both China and Japan abstained from outward hostility toward each other. In this truce, which lasted until 1894, Japan engaged in the development of her economic interests in Korea, and China made rapid progress in asserting her political influence there. Through the efforts of Yuan Shih-kai, the Chinese Consul at Seoul, Chinese influence was paramount in the Korean court. China controlled all telegraphic communications from Seoul. Loans to the Korean government were likewise monopolized by China through its subsidized China Merchant Steamship Company.[135] After 1885 the Korean customs service was converted into a branch of the Chinese customs service.[136] China even attempted to subordinate Korean representatives abroad to her own.[137]

During this period Chinese influence was in the ascendency and promised to accentuate further China's claim that Korea was her tributary vassal. Although Japan watched this ascendancy closely, she refrained from countermeasures until a propitious time. When, under the influence of Yuan Shih-kai, the King of Korea called for Chinese intervention, he simply overplayed his hand and Li Hung-chang sent in troops. Li had stated to the Austrian Consul General to China that Japan would not act.[138] However, Japan proved to be ready and willing.

While the European powers were just getting ready to initiate their mild form of "advisory" mediation, Japan launched her plan. On July 19, 1894, Otori, the Japanese Minister to Seoul, presented to the Korean government an ultimatum which included a demand for the expulsion of Chinese troops from Asan and the abrogation of all Sino-

Korean treaties. The Korean reply arrived within the set three-day limit, but it was rather vague. On the twenty-third, Japanese troops entered the capital and stormed the palace. A pro-Japanese minister was raised to power, and in the name of the King he abrogated all Sino-Korean treaties and formally asked Japan to drive the Chinese out of Asan.[139] In last-minute preparations Li Hung-chang sent reinforcements by sea from Tientsin, but these were intercepted and scattered by Admiral Togo's squadron, and the leased, British-owned transport *Kowshing* was sunk, with heavy loss of life.[140] Open hostilities followed, and Japan declared on August 1 that a state of war with China existed. China then declared war also.[141]

Li Hung-chang, caught unprepared, became thoroughly alarmed.[142] Once more he appealed for international mediation and suggested that China, Japan, and all the powers which had agreed to join in "advisory" mediation—Russia, England, France, Germany, and Italy—plan reforms for Korea in a conference to be held at either Tientsin or Peking.[143] In a telegram to Cassini, Giers could only point out that Russia would continue to act in concert with England in an effort to restore peace.[144] France, however, seemed ready to break away, for she said she doubted whether advice to Japan to return to the *status quo ante* would be completely impartial in view of the advantages already gained by that country in the first few days of the war.[145]

On August 21, by order of Alexander III, a Special Conference of Ministers was called to discuss the Far Eastern crisis and to formulate a policy for Russia.[146] The conference reviewed events leading to the opening of hostilities, and the ministers exchanged views. They found no problem which called for immediate attention or a change of policy. Giers declared that he was for maintenance of the status quo in Korea, an opinion which echoed the views of P. S. Vannovskii, the Minister of War.[147] Witte foresaw the possibility that England would intervene at the end of the war in order to acquire some advantage and argued that this "interference must not be permitted, and therefore we ought to prepare to oppose England in case she reveals her selfish plans." In answer to Witte, N. M. Chikhachev, Acting Minister of the Navy, emerged with a traditional navy plan and suggested that in the event of British interference Russia should seize the island of Goncharov off the coast of Korea. But he did not advise taking such action without proper cause, because "any extension of our possessions at the expense of Korean territory would hardly bring us great advantages and would at the same time demand great expenditures for the fortification of the annexed place."[148] General Vannovskii foresaw a victory for Japan and feared that at the termination of the conflict China would seek an alliance with England. He felt that Russia should begin making some military preparations, particularly because of the long time required for any undertaking in the Russian Far East. But Giers and Witte saw no immediate necessity for making such preparations.[149]

The conference came to the conclusion that Russian interests would not be served by active interference in the Sino-Japanese War, and that Russia should continue to act in conjunction with other powers in an effort to settle the conflict by diplomatic means. It set the *status quo ante* in Korea as the desired objective for Russian policy and advocated that China and Japan be urged to respect Russian interests and advised to refrain from any action that might affect the Russian-Korean frontier.[150] The conference did not mention any Russian interests in Korea and actually did not formulate any positive policy. It merely expressed clearly its conclusion that Japan should not be left in possession of Korea, and the ministers trustfully accepted the repeated assurances of the Japanese government in July that the Japanese troops would be withdrawn.

In September the course of the war was decided. The Chinese land forces suffered a defeat at Pingyang (on September 15) and the prized northern Chinese squadron was almost annihilated at the naval battle of the Yalu on September 17. The Japanese won control of the Yellow Sea, landed on the Liaotung Peninsula on October 24, and stormed the fortress of Port Arthur on November 20 and 21. The port had recently been fortified by European engineers.[151]

During these developments the projected concert grew weaker. On October 6 England proposed a joint intervention by England, Germany, France, Russia, and the United States and a settlement on the basis of an independent Korea and an indemnity for Japan. However, the United States refused to participate, and Germany felt that any attempt to intervene would be futile at this time.[152] Prince Kung, who now headed the Chinese government, invited the ministers of these five powers to the Tsungli Yamen on November 3 and formally asked them to transmit to their governments the Chinese official request for intervention on the same basis as the English *démarche*.[153] This attempt also failed.

The inactivity of Russian diplomacy at this critical time is hard to understand, for Russia was clearly the nation most interested in a European concert. The reason may lie in the affairs of Russian succession. In September and October, Alexander III was dying. Even on his deathbed he continued to rule, though he was frequently incapable of understanding the reports of his ministers. His stubborn nature and hatred of even the "regent" would not permit him to relinquish the reins of government.[154] The interest he had earlier exhibited in the affairs of the Far East now naturally declined.[155] On November 1 the Tsar died at Livadia.

The new Tsar, Nicholas II, had his hands full. Besides all the complications attendant upon his ascending the throne there were the preparations for his marriage, which, according to the dying wishes of his father, took place on November 26 as had been planned.[156] Giers, too, was dying, but did not relinquish his office. He had been seriously ill since 1892 and wished to retire but was persuaded to remain in office by Alexander III. He died on January 26, 1895, and Shishkin was appointed minister of foreign affairs ad interim.[157] The situation was not conducive to the development of a strong foreign policy.

The Third Japanese Army landed in Shantung in January and quickly captured Wei-hai-wei. China sued for peace after several vain attempts to invite mediation or intervention.[158] Chinese plenipotentiaries met the Japanese at Hiroshima on February 1, but the conference broke down when the Japanese discovered that the Chinese diplomats lacked full plenipotentiary powers.[159]

On the same day, the new Tsar called the second Special Conference of Ministers to deal with the Far Eastern crisis.[160] The conference was apparently brought about by the dissatisfaction of the Tsar with the policy of acting in concert with the European powers in unofficial mediation. The stumbling block of the conference was the lack of knowledge of Japanese intentions in the coming peace negotiations. The prevailing opinion was that any action taken by Russia at that time would be premature. It was considered that Russia's vital interest lay in the independence of Korea, and the conferees seemed satisfied that Japan would fulfill her promises and respect that independence. The conference examined several contingencies. General Vannovski proposed that if Japan should violate Russian interests, a force should be sent to occupy some island in Korea Strait, such as Kargodo. On this point, Admiral N. M. Chikhachev stated that the occupation of this island would be an advantage in that it was unlikely that Japan would make any objections, whereas an occupation of Port Lazarev would arouse protests.[161] General N. N. Obruchev, the Chief of Staff, opposed the occupation of any area cut off from continental Russia, because of the difficulty of defending such an outpost.

Questioned whether Russian interests would be affected by the

Japanese annexation of such ports in the Gulf of Pechili (now the Gulf of Chihli) as Port Arthur and Wei-hai-wei, Shishkin answered vaguely: "As the Gulf of Pechili is more or less included in a Russian sphere of influence, the establishment of the Japanese on the shores of this gulf, at Port Arthur and Wei-hai-wei, obviously must affect our interests to a certain degree."[162] Admiral Chikhachev suggested that in that contingency Russia should occupy a part of Manchuria, and that "then the acquisition by Japan of the ports of Port Arthur and Wei-hai-wei would not have any significance for Russia."[163]

General Obruchev suggested that Russia abstain from any territorial annexation lest a precedent be given to England, and Witte proposed strengthening the Russian squadron in the Far East not only to make it ready to meet any emergency on better terms but also to arouse English anxiety in regard to Far Eastern trade and prompt the English to take steps to terminate the Sino-Japanese War.[164]

There was little difference of opinion on the course to be followed. The conferees considered British interests analogous to Russian interests and, since Russia could not act alone, found it advisable to act with England. Count D. A. Kapnist stated:

Only by acting in this course is there some possibility of averting the disastrous consequences of the Sino-Japanese conflict and of gaining the time necessary for the completion of the trans-Siberian railroad, when we will be in a position finally to bring forth all our material resources and to occupy a commensurate position in the affairs of the Pacific.[165]

The conference reached the following conclusions:

1. To strengthen our squadron in the Pacific to such an extent that our naval forces in those waters will be superior to those of Japan....

2. To instruct the Ministry of Foreign Affairs to attempt to form an agreement with England and other European powers, principally France, in regard to collective action against Japan if the government of Japan at the conclusion of the war with China should make demands which would violate our vital interests.... The principal aim which we must pursue is the maintenance of the independence of Korea.

3. If the attempt for an agreement with England and other powers concerning the above conditions should not be crowned with success, and if it should be necessary to accede to a mutual guarantee for Korean independence by foreign powers, the question of our further course of action ... will be submitted for consideration at a new conference.[166]

The decisions of the conference were put into effect. The strong and modern Russian Mediterranean squadron was sent to the Far East and was incorporated in the Far Eastern squadron, making it temporarily the most powerful naval force in the Far East.[167] Conversations in London, Paris, and St. Petersburg in February and March established a general agreement that the governments of these capitals should act in concert and insist on the preservation of the territorial integrity and independence of Korea.[168] Beyond that, nothing was done. By April the English had veered from the agreement, influenced by public opinion favoring the Japanese, and by the growing idea in governing circles that the success of Japan and her establishment as a power in the Far East was beneficial to the British policy of checking Russia.[169]

Russian policy, established by the conferences of August 21, 1894, and February 1, 1895, had completely failed. The idea of a concert of European powers had to be abandoned, since not even Germany could be brought to express her views.[170] By the end of March, Russia began to suspect the nature of the demands Japan had presented to the Chinese peace plenipotentiaries at Shimonoseki on April 1.[171]

Russia then groped for another policy. Behind the scenes, the notorious Badmaev, who had not yet fully launched his plan of preparing the "bloodless" annexation of Tibet, Mongolia, and western China, but who had meanwhile gained access to Nicholas II, strongly urged the new Tsar to pursue the Badmaev plan, which ostensibly had been supported by the late Tsar. In a memorandum written directly to the Tsar, dated March 6, 1895, Badmaev warned that infiltrations by Japanese individuals into Mongolia and western China were evidence of further intentions of aggression.[172] He needed time for the fruition of his scheme and urged the Tsar to adopt a strong policy. He wrote:

Fully realizing the uncertainty of the results of the war of Japan with China, I am certain that without recourse to military intervention, which would be damaging to our prestige in the Far East, we could find the means to persuade Japan to accept for its victories an indemnity as large as she desires, and the remainder of the Chinese fleet, but to give up claims on territory on the continent and her interference in the internal affairs of Korea and China.[173]

The importance of this opinion lies mainly in the fact that Badmaev was becoming *persona grata* on the political scene and behind the scenes. In the months that followed, his prestige rose, and by May 11 he had grown so bold as to write quite informally to the Tsar and presume to suggest to him what kind of diplomats were suitable for Far Eastern posts. He designated some as "unsuitable," "dangerous," or "lacking in character." He even had the temerity to recommend his erstwhile patron, Prince Ukhtomskii, for the post of Director of the Asiatic Department.[174]

The Tsar was now convinced of the need for an ice-free port, but he saw it this time not as a countermeasure intended to force an opponent to relinquish his annexation, but as a definite project. In 1894 Japan had passed a regulation for visiting foreign warships by which only two vessels belonging to any one nation could remain in Japanese ports at one time.[175] This measure seriously affected Russian naval strategy in the Pacific. Because the Russian Far Eastern squadron had always been weaker than the British South China squadron, Russia planned to conduct a war against commerce, using Japanese ports for temporary security, refitting, and supplies, particularly during the four months when Vladivostok was icebound. The new regulations would seriously hamper this type of strategy and would either immobilize Russian ships or leave them without a base during the winter months. Furthermore, even in time of peace, Russia used Nagasaki as a winter station from which her ships could go out for tactical and training purposes.

In an attempt to evolve a Russian policy, Prince A. B. Lobanov-Rostovskii, the new Minister of Foreign Affairs, wrote a memorandum to the Tsar on April 6, 1895,[176] in which he stated that, at the conclusion of the Sino-Japanese War, Russia must decide whether to pursue a passive or an aggressive policy. Lobanov argued that if Russia adopted a passive policy, China would be the ideal ally. Russian frontiers would be secure, and even if projected reforms were undertaken in China it would be some time before China could recover sufficiently from the war to be dangerous. But if Russia adopted an aggressive policy, the aim would be twofold: "our acquisition of an ice-free port on the Pacific and an annexation of a certain part of Manchuria necessary for a more convenient routing of the trans-Siberian railroad." Opposite the quoted passage on the original document, the Tsar wrote the word "Exactly,"[177] and elsewhere on it: "Russia unquestionably needs an open port, free from ice all the year round. This port must be on the continent [southeast Korea] and must be definitely connected with our present possessions by a strip of land. Communicate this to the Grand Duke General-Admiral."[178] Lobanov argued further that "unquestionably" Russia's most dangerous enemy in Asia was England; and the Tsar annotated, "of course." Lobanov argued that, in spite of her recent victories, Japan would have to lean on some alliance for some time, and that her natural enemy in the Far East was England. Hence, though Russia might act with other powers—principally England—to restrain Japan at the end of the Sino-Japanese War, she must refrain from any action hostile to Japan lest she prejudice future Russo-Japanese friendship.[179] On this basis Russia made another *démarche* for collective advisory action on April 8.

Meanwhile, both China and Japan were active in propagating their cause in the capitals of Europe. Li Hung-chang through the Tsungli Yamen, and the Tsungli Yamen through foreign representatives in China, kept the world informed of the course of negotiations. They argued that the Japanese acquisition of Port Arthur would put Japan in control of the Gulf of Pechili, drive a wedge between China and Korea, and lead to Japanese domination of the Chinese court because of Japan's proximity to the capital.[180] The Japanese, on their part, virtually suggested a dismemberment of China. The Japanese Ambassador to Berlin hinted to the German Foreign Office that Japan would not object to Russia's acquiring northern Manchuria through a separate agreement with China, if England compensated herself with the Chusan Archipelago, or if Germany took a province in southeastern China.[181]

A scramble for compensation in China, however, did not appeal to Germany. German imperialistic ambitions in the Far East had not yet matured, and, although in November, 1894, the Kaiser had expressed vague ideas about acquiring territory in Formosa and elsewhere, the German Foreign Office, particularly its expert on the Far East, Herr Max von Brandt, counseled that a naval and coaling station in the Far East could best be acquired through joint action with Russia.[182] France also was not ready for the scramble, and she was more interested in keeping Japan from the Pescadores than in her own minimal program of acquiring a small island off the coast of Hainan.[183]

On April 8, 1895, in an attempt to have a concrete starting point for a European concert on "friendly advice" to Japan, Lobanov presented his *démarche*. He suggested that the European powers through their representatives in Tokyo state that "the annexation of Port Arthur by Japan would be a lasting obstacle to the establishment of friendly relations between China and Japan and a serious threat to peace in the Far East."[184] Germany and France accepted this suggestion,[185] but, on April 10, England refused to make such a statement.[186] On the same day, Li Hung-chang, negotiating peace terms at Shimonoseki, was informed of the Russian, German, and French views.[187]

The *démarche* was a starting point for a joint representation; it cannot be considered an embodiment of Russian policy. It contradicted the opinions of the Tsar on the course of Russian policy and made even more necessary a new Special Conference of Ministers, which met on April 11.[188]

At this conference the Grand Duke General-Admiral Alexei Alexandrovich announced the views of his Imperial nephew (Nicholas II) that "it was necessary to preserve friendly relations with Japan" and that "under present conditions it would be more advantageous for us to shift quietly over to the side of Japan, and without hindering her further progress, to enter into an agreement with her concerning the preservation of our interests."[189] The General-Admiral supported the Tsar's view that the matter of an ice-free port was of paramount importance, but he felt that the occupation of Port Lazarev without Japanese consent would be difficult until the trans-Siberian railroad was completed. Furthermore, he preferred Port Shestakov over Port Lazarev because the latter would require extended defense lines.[190]

The expression of views which followed was virtually a revolt of ministers against the policy suggested by the Tsar. The ministers regarded Japan's foothold in Manchuria as a great menace. Lobanov declared that Russia could not count on Japan's friendship, because the war in the Far East "was aimed not so much against China as against Russia, and then all of Europe." Japan, he claimed, would expand northward from her southern Manchurian foothold.[191] General Vannovskii saw in this not only a military menace to Russian frontiers but also a future obstacle to the essential rectification of the Amur River boundary. He felt that Japan must be kept out of Manchuria, even at the price of yielding to Japan all of southern Korea. Japan must diplomatically be persuaded to relinquish her foothold in Manchuria, but if persuasion failed, Russia should use force.[192]

Although Obruchev felt that only diplomatic means must be used, since Russian forces remote from their bases would encounter difficulties in military operations, General Vannovskii felt that Russia could be equal to the task. To be sure, Russian forces were weak, consisting of only 30,000 men, which were to be reinforced in six months to a total strength of 50,000, with an initial field force of 12,000; but Japanese forces were also weak and widely scattered. With the assistance of a superior navy, a military solution promised success.[193]

Witte outlined a broad policy comparable to Badmaev's suggestions of March, 1895. He, too, felt that the Japanese foothold in southern Manchuria was only a beginning. In time, strengthened by the huge indemnity from China, Japan would seize Korea, extend her influence over the warlike Mongolians and Manchus, and begin a new war with China. In that event, Witte stated, "it would not be improbable that after a few years the Mikado will become the Chinese Bogdokhan [Emperor]." To Witte the question was whether to take action at this time or wait until the completion of the trans-Siberian railroad would make Russia's position stronger, and then seek compensation from Japan. He advised immediate action without recourse to any annexation, so as not to antagonize Japan and China at the same time. Japan must be told that Russia would not tolerate her occupation of southern Manchuria. He did not expect that this would lead to war; but said that if, contrary to expectations, Japan does not yield to diplomatic insistence, the Russian squadron must be ordered to begin operations against the Japanese fleet and bombard Japanese ports, without occupying any. Russia would thus acquire the role of a saviour of China, who would appreciate the aid given her and would later agree to a rectification of the boundary by peaceful means.

Speaking for the second time at the conference, Witte added that Russia must refrain from taking any part of China, because such a seizure would bring about new conflicts and would result in the dismemberment of China by other powers. He suggested: "We could allow Japan as a victorious nation to take Formosa, the Pescadores, even Port Arthur, and the southern part of Korea, in the extreme case, but not Manchuria."[195] He then proposed that the Ministry of Foreign Affairs begin negotiations along that line.[196]

The conference made the following decisions: (1) Russia would attempt to restore the *status quo ante* in northern China and would suggest to Japan in a friendly manner that she abandon her intentions of annexing southern Manchuria; if Japan categorically refused to abandon them, she would be notified that Russia considered herself free to act according to her own interests. (2) Russia would inform China and the European powers that she had no intentions of annexing any territory, but that she considered it vital to her own interests that Japan's hold on southern Manchuria be relinquished.[197]

This special conference ignored the views of the Tsar. Incomprehensibly, the divergence became even greater when, on April 14, Lobanov, knowing the decisions of the conference, wrote a memorandum to the Tsar describing his conversation with the French Ambassador to St. Petersburg. The second subject of the conversation centered on the possibility that the Russian and French governments would not oppose the conditions of the Sino-Japanese peace but would demand compensations instead. Lobanov did not venture to name the place or extent of a possible Russian compensation, stating that this question rested principally on the decision of the Russian Naval Ministry.[198] This document Nicholas II annotated: "I agree with the second proposition, i.e., with the agreement not to oppose the execution of the Sino-Japanese peace treaty, but by all means to receive the compensation desired by us in the form of a [an ice-] free port."[199]

The continued divergence of policies may have been due to the fact that Lobanov hesitated to submit to the Tsar the journal of the conference, which disagreed widely with the Tsar's views and even violated his wishes. However, he could not withhold so important a document for long. On April 15 he submitted the journal, and the storm broke.[200] The Tsar ordered another conference, which was held on April 16 in his palace. It was attended only by Witte, Vannovskii, Lobanov, and the Grand Duke Alexei.[201] No journal was kept at this conference. Since the decisions of April 11 were founded on Witte's views, he defended them, while the other members of the conference said little or nothing. In the end, Witte persuaded the Tsar to approve the decisions of the April 11 conference.[202] Witte thus laid the basis of a new policy which, however, did not preclude further collective action, though the conference of April 11 did not seek or foresee such action.

On April 17 Lobanov officially asked Germany, France, and England to support Russia's protest against the Japanese claim to Port Arthur.[203] France agreed, with distaste, merely following the principle of solidifying the Franco-Russian Alliance.[204] Germany accepted with alacrity,[205] and on the same day, Wilhelm II ordered the German squadron in the Far East to make contact with the Russian squadron.[206] England did not reply immediately, but after a heated cabinet meeting let it be known that she would continue her policy of noninterference. On April 18, Cassini, at Peking, was ordered to advise the Chinese government to delay the ratification of the Treaty of Shimonoseki, which had been signed on April 17, 1895.[207]

On April 23, the "Triplice" (Russia, Germany, and France) handed to the Japanese Acting Minister of Foreign Affairs identical notes stating that "the possession of the peninsula of Liaotung, claimed by Japan, would be a constant menace to the capital of China, would at the same time render illusory the independence of Korea, and would henceforth be a perpetual obstacle to the peace of the Far East."[208]

The Japanese government did not reply immediately, and for a time the diplomats and admirals of the Triplice nervously expected an outbreak of hostilities.[209] The Japanese General Staff realized that Japan could not fight the combined forces of the Triplice, and Japan yielded to the demand on May 5. On May 8 the amended Treaty of Shimonoseki was ratified at Chefoo. Japan was placated by a larger indemnity.[210] On November 8, 1895, Japan formally renounced her claim to gains in Manchuria by the Declaration of the Retrocession of Liaotung.

The success of the Triplice was a triumph of Russian policy.[211] Russia had won all her short-term aims. According to the Treaty of Shimonoseki, Korea remained independent, and the existence of the Triplice insured Japan's evacuation of Korea. The Japanese were removed from the continent as Badmaev had hoped they would be. China, defeated and still isolated, was an ideal neighbor for Russia and soon became more than willing to accept Russian financial assistance at the price of Russian political influence.

The Sino-Japanese War and the intervention of the Triplice had far-reaching effects on the history of the Far East. The Far East became prominent in world politics. Germany had taken an interest in it and Japan had taken an interest in the affairs of Europe. The dormant hostility of the Japanese toward the Russians was aroused.[212] Japan immediately began preparations to safeguard herself from any repetition of such an indignity as the Retrocession of Liaotung.[213]

After the Sino-Japanese War and the resulting Treaty of Shimonoseki and the Retrocession of Liaotung, Russia adopted a positive Far Eastern policy for the first time since 1860. Before 1895 Russia had been content with the status quo, because no power had entered her security zone—Korea, Manchuria and neighboring areas. Whenever the matter of obtaining an ice-free port was considered, it was only as a countermove to actions of other powers and was aimed at forcing those powers to retract their claims. In 1894–1895 special attention given to the affairs of the Far East brought forth three general unmistakable policies. First, the question raised in the special conferences, whether to rely on a Chinese or a Japanese alliance, was settled when the hostility of the Japanese was aroused by the actions of the Triplice. A Russo-Chinese alliance then naturally suggested itself. Secondly, a new version of the idea of the ice-free port envisaged by Nicholas II was brought forward. With the increase of Russian naval power in the Far East it became important for the first time. Finally, the need for a railroad to the Far East became associated with the strategic problem of the defense of the Amur River frontier. The military members of the special conferences foresaw northern Manchuria as an outpost—or, to use a modern term, "a zone of security"—for the protection of Russian territories in the Far East.[214] This suggested a policy of Russian domination of northern Manchuria in one way or another.

Although none of these policies was yet clearly formulated, they were alive in the minds of men. Russian statesmen, diplomats, the Tsar, and adventurers such as Badmaev were vitally interested in phases of these policies. There was no need for any group, such as the earlier Vostochniki, to call the attention of the Russian people to the events in the Far East, because these events became important enough to attract their attention. The realization of the importance of the changing East can be seen also in certain administrative and diplomatic changes. Before 1895 Russia was satisfied to have one man serve as both military attaché to China and military agent to Japan, which shows that Japan was regarded as relatively unimportant. In February, 1896, the post of military attaché to Japan was created.[215] Earlier, in June, 1895, the Asiatic Department of the Ministry of Foreign Affairs had been abolished as a semi-independent organization—Far Eastern affairs had become important enough to deserve the direct attention of the Minister of Foreign Affairs.[216] It can be said that by 1896 Russia had completely recognized the importance of the Far East.

IV

RUSSIAN PENETRATION OF MANCHURIA AND THE ASCENDANCY OF RUSSIAN INFLUENCE IN KOREA, 1895–1897

EVEN BEFORE the terms of the Retrocession of the Liaotung Peninsula were agreed upon, China became concerned over the indemnity of 200,000,000 Kuping taels (*ca.* $150,000,000), one-half of which was to be paid in two semiannual installments.[1] The unpaid portion carried a 5 per cent interest and was guaranteed by the Japanese occupation of Wei-hai-wei, which cost China an additional 500,000 taels annually.[2] These sums were immense for China to raise, and the payment required drastic action on her part. At first China attempted to raise the money from internal sources. In April, 1895, she asked permission to increase her tariffs (then generally 5 per cent ad valorem), but this measure was immediately blocked by England,[3] who was then enjoying the lion's share of Chinese markets.[4] China even considered raising the already burdensome salt tax 100 per cent and allowing the importation of salt; but Sir Robert Hart, the British Director of the Chinese Maritime Customs, foresaw complications in such a solution.[5]

China then sought relief in a foreign loan. Her foreign debt was small,[6] consequently her credit was good. Within a week after the signing of the Treaty of Shimonoseki the Chinese government approached financial circles in Great Britain, France, and Germany with a request for a joint loan. Once again the idea of collective action contradicted the plans of individual powers. Germany was not satisfied with the guarantees offered for receipts of the Chinese Maritime Customs and wanted to set up a special customs administration. The British demanded a revision of tariffs. France was cautious about the British proposal, however, fearing that in an international commission she would be isolated.[7] Consequently, negotiations for the loan were checked by this petty international rivalry.

RUSSIAN PENETRATION OF MANCHURIA, 1895–1897

The negotiations were not held in strict secrecy; Witte heard of them on April 26 from the Russian chargé at Berlin.[8] On the following day he made further inquiries of his friend V. Mendelsohn, an international financier of Paris and St. Petersburg, and from him obtained a clearer

---

[1] For notes to chap. iv see pp. 273–280.

picture of the international scope of the negotiations.[9] But Russia was not in a position to suggest that she herself participate in the projected loan, for she was encumbered by the mounting expenses of the Trans-Siberian Railway, the building of which had been stepped up since the Sino-Japanese War.[10] She was also recovering from the effects of the prolonged famine of 1891–1893.

Russian participation was first suggested by the Paris-Netherlands Bank in the beginning of May, but Witte was unwilling to accept as indispensable the provision that a special commission for the financial control of China be set up by the participating powers.[11] Several financial negotiations continued simultaneously through May. The Chinese negotiated for loans from combinations of powers as well as from single powers.[12] France had a surplus of capital and considered Russia a good risk because of her recovery from the depression of 1893, her increased gold production, and the growing reputation of Witte. In negotiations with Russia she suggested that she participate in the Chinese loan or make a new loan to Russia.[13] Apparently, Witte was not interested in an international loan[14] and came to favor the idea of a joint Franco-Russian loan, especially after his agent, A. G. Rafalovich, telegraphed from Paris that the French bankers were willing to subscribe the whole amount of the loan with only nominal participation by Russian banks and with a guarantee from the Russian government.[15]

Reports that the Franco-Russian loan would probably be forthcoming were current in St. Petersburg by June 17.[16] On June 21 Witte invited representatives of a number of French banks to meet with him in St. Petersburg. On July 6, 1895, at the Russian Ministry of Foreign Affairs, in the presence of Witte and the new Russian Minister of Foreign Affairs, Prince A. B. Lobanov-Rostovskii, the Chinese representatives signed a loan agreement with the representatives of six French and four Russian banks.[17] The contract stipulated that China was to receive 400,000,000 gold francs at 94 per cent face value and bearing 4 per cent interest, the lowest interest rate hitherto granted to China. Russia guaranteed the loan. But under Article III, China pledged to give, in the event of default, an unspecified "additional security," and under Article IV, promised not to accept financial supervision from any power without extending equal rights to Russia.[18]

In this transaction Russia played the part of an "honest broker." Franco-Russian financial and political ties were strengthened, and Russia could rest assured that no other nation would gain a dominant position in Chinese financial affairs. Witte then quickly pressed his advantage. Immediately after the signing of the contract and before the signers left the room, he outlined to the French financiers his plan for a Russo-Chinese bank to be founded by the participants in the same syndicate which made possible the loan to China, and whose investment in the bank would again be guaranteed by the Russian government.[19]

The proposal came as a surprise, and time was required for further consultations. The plan for the activities of the bank was ambitious. It envisaged the creation of subsidiary commercial and industrial enterprises in China, participation in further Chinese loans and in banking operations connected with such loans, railroad concessions in any part of China, construction of telegraph lines, and even the issuing of money.[20] The French financiers were encouraged to accept the plan under the terms of the Peking Convention between France and China signed on June 20, 1895, which opened three southern Chinese provinces adjacent to French Indochina to French railroad interests and to commercial and mining enterprises.[21] Participation in these would be at the financiers' own risk; whereas, at the conference of July 6, Witte apparently pledged the support of the Russian government in the event that the planned Russo-Chinese bank should encounter international complications.[22] On July 7, Russian newspapers received with acclaim the Imperial ukase announcing the Chinese loan. They mirrored a general enthusiasm in Russian financial circles for the "new era" in the Far East which they thought would be initiated by the loan.[23]

However, for several months French financiers objected to the bank's management plan. In the initial capitalization of six million rubles the French were assigned five-eighths participation but were to receive only three of the eight directorships.[24] Nevertheless, the French financiers finally agreed to the plan and on December 5, 1895, signed the charter of the Russo-Chinese Bank, which was sponsored by the Committee of the Trans-Siberian Railway and was approved by that committee on December 22.[25]

There was an actual need for a Russo-Chinese bank. Russian tea merchants in the Far East had in 1894 petitioned the Ministry of Finance for the establishment of a bank to facilitate their large financial operations, which were then in the hands of British banks.[26] But the bank planned by Witte would have a greater scope of activity. In a report to the Tsar on July 26, 1895, Witte suggested that the bank, in addition to strengthening Russian economic influence in China, "may prove to be a very useful instrument in the hands of the Russian government for carrying out measures closely connected with the completion of the construction of the Trans-Siberian Railway."[27] In this Witte hinted at his growing conviction that this railroad should take a short

cut across Manchuria, for the original plan of the railway constructed
on Russian territory would certainly not have required the services of a
Russo-Chinese bank. On November 11, three days after the signing
of the Retrocession of Liaotung, Witte had already formulated a project
for a railway across Manchuria, which he submitted to the Tsar on
December 9, 1895, four days after the signing of the charter of the
Russo-Chinese Bank. In this project he suggested that one of the first
functions of the bank should be that of providing the Russian Minister
to China with a special fund to finance the customary bribes to Chinese
statesmen in order to gain their approval for a Russian railway concession across Manchuria.[28]

Plans for the extension of the Trans-Siberian Railway through Manchuria had recurred from time to time since 1887 when Rear Admiral
Kopytov had suggested a short cut which approximated the route finally
adopted.[29] His plan was rejected in 1891 by A. Ia. Hubbenet (A. Ia.
Gubbenet), the Russian Minister of Communications, and by Witte in
1892.[30] The survey reports made in the summer of 1894 on the originally
proposed route along the Amur River, between Sretensk and Khabarovsk, prompted Witte to reconsider the plan of constructing the
railway through Manchuria. These reports indicated that the construction of the railroad along the Amur would encounter many technical
difficulties. Spurs of the Yablonovoi and Stanovoi ranges descended to
the Amur River and required many tunnels. Many large affluents of the
Amur required bridges between the spurs.[31] In the section between
Khabarovsk and the Zeya River, 50 per cent of the route was swampy
and would necessitate costly technical construction.[32] In addition, a
railroad along the Amur River would lessen the usefulness of the steam
navigation which had hitherto satisfied the requirements of the settlements along the river.[33]

In February, 1895, Witte suggested to the Ministry of Foreign Affairs a limited concession for a railroad running from the Russian
frontier post of Novo-Tsurukhaitui, through Mergen to Blagoveschensk,
which would avoid the "big bend" of the Amur River and the spurs
of the Yablonovoi range.[34] Witte did not follow up his suggestion,
which was reported to the Tsar as one of the essentials of Russian
policy in the Far East in Lobanov-Rostovskii's "Memoir" of April 6,
1895.[35] In May, Prince M. T. Khilkov, the new Minister of Communications, took up the plan and, without informing Witte or Lobanov,
obtained permission from the Tsar to begin a reconnaissance of the
Manchurian cutoff.[36] Witte and Lobanov were completely ignorant of
this measure; when, in October, Lobanov received news that the Chinese

were alarmed at the presence of Russian engineers in Manchuria, Witte thought the report referred to some of "Badmaev's boys."[37]

In November, Witte's attitude changed radically. Japan was out of Manchuria, and the Russo-Chinese Bank provided the medium by which money could be obtained from France. The personnel of the bank, particularly the managers of its Far Eastern branches, was closely integrated with the personnel of the Ministry of Finance; the bank thus served as an unofficial agency of Witte.[38]

The political situation was also favorable. German and British financial circles, in March, 1896, sought to counteract the Russian and French influence by raising a loan to China of £16,000,000 at 5 per cent.[39] The governments of Germany and England were eager to see the development of Russian interests in the Far East. In a number of personal letters to the Tsar in 1895, William II expressed his approval of and encouraged a positive Russian policy in the Far East, hoping that Russia's entanglement there would give him a freer hand in Europe.[40] In November, 1895, Lord Salisbury frankly told the German Ambassador that he welcomed Russia's involvement in the Far East, for he thought it would deny her the opportunity to interfere in the Near East.[41]

The strongest opposition to Witte's Manchurian railway plan came from some Russian statesmen and from China. Before Witte's project and political memorandum of December 9 were sent to Cassini at Peking, Count D. A. Kapnist hurriedly made a strenuous objection to the project. Apparently Witte's memorandum was expressed in guarded terms and consequently appeared incomplete. Kapnist criticized the two documents for ignoring strategic and political considerations and for emphasizing economic advantages "which at the present time are but a question for the future." Kapnist feared that an economic exploitation of the railroad would require Russia's taking over the entire internal administration of northern Manchuria, and that such a step could not be taken without military occupation. This would lead to the partition of China and to British occupation of ports on the Yellow Sea. Kapnist then suggested a minimum project for a railroad on the route suggested by Witte in February, 1895. He believed, as Witte had in February, that the plan could be carried out by solely diplomatic means without incurring international repercussions.[42] Although not mentioned by its proponents, the underlying reason for the minimum plan was that the Chinese population and Chinese interest in the three Manchurian provinces were disproportionate. Heilungkiang, the northwestern province, was largest in area but smallest in Chinese population

(400,000) ; Kirin, in the northeast, was slightly more populated (626,-000) ; and Mukden (Fengtien), in the south, had absorbed most of the recent Chinese immigration and was by far the most heavily populated (4,724,000). Mukden was also the most important.[43] There would be little opposition to a Russian railroad running through the comparatively waste lands of Heilungkiang.

The Kapnist memorandum did not convince the Foreign Minister, who in December sent Witte's project and "political memorandum," approved by the Tsar, to Cassini in Peking. Copies of the two documents apparently were also sent to other statesmen directly interested. On January 23, 1896, Lieutenant General S. M. Dukhovskoi, Governor General of the Priamur region, objected to Witte's projected route in a note addressed to Witte and referring to the two documents.[44] In general, Dukhovskoi followed the line of criticism taken by Kapnist. In addition, he argued that the line across northern Manchuria would be impossible to defend and that Witte's project would deprive the Priamur region of the opportunity to develop its resources.[45] Dukhovskoi's arguments were erroneous and weak. He considered the Priamur region the Russian military supply base for the Far East, although in food supplies, population, and strategic position the Primorsk region was vastly superior to it.[46] He argued for the minimum program in order to avoid international jealousy, but at the same time he suggested that a branch railroad could be directed to Newchwang, on the Gulf of Pechili, to link up with the Chinese railroad, which was slowly being constructed from Peking to the north.[47] Because both Kapnist and Dukhovskoi failed to realize that Witte's two documents were of necessity reserved and incomplete, both critics underestimated the broad scope of the project. On Dukhovskoi's query "will it not be a great historical mistake to build a sector of the Trans-Siberian Railway, 2,000 versts in length, in a region which shall be foreign for a long time," Nicholas II cryptically annotated, "No."[48]

Witte, in his memorandum of April 12, 1896,[49] challenged Dukhovskoi's criticism. He easily exposed the blunders in Dukhovskoi's arguments and statements. The "2,000 versts" in Dukhovskoi's note were in reality 1,100 to 1,300; it would be just as difficult to defend the minimum route as the route across all northern Manchuria; the real base for the Russian Far East was of course the transbaikal region and not the Priamur region.[50] But Witte's note had greater significance. It was the first, if not the only, authentic and clear exposition of his broad economic, political, and strategic plans for the Manchurian railroad. Witte incorporated in his memorandum the opinion of Cassini, which he shared, that all efforts must be directed to the main goal of acquiring the concession for the railroad through Manchuria. He saw that the difficulties which must be overcome to achieve this objective were so great that it was useless to discuss details at this time, particularly such details as the plan recommended by Dukhovskoi for the acquisition or purchase of a strip of territory along the railroad to be settled by Russian colonists, or the use of eight battalions of infantry recently designated for service in the Far East in the construction of the railroad.[51]

Witte saw in the trans-Manchurian railroad merely a beginning. Branches to the south would certainly be necessary and "would follow soon in the course of events." With the completion of the railroad and the closing of the *porto franco* at Vladivostok, the railroad would become a great artery of import and export trade for Manchuria.[52] Witte also attacked Dukhovskoi's argument that the minimum railroad plan was necessary for the development of the Priamur region. The gold-mining districts, he argued, were increasing their production without the railroad, and the Amur River navigation for the riparian settlements seemed adequate.[53]

On the political and strategic role of the railroad, Witte wrote:

> On the political and strategic side this railroad will have the importance of offering to Russia the opportunity of transporting her military forces to Vladivostock, at all times and by the shortest route, of concentrating them in Manchuria, on the shores of the Yellow Sea, and in the proximity of the capital of China. Even the possibility of sizable Russian forces appearing in the places mentioned would immensely strengthen the prestige and influence of Russia, not only in China but generally in the Far East, and would contribute to a closer relationship between Russia and the nationalities subject to China.[54]

Witte did not amplify this statement, for it was too early to have concrete plans, but he intimated in this passage the broad scope of the plan for Russia's position in the Far East once the trans-Manchurian railroad was completed. Russia could use the railroad against either Japan or China. Either as a direct threat to the capital of China or as an indication of China's strategical weakness, it might well affect the loyalty of Mongolians, Dungans, and other nationalities subject to China on the northern fringes of her empire. Witte claimed that once this railroad was completed, Russia's position in all of Manchuria would be assured, for "afterward no other railroad or branch line would be built in northern China without the approval of Russia."[55]

Witte also indicated that he did not fear serious international complications, so long as the railroad concession was acquired through proper diplomatic channels. He recognized the disunity among the powers in their rivalry for concessions and privileges in China, and he felt that the partitioning of China had already begun. Russia would follow the course already adopted by other powers. Even during the Sino-Japanese War, Japan had negotiated for a railroad concession along the western shore of Korea to the Liaotung Peninsula, and France had obtained the right to build a railroad from Indochina to an undefined point in southern China and had extended a similar privilege to Great Britain under Article IV of the Anglo-French convention of January 15, 1896. Germany at the same time had obtained monopolies for contracts for rails and rolling stock for the Chinese-owned Peking-Tientsin railroad and had acquired settlement concessions in Tientsin, Shanghai, and Hankow.[56]

The result of the discussions and interchanges of notes within Russia regarding the trans-Manchurian railroad created a solidarity among the more influential Russian statesmen, which permitted the project to become a reality through coöperative and energetic action. The Tsar, judging by his annotations on the Dukhovskoi and Witte memoranda, heartily approved Witte's plan. Prince Lobanov-Rostovskii by accepting the two Witte memoranda and bringing them to the attention and approval of the Tsar also indicated his own adherence to the plan. Yet all three accepted the advice of Cassini in Peking with respect to the limitations of the demands and the proper time to suggest them.[57] The four authors of the plan for the trans-Manchurian railroad worked in amity and coördination.

The route directly across Manchuria was therefore accepted, and the plan for a branch to the Yellow Sea was postponed till the achievement of the main goal. In March, 1896, a special committee, of which A. N. Kulomzin, the general manager of the Committee of the Siberian Railway, was chairman, and which included Prince Khilkov, General Dukhovskoi, and representatives of the Ministries of War, Navy, Finance, Commerce, and Internal Affairs, agreed that for the purpose of security and convenience Vladivostok represented the best terminal point of the Trans-Siberian Railway. The representatives of the Naval Ministry stated that Vladivostok was adequate for the needs of the Russian fleet and for such naval expansion as was contemplated in the near future.[58] The conclusions of the special committee were approved by the Committee of the Siberian Railway in a session presided over by Nicholas II on May 22, 1896.[59] Measures were immediately taken to improve the commercial and naval port of Vladivostok, which experiments with the rather primitive icebreaker Silach in the winter of

1893–94 had proved to be closed by ice only fifty-two days of the year.[60] In June, 1896, more than 17,000,000 rubles (an impressive sum in that day) was assigned for the fortification of Vladivostok.[61] Everything pointed to a normal, gradual, and unobtrusive development of Russian power in the Far East.

Meanwhile, Cassini in Peking broached the subject of the trans-Manchurian railroad to the Chinese authorities. Apparently, until April, 1896, his conversations were unofficial.[62] In Peking during the winter of 1895–96 there was intense rivalry among the powers for railroad concessions, and even the solidarity of the French and Russian interests was broken.[63] The Chinese government vacillated in its Russian policy. On the one hand, in December, 1895, the Chinese government dismissed German advisers and military instructors, who had penetrated as far west as Hami in eastern Sinkiang, and agreed to Cassini's suggestion that several hundred Chinese officers be sent to Russia for training while serving in the Russian army.[64] Also, Chinese newspapers expressed the idea that in return for Russia's aid in forcing the Japanese to withdraw from the continent and promoting the loan of July 6, 1895, China would satisfy two major Russian requirements: the desire for the transit of the Trans-Siberian Railway across Manchuria and the right to winter the Russian squadron in some northern Chinese port, presumably Kiaochow.[65] On the other hand, China veered to the financial support of the Anglo-German consortium, and Li Hung-chang, considered a proponent of the pro-Russian policy, fell into disgrace temporarily.[66]

Li's disgrace may have been the determining factor in causing Cassini, who since December, 1895, had been armed with Witte's general memoranda on the demands for the trans-Manchurian railroad, to delay making an official presentation of the Russian demands to the Chinese government. International competition forced the pace. In January, 1896, Li Hung-chang, who had been reinstated, obtained the Imperial approval for the resumption of construction of the Chinese Imperial Northern Railway from Peking to Shanhaikwan, now projected to Mukden and Kirin.[67] In February and March, an American citizen named Bush, who claimed that he represented a $250,000,000 syndicate of American financiers backing a commercial house known as the American China Development Company, approached Cassini, Li Hung-chang, and others. He offered to finance the Peking-Hankow-Canton railroad and to coöperate with the Russians in Manchurian railroad enterprises.[68]

On April 18, 1896, Cassini officially opened negotiations with the

Tsungli Yamen for a railroad concession across Manchuria.[69] Since his instructions from Witte and Lobanov were in general terms, he may possibly have formed on his own initiative a more detailed sketch of an agreement, so as to be prepared for practical considerations. His conversations never reached the stage of discussing details, and his sketch remained unofficial and unused. However, on October 30, 1896, the *North China Herald* published the text of a "Special Convention between China and Russia," which became known as the "Cassini Convention."[70] In the opinion of B. A. Romanov this "convention" was an illicitly copied preliminary report, an unauthorized sketch made by Cassini before his conference of April 18. Romanov indicated four points of internal evidence confirming his interpretation. In the opening paragraph concerning the plenipotentiaries, only Cassini's name appeared, and blanks were left for the names of Chinese plenipotentiaries. Similarly, there were no signatures. The text does not enumerate the articles, and they do not follow in logical order. Finally, the wording of the provisions is curt and crude compared with that of most diplomatic documents.[71]

Other evidence substantiates Romanov's opinion. In February, 1896, the Chinese government had decided to send Li Hung-chang to Russia as its representative at the coronation of Nicholas II. Acting as though the Chinese government was completely reconciled to the prevailing idea that Russia would seek some *rapprochement* with China, or some concession, Li Hung-chang left Shanghai on March 28 already provided with wide plenipotentiary powers.[72] Meanwhile, in St. Petersburg, Witte and Lobanov made plans to receive Li Hung-chang and negotiate with him directly on their plans for a Russian railroad across Manchuria.[73] If the "Cassini Convention" had actually been signed, Li Hung-chang's and Witte's preparations and subsequent discussions would not have been necessary and certainly would not have led to the clash of views which preceded the signing of the Russo-Chinese Treaty of June 8, 1896.

Cassini's discussions with the Tsungli Yamen in April, 1896, were perhaps superfluous. However, they may have been considered necessary in order to prepare the Tsungli Yamen to receive favorably the terms of the Russo-Chinese agreements planned in St. Petersburg. From December, 1895, Russian policy aimed at obtaining Chinese consent in principle to the Russian railroad penetration of Manchuria; the details would be worked out later. On that basis, Cassini opened negotiations with the Tsungli Yamen. At the first conference, on April 18, following his instructions, Cassini tried to gain approval for a Russian railroad concession across Manchuria with feeder lines within

Manchuria which would make it possible for Russia to protect China "from the danger of new conflicts with Japan or generally with any other power."[74] The Chinese statesmen asked for a twelve-day postponement to allow them to consider the proposal; but when negotiations were resumed, on April 30, they flatly refused to give railway concessions in Manchuria to any foreign power. After three hours of general and futile arguments Cassini realized his failure and ended the negotiations. On the following day he reported to St. Petersburg that only a threat of "dire consequences" might persuade the Chinese statesmen.[75]

On April 30 Li Hung-chang arrived at St. Petersburg. Originally he had planned to visit some European capitals on his way, but in Shanghai, D. D. Pokotilov persuaded him to transfer to the crack liner of the Russian Volunteer Fleet at Alexandria, in order to travel with Prince Ukhtomskii to Odessa and then go directly to St. Petersburg, so as to arrive there three weeks before the coronation and with ample time for the negotiations which Witte had in mind.[76] After a few formal and informal visits, Li Hung-chang's mission turned "from problems of ceremony to business."[77] Witte and Lobanov negotiated with Li Hung-chang, and at the same time A. Iu. Rothstein negotiated with Li's interpreter and advisor, Victor Grot, a Russian subject previously employed in the Chinese Maritime Customs.[78]

In order to obtain the desired railway concession through Manchuria, Witte used two persuasive arguments: a secret defensive alliance between Russia and China, and a bribe of three million rubles to be paid to Li Hung-chang in installments.[79] Li had no objections to the alliance, which must have been proposed early in the negotiations. The Russians consistently stressed the necessity for the trans-Manchurian railway in connection with military aid to China.[80] However, on the details of the trans-Manchurian railway Li yielded only gradually and on some points not at all. He categorically refused to accept the plan that the Russian government construct the railroad, just as Witte refused to have the railroad a joint Russo-Chinese enterprise. Eventually a compromise was reached by giving the concession to the Russo-Chinese Bank.[81] Witte insistently urged that the bank be authorized also to build a branch line from the trans-Manchurian railroad to some port on the Yellow Sea, but Li adamantly refused this unless the road could be constructed on the European gauge of four feet nine and a half inches, the gauge then used on Chinese railroads.[82] On this point the negotiators could not agree, even after they moved to Moscow to prepare for the ceremony of the Tsar's coronation.[83] It is not clear whether the negotiators discussed the lease of an ice-free port within the confines of the Chinese Empire.[84] However, it is significant that the Tsar, on May 22, approved the findings of the special committee which dealt with the future plans for the port of Vladivostok. In all probability the approval of the Tsar signified the end of negotiations concerning the ice-free port.

On June 3, 1896, Witte, Lobanov, and Li Hung-chang signed the secret Treaty of Alliance between China and Russia.[85] This defensive alliance provided that the two contracting powers would come to each other's aid in the event of a Japanese attack on Russia in the Far East, on any Chinese territory, or on Korea (Art. I). Under Article III, all Chinese ports would be opened to Russian warships during military operations against Japan. Article VI provided that the treaty would be in effect for fifteen years. The price China paid for this added security was contained in Article IV:

> In order to facilitate the access of Russian land troops to the menaced points, and to ensure their means of subsistence, the Chinese government consents to the construction of a railway line across the Chinese province of the Amur [i.e., Heilungkiang] and of Kirin in the direction of Vladivostock. The junction of this railway with the Russian railway shall not serve as a pretext for any encroachment on Chinese territory nor for any infringement of the rights of sovereignty of His Majesty the Emperor of China. The construction and exploitation of this railway shall be accorded to the Russo-Chinese Bank, and the clauses of the contract which shall be concluded for this purpose shall be duly discussed between the Chinese Minister in St. Petersburg and the Russo-Chinese Bank.[86]

Article V stated that in time of peace Russian troops in transit over the railway should have the right to stop only when justified by "the needs of the transport service."

On June 4, to assuage Li Hung-chang's fears that he would not be paid his well-earned bribe, Witte authorized Prince E. E. Ukhtomskii, A. Iu. Rothstein, and P. M. Romanov to sign a protocol promising Li three million rubles, the first million to be paid when the concession was approved by the Emperor of Russia. This amount was to be borrowed from the Russo-Chinese Bank and eventually debited as a construction cost of the Chinese Eastern Railway Company, the name given to the company constructing the trans-Manchurian railway.[87]

Witte was all ready to go on with the details of the project. On May 30 he had received the Imperial approval for his own draft of the contract for the Chinese Eastern Railway (hereafter referred to as the C.E.R.), but technical difficulties delayed the acceptance of the contract by China. Shu King-chen, the Chinese Minister to St. Petersburg, named to negotiate the contract, was at the same time Minister to Berlin, and though Witte's financial aide, Rothstein, conducted negotiations in person, a good deal of time-wasting correspondence took place.[88] Furthermore, the Chinese statesmen of the Tsungli Yamen, and particularly its chairman, Prince Kung, vehemently opposed the concessions made by Li Hung-chang.[89] After several months Li restored his own reputation, possibly by using bribes, but by that time his influence was not necessary, for the Tsungli Yamen had approved the concession before his return.[90]

On September 8, 1896, the contract for the construction and exploitation of the C.E.R. was signed in Berlin by Shu King-chen, as the Chinese plenipotentiary, and by Rothstein and Prince Ukhtomskii as the representatives of the Russo-Chinese Bank.[91] Under the contract, China would receive the railroad after eighty years and had the right to purchase it after thirty-six years upon completion of payments on all funded and unfunded debts (Art. XII).[92] The railroad was to be free from all taxes and was to have the right of administration and of any type of construction on the land used by the company adjacent to its railway line (Art. VI). To encourage Russian and Manchurian freight transits, Russian and Chinese tariffs on goods carried by the railroad were reduced by one third (Art. X). The determination of charges on freights and passengers was left entirely to the company (Art. XI).

Some points were left vague, perhaps purposely. Article V stipulated that the company had the right to hire any employee. This general provision permitted Witte to appoint his own agents to the most important positions in the C.E.R. as soon as the Russian government (i.e., the Ministry of Finance) purchased the controlling bloc of shares. The article also stipulated that all crimes committed on the lands or on the right of way of the C.E.R. would be under the "jurisdiction of the local administration on the basis of the terms of international treaties." In conjunction with Article VI, this stipulation could be, and was, interpreted as the right of the C.E.R. to establish a sort of a "settlement administration and police force" whose authority extended throughout all the territory leased by the C.E.R.[93] On only one point was the C.E.R. at a disadvantage: the Chinese refused to yield to it the right to exploit coal mines adjacent to the railway, claiming that mineral rights were part of the Imperial regalia and thus required a special convention.[94] Article VI promised that such a convention would follow, and in a special letter, September 8, 1896, Shu King-chen promised to add his influence in Peking in order to obtain this convention.[95]

On December 16, 1896, Nicholas II approved the charter of the C.E.R.[96] and there remained only the business of financing the original modest capitalization of 5,000,000 rubles. Witte's draft of August 30 in Article IV prescribed a capitalization by which 700 of the 1,000 shares would be bought by the Russian government.[97] But this article was deleted because it made it obvious that the control of the C.E.R. was in the hands of the Russian government. Witte and his financial agents then turned to a subterfuge. A public sale of the shares was announced in the official newspaper, *Pravitel'stvennyi Vestnik*, on the morning of December 29, to take place on the same morning at nine o'clock.[98] With so short a notice, the high cost of individual shares (5,000 rubles), and the decidedly early hours for bankers—particularly Russians and particularly in St. Petersburg, the city of "white nights" and midnight suppers—the results of the sale were as expected. On the same day, Rothstein wrote Witte that "there was not even a shadow of the public" and that a few minutes after the opening of the sale it was officially closed.[99] The Russian government bought less than 25 per cent of the shares outright and obtained an option on the rest, which were held for that government by the Russo-Chinese Bank. Not until 1902 did the Russian government purchase enough shares to control 53 per cent of the company; nevertheless, with an actual investment of about one million rubles, the government, under the Ministry of Finance (actually Witte), controlled the C.E.R. directly.[100] In a purely honorary capacity Shu King-chen was made president of the company, with vague additional duties of supervising Chinese interests in company affairs.[101]

Before 1895 Manchuria was rarely visited by Russians. Although, by agreements with China, Russian nationals could trade in Manchuria in a zone one hundred versts in depth, the privilege was seldom used. Before 1895 there were French, Belgian, and English missionaries in Mukden and Kirin and English merchants resident in Port Arthur, but there was not one Russian missionary or merchant anywhere in Manchuria.[102] The "secret" publications of the Russian General Staff which contain accounts of Russian explorations and special investigations in Asiatic territories adjacent to the Russian frontiers have no comprehensive accounts of Manchuria before 1895.[103] Manchuria was visited mainly by expeditions going to or from Korea or northern China.[104] When such an expedition appeared in Mukden in 1895 it caused a sensation.[105]

In 1895 the Russians made a few attempts to come into closer contact with Manchuria. The Imperial Russian Geographical Society sent a geological and botanical expedition to Korea and northern Manchuria under E. E. Ahnert and V. L. Komarov.[106] And two merchants from

Khabarovsk—Bogdanov and Tifonov—on their own initiative sent a chartered steamer up the Sungari to establish trade relations with the riparian settlements.[107] In April and May, 1896, in anticipation of the opening up of Manchuria by a Russo-Chinese treaty, several topographical and surveying expeditions were sent to the borders of Manchuria and awaited permission to cross the border and begin their assigned work.[108] When permission arrived and the group from the Primorsk region crossed the border on June 29, work was further delayed by the "Khunhuz War of 1896."[109] Throughout the summer of 1896, groups of Manchurian bandits (*khunhuzes*), numbering at times as many as three hundred men, raided Chinese settlements in northeastern Manchuria and several times crossed the border into Russian territory, where they were defeated and driven out by sotnias (squadrons of one hundred men) of the Ussuri cossacks.[110] This endemic summer banditry in Manchuria so delayed the work of the expedition in 1896 that the real survey of a possible trans-Manchurian railroad could not be carried out until 1897, and with the exception of some simple preliminary work, the construction of the C.E.R. did not begin until the spring of 1898.[111]

Consequently, in 1896 and 1897, Russian penetration of Manchuria was more theoretical than actual. Though some stores for the future construction of the railroad were deposited along the Sungari River, neither the Russo-Chinese Bank nor the C.E.R. established offices or branches in Manchuria until 1898.[112] Other unforeseen factors delayed the execution of Witte's plan. The sudden death of Prince Lobanov-Rostovskii in August, 1896, and the departure of Cassini from Peking on September 30, 1896, because of ill health, deprived Witte of two friendly collaborators in his plan for a trans-Manchurian railroad. Shishkin, the Acting Minister of Foreign Affairs, and the not very active A. I. Pavlov, who for one year held the post of chargé in Peking, proved to be less competent aides.[113] In 1897 Witte had to rely more on his direct agents in the Russo-Chinese Bank, Pokotilov and Ukhtomskii. Several other matters caused delays. And when in the spring of 1897, Victor Grot, now transferred from the service of Li Hung-chang to the Russo-Chinese Bank, obtained a gold-mining concession in northeastern Mongolia, breaking down for the first time the Chinese insistence that mineral rights were reserved for the Imperial regalia, he was given no assistance for his enterprise.[114] A "Syndicate for the Exploration of Mineral Riches in China" was formed in the same year with the help of the Russo-Chinese Bank and the personal participation of Grot, Rothstein, Pokotilov, and other investors interested in the Russo-Chinese Bank. No practical work, however, was begun in Mongolia until the spring of 1900.[115] The publication of the alleged "Cassini Convention" also caused delay. The secrecy shrouding the actual Defensive Alliance of June 3, 1896, and the Agreement of September 8, 1896, together with the public declaration of the statutes of the C.E.R., led to the suspicion that the "Cassini Convention" represented, in the main, Russia's true intentions.[116] Hence Russia's activities in the Far East were looked upon with suspicion and alarm. Then, in 1896–1897, an opportunity occurred for Russia to enhance her prestige and position in Korea, and Russian energies were further distracted by this Korean "interlude."

RUSSIAN INFLUENCE IN KOREA, 1895–1897

Following the policy established by the Special Conference of 1888 and the conferences of 1894–1895, Russia showed little interest in Korea as long as its territorial integrity and, after 1895, its independence were not menaced by any other power. Russia witnessed the increase of European, American, and Japanese contracts with Korea with apparent indifference and made no effort even to begin establishing Russian contacts. By 1890 there were 150 Protestant missionaries in Korea,[117] while the Russian Greek Orthodox Church had none. In 1892 there were 13 Russian subjects in all of Korea, including Russian diplomatic representatives, as compared with 9,132 Japanese, 78 American, 51 British, 28 French, and 25 German subjects.[118] Although Russian economic relations with Korea showed the most rapid increase from 1886 to 1894, the increase was mainly due to the increase in the population and the military garrison of the Primorsk region and the consequently greater dependence on imports from Korea. In quantity and in comparison with other countries this trade remained insignificant, the total imports and exports amounting to $218,000 as compared with $2,697,000 of Japanese-Korean trade and $2,226,000 of Chinese-Korean trade,[119] not to mention British trade, which in 1892 represented 57 per cent of Korean imports.[120]

In 1894 Korea became the haunt of concession seekers. By the end of 1895 China had absolute control over the telegraph franchise; Japan had obtained vast fishing rights as well as the monopoly of paper production, the mint, glassworks, and other enterprises; citizens of the United States held concessions in coastal trade, pearl fisheries, electric power in Seoul, timber grants, and a gold-mining concession in the entire Unsan district of the province of Pyongan, which for forty years proved to be the most profitable and the largest of the concessionary enterprises in Korea.[121] In this grab for concessions Russia was not represented, and there is no evidence that she attempted to gain any concessions.

In October, 1895, events in Seoul placed Korea under Russian influence. The Japanese, apparently dissatisfied with the slow progress of their influence in Korea and blocked by the King of Korea in their desire to obtain a railway concession from Fusan to the Yalu River,[122] recalled Count Inouye, their moderate Minister to Seoul, and replaced him with a blunt former soldier, the politically and diplomatically immature General Miura.[123] On the night of October 8, 1895, Miura, after consulting with his more experienced advisers at the Japanese Legation, engineered a coup d'état in which a mob of Japanese *soshi,* Korean adherents, and members of the *Kurentai,* a Japanese-trained army unit, protected by a screen of regular Japanese soldiers, stormed the palace and murdered the Queen of Korea and members of her family whom she had brought to power in an anti-Japanese movement.[124]

The coup d'état was an immediate success. The King of Korea yielded "in panic" to all Japanese demands, repealed the reforms of the previous year, published an edict degrading the Queen, and generally acted as a "tool" in the hands of the Japanese.[125] The complicity of the Japanese envoy in the coup of 1895 was so obvious that the diplomatic representatives of foreign powers formed a "united front" against their Japanese colleague. They conferred mutually in the absence of Miura, befriended the refugee partisans of the Min family, and brought to Seoul small detachments of marines.[126] Closely coöperating in this policy and assuming a leadership over the other representatives were Carl Weber, the Russian Minister to Seoul, and Dr. Horace N. Allen, a missionary and then secretary and actual chargé of the American legation, who was acting in defiance of instructions to abstain from any influence on the political events in Korea and particularly from any joint action with another power.[127]

The momentary Japanese success soon vanished. Miura was recalled. He was tried at Hiroshima by a Japanese court and, though acquitted of direct guilt, was compelled to admit an error in policy.[128] The moderate Inouye once more was sent to restore Japan's position and was readmitted into the councils of foreign representatives. On November 1, 1895, he approached Dr. Allen to effect a reconciliation with Weber. Allen, who favored a Russo-Japanese condominium in Korea in view of the unwillingness of the United States to commit itself to a positive policy there, brought the two together.[129] Inouye influenced the King of Korea to withdraw the decrees of October, particularly the decree degrading the Queen ;[130] but the King still remained a virtual prisoner of the Japanese-trained and Japanese-led army group. On November 28, a Korean counterrevolution failed to free the King, but the counterrevolutionary movement continued.[131] The rebels in the provinces defeated the troops sent to crush the revolt, and by February, 1896, Seoul was again in danger from the approaching rebels.[132] On February 9, Russian sailors were landed and rushed to Seoul, reinforcing the legation guard to 150 men.[133] On the following day, the King of Korea asked Dr. Allen whether it would be safe for him to take refuge with the Russian minister. Dr. Allen assured him that it would be and personally aided his plan by bringing Weber in touch with the officer in charge of the King's bodyguard. On the morning of the eleventh the King of Korea, the Crown Prince, and some of their loyal attendants fled to the Russian legation, and the King remained there for more than a year.[134]

An anti-Japanese reaction began immediately. On February 11, the pro-Japanese ministers were massacred almost to a man, and the King performed penance for having associated with them.[135] Although Russia was placed in an extraordinarily favorable position for influencing a pro-Russian orientation of Korean affairs, Weber refused to take advantage of his position.[136] The immediate gains were reaped by Dr. Allen; the anti-Japanese, and later anti-Russian, Korean Independence party of Philip Jaisohn, an American-educated Korean adviser to the King; and J. McLeavy Brown, the British Director of the Korean Customs, who became the leading political figures in Seoul.[137] On the advice of Dr. Allen the King selected a new ministry predominantly of men who had sought refuge in the American legation, and through them Allen obtained an extension of the lucrative Unsan franchise and the Seoul-Chemulpo railroad concession for American interests.[138]

Meanwhile, in Japan, Premier Ito Hirobumi, General Marquis Yamagata, and Count Inouye, the proponent of a moderate policy in Korea, came to the conclusion that to avert Russian ascendancy in Korea and to prevent a clash of Russian and Japanese interests there, Japan must come to an agreement with Russia.[139] Negotiations were started in Seoul between Weber and Komura, the new Japanese Minister, which resulted in the signing on May 14, 1896, of a joint memorandum, known as the Seoul Protocol.[140]

This agreement, though presumably a *quid pro quo* agreement, was in reality a Russian victory. Under Article I, the representatives of Russia and Japan were to advise the King of Korea to return to his own palace "when no doubts concerning his safety could be entertained." This decision was to rest entirely upon the discretion of the King, but his presence in the Russian legation naturally made him more likely to accept the Russian minister's interpretation of what would be the safe time. Under Article III, Russia acknowledged that it was necessary for the Japanese to maintain a force of two hundred "gendarmes" along the Japanese telegraph line from Fusan to Seoul, but this was much less than the three companies of infantry which previously were deployed along this line. Under Article IV, Japan was allowed to maintain two companies of soldiers in Seoul, one in Gensan and one in Fusan, for the protection of her settlements, each company not to exceed two hundred men; and Russia had the right to have a corresponding force for the protection of her legation and consulates. In view of the great disparity of Japanese and Russian interests in Korea, and of Russian and Japanese forces in Korea, the article meant that Japan must reduce her forces, whereas Russia had Japan's consent to increase hers. Furthermore, Article I practically represented an admission of Japanese complicitiy in the coup of October 8 by including the provision that "the Japanese representative on his part gives the assurance that the most complete and effective measures will be taken for the control of the Japanese *soshi*."[141]

Japan then planned a broader agreement with Russia. Late in April, 1896, Marquis Yamagata left for Russia to represent Japan at the coronation of Nicholas II,[142] and in the latter part of May and in June he negotiated with Lobanov on Korean affairs. Yamagata proposed a division of Korea into Russian and Japanese spheres of influence, the line of division to be the thirty-eighth parallel of latitude;[143] but Lobanov rejected the proposal, possibly because Russia was already pledging to preserve the territorial integrity of Korea in the negotiations of the secret Russo-Chinese Treaty of June 3, and possibly because, as a later Minister of Foreign Affairs argued in a memorandum in 1903, "by yielding to Japan the southern part of the Korean peninsula by an agreement, Russia would have formally, and forever, abandoned the most important part of Korea in the strategic and military-naval sense, and thus, voluntarily, would have compromised her freedom of action in the future."[144]

The best that Yamagata was able to achieve was the negotiation of the Lobanov-Yamagata Agreement, also known as the Moscow Protocol of June 9, 1896,[145] which, like its Seoul predecessor, was open to various interpretations and equivocations. Article I of the agreement bound Russia and Japan to come to an accord if Korea required a foreign loan. However, Article II made no provision for a mutual accord in the event Korea required foreign assistance in creating an army or a police force. The article read: "The Russian and Japanese governments will endeavor to leave to Korea, as far as the financial and economic situation of that country will permit them to do so, the creation and maintenance of an armed force and of a native police in sufficient proportions to maintain order without foreign aid." In accordance with this article Russia could—and later did—consider that the financial and economic condition of Korea did not permit Russia to "leave to Korea . . . the creation of an armed force"; consequently Russia later arranged a military mission for the training of the Korean army. The final interpretation of this article lay in the hands of the King of Korea, who was still in the Russian legation.

The narrow scope of the Moscow Protocol made it merely an extension of the *modus vivendi* agreement at Seoul, from which were eliminated a few more points on which Russia and Japan disagreed. Several secret clauses were added, which provided that neither Russia nor Japan would send troops into Korea unless the other nation gave its consent, and if such a measure should be necessary, the two powers would agree beforehand on the zone of operations of their troops and the neutral zone between the forces of the two powers.[146]

The Russo-Japanese agreements of 1896 have frequently been considered to have established a condominium of Japan and Russia in Korea. It is clear, however, that Russia had no intention of forming a condominium (joint sovereignty). The Japanese envoy wanted an agreement. He was given one, but of a scope so restricted that the freedom of interpretation and action reserved for the Russians could hardly have been missed by the Japanese statesmen. Far from considering the agreements as the beginning of amicable relations between Russia and Japan, the Japanese Diet in 1896 voted even larger sums for the military and naval expansion which had begun in 1895.[147] Furthermore, it was an open secret that, in addition to the suspected Russo-Chinese negotiations and the Russo-Japanese negotiations, the Korean envoy to the Tsar's coronation was also conducting talks.

The Korean envoy was the brother of the murdered Queen. His mission was arranged by Weber, and he was escorted from Seoul to Moscow by Russian agents.[148] The Korean proposals in the Russo-Korean negotiations are not known, but they can be judged from the final Russian reply.[149] It is doubtful, in view of the text of the reply and the desire of the Koreans in general to maintain their independence, that the Korean envoy, in a private audience with the Tsar, asked for or was promised a Russian protectorate over Korea.[150] However, the Russian reply (in point 1) did promise "protection" to the person of the King while he was in the Russian legation and after his return to his own palace. Point 2 indicated an extension of Russian influence:

In order to solve the question of instructors [for the army] there will be sent to Seoul in the near future a high-ranking and experienced Russian officer, who will be empowered by the Russian government to enter into negotiations with the Korean government on this matter; the said officer will be instructed to take up, first of all, the question of creating a detachment of bodyguards for the King. An equally experienced person will be sent from Russia for the investigation of the economic condition of Korea and for the determination of necessary financial measures.[151]

Point 3 stipulated that the persons mentioned in point 2 would also act as advisers to the King of Korea under the direction of the Russian Minister to Seoul. Point 4 was equivocal and stated that a loan to Korea "would be taken into consideration as soon as the economic condition of the country and the requirements of the country are determined."[152]

Within a month after the signing of the Lobanov-Yamagata Agreement the Russian government was undermining the idea of a Russo-Japanese condominium. In July, negotiations were begun to bring in Russian instructors for the army. In August, Colonel Strel'bitskii arrived at Seoul as the Russian military agent, and D. D. Pokotilov as the financial agent of the Russian General Staff arrived with three officers and ten noncommissioned officers and began the reorganization of the Korean army, starting with the palace guard. On February 20, 1897, the King of Korea felt sufficiently safe to leave the Russian legation and move to the Chong Dong Palace, practically next door to the legation, where Colonel Putiata and a group of Russian officers were also stationed as commanders of the Royal Bodyguard.[153] It was also during this period, on September 9, 1896, that Iulii Ivanovich Briner, a prominent merchant of Vladivostock, received a concession from the Korean Minister of the Household to exploit timber and mineral resources on the Korean banks of the Yalu and Tumen rivers.[154]

The Japanese government viewed this Russian ascendancy with considerable misgiving and inquired of Russian diplomatic representatives in Tokyo and Seoul concerning the right of Korea to employ Russian instructors.[155] The inquiries did not check Russian intentions of gaining control of the Korean army. In April, 1897, Weber suggested to the Korean government that 160 Russian officers and men be employed as instructors for the Korean army. On May 8, 1897, the Korean Minister of Foreign Affairs refused the offer.[156] In St. Petersburg, the Russian Ministry of Foreign Affairs attempted to quiet Japanese indignation by giving assurances to Hayashi Todasu, the Japanese Minister to St. Petersburg, that Baron R. R. Rosen, the newly appointed Russian Minister to Tokyo, would iron out the difficulties upon his arrival in Japan, and that until that time no new steps would be taken in Korean affairs.[157] This assurance was also treated in an equivocal manner, and on August 3, 1897, thirteen additional officers arrived in Seoul to train Korean troops.[158]

In matters of financial assistance to Korea there were some delays. Witte, busy with Li Hung-chang in May and June, 1896, did not take part in the negotiations on Korean affairs.[159] His interest in the trans-Manchurian railroad was paramount. In June he postponed the decision of a loan to Korea by which the Korean government hoped to buy out the Japanese telegraph line and thus render unnecessary the small Japanese garrisons along this line.[160] Weber, from Seoul, and Lobanov, in St. Petersburg, urged Witte to take measures because a French firm, Cie de Fives-Lilles, was secretly offering a loan to Korea and the Hong Kong and Shanghai Banking Corporation was about to establish a branch in Seoul.[161] Witte refused to be distracted from his program. He compromised by sending Pokotilov to Korea to investigate its economic conditions. Pokotilov joined Weber in urging immediate action in establishing a Russian bank in Korea and creating a stronger Russian influence there through the medium of a loan to the Korean government.[162]

Witte was directly responsible for the delays. He replied to Pokotilov with a categorical refusal to do anything until November, and in November he announced that he was in favor of a loan to Korea only "when it will be found to be timely."[163] He furthermore insisted on Russian control of the Korean customs, a measure difficult to effect in view of the strong position held by McLeavy Brown in the Customs Department.[164] In December he turned down a project of G. P. Möllendorff, supported by many Russians, to form a Russo-American syndicate for the purchase of the existing railroads, and for the construction of future railroads in all parts of Korea.[165] In February, 1897, Witte delayed the appointment of a Russian financial agent to Korea by raising the irrelevant question who was to pay the agent's salary.[166] In June he let pass the opportunity to purchase the lapsing American concession on the Seoul-Chemulpo railway, which then was mortgaged to the Japanese and later was bought by them.[167]

The only Russian victory in the economic and concessionary developments was the work of Pokotilov, who in October, 1896, persuaded the Cie de Fives-Lilles to use the Russian railroad gauge on their concession of the Seoul-Wiju railway.[168] After Pokotilov's departure in November, 1896, opportunities to establish financial control of Korea decreased. In January, 1897, McLeavy Brown persuaded the King of Korea to issue an edict proclaiming that in the future all railroads in Korea would be built by the Korean government.[169] In March the Japanese government, anxious to check the ascendancy of Russian influence, revealed to the Korean government the public and secret terms of the Moscow agreements[170] and thus further undermined Russian prestige. McLeavy Brown then easily persuaded the Koreans to try to pay off the Japanese loan with Korean funds.[171]

However, by this time Witte had begun gradually to change his views on Korean affairs. Constantly urged by Pokotilov and now by Count M. N. Muraviev, the new Russian Minister of Foreign Affairs, to take positive action in Korea, Witte began conferring with Rothstein on the formation of a Russo-Korean bank.[172] Witte's plans to obtain a right to construct a branch from the C.E.R. to an ice-free port in southern Manchuria were at their lowest ebb in March, 1897. On March 20, P. M. Romanov, Director of the Chancellery of the Ministry of Finance and a member of the Board of Directors of the C.E.R. and the Russo-Chinese Bank, submitted to Witte a memoir containing some convincing arguments. Romanov wrote:

> In my opinion Korea has the greatest importance for us; northern Manchuria is important to us only inasmuch as it provides us with access to Liaotung or to Korea. But the Chinese in the near future will hardly permit us to bring our railroad to one of the ports of the Liaotung Peninsula, as they understand that this would place Peking in our hands; on the other hand they will not oppose strongly our routing of the railroad from Bodune through Kirin to one of the ports of Korea, as this would safeguard them from a Japanese seizure of Korea. But in order to gain the consent of Korea we must first acquire an influence in her financial affairs, and in this respect we must not hesitate even before financial sacrifices. . . .[173]

Witte accepted Romanov's plan without enthusiasm.[174] He still hesitated, delayed, and shared with Muraviev the opinion that the favorable situation that had existed in 1896 had changed.[175] Nevertheless, on May 21 he obtained the permission of the Tsar to send a financial agent to Korea.[176]

After another month of delay the choice fell on K. A. Alexeev, an official in the Russian customs service. Alexeev was instructed by Witte to act cautiously, to make a thorough investigation of Korean finances and the opportunities for establishing a Russian bank in Korea, and to find means of taking over the Korean customs service. Traveling by the long sea route, Alexeev arrived in Korea in October, 1897,[177] in time to participate in a strong, though temporary, resurgence of Russian influence in Korean affairs. Meanwhile, Russian interests turned to Manchuria, where, in consequence of international developments, the acquisition of an ice-free port was once more feasible.

V

PENETRATION OF SOUTHERN MANCHURIA AND LIMITATIONS ON RUSSIAN EXPANSION, 1897–1900

SIX DAYS after the signing of the Russo-Chinese contract for the Chinese Eastern Railway, Ukhtomskii and Rothstein concluded that it was timely to arrange the payment of the first million rubles promised to Li Hung-chang for his coöperation in the May and June negotiations of 1896. Feeling that a delay might turn Li and his supporters against the acceptance of the contract of September 8, and that the payment had to be handled with circumspection, they suggested that Ukhtomskii be sent to China to transmit the payment in person.[1] Witte, however, counseled delay and telegraphed Ukhtomskii from Yalta on September 15 that undue haste might affect the negotiations adversely. He also hinted that a later mission might have an additional purpose.[2]

ACQUISITION OF PORT ARTHUR AND PENETRATION OF SOUTHERN MANCHURIA, 1897–1898

The additional purpose which Witte had in mind was to negotiate a project for the penetration of southern Manchuria by a railroad branch from the C.E.R. The proposal was presented at the first conference of the Board of Directors of the C.E.R. on February 3, 1897.[3] This conference was attended by the directors and engineers of the C.E.R., who were predominantly Witte's friends and appointees,[4] and who showed considerable knowledge of his plans and negotiations of May through June, 1896.

At the conference, S. I. Kerbedz, the acting chairman, proposed that the C.E.R. take advantage of the intended mission of Ukhtomskii and empower him to conduct negotiations with Li Hung-chang for a Russian railway concession to "one of the ports on the Yellow Sea." Kerbedz suggested that if the Chinese authorities opposed the construction of a broad Russian five-foot-gauge track, which Li Hung-chang had opposed in the May and June negotiations, Russia could agree to the narrow European gauge of four feet nine inches, which had been acceptable to Li in May and June, and build the roadbed to accommodate the larger gauge. "Under such conditions the transformation of this

---

[1] For notes to chap. v see pp. 280–286.

branch from a narrow to a broad gauge could be carried out whenever needed in the course of a few days."[5]

P. M. Romanov, supported by E. K. Tsigler, opposed the narrow-gauge subterfuge on the grounds that negotiations with the Chinese must be firm, and that Russian insistence that foreign concessionary railways in Korea be built on a broad gauge would render the subterfuge transparent.[6] The conference adopted the general policy that any negotiations that took place should be handled cautiously so as not to arouse increased opposition by foreign powers and China; that thorough preparations should be made for the negotiations, to lessen the likelihood of a refusal; and that the work on the branch line to southern Manchuria should proceed slowly, for haste would overburden the C.E.R. with additional expenses. The conference also adopted another suggestion by Kerbedz that the C.E.R. should negotiate for a concession of a branch railroad to the coal deposits in the vicinity of Mukden, on the grounds that the fuel was needed for the C.E.R. Later, the extension of this railroad to the Yellow Sea would be a logical development and permission for it would be easier to obtain.[7]

The recommendations of this conference were combined with the decisions made by Witte, after his conference with Rothstein, to seek a terminal for the southern branch of the C.E.R. in Korea, and they formed the basis of the main instructions given to Ukhtomskii for his negotiations with the Chinese government.[8] Ukhtomskii was directed to obtain theoretical approval from the Chinese government for the construction of the C.E.R. branch to the south, and more specifically to elicit Chinese reaction to a plan for a Russian railway from the C.E.R. to a Korean port, and from the C.E.R. to Chinchow (now Chinhsien), where it would form a junction with the Chinese Imperial Northern Railway advancing toward Manchuria. Other instructions dealt with increasing the power of the agents and agencies of the C.E.R. Ukhtomskii was to obtain for the chief engineer of the C.E.R. the right to negotiate directly with the governors general of the three Manchurian provinces, and the Russo-Chinese Bank asked that its right to coin silver and issue paper money be implemented by Chinese legislation enforcing its circulation.

Ukhtomskii reached Shanghai in the middle of May and, through Pokotilov in Peking, transferred the one million rubles to Li Hung-chang. At first Li appeared quite willing to take up new negotiations, but his attitude changed as soon as the money was in his hands. In June, in the first conversation with Ukhtomskii at the Tsungli Yamen, Li assumed an offended tone, remarking that "we have allowed your entrance into our courtyard, but you want to shove your way into our private rooms where we have our wives and little children."[9] In discussing a Russian branch to Chinchow, Ukhtomskii even compromised Li Hung-chang in the Tsungli Yamen and made him the object of verbal attacks and the accusations of interested Russian parties.[10] Ukhtomskii then decided to drop the subject and asked only for a guarantee of "nonalienation" of Manchurian railroads. The Tsungli Yamen also refused that and would not even discuss a branch railroad to a Korean port.[11]

Ukhtomskii's mission was therefore a complete failure. What was even worse, from the Russian point of view, it prompted Li Hung-chang to take countermeasures against Russian plans in southern Manchuria. On July 31, 1897, Li Hung-chang obtained the Imperial consent to his project of further railroad expansion into Manchuria and appointed as its executor a former employee of the Hong Kong and Shanghai Banking Corporation, who was also under the influence of C. W. Kinder, the British engineer who had long been connected with Chinese railroads.[12] Witte attempted to persuade Muraviev to oppose this appointment by diplomatic means and to secure, through the Russian diplomatic representatives, a promise from China that either no railroads would be constructed in Manchuria at all or, if any were constructed, they would be built by Russia;[13] but Muraviev saw no possibility of exacting such a promise from China.[14] Li Hung-chang took advantage of his favorable position and obtained two small loans from the Russo-Chinese Bank, which the bank did not dare refuse; and in September, 1897, he permitted an Anglo-American group of mining engineers to begin a survey of mineral deposits in southern Manchuria with a view toward their eventual exploitation.[15] Further successes in Li Hung-chang's policy of independent Chinese action were halted by the developments of the Kiaochow and Port Arthur crises of 1897–1898.

Since 1895, Germany had shown an interest in acquiring a coaling station or a naval base in the Far East; in that year William II suggested a base in China, where the trade interests of Germany were second only to those of Great Britain.[16] After Germany's participation in the Triplice of 1895, realization of her desire seemed possible. On October 29 she asked China, through the Chinese ambassadors to Russia and Germany, to lease a harbor to her;[17] but the Chinese, avoiding a direct refusal, pointed out that such a lease might lead to a general attack on China's territorial integrity.[18] In the spring of 1897 Admiral Alfred von Tirpitz, the commander of the German squadron in the

Far East, and Baron von Heyking, the minister to China, accepted the report of Georg Franzius, a noted German harbor expert, and agreed that the port of Kiaochow was the port most suitable for German naval requirements.[19]

Before proceeding with Chinese negotiations concerning the lease of Kiaochow, Germany made inquiries about Russian interests in Kiaochow Bay. She feared that Russia had a lien on the bay, because in the winter of 1895–96 the Russian squadron had used it for a winter station.[20] Furthermore, the so-called "Cassini Convention" stated that Russia was to have the exclusive use of the port for fifteen years.[21] When Li Hung-chang passed through Berlin in June, 1896, he was asked directly by Baron Marschall von Bieberstein, the German Foreign Minister, whether Russia had any rights on Kiaochow; Li Hung-chang answered emphatically that she did not.[22]

Germany then canvassed various Russian authorities. Heyking approached Admiral Alexeev, the commander of the Pacific squadron, who informed him that the port had once been considered by the Admiralty but had been rejected.[23] The German Ambassador to Russia, Radolin, conferred with Muraviev and received the discouraging advice that Germany should seek a port farther south because Russia intended to use Kiaochow as a winter station for 1897–98.[24] In Peking, however, Count Cassini told the German minister that, although "he could not say for certain," the port of Kiaochow would definitely be free of any liens if Russia could find a port in Korea.[25]

From August 2 to August 11, 1897, William II was in Russia on a visit of state, and one day while returning in a carriage from a parade at Tsarskoe Selo to Peterhof, William II broached the subject of Kiaochow to Nicholas II. In conversations as early as 1900,[26] in his memoirs,[27] and in materials he supplied to the historian E. J. Dillon,[28] Witte circulated the story that during this trip the Tsar gave unqualified assent to William II for the German occupation of Kiaochow, and that presumably either Nicholas II was ignorant of Russian priorities in regard to the port, or the "weak-willed" Tsar simply could not resist the appeal of the German Emperor, who "was too insistent."[29] From such accounts of the "Peterhof agreement" arose the interpretation that Nicholas II was an admirer of William II and was easily influenced by him.

In all probability the opposite is true. Although Nicholas II acceded politely to the appointment of William II to the rank of a Russian admiral, he did it with distaste. He wrote to his mother on the same day, "It makes me sick just to think of it!"[30] And when the Kaiser left Russia, the Tsar wrote to his mother, "Thank God the German visit is over.''[31] Actually, after the ride from Tsarskoe Selo to Peterhof, the Tsar reported the gist of their conversation to Muraviev, and William II reported it to Chancellor von Bülow, who accompanied him to Russia. From the German account it is evident that the Tsar gave assent only to a temporary visit of the German squadron to Kiaochow Bay in time of need and with the permission of the Russian naval authorities in the Far East. To the question whether Russia had any future intentions in regard to Kiaochow, the Tsar answered that "Russia is interested in reserving her rights to the use of this port, the acquisition of which she has already contemplated.''[32]

Germany then decided to force the issue. Radolin informed Muraviev on September 21 that Germany would avail herself of the Tsar's approval of a temporary visit, and Muraviev promised to inform the Tsar of the German decision. On October 1 the German Minister to China informed the Tsungli Yamen that the German squadron would station itself in Kiaochow; he mentioned having the assent of the Russian government, which actually had not been expressed; and he omitted any reference to the length of the stay.[33] Before taking further steps, Germany once more tried to get some sort of consent from Russia. The *démarche* was timed with Muraviev's trip to France. On October 14, Tschirsky, the German chargé at St. Petersburg, informed Count V. N. Lamsdorf, the Assistant Minister of Foreign Affairs, that Germany would take advantage of the Tsar's previous promise.[34] Lamsdorf was thus placed in a predicament. He could hardly refuse the German request, for at the time there were no Russian ships in Kiaochow, nor could he give his assent, as that would establish a precedent and German warships would from then on claim the right to anchor in Kiaochow. He evaded the issue by accepting another alternative, expressing the opinion to Tschirsky that Russia herself had the right to remain in Kiaochow only for the winter of 1895–96, and therefore was unable to grant Germany the rights she asked for.[35]

On November 2, 1897, the murder of two German missionaries in Shantung gave Germany a pretext for taking further steps. On November 6, William II ordered his Pacific squadron to go to Kiaochow and demand an indemnity from the Chinese government.[36] On the same day, he telegraphed Nicholas II of his intentions, adding a reference to the Peterhof conversations:

I hope, that in accordance with our personal conversation in Peterhof, you will approve the movement of my squadron to Kiaochow, for that is the only port from which it can operate against marauders, and I am under obligation to the Catholic party in Germany to show that I am in a position to come to the defense of their missions. Punishment is necessary, and it will bring advantages to all Christians.

To this the Tsar replied on November 7: "Cannot approve or disapprove your sending German squadron to Kiaochow as I have lately learned that this harbor was ours only temporarily in 1895–96."[38]

This reply gave Germany the opportunity to claim that the Tsar's statement annulled all previous declarations in regard to Russian priorities in Kiaochow; but on November 9, Baron F. P. Osten-Sacken, the Russian chargé in Berlin, delivered to the Foreign Office two telegrams from Muraviev, which renewed Russian claims.[39] The telegrams expressed Muraviev's willingness to undertake to induce China to give satisfaction for the murder of the two missionaries. They also set forth for the first time a concrete Russian claim to Kiaochow, based on the fact that Russia, by wintering in Kiaochow in 1895–96, automatically received from China "a right of first anchorage" (*droit de premier mouillage*), which amounted to a priority if ever the port were to be alienated to another power.[40] He added that the Russian admiral in the Far East had instructions to send his ships into Kiaochow Bay if the German squadron entered it.

From November 10 to November 24, C. K. von Hohenlohe and Chancellor von Bülow discussed this deadlock with the Russian chargé. They refused to recognize any earlier arrangements made by Russia concerning Kiaochow and refused to accept Russia as a mediator in getting satisfaction from China. They pointed out to Osten-Sacken that Russia ought to be glad to have Germany as her neighbor in the Far East, that Russia could get a port of her own, and that Russian ships could still use the port of Kiaochow with German permission.[41] In applying pressure on the Russians to get them to accept their stand, the German statesmen threatened to "turn to the West" because British statesmen had no objections to Germany's occupation of Kiaochow, since it would be a counterbalance to Russia in the north.[42]

On November 14, Admiral Diederichs entered Kiaochow Bay with the German squadron. Four days later, Pavlov, the Russian chargé in Peking, was informed that the Russian squadron had received orders to follow the German squadron into Kiaochow Bay.[43] Although Russia seemed to stand behind China and had unofficially advised procrastination in the German-Chinese negotiations,[44] the fate of Kiaochow was not in doubt. On November 20 the orders to the Russian Pacific squadron were countermanded,[45] and on November 23 Muraviev admitted that Kiaochow would eventually go to the Germans.[46]

The loss of priority rights in Kiaochow was not a serious blow to Russian interests. The Russian squadron had made little use of the station. Although Japan had had restrictions on the use of her ports by foreign warships since 1895, granting such use on sufferance and only in time of peace, the Russian squadron could still use the ports of Japan, chiefly Nagasaki. It usually found a warm welcome in these ports and used the only large dry-dock facilities in the Far East besides those at Hong Kong.[47] Furthermore, the prospect arose that Russia might acquire a more desirable port.

On November 15, when news came to Peking that the Germans had landed at Kiaochow, Li Hung-chang "immediately rushed to the Russian legation with an appeal for Russian assistance, and he did not leave it until he received a ciphered telegram to be sent to St. Petersburg from the Russian chargé d'affaires."[48] A hint on the nature of this appeal can be gained from an excerpt of this telegram, or another telegram sent by the chargé on the same day. "The [Chinese] ministers declare their unconditional consent to open all ports not open to foreigners, to our vessels at once, and for any desired time, without exception, with an offer to use Chinese government arsenals, stores, etc., in case of need."[49] This appeal seems like an attempt to invoke the Russo-Chinese Treaty of June 3, 1896, against Germany. It was also a direct invitation to Russia to occupy temporarily some port in China as a countermeasure to the German occupation of Kiaochow.

In favor of this occupation, on November 23, 1897, Muraviev submitted a lengthy memorandum to the Tsar outlining Russia's political and naval situation in the Far East and reviewing Russian claims to Kiaochow, which had already been abandoned. Muraviev considered Kiaochow lost, but he considered the loss of no great importance, since the port was unsuitable for a Russian naval station or base because of its remoteness from spheres of Russian interests.[50] In fact, he saw in the German occupation of Kiaochow a "favorable" turn of events[51] which gave Russia an opportunity to acquire an ice-free port.[52] The main problem was what ice-free port to take. Muraviev eliminated from consideration the ports on the eastern coast of Korea because they could be easily blockaded by the Japanese fleet and would thus be a trap for Russian ships.[53] For similar reasons he disapproved of the interest of the Navy in the port of Fusan.[54] The Navy Department, as the department most interested in the matter and the one most competent to select the port, had not yet told Muraviev of its choice.[55]

Therefore, Muraviev suggested the acquisition of a port on the Liaotung Peninsula, preferably Talienwan, which had been explored and found suitable for Russian naval needs.[56] In the acquisition of this port, Muraviev counseled haste and determination—haste because some other power might follow the example of Germany and occupy

Talienwan, and determination because that is the only way to deal with "oriental peoples."[57]

Nicholas II approved the memorandum on the same day, and wrote to Muraviev:

> I fully agree with the conclusions drawn in this memorandum, and considering that we must not lose time I am calling a conference this Friday, November 26, at two o'clock. I ask you to inform and invite in my name: the Minister of War, the Director of the Navy Department, and the Minister of Finance. I have always held the opinion that our future ice-free port should be on the Liaotung Peninsula or in the northeastern corner of the Bay of Korea.[58]

On November 26 the proposed conference took place, attended by the Ministers of War, Finance, and Foreign Affairs and the Director of the Navy Department.[59] In discussing the measures proposed by Muraviev, the ministers were divided in their opinions. Muraviev upheld the views expressed in his memorandum that the time was opportune for Russia to occupy an ice-free port, such as Talienwan or Port Arthur, but he also stated that he was incompetent to judge whether Russia needed such a port and where such a port should be.[60]

Witte opposed the policy of compensation. He argued that if Russia did not need Kiaochow, the German occupation of that port could be ignored. A policy of taking compensation, Witte stated, would violate the spirit of the Russo-Chinese Alliance of June 3, 1896; for by taking compensation Russia would be doing exactly what she had pledged to prevent Japan from doing. Furthermore, Japan might seek to follow the example of Germany and Russia and seize some port and thus bring about a situation in which Russia would have to go to war with Japan in accordance with the Treaty of June 3.[61]

The Minister of War, P. S. Vannovskii, had little to contribute. He deemed the acquisition of an ice-free port in the Far East necessary; consequently, if the time was opportune, Russia should take Port Arthur. But he felt that the decisive vote should rest with the Director of the Navy Department.[62]

Admiral P. P. Tyrtov, the Director of the Navy Department, was not quite certain that Port Arthur would satisfy the needs of the Russian squadron of the Pacific. He still considered the ports in Korea more suitable but realized that politically the time was not ripe to take them. Hence, he advised that Russia take no part at that time and that she content herself with the use of Vladivostok for two or three more years. He felt that the future would bring another opportunity for obtaining a Korean port.[63]

The final decision of the conference was not to occupy Port Arthur or any other port. The desire to obtain an ice-free port was once again made secondary to the policy of restraining other powers from a scramble for territory and spheres of influence in China and Korea. This dominant policy was particularly desirable to Witte, who since September, 1897, had vigorously advanced a policy of economic penetration of Korea by means of the newly established Russo-Korean Bank.[64]

Sometime between November 26 and December 11, 1897, Nicholas II and Muraviev reversed the decision of the Special Conference of November 26. No documentary evidence has come to light to explain the motives and course of the reversal. Witte in his memoirs attributed the reversal to Muraviev's jealousy of Witte's and Lobanov's successful negotiations in May and June, 1896, and to Muraviev's desire to "distinguish himself" in some similar achievement in the Far East. Witte also accused Muraviev of instilling in the Tsar the fear that the English would take advantage of the German seizure of Kiaochow and take Port Arthur.[65] The change of policy required the approval of the Tsar; consequently, even if Witte's later analysis of the motives for the change is correct, the responsibility was shared by Nicholas II. It was not within Muraviev's province to order the occupation of Port Arthur. On December 11, he notified Pavlov in Peking through the Russian Foreign Office: "In view of our acceptance [of the Chinese proposal of November 15], a squadron of our ships, under the command of Rear Admiral Reunov, has been immediately dispatched to Port Arthur. Instructions must be given for a friendly reception of the squadron."[66]

The decision to occupy Port Arthur was communicated to William II on December 14 through the Russian embassy. Muraviev stated that with the "consent" of the Chinese government a Russian squadron would be temporarily stationed at Port Arthur until further order. He added that the Tsar issued this advance information, "being convinced that Germany and Russia could and should act hand in hand in the Far East."[67]

William II was delighted. On December 17 he conveyed his approval of the action through the Foreign Office.[68] On the nineteenth he himself telegraphed to the Tsar: "Please accept my congratulations on the arrival of your squadron at Port Arthur."[69] On the same day, he charged Baron Osten-Sacken to convey to Nicholas II the message: "Your enemies, whether they be called Japanese or English, now become my enemies; and every troublemaker, whoever he may be, who wishes to hinder your intentions by force, will meet the German squadron side by side with your warships."[70] It must be noted that the method of sending this message, through the Russian chargé, safeguarded Germany from being bound by it, whereas the direct telegram of Nicholas II to William II on November 7, 1897, had permitted Germany to ignore previous statements of Russian prior claims on Kiaochow.

It is not certain that the "temporary" occupation of Port Arthur was intended from the beginning to lead to the establishment of a permanent Russian base at Port Arthur. The Russian squadron which entered the harbor on December 19, 1897, acted in a "correct" manner.[71] It did not land troops, and for two months it made no attempt to establish any land installation. When on December 25 two British cruisers entered Port Arthur with the intention of wintering there side by side with the Russians, the Russian admiral made no protest, though apparently he urged the Chinese authorities to do so.[72]

Another opportunity to obtain an ice-free port came on December 14, 1897, when Li Hung-chang approached Russia for a loan of one hundred million lan (*ca.* $150,000,000) with which to pay the last of the indemnities of the Sino-Japanese War. On the sixteenth, Witte agreed to sponsor this loan on condition that China would sign an agreement with Russia which would stipulate that (1) only Russia would have the right to build railroads in Manchuria and Mongolia and to conduct mining and industrial enterprises there; (2) the C.E.R. would have the right to build a branch railroad to the Yellow Sea to any port east of Inkou (near the mouth of the Liao); (3) Russia could build a port in any chosen harbor and have the right of entrance for all ships flying the Russian flag.[73]

Repulsed by such demands, China turned to Britain, but the British terms were also "none too modest," including the rights for a railroad from Burma to the Yangtze River, the "nonalienation" of the Yangtze basin, and the opening of the port of Talienwan as a treaty port.[74] After failing to raise the money by a domestic loan,[75] Li Hung-chang again turned to Russia. He was adamant against those points of the Russian proposals which would surrender Mongolia and Manchuria to a Russian monopoly, and also against the terms which would permit Russia to keep Port Arthur. He attempted to interest Russia in a port at the mouth of the Yalu River and to extract a written promise that Russia would evacuate Port Arthur.[76] Failing in his counterproposals, Li Hung-chang reverted to the idea of a British loan.

The advantages to be derived by Russia from the acceptance by China of the terms accompanying a Russian loan outweighed those to be gained by a temporary and uncertain occupation of Port Arthur. To promote the loan negotiations, Muraviev yielded whatever plans he

may have had to keep Port Arthur, and on January 4, 1898, he telegraphed Pavlov to inform the Tsungli Yamen:

We never had any intention of a territorial acquisition and will leave Port
Arthur and Talienwan as soon as political circumstances and the interests of Russia
and China will permit us to do so.

In view of our friendship with China, we rely on the Peking government to
offer for our use a thoroughly secure station in the Gulf of Pechili or in Korea,
so as to spare us from the necessity of using the Nagasaki station.

[We would require] a written guarantee of the verbal promises on the subjects
of [military] instructors and railroads, with a guarantee of a concession for a
linking railroad (from the C.E.R. to Chinchow).[77]

Thus after a two-week occupation of Port Arthur, Russia was ready
to withdraw in order to put through the Chinese loan and attain her
now modified and reduced objectives.[78]

The vacillation between the plan of acquiring an ice-free port at
Port Arthur and Witte's plan of primary insistence on a railroad into
southern Manchuria began anew in January when Muraviev lost faith
in the success of his colleague's plan. On January 20 Muraviev by
telegraph directed Pavlov to ask the Chinese government to lease Port
Arthur to Russia, but to "make the request very cautiously so as not to
injure our negotiations concerning the loan."[79] On the same day, Pavlov
discovered that the British had offered a substantial bribe to the statesmen of the Tsungli Yamen for the right to handle the loan.[80] Witte
followed this example and directed Pokotilov to offer 1,000,000 rubles
to Li Hung-chang if he would promote the acceptance of the Russian
loan and its accompanying conditions, and 1,000,000 rubles more if
China would send a suitable pro-Russian delegate to St. Petersburg
for the signing of the loan agreement.[81] With typical craftiness, Li
Hung-chang did not refuse directly—he even intimated his consent[82]—
but on February 1, Witte's hopes and plans were shattered when the
Chinese Minister to St. Petersburg notified the Russian Foreign Office
of China's definite refusal of the Russian loan.[83] China accepted from
the Hong Kong and Shanghai Banking Corporation and the Deutsche-
Asiatische Bank the required 16,000,000 pounds sterling and yielded
to the British demand of "nonalienation" of the Yangtze basin.[84] China
promised that only Englishmen would be selected for the post of inspector general of the Chinese Customs as long as British trade in
China was greater than that of any other country.[85] Germany, at the
same time, received a reassurance about the lease of Kiaochow.[86]

After February 1 the acquisition of an ice-free port became the
predominant plan. General A. N. Kuropatkin, the Acting Minister of

War, openly argued for the retention of Port Arthur, and even Witte gave up his opposition. Although he still disliked the plan and feared that the retention of Port Arthur might lead to a break in Russo-Chinese relations, he thought it better to join the movement and moderate its objectives in the Far East rather than withdraw from it altogether.[87] A special committee was constantly in session from the middle of February on, working out the problem of the proper demands to be made on China for the lease of Port Arthur.[88] One of these special conferences, held in the middle of February,[89] brought together the most important authorities on the matter: the Grand Duke General-Admiral Alexei Alexandrovich, Witte, Muraviev, General Kuropatkin, Admiral Tyrtov, Admiral Avelan, the Navy Chief of Staff, and General V. V. Sakharov, the Army Chief of Staff. This group adopted practical and specific resolutions, which directed that Russia (1) demand a lease of the southern part of the Liaotung Peninsula, the northern part to form a neutral zone; (2) demand the right to build a railroad from the C.E.R. to one of the ports of the Liaotung Peninsula; and (3) send an amphibious force to Port Arthur to implement those demands.[90] The adopted resolutions also included many minor details dealing with the problems of administration of the leased territory by Chinese, the rights of Chinese military forces in relation to the leased territory, and boundaries of the territory. The specific nature of the resolutions indicates that the majority of the participating members of the special conference were in complete agreement.

On February 20, 1898, Muraviev renewed negotiations with China for a lease of Port Arthur.[91] To expedite matters, on March 3 negotiations were transferred to Peking, where Pavlov and Pokotilov conferred directly with the Tsungli Yamen. China turned to England and Japan for support, but Russia applied the usual tactics of bribery to speed the negotiations.[92] On March 21 Pavlov and Pokotilov carried out the instructions from St. Petersburg and offered to pay the two Chinese negotiators, Li Hung-chang and Chang Yin-huan, a bribe of 500,000 taels each if the lease should be signed in the next few days.[93] Li Hung-chang protested against granting the lease, but this time not too strenuously.[94] Acceptance by the Chinese was definitely expected by the foreign diplomatic corps.[95] On March 27, 1898, the final lease was signed,[96] and Russia at last received the ice-free port she had long desired. The terms of the lease closely followed the resolutions of the February conference. The area later known as Kwantung was leased for twenty-five years, the lease to be subject to renewal on consent of both parties. Under Article VIII, a branch of the C.E.R. could be constructed to Talienwan under the conditions of the contract of the C.E.R. of September 8, 1896. Furthermore, Russia was given the right to build branches from the main line of this railroad east to the Yalu River and west to Inkou, near the mouth of the Liao. The neutral zone, the boundaries of the leased territory, and the limited rights of Chinese forces in the leased territory were all included in the lease in accordance with the resolutions of the special conference.

Before acquiring the ice-free port, Russia found it necessary to placate the two inveterate foes of her Far Eastern expansion—England and Japan. Soon after the entrance of Russian warships into Port Arthur, British and Japanese squadrons carried on naval demonstrations in and around Korea. By December 30, the strong British Far Eastern squadron was concentrated at Chemulpo, ostensibly to influence the Koreans and to add indirect opposition to the Russian attempt to oust the English Director of Korean Customs, but actually with secret orders to watch the Russian squadron and be ready for any eventuality.[97] The Japanese fleet concentrated at Tsushima, where it would be in a position to control Tsushima Strait or intercept the Russian units still in Nagasaki.[98] This naval tension continued until the beginning of February, when the decrease of diplomatic tension led to the gradual abatement of the Port Arthur "crisis."

In January, 1898, a *rapprochement* between England and Russia was in evidence. Muraviev in St. Petersburg and Baron E. E. de Staal, the Russian Ambassador to London, complained to the British government that the continued presence of British cruisers in Port Arthur might be interpreted as evidence of unfriendliness.[99] Although Lord Salisbury stressed the right of the cruisers to remain there, he ordered their withdrawal before January 14.[100] A more striking feature of this *rapprochement* was the English attempt to compromise with the threat of Russian economic penetration into Manchuria. On January 17, 1898, Salisbury wrote to the British Ambassador in St. Petersburg:

> If practicable, ask Monsieur Witte whether it is possible that England and Russia could work together in China. Our objects are not antagonistic to any serious degree; on the other hand we can both do each other a great deal of harm if we try. It is better therefore we should come to an understanding. We could go far to further Russian commercial objects in the north, if we regard her as willing to work with us.[101]

Judging by Salisbury's actions toward the end of January, England did not fear Russian economic predominance in the north nor the consequences of a Russian occupation of Port Arthur. What England feared most was the much larger scope of Russian influence as envisaged by Witte's program of December 26, 1897. This larger program had also found expression in a *note-mémoire* written by the Russian Ambassador to Berlin for the German Chancellor on January 2, 1898. The note contained the following sentence:

Starting with the principle, virtually recognized by the German government, of our exclusive sphere of action in the provinces of northern China, comprising the whole of Manchuria, the province of Chihli, and Chinese Turkestan, we cannot admit there any foreign political influence, and all the efforts of the Imperial government will be directed to asserting and consolidating its influence.[102]

This policy meant a Russian monopoly in northern China. Either through Chinese or German sources, the English were made aware of the Witte–Osten-Sacken conception of a Russian "sphere of influence." On January 22, the German Ambassador to London expressed his opinion that the British clearly understood that the matter for concern was not "Port Arthur or the Siberian [trans-Manchurian] railroad" but Russia's attempts "to lay a hand on a considerable part of the Chinese Empire and to completely withdraw it from the trade of the world."[103] This was directly contrary to British interests. In the same month, Sir Michael Hicks-Beach, the Chancellor of the Exchequer, announced the British stand in a speech in which he declared that "the Government is firmly decided to keep open the market of China at any price and whenever necessary."[104] And the British were so little alarmed about Port Arthur that Salisbury even stated that "Russian policy up to now has been absolutely correct."[105]

In February, 1898, the successful conclusion of negotiations for an Anglo-German loan removed the danger that the objectionable features of Witte's broad plan of December 26, 1897, would be carried out. In March the British government learned of Russia's decision to keep Port Arthur, and the "Port Arthur crisis" was momentarily revived.[106] On March 25 the British concluded that Port Arthur would fall to the Russians and decided that the best solution to counteract the increased Russian influence in the Far East would be to lease Wei-hai-wei. Salisbury notified the Russian government of England's "grave objections" to the expected Russian lease of Port Arthur and reserved for the British the right "to take what steps they think best to protect their own interests."[107] On April 19, 1898, the English leased the port of Wei-hai-wei, practically at the request of the Chinese government, and with no opposition from the Russian, French, or German diplomats.[108]

The necessity of placating Japan for the acquisition of Port Arthur influenced Russian actions in Korean affairs in 1897–1898. On September 7, 1897, Carl Weber, the amenable Russian Minister to Korea, was replaced by Alexis de Speyer, a young and aggressive imperialist, whom H. N. Allen characterizes as "an impudent pup," and "a most arrogant and boisterous man."[109] Speyer had a grandiose program in mind. He evolved plans for timber, mining, and railroad enterprises and aimed at Russian domination of the army, the customs service, and a Russian naval base at Deer Island off the port of Fusan.[110] In September, Speyer persuaded the King of Korea to dismiss all his American advisers and to have only Russian advisers. The only American adviser who remained was, in Allen's words, "an alcoholic Russophile employed by Chosen as a legal expert."[111] A change of the cabinet followed, and new ministers were selected from the pro-Russian groups.[112] In return for this "friendly attitude," the King was promised Russian recognition of his imperial title in October, 1897.[113]

Although the King seemed powerless to oppose Speyer's plans, others did oppose them. Speyer failed to influence the Korean Minister of Finance in the attempt to have K. A. Alexeev appointed Director of the Korean Customs. On October 25 Speyer succeeded in gaining this appointment, this time through the Minister of Foreign Affairs, a noted pro-Russian member of the cabinet.[114] On the following day the King dismissed McLeavy Brown from all of his Korean appointments; but Brown refused to leave his post, disregarded the dismissal, and continued to act in his customary capacity.[115] Alexeev then tried to alienate the employees of the customs service from their chief by doubling their salaries and making himself popular with them. But Brown, in spite of the general hostility toward him, still refused to budge.[116] This rather absurd deadlock continued until December 31, 1897, when, ostensibly in protest of the dismissal of Brown, Admiral Büller's squadron of eight warships anchored at Chemulpo. In consequence of this demonstration and the diplomatic protest made by J. N. Jordan, the British consul at Seoul, Brown was officially restored to his office and Alexeev had to accept a subordinate position under him.[117]

Either St. Petersburg delayed too long in taking advantage of the opportunities opened up by Speyer's aggressive diplomacy in Seoul, or events in the Far East progressed too rapidly for Speyer to complete his program. Although Witte enthusiastically approved the formation of the Russo-Korean Bank on October 28, 1897, the charter of the bank passed slowly through the various bureaucratic channels and did not receive the Emperor's approval until December 17. On December 23, the bank petitioned for the right to open its first branch at Seoul and late in February, 1898, actually established it.[118] Muraviev by December 11 had adopted a "Port Arthur orientation" and failed to support

Speyer. On December 19, the day the Russian squadron entered Port Arthur, the Japanese submitted a protest to the Russians against the dismissal of Brown and the appointment of Alexeev, referring to the Moscow Protocol of June 9, 1896.[119] The Japanese protest was debatable, but Muraviev, wholeheartedly interested in Port Arthur, chose to appease the Japanese on the one point raised by them, because, he said, "in the present political circumstances we are faced with the unquestionable necessity of preserving friendly relations with Japan."[120]

The need for taking cognizance of Japanese reaction to the actions of Russia was greater in 1897–1898 than during the 1895 crisis over Liaotung. The Russian Pacific squadron still retained a slight margin of technical superiority over the Japanese fleet, having two battleships, six armored cruisers, and one unarmored cruiser in the spring of 1896, against Japan's three battleships, no armored cruisers, and twelve unarmored cruisers most of which were old.[121] Both nations were engaged in a naval construction race started by Japan in September, 1895, when the Japanese voted for the construction of four 15,000-ton battleships of the recent *Majestic* type.[122] This program, commenced in 1896, was answered by the Russian naval program of 1897, which also contemplated the building of four battleships, and the number was increased to six by the Imperial ukase of March 10, 1898.[123] Due to the slow rate of warship construction, neither of the two naval programs could have had any effect on the situation in 1898. The British Ambassador to Tokyo, Sir Ernest Satow, reported to his government after a conversation with the Japanese Chief of Staff, that Japan was definitely preparing for war against Russia, but that the Japanese armed forces would not be ready until 1902.[124]

Japan was probably prepared not only in naval matters, for in 1895, after the Triplice had ousted Japan from her continental gains, the Japanese peacetime army had been expanded threefold.[125] In contrast, Russian forces east of Lake Baikal were increased on a very gradual scale, with the result that in November, 1897, Russia had some 40,000 men at her disposal in the Far East, in contrast to 170,000 in the Japanese peacetime army.[126] The disparity of forces was even more accentuated by the changes in strategical deployment. In April, 1895, the Russian Minister of War considered that, even with a field force of only 15,000 men, Russia was secure in the Far East because the Japanese army of 70,000 men was scattered in Japan, Korea, Manchuria, and northern China, and that in the event of a Russo-Japanese conflict Russia could hope for Chinese and Korean assistance. In 1898, however, the Japanese forces were concentrated, while the Russian forces

were encumbered with secondary missions such as guarding the construction of railroads, providing garrisons for Vladivostok and later
Port Arthur, and screening the Ussuri border against the attacks of
khunhuzes.

The indignation of the Japanese people against the Russian occupation of Port Arthur in December, 1897, would have made an attack
on Russia popular, but wiser counsel prevailed. The Japanese could
not determine whether the Franco-Russian Alliance extended to the
Far East, or whether behind the German occupation of Kiaochow
there was also an alliance—or at least agreement—for joint action.[127]
Muraviev, however, when in Paris a short while before, had been informed that Russia could expect only diplomatic assistance from
France. He found that Russia could hardly hope for French military
aid in the Far East, particularly in view of the weakness of the French
Far Eastern squadron, consisting of an old battleship and five unarmored cruisers.[128] Germany was certainly not an ally; for though her
actions in the Kiaochow affair had been helpful in Russia's penetration
of southern Manchuria and the acquisition of Port Arthur, and although William II flattered and encouraged the interests of Nicholas
II in the Far East, it was Germany and England who worked hand in
hand in financial rivalry against the Franco-Russian combination in the
Far East.

The obscurity of political alignments, the numerical superiority of
the Japanese army over the Russian forces in the Far East, and the
delicate balance in naval forces, influenced Russia and Japan to act
cautiously and pushed them toward a compromise on Korea. On February 16, 1898, the Japanese Ambassador to St. Petersburg presented
to the Russian Ministry of Foreign Affairs a project for a new agreement on Korea by which (1) Japan and Russia would guarantee the
independence of Korea, (2) Russia would appoint military instructors
for the Korean army, (3) Japan would appoint the financial advisers,
and (4) Russia and Japan would come to a preliminary agreement
before taking any new measures in commercial and industrial matters.[129]
The proposal was strongly opposed by Witte, whose scheme for Russian hegemony in Mongolia and Manchuria had just suffered a defeat,
and who had recently begun to be actively interested in Korea after
the Russo-Korean Bank had established a branch at Seoul.[130] However,
Muraviev's policy of concentrating every effort on the Manchurian
project prevailed. Although Muraviev did not accept the offer of February 16, he withheld his support from Speyer in Korea. In January,
Dr. Allen reported from Seoul that Russia was losing her grip on

Korea, and in March, Allen considered that Speyer's influence in Korean affairs was definitely on the decline.[131]

On March 17, 1898, Muraviev made a counterproposal in regard to Korea, in which he expressed Russia's intention to lease Port Arthur and Talienwan and to give Japan a pledge that Russia would not interfere in the internal affairs of Korea. Two days later, Marquis Ito suggested an agreement by which Russia would recognize Japan's freedom of action in Korea and in return Japan would regard Manchuria as lying outside Japanese interests. This "exchange policy," as it was termed in Japan, was endorsed by Marquis Yamagata and the leading Japanese statesmen, such as Nishi, Komura, and Hayashi.[132] This proposal also was apparently ignored or circumvented. Instead, Russia made a withdrawal from Korea without committing herself to a definite promise of surrender of her interests. Early in March, Speyer made a final bid for the preservation of Russian interests in Korea. He asked the leading Korean statesmen whether they wanted Russian aid and advice, and five days later he received an unexpectedly blunt negative answer.[133] On April 12, Russian military and financial advisers resigned in a body, and the Russo-Korean Bank was liquidated after a month and a half of operation. Speyer was replaced by the more amiable and easygoing N. G. Matiunin.[134]

In the following month Russian influence further declined and Japanese influence increased. Matiunin allowed one of Russia's best Korean agents, a Korean interpreter to the Russian legation, to be executed during the anti-Russian reaction. Witte showed renewed interest in the Manchurian project and discouraged any Russian business enterprises in Korea.[135]

On April 25, 1898, Baron R. R. Rosen, the Russian Minister to Tokyo, and Nishi, the Japanese Minister of Foreign Affairs, signed a convention regarding Korea known as the Nishi-Rosen Convention.[136] This "rather lame and pointless convention"[137] stated in Article I that both signatory powers recognized the independence of Korea and pledged themselves not to interfere in her internal affairs. Article II provided for a mutual agreement "not to take any measure regarding the nomination of military instructors and financial advisers, without having previously arrived at a mutual accord on the subject." The most important article was Article III, which stated: "In view of the great development of the commercial and industrial enterprises of Japan in Korea and also of the considerable number of Japanese subjects residing in that country, the Russian Imperial government shall not obstruct the development of the commercial and industrial relations between Japan and Korea." This was the first recognition of the particular interest of Japan in the economic development of Korea.

The period from 1896 to the middle of 1898 saw the attainment of the Russian Far Eastern policy that was evolved in the special conferences of 1894–1895. The routing of the Trans-Siberian Railway through Manchuria solved many problems of the Russian Far East. The C.E.R. provided a more rapid strategic rail connection between the Russian Far Eastern base in the transbaikal region. It tapped the resources of northern Manchuria and created a new food base for the Russian Far East, and the theoretically assured monopoly of the C.E.R. permitted the Russians to regard the Manchurian borderlands as a secure defense zone. The second attainment was the acquisition of an ice-free port in the lease of Port Arthur and Talienwan. The military and naval authorities considered this lease undesirable.[138] At the conference of November 26 the admirals rejected the choice of Port Arthur. Nevertheless, they could not make up their minds what port would be desirable because they were uncertain why such a port was necessary. Even Nicholas II, an ardent supporter of the policy of obtaining an ice-free port, had hazy and contradictory conceptions in regard to the location that would be advantageous. In 1895 he wanted a port in northeastern Korea; in the summer of 1896 he rejected the idea of any Korean port;[139] in November, 1897, he was strongly in favor of Pingyang (Heijo) in central western Korea; and by December 11, against the advice of the special conference of November 26 and possibly even without informing Muraviev,[140] he made the decision to occupy Port Arthur.

The success of the policy of obtaining an ice-free port led to the rapid evolution and success of a third policy, namely, to connect by a branch railroad the far-flung outpost and the Russian strategic axis of the Trans-Siberian Railway, and the C.E.R. Russian policy never deviated from an insistence upon that connection. Whether the ice-free port was contemplated in northeastern Korea, at the mouth of the Yalu, at Pingyang, or at Port Arthur, either in the form of a railroad concession or direct cession of a strip of territory as in the plan of Nicholas II in 1895, this connection was an integral part of the plan. It was because of the difficulty or the impossibility of such a connection that General P. S. Vannovskii objected to the navy's plan of selecting the island of Kargodo in 1895. In the November Memorandum of 1897 Muraviev eliminated the navy's choice of Fusan also because of this. The same reason probably influenced the abandonment of the priority claims on Kiaochow. After the acquisition of Port

Arthur it was only a matter of the "logic of railroad expansion"[141] that
on July 6, 1898, Russia and China signed an agreement for the construction by Russia of a branch railroad from the C.E.R. to Port
Arthur and Talienwan.[142] This branch was called the South Manchurian Railway (hereafter referred to as the S.M.R.). The three
facets of the Russian policy then became integrated. Port Arthur was
to protect the Russian economic penetration of rich and heavily populated southern Manchuria by the S.M.R., while the S.M.R. was to
support and feed Port Arthur; the C.E.R. was to link the Russian
Far East with the source of power in European Russia; and the
C.E.R. and S.M.R. through the power of the Russians in Port Arthur,
would make the policy of St. Petersburg felt in Peking and in the
Far East in general.

The diplomatic struggles connected with the evolution and success
of the Russian Far Eastern policy also brought forth the Russian
maximum and minimum plans. As envisaged by Witte in his demands
of December 16, 1897, the maximum plan amounted to the formation
of a Russian sphere of influence in Mongolia, in practically all of
Manchuria, and more vaguely, in Korea. However, Muraviev in the
diplomatic field and Witte in the economic field could not cope with
the outlined maximum program. Retreats were distasteful to such
men as Nicholas II, Muraviev, and Witte; yet they all approved the
minimum program, by which Russian interests would withdraw from
Korea. Only the Nishi-Rosen convention on Korea, the vague "nonalienation" understanding implied in the negotiations with China over
the S.M.R., and the remoteness of Mongolia and Chinese Turkestan
guaranteed the "security zone" Russia envisaged in the maximum
program and reserved for Russia the opportunity to try again, in the
future, for a more definite realization of such a program.

LIMITATIONS ON RUSSIAN EXPANSION, 1899–1900

Witte's maximum plan was twice overthrown in 1897–1898 by Muraviev, who, though inexperienced and considered inept, had the knack
of presenting proposals which he knew beforehand would be acceptable to the Tsar.[143] In 1898 Witte renewed his plans of economic aggression in China and once more came into conflict with Anglo-Chinese
interests and Muraviev's policy of limited expansion.

On June 7, 1898, it was announced in Peking that an English syndi-
cate had been formed to construct some 250 miles of railroad from
Shanhaikwan on the Gulf of Pechili at the end of the Great Wall to
Newchwang and Hsinmintun, 50 miles from Mukden. The syndicate

offered China a loan of 16,000,000 taels (8 per cent at 92), to be guaranteed by a mortgage on the equipment of the railroad, and the managerial rights of construction.[144] On the same day, Pavlov protested to the Tsungli Yamen that the preliminary convention which established this syndicate violated Article III of the Additional Protocol of May 7, 1898, between Russia and China, which stipulated that no foreign power except Russia would be allowed to build, operate, or own railways in Manchuria.[145] At practically the same time, however, the Russo-Chinese Bank was participating secretly in the Franco-Belgian syndicate for the concession of the Peking-Hankow line, which was infringing on the British sphere of influence established by the Anglo-Chinese agreement on the nonalienation of the Yangtze valley.[146] Sir Nicolas O'Conor, the British Minister to China, protested to the Chinese but was diverted by the statement of the Tsungli Yamen that the Russians had nothing to do with the plan for the Peking-Hankow railway.[147]

This version was definitely untrue ;[148] it probably originated with the group of Chinese statesmen who followed the pro-Russian policy of Li Hung-chang, who was still in power. In the middle of August the Tsungli Yamen ratified the Peking-Hankow concession and refused to authorize the loan from the British syndicate.[149] This pro-Russian turn of events had immediate repercussions. The majority of the Chinese ministers turned against Li Hung-chang and his small pro-Russian group. Li was dismissed in August, and his cosigner of the lease of Port Arthur, Chang Yin-huan, was exiled to a remote province in the following month. The remainder of the pro-Russian group rapidly changed their policies.[150]

However, the limitation of Russian activities in the Far East began independently of the internal change in the Tsungli Yamen. On August 10, Muraviev, the proponent of a limited-objective policy, instructed P. M. Lessar, the Russian chargé in London, to open conversations with Lord A. F. Balfour, the British Minister of Russian Affairs, on the subject of delimitation of Russian and British spheres of influence in China. On August 12, while Lessar and Balfour discussed the question in London, Muraviev conversed in St. Petersburg with the British Ambassador, Sir Charles Scott.[151] The conversations led only to an exchange of opinions. The British stoutly maintained that their participation in the Shanhaikwan-Hsinmintun railroad project was purely a private, financial affair and did not represent a penetration of Manchuria by British interests. On the Russian side, Muraviev now had less reason to seek an accord with the British, for shortly before August 10, Pavlov obtained from the Tsungli Yamen, which was still

pro-Russian, a promise expanding Article III of the Additional Protocol of 1898, which stated that the Shanhaikwan-Newchwang railroad would not become a guarantee for any foreign loan.[152]

However, the British refused to drop the negotiations and, through
Ambassador Scott in St. Petersburg, proposed in September that Russia recognize a British railroad monopoly in the Yangtse basin in
return for a similar British recognition of a Russian monopoly in
Manchuria, that the two powers establish no preferential rates and
tariffs on their railroads, and that the Shanhaikwan-Hsinmintun railroad be permitted to accept the British syndicated loan.[153] Through
November and December, 1898, the British attempted to get Russia
to accept these terms, but neither Witte nor Muraviev considered
them acceptable. Muraviev wanted a definite division of railroad
spheres of influence, preferably by a demarcation line running through
Peking.[154] Witte had greater objections. He saw in the British plan
a one-sided British victory by which an open-door policy would be
established in Manchuria and the S.M.R. would carry British goods
into the interior of Manchuria. The British would have the nonalienation agreement of the Yangtze, where British railroads had not yet
been built. The division of the spheres of influence for railroad construction at Shanhaikwan would give the British a much larger sphere
of influence than the Russians, and besides, the Chinese government
had already twice promised the Russians a nonalienation agreement
for Manchuria.[155] Furthermore, the acceptance of the British proposals
would mean a "retreat" for Russian interests, which through the Russo-
Chinese Bank had now penetrated to the Yangtze by participating in
the Peking-Hankow syndicate, and westward to Shansi by participating in a Russo-German syndicate.[156]

Witte attempted to marshal support for his opposition as Muraviev
and Nicholas II became more and more inclined to accept the British
proposal. He asked General A. N. Kuropatkin for his opinion and
submitted for his perusal the entire file of documents on the railroad
problem. Kuropatkin's reaction was unexpectedly hostile and adverse.
On January 8, 1899, he wrote in a personal letter to Witte:

> Since last year the Russo-Chinese Bank has begun to scatter its activities. As the
> Russian government is responsible for the actions of this bank, we could be drawn
> into very unpleasant affairs in regard to concessions on the middle Yangtze
> [Hankow] and lower Yangtze [to Chinkiang], or the concession between Cheng-
> ting and Taiyuan. I can understand the necessity of defending Russian interests
> in Manchuria, which has a common boundary with Russia for thousands of versts.
> But I consider it incomprehensible and disastrous for Russia to be required to

defend with Russian blood the interests of the Russo-Chinese Bank on the Yangtze, or generally south of Peking.[157]

Meanwhile, Russian prestige in the Far East was growing weaker. Li Hung-chang was out of office, and in October, 1898, the anti-Russian group in the Tsungli Yamen authorized the acceptance of a modified but essentially similar railroad loan from the British syndicate for the construction of the Shanhaikwan-Hsinmintun railroad.[158] Even in its political orientation China began to shift. From the autumn of 1898 a *rapprochement* between China and Japan was in evidence. Marquis Ito appeared in Peking on a special mission and was cordially received by the Tsungli Yamen and even by the Emperor. In subsequent months arrangements were made for the employment of Japanese instructors in Chinese military schools, for Chinese students to study in Japanese schools, and for the establishment of a propaganda bureau to eradicate the popular hostility engendered by the Sino-Japanese War.[159]

Under such circumstances, and pursuing the policy of limited objectives, Muraviev reopened negotiations with the British in February, 1899, and in the course of two months came to an understanding with the British which in an interchange of notes on April 28, 1899, constituted the Scott-Muraviev Agreement.[160] The terms of this agreement represented a triple compromise. The British gained the Russian recognition of their railroad sphere of influence in the Yangtze in return for similar recognition of the Russian sphere in Manchuria; and through additional notes interchanged on the same day, Russia accepted the loan of the British syndicate and British management of construction of the Shanhaikwan-Hsinmintun railroad. Muraviev's point on a definite division was accepted, with Shanhaikwan as the dividing point, and, to please Witte, included all Chinese territory north of the Great Wall, including Mongolia and possibly Chinese Turkestan. Witte's opposition also caused the exclusion from the agreement of binding terms on rates and tariffs which would have seriously hampered his plans for the exploitation of Manchuria for Russian capital and industry. Although the Russo-Chinese Bank eventually had to abandon its plans in regard to central China, where Russian diplomacy was obligated not to interfere in the development of British interests, by this compromise Witte still retained a part of the maximum program for northern China.

The Scott-Muraviev Agreement did not end railroad rivalry, or plans of rivalry, between the British and the Russians. No sooner had the exchange of notes taken place than the Russo-Chinese Bank began to probe for an opportunity to buy out the British loan to the Shanhaikwan railroad and become the sole arbiter of Chinese railroad development north of the Great Wall.[161] This measure was vigorously opposed by British interests. The opposition of the Chinese was greatly weakened by the sudden and fearful thought that the Scott-Muraviev Agreement was an outward manifestation of a secret plan for the partition of China between England and Russia.[162] When pressed by M. N. de Giers, the new Russian Minister to China, the Tsungli Yamen gave written guarantees on June 1 and July 21, accepting the Russian demands that all new railroads to the north and northeast of Peking be built by Russia or China.[163] By this Russia obtained virtually the Muraviev line of demarcation between English and Russian railroad interests.

Rivalry and fears of rivalry still continued. In Parliament, British leaders were compelled on many occasions to define the "basin of the Yangtze" mentioned in the agreement, and these interpretations were frequently challenged by the Russian Ministry of Foreign Affairs.[164] British papers in the Far East and in London gave prominent place to the rumor of a project of a Russian railroad from Kiakhta through Urga and Kalgan to Peking, and another rumor of a railroad to Singan (Sian), the capital of the province of Shensi, to which the Chinese Imperial Court was supposed to have intentions of withdrawing.[165] Events outside the Far East eliminated the possibility of intense rivalry. The British were drifting toward war with the Boers in South Africa and, because of the pronounced hostility of Germany and the general pro-Boer sympathy of the entire world, had to act cautiously in the Far East. In June the first British expeditionary force was sent to South Africa, and a few months later, the Tsar and Muraviev launched their project of a World Peace Conference at The Hague. A policy of nonaggressive development in the Far East was desirable.

On September 6, 1899, John Hay, the American Secretary of State, dispatched to London, Berlin, and St. Petersburg and later to Tokyo, Rome, and Paris a circular note outlining the policy of the open door in China.[166] The government of the United States asked the powers which held "spheres of influence" in China to declare that these powers would not "interfere with any treaty port or any vested interest within any so-called 'sphere of interest,'" and "that the Chinese treaty tariff shall apply to all merchandise landed or shipped to all such ports . . . no matter to what nationality it may belong." The third point renewed the assault on the Russian hopes for the future prosperity of the C.E.R. and the S.M.R. so strongly defended by Witte in the Anglo-Russian negotiations of 1898–1899. It asked the afore-mentioned powers to declare

That it will levy no higher harbor dues on vessels of another nationality fre-quenting any port in such "sphere" than shall be levied on vessels of its own nationality; no higher railroad charges over lines built, controlled, or operated within its "sphere" on merchandise belonging to citizens or subjects of other nation-alities transported through such "sphere" than shall be levied on similar merchan-dise belonging to its own nationals transported over equal distances.[167]

The application of this provision to the Russian railway enterprises in Manchuria was a form of discrimination and can be considered hostile to Russia.[168] Although China had been partitioned into spheres of influence and committed by agreements to permit foreign nations to build railroads in China, only Russia had actually started such railroad enterprises on a large scale, other railroads being still in the "planning" stage. Consequently the practical application of point three would affect only Russia, and Russia, under Article II of the C.E.R. Agreement of September 8, 1896, had the right to levy discriminating railroad charges. Furthermore, the Trans-Siberian Railway, the C.E.R., and the S.M.R. were at that time being constructed simultaneously from several points—from Port Arthur northward and from Nikolsk-Ussuriisk westward,[169] for instance. Until the linking of the Manchu-rian railroads with the Trans-Siberian, which reached the Ob River in 1899, the railroads from Talienwan in Kwantung and from Vladi-vostok would serve principally as carriers of foreign trade. The major powers were in better position to approach the Far East with sea-borne trade than was Russia. The easy access of competitive trade was even further accentuated by the Imperial ukase of July 12, 1899, which made Talienwan a *porto franco*.[170] Vladivostok was also a *porto franco* and according to the declaration of August, 1898, was to con-tinue as one until January 1, 1901.[171] The acceptance of Hay's doc-trine would have been disastrous to Russian financial and economic interests in Manchuria. The doctrine as applied to Russia in the Far East was much too one-sided.

Apparently Muraviev and Cassini, who was now Ambassador to the United States, failed to see clearly the economic implications of Hay's note. However, Witte was quick to grasp its significance if not its intent and prevailed on Muraviev to await the reaction of other major powers and later to accept Witte's edition of the answer to the circular.[172] In November and December, 1899, England, France, and Japan gave their consent to the open-door doctrine with the reservation that "all the powers interested give an assurance of their willingness to act likewise."[173] In January, 1900, Italy gave its consent without reservation, since she had no "sphere of influence"; in February, Germany consented, with the same reservation as the other three powers.[174]

On December 30, 1899, Muraviev transmitted to Charlemagne Tower, the American Ambassador to Russia, the Russian reply to Hay's note. The reply lamely pointed out that the declaration of the *porto franco* at Talienwan, renamed Dalny, was proof of Russia's "firm intention to follow the policy of the 'open door' "; it accepted the second point of Hay's circular dealing with tariffs in treaty ports, but it completely ignored the third provision, which dealt with railroad tariffs.[175] Therefore it amounted to a rejection of Hay's open-door policy, and this led to its rejection by all the other powers, whose acceptance was based on the reservation that all powers "act likewise." Hay's circular note of March 20, 1900, stated that the consent given to the original note was considered by the United States government to be "final and definitive" on the ground that compliance with the reservation had been expressed by the various powers. This was only a "face-saving" concluding remark on the *démarche*.[176] The open-door doctrine remained merely a doctrine and a policy unaccepted by most nations and definitely denied by Russia.

Russian economic expansion in the Far East, limited by the Scott-Muraviev Agreement and threatened by further limitation under the doctrine of the open door, was still further hampered by the course of Russian internal affairs and the unexpected difficulties encountered in the Manchurian railroad enterprises. In 1899–1901 European Russia underwent a financial and industrial crisis.[177] The hurried expansion of heavy industries in the industrial boom of 1890–1900 brought with it overcapitalization and speculative investments which in the period 1899–1900 brought about frequent bankruptcy in private railroads and other ventures.[178] The Ministry of Finance was encumbered by tremendous extra expenditures connected with the construction of a huge fleet in accordance with the 1898 program, the complete rearmament of the artillery arm of the military forces, and the increased expenses for the simultaneous and accelerated construction of the Trans-Siberian and Manchurian railways.[179]

In Manchuria the Russians encountered new and unexpected difficulties. More than 6,000 Russian soldiers and workmen and 60,000 Chinese and Manchurian workmen were engaged in railroad construction;[180] yet innumerable incidents produced delays and added new expenses. In 1898 the Chinese authorities and population seemed to be willing to coöperate with the Russian authorities in charge of construction; but between 1898 and 1900, sporadic opposition, especially in southern Manchuria, made itself felt. There were repeated attacks on Russian officers, engineers, and workmen, and on Chinese laborers.[181] In 1899 the Chinese assailants, abetted by the local Chinese administration, even went so far as to use artillery.[182] There was staunch opposition to Russian purchases of rights of way and of land for installations and stations. In Kwangtung, the Chinese population was secretly encouraged to refuse to pay taxes. Ignoring the spirit of the Scott-Muraviev Agreement, British firms in Newchwang accepted the lease of the Yentai coal fields, north of Mukden, offered to them by the anti-Russian Governor General of Mukden. In Kirin and Tsitsihar, the governors general who were friendly with the Russian authorities were recalled and new men were selected and appointed in their places by the anti-Russian group of the Tsungli Yamen.[183]

The C.E.R. fought against this opposition with every means in its power. Additional guards, money, workmen, and equipment were directed to Manchuria without stint. In order to expedite the construction of the Manchurian railroads, rails, rolling stock, and other equipment were brought from the United States at high prices, violating Witte's plan to have the railroad enterprises provide business exclusively for Russian heavy industry.[184] During the short period when the Tsungli Yamen was frightened by the belief that the Scott-Muraviev Agreement indicated an Anglo-Russian plan for the partition of China, Witte secured for the chief engineer of the C.E.R. the right to negotiate directly with the Chinese governors of the three Manchurian provinces on matters already specified in agreements with China. Under special agreements of May 31, 1899, with the Governor General of Kirin province,[185] and December 2, 1899, with the Governor General of Heilungkiang province,[186] the C.E.R. established a Central Bureau for International and Railroad Affairs. This bureau expedited matters such as the hiring of workmen, receiving of complaints, purchase of land, and other vexatious business without having to refer them to the Chinese central government.

During the development of Kwangtung, the port of Talienwan (Dalny), and Port Arthur, the naval base, other troublesome problems arose. It was found that the southern part of the Liaotung Peninsula was short of water and the supply to the garrison had to be supplemented by the use of condensers.[187] There were many criticisms of Port Arthur: it was too small; because some parts of the bay were frozen in the winter of 1898–99 the greater part of the Russian Far

Eastern squadron had again wintered in Nagasaki.[188] Despite the money poured into the improvement of its facilities, Dalny was unpopular. Business enterprises preferred to establish themselves in Port Arthur, where the trade of the garrison was a certainty. The Russo-Chinese Bank hoped to reap a huge profit from sales of lots in the newly created port, but its hopes were not realized.[189] For these and many other minor reasons Russian imperialism in the Far East was established at a heavy price and continued at a heavy cost. Together with the financial crisis in Europe, the heavy financial outlays in the Far East prompted ideas of retrenchment.

Sometime at the end of January or the beginning of February, 1900, Muraviev submitted to the Tsar a "most secret" memorandum on problems of Russian foreign policy.[190] The memorandum was prompted by the events in South Africa, where England had already suffered initial setbacks in the war against the Boers. Muraviev discussed the possibility of taking advantage of England's preoccupation and of the decline of British prestige in Asia as a result of these initial setbacks.[191] He analyzed Russian problems in a comprehensive manner and suggested a course of immediate policy in regard to Turkey, Persia, Afghanistan, and the Far East. His general conclusions were that Russia should retrench in the Far East and turn toward the Near East. He suggested measures for the increase of Russian influence in Afghanistan, Persia, and Turkey; but his most emphatic suggestion was that Russia should clarify her plans for the seizure of the Bosphorus in the near future.[192]

Muraviev stressed the necessity of awaiting the completion of the Trans-Siberian Railway before taking any further steps in the Far East or seeking compensation there for the British gains in Africa. Following the argument of naval authorities against a project of purchasing Ceuta from Spain or establishing a Russian naval station in the Gulf of Persia,[193] he declared himself against any occupation of a detached naval station in the southern part of Korea, such as the island of Kargodo.[194] He claimed that the establishment of a coaling station there would be of little value unless it was well fortified and well garrisoned, and to make it so would entail heavy expenditures.

In his conclusion Muraviev recommended the following measures for the Far East:

7. To continue the preparation for active service of the troops of the Priamur military district and of the Kwantung peninsula which was begun by the Minister of War last year.

8. To expedite the fortification and equipment of Port Arthur and the construc-

tion of the railroads to the Kwantung peninsula which would link that peninsula with the Trans-Siberian Railway.

9. Not to ignore the fact that the main factor for the support of Russian power in the Pacific Ocean at its desired height is the maintenance of a powerful squadron supplied with all the stores necessary for combat.[195]

Admiral P. P. Tyrtov in a "most secret" letter on February 27, 1900, replied that he also opposed the establishment of any coaling station outside the Empire;[196] yet he said that from the naval standpoint it was necessary to have a coaling station in southern Korea. He considered that Port Arthur would be an inefficient base for operations against Japan and pointed out that the 1,100 miles separating Vladivostok and Port Arthur represented a strategical weakness for the Russian naval forces in the Far East. He considered Japan a natural enemy of Russia and suspected that her military and naval plans were aimed at Russia. He also suspected that the Japanese had evolved some plan for the immediate seizure of Korea, just as Russia was making plans for the seizure of the Bosphorus.[197] Tyrtov concluded illogically:

Russia, of course, has no need for any territorial seizures, as it is correctly pointed out in the [Muraviev] memorandum, and we will not pursue an aggressive policy in the Far East; but Japan can only be held back by the threat of actual force.

For this peaceful goal, the Emperor has graciously opened special credit for the formation of a fleet which will be 30 per cent stronger than the Japanese in the waters of the Pacific Ocean; for this goal it is also necessary that we have a port in southern Korea, and it has been contemplated in the bay of Masampo and the adjoining island of Kargodo.[198]

Tyrtov stated that the acquisition of this base should be the object of unrelenting Russian diplomatic efforts; then he admitted that "unfortunately, the last year's incident in which Korea disrespected our rights in Masampo indicates that the influence of Japan in Korea is apparently stronger than ours."

Witte in his reply of February[199] opposed all aggression. He referred to the heavy burdens on Russian finances created by military, naval, and railroad-construction programs and stated that any aggressive move would be in violation of the Imperial circular of August 24, 1899, addressed to all powers, for the calling of a peace conference. He opposed the views expounded in points 7 to 9 of the Muraviev memorandum on the grounds that military and naval preparations only create an armaments rivalry and that to engage in such rivalry with Japan and the wealthy British Empire would be financially disadvantageous for Russia. Witte reminded Muraviev that in previous conferences he had considered the maintenance of 12,000 men in Kwantung excessive. In short, Witte also counseled retrenchment.

In a summary of the replies of the ministers,[200] Muraviev again revealed the policy of retrenchment for the Far East. He explained more fully the meaning intended in points 7 to 9 of the basic memorandum. The preparation for active duty and the strengthening of the fleet were to be accomplished through redeployment and improvement and not by an increase of forces. The remainder of the summary was concerned with the renewed interest in the Near East and central Asia.

In the light of the Muraviev memorandum and Admiral Tyrtov's reply, the Russian lease of a coaling station at Masampo on March 30, 1900,[201] was neither an act of aggressive policy nor a secret move to infiltrate into a strategic position. Light Russian vessels, such as destroyers and torpedo boats, were unable to move from Vladivostok to Port Arthur on the coal supplies of their bunkers and required either a difficult coaling operation at sea or entrance into a Japanese coaling station. The coaling station at Masampo would therefore be a convenient answer to their needs. The lease was apparently restricted in its usefulness. It provided for the establishment of a coal depot and for a naval hospital on a practically uninhabited stretch of the coast outside the town of Masampo, extending for about a mile and a half along the shore and half a mile inland.[202] Such an area would preclude the necessity of developing a defensive area. Furthermore the lease was accompanied by the Russian pledge "never to demand either for the use of the Russian government, or for the use of its subjects' trading or commercial companies, any concessions or cessions or leases of any plots of land on the island of Kargodo, or on the opposite shore as far as the city limits of the port of Masampo, or on any of the surrounding islands."[203] The Korean government made a similar pledge not to give over this territory to any foreign power.

By this additional provision Russia restricted her freedom of action for the immediate future. Only in the remote possibility of a decided superiority of the Russian fleet over the Japanese fleet could the Russians use Masampo strategically. By stationing the fleet in the open harbor and utilizing large coal reserves built up in peacetime, the fleet could maintain a closer blockade of the western coast of Japan and Shimonoseki Strait. Should the Japanese fleet be stronger than the Russian fleet initially, the Masampo coaling station would fall an easy prey to the Japanese, and any Russian vessels stationed there would be hopelessly trapped. Apparently the Japanese were aware of the real significance of the Masampo lease; Japanese newspapers made an outcry against this "menacing" move; during the period of uncertainty before the publication of the terms of the lease, the Japanese fleet was mobilized on a war footing.[204] However, Japan's influence was again ascending in Korea and Japan made little effort to dislodge the Russians or to prevent the lease.

In the spring of 1900 Russia had established a new policy in the Far East. The aggressive aims of the policy of 1895 had been attained; now they must be secured and justified by economic returns. Russia had resisted attempts by England and the United States to penetrate economically into her sphere of influence in Manchuria. For a time Japan had been placated by a Russian retreat in Korea. The new policy called for a period of retrenchment—which all Russian statesmen connected with Russian interests in the Far East felt was desirable—to last at least until 1902 when the Trans-Siberian, Chinese Eastern, and South Manchurian railways would be completed and linked. As all the ministers had stated on numerous occasions from 1894 to 1900, Russia would then be able to have a free hand in the Far East and take her proper place on the shores of the Pacific.

VI

RUSSIAN POLICY IN THE BOXER REBELLION

IN THE FALL of 1899 a Chinese secret society, whose members were later termed "Boxers" by Occidentals, manifested itself in the province of Shantung. This group used marked antidynastic and antiforeign slogans and made demonstrations.[1] Encouraged by the inaction of the governor of Shantung and inflamed by the belief that foreigners were responsible for the severe famine in that province and in other areas of northern China and southern Manchuria, the Boxers spread through Shantung, attacking European missionaries and their converts.[2]

RUSSIAN PARTICIPATION IN THE INTERNATIONAL INTERVENTION IN NORTHERN CHINA

The Chinese government acted promptly upon the suggestions made by the European diplomatic representatives at Peking in their protests against these outrages: the governor of Shantung was replaced by Yuan Shih-kai,[3] a more determined man, and an honest effort was made to rescue the Reverend S. M. Brooks, a captured missionary.[4] However, the stern measures of the new governor and a further deterioration of economic conditions only served to spread the Boxer movement into the province of Chihli during the winter of 1899–1900. Disorders became so frequent and so serious that, on January 27, the British Minister, Sir Claude MacDonald, backed by his American, German, French, and Italian colleagues, with the notable exception of the Russian Minister to China, M. N. de Giers, presented a harsh note to the Chinese government demanding the suppression of antiforeign societies.[5] This note was not answered, possibly because on January 24, 1900, the day before the Chinese New Year, the customary annual appointments in the Court placed several Boxer sympathizers in positions of power and authority.[6] Subsequent protests by the European ministers[7] were met with evasion and procrastination.[8] The Boxer menace increased, and Boxers were soon reported drilling openly in Peking and Tientsin.[9]

Toward the end of March the European nations became acutely aware that a crisis was forming, and they dispatched reinforcements to their Far Eastern squadrons.[10] In May the Boxers were burning,

---

[1] For notes to chap. vi see pp. 286–292.

looting, and killing in the vicinity of Peking; but the ministers did not consider the legations in any danger as yet and opposed the proposal to bring up some forces from Taku. They considered a naval demonstration off the mouth of the Pei-ho adequate for the time being.[11] The Russian gunboat *Koreets,* although present off the Taku bar, did not take part in this demonstration, because of a request by Giers to Admiral E. I. Alexeev, Commander of the Russian naval forces in the Pacific and of the Kwantung garrison.[12]

Until the joint note of May 21, Russia abstained from formal participation in the European concert of protests and demands to the Chinese government. The Russian Ministry of Foreign Affairs had kept a detailed chronicle of antiforeign outbreaks in China from 1891 on, and in Manchuria from February 1899,[13] and was consequently fully aware of the magnitude of these disturbances. From reports it was apparent to Russian statesmen that the enmity of the Boxers was directed primarily against missionary activities of Europeans and was aggravated by economic competition brought about by the penetration of European commercial and railroad interests in to the hinterland of China. Russia did not participate to any great extent in either of these activities in China. There was a Russian church in Shanghai, a Russian religious mission in Peking, and a small church in the suburbs of Peking at Duntinan; but these churches did not engage in proselytizing.[14] At the end of 1899 there were only 250 Russian subjects in all of China.[15]

Warnings that the Boxer movement might have serious consequences reached Giers through his subordinates, such as N. Shuiskii, the consul at Tientsin, and Ostroverkhov, the consul at Inkou. Colonel K. A. Vogak, then military agent for China and Japan and perhaps the most active and energetic Russian diplomat in the Far East at the time, sent Giers several warnings.[16] However, Giers considered Vogak "an alarmist" and was generally opposed to his views.[17] In St. Petersburg, Muraviev also took the situation calmly. He was noted neither for energetic action nor for perspicacity,[18] and as he later admitted, he kept such unpleasant information from Nicholas II "so as not to disturb the Tsar."[19] Furthermore, the underlying policy of friendship with China inherent in the secret treaty of 1896, and the adoption of the nonaggressive policy in the Far East as a result of the Muraviev memorandum of February, 1900, precluded Russia's taking the initiative in the uncertain situation around Peking.

Apparently sharing the views held by his British colleague Sir Claude MacDonald that "energetic measures would at last be taken [by the Chinese government] against the Boxers,"[20] Giers telegraphed the Russian Foreign Office on May 27:

During yesterday's meeting, the German minister declared more openly that the debarkation of landing parties was not an adequate measure and that the time had come for a more active intervention by the Powers. I believe, however, that he will not succeed in leading his colleagues onto this dangerous path which threatens to partition China and that things will go no farther than the summoning of the landing parties.[21]

Policy or no policy, because the lives of the European residents of Peking were at stake, Giers joined his British, American, German, and French colleagues in telegraphing on May 28 for the dispatch of a detachment of sailors to reinforce the legation guards in Peking.[22] Although the Boxers cut the Tientsin-Peking railroad line on the twenty-ninth, the guards reached Peking on the thirty-first, 337 strong, including 74 Russian officers and men.[23] They disregarded the numerical restriction demanded by the Tsungli Yamen that no more than thirty men for each legation be sent.[24] When the railroad was again out, on June 4, Giers joined the British and Austrian ministers in a plan to telegraph their respective governments a request that the admirals in the Far East "take concerted measures" if Peking should be besieged.[25]

On June 5, Giers took the initiative. Acting independently of his colleagues, he addressed a letter to the Empress Dowager of China demanding that immediate action be taken against the Boxers. To Prince Ching, his intermediary with the Empress, Giers added that if the telegraph line to Tientsin were destroyed, Russian troops would be sent to Taku.[26] However, this threat proved to be of no avail. Insults to Europeans and attacks on Christian converts continued, although some feeble efforts were made by General Nieh on June 7 to clear the Peking-Tientsin railroad with Chinese regulars, and with Russian Colonel Voronov acting as his adviser.[27] Some time before that date the Russian church buildings at Duntinan were burned down, and several Russian tea merchants at Kalgan reported that their lives were in danger.[28] By this date Giers was convinced that mere reinforcement of the legation guards would not be sufficient, for "there can be no doubt that the Chinese army is on the side of the Boxers."[29]

Acting on the dispatches of Giers and Alexeev, on the same day, Muraviev wrote a memorandum to the Tsar suggesting that 4,000 men from the Port Arthur garrison be dispatched to the scene of disturbances. This was partly to forestall the dispatch of Japanese or other troops. "It seems" wrote Muraviev, "that the suggested measure . . .

will serve toward the enhancement of our prestige in the Far East and will present a new proof of the value of the Russian occupation of the Kwantung territory."[30] The Tsar approved the measure on the same day and ordered Muraviev to confer with General V. V. Sakharov, the Chief of Staff, in order to expedite its execution.[31]

On June 9, despairing of any other solution, the European representatives at Peking telegraphed their admirals in the Far East to march their landing parties on Peking.[32] On the same day, Giers telegraphed St. Petersburg: "In my opinion, the role of the ministers has come to an end, and the admirals must take charge of the situation. Only the prompt arrival of a strong force can save the foreigners in Peking."[33] On the morning of June 10, Admiral E. H. Seymour, the senior naval commander present, with an international force of 2,066 men, including 312 Russians, marched out of Tientsin to raise the investment of Peking.[34] That evening, the Twelfth East Siberian Rifle Company of about 4,000 men embarked at Port Arthur for Taku:[35] the first echelon of some 2,000 men reached Tientsin on June 12, after two small skirmishes with the Boxers in their march from Taku.[36]

By the middle of June, therefore, the Russians were deeply involved with other interested powers in both diplomatic and military activities having to do with the Boxer uprising. In fact, by virtue of the geographical and strategic proximity of Port Arthur, with its garrison of 12,000 men,[37] and the assumed preëminence of Russian diplomats in relations with the Chinese Court, Russia was in an admirable position to take the leadership in the ensuing action. However, Russia made no claim to this leadership. Fear of loss of prestige drove her to take a prominent part in these and subsequent actions because neither she nor the world at large could easily countenance inaction from a nation in her preëminent position.

But the military leadership of British Admiral Seymour was not to pass unchallenged. On June 16 Admiral Alexeev telegraphed the Viceroy of Pechili to block the movement of foreign troops from Tientsin to Peking and informed him that telegraph communications with the ministers at Peking had been cut. According to Alexeev, the situation demanded that someone with military and political authority be on the spot. Admiral Seymour was attempting to assume a leading position and Alexeev thought Russia should have someone to counterbalance him.[38] On June 17, however, Muraviev submitted another memorandum, which had been approved by the Tsar and which was to serve as the basis of Russian policy with reference to the Boxer crisis.[39] He predicted that the hostility of the Chinese government troops would turn international intervention into an outright war with China. In view of the special relationship between Russia and China because of their long contiguous frontiers and traditional friendship, he advised (1) that Russia should not seek the leadership of the international forces, lest she appear before the Chinese as the party responsible for whatever aggressive incidents might take place, and (2) that the Russian expeditionary force participate in the joint action of the powers only to the extent of freeing the legations and of guaranteeing the safety of Russian subjects and their property in northern China. The presence of a Russian expeditionary force would also act as a check on the political actions of other participants. Russia should continue to show a friendly attitude toward the Chinese government, regarding the Boxer uprising as a "revolution" against the throne which the Russians would help crush. Secret directives to this effect were sent to Admiral Alexeev and General Sakharov the following day.[40]

Events in the Far East complicated the Russian position. Seymour's column found itself in a precarious position after reaching a point halfway to Peking. The Boxers gathered in strength both in front of and across the line of communications, especially at the Taku forts guarding the entrance to the Pei-ho. In order to reopen the river route, the admirals of the European squadrons decided to seize the forts.[41] An ultimatum was presented to the commanders of the forts. When this was refused,[42] the attack was launched on the morning of June 17. Firing provoked from the Chinese forts became a justification for the assault when gunboats and other light vessels of the international flotilla helped in the capture of these forts from the landward side. The Russians participated in this operation with three powerful gunboats out of a total of eight.[43]

The bombardment and capture of the Taku forts incensed not only the Boxers but also the Chinese government. After June 17, regular Chinese troops fought on the side of the Boxers, and the problem of relieving the Peking legations became increasingly difficult. Seymour's column was stopped and was forced to retire. The Tientsin concessions were attacked by large bands of Boxers and were shelled by artillery of the regular Chinese Army. Repeated attacks were repulsed with great effort, principally by the recently arrived Russian troops.[44] In Peking, incidents between the Boxers and Europeans increased, culminating in the murder of Baron von Ketteler, the German Minister, on June 20.[45] The Peking legation, until that time merely invested, was now actually besieged. On the following day, the Chinese government declared war on the nations engaged in the intervention, though these nations did not definitely learn of the declaration until two months later.[46]

On June 21 Muraviev died suddenly, and Count V. N. Lamsdorf, probably nominated by Witte,[47] was appointed acting minister of foreign affairs.[48] Lamsdorf's initial acts were to follow the policies of his predecessor as set down in the memorandum of June 17. He emphasized this in his telegram to Alexeev on June 28 and again in a memorandum to the Tsar on July 13.[49] However, his leadership of the Russian Foreign Office was bound to differ from that of his predecessor because he probably was already under the influence of Witte, whose plans for the expansion of Russian influence in the Far East through the agency of the Chinese Eastern Railway would be affected by the spread of the Boxer movement. On August 1, to meet this and other contingencies, Lamsdorf added to the established policy a "wait and see" provision with the query: "Shouldn't we wait until a time when the numerous uncertainties of the present moment will give way to a somewhat more definite situation?"[50]

The first important diplomatic problem encountered by Lamsdorf in reference to the Far Eastern crisis was the Japanese offer to send a contingent of 30,000 men to northern China. The Japanese Minister of Foreign Affairs made this offer to the diplomatic representatives at Tokyo[51] on June 11. The Russian government replied almost immediately, through its representative, Count A. P. Izvolskii, that it saw no reason for interfering with Japan's liberty of action.[52] The matter would have ended there had not Japan been mindful of her experience in 1895 with the Triplice of Russia, Germany, and France; she therefore desired from England "some assurance that there were no objections on the part of governments having interests in the Far East."[53] To obtain these assurances, Salisbury approached the German government.[54] But Emperor William II still entertained the "yellow peril" bogey;[55] he also hoped to avenge the murder of Baron von Ketteler with German troops,[56] and above all, he wanted to earn Russia's gratitude by refusing Salisbury's proposal of large-scale Japanese participation in the Far East.[57]

Salisbury soon realized his failure and abandoned the attempt in exchange for a guarantee.[58] He represented Japanese intervention as an obligation of Japan to the European nations. In a secret circular telegram of July 9 to the Russian representatives abroad, the Russian Foreign Office, although it again affirmed the acceptance of voluntary

Japanese participation, objected to the idea of a European "mandate," in the following passage:

This interpretation, in our opinion, could to some extent violate those principles which have already been accepted by the majority of powers as the guiding principles in relation to the events in China; namely the maintenance of unanimity among the powers, the maintenance of the established system in China, the avoidance of anything that could bring forth the partition of the Celestial Empire, and finally, the restoration by common efforts of the legal central government in Peking . . .[59]

The problem resolved itself for reasons not unlike those which had motivated Russian participation. The strategic position of Japan with reference to events in northern China favored participation, and the opportunity for Japan to play a prominent role in international affairs was too good to miss.[60] At the conference of admirals at the Taku bar held on July 4, the Anglo-Japanese proposal to bring in a division of Japanese troops was accepted by all powers, including Russia, whose representative, Admiral Hildebrand, apparently accepted the proposal on his own initiative.[61] At the beginning of July, Japanese troops dribbled into the Tientsin area in time for the final battles around that city, and also in time to take a prominent role in the August advance to relieve the Peking legations.

The second problem encountered by Lamsdorf was that of the supreme command. Once again the events at the scene of operations were foremost. At the end of June, 1900, Russian troops forming the numerical majority of the international forces on the Tientsin-Taku line were inscribing a glorious page in Russian military history. Under the command of Colonel S. Anisimov, the Russians took charge of the defense of Tientsin throughout its six-day siege and probably saved the Europeans of the Tientsin concessions from a general massacre.[62] On June 24, General A. M. Stössel, with a force of 2,000 men including 1,500 Russians, penetrated the Boxer lines and relieved the besieged legations.[63] Two days later, Russian troops led the attack on the northern arsenal from which the Boxers had menaced the concessions with artillery.[64] On the same day, Lieutenant Colonel Shirinskii with 1,800 men, including 900 Russians, relieved the Seymour column, in the Hai-ku arsenal eight miles north of Tientsin.[65]

In view of the actual leadership exercised by the Russian forces and commanders, it was natural for Russia to seek an official recognition of this leadership. On June 19 Kuropatkin made arrangements for Admiral Alexeev to hold the rank of corps commander, making him the senior land commander in northern China. He had pressed for the appointment of Alexeev as the supreme commander of the forces of the intervention in his letter to the Tsar of July 12.[66] However, considerations of higher policy prevailed in accordance with the accepted Muraviev program. In diplomatic discussions concerning the matter of supreme command, European powers objected to the British, French, and Japanese commanders[67] that were suggested. On August 6 the Kaiser, in a personal telegram to the Tsar, suggested that Field Marshal Count Alfred von Waldersee was available and suited to this post.[68] Nicholas II gladly accepted this nomination, insisting only that the authority of the commander in chief be limited to the province of Chihli.[69] Within the next few days, using the Russian acceptance as a lever, the Kaiser obtained the approval of England and France.[70] However, until the arrival of Waldersee in October, operations of the intervening powers were effectively conducted under a joint council of war, and administration of the conglomeration of troops in the Tientsin base area was in the hands of a council of three powers—England, Japan, and Russia.[71]

A new turn of events came when, toward the end of June, the Boxer rebellion spread to Manchuria, and in the three days July 5 to 7 the Boxers attacked construction workers along the southern branch of the C.E.R.[72] This new problem made Witte and his friend Lamsdorf even more opposed to the idea of taking an active part in subsequent operations in the Chihli province.[73] Kuropatkin argued the point that Russia should first "finish with Peking";[74] but Witte succeeded in impressing Lamsdorf and the Tsar with the necessity of holding back the advance on Peking until all other measures had failed. He pointed out to Kuropatkin that the Russians should have sixteen additional battalions of infantry in the theater of operations before launching the advance.[75] The real cause of the delay was the heavy summer rains, and Witte's efforts to hold back the march on Peking were needless.[76]

The unspecified "measures" in Witte's mind were possibly those having to do with the appointment of Li Hung-chang, then Viceroy of Canton, to the post of Viceroy of Shantung and Chihli, and his orders to come north and advise the Imperial Court about its relations with the European powers.[77] Li telegraphed Witte from Canton on June 26, informing him of his appointment. On the same day, two telegrams were sent to Li. One, from Witte, carried a promise that Russia would not declare war on China and would support Li Hung-chang with Russian troops if Li, in return, would support the normal situation in Manchuria. The other, from Prince Ukhtomskii, notified Li that Ukhtomskii would be in Canton at the end of July to confer with him on future Russo-Chinese relations.[78] However, Witte's hopes for a separate peaceful arrangement through negotiations with his presumed friend did not materialize. Military events moved too rapidly, and furthermore, England—even before Witte—began to negotiate with and back Li Hung-chang in the hope that he might bring order out of chaos,[79] preserve British interests in central China, and save the lives of besieged and isolated British subjects.[80]

On July 13 and 14, 1900, the international forces stormed the native city of Tientsin in their first strictly offensive action against China.[81] On the nineteenth, through a personal message from the Emperor, China appealed to the political heads of all the European powers, begging them to take steps to come to her assistance and to destroy the menace to the Empire.[82] The appeal fell on deaf ears. The governments of Europe reiterated their demands for the immediate suppression of the Boxer movement.[83] The Russian answer merely repeated once more Muraviev's policy in general terms:

The efforts of Russia have only one objective in view: namely, to assist in the reëstablishment of order and tranquillity in the Chinese Empire and, inspired by its traditional friendship toward China, the Imperial Government has decided to render to the Chinese Government every assistance with a view to suppressing the present troubles.[84]

In this manner the policy of "traditional friendship toward China" was made subservient to the joint policy of restoration of order as expressed by the European powers. The matter of prestige would not permit any other course.

Despite the desire of the English and the Germans to hold back the advance on Peking until 40,000 to 50,000 men would be able to take the field,[85] the relief force began its advance on August 4 with 18,800 men,[86] acting as a result of the information imparted by the Japanese and Russian military intelligence that the Chinese would not offer any serious resistance.[87] After a series of skirmishes, the relief force reached the outskirts of Peking on August 13. Unwilling to pause for reorganization before the completion of the relief operation, and no doubt inspired by a spirit of rivalry which was shared by all the international contingents, the Russian forces commanded by General N. P. Linevich broke the agreement to rest until August 14 before attacking the walls of Peking,[88] and assaulted the Tungpien gate on the night of August 13–14.[89] This brought on a general engagement, during which the other expeditionary forces entered the Chinese City, the southern part of intramural Peking, and on the fifteenth relieved the legations, while the Russians and Japanese coöperated in clearing the Tartar City and its immediate suburbs.[90]

After the relief of the Peking legations, discord among the representatives of the nations participating in the relief became more marked. The English and American commanders took the attitude that the Russians were not "playing the game" when they precipitated the assault on the walls of Peking.[91] There were other points of discord—some serious, some trivial, and others somewhat ridiculous. There were petty contentions between the Russian and the Japanese commanders over the order of precedence in the triumphal march through Peking on August 25,[92] and an intentional disregard of military courtesy to the British forces by General Linevich, the senior commander present, when he reviewed the international contingents.[93]

Ridiculous, but still important, was the refusal of the English and German representatives to allow Li Hung-chang to go through Peking.[94] He had been appointed on August 7 by the Chinese Court to act as their representative in the forthcoming negotiations.[95] The decision to detain Li Hung-chang was made jointly by the German, English, Japanese, and French admirals of the Far Eastern squadrons on their own authority,[96] and Li had to cruise between Shanghai and the Taku bar at the mouth of the Pei-ho until permission was given him to proceed to Tientsin on September 12.[97] The action of the admirals in detaining a Chinese plenipotentiary raised a curious legal point. Li Hung-chang had been accepted in his official capacity by the Russian and American governments.[98] Furthermore, as a civilian Chinese official, Li Hung-chang had the right of transit through Chinese territory. However, William II feared that the objective of the experienced Chinese diplomat was to sow dissension among the European powers by playing them off one against the other.[99] In a verbal statement to Sir Frank Lascelles, the British Ambassador to Berlin, the Kaiser said that Germany was "most certainly" at war with China,[100] and that Li Hung-chang was liable to arrest and internment as a subject of an enemy country. An accredited plenipotentiary, accepted by two of the powers, was a refugee from a third power either in the International Settlement of Shanghai or on a neutral vessel.

A serious disharmony between the Russian policy and that of the other powers arose from the Russian suggestion of removing the diplomatic missions from Peking to Tientsin for the conduct of negotiations with China.[101] On August 22 Lamsdorf still thought that Peking would be the logical place for the negotiations;[102] but in the circular of August

25 which he sent to the capitals of the principal countries concerned, after reiterating the basic Russian policies, he presented the argument that since the Chinese Court had fled to Sian-fu there was no purpose in keeping the diplomatic missions in Peking. In fact, their presence there even complicated matters. The powers should consequently withdraw their troops and their legations to Tientsin and postpone all attempts to make a settlement with China until the return of the Imperial Court to Peking would make possible the reëstablishment of normal diplomatic relations.[103]

Orders for the Russian legation to prepare to withdraw from Peking were telegraphed to Giers and Linevich on August 25,[104] and their intention was made known to all the powers by August 28, 1900.[105] However, General Linevich publicly maintained the attitude that Russian troops were to winter in Peking and in the province of Chihli in their "present" strength of 15,000 men.[106] On September 12 England initiated a refusal on the part of the other powers to follow the example of Russia.[107] Nevertheless, Russian troops began to withdraw from Peking on September 13,[108] and on the twenty-ninth Russia set a futile example by withdrawing her legation and all troops from Peking[109] with the exception of a reinforced legation guard of 1,200 men.[110]

The last important action of Russian troops in the Chihli theater of operations was the overland march of some 5,000 Russians to Shanhaikwan in late September. During this march, intended to clear the Imperial Northern Chinese Railway from Tientsin to Shanhaikwan, the Russians fought two petty and nearly bloodless engagements;[111] and on September 30 the Russian force, together with representative landing parties of other powers, occupied the various fortified points at Shanhaikwan.[112] In subsequent military and punitive expeditions in Chihli and Hupeh, beginning with the march on Pao-ting-fu on October 4, 1900,[113] and lasting until the end of April, 1901,[114] Russian troops did not participate. Their active role had ended.

The military solution of the Boxer crisis brought forth expressions of unqualified satisfaction from Witte, Lamsdorf, Alexeev, and the Tsar. As early as July, and certainly in August, when Linevich superseded him in command of the Russian troops in northern China, Alexeev expressed his unwillingness to become involved in the decision to march on Peking. Sometime in July he had stated:

Our interests are in Manchuria; our political center is there: and all our efforts must be directed to the security of our position in that region. Circumstances brought us to Chihli, but the sooner we get out of there the better. I am sorry about the ministers, but they themselves are responsible for their situation, and the losses now suffered by Russia have been brought on by their own lack of foresight.[115]

The Tsar, in a personal letter to his mother on August 24, 1900, wrote that "the happiest day of my life will be when we leave Peking and get out of the mess for good."[116] Witte grew more and more concerned with the developments in Manchuria and hoped that the crisis around Peking would resolve itself in the course of time. As for Lamsdorf, the August events in northern China did not affect his policy. He had guided Russian policy away from any premature commitments, except those of joint action in the preservation of the integrity of China and the restoration of Chinese sovereignty in northern China and Manchuria at the end of the disturbances. Both commitments were dependent on the course of events and on those "uncertainties" of which he wrote on August 1.

Even General A. N. Kuropatkin, the proponent of a vigorous and aggressive stand in northern China, showed no regret that the war in that area was over. As a military man immediately concerned with the operation of troops he had pressed for positive action in northern China. Now that the military aims of the expedition had been achieved, he eagerly turned his interests to the developing campaign in Manchuria. At least there is no record of his opposition to the withdrawals in northern China which occurred in September, 1900. The interest of the Tsar and his leading ministers naturally turned to developments in Manchuria which created new problems out of the previous "uncertainties." These more specific problems were to dominate the course of Russian policy in the Far East down to the outbreak of the Russo-Japanese War.

THE "CONQUEST" OF MANCHURIA, JUNE 30–OCTOBER 6, 1900

In June, 1900, the Boxer rebellion spread into Manchuria. At first little was heard of the Boxers and no special interest was shown in their activity[117] since the first outbreaks of the movement were hard to distinguish from the periodic operations of the *khunhuzes*.[118] About the middle of June, Boxer propaganda was more in evidence. A few leaders from Shantung arrived in Mukden seeking recruits, but they achieved only small success as the stable population of the city condemned the policies of the rebellion. The Boxers, however, did find recruits in the poorest sections of the city, among beggars, outcasts, and the desperately poor.[119] Even among the 60,000 Chinese workmen—more than half of whom were recent arrivals from Shantung[120]—engaged in the construction work of the Chinese Eastern Railway and its southern branch, the Boxer agitators had little success. In northern China the railroads constructed by Europeans increased the economic hardships of the population by taking work from tens of thousands previously engaged in the carrying trade, whereas Russian railroads in Manchuria did not similarly dislocate workers. On the contrary, because of their magnitude, they supported not only the 60,000 Chinese engaged in construction work but tens of thousands more Manchurian settlers who were able to conduct a profitable catering trade with the railroad workers and employees. In Manchuria, especially in the northern provinces, distances were too great for the conduct of a large carrying trade by primitive methods, except on the Liao and Sungari rivers, and this trade was almost unaffected by the competition of the railroads, which were still unfinished. As in China proper, the Russian church in Manchuria had no proselytizing missionary activities.

The Boxer rebellion and its suppression in Manchuria differed from similar events in northern China, chiefly because of the different status of European economic interests in Manchuria. European economic interests in Manchuria—with the exception of the open port of Newchwang—were almost exclusively Russian. These interests consisted of the advanced stage of construction of the Chinese Eastern Railway, which was 960 miles long, and its southern branch from Harbin to Dalny and Port Arthur, which was 650 miles; the operations of the Russo-Chinese banks at Harbin, Kirin, Newchwang, and Mukden; the exploitation of the coal mines at Yentai and Wu-fand-yang by the C.E.R. Company; navigation on the Sungari; and the administration of the railroad and its sundry trade engagements at the construction headquarters of the railway in the growing Russian quarter of the Chinese city of Harbin.[121] About 1,500 Russian civilians and 4,500 railroad guards[122] were engaged in these enterprises in Manchuria. The homogeneous nature of foreign interests in Manchuria made the pacification of its three provinces, in default of a Chinese solution, solely a Russian problem; and in view of the considerable number of Russians involved and the enormous capital outlay on the Russian railroads, it was a very serious and pressing problem.

The original military situation was also quite different from that in northern China. The relatively small force of Russian railroad guards was more than ten times the size of the garrison which defended the legations in Peking throughout the two-month siege, whereas the noncombatants in the railroad area and in Peking were approximately equal in number. The Russian groups which were attacked thus had a large degree of mobility and could fight their way out of Manchuria or into the besieged quarter of Harbin with relative ease; furthermore, reinforcements were available and forthcoming. As soon as news of the beginning of unrest reached Witte he appealed to Kuropatkin, the Minister of War, for an increase in the number of railroad guards, of whom there were 11,000 by the end of the first week of July,[123] recruited from reservists and currently discharged soldiers. Within immediate call, in its Maritime and Priamur provinces and in the Irkutsk *guberniia,* Russia had for its relief forces large numbers of troops, especially cossacks, admirably suited for the type of campaign later undertaken in Manchuria. These troops had organized transport facilities and could operate with a helpful unity of command and without diplomatic hindrances or the disturbing influence of intense international rivalry and suspicion.

The conduct of diplomatic affairs in matters pertaining to Manchuria also differed from that shown in matters pertaining to the crisis in northern China. The firm hand of Witte, the presiding genius of the Chinese Eastern Railway Company, was evident from the start. On hearing from his agent, A. I. Iugovich, the chief engineer in charge of construction of the railroad, of the possibility of serious trouble in Manchuria, Witte asked for and received on June 13 a promise from Alexeev not to send troops into Manchuria until Witte asked him to do so. On June 29 he received a similar promise from Kuropatkin, and on July 1, one from the Tsar.[124] Meanwhile he resorted to private diplomacy in a manner quite common with him. On June 28 he instructed Iugovich to open a credit of 100,000 lan (about 150,000 rubles) for the governor of each of the three Manchurian provinces as a first payment to them if they could keep their provinces under control and suppress the Boxer troubles where they had begun.[125] After the opening of military operations the control quite naturally fell into the hands of the military, but it was Witte who gave the signal to issue the order for Russian mobilization in the Far East, who reported on the situation in Manchuria to the press during the months of July and August, and who finally offered the solution accepted for "conquered" Manchuria.

The final important point of difference between the events in Chihli and those in Manchuria is one of military strategy and tactics. In Chihli the heaviest fighting was between the relatively small bodies of European troops and bands of Boxers who were fanatical elements of the Chinese civilian population and disbanded soldiery. At no time, it has been stated, did the Chinese forces number more than 20,000 men or take the field as a complete unit.[126] In Manchuria, the fanatical element was insignificant. Almost from the beginning, the military operations of the Chinese were conducted with regular troops and their auxiliary bandit irregulars, who were commanded by regular officers. They took the field with their full complement of artillery. The operations in Manchuria had the character of a real war. A Russian town was bombarded and an invasion of Russian territory projected. The disparity between the heavy losses suffered by the interventionists in Chihli and those incurred by the Russians in their conquest of Manchuria was due not so much to the difference in the fighting quality of the Chinese forces engaged, or to the scale of operations in the two theaters of war, as it was to the difference in terrain. In Chihli, the flat, densely settled country, with narrow and limited horizons, lent itself admirably to the primitive tactics used by the Chinese in rushing and ambushing advancing troops. In Manchuria, especially in the north, the vast plains, the gradually sloping hills, and the sparse population allowed the Russians ample opportunity to execute strategic maneuvers with their better-trained troops and to exploit their great advantage in armament by using maximum ranges of infantry and artillery fire.[127]

The Boxer outbreak in Manchuria began with disorders, which were not armed nor violent, in Mukden, Liaoyang, Inkou, and Haicheng, the largest cities of the Mukden (Fengtien) province.[128] On June 30, with the connivance of the Lieutenant Governor of Fengtien,[129] the Boxer mobs led by Chinese officials[130] attacked the Roman Catholic mission in Mukden, killing five Europeans. The mobs pressed on to the Russian railroad station, which, according to the Russian custom, was constructed several miles away from the walls of the Chinese city, burned it, set fire to the nearby Russian barracks, and then dispersed.[131] This display of hostility was so unexpected and so uncommon that the Russian authorities did not attach any special significance to it. On July 4 Iugovich telegraphed Witte from Harbin that the three governors general of Manchuria would guarantee the safety of Russian subjects and railroads in Manchuria if the Russians would refrain from taking active military measures.[132] On the same day, however, the Boxers descended in great force on all stations along two hundred miles of the railroad south of Mukden, and within three days they drove the Russian railroad guards and a few civilians northward from Tienling and southward from Liaoyang.[133]

About July 6 or 7 an imperial edict was posted in Kirin and in Tsitsihar ordering regular Chinese troops to unite with the Boxers and attack the Russians.[134] After the proclamation of this edict events took on the character of an open war with Russia. In the north there were no manifestations of fanatical excesses. Shoi, the Governor General of the Heilungkiang province, moving his troops to the siege of Harbin, suggested to Iugovich on July 8 that Iugovich evacuate from Harbin all women and children and send them by the open river route to Khabarovsk.[135] On the tenth, the regular Chinese troops advancing on Hailar gave the Russian refugees there an advance warning to evacuate the town and retreat along the unobstructed railroad toward the Russian frontier.[136] As a result, when Russian troops entered Manchuria, there were no official reprisals, punitive expeditions, or other manifestations of vengeance on Chinese civilians or officials implicated in the Boxer movement. To be sure, there were many incidents of violence, wholesale looting, and kindred concomitants of war. After the declaration of mobilization among the Ussuri and the Amur cossacks on June 24, 1900, robbing and killing of lone Chinese in out-of-the-way places was rather frequent.[137] During the "conquest" of Manchuria there was a profusion of incidents of wholesale looting with the connivance—if not by orders—of the military authorities.[138] The behaviour of the Russian troops in these incidents in no way differed from that of the participants in the relief of Peking. However, conditions were so unsettled at this time that even peaceful villagers derailed trains and looted them down to the copper tubing in the boilers of locomotives, and even more peaceful Koreans staged bloody "pogroms" against the Chinese in Hunchun (Manchuria).[139] And in engagements from which the Russians had to withdraw it was impossible to tell whether the attackers were *khunhuzes,* Boxers, regulars, local villagers, or any combination of these.[140]

The type of war fought between the Chinese and Russians in Manchuria is well illustrated by the incident of the bombardment of Blagoveschensk.[141] On July 12, when Blagoveschensk was almost denuded of its garrison troops, having sent reinforcements to the columns destined to operate in Manchuria, Chinese artillery opened fire on Russian military transport steamers going down the river past Aigun.[142] On the following day, Chinese artillery began the bombardment of Blagoveschensk from the Manchurian side of the Amur,[143] and General Gribskii, Ataman of the Amur cossacks, received a telegram from the Governor General of Tsitsihar informing him that, because Russian troops were advancing into Manchuria, he had ordered the bombardment of the Russian city.[144] The bombardment of Blagoveschensk was not severe. For two weeks the Chinese sporadically shelled the town,[145] but because of the small caliber of their guns and poor gunnery, most of the shells did not reach the town and only some fifteen to twenty persons were killed or wounded throughout the entire bombardment.[146] Nevertheless, the heavy shelling of July 14 to 16, together with rumors of possible Chinese invasion and revolt among the Chinese population of the town, produced a state of panic among the Russians.[147]

The vague military threat to the town was especially menacing because of a large unstable population among the Chinese—itinerant workers, petty tradesmen, and manual workers—resident in the city, who in the event of a Chinese attack could easily influence the outcome by turning against the Russians. Consequently, on July 14, the military authorities defending the city decided upon the drastic measure of deporting the Chinese population across the river into Manchurian territory, despite the assurance given to a deputation from the Chinese residents by General Gribskii that they might "remain where they were without fear, as they were on the soil of the great Russian Empire whose government would never allow peaceful foreigners to be molested."[148]

Various reports of "eyewitnesses" do not agree on the actual incidents of the expulsion. It is generally accepted that from July 14 to 16 some 3,000 Chinese were rounded up, with considerable brutality, and a few were killed. The Chinese were driven to an abandoned cossack village a few miles up the river from Blagoveschensk. Early in the morning of July 17, they were forced to cross the river, which at that point is more than half a mile wide.[149] There are no published reports of actual eyewitnesses of the crossing. Leo Deutsch, the most important non-Russian source of information about this event, possibly influenced by his general critical attitude toward all things Russian, alleged that his informants, eyewitnesses of the event, saw the Russians force the Chinese men, women, and children to swim across, and that when the refugees were swimming, the Chinese troops on the opposite bank opened fire on them and the Russians followed suit in sport. As a result, only a few of the strongest swimmers succeeded in gaining safety on the Manchurian bank.[150] However, another non-Russian "witness," Captain Smith-Dorrien, artist-correspondent of the London *Times* and the *Illustrated London News,* reported on the authority of his informants that the passage of the river was negotiated on rafts built by the Russians, and that when the Chinese troops vaguely saw through the morning mist the approaching rafts filled with unidentified occupants, they imagined that the Russians were forcing the river and opened fire on their compatriots, who, thrown into a panic, capsized the rafts, and as a result "many hundreds were drowned."[151]

The menace to Blagoveschensk did not end with the expulsion of the Chinese. On the Manchurian bank of the river, between Sakhalin, a village opposite Blagoveschensk, and Aigun, twenty miles downstream, a concentration of 18,000 men with 45 guns was reported,[152] and on July 18, the Chinese in considerable strength with artillery crossed the Amur into Russian territory and burned several deserted villages.[153] However, on July 27, water-borne Russian reinforcements from Sretensk, which had been held up by the low waters of the Shilka River, arrived to relieve the city. On August 2 the Russian forces assumed the offensive and crossed the Amur at Blagoveschensk.[154]

The Blagoveschensk incident is only a conspicuous and widely publicized example of the panic and chaos which prevailed in official circles as well as among the populace. Widely divergent reactions of the chief responsible administrators aggravated the confusion. Sometime in the middle of July, General Gribskii published in the newspaper *Amurskii Krai* of Khabarovsk a "Call to the Amur Cossacks" in which he invited "the stalwart sons of the Amur to take up arms, and in cossack fashion, decisively and quickly, settle with the violators of the peace . . . without losing time on questions and permissions unnecessary in this case."[155] An order was issued that this "call" be read in all stanitzas (cossack settlements) immediately upon its receipt. On the other hand, General N. I. Grodekov, Military Governor of the Priamur province and Gribskii's indirect superior, published in *Vostochnoe Obozrenie,* another Khabarovsk newspaper, on July 22 and 28 and August 18, stern warnings against excesses committed by the inhabitants of Blagoveschensk and others who were taking unauthorized measures against the peaceful Chinese and Manchus. His proclamation stated that "those guilty of murder, robbery, and other acts of violence against peaceful and unarmed Chinese will be subject to trial and be liable to punishment according to the full severity of martial law."[156]

The confusion created by such official contradictions produced further excesses. In Blagoveschensk there were other mass deportations of Chinese even after the "massacre";[157] and along the Amur and Ussuri rivers there were "pogroms" and attacks on the widely scattered and defenseless Chinese and Manchu agricultural settlements in which scores, if not hundreds, of inhabitants were killed.[158] Even in Vladivostok, where order prevailed among most of the residents, there was a panic and a mass exodus of Chinese—more than 4,000 Chinese fled from the city and its suburbs in July and August.[159] The high point of unauthorized and highhanded official actions came on August 17 when the chauvinistic Gribskii issued a bombastic proclamation annexing the right (Manchurian) bank of the Amur River.[160] Though this action and all similar intentions were officially disavowed by the circular of August 25, the idea of annexation was also echoed in a memorandum of General N. I. Grodekov, who argued that Russia must demand the Manchurian banks of the Amur and the Ussuri as far inland as the watershed separating the Amur basin from the Manchurian plains. In his opinion the return of the Manchurian bank to China would eventually spell a "death sentence" to the Russian possessions along the Amur River.[161]

Further evidence that the unauthorized actions on the Amur were disapproved is to be found in subsequent circulars and declarations and also in the courts-martial of local officials which took place in May, 1901. The investigation and the trials did not end until February, 1902, when by an agreement between the Ministers of the Interior, Justice, and War, the matter was closed. Lieutenant General Gribskii was found responsible for the mismanagement of the deportation, but in view of his past services, he was merely transferred to the General Staff. The military commander at Blagoveschensk was sentenced to an imprisonment of three months and then dismissed from the service. The assistant chief of police actually in charge of the crossing was sentenced to three months' confinement. All other charges were dismissed.[162]

On July 9, 1900, at Witte's request, Kuropatkin ordered Russian troops to invade Manchuria and crush the Boxer rebellion.[163] On the same day, General Sakharov with four battalions of infantry, three sotnias of cossacks, and twenty-six guns, left Khabarovsk by steamer and barge for the relief of Harbin. The general offensive was delayed until the last week of July by the necessity of mobilizing a sufficiently large military transport service. When this advance began, it was executed by five columns (later seven) converging on the main centers of Manchuria from the east, west, south, and north.[164] The first main objective in the north was the relief of Harbin, which had been defended since July 10 by the energetic efforts of General A. A. Gerngross, the commander of the Manchurian railroad guards, and Iugovich, the chief engineer.[165] The city was relieved just in time, on August 2, by the column of General Sakharov moving up the Sungari River. Without a single reverse, Russian columns in the north reëstablished Russian control along the trans-Manchurian line by September 1 and were prepared to move south to join hands with the forces of General D. I. Subbotich, who commanded several columns sent out from the Kwantung territory to effect the capture of Mukden.

The progress of the Russian advance was favored by the disunity and strife in the ranks of the Chinese officials. In Kirin, the Governor General had been successful in preventing his troops from engaging the Russians and had kept down the Boxer movement among the population.[166] In fact, he even offered a regiment of his troops to the Russian authorities at Harbin; but the offer was declined.[167] In Mukden, Tseng Chitchze, the Governor General, had been pro-Russian from the start. On July 4, the day the Boxer movement was directed against the C.E.R., Tseng Chitchze was overthrown by a revolt of the Boxer leaders led by his subordinate, Lieutenant General Fudutun.[168] He was kept a virtual prisoner in his own yamen.[169] On August 11, when the Lieutenant Governor was away in the south fighting the Russians, Tseng-Chitchze engineered an anti-Boxer revolution and commanded his soldiers to exterminate the Boxers. In the course of the massacres which followed, many Boxer leaders were killed, many fled from Mukden, and the rest went into hiding by merging with the general populace.[170]

This revolution broke the back of the Boxer movement in southern Manchuria. Although on September 29 Tseng-Chitchze and his faction had to flee from Mukden at the approach of his rebellious lieutenant governor, the Boxer control was never reëstablished. The looting and burning which broke out in the city on the thirtieth was the work of disorganized and defeated Chinese soldiers and uncontrolled mobs.[171] On October 1, 1900, a reconnaissance detachment of 300 cossacks entered Mukden by the south gate, without opposition, while Chinese soldiers fled into the country by the north gate. In the afternoon, General Subbotich and his force entered Mukden,[172] and the Russian "conquest" of Manchuria was ended. Subbotich then took up his residence in the Imperial Palace and began to restore order. On October 6 the northern and southern expeditions joined forces north of Mukden, and Russian control was reëstablished along all the railroad lines of the C.E.R.

Immediately after the capture of Mukden, orders were issued for the demobilization of Russian troops in Manchuria.[173] The maintenance of large forces was undesirable because of the scarcity of the previous year's crops, which would render the maintenance costly and objectionable to the native populace. However, demobilization was hindered by circumstances independent of the will of the commanders. The approach of cold weather necessitated the establishment of road barracks and rest stations for marching troops, the railroad was still unrepaired, and the freezing of the Sungari and Amur rivers closed the navigation system by which an evacuation of Manchuria could best be carried out.[174] Furthermore, in November, the former

Boxers began to appear as out-and-out brigands in such numbers that the railroad guards could not cope with them without the assistance of the regular forces.[175] In December, twenty-eight out of the forty-two infantry battalions brought into Manchuria were still there,[176] and they were held over through the spring of 1901, mainly for the suppression of banditry. The excellent harvest of 1901 worked miracles in returning the brigands to their peaceful occupations,[177] and then the last nonpolitical reason for the maintenance of Russian troops in Manchuria vanished.

News of the end of the military phase of the suppression of the Boxer rebellion was received with great satisfaction in St. Petersburg. The intervention of the European powers was never popular. In contrast to the German press,[178] Russian newspapers took a sympathetic stand toward China. Although on occasion there appeared insignificant pamphlets representing the events in the Far East as a manifestation of the "yellow peril"[179] the leading newspapers abstained from sensationalism and chauvinism. The *Promyshlennyi Mir* felt that the military operations would bring more harm than good in future relations with China. *Novoe Vremia* warmly espoused the idea of an alliance with Turkey and China, the underprivileged nations. The *Grazhdanin* went as far as to announce that all its sympathies were on the side of the Chinese, who were "defending their civilization against that of the Westerners." Even the ultraconservative *Moskovskie Vedomosti* took a sympathetic stand by stating that it stood for the suppression of the Boxers only because they were anarchists; the paper was in favor of all measures maintaining order.[180]

Witte and Lamsdorf were naturally pleased to have Far Eastern Affairs taken out of the hands of the military and returned to normal diplomatic channels.[181] Even Kuropatkin grudgingly had to agree with that.[182] On October 6, the date of the reëstablishment of Russian control over all Russian railroads in Manchuria, the Tsar wrote from Livadia to his mother:

The glad news has just arrived that our forces have taken Mukden. . . . That will, thank God, be the end of our military action in northern China; and all that is left to do is to organize the defense of the railway, to pacify the country, and to clean up the robber bands. The occupation of Mukden is for us just as important as, at the time, was that of Peking. We cannot thank God enough for such a speedy and unexpected end to our actions in the Far East.[183]

However, the Tsar's fervent jubilation was premature. It was just this matter of the "defense of the railway" that was to be the vital and insurmountable problem for Russian Far Eastern diplomacy.

VII

DIPLOMATIC SETTLEMENT OF THE BOXER CRISIS—THE JOINT AND SEPARATE AGREEMENTS WITH CHINA

AT THE HEIGHT of operations by the forces engaged in the suppression of the Boxer uprising in Chihli and Manchuria in August, 1900, the prevailing British suspicions of Russian aims and motives were once more aroused. German and American diplomatic representatives at times admitted Russia's right to invade Manchuria in order to protect her paramount interests by force, if necessary.[1] Although noncommital on the subject of Manchuria, France gave the Russian conduct a sign of tacit approval by repeated expressions of her complete accord with Russia in the Far Eastern situation.[2] England, however, continued to look critically on every Russian move in the Far East.

THE CONFLICT BETWEEN RUSSIAN AND INTERNATIONAL POLICIES IN THE SETTLEMENT WITH CHINA TO DECEMBER 27, 1900

One of the first moves objectionable to the British was the Russian occupation of the open port of Newchwang on the "pretext of an alleged attack" by the Boxers on the foreign quarter of the town.[3] The "alleged" attack of August 4 was quite real to the defending Russian and Japanese naval detachments; it took a whole day's fighting to repel.[4] The occupying garrison was relieved on August 12 by Russian naval units, which landed reinforcements. At the same time, Japanese naval units, which did not participate in the bombardment of the forts guarding the river entrance to the town, also landed naval detachments.[5] A point too often ignored is the fact that the Japanese detachments remained in Newchwang at least until March 1902,[6] and that nowhere in published correspondence on the subject of the Newchwang incident is there any evidence that their presence aroused protests or comments from any side.

As was commonly done by all participants in the suppression of the Boxer rebellion, the Russian military took over the administration of Newchwang, which had been deserted by the Chinese authorities, and installed their headquarters in the building of the Imperial Chinese Customs, raising a Russian flag over this headquarters.[7] This led to a series of protests and much diplomatic correspondence indica-

---

[1] For notes to chap. vii see pp. 292–299.

[145]

tive of extreme British watchfulness of every minor action of the Russians in the Far East and extreme sensitivity to such actions.[8] When, late in August, 1900, Admiral Alexeev visited the port on a Russian cruiser, he frankly told the foreign consuls that the Russians intended to establish a temporary civil administration for the town. For that purpose a Russian diplomat, I. Ia. Korostovets, conferred with the foreign consuls and Cecil Bauer, the English-born local director of the Chinese Maritime Customs. An effective administration was devised by mutual consent, Bauer was persuaded by Korostovets to remain in his post under Russian supervision,[9] and the customs administration operated as effectively as before.[10] In July, 1901, the British decided to send a gunboat to Newchwang to demonstrate more strongly their interests there.[11] With the arrival of the insignificant gunboat *Plover* on July 31 and a Japanese gunboat a few days later, the Newchwang "incident" came to an end.[12]

It was probably in view of the suspicions aroused by Russian actions in Manchuria, expressed chiefly through the English press, that the Russian Minister of Foreign Affairs decided to include in the circular of August 25 a statement that the military occupation of Manchuria had been dictated solely by the absolute necessity of repelling attacks of Chinese insurgents on the C.E.R., and that as soon as peace was restored and the security of the railroad assured, "Russia would not fail to withdraw her troops from Chinese territory, provided such action did not meet with obstacles caused by the proceedings of other Powers."[13] About August 27, Witte, through Iugovich, proclaimed to the population of Manchuria that Russian occupation was only temporary and was due solely to the desire of the Russian government to restore order in the territories of the Chinese Empire.[14]

Russian activities in the Chihli area, however, did not help to allay the fears of the British government regarding Russian aims in the Far East. On October 4 the British discovered that the Russian encampment on the east side of the Pei-ho at Tientsin had been converted into a Russian concession.[15] An appeal to the Tientsin provisional government brought no satisfaction, because the Russian military commanders claimed that the order for seizure of that land was given by Alexeev, who was then out of reach in Manchuria.[16] On November 6, General Linevich issued a circular expressing the legality of the seizure in the following terms:

... on the 23rd of June Russian reinforcements, which came to raise the blockade, swept the left bank of the Pei-ho and established themselves there by right of conquest, having taken possession by force of arms and at the price of Russian blood spilled, in order to prevent the Chinese from returning and resuming fire. His Excellency [Lt. General Linevich] considers this entire tract of land to have become the property of the Russian troops on the twenty-third of June by act of war.[17]

British and American representatives in China protested against this circular,[18] but Giers disclaimed any responsibility for it, stating that all questions concerning the matter must be addressed to the military authorities and that "there is no question whatever of acquiring territory by conquest on the part of Russia."[19] The position of Russia was made stronger by the fact that other powers followed the policy of "grabbing" justified by the Russian circular. On November 7 a Belgian circular announced the appropriation of a concession;[20] on the twentieth, a French circular announced a similar action;[21] then in succession, the Italians, Austrians, and Japanese made their appropriations.[22] The crux of the British objection to the Russian moves lay in the belief of members of the British cabinet that, despite assurances from St. Petersburg to the contrary, "they are taken not merely as a concession, but as a territorial acquisition."[23] In the second place, this Russian step was looked upon as an attempt on the part of Russia to bring the land and water communications between Peking and the sea under her control.[24] Later in November the legality of the Russian seizure was put to a test when the British military authorities ordered the construction of a railroad siding on ground which came within the boundaries of the new Russian concession. The Russians immediately mounted guard on the rising embankment to prevent further construction, and for several weeks Russian and British guards faced each other over barricades separated by only a few yards.[25] In December and again in March, 1901, the dispute over the railroad siding was submitted for arbitration to Field Marshal von Waldersee,[26] who adjudicated the question in favor of the Russians. The English withheld their objections but reserved the right "to question the validity of the concession as a whole or the proprietory rights within it" at some future time.[27]

The incident of the Tientsin railroad siding was aggravated because it appeared for a time as part of a broader Russian scheme to control the railroad from Peking to Taku and also the northern line of the Imperial Chinese Northern Railway from Tientsin to Newchwang. This railroad was owned and operated by the Chinese government, but its bonded debt had been financed by British banks.[28] The task of recapturing the line from Boxer control had been undertaken by the Russians in their march from Tientsin to Shanhaikwan, September

20–30, 1900, and again in the march of Colonel N. G. Volkov's column from Shanhaikwan to Kinchow, October 2–6, 1900.[29] Throughout the winter of 1900–1901 the Russians were in exclusive occupation of the railroad line with the exception of the town of Shanhaikwan, where a small international force had previously shared the control of the several forts.[30] The occupation of the railroad was very convenient for the Russians from a military standpoint because the Russians redeployed their troops from the Chihli theater of operations to Manchuria and later to Kwantung.[31] At first British interests were little affected by Russian control. In fact, W. C. Hillier, the Director-Manager of the Shanghai and Hong Kong Banking Corporation, offered to sell the British loan to the railroad to the Russo-Chinese Bank; but at the time Witte considered the price too high for the political importance such an investment might bring.[32]

Besides the strategic reason for retaining control of the railroad, Alexeev, on October 8, recommended it because German intrigues were attempting to effect the seizure of the Kaiping coal mines, which were the most productive in northern China, and also the port of Chinwang-tao. His telegram added: "I consider it my duty to express my firm conviction that the railroad, as property of the Chinese government, occupied and defended by our troops with unavoidable loss of life, must unquestionably remain in our hands at least until the final solution of the present crisis."[33]

Alexeev's suggestion was carried out. On December 26 the Russian management of the railroad was confirmed by Field Marshal von Waldersee, who removed the British despite objections, leaving the railroad in the absolute control of the Russians.[34] The British remonstrances forced the Russians to hand over the part of the line south of the Great Wall to Field Marshal von Waldersee for restitution to the Chinese-English management,[35] but the section north of the Great Wall remained under Russian occupation and control until after the international settlement with China on September 7, 1901.

British suspicion and hostility were also aroused by the actions of the Russian Minister to China in the negotiations with the Chinese plenipotentiaries Li Hung-chang and Prince Ching,[36] which began on October 4, 1900, with a discussion of a note presented by France, establishing six basic principles for future agreement.[37] On October 22, Giers returned to Peking with the Russian legation and gave his attention to the note. On October 26, on the initiative of Giers, the diplomatic corps met in the first conference to the final note.[38]

Throughout subsequent negotiations Russia was the leading advocate of mild punishment for China. Russia's main opponent was Germany, who proposed severe terms. Russia opposed the German demands for the "execution" of the high Chinese officials implicated in the Boxer movement but compromised on the demand for their "punishment."[39] The Russians took an especially firm stand in opposing the German proposal to include a provision for a Chinese mission of apology to Berlin, and the erection in Peking of a monument to the murdered Baron von Ketteler.[40] The Russians maintained:

Proposals of this nature, serving principally as a satisfaction to be given to the private views of one State, ought not to enter into the common program of collective demands, which had as their main object the interests of all powers collectively, and the reëstablishment of a normal state of affairs in the Celestial Empire.[41]

The Russian government continued to express its dissatisfaction with the policy of Field Marshal von Waldersee in ordering new punitive expeditions, and it violently opposed his proposal to march on Sian-fu and bring the Chinese Imperial Court back to Peking by force.[42]

Opposing the British, French, and American policies, Russia stood against the attempts made to exact indemnities for the massacred Chinese Christians[43] and even mildly opposed the whole matter of indemnity for the missionaries in China.[44] In general, there was no marked discord between the views of Russia and those of France, both nations being eager to have each other's support in all matters,[45] and both being interested in bringing the negotiations to an end as soon as possible.[46]

On December 21 the ministers of the foreign powers at Peking signed a collective note,[47] which was submitted to the Chinese plenipotentiaries three days later[48] and was accepted in full by the Chinese government on December 31, 1900.[49] This note, containing twelve articles, made no mention of Manchuria, although there is no evidence in available sources that Giers or Lamsdorf made any attempt to restrict this subject to separate negotiations between China and Russia, nor did they seem to wish to include Manchuria in the general negotiations. It can therefore be assumed that a tacit agreement was reached whereby individual nations would conduct separate negotiations with China on matters dealing with their own specific interests— a principle which was followed in practice by all the major powers.

On December 22, after Russia had signed the collective note, Lamsdorf sent Giers a telegram indicating Russia's new attitude toward the Far Eastern situation.[50] After stating that with the signing of the collective note "our role in Pechili can be considered finished," and

that "we do not seek to contest the acceptance of the proposal suggested by the English minister that the international troops remain
in the Pechili theater of operations until China submits to the demands
placed before her," Lamsdorf added for the "exclusive information"
of Giers:

> I consider it my duty to note that the continued occupation of Pechili arouses
> the enmity of the Chinese against the remaining foreign contingents, which can
> hardly bring any loss to the intrinsically Russian interests in that province; and
> in the meantime, such a condition of affairs will offer to us a completely legal
> basis to prolong, in agreement with the declaration announced in the circular
> of August 25, the occupation of Manchuria, the internal organization of which
> still demands from us considerable care and effort.
>
> We have promised to withdraw our troops from Manchuria only on the restora-
> tion of complete order in China, and only if the actions of other powers will not
> serve as obstacles to this withdrawal. From our point of view, we cannot consider
> the restoration of normal order guaranteed until the Court returns to Peking,
> which, in turn, will be possible only in case foreign troops quit the capital of the
> Empire.

The new policy was therefore to utilize the situation in Pechili and
the negotiations of the European powers with China to Russia's advantage in her separate negotiations with China.

After December 22, Russia seemingly took a minor part in the
Peking negotiations.[51] Although Lamsdorf and Witte made suggestions
with reference to such matters as the means of collecting the Boxer
indemnity, the rate of interest on the indemnity bonds, and the currency evaluations,[52] Russia showed little concern over the acceptance
or rejection of the suggestions. In the negotiations of the final Boxer
Protocol of September 7, 1901,[53] Russia found strong support for her
policy in Manchuria. First, there was the presence of the large armies
of the intervening nations in northern China, which in April, 1901,
numbered (by one account) 173,000 men,[54] as compared with some
100,000 Russian troops in Manchuria and the Kwangtung territory.[55]
This great force could always serve as partial justification for the
presence of Russian troops in Manchuria. Other support came from
the increased possibility of making greater financial demands upon
China. As Russian negotiations for a separate agreement with China
concerning Manchuria wavered, this pressure was brought to bear.
When an advantageous agreement seemed impossible, Russia increased
her demands from the modest sum of 18,000,000 Haikwan taels (about
£6,000,000) demanded on February 5, 1901,[56] to 130,371,120 taels, or
28.97 per cent of the total.[57] This sum fully compensated Russia for the
losses incurred in the Boxer rebellion. It paid generously for the

Russian military expenditures in the occupation of Chihli and Manchuria and left a handsome profit in addition.[58]

EVOLUTION OF A PLAN FOR A SEPARATE AGREEMENT WITH CHINA

The idea of a separate agreement with China appeared in Russian diplomatic correspondence about the end of September, 1901, when the advanced stage of the "conquest" of Manchuria made apparent the great difference between the Russian problems in Manchuria and those in northern China. In a telegram to Giers on September 26, Lamsdorf clearly pointed out the presence of the divergent policies.

In the coming negotiations with the Chinese Government we differentiate two questions: the first a collective one, touching all the powers combined; the other, a private one, the question of regulating the future relations of Russia and China, in which we cannot by any means allow the interference of other nations.[59]

From the same telegram it is also evident that no official steps had been taken to approach the Chinese government on the matter of a separate agreement.[60]

On September 29 a separate agreement was projected through unofficial channels by Witte through Ukhtomskii. In the telegraphic communications of June 26, between Witte, Li Hung-chang, and Ukhtomskii, it was stated that the purpose of Ukhtomskii's voyage to the Far East was to arrange an agreement for the preservation of Russian interests in Manchuria.[61] On September 29, when Ukhtomskii arrived at Shanghai, the project took on a different connotation. In the absence of Li Hung-chang, who was then in northern China, Ukhtomskii was met by Li's son, Li Tsin-fan, who as his father's deputy stated that in return for Russia's voluntary relinquishment of Manchuria, China was ready to pay all indemnities demanded and to grant to Russia the sole right of exploitation of Mongolia and Kashgar through intermediary private companies.[62] However, Ukhtomskii decided that it was not worth while to negotiate with Li Tsin-fan, whose authority could be questioned, and continued to Peking,[63] from which city, on November 5, he telegraphed Witte one of his brilliant but, as usual, impracticable projects. It was to give asylum to the Chinese Imperial Court at Mukden.[64] This project was acceptable to Witte[65] but was categorically refused by Li Hung-chang on November 19.[66] Li once again attempted to divert Russian ambitions, real or imaginary, to the outlying provinces of Mongolia and Kashgar.[67]

Ukhtomskii's negotiations were brought to a close on November 23 when Witte telegraphed him a directive, ending with the comment that "we cannot conclude a separate agreement [with China] not knowing what the other powers will do, otherwise we will tie our own hands."[68]

Another move toward a separate agreement originated with Kuropatkin,[69] who on October 6, on his own initiative, sent a telegram to Pokotilov, Witte's financial agent at Peking, setting forth the advantages of such a step.

The policy for a separate agreement had to be abandoned for a time because of the considerations expressed by Witte in his telegram of November 23. The originators of the policy bided their time. Meanwhile, it became apparent that the pacification of Manchuria was not progressing very satisfactorily, and that it was imperative to conclude some sort of *modus vivendi* with the local authorities concerning that province, for the Russians found the task of chasing elusive bandits into the interior an arduous and a thankless one, which made them increasingly unpopular with the populace. The lack of trained personnel with knowledge of the local languages made Russian operations dependent on close contact with local Chinese officials.[70] Consequently, on October 18, 1900, General Grodekov and Alexeev received orders to hand over the administration of the occupied provinces to Chinese authorities as soon as possible.[71] Encouraging this step was the Russian opinion that the governors general of Manchuria had been authorized by the Chinese government to deal with the Russian generals on matters of local administration.[72]

The temporary local character of the negotiations for the *modus vivendi* agreement was apparent throughout their various stages. It was Li Hung-chang who suggested that Alexeev, not Giers, be empowered to negotiate for the Russians.[73] This met with general approval in St. Petersburg because in the uncertain stage of the diplomatic negotiations being conducted by Lamsdorf with Peking, and by Witte with Li Hung-chang, the Ministry of Foreign Affairs seemed reluctant to take the responsibility for an agreement.[74] It was therefore the Ministry of War which launched the negotiations as a measure in the general program of pacification of Manchuria. The lack of a political program of the Ministry of War is evident from the fact that Kuropatkin telegraphed Alexeev on October 8 for his views on the most elementary and essential questions, such as whether the governors general of Manchuria had the right to maintain horse and foot police though they had not the right to maintain regular troops, and whether the governors general should be retained, and if so, whether Russian commissars should be appointed to supervise their administration. In fact, Kuropatkin had not even decided whether or not the negotiations should be conducted independently of those in Peking.[75]

Alexeev replied to this query on October 11 with suggestions which although vague on some points, clearly indicate that he felt that Russian control over the administration of Manchuria should be limited in its scope. He argued for the retention of the Chinese administrative structure, keeping the same governors general, with a limited police force. On the key question of supervision, he answered vaguely:

"To establish our control and to guide him [the Governor General], there should be on his staff a representative from the War Department and one from the Ministry of Foreign Affairs. The activities of these persons could be similar to that of the British advisers to the native rulers in India."[76]

Alexeev was given plenipotentiary powers for this program and appointed I. Ia. Korostovets, who represented the Ministry of Foreign Affairs and who was then attached to Alexeev's staff, and P. G. Tideman, representing the Chinese Eastern Railway Company and the Ministry of Finance. They conducted the negotiations.[77] The Governor General of Mukden, Tseng Chitchze, then virtually a prisoner of the Russians in Hsinmintun, appointed three members of his staff.[78]

The negotiations, which opened on November 4, 1900, at Port Arthur, were conducted with extreme haste and were further hurried by Alexeev. When a Russian draft was prepared, Korostovets advised Alexeev to get in touch with St. Petersburg or Peking in view of the political nature of the agreement. However, Alexeev refused to do so and argued that "we must strike while the iron is hot," that he was empowered to act "according to his own discretion," and that "the projected agreement will be temporary."[79] The Chinese envoys protested the terms and stated that some of the articles violated Chinese sovereignty. They feared that they would be tried for treason and executed if they signed the agreement, and asked to communicate with Li Hung-chang or the Governor General of Mukden. They even claimed that the Governor General had no authority to sign such an agreement. But Alexeev was adamant and insisted that they sign the Russian draft without further consultation, and even threatened to send the Chinese plenipotentiaries back to Hsinmintun under escort and to place the Governor General under arrest. At the same time, he would not permit Korostovets to telegraph the terms of the treaty to Giers for fear that last-minute intervention by the Russian Minister to China would force some changes.[80] Under such pressure, on November 9, the agreement was signed by Korostovets and a Chinese official acting for Tseng Chitchze, the Governor General of Mukden.[81]

The agreement encountered further difficulties. The treaty was sent to Hsinmintun for ratification by Tseng Chitchze, who deliberated over the matter for almost a month. He, too, feared for his life if he signed the agreement,[82] and he wanted to discuss with Alexeev some of the points of the agreement, such as the disarmament of Chinese regular troops in Manchuria. Alexeev let him know that he would not be permitted to return to Mukden unless he signed the ratification.[83] On November 26 Tseng Chitchze signed, submissively.[84]

The terms of the Alexeev–Tseng Chitchze agreement were not revealed at the time. Perhaps the reason was that this semimilitary, roughhewn agreement contained terms which were so explicit that it would be unwise to publish them, for the use of such ironclad clauses in a mere *modus vivendi* agreement was bound to draw unfavorable publicity and criticism. Perhaps the Russians did not give it so much importance because it was for them merely a temporary agreement and certainly a minor one. In December they took serious steps to formulate a separate agreement with China. At all events, the secrecy resulted in a great deal of adverse publicity and comment when Dr. Morrison, a correspondent of the London *Times*, revealed on January 3, 1901, the existence of the agreement by publishing a somewhat garbled version of its terms in the *Times*.[85] Because of this, the Russian government finally announced the gist of the agreement, stressing its temporary nature and the necessity for an agreement, in the *Pravitel'stvennyi Vestnik* of April 5, 1901.[86] Nevertheless, throughout 1901 and 1902 adverse comment on supposed Russian intrigues in the Far East was prevalent in the Far Eastern press. Between July, 1901, and April, 1902, seventeen different versions of alleged Russo-Chinese secret agreements were reported in many journals. All these versions were examined by the Vladivostok Oriental Institute and summarized in the Chronicle of the Institute's journal (*Izvestiia Vostochnago Instituta*).[87]

Perhaps the Russians felt it unnecessary to publish the Alexeev–Tseng Chitchzi agreement because Dr. Morrison's version was comparatively accurate, although its form of expression was "fantastic," as B. A. Romanov has termed it.[88] Both versions set forth the conditions required for the Russian evacuation of Manchuria in the manner in which the collective note of December 22 to China had listed the major points of the larger and more explicit Protocol of September 7, 1901, for the powers in northern China. Dr. Morrison's version omitted the essential "temporary" terms and clauses of the text and also the preamble respecting the sovereignty of China, and it made the agreement appear to be an actual seizure of Manchuria as a protectorate of Russia.

The terms of the agreement contained very little of an alarming nature when one considers the special conditions of the Boxer movement in Manchuria, and when one compares them with the terms of the Collective Note, or the Boxer Protocol. The disarmament and demobilization of Chinese troops in Manchuria (Art. III) was a natural *sine qua non,* considering that the Boxer movement in Manchuria had caused the greatest damage to Russian interests mainly through their alliance with regular Chinese forces. The provisions for temporary occupation (Art. II) and the destruction of fortifications where no Russian troops were to be stationed (Art. IV) found counterparts in the Boxer Protocol. Perhaps the only alarming features were the vague statements about the Russian occupation "depending on the actual pacification of the country" (Art. V) and the establishment of political "commissars" at the court of the Governor General for liaison with the Russian commander of the Kwantung territory (Art. VII). Again, the inherent danger lay in the indefinite nature of the commissar's powers. These points could easily have been defined and modified to the satisfaction of both China and Russia without changing the purport of the agreement. China could have effected an evacuation agreement with Russia soon after December 31, 1900, when Russian diplomacy was once again freed by the acceptance of the Collective Note by China. But the Alexeev–Tseng Chitchze agreement was not ratified by the Chinese government,[89] nor did the Russian government press China for its acceptance, because the originators of the idea of a separate agreement with China were then out for bigger stakes.

On December 11 Giers telegraphed Lamsdorf stating that an agreement could then be reached between the Russian legation and the Chinese ministers for the exclusive right of railroad and mineral exploitation in Manchuria, as well as "perhaps in all our sphere of influence," and that "we should stipulate now the rights we want to secure in Manchuria, for it would be difficult to secure them later."[90] Lamsdorf then asked Witte and Kuropatkin for their views on the rights to be secured from China. The three ministers, in November and early December, had discussed the desirable concessions to be extracted from China and had put their views together in a rather loose form in a memorandum elucidating points to be made concerning the temporary occupation of Manchuria. This memorandum, entitled "The Establishment of Russian Supervision in Manchuria," received the approval of the Tsar on December 17.[91] However, it fell short of outlining a broad policy in regard to Manchuria and other territories of China adjoining Russia where Russia had been invited to stake concessionary claims.

Some of the fundamental views expressed in the replies to Lamsdorf were to be held by the ministers throughout their tenure of office. Kuropatkin, in a letter to Lamsdorf on December 16,[92] stated that he shared the view held by his colleagues that Russia should evacuate Manchuria; but as Minister of War, charged with the defense of Russian interests in Manchuria, he felt that he could not guarantee the safety of these interests if Russian troops should be withdrawn completely, and he urged that Russia retain the right to hold at least eight battalions of infantry in northern Manchuria and four battalions in southern Manchuria even after the completion of the railroad. He therefore urged the return of Manchuria to China with a reservation for a right of military occupation. This was a truly equivocal stand.

Witte's terms in his reply of December 18 aimed at strengthening the monopolistic position of the C.E.R. in Manchuria. In addition to some minor financial and administrative points, Witte suggested transferring the Chinese customs administration at the points where the C.E.R. crossed the border, to the C.E.R. Company and the complete transfer of the section of the Imperial Northern Railway north of the Great Wall to the C.E.R. Company in return for a payment to the Hong Kong–Shanghai Bank of a suitable sum covering the obligation of China "not to construct by her own means any railroad lines without our consent and not to give either railroad or any other kind of concession to foreigners in any part of our sphere of influence," that is, "in Manchuria, all parts of China north of the Great Wall, Mongolia, the Ili region, and Kashgaria."[93] Witte considered it unnecessary to demand any other special concessions, since the exclusion of foreign concessions would guarantee the existing Russian interests. In regard to the rights of exploitation of mineral resources in Mongolia and Sinkiang (Kashgaria), so generously offered to Russia by Li Hung-chang,[94] Witte realistically wrote that "it can have practical importance to us only in the distant future, as at the present time Russia is experiencing a lack of capital for the exploitation of even her own natural resources, and consequently it is hardly possible that we can find the means for the exploitation of mineral deposits in China."[95]

Even with Lamsdorf's proposal that China should not engage foreign instructors for her troops and her navy in northern China,[96] these views still did not form a concrete policy for Manchuria. Additional views were exchanged, Kuropatkin amplifying his ideas in a letter of January 15, 1901.[97] He advocated that even after the restoration of Manchuria, China should not have the right to station troops or establish arsenals in Manchuria, that the number of the Chinese police forces in Manchuria be determined by an agreement, and that all railroads in Manchuria be operated by Russia. These views, in a milder form, were accepted by the other ministers.

On January 22, 1901, Yang Yu, the Chinese Minister to Russia, notified Lamsdorf that he had orders to begin discussions concerning a separate agreement on the basis of additional concessions to Russia. Lamsdorf was caught unprepared and could not submit a concrete proposal; but on the same day, and again two days later, Witte gave Lamsdorf two fully prepared drafts—one of a general Russo-Chinese agreement, the other of an agreement between the C.E.R. and China.[98] From these draft proposals, the three ministers drew up their first formal proposal to China after a series of conferences on January 29, and February 4, 7, and 8, 1901, during which the C.E.R. draft proposals were relegated to a later period.[99]

The proposals of February 8[100] must be regarded as the optimum, not basic, Russian demands. They were the starting points of the negotiations and consequently included items which might have been inserted as bargaining points to be yielded during the course of the negotiations. They contained most of the demands projected by Witte, Lamsdorf, and Kuropatkin in their correspondence since December 11, 1900, now modified and couched in diplomatic terms. They added and moderated considerably some of the terms proposed in Witte's general agreement draft of January 22.[101]

The terms are important chiefly as a summary of previously expressed views. In the course of negotiations with China these terms shrank and then, under mounting pressure, were completely abandoned in favor of an entirely different evacuation agreement. They provided for recognition of Chinese sovereignty in Manchuria (Art. I), temporary military occupation (Art. II), the demilitarization of Manchuria until a later agreement (Art. IV), and the establishment of a numerically limited native police force (Art. V), and required a promise from China not to engage foreign instructors for the army or the fleet of northern China (Art. VI). Six articles dealt with compensations for losses suffered by the C.E.R., the Russo-Chinese Bank, and private Russian subjects as a result of the Boxer rebellion (Art. IX, XI, XIII, XIV), and one (Art. VII) with an administrative-territorial adjustment of the Kwangtung territory.

The interesting articles were the eighth and ninth. Article IX gave the C.E.R. as compensation an additional railroad from its southern branch to the Great Wall on the same condition as the C.E.R. contracts. Article VIII established a large and effective sphere of influence in China:

> The Chinese Government will not grant in all the area of the provinces adjacent to Russia, namely Manchuria and Mongolia, as well as in the area of the districts of Tarbagatai, Kuldja [Ili], Kashgar, Yarkend, Khotan, and Keri, in the provinces of Kansu and Sinkiang adjacent to Russia, any concessions for the construction of railroads, exploitation of mineral deposits, or any industrial enterprises whatsoever, to foreign powers and their subjects without the consent of the Russian Government. In all the territory of the above mentioned provinces the Chinese Government will not build railroads by its own means, and will not grant parcels of land for the use of foreigners without the consent of the Russian Government, except in the open port of Newchwang.[102]

In the presentation of these maximum demands on February 8, Russian diplomacy made one serious miscalculation. It had played a double game in acting as a "friend of China" in the Peking negotiations while at the same time it was attempting to exact Chinese acceptance of its maximum terms. But in February, 1901, the situation was different. For China, after the presentation of the Collective Note of December 22, 1900, the worst was over. Thereafter it was Li Hung-chang who could play a double game, relying on Russian support to modify the extreme demands of the other powers, and at the same time mitigating Russian pressure by promoting the opposition of the powers to alleged Russian demands. This he could do by merely hinting at the actual Russian demands, as he apparently had done with respect to the terms of the Alexeev–Tseng Chitchze agreement. In this, he was inadvertently aided by Witte, who for some reason of his own—possibly in order to launch a "trial balloon"—mentioned some of the debated and rejected terms of his projects to the Japanese minister to St. Petersburg even before the presentation of the Russian terms to the Chinese minister.[103] At any rate, the negotiations were a badly kept secret. The British Foreign Office had a reasonably correct version of the Russian demands within a month of their presentation, from the telegraphic dispatches of their minister to China.[104] Apparently similar, if not exact, copies of the projected agreement were dispatched to other capitals.[105]

In January and February, 1901, the powers were not unified in their reaction to the Russian plans for a separate agreement with China, even after the adverse publicity received through the publication of Dr. Morrison's alarming version of the Alexeev–Tseng Chitchze agreement. Perhaps that was due to the instructions sent to the Russian representatives abroad ordering them to inform the governments to which they were accredited of the true nature of the agreement.[106] At any event, the long-established Franco-Russian and Russo-German friendships in the Far East once again stood the test. In the last days of January, the Duc de Montebello, the French Minister to St. Petersburg, and Lamsdorf came to a verbal understanding according to which the French would regard with equanimity Russian activities in Manchuria, and Russia would take a similar attitude toward the French efforts to promote their interests in the Yünnan railroad and the French solution of the missionary problem.[107]

For a short period it might have appeared that Russo-German friendship in the Far East had been shaken by the signing by Great Britain and Germany of the agreement of October 16, 1900, which confirmed their support of the open-door policy in China.[108] Later discussions and comments made it doubtful whether the agreement extended to Manchuria,[109] and on January 21, 1901, the Kaiser stated that he "quite understood that Russia had interests in Manchuria which might make it necessary for her to conclude separate arrangements with the Chinese. He had no desire to interfere with such arrangements."[110] Finally, on March 15, 1901, the German Chancellor, Bernhard von Bülow, made the point clear by stating in the Reichstag that the Anglo-German agreement definitely did not extend to Manchuria.[111]

In opposition to the Russian-French-German view, the British attempted to unite the other powers in a joint declaration by suggesting that "the powers should arrive at a general agreement neither to recognize the pending agreements among themselves nor the validity of any concessions of settlements obtained since the outbreak of the Boxer disturbances and the siege of legations."[112] The Japanese were worried over Manchuria and expressed a general approval of this principle in a note of January 29 from their minister in London to the Marquess of Lansdowne, the British Minister of Foreign Affairs.[113] The position of the United States was not clearly stated until February, 1902, when John Hay finally expressed disapproval of the Russian policy in a note to the Russian Ministry of Foreign Affairs in which the policy of the open door was again restated.[114]

Thus, in January and February, 1901, two conflicting views were expressed respecting the separate Russo-Chinese negotiations. This was enough to cause Li Hung-chang and his colleagues to take heart and assume a firmer stand. The negotiations, which opened on February 22, encountered opposition from the start. To promote Chinese acceptance of the Russian demands Witte telegraphed Pokotilov on February 23, instructing him to promise Li Hung-chang 500,000 rubles from the unexpended fund created for the bribery of Chinese officials in 1898. Witte telegraphed:

> I give you the authority to inform Li Hung-chang that immediately upon the conclusion of our agreement, you will give him or any person designated by him, a sum of 500,000 rubles as a sign of our gratitude. Besides, tell him that with the permission of His Imperial Majesty, I will be in Port Arthur and possibly in Peking in December, and if our affairs are doing well, I will again give him or to anyone he designates, a fitting sum.[115]

This time Li Hung-chang could not be bribed. The Chinese did not make a counterproposal to the Russian terms but merely rejected most of them. The second Russian project, launched on February 28, left out the rejected points, making a considerable concession to the Chinese stand.[116] Nevertheless, this project was also rejected, and Yang Yu was ordered to drop the negotiations.[117] So ended the first Russian attempt to take advantage of the Boxer rebellion by making a separate agreement with China. But the storm aroused by the reports of these negotiations persisted. On April 5, 1901, the Russian government issued in the *Pravitel'stvennyi Vestnik* a long explanatory and rather apologetic statement entitled "The Survey of Russian Policy in the Boxer Uprising,"[118] which attributed the failure of the Russo-Chinese negotiations to "obstacles" put in their way. The statement ended with this resolution: "Maintaining the temporary military occupation of Manchuria in order to preserve order in the vicinity of the extensive frontiers of Russia, and remaining at the same time true to the clearly expressed political program, the Imperial Government will calmly await the further course of events."[119] But prospects for this "wait and see" policy remained dim in the course of diplomatic events.

FAILURE OF THE PLAN FOR A SEPARATE AGREEMENT WITH CHINA— CONCLUSION OF THE EVACUATION AGREEMENT OF APRIL 8, 1902

The launching and subsequent failure of the first project for a separate agreement with China coincided with three other diplomatic events which, if accepted at their face value, would indicate a general Russian diplomatic offensive in all of Asia bordering the Russian Empire. Russian influence in Persia had been on the increase during the last years of the nineteenth century, and when, in June, 1900, Russia gave Persia a loan of some 5,000,000 rubles for the conversion of previous loans, British anxieties were at once aroused.[120] The so-called Persian State Bank (neither Persian nor State) had the same relation to the Russian Ministry of Finance as the Russo-Chinese Bank. It was to all purposes Witte's agency for the promotion of Russian interests in Persia, a fact readily recognized by one English contemporary observer, who remarked that the bank's manager "plays in Persia a part similar to that filled by Mr. Pokotilov, the manager of the Russo-Chinese Bank in China. Indeed, since he is a protégé of Mr. Witte, it is not certain that he does not indirectly wield a greater power than the present occupant of the Russian legation."[121]

Russian trade had natural advantages in northern Persia, where at this time Persia's wealth and population were concentrated. The proximity to the Russian manufacturing centers and the availability of the inexpensive Volga-Caspian trade route naturally tended to cause Persian trade to gravitate into Russian channels. Also, Russian export trade to Persia compared favorably with that to China and Mongolia, being almost equal to it in value.[122] Hence there was nothing aggressive or spectacular in the ordinary promotion of that trade by the Russian government, which from March to November, 1901, negotiated a more favorable tariff agreement with Persia and thus further strengthened Russia's commercial position there. By 1903, Russia's exports to Persia amounted to 56 per cent of the total Persian imports.[123] Nevertheless, perhaps from sheer envy, the British viewed this development with alarm.[124]

A rather eccentric diplomatic development arose in 1900–1901 from the mission to Russia of a Tibetan high official, possibly of Russian-Buriat origin, Aharamba Agvan Dorzheev (spelled also Dorjief, Dorojiev, and Doroshiyeff).[125] This mission of seven Tibetan officials arrived in Odessa from India on a steamer belonging to the Russian Volunteer Fleet in July, 1900, and was received by the Tsar in his palace at Livadia in the Crimea in October. On July 1, 1901, the mission arrived in St. Petersburg, where it visited the Ministry of Foreign Affairs and the Ministry of Finance.[126] This mission from the "Forbidden Kingdom" created a stir in Russian society and the press, but its purpose and achievements remained uncertain. From later developments it appears to have been an attempt by Tibet to assure itself of some sort of vague international recognition, to bolster its position of independence against the Chinese claims of suzerainty, and to counter the current (later more pressing) demands by the government of India with respect to the Chumbi Valley, which in 1904 led to the British military expedition to Lhasa.[127]

Whatever the true nature of the mission, its diplomatic repercussions were the result of further suspicions of Russian activities in Asia. Lamsdorf, in answer to a British document of the "Dorjief mission" by an official of the Russian Ministry of Foreign Affairs,[128] strongly confirms the assurance given to Lansdowne in August, 1901, and even ridicules British fears.[129] However, more striking evidence of the lack of Russian official interest in the Tibetan question is found elsewhere.

Of course, Russian geographers were interested in the little-known country no less than other geographers. Its relative proximity to the Russian border had prompted several expeditions of the Russian Imperial Geographical Society of St. Petersburg toward the exploration of the northern borderlands of Tibet, the last expedition of M. N. Prjevalskii almost reaching Lhasa in 1879.[130] In 1900–1901 another Geographical Society expedition, headed by P. K. Kozlov, was on the border region of Sinkiang and Tibet, unable to penetrate into Tibet because of the hostility of a local Tibetan tribe; this was a curious manifestation of the reputed Tibetan friendship for Russia. At that time there were some contacts between Russia and Tibet through the pilgrimages of the Russian Buriat Mongols of the Buddhist Lamaist faith to Lhasa and other holy places of their faith.[131] Also, from 1899 to 1901, a Russian Buriat, Gonbo-Ghzab Tsybikov, educated in the Department of Oriental Languages at the St. Petersburg University, with some financial aid from the Imperial Geographical Society lived and studied Tibetan in Tibet, living for eighteen months in Lhasa. He regularly corresponded with the Oriental Institute at Vladivostok.[132]

During Dorzheev's stay in St. Petersburg, it was found, to the dismay of the Russian Ministry of Foreign Affairs, that there was no one in St. Petersburg who knew Tibetan well enough to translate the letters of the Dalai Lama of Tibet to the Emperor. Fortunately, Professor A. M. Pozdneev, Director of the Oriental Institute of Vladivostok, was at that time in the capital on a vacation, and his services were enlisted to translate the letters and also draft a reply in Tibetan to Dorzheev, who apparently did not know the Russian language, although Pozdneev's Tibetan was, in his own words, "practically self-taught and even then only theoretical."[133] Apparently, even the previously mentioned "Tibetan doctor," Badmaev, who was then in St. Petersburg and who ventured to give his "learned" opinions on the mission to the newspapers, could not read or write the Tibetan language.[134]

There is further evidence of a lack of Russian official interest. Pozdneev, realizing that "after the death of Professor Vasiliev, Russia hasn't a single person who knows Tibetan," sought to establish Tsybikov, then in need of a job, as a professor of Tibetan in his Institute. This required an authorization from the Ministry of Education[135] for the expenditure of 4,000 rubles annually for the salary of Tsybikov and 1,500 rubles for his assistant and books. A request for these amounts was submitted to the Minister of Education; it was rejected in October, 1900. Accompanying the refusal was a letter from Witte, an official message between the two ministries, which refused the sum requested and added:

> The study of Tibetan appears to be largely of academic interest, and can hardly be considered of sufficient practical value to warrant the establishment of a special chair at the Oriental Institute ... Concerning its [the chair's] value for the opening of Tibet to the world ... it must be noted that, aside from the fact that this would hardly be in our interest, at present, due to many circumstances we have no indication that we can count on the possibilitiy of realizing such assumptions in the near future.[136]

At the time, Russian interests in Tibet did not seem to warrant the investment of 5,500 rubles per year.

A far more important diplomatic development arose between Russia and Japan concerning Korea. Japan would be in a disadvantageous position in 1901 if China should be partitioned. If Russia succeeded in establishing her political hegemony in Manchuria by a separate agreement with China, Germany and England might take similar actions in their vaguely designated spheres of influence, a course implied in Article III of the Anglo-German Agreement of October, 1900.[137] With Chihli under what was tantamount to international control, the Japanese would find themselves left out in the partition. There was, of course, Korea, where merely in the course of natural developments Japanese economic interests had been expanding rapidly since the signing of the Nishi-Rosen Convention of April, 1898. In fact, the concessionary rights and privileges obtained by Japan in Korea were far in advance of her ability to take full advantage of them. For example, though the concession for the Seoul-Fusan railroad, the largest single foreign enterprise in Korea and the most promising means of Japanese influence in southern Korea, was obtained in 1898, the railroad did not pass the surveying stage until the approach of the termination date of the contract, September, 1901, forced the opening of construction work in Seoul and Fusan. This was begun in August and September, 1901, with rather elaborate ceremony.[138]

Japanese influence on the Chinese Court was of little importance, although Japan had attempted to represent herself as a "friend of China" in advising China against making a separate agreement with

Russia.[139] Since as a *coup de main* in Korea like the ill-fated attempt of 1896 was out of the question in 1900, Japan had two courses open to her. She could join the Anglo-German agreement and thus be party to the possible partition of China with the support of those signatories. Or she could make an arrangement with Russia, to the effect that if Russia should establish herself in Manchuria, Japan would be given corresponding advantages in Korea.

Within Japanese diplomatic circles there was a marked cleavage of opinion. Premier Ito and Count Inouye, a member of the Genro (Council of Elder Statesmen), as well as Kurino, the Minister to Russia, favored a Russo-Japanese agreement. On the other hand, Kato, the Minister of Foreign Affairs, led a group favoring an Anglo-Japanese agreement.[140] Only on one point was there a complete accord: there should be an end to Japanese isolation.[141]

It is not clear, from the available sources, who started the conversations on the subject of a Russo-Japanese agreement concerning Manchuria and Korea. R. H. Akagi states that V. N. Lamsdorf and A. P. Izvolskii initiated them; A. Galperin ascribes the initiative to Korea.[142] Neither writer gives the dates or the sources of his statement. The idea might have originated with Witte, who on or about October 1, 1900, wrote to his friend D. S. Sipiagin:

"I do not expect any complications with Europe [over the expected Russian occupation of Mukden] . . . Japan—I am afraid she will get into Korea—and though the Emperor said that even then he will not start anything, nevertheless it will be very unpleasant . . . it may arouse us. I advise making a proposal of neutralization of Korea."[143]

It is evident that at the time this letter was written Japan had not yet approached anyone on the subject. It is also evident that Witte, who after all had the greatest influence on Russian affairs in the Far East, was willing to further compromise Russia's freedom of action in regard to Korea, where Japanese economic interests had already been recognized as predominant. However, it is difficult to understand why Russia would take the initiative in the *pourparler* on the Korean question when she was quite satisfied with the status quo.

It is most likely that the Japanese brought up the matter, hoping to restrict Russia's action in Manchuria. They could not question the actions of Russia in Manchuria merely on the evidence of Dr. Morrison's revelation of the Alexeev–Tseng Chitchze agreement; but by tying in the Manchurian question with Korea they could hope to ascertain Russia's intentions.[144] Probably a few days before January 17, 1901, Ito therefore informed Izvolskii confidentially that Japan was ready to enter into negotiations with Russia for a "neutralization of Korea." But the discussions ended almost as soon as they had begun, because on that date Kato told Izvolskii that Japan could not make an agreement concerning Korea until the fate of Manchuria was definitely settled.[145]

The main concern of the Japanese was over the future status of Manchuria, and this became apparent when, on January 22, the Japanese Minister to St. Petersburg presented to the Russian Ministry of Foreign Affairs a mild note expounding the Japanese view that in order to avoid misunderstandings of Russian intentions in the reported Russo-Chinese separate negotiations, Russia should postpone such negotiations until the restoration of the *status quo ante* in Manchuria.[146] Lamsdorf's answer to the note completely ignored the Manchurian issue and merely stated that Russia was quite satisfied with the conditions of the Nishi-Rosen Convention on Korea and apparently with Kato's decision to postpone any further discussion about the neutralization of Korea raised by the government of Japan.[147] This created an awkward impasse, since the Japanese meant the *status quo ante* in regard to Manchuria and Lamsdorf referred to Korea. Additional assurances of the temporary nature of the terms under consideration in the Russo-Chinese negotiations did not allay the Japanese concern.[148]

On March 25 Kurino presented to Lamsdorf a much stronger note in which it was mentioned that Japan felt that some of the terms of the proposed Russo-Chinese agreement "violated the sovereign rights and territorial integrity of China as well as some treaty rights of other powers."[149]

Thereupon a "diplomatic incident occurred." Lamsdorf officially refused to accept the note or to discuss the matter, stating that as a minister he "could not recognize the right of a third power to interpolate and interfere in a matter which is being conducted by two independent countries."[150] However, he added privately that the negotiations were held merely to establish a *modus vivendi* and Japan could rest assured that Russia would respect the territorial integrity of China.[151]

Seeing through the diplomatic euphemisms, Japan realized that she had been told "to mind her own business." A furor of anti-Russianism appeared in the Japanese press,[152] and the notoriously chauvinistic anti-Russian "Black Dragon Society" published a forecast of a Russo-Japanese war in which a Japanese victory was predicted.[153] In the Japanese Parliament inflammatory speeches were frequently directed against Russia.[154] An atmosphere of war crisis was apparent in diplomatic circles and in diplomatic correspondence. In all probability Japan had no real intention to avenge the diplomatic "insult" and settle the problems of Manchuria and Korea by war. Marquis Ito realistically counseled moderation. Japan was not prepared to challenge Russia singlehanded. Her financial, military, and naval unpreparedness were manifest, and Russian military and naval agents in Japan could see no signs of any special preparations by the armed forces.[155]

The actual military situation must have given weight to the arguments for peace. Russian troops in the Far East, mobilized to a strength of 3,900 officers and 173,000 men by mid-October, 1900, were just beginning their demobilization.[156] The troops were in peak condition and their morale was probably high after their victorious and swift campaign in northern China and Manchuria—a campaign which brought them relatively light losses and much experience.[157] The performance of these troops in the field had been closely followed by foreign observers, who were much impressed by the military prowess displayed.[158] Furthermore, these troops were in an advanced stage of deployment throughout the potential theater of operations, with ready or available transport and organized supply and forage—all factors which could prove of great advantage to the Russians.

On the naval side, the situation was equally favorable to the Russians. The Russian "Pacific squadron" consisted of five battleships and six first-class cruisers, all of recent construction, as opposed to the Japanese naval force of five battleships and four armored cruisers. These were the essential factors for naval strategists to consider. The Japanese superiority of ten light cruisers to two Russian, and a far greater superiority in light craft of all sorts, were not to be taken into consideration.[159] Of course it could have been argued—and it probably was—that the Japanese vessels, ship for ship, were superior to those of Russia. They had all been built recently in England and were considered the best in naval construction. Russian ships were of Russian origin and presumably were of inferior quality, but this did not become apparent nor prove important until their test in the Russo-Japanese War.[160] In April, 1901, the Japanese navy was expecting a planned reinforcement of two battleships ordered from England. One had already been launched and another was still on the ways. Russia, on her part, had six more battleships and two first-class cruisers in European waters, most of which could be sent to the Far East as reinforcements.[161] At that time, neither the strength of the Japanese naval force nor the prospect of reinforcements could give the Japanese naval command hope for an easy victory.

Ito's influential position as prime minister and a member of the Genro probably was the decisive factor in the matter of peace or war. Hotheaded and probably piqued, Kato wanted to send to St. Petersburg an even stronger note than the rejected one of March 25; but after several days he calmed down considerably. The Supreme War Council of Japan, consisting of Marshal Yamagata (the President of the Council), Prince Komatsu, and Admirals Saigo and Ito, called Kato before it and apparently ordered moderation.[162] In the cabinet, Kato was curbed also, so that instead of sending his original strong protest, Japan was content to issue an innocuous statement on April 6: "The Imperial (Japanese) Government is unable to accept the answer of Count Lamsdorf of March 25, and reserves its opinion under the present circumstances."[163] With that the "crisis" subsided.

The "war crisis" of March–April, 1901, had a number of consequences. It tended to unite the undecided Japanese statesmen with the proponents of the Anglo-Japanese alliance. It helped to overthrow Ito's government and brought in the government of Viscount Katsura on May 10, with Komura, a former minister to China, as Minister of Foreign Affairs. It brought about almost immediately a diplomatic move by Japan, first to ascertain England's position in regard to an Anglo-Japanese alliance and then to propose such an alliance.[164] In Russia it led to a reëxamination of the problem of the evacuation of Manchuria and the guarantees and privileges demanded from China, now with a view to the immediate and final hostility of Japan.

Lamsdorf clearly envisaged this hostility and on June 5 sent a circular to the Ministers of War and Finance and the Director of the Department of Navy, aimed at eliciting their views on whether Russia was prepared for a war with Japan. He indicated that the Japanese official circles had been showing evidence of hostility to Russia since the beginning of 1901, and that "if in March [April 6, N.S.] there had not followed the circular of the Imperial [Russian] Government on its refusal to conclude a separate agreement with China, Japan would not have hesitated then to open hostilities against Russia."[165] He felt that a clash with Japan could result from any insignificant incident, and that negotiations with Japan could not be relied on to avert complications, "as in the eyes of the Japanese Government a break with Russia is not a means [to prompt Russia to withdraw from Manchuria] but more likely a direct goal."[166]

Witte's reply on June 6 and his supplementary letter of June 10 stated the only aim of Russia must be to avoid war with Japan, and that the best means of solving the Manchurian problem would be to renounce any political intentions in Manchuria and limit Russian interests there to the protection of the interests of the C.E.R. as a private company. In regard to Korea, he felt that if Japan demanded annexation of that country, the proper course would be to bring out the matter on an international level; but even if Japan seized Korea, Russia should not consider it a *casus belli*.[167]

There are no published records of other responses to the Lamsdorf interministerial circular of May 5, nor of the interchanges of opinion that must have taken place between the high officials concerned. At all events, Witte's comments were accepted as the basis of a plan for evacuation of Manchuria, which was worked out by Witte by June 24, discussed by other ministers without opposition at a special conference on July 11, and approved by the Tsar on July 18. This was but a minor plan, calling for an immediate return of the railroads occupied by the Russians in southern Manchuria and Chihli to their Chinese administrations, in return for compensations, guarantees, and the right to build a Russian railroad from the C.E.R. southern branch to the Great Wall.[168] On the over-all matter of Manchuria there was no decision.

However, the idea of evacuation of Manchuria was still paramount in the minds of the Russian statesmen. On August 1, Lamsdorf again wrote a circular to the ministers concerned calling for their views. He stated that the Tsar wanted to start the evacuation of Manchuria by independent action, and that it was impossible to drag out the matter of the evacuation indefinitely. Specifically, Lamsdorf wanted to know whether the ministers thought that Russia should continue the occupation of all Manchuria or of only one of its provinces.[169]

To this query Witte gave the categorical answer that the annexation of Manchuria would not be in the interest of Russia, either in a general or an economic sense, even if no other nations seriously opposed it. However, since Japan was seriously opposing the annexation, Russia should evacuate Manchuria. He considered that a complete administrative and military evacuation was essential and that the railroad guard was sufficient to guarantee the safety of the railroad.[170]

Kuropatkin's detailed exposition sent on August 12 is interesting because of the discussion of the value of Manchuria from a strategic standpoint.[171] It also expressed the ideas underlying the position Kuropatkin maintained throughout later conferences on the Manchurian question. For immediate action Kuropatkin counseled neither annexation nor complete withdrawal. Yet he felt that the occupation of even northern Manchuria was neither advantageous nor timely. The Amur River was a poor defensive barrier against China because the absence of roads along the Amur made defense difficult, and the occupation of northern Manchuria would improve the defensive position against China. By occupying all of Manchuria, Russia would have a complicated front against China and Korea (i.e., Japan). Kuropatkin proposed that "it would be advantageous for Russia to form out of northern Manchuria either an independent state or a province nominally dependent on China, governed by, and subject to the influence of Russia approximately on the same basis as the Khanate of Bukhara." To avoid international opposition to this step he counseled an immediate restoration of the Mukden region and the southern part of the province of Kirin, and continued temporary occupation of the north. Furthermore, he hoped that in future years Russia might have a better opportunity to lease northern Manchuria on a basis similar to the lease of the Kwantung territory.[172] This interesting program was supported neither by Witte nor by Lamsdorf, who had meanwhile evolved a new project for the evacuation of Manchuria.

This was occasioned by the renewal of direct negotiations with China by Li Hung-chang, who on August 2 notified A. M. Pozdneev, the representative of the Russo-Chinese Bank in Peking, that China was ready to come to terms with Russia on Manchuria and the sooner the better.[173] Perhaps Li Hung-chang's willingness was prompted by the fact that the Chinese Court was soon to return to Peking, and that some individuals of the Court would take over Li Hung-chang's unique position in negotiations with the foreign powers. Li therefore was in haste to earn the 500,000 rubles promised him in February, 1901.[174] He had hoped that the Russian proposals would be based on the terms of the March 12 proposals, which indeed they were for the most part, except that Russia did not appear anxious to evacuate Manchuria.

The March–April "crisis" and the period of strained relations between Japan and Russia were over, although the Japanese concern over the Manchurian situation continued. In a dispatch of August 7, 1901, Izvolskii warned that even though Japan was in financial difficulties and had an unprepared expeditionary force, she would go to war with Russia if Russia should annex Manchuria. However, at the same time, he suggested a measure somewhat similar to one of Kuropatkin's views of August 12.

If in Manchuria the Russian occupation should be extended in point of view of time without a proclamation of any official act, we can most likely expect that Japan will in time accustom herself to the established fact, although even in this case, we can expect periodic outbursts of warlike expression and attempts by the Tokyo cabinet to arouse an international protest against such an occupation.[175]

This was in line with Lamdorf's opinion, expressed earlier, that Russia should avoid agreement with Japan on the Manchurian matter lest the Russian evacuation of Manchuria appear to be a concession to an Oriental nation, which would be a bad precedent.[176]

Thus the idea of delay by adopting a periodic evacuation program gained greater authority. In the terms sent to Li Hung-chang on August 14, Article II projected an evacuation of Manchuria by Russian troops in three six-month periods. Other articles allowed for the immediate transfer of the administration into Chinese hands (Art. I); the reintroduction of Chinese troops into the provinces in limited, though unspecified, numbers (Art. III); the restoration of the Chinese Imperial Northern Railroad to its former administration (Art. IV). The text ended with the now-stereotyped reservation that Russia would carry out these measures "if no new complications should arise, and if the actions of other powers would not hinder their execution."[177]

These terms were in general quite suitable to the Chinese negotiators Li Hung-chang and Prince Ching, but there were still many debatable points in the specifications of the articles. But the most important cause of the delay in the negotiations was now Witte's attempt to promote a separate agreement between the Chinese government and the Russo-Chinese Bank, which would give the bank large-scale mining concessions in Manchuria.[178] The inability and unwillingness of the negotiators to express their desires in concrete terms, together with the unavoidable delays in coding, decoding, and transmitting telegrams between Peking and St. Petersburg, caused the negotiations to move with extreme slowness. Witte had even directed Pozdneev "not to let him [Li Hung-chang] get the notion that we are especially anxious for an agreement or that we are in a hurry to conclude it."[179] Then, too, international suspicions and pressures tended to delay the settlement of the remaining minor points. And on November 7, 1901, in the midst of these negotiations, Li Hung-chang died.[180] This unprepared for, although by no means unexpected, event caused the complete collapse of the negotiations which had been conducted on a person-to-person basis—Li Hung-chang to Witte through Pozdneev.

Meanwhile, the possibility of a Russo-Japanese agreement once more came to the fore, this time Russia clearly taking the initiative. Late in September, 1901, Marquis Ito left Japan for a trip to Europe to negotiate a much-needed loan with French or British banks.[181] It was suspected that the influential statesman had even more important plans.[182] In the beginning of October, 1901, Komura, who had been Minister to the Court of Peking for six months and, before that, Minister to St. Petersburg for three years, took office as Minister of Foreign Affairs, a position which had been vacant for five months, since the fall of Ito's cabinet.[183] Komura had been known as a protagonist of a Russo-Japanese alliance; soon after the first official reception Izvolskii had occasion to expound his views to Komura on this subject.

Izvolskii argued that Japan and Russia were not rivals in the Far East—that they had vital interests quite different from those of the other powers which looked on the Far East as a colonial market. As Far Eastern powers they were both, in fact, vitally interested in the preservation of peace in the Far East.[184] According to Izvolskii's account, Komura was in complete accord with the ideas expressed in these and similar arguments and stated that he would exert all his powers to promote firm friendship between Russia and Japan. However, Komura refused to be drawn out on the subject of an agreement on the matter of Korea, falling back on the previous argument used by Kato that Japan could not deal with that subject until Russia had evacuated Manchuria.[185]

There is no evidence connecting this *démarche* with Ito's subsequent actions in Europe, nor is there any evidence in published documents that Ito had any authority to discuss the Korean situation with Russia while he was in Europe. It is possible that, just as in the development of the Anglo-Japanese Alliance, Ito, like his compatriots, was officially instructed to open unofficial negotiations as a *ballon d'essai*. But again it seems that the initiative was not Japan's. While Ito was in Paris, Théophile Delcassé, the French Minister of Foreign Affairs, offered his services to Lamsdorf in feeling out Ito on the possibility of a Russo-Japanese understanding in regard to the problems of the Far East and asked Lamsdorf to send him a statement of Russian policies in the Far East for his orientation.[186] On October 30 Lamsdorf sent Delcassé an outline of Russian policy in the Far East, with a suggestion that Russia would be quite willing to enlarge on the previous treaties relative to Korea, and repeating the official diplomatic announcement concerning Russian intentions of evacuating Manchuria.[187] This apparently was enough to attract Ito to St. Petersburg.

Ito arrived in St. Petersburg on November 23 and remained in the Russian capital for eleven days, during which he was honored, feted, and well received by the Tsar and the Russian diplomatic corps.[188] On December 2, Ito and Lamsdorf held an informal conversation concerning a possible Russo-Japanese agreement. The record of this conversation can have only academic interest.[189] The two spoke through an interpreter and in languages foreign to them. Ito spoke in bad English with interjections in Japanese the result was translated into Russian by his interpreter, Suzuki. Lamsdorf replied in poor German, which the Japanese interpreter translated into Japanese. Between what was meant and what was said, how it was translated and how later remembered and recorded by Witte, there could have been considerable difference.[190] Fortunately, Lamsdorf asked Ito at this first meeting to draw up a project for a Russo-Japanese agreement. Ito presented such a project at their second meeting on December 3.

Ito's project, written in English,[191] contained little to satisfy Russia except a provision pledging both parties not to utilize the coast of Korea in any way that might threaten free passage of Korea Strait— this was a shallow concession to a basic Russian demand, since Japan could freely utilize her own shores for that purpose. Lamsdorf's comment to Ito on the project was quite valid: it was not a *quid pro quo* agreement but merely a statement of Japanese aspirations, concentrated in Article IV, which would give Japan political domination in Korea. Ito seemed surprised at this comment.[192]

Since Ito was scheduled to leave the next day and Lamsdorf was unable to confer with the Tsar or any of his colleagues in regard to these proposed terms, Lamsdorf promised to send the Russian counterproposals to Ito in Berlin.[193] Most of this counterproject was formulated by Witte with the assistance of Kuropatkin; using Ito's terms as a basis, it was sent to Ito through the Japanese Ambassador at Berlin on December 13.[194] Besides small changes in the wording of Ito's terms, it included major alterations of Article IV by limiting Japan's freedom of action to "industrial and commercial aspects." Japanese "exclusive" rights of friendly intervention were likewise changed to "preferential rights of Japan to come, in agreement with Russia, but alone, to Korea's assistance. . . ." But an entirely different aspect was given to the agreement by an article (VI) added by the Russians: "On her part, Japan recognizes Russia's preferential rights in the districts of the Chinese Empire adjacent to the Chinese border, and promises in no way to hinder Russia's liberty of action in these districts."

This changed the meaning of the project completely. Instead of giving the Japanese a free hand in Korea for a nominal concession, the Russians now demanded a free hand in Manchuria and other places as well, in return for a slight improvement of the Japanese position in Korea over the status quo. Of course neither project in its original form was acceptable to the other party; but it must be remembered that these were starting points and therefore included broad terms which in the process of negotiations would inevitably be reduced. There was still possibility for agreement. At least Ito believed so, and he telegraphed Komura in Japan words to that effect on December 13.[195] But by that time Japan had committed herself officially to the last stages of negotiations of the Anglo-Japanese Alliance.[196]

The history of the origin, negotiations, and significance of the Anglo-Japanese Alliance of January 30, 1902, are too well known to warrant any discussion here.[197] Suffice it to say that the community of Japanese and British interests had been frequently pointed out, especially since 1895; that suggestions for an Anglo-Japanese understanding in the Far East had been periodically expressed by statesmen of both nations and the press of both countries since 1898; and that England's signing of the alliance was a radical step from her policy of "splendid isolation"—which had not appeared so "splendid" during the complications of the Boer War (1899–1902) and during the abandonment of the idea of an Anglo-German *rapprochement* in the Moroccan crisis in 1901.[198] For Japan, however, it signaled the end of a period of what might be called "pathetic isolation"—an isolation which had been much in evidence in 1895 when the "Triplice" forced her to accept the humiliating changes in the Treaty of Shimonoseki.

By Article I of the Anglo-Japanese Alliance, Japan's special political as well as commercial interests in Korea were recognized; if these interests should be threatened and Japan should take measures to defend them by force of arms and thus be involved in a war, England would remain benevolently neutral. If, however, a third power should attack Japan, England would come to the aid of her ally (Art. III.). The same provisions of course applied to British interests in China.[199]

The announcement of the Anglo-Japanese Alliance on February 12, 1902, came as a complete surprise to Lamsdorf, Witte, and Izvolskii and produced much consternation in Russian diplomatic ranks.[200] What made it all the more galling was that it was officially announced to the Russian Ministry of Foreign Affairs by the presentation of a *note verbale* by the Japanese ambassador on the day of its publication in the press.[201] Furthermore, it came directly on top of two other diplomatic setbacks. On the eleventh Witte learned that the negotiations with China, which had been renewed by Prince Ching through Pozdneev on December 11, 1901, and had been slowly grinding through the details of a preliminary separate agreement between China and the Russo-Chinese Bank, had been broken off because of American and Japanese pressure.[202] Previously, Secretary of State Hay had sent a circular telegram addressed to the governments of China, Japan, Great Britain, Russia, and France, which embodied a strong objection to

the continuation of the Russian occupation of Manchuria and especially
to the reported Russian attempts to negotiate a secret agreement with
China which would establish a monopoly of the Russo-Chinese Bank
and the C.E.R. in Manchuria.[203] All these almost simultaneous developments created an impression of Anglo-Japanese-American solidarity
with respect to Manchuria.

In an attempt to counteract the influence of the Anglo-Japanese
Alliance, Lamsdorf, on February 18, instructed the Russian Ambassador in Paris, Count Urusov, to begin negotiations for a Franco-
Russian agreement which would extend the Franco-Russian Entente
to the Far East.[204] Lamsdorf also wanted to bring Germany into some
alignment with Russian interests, but Chancellor von Bülow declined
to take steps in that direction, although he instructed the German
Ambassador to Russia, Alvensleben, to take no measures which might
hinder the progress of the Franco-Russian negotiations.[205]

In the Franco-Russian negotiations, Lamsdorf wanted a counterpoise
to the Anglo-Japanese Alliance, but the result fell short of that mark.
The Franco-Russian declaration issued on March 16, 1902,[206] did not
extend the Franco-Russian Alliance to the Far East; but in the manner
of the Anglo-German Agreement of October 16, 1900, it asserted that
the two powers reserved for themselves the right to come to a preliminary understanding should a third power, by its actions, threaten to
disturb the status quo of the Far East. Such a statement in negotiations between two friendly powers was hardly necessary and therefore
was practically meaningless.

Under pressure of the diplomatic developments of February, Russia
turned in haste to conclude an agreement with China on terms which
left not a shadow of the aggressive tendencies of the first program of
January, 1900. The last remaining obstacle and one which led to the
collapse of the negotiations in the beginning of February, 1902, was
one clause in the proposed secret agreement between the Russo-Chinese
Bank and the Chinese government. This clause stated that commercial
and industrial enterprises in Manchuria could be undertaken by the
Chinese government or by Chinese companies or individuals without
the participation of foreigners or foreign capital, but that the financial
affairs of these enterprises must be in the hands of the Russo-Chinese
Bank. Furthermore, all concessions must be offered first to the bank,
and only if the bank refused to undertake the enterprises could they
be offered to others, and then only on the same terms as those offered
the bank.[207] This monopolistic clause was discarded; negotiations were
resumed on February 25 and continued uninterrupted to the signing

of the Russo-Chinese Convention on the evacuation of Manchuria on April 8, 1902, in Peking.[208]

This convention provided for the Russian evacuation of Manchuria in three six-month periods beginning with the date of the convention (Art. II). In the first six months Russian troops were to evacuate the Manchurian territory west of the Liao River, in the next six months they were to evacuate the rest of the province of Mukden (Fengtien) and the province of Kirin, and in the final six months all the rest of Manchuria. Limited numbers of Chinese troops would be permitted by a subsequent agreement between the Chinese government and Russian military authorities while Russian troops were still in occupation. When the evacuation was complete the Chinese government could increase or decrease its forces in Manchuria at will, but it pledged itself to notify Russia of such changes (Art. III). Other articles of lesser importance were concerned with compensations for the return of the Shanhaikwan-Inkou-Hsinmintun railroad and guarantees that China would not build extensions or branches of the Imperial Northern Railroad without the consent of Russia. All these terms were quite reasonable, but they were subject to the usual elastic provision that these terms of evacuation would be carried out only "if there were no uprisings, or actions of other powers preventing this." A loophole was thus provided.

The honest intentions of the Russian government to carry out the terms of this convention can be judged by the execution of the measures. In the first six months, Russian troops carried out the evacuation west of the Liao River ahead of schedule. On April 29, 1902, the Shanhaikwan-Inkou-Hsinmintun railroad was handed over to the Chinese administration by a special agreement.[209] Since there was little strategic value in the presence of Russian troops west of the Liao after the transfer, they were immediately withdrawn. In the second period of evacuation, although some measure of Russian intent to evacuate was still apparent, it was also evident that the Russian attitude toward the evacuation had undergone a change. In most places the evacuation consisted of moving troops to barracks constructed near the railroad stations, which classified them technically "en route" from the provinces.[210] During the third period there was not even the pretense of an evacuation.

This change of policy was an outward manifestation of a great change which occurred in the leadership of Russian Far Eastern affairs in 1902 and the first half of 1903. This change had been slowly brewing "behind the scenes" of the Russian Court. It was felt in internal politics as well as in the minds of a number of prominent statesmen who hitherto had been willing to follow the leadership of Witte in formulating Russian policy in the Far East, and who were now ready to question both that leadership and the established policy, so laboriously evolved, of returning to the status quo before the Boxer uprising.

VIII

THE RISE TO POWER OF THE BEZOBRAZOV GROUP AND THE DECLINE OF WITTE

THE CHANGE in the leadership of Russia's foreign policy in the Far East was closely connected with the rise of the so-called Bezobrazov group, which revolved around an insignificant enterprise generally known as the Yalu concessions. Neither the group nor the concessions were of great importance in the change, but their egregious appearance in the press, court circles, and later in the historiography of the causes of the Russo-Japanese War, gave them a far greater importance than they actually deserved. If only because of the erroneous emphasis given to their role, a reëxamination of their historical importance is required. However, the Bezobrazov group also helped to promote and crystallize the opposition to Witte and the policy of evacuation of Manchuria. It also contributed to forcing Russian policy in the Far East into the state of indecision and procrastination which exasperated the Japanese and provided them with a plausible *casus belli* for the opening of military operations against Russia.

EMERGENCE OF THE BEZOBRAZOV GROUP

On September 9, 1896, during the period when the King of Korea was a refugee in the Russian legation at Seoul, Iu. I. Briner, a prominent Russian merchant and "entrepreneur" of Vladivostok, secured through the agency of Weber, the Russian Minister, and Polianovskii, the Vice-Consul, a concession for the exclusive right to cut timber on the Korean side of the watershed of the Yalu and Tumen rivers.[1] Until 1900 this was the only Russian concession in Korea,[2] and it was in a form of an option which would expire after five years if no exploitation was undertaken.[3]

Briner was not particularly enthusiastic about the concession. His commercial ventures and a timber concession being exploited in the Suchan Valley near Vladivostok kept him occupied.[4] After failing to interest other Vladivostok merchants in a company to exploit the Korean concession (in spite of the proximity of the Tumen River to Vladivostok), Briner, during a trip to St. Petersburg in the fall of 1897, tried to interest A. Iu. Rothstein, a director of the Russo-Chinese Bank and chairman of the short-lived Russo-Korean Bank, which at the time

---

[1] For notes to chap. viii see pp. 299–305.

had some funds but no investments.[5] Rothstein was not interested, but he discussed the concession with N. G. Matiunin, who had had twenty-five years diplomatic experience in the Far East as border commissioner on the Korean frontier and as vice-consul in northern Korea.[6] Matiunin had just been appointed chargé d'affaires in Korea. Before leaving to take up his post, Matiunin brought the matter of the concession to the attention of his one-time school (lyceum) friend V. M. Vonliarliarskii, formerly a colonel of the Chevalier Guards[7] and an energetic promoter. He had a string of concessions: gold mining in the Urals and the Chukchi Peninsula, interests in the Vologda–St. Petersburg railroad concession, and a number of promotion syndicates.[8]

The Korean concession was probably a minor affair to Vonliarliarskii; but promoters thrive on remote opportunities and are prone to clothe them with a past, present, and future importance far above their actual interest in the matter. Vonliarliarskii seized one of Matiunin's minor suggestions about not letting the concession get out of Russian hands[9] and expanded it. By metamorphosis the concession became the nucleus of a "great Russian industrial[10] company after the pattern of the East India Company."[11] The crux of Vonliarliarskii's scheme was the establishment of a powerful Russian company which would "enter into relations with American and French capitalists to attract their capital to the company's branch establishments, and in case of inevitable complications in the Far East, to invoke the protection not only of the Russian flag but also of the French and American flags."[12]

Besides conducting his private commercial affairs, Vonliarliarskii in 1897 was also acting as a privy counselor in the State Council, and as assistant secretary to the head of the Chancellery, Secretary of State V. K. Plehve.[13] This position brought him into contact with the highest officials of the government, as even ministers were required to submit projects of their proposed laws for discussion in the State Council branches, through its central office. His official position, therefore, made it relatively simple for him to bring the Korean concession to the attention of the Minister of Foreign Affairs, M. N. Muraviev. After first broaching the subject through Matiunin, Vonliarliarskii had several talks with Muraviev, who received his views with "favor" but not encouragement.[14] Vonliarliarskii foresaw that his idea would not find favor with Witte, because Rothstein, Witte's appointee, had rejected it. Vonliarliarskii was about to drop the whole matter, when he brought the concession, perhaps only in a incidental way, to the attention of a regimental acquaintance, a retired captain of the Chevalier Guards, Alexander Mikhailovich Bezobrazov.[15]

Bezobrazov was a veteran of officialdom and bureaucratic service. From 1881 to 1897 he had served in various capacities under the very wealthy and popular Count I. I. Vorontsov-Dashkov, Minister of the Imperial Court. In the years 1897–1898 he had been a special assistant to Count A. P. Ignatiev, Governor General of Western Siberia.[16] Bezobrazov was already a man of wealth, social position, and some influence. Prone to speak in unequivocal terms, he had an undeniable appeal for those who accepted his outspoken opinions as a sign of deep conviction and frankness. He probably later gained the favor of the Tsar in that manner. Many saw in his unreserved statements a sign of "genius,"[17] and even Witte, his main opponent and personal enemy, had to admit that he was personally "honest" and sincere.[18] He was also vain, ambitious, and self-assured.[19]

It was soon after Matiunin's departure for the Far East, sometime in January or early February, 1898, that Vonliarliarskii spoke to Bezobrazov. Bezobrazov then undertook to expound the political-economic value of the Korean concession to Count Vorontsov-Dashkov, who then asked the promoters to draw up a memorandum on the subject and also statutes for the proposed company.[20] The memorandum, dated March 12, 1898, and the statutes, which were the work of Vonliarliarskii and Bezobrazov, were presented to the Tsar by Vorontsov-Dashkov. The memorandum emphasized the importance of promoting Russian influence in Korea and the perfect feasibility of acquiring a predominant position in Korea through a private, but actually semiofficial, company by bringing in American and other capitalists into the company on a commercial basis.[21]

Nicholas II apparently approved of the plan, though the word "approved" as used by Russian writers on the subject does not necessarily mean that he wholeheartedly approved of the entire scheme.[22] To look into the matter, he appointed the Grand Duke Alexander Mikhailovich, who was then holding the sinecure of the chairmanship of the Volunteer Fleet, and who had been interested in the development of Russian interests in the Far East since his "Naval Memorandum" of 1897.[23] The Grand Duke worked under a disadvantage because Russian policy toward Korea definitely retreated after the Nishi-Rosen Convention of April 25, 1898. Nevertheless, on May 12 he submitted a favorable memorandum to the Tsar, accompanied by a copy of the text of Briner's concession.[24] It was a plan for an expedition to Korea and a report on conditions there written by a recent traveler in that country, S. N. Syromiatnikov, known in St. Petersburg by his journalistic pseudonym, "Sigma." He was also a promoter of gold-mining schemes in northern Korea. The memorandum was also accompanied by a fantastic project, probably written by Bezobrazov, in which the writer envisaged enterprises which could be a vanguard of Russian military power by disguising twenty thousand men as guards, workers, and general employees of the enterprises.[25]

There is no evidence that the Tsar was attracted by the military angle of the project, but it appeared to him that the unwanted concession was worth something. An option for 20,000 rubles was accordingly taken, on May 23, 1898, on Briner's concession. It was in the name of Privy Councilor N. I. Neporozhnev and contained reasonable terms for a purchase of all Briner's interests.[26] Since the option was to terminate on February 13, 1899, there was no time to lose. It was necessary that an organization be created immediately. The enterprise was to be presided over by the Grand Duke Alexander Mikhailovich and the executive management entrusted to Bezobrazov and Vonliarliarskii. To keep the Tsar's anonymity in the enterprise, the progress of the company was to be reported to the Tsar by the Minister of the Imperial Court, Baron V. B. Frederiks. At the Tsar's expense an expedition was fitted out to survey timber, mineral, and other resources of the area included in the concession. A lieutenant of the Chevalier Guards, A. I. Zvegintsev, was the nominal head. The group included Neporozhnev and G. Tikhonov, an inspector of forests.[27] This expedition left almost immediately and was soon joined by an independent expedition sent by M. O. Albert, director of the Neva Shipbuilding Company and a railroad promoter, who had recently been thwarted by Witte in a concession dispute concerning the Vologda–St. Petersburg railroad.[28] In July, 1898, Albert planned to recoup his fortune or take revenge on Witte by opposing Witte's plan of a southern branch of the C.E.R. to Port Arthur. He proposed a counter plan envisaging a Vladivostok–Port Arthur railroad running through the Briner concession area.[29]

The participants in the Korean venture acted with surprising speed. On July 4, 1898, when the "independent" expedition left St. Petersburg to survey the planned railroad, a report was submitted to the Tsar, through the established channels, concerning the advantages of the Port Arthur–Kirin–Port Shestakov–Vladivostok railroad route and the necessity for coördination and complete harmony among all governmental departments.[30] In the Far East the expedition broke up into eight parties. It quickly traversed the concession area[31] and by the end

of October was ready with new schemes. Neporozhnev at Seoul obtained a vague promise from the King of Korea to form a board of administration for Korean crown lands.[32] However, the important contacts the group had with both Korean and Russian authorities were lost when Matiunin was appointed consul to Melbourne, Australia, late in August, and the Russian legation in Seoul was left in the charge of A. I. Pavlov, a proponent of Russian expansion in China.[33] Neporozhnev telegraphed his backers in Russia for a 200,000-ruble credit to provide the customary bribes, but a refusal from Baron Frederiks came on November 18 from Livadia, the winter vacation palace of the Tsar. The promoters of the enterprise protested in vigorous terms.[34] Bezobrazov in a memorandum on November 23, Neporozhnev after his return on December 26, and Vonliarliarskii on December 31 complained that the opportunity was being allowed to slip by, but the most they could do was to prolong the option until May 17, 1899.[35]

In February, 1899, the route of the southern branch of the C.E.R. was determined, and the plans for the Korean concession began to fall apart. To rescue the funds already expended, Vonliarliarskii bought out all Briner's rights for an additional 65,000 rubles of Imperial Cabinet funds.[36] He obtained permission to draft the statutes of a projected East Asiatic Development Company, a kind of holding company which would promote mining, railroads, lumber, and other enterprises in the Far East.[37]

Since the company's only assets were the Briner concession, on which no work had been done, and the vague promise of the King of Korea in regard to control over the mining rights on the crown lands, Bezobrazov tried to get the Volunteer Fleet to take over the concession. However, he failed to persuade the Grand Duke Alexander Mikhailovich. Vonliarliarskii tried the Navy Department, but the Grand Duke stopped him once more by stating that he declined to have anything more to do with the concession.[38] Finally, Vonliarliarskii tried to transfer the concession to the Department of Imperial Domains, and here again he met refusal.[39] On August 13, 1889, the timber concession was transferred fictitiously from Neporozhnev to N. G. Matiunin and M. O. Albert for the nominal sum of 30,000 rubles. On October 27, 1899, the vague mining rights were also transferred.[40] Vonliarliarskii, having arranged this transfer, concerned himself with his private interests in a joint Russian-American enterprise for the exploitation of gold fields on the Chukchi Peninsula.[41]

In the winter of 1899–1900, Matiunin, who apparently had not gone to Melbourne or resigned from diplomatic service, attempted to develop the concession into a paying proposition. He negotiated with Witte personally for a loan from the Russo-Chinese Bank, but he was politely refused. He attempted to link the nebulous concessionary rights for establishing a department of mines in Korea with similar vague and unratified concessions for the mineral exploitation of Korean crown lands held by an American promoter named Hunt, who seemed to have financial backing.[42] Matiunin failed in all these schemes. On November 5, 1899, he received Witte's reply stating that the Tsar's decision was that "the participation of the Treasury in the matter of Korean mining concessions, in whatever shape or form, is to be refused."[43] The matter rested, with the "orphaned" concession begging for a sponsor. Yet it was a perfectly legal concession and had sound economic prospects. In the construction of the South Manchurian branch of the C.E.R. and the building of the terminal city of Dalny, Korean lumber would have a ready market, if only the principal buyers, the C.E.R. and Witte, would favor it with patronage of some sort, or if the real owner of the concession, the Tsar, would condescend to give it an official sign of his favor, which would in turn influence the C.E.R. to favor the lumber enterprise.

Bezobrazov did not abandon the politico-economic schemes aroused by his connections with the concession. In March, 1900, he submitted to the Tsar a complete project for the East Asiatic Development Company.[44] It was a typical promotion scheme based on important names, Imperial patronage, and promises of quick and sizable returns. The financing of the company was to be accomplished by the issue of four hundred subscription shares at a par value of 5,000 rubles, but it was to be paid for in installments subject to call. Two hundred shares were to be subscribed by the Cabinet (Personal Treasury) of the Tsar, but without any cash outlay, since one hundred shares were to be given the Cabinet for its rights on the Briner concession and one hundred shares were to be given for the sale of a part of the concession—the timber rights on Dajelet Island off the western coast of Korea, from which the company hoped to realize 150,000 rubles. Thus, by a stroke of a pen, the Tsar would theoretically receive a profitable return on the 250,000 rubles spent by the Cabinet for the purchase of the Briner concession and the exploration work.[45] In addition, the company would have 150,000 rubles with which to begin its operations. This was essential because, like promotion ventures in all parts of the world, the subscribed shares did not have to be paid for in full, but only at a rate of 1,000 rubles per share, when the company needed the money.

Apparently Bezobrazov had done a good deal of groundwork, for he submitted a list of "founders" and "specialists" who had promised to subscribe to the venture. It is impossible to determine whether the persons listed joined the project because of its political angle, or because of the absolutely certain profit under the conditions mentioned above, or perhaps just because they wanted to help a fellow guardsman or club acquaintance. Many of them were so immensely rich that the small financial outlay needed for the first call on the shares must have been an insignificant item in their minds. The names of such immensely wealthy people as Count Vorontsov, Prince Yusupov, Count Orlov-Davydov, Count Nostits, Count Sumarokov-Elston, and Colonel Serebriakov were included in the list of subscribers. Other founders were also men of prominence in state affairs, including Colonel Vonliarliarskii and Captain A. M. Abaza, a cousin of Bezobrazov.[46] The list of "specialists" included N. G. Matiunin and M. O. Albert.[47]

For reasons of his own, the Tsar was attracted to the scheme. There was nothing wrong with the organization of an enterprise under such prominent founders. It was somewhat unethical for the head of a state to give his name to a promotion scheme, but that obstacle could easily be circumvented by having the Tsar's shares held by another person. Whether the Tsar completely subscribed to the political program so often expounded by Bezobrazov cannot be determined. Later events proved this to be very doubtful. However, it is important to note that the Tsar had absolute confidence in the financial outcome of the project. This fact was brought out in his note of approval sent to the Ministers of Finance and Foreign Affairs and to the Imperial Court, in which he made provision for the disposition of his profits: "It is desirable to limit the profit of the Cabinet [of his Imperial Majesty] to a legal rate of interest on capital really spent and to employ all the remainder of the financial profit in satisfying the needs of far distant places, in the work of educating the people, and the building of churches."[48]

In June, 1900, the fate of the East Asiatic Development Company came up for decision. The Tsar received a memorandum from the Ministry of Finance criticising the structure of the company, and at the same time he received one from Count Vorontsov urging that he make a definite decision because the Count was scheduled to leave on a trip to western Europe.[49] In haste, on June 18, the Tsar decided in favor of the company, and on a plain sheet of paper he wrote in pencil his resolution to have the organization of the company examined by the

Committee of Ministers.[50] He added that "the Cabinet will be ordered to purchase 200 shares of the East Asiatic Company in the name of Captain of the First Rank Abaza." This note was apparently given to Vorontsov. Vorontsov gave it to Vonliarliarskii, who gave it to Bezabrazov; he in turn submitted it to the Ministry of Finance.[51] The matter was blocked again by Witte, who persuaded the Tsar not to let the statutes of the company be brought up before the Committee of Ministers until the end of the troubles in the Far East. The Boxer rebellion was at that time assuming threatening proportions.[52]

Bezobrazov was furious. In a letter to Count Vorontsov-Dashkov, on June 28, he fulminated against Witte's opposition. He bitterly berated Witte, the Manchurian railroad, and its "Jewish speculators" as the cause of Russian diplomatic difficulties in the Far East and denounced Witte's system in general as failing in peacetime and threatening Russia with bankruptcy in the event of war.[53] In subsequent memorandums to the Tsar on August 5 and August 8, Bezobrazov again stressed the political importance of the project and the necessity of its rapid realization.[54] However, the Tsar remained at least "correct" in his relations with his responsible ministers and refused to lend his influence in promotion of the project.

In the fall of 1900 there might have been another reason for a temporary submerging of the matter of the Korean concession. In October, Dajelet Island was visited by the Russian cruiser *Kornilov*, with Kochetkov, an inspector of forests, on board. On Kochetkov's return to Port Arthur he reported that most of the timber stand on the island had been burned, and that the island had no suitable harbors for loading operations. Then attempts were made to sell the concession rights on this island to the Japanese, who appeared interested and who, presumably, made a tentative offer of 200,000 rubles for a fifteen-year lease of the island. The Japanese at that time were large-scale suppliers of lumber in the Far East, and no doubt supplied it to the Russians in Manchuria.[55] They were interested in such prospects as the Dajelet Island timberlands. However, in time their offers were reduced to a pittance, and the possibility of the disposal of the timber concession on the island with profit vanished. Japanese interlopers—individuals and groups—continued to cut down such timber as they could carry away on their junks, just as they had done before the negotiations.[56]

Sometime before June 30, 1901, Bezobrazov made another attempt to overcome Witte's opposition, but to no avail. Witte insisted that the two hundred shares designated for the Cabinet be taken over by

the Treasury under Witte's control, in return for the Suchan concession, once held by Briner and now in the hands of the Treasury. Secondly, he insisted on the removal from the list of promoters the names of certain persons who held important positions in the government: Yusupov, Vonliarliarskii, Count V. A. Gendrikov, and M. A. Serebriakov.[57] This would have changed the entire aspect of the enterprise. Instead of Imperial patronage there would be cold and impersonal business supervision and the participation of the Treasury; instead of an economic-political penetration of Korea there would be merely another timber enterprise in the Primorsk region, actually controlled by Witte. It was a completely unsatisfactory arrangement for Bezobrazov and his supporters, who began to drop away as soon as they heard of the new attitude toward the project. The Grand Duke Alexander Mikhailovich led the deserters; others followed. They had lost nothing but their time, whereas the Tsar's Cabinet was out 112,000 rubles, although still holding title to the unwanted concession. Bezobrazov had been thwarted in whatever schemes he might have had. On February 2, 1902, Bezobrazov was ordered to liquidate the project of the East Asiatic Development Company.[58] This was another blow to his ambitious and proud nature.

Perhaps unwittingly, Bezobrazov had gained a great deal in prestige and position. The affairs of the concession had enabled him to get into close touch with the Tsar, his ministers, and with prominent members of the Court and the capital. He was very much in the limelight and was widely talked about. Although his acid comments and intransigent views on the true role of Russia in the Far East may not have been accepted by many of his listeners, they were at least listened to in circles where his anti-Semitism and dislike of Witte were heartily approved. Bezobrazov became the most vocal of Witte's critics and opened his attack on him at an opportune time, when Witte was open to criticism in consequence of the mounting economic depression in Russia, and when a great many errors in policy and the conduct of affairs became increasingly apparent. The Far Eastern situation, the internal opposition to Witte, the revelations of Witte's missteps and of some of his unquestionable trickery in the conduct of affairs, the growth of the inherent autocratic aspirations of the Tsar, and the increasing advice in favor of stronger autocracy offered to the Tsar by some of his closest advisers—all merged with Bezobrazov's political criticisms and served to make Bezobrazov's position, even as an unattached member of the Court, one to be reckoned with.

Witte clearly recognized the strong position of Bezobrazov, although perhaps not its origins and implications, when he wrote to his friend and colleague Sipiagin on July 25, 1901:

I wrote you that everything is quiet here except that Bezobrazov is scheming something. In the last few days what he is scheming is made more clear from various conversations of the Emperor with Ermolov [Minister of Agriculture and State Properties], Count Lamsdorf and P. P. Hesse, and from various incidents. Bezobrazov, behind whom stands Vonliarliarskii ... and Albert, have come to the conclusion that they cannot do business with me, and hence consider that they must clear the way. ... As Bezobrazov visits the Emperor at least twice a week and stays with him for hours, he of course tells him all sorts of nonsense and all kinds of ephemeral plans. ... Bezobrazov suddenly announced to Ermolov the Imperial desire that all mineral deposits in the Amur region be turned over for exploitation to the East Asiatic Company and that all present companies there must be liquidated. ...

We are going through a bad economic period. ... On this matter the Tsar is being persuaded that we must therefore change our financial policy;—that this is a result of my policy. But how to change it? Of course, they do not know. The problem for him [Bezobrazov] consists only in clearing the way for himself and fishing in troubled waters. . . . The Tsar does not confer with me. I drum out my report and that is all. ... At one time he said, "Shouldn't we transfer the C.E.R. to the Ministry of Communications?" I do not know where this idea originated. I answered, "Yes, in three years that might be convenient."[59]

However, Witte at that time was not alarmed. He concluded the letter quoted above: "As far as I personally am concerned, I am not alarmed in the least about the state of affairs. One cannot expect that at all times everything will go satisfactorily."

However, Witte greatly underestimated the situation. The roots of criticism lay deeper than the attacks apparent in Bezobrazov's schemes or in the vacillation of the Tsar. He also overestimated the security of his position, which at that time appeared unassailable, and he underestimated the strength of the forces being marshaled to remove him from his position.

ECONOMIC WEAKNESS OF THE RUSSIAN FAR EASTERN PLANS

The encouragement of heavy industry was prominent among Witte's economic policies for Russia. Light industries were not neglected and were even greatly favored by the Russo-German tariff agreement of January 1894,[60] but the promotion of iron and steel industries was particularly favored in the great railroad expansion program undertaken by the Ministry of Finance. The stability of the Russian market for consumer goods and heavy metallurgical goods attracted an influx of foreign capital, and the establishment of the gold standard in 1897 as well as the general reorganization of Russian finances helped by

French loans made Russia a profitable and secure market for capital investments.[61]

Profits of steel and iron works soared; companies paid dividends averaging 50 per cent from 1896 to 1900. This caused a natural expansion of the iron and steel industry, especially in the Don basin of the southern Ukraine. From 1896 to 1900, pig-iron production in Russia increased from 1,595,000 tons to 2,821,000 tons. The government bought the greatest share of the production—1,000,000 tons in 1899, and 970,000 tons in 1900[62]—and a large part of this went to the railroads. It has been estimated that the needs of the railroads, principally for construction purposes, took 43 per cent of all pig-iron production in 1899.[63] The greatest railroad builder at the time was the State Railroad Administration, within which were the Trans-Siberian Railway and the C.E.R.[64]

This artificial stimulation of production could not continue unchecked. It can be claimed that Witte's policy had not been properly integrated and planned far enough in advance, for the financial situation changed markedly at the beginning of the twentieth century. There was a natural recession caused by the overexpansion and the tightening of credit abroad. In 1900 Russia began to experience a financial and industrial crisis which probably originated in the bankers' and brokers' panic in western Europe and the United States in the same year.[65] Within Russia and on the stock exchanges abroad, Russian bonds and industrial shares fell sharply, with an average decline of almost 50 per cent in the leading industrial enterprises. Even such gilt-edged securities as the shares of the Russo-Chinese Bank fell more than 10 per cent.[66] The situation did not improve in 1901, when Witte was forced into a policy of retrenchment by the partial failure of the grain crop, the difficulty of raising even a relatively small loan in France,[67] and the unexpectedly heavy expenditures connected with the Boxer rebellion. The railroad construction program in the Far East had been almost completed as far as purchases from the iron and steel industry were concerned. Purchases of pig iron by the government fell to 400,000 tons in 1901,[68] and this aggravated the depression. This depression or recession, although not in an acute form, persisted till the Russo-Japanese War.

Under these conditions the huge expenditures in the Far East were a great burden on the economy of the country as a whole. Of course, since Witte had tight control over the Ministry of Finance and the State Comptroller's Office, the real cost of the Far Eastern program was not known at the time: its magnitude was hardly suspected. The

prosperity that normally surrounds any large construction boom created among the Russians engaged in the Far Eastern enterprises a feeling of great optimism which did not tolerate any criticism. However,
besides being of concern to such critics as Bezobrazov, the question of
the vast expenditures vitally concerned others, such as Kuropatkin,
who was frequently at odds with Witte and other ministers for their
stress on economy at the expense of the Ministry of War.[69]

At the meeting of the State Council on January 12, 1903, Witte
raised the matter of railroad costs; he estimated the deficit of the
Ministry of Communications to be 60,000,000 rubles a year, as contrasted with a profit of 11,000,000 rubles when he was in charge in
1893.[70] This led Kuropatkin to make an estimate of the cost of the
C.E.R. in particular, which he placed at 400,000,000, with an annual
deficit of 40,000,000.[71] These figures, however, do not give a true picture
of the cost of the Far Eastern developments as a whole, when the increased cost of military and naval establishments, caused principally
by the new course of Russian policy in the Far East, are also taken into
account.

Later in 1903, the Ministry of Finance was asked to submit an account of the expenditures and income of the government in the Far
East,[72] and presented the following summary.

EXPENDITURES AND INCOME OF THE RUSSIAN GOVERNMENT IN THE FAR EAST
(In Thousands of Rubles)

Year	Revenue	Expenditures	Difference	C. E. R. expenditure
1897	9,601	92,726	83,124	5,000
1898	12,573	123,952	111,378	26,300
1899	15,753	201,030	185,277	69,200
1900	21,914	263,592	241,677	84,500
1901	29,846	247,647	217,801	73,111
1902	196,885	220,816	_23,931	69,417
Total	286,574	1,140,765	863,190	327,529[73]

According to this calculation, the administration, construction work,
and other expenditures in the Far East from the beginning of the Construction of the C.E.R. through 1902 had an average yearly deficit.[74]
This table is, of course, incomplete, for it probably does not take into
account some of the extraordinary expenditures of the Treasury in
connection with the suppression of the Boxer rebellion. To what fund
or item, for example, should one assign the gifts of 200,000 rubles each

to Kuropatkin, Lamsdorf, and Witte, ordered by the Tsar in December, 1900, for their successful work in the suppression of the Boxer rebellion?[75] Furthermore, the revenue item of 196,885,000 rubles in 1902 is a fictitious sum because it no doubt includes the share of the Boxer Indemnity bonds assigned to Russia, which were payable sometime in the future. The more normal increase of revenue in 1901 and probably a similar increase in 1902 were due to the movement of troops in the Far East, the C.E.R. and its subsidiary shipping company charging high rates for transportation. Consequently, taking the revenue of 1902 at about 36,000,000 rubles, the average annual deficit would be closer to 171,000,000 rubles.[76]

If the true figure was close to 171,000,000, it was an enormous amount at a time when national budgets were still computed in millions. In comparison, the total Russian budget for 1903 was only 1,296,000,000 rubles, of which 289,000,000 rubles, or 22 per cent, were allocated for interest and repayment of loans, 465,000,000, or 36 per cent, for the Army and Navy, and 542,000,000, or 42 per cent, for all other expenditures.[77] Again, in comparison, the entire budget of the Navy Department in 1902 was 98,000,000 rubles, and in 1901, 93,000,000 rubles.[78] When the titular head of the Navy Department, Grand Duke Alexander Mikhailovich, and later the Tsar projected in 1902 an eight-year program of naval construction for Russia, which would cost 40,000,000 rubles a year, both Witte and Kuropatkin were aghast at the audacity of the plan and eliminated it for reasons of economy.[79] Compared with the expenditures on the C.E.R. and its installations, the sums expended on such purely military projects as the fortification of Port Arthur were modest indeed. In 1899 the Tsar and Witte finally approved the Port Arthur fortification project for a total of 8,927,000 rubles to be expended in two five-year periods, ending in 1909. When the Russo-Japanese War broke out, of 4,631,000 rubles allocated for the first period, 550,000 rubles were still unexpended.[80] The fortification of Port Arthur had cost the Treasury less than 1,000,000 rubles a year.

If these large expenditures had passed into the hands of Russian industry and Russian workmen and into the domestic market, they would have been theoretically justified. However, as tempo in the construction of the Trans-Siberian Railway and the C.E.R. increased after the events of 1898, and particularly the Boxer crisis, the available means of construction and equipment for the enterprises in Russia fell short of the demand, and more foreign help, foreign contractors. and foreign equipment had to be brought in to finish the task. Some 60,000 Chinese from northern China, contracted through Chinese agents and

brought to Port Arthur, Newchwang, or Dalny chiefly on Japanese
ships, worked on the railroad in Manchuria;[81] and thousands more
worked on the railroad sector around the southeast end of Lake Baikal,
where construction continued until 1905.[82] American and Italian hard-
rock drillers were hired until mid-1904 for work on the scores of tunnels in that sector and on the mile-long tunnel through the Great
Khingan range.[83] Locomotives and other rolling stock were bought in
France, Belgium, and the United States;[84] railroad ties for the southern
branch of the C.E.R. were bought in Canada and the United States;[85]
coal for the C.E.R. steamers and the railroad was bought from the
Mitsui firm in Kyushu, Japan,[86] and cattle for food for the garrisons at
Port Arthur and Vladivostok was bought in Shantung, China, and at
the Treaty Port of Chefoo.[87]

More examples can be cited, but suffice it to add that the southern
branch of the C.E.R., the treaty port status of Newchwang, and the
porto franco of Dalny permitted Chinese, Japanese, American, and
western European goods to penetrate into Manchuria and find a lucrative market among the 60,000 workers and their numerous dependents
and "caterers" who were supported by the C.E.R.—that is, at the
expense of the Russian Treasury. It was therefore no wonder that as
early as 1900, before the Boxer uprising, some writers looked upon
the situation in northern Manchuria with alarm and foresaw in the
construction of the C.E.R. and its branch enterprises a triumphal
march of the yellow race, specifically the Chinese, into the north and
into the eastern parts of the Russian Empire.[88] This "yellow invasion"
also took place in the region around Vladivostok. If a certain Japanese report is credible, 40,000 Chinese, mostly from Chefoo, went annually to Vladivostok in the spring and returned in the autumn. They
were recruited for seasonal work by the Russo-Chinese Bank and its
subcontractors, traveled in Japanese ships, worked in organized gangs,
and returned to China with most of the money they earned.[89]

The C.E.R. was opened for commercial exploitation in 1901, although
the first passenger service was officially inaugurated by the arrival of
the "Oriental Express" passenger train from European Russia in
Dalny on March 8, 1903.[90] The relatively short period of operation of
the railroad before the Russo-Japanese War did not permit the accumu-
lation of enough evidence of the soundness of the commercial value of
the railroad. It is now generally admitted that the railroad was over-
capitalized and overstaffed and its employees were overpaid. Even
in the few years of operation before the Russo-Japanese War, it began
to show signs of weakness. Freight rates were high; a shortage of roll-

ing stock caused congestion of freight; passenger and troop trains had impeded the normal operations of freight transit. Small cargo vessels and junks with freight for the hinterland of Manchuria avoided Dalny and the Russian branch railroad port of Inkou, and transferred goods to river boats going up the Liao River.[91] Because of the high cost of handling goods due to the interruptions in the lines of the Trans-Siberian and the C.E.R., direct freight from Europe to the Far East was negligible. According to one contemporary writer, shipping costs from Bremen to Dalny by train amounted to 220 marks a long ton, whereas the steamers of the North German Lloyd would deliver the same freight there for 22 to 23 marks per ton.[92] Even more serious, of course, was the lack of the necessary cheap merchandise, which apparently was not available to the Russian industries. Neither did they have in Manchuria the agencies necessary for distribution; thus, in 1902, even in the northwest province of Tsitsihar, Japanese, American, and English merchandise was brought in by the railroads and found a ready market. But aside from that in the immediate railroad zones, there seems to have been no sale of Russian merchandise, except of vodka and tobacco.[93]

Next to the movement of troops, the largest amount of revenue for the Manchurian railroads came from the vast amount of government freight carried to or through Manchuria. From 1901 to 1904, government freight, paid for by the various agencies of the Russian government, amounted to ten times the private freight;[94] whereas the usual ratio on Russia's European railroads was the reverse. Of course, as far as the C.E.R. was concerned, it made no difference what freight it carried. The government paid and the C.E.R. Company shareholders, the Russo-Chinese Bank, the Minister of Finance, and the French holders of Russian bonds were satisfied. However, the condition could not be considered normal when it depended on extraordinary movements of traffic without much regard to expense.

The crucial test of the economic value of the C.E.R. was in the matter of express freight, since even with the interruptions in the Manchurian and Trans-Siberian railways, the land route was much faster than the sea route; and the one item of express freight which was ideally suited for this service was Chinese tea, traditionally packaged in south-central Chinese ports, brought to northern China by sea, and then routed overland to Kiakhta in Siberia and then to European Russia. Of this trade Alexander Ular wrote in 1904: "the Manchuria route is of such slight commercial importance that it is completely ignored by those most interested, the businessmen of Kiakhta. They do not reckon upon proceeding with the smallest change in the organization of their trade."[95] Such a statement is of course an exaggeration, but according to the official records of the year 1903, the best year of commercial traffic on the C.E.R. until 1907, the Manchurian railroads carried 734,000 poods of tea to Russia, while 685,000 poods entered Russia through Kiakhta by the old caravan route.[96] Yet in 1900 and 1901 the overland route was disrupted, and at one time completely closed, by the Boxer rebellion and later uprisings in the Kansu region.

In order to bolster the economic position of the C.E.R. and its subsidiaries, Witte exercised his wide powers in the government. Previously he had tried to place the Imperial Chinese Customs in the hands of his C.E.R. agents at the border stations, but he was foiled in this attempt in the spring of 1901. However, he did succeed in arranging a reduction of one-third in import and export tariffs with the Chinese government along the stations of the Manchurian railroads. From 1901 to 1903, on goods destined for the Russian workers and troops guarding them, the Chinese tariffs were completely withdrawn at stations of the C.E.R.[97] He also succeeded in lifting the Chinese prohibition on export of grains from Manchuria to the Russian Maritime Province, at first by local arrangement and later by ratification.[98] This prohibition was to a large degree ignored on the border, where the contemporary trade was fluid. However, such measures were still not sufficient to attract large import and export trade along the C.E.R. even with the facilities for unloading, loading, and storage offered by the entrepôt port of Dalny, which had been made a free port by an Imperial decree on August 11, 1899.[99]

To channel trade to and from Dalny, Witte exercised his power as head of the Merchant Marine and head of the Volunteer Fleet, the ships of which were, in effect, the direct competitors of the Russian railroad ventures in Manchuria. In 1901 he directed shipping to the Persian Gulf and India to engage in a search for cargoes, which proved unremunerative.[100] The Volunteer Fleet became used less as a link of transportation between European Russia and the Far East and more as an auxiliary service to bring Far Eastern products to the entrepôt of Dalny. The result was that Far Eastern trade with Odessa decreased yearly,[101] while cabotage and general freight carriage by Russian shipping in the Far East correspondingly increased.[102] In 1900 Witte also succeeded in closing the sea route to the Resettlement Administration, so that the settlers going to the Far East had to use Witte's railroads. This was hardly a great saving in time, for the trip averaged twenty-seven to thirty days.[103] These measures, of course, improved the financial position of both the Trans-Siberian Railway and the C.E.R., but they were hardly sound economic measures in the interests of the state. Long-distance cargo shipments are the most profitable and economical in merchant shipping; the Volunteer Fleet, representing Russia's finest, fastest, and newest merchant vessels, was best suited for long transfers of passengers and cargoes and not for stimulation of local trade or for short hauls between Far Eastern ports and Dalny.

The conclusive proof that the trend from sea to railroad transportation was artificially promoted by Witte, and not a natural shift, is evident in Witte's juggling of the Russian customs in the interests of imports coming through Manchuria. Numerous examples can be found in table 12 of the *Obzor vneshnei torgovli* for the year 1903 (pp. 598–685) which prove his intentions. For instance, the tariff on rice entering Odessa was 88 per cent ad valorem, while that on rice entering Russia from Manchuria was a mere one-fortieth of one per cent.[104] On rice coming through Vladivostok, however, the duties were more reasonable, the tariff being 18 per cent ad valorem. Thus the Manchurian railroads, though imposing staggering freight charges, reaped the benefit from the discrepancy in the tariff system.

A second example of the same favoritism is found in the tea trade. Making a bid for this long-distance express cargo, Witte set the tariff on the Asiatic frontiers at 25 rubles 50 kopeks per pood, while at Odessa the charge was 31 rubles 50 kopeks.[105] The 6-ruble difference per pood was no doubt sufficient to take care of the heavy charges on the railroad, yet more than 71 per cent of all fine teas still went to Russia through Odessa.[106]

The development of the Russian city of Harbin was an apparently successful enterprise of the C.E.R. This railroad center was chosen from the start as construction headquarters of the C.E.R. and grew rapidly beside the old Chinese city. The presence of many well-paid engineers, contractors, workers, and railroad guards attracted a commercial population; the two Russian quarters of New Harbin and Pristan thus had a population of 20,000 Russians and Chinese by 1902. Among them were more than 500 Japanese.[107] Besides being a logical place for railroad shops, the city also profited from the river trade on the Sungari, which helped to feed the railroad, as well as by the tariff changes instituted by Witte.

On June 23, 1900, Witte ended the *porto franco* privileges of Vladivostok and of Nikolaevsk on the Amur.[108] He did this in the interests of the Manchurian grain trade, the C.E.R., and its subsidiary flour mills in Manchuria. In the 1890's the failure of the Maritime Province to provide grain products for local needs was clearly recognized. The Governor General, Baron Korf, attempted to encourage local grain production by ordering the army intendants to buy grain directly from the peasants at prices 30 to 40 per cent higher than the market price of imported grain; but this had little effect on production. Peasants contrived to purchase Korean and Manchurian grain and sell it as their own rather than engage in the more arduous task of growing grain.[109] Under the *porto franco* arrangement, American flour predominated in the market. After this, a tariff of 30 kopeks per pood was placed on flour entering Vladivostok by sea, while the imports by land remained free from tariff. This favored Manchurian wheat production, mainly concentrated in north Manchuria along the Sungari River. This also made profitable the establishment of a milling industry centered in Harbin. A Chinese law dating from the eighteenth century prohibited exportation of grain from Manchuria, but nothing was said about flour. Consequently, a large-scale milling industry boomed in northern Manchuria, started and operated by the Russo-Chinese Bank and the C.E.R. subsidiaries. In 1900 one large flour mill produced some 750,000 poods per year. By 1903 there were five mills with a total production of 12,000,000 poods.[110] This of course helped both the C.E.R. and the development of Manchuria and proved of inestimable value in feeding the army during the Russo-Japanese War; the economic frailty of the enterprise became apparent later. When, after the war in 1905, Manchurian flour was placed on a competitive basis in the Russian Far East with a uniform tariff on land and sea of 45 kopeks per pood, and in addition the flour export of Manchuria carried a Chinese export tariff of 6 kopeks per pood, American flour once again could favorably compete with that produced in Manchuria.[111]

The ending of the *porto franco* regulations in Vladivostok also seems to have been intended to promote Dalny. The brief period of Russian exploitation of Dalny does not permit a thorough examination of its value to Russian Far Eastern commercial developments. From 1900 to 1903 the town was still in the building stage, but by 1903 some doubts were clearly apparent concerning its future role. There were two schools of thought: one claimed that Dalny was financially insecure and was unnecessary because Port Arthur, which was near by, also had a commercial harbor, good railroad facilities, and a ready local market in the large garrison; the other school of thought firmly believed in the future of Dalny.[112] Of course the optimists at first had everything in their favor. Large sums of money were being spent on construction work in Dalny—far larger than the sums spent on the fortifications of Port Arthur. The growth of Dalny was unhampered by military needs, and the town had many privileges not accorded to Port Arthur. For example, in Dalny, Russian Jews were allowed to purchase real estate and to engage in all types of business activities, whereas in Port Arthur they were under restrictions then common in most Russian possessions outside the pale of settlement.[113]

Nevertheless, by 1903, Dalny began to appear disappointing. The town had been laid out to provide for great expansion. Suburbs of luxurious villas had been plotted out along the outlying bays, and roads had been built leading to them. The sale of lots which was supposed to bring 15,000,000 rubles had gone badly and by the middle of 1903 had brought in the paltry sum of 500,000 rubles.[114] The large Russian private commercial enterprises in the Far East, such as Churin and Company and Kunst and Albers, refused to be attracted to Dalny and established their permanent branches in Port Arthur. They were followed there by private Russian banks, which helped the trade at Port Arthur.[115] Even more astonishing is the fact that Russian shipping in the Far East, a good deal of it directly under the control of the C.E.R., preferred Port Arthur to Dalny, because of the incomplete condition of the latter port.[116] Perhaps the most discouraging disaster of all came in 1903, when the protective mole was completed: that winter the harbor froze.[117]

By the end of 1903 the rivalry between Port Arthur and Dalny was practically over. The almost general preference for Port Arthur was recognized. Perhaps the rumors of war had something to do with this situation; but the presence of a ready market in the form of the increased Russian garrison was a more direct cause. The large warehouses, the available shipping berths, and the many railroad sidings were little used. The doubts regarding Russian commercial enterprises in Manchuria were widely recognized. One observant eyewitness reported, apparently just before the Russo-Japanese War:

As yet all Russian undertakings in Port Arthur, as well as in the rest of Manchuria, have an unsolid character. Without troops, with the cessation of all further government undertakings, the Russian entrepreneurs as well as all Russian workers engaged in these activities ... would have nothing to do. In order that Russian entrepreneurs could open up their activity in Manchuria it would be necessary to fence them in from all foreign competition, to stop foreign access, to surround the region with customs guards. . . . And all this can be done only on the condition that all Manchuria becomes the property of Russia. Consequently, until this occurs, all expenditures by Russia bring gain only to foreigners with whom our entrepreneurs cannot compete without government protection.[118]

This, in brief, is the essence of criticism of Witte's scheme for an

economic penetration of Manchuria and the Far East, and the basis
of the main attack on Witte in 1902–1903, as well as the basis of the
reëxamination of Russia's role in the Far East which then took place.

The Failure of Witte's Diplomacy

The spring of 1902 brought Witte many unpleasant surprises. The
strong stand taken by China and her final refusal to come to a separate agreement with Russia before the evacuation of Manchuria were
unexpected in view of the moderate Russian demands. This, together
with the announcement of the Anglo-Japanese Alliance had hastened
the signing of the Evacuation Agreement of April 8, 1902. On April
15, D. L. Sipiagin, Minister of the Interior, who was a personal friend
of Witte and a staunch supporter in the government, was assassi-
nated.[119] In choosing a successor, Witte persuaded the Tsar to pass
over the candidacy of N. V. Muraviev, the Minister of Justice, and
thus incurred Muraviev's enmity.[120] Witte failed to block the appointment of V. K. Plehve, his own archenemy. At this crucial point, therefore, he lost a staunch friend and gained two powerful enemies in
higher governmental circles.

The personal and political struggle between Witte and Plehve was
both profound and important.[121] It arose from their differences of
opinion on the role of autocracy in the Russian government and on
the role of the zemstvo in the agrarian reforms discussed by a special
committee established in February, 1902. It manifested itself in jurisdictional disputes about whether control of the factory police was to
be with the Minister of the Interior or the Department of Manufactures
under the Ministry of Finance. Some of the personal enmity may have
arisen from the fact that Plehve was an outspoken anti-Semite and
Witte was married to a Jewess. The important point in regard to
Russian policy in the Far East was that Plehve, as an important minister, was now in a position to oppose Witte in any conference in which
he participated.

With the failure of the separate agreement with China, Witte had
an alternate course, which he adopted in 1902. This was to buy on an
optional or provisional basis all concessions and land sites directly
through his agencies, the C.E.R. and the Russo-Chinese Bank, or
through trusted individuals connected with them.[122] This step had already been taken on a provisional basis by the Russo-Chinese Bank
in negotiating with the governors general of Kirin and Tsitsihar (Heilungkiang) provinces from July to September, 1901. However, many

of the concessions obtained were on options giving only exploratory
rights, or rights to exploit minerals and forest resources *in* (not *of*)
certain areas.[123] On March 17, 1902, the Chinese Imperial Government
issued a series of new mining laws, applicable to Manchuria, which
demanded that concessionaries specify the exact location of their concession and the specific metal they intended to work. The laws limited
the area of the claims by numerous restrictions.[124] This made the previously established claims, which are graphically presented by B. A.
Romanov in the map appended to his *Rossiia v Manzhurii,* so much
theoretical planning.[125] Actually, most concessions carried time limitations which demanded periodic expenditures or work, and little if any
work was done on many of the Russian concessions in Manchuria at
the time. In all probability most of the concessions were not legal, for
they had not been ratified by the Chinese central authorities; but, as
it will be shown later, that did not necessarily preclude some Russian
work on them.

The main obstacle to the work on the concessions was the absence of
trained personnel for exploitation: engineers, surveyors, technicians,
foremen, and other Russian workmen who would lend the enterprises
the appearance of a Russian enterprise. The Yentai coal mines operated
by the C.E.R. in conjunction with Chinese shareholders were all sub-
leased to Chinese contractors.[126] The great quarries near Tsitsihar, em-
ploying more than 6,000 workmen, were also let out to a group of
Chinese contractors in northern Manchuria, who in turn worked the
quarries with subcontractors.[127] In June, 1902, D. D. Pokotilov wrote
Witte from Port Arthur that there was no hope of starting the work
required on the concessions unless competent engineers were sent to
Manchuria.[128]

To facilitate this exploratory work, Witte organized on July 18, 1902,
the Manchurian Mining Company, which was to take over the concessions from the Russo-Chinese Bank. As a holding company with a
staff of engineers hired or borrowed from the C.E.R., it was to conduct
exploratory work on all the concessions.[129] This system would effect
considerable saving in personnel as well as expenses; for the board of
directors was composed mostly of men from the board of directors of
the C.E.R. Company or the Russo-Chinese Bank or both; it included
some persons of long association with Witte, such as A. I. Putilov, A. Iu.
Rothstein, and L. F. Davydov.[130] The work did not progress rapidly.
Though actually a branch of the Russo-Chinese Bank, the Manchurian
Mining Company had a limited working capital of 1,000,000 rubles

until 1902. It financed some expeditions, took over some options, and operated one quarry and one coal-mining and one gold-mining enterprise in the Mukden region.[131]

Times were inauspicious for expansion. Not enough money was to be found for the new Manchurian enterprises. On July 5, 1902, at a shareholders' meeting of the Russo-Chinese Bank it was decided to issue an additional 20,000 shares of stock valued at 3,750,000 rubles; but the prospect of selling them on the open market was so bleak that the entire amount—actually a mere trifle in comparison with previous issues—was taken up by Witte for the Ministry of Finance.[132] With diminishing resources Witte did not have the opportunity to block off the best prospects in Manchuria for Russian or Russian-controlled capital. The Russo-Chinese Bank bought out the English-owned shares in the Anglo-Russian Exploration Company in July, 1902. The company was operating marginal gold properties in the vicinity of the Shanhaikwan-Newchwang railroad, so that the bank acquired a 90 per cent control; but these properties proved to be no asset.[133] Meanwhile, English and American engineers appeared on the Manchurian bank of the Amur River to examine mining and timber properties.[134] The situation looked ominous. Militarily Russia was evacuating Manchuria without leaving a firm economic hold on the country. Not only was the future position of Russia in Manchuria threatened, but competitors were already in the field. At this point Witte was almost ready to accept any measures to preserve Manchurian resources for future Russian exploitation. At this time Bezobrazov and the Yalu concession reappeared on the scene.

In the summer of 1902, when the C.E.R. and the Russo-Chinese Bank were more amenable to Russian private enterprise in Manchuria, there suddenly appeared not one, but three, Yalu concessions. Although the East Asiatic Development Company had apparently been dissolved by order of the Tsar in February, 1902, the Tsar still held the timber concession on the Korean bank of the Yalu and Tumen rivers, and its nominal owner, Matiunin, was in Manchuria with credit—from somewhere—of 75,000 rubles.[135] Matiunin was then a civilian and he might have been genuinely trying to sell the concession locally, but in order to preserve the rights on the concession he had to undertake annually some minor work of exploitation. It might have been that this credit was extended to him by the Tsar in order to get rid of the concession for some sum that would cut down the otherwise complete loss to the cabinet. Matiunin came in contact with two other promoters of concessions in Manchuria. Lieutenant Colonel A. S. Madritov of the General

Staff, then attached to Admiral Alexeev's staff, had obtained a timber concession on the right (Manchurian) bank of the Yalu by dubious means. According to the most nearly complete account of the transaction, in 1900 Madritov was in command of Russian troops which occupied the Mukden arsenal; he had traded the guns he had confiscated for a timber concession from the Governor General of Mukden.[136] This concession, like most of the others, was not properly delimited, was not ratified, and was not worked. But these "trifles" did not daunt the intrepid promoter. He had been inspired by P. A. Lvov, the holder of the third concession.

Lvov, by his own admission, had lost a million rubles in the financial crisis of 1899–1900 in industrial enterprises in southern Russia. In 1900 he had come to Manchuria to make a fortune.[137] He became an agent for a number of entrepreneurs and was backed by funds of the Ministry of Foreign Affairs, according to his own account.[138] At any rate, he obtained concessions on the right bank of the Yalu after spending some 107,000 rubles on bribes. These concessions were also unratified, undelineated, and unworked at the end of 1903. Lvov hit on the expedient plan to unite all the concessions into one company, in order to cut expenses and avoid competition. He suggested this to Madritov and Matiunin and perhaps others.[139] At the time, however, none of the concessions had a company to back it. They were still paper projects, frowned upon even by Alexeev,[140] and without representation in Peking to help the ratification of the local grants, or to promote in St. Petersburg the rather modest financing of a project which now was in keeping with Witte's policy in Manchuria and could therefore find funds for its realization. It must be recalled once more that the timber concessions on the Yalu had every chance for success and expansion, given reasonably honest and efficient exploitation.

Lvov returned to St. Petersburg in December, 1902, because of illness, but he still represented the promoters unofficially.[141] In the same month, Bezobrazov came to Manchuria on a special mission for the Tsar. He was apparently armed with a secret promise of the Tsar's support of state funds for promotion of "private" enterprises in Manchuria. With this support, and particularly after the state credit was given to him, Bezobrazov was able to change Alexeev's attitude, encourage the promoters of the Yalu concessions, and launch the Yalu concession scheme on the basis of actual exploitation for the first time since its inception.[142] The interests of all concerned were then converging upon the Yalu concession. Witte wanted private entrepreneurs with limited government aid, preferably through the Russo-Chinese

Bank, to obtain concessions in Manchuria. The Tsar wanted to maintain Russian prestige there and to convert his useless concession into a profitable enterprise. Bezobrazov resurrected his scheme for a holding company in which the Yalu concessions would be but one integral part. The Lvov-Madritov group held concessions which could be attached to the Matiunin (Tsar's) concession and which would render the Yalu concession free from dangerous competition. The actual launching of the project had to wait until Bezobrazov's eventful return to St. Petersburg.

In August, 1902, Witte was faced with a momentous decision in regard to the role of Russian enterprises in Manchuria. Probably at the suggestion of the Tsar, Witte made a personal visit to Manchuria and was away from the capital for two months.[143] On his trip to the Far East he visited only Manchuria, spending most of the time in Harbin and making only short visits to Dalny and Port Arthur. In October he returned with a long written report for the Tsar, most of which was soon made public.[144]

The report presented very little that was new in elucidating Russian policies in the Far East. It contained a large number of redundant platitudes on the great role of Russia in the Far East, the "world importance" of the Trans-Siberian and Manchurian railways, which "open the door between Europe and Asia," and similar fatuous phrases. It is no wonder then that Nicholas II, as Witte later claimed, paid little attention to it.[145] It glossed over or ignored all the points of criticism that could be leveled against the C.E.R. at the time, or against the current Russian policies in Manchuria. However, because the report was published soon after its presentation to the Tsar, it ranks as an official document indicating the latest Russian view on immediate and far-range policy in the Far East, and it deserves more than casual mention.

Witte considered the withdrawal from Manchuria essential because he felt that the country could not be properly colonized by Russia even in the distant future. The necessity of settling Siberia first, and the success which accompanied the settling of western Siberia precluded any large-scale settling of Manchuria, which Witte considered for many reasons impractical and impossible.[146] Russian policy toward Manchuria should consist of carrying out the Evacuation Agreement to the letter. The presence of the Russian army in Manchuria was not only creating international problems but was undermining Russian prestige and alienating the populace. Witte cited a number of instances which were detrimental to Russia's position, such as the occupation of large public buildings and private Chinese commercial buildings for the use of Russian troops and the refusal of the Russian controlled telegraph lines to send any messages in Chinese codes.[147] He recognized that the security of Russian railroads in Manchuria was still in jeopardy. Large bands of *khunhuzes,* perhaps 8,000 to 9,000 in Kirin province alone, were still rampant in the countryside, and the Chinese authorities alone could not cope with them successfully. Many of the bandits were the demobilized Chinese regulars of 1900 and many of them were better armed than the provincial police, whose rearmament had been closely controlled by the Russian military authorities.[148] However, Witte felt that the proposed increase of the Russian railroad guards to 25,000 men would solve the problem of security, for he found them very efficient. He personally directed one minor operation of these guards against the bandits, with "brilliant success."[149]

Witte recognized that there was a wide difference of opinion about whether Russia should evacuate Manchuria completely. He dismissed the argument with the statement that, after all, in case of need, Russia could immediately reoccupy Manchuria and have an excuse to establish a "normal Russian administration."[150] According to Witte, the most pressing problem was that of relations with Japan. He considered that in the event of war with Japan, Russia would of course be victorious, but a war would bring "dire" consequences to both countries. Therefore he felt that it would be better to "compromise" with Japan or Korea.[151] The report was very sketchy on the subject of Japan.

Witte presented no solution to the Manchurian problem and yet indicated the necessity of finding one. All previous policies had suffered defeat. The Chinese government would not sign a desirable separate agreement with the Russian government or with the Russo-Chinese Bank. The agencies of the Ministry of Finance were unable to guarantee Russian domination of the economic wealth of Manchuria through the exploitation of concessions. Private Russian enterprises fought shy of the region without official backing. There remained one other method—colonization. At all events, the whole question of Russian policy in the Far East was ready for revision.

The first step toward reconsideration of the problem of Manchuria was taken in a conference on November 9, 1902, at Yalta, where the Court and some of the ministers were spending their usual winter vacation. This conference was attended by the Ministers of Finance, War, Foreign Affairs, and the Interior. From the first, the ministers discarded the possibility of colonizing a strip along the C.E.R. unless Manchuria belonged to Russia or was bound to it by firmer ties. They agreed unanimously that in the future Manchuria must be annexed to Russia or be dependent upon it. This reopened the whole Manchurian problem. The journal of the conference further records:

But, in the opinion of the Minister of Finance, we must allow this process to take place in the course of historical events, without haste, and without forcing the natural course of events.

The Minister of War ... expressed the opinion that the longer we postpone the decision ... on the Manchurian question, the more difficult it will be to carry out this decision.[152]

The conference did not reach any agreement as to a policy, but the vagueness of the terms used in the journal implied the necessity of reëxamining the situation of Manchuria.

A thorough reëxamination of the problem took place first at a preliminary conference held by Lamsdorf at the Ministry of Foreign Affairs on January 24, 1903. By accident or design, all the three Russian ministers to the Far Eastern countries were present in the capital: A. I. Pavlov, the newly appointed R. R. Rosen, and P. M. Lessar,[153] ministers to Korea, Japan, and China, respectively. At this strictly ministerial conference there was unanimous agreement that the Evacuation Agreement of April 8, 1902, should be carried out, and almost in direct contradiction to this, that the evacuation could be delayed until the acceptance by China of certain guarantees of Russian rights and security in Manchuria. Lessar drew up a list of these guarantees, classifying them in two categories—essential and merely technical.[154] The subject of Korea apparently was not even brought up.

A reëxamination of the Far Eastern policy as a whole was then taken up at a special conference on February 7, by an imposing array of ministers, diplomatic envoys, and experts of the Ministry of Foreign Affairs. Lamsdorf presided, and in attendance were Witte, Kuropatkin, Admiral Tyrtov, Pavlov, Rosen, Lessar, and Prince Obolenskii, the Director of the Chancellery of the Ministry of Foreign Affairs.[155] This conference represented the highest policy-making body that could be selected for Russia's Far Eastern policy. The journal of the main views and resolutions of the conference, which was signed by the four ministers present and Prince Obolenskii, was approved by the Tsar and can therefore be considered the statement of the basic Russian policy in the Far East in the spring of 1903.

In the first place, the conference discussed Russia's relations with Japan. Lamsdorf revealed that on August 4, 1902, Japan had suggested to Russia, through her minister at St. Petersburg, that the previous Russo-Japanese agreements be annulled and a new agreement formulated on the basis of the recognition of Japan's paramount interest in Korea in return for Japan's recognition of Russia's paramount interests in Manchuria.[156] The journal does not reveal what the Japanese terms were in regard to Korea. Lamsdorf felt that they were too demanding, "in view of the great importance which Korea will unavoidably have for Russian national interests in the future."[157] Witte then brought forth his former thesis of "neutralization of Korea," which Kuropatkin rather indelicately ruled as immaterial in view of the Japanese proposal for a mutual obligation not to utilize any Korean territory for military or strategic purposes. Tyrtov was also against any concessions to the Japanese which would restrict the Russians' use of Masampo as a temporary naval station for training purposes when climatic conditions hindered training at Port Arthur. Rosen strongly counseled against any attempts to acquire Korean territory, because that inevitably would lead to war, and he expressed the opinion that, under the existing circumstances, seizure of Korea by the Japanese was unlikely. It was finally agreed that an agreement with Japan would be desirable, and that the most pressing needs of the moment were the establishment of a clearly defined policy toward Korea, and "a complete unanimity in the actions of all ministries and their local representatives and agents." It was furthermore agreed that the best results in negotiations would be attained if Russia would wait for Japan to reopen the negotiations even on the basis of the note of August 4.[158]

On the subject of Manchuria, widely different opinions were expressed during the discussion. The principal purpose of the conference was to discuss the guarantees of Lessar's project, which had already been adopted by the Conference of January 24. In a discussion of the possibility of including with the guarantee a provision forbidding additional Chinese settlers to buy land within a prescribed distance of the Russian railroads in Manchuria, Witte came out strongly against its inclusion on the grounds that this would be impossible to enforce, and that the forbidden strip could not be settled by Russian colonists even in the foreseeable future.[159] He counseled that this question be scrupulously avoided, as its mere mention might lead the Chinese government to take measures to settle northern Manchuria and Mongolia merely to forestall future Russian colonization. In general, Lessar agreed with Witte and regarded as necessary only the measures dealing with the security of the Russian railroads in Manchuria.

Then Kuropatkin brought up opinions that were undoubtedly distasteful to Witte. He claimed, quite needlessly, that the Chinese settlement of northern Manchuria had been hastened by the Russian

railroads in Manchuria and stated that he feared that in the near
future even the Maritime Province would become mostly Chinese. The
C.E.R. had been actually serving Chinese interests by furthering the
settlement of northern Manchuria and helping to develop the country,
and it had made the defense of Russian Far Eastern possessions more
difficult. Kuropatkin spoke strictly as Minister of War charged with
the problem of the defense of the Empire, emphasizing that this was
the most important of all his duties, and that in such a position he
must look upon Manchuria as partly Russian.[160] The complete security
of the trans-Manchurian railroad must be his first consideration, otherwise Russia must build a railroad along the Amur River to its possessions in the Far East, an enormous task of construction and defense
stretching over 2,400 versts as compared with 1,200 versts of the trans-
Manchurian line. He saw no other solution than to absorb northern
Manchuria; that is, all of the province of Heilungkiang and the better
part of the province of Kirin from—and including—the Korean-
Chinese town of Hunchun to the junction of the Nonni and Sungari
rivers. This absorption was to take the form of direct annexation or an
establishment of a protectorate like the one over Bukhara. Southern
Manchuria could be given up because, even if Kwantung were cut off
from Russia, it was well supplied and could stand a siege of eighteen
months.

As for immediate policy, Kuropatkin considered it vitally necessary
to delay the evacuation of the southern part of the province of Kirin,
which was scheduled for completion by April 8, 1903, because of winter
conditions unfavorable to the movement of troops. This stage of the
evacuation was to be delayed for at least several months. The evacuation of northern Manchuria would depend upon the results of the evacuation of the southern area. At all events, however, Russian military
detachments[161] should be retained along the railroad and small ones
kept in some places along the Chinese bank of the Amur and Ussuri
rivers. Because of this requirement, Kuropatkin considered the Russian demand of guarantees "too modest."[162]

Lamsdorf completely disagreed with the General, because such a
policy would inevitably arouse the hostility of China and Japan, which
was already evident in their displeasure over the slow progress of
Russian evacuation. And at this point Witte took the opportunity to
criticize Kuropatkin by stating, rather indelicately, that there could
be no comparison between the situation in Bukhara and that in northern
Manchuria, since Bukhara was at the time of its absorption completely
isolated and independent. Lessar also supported the Lamsdorf-Witte

opposition by pointing out that even a temporary prolongation of the occupation period would arouse as much hostility as the occupation of all of Manchuria. He also counseled strict adherence to the Evacuation Agreement because otherwise negotiations with China on the guarantees would be rendered more difficult, and because, if the evacuation was not carried out in time and was completed later under a storm of international protests, it would appear as though Russia had been forced out of Manchuria.[163]

It seems as though the Conference disagreed on the Manchurian question, but actually the basic disagreement was on an entirely different matter. Kuropatkin spoke as Minister of War charged with the defense of Russian territory in the Far East, and as such, he saw the major danger to Russia's position in the progress of Chinese settlement of northern Manchuria, a concern held by Russian military analysts since the 1880's. Lamsdorf and Witte, discussing the Manchurian question on an immediate and international level, refused to consider the remote, though perhaps inevitable, menace from China.

On the problem of guarantees to be demanded from China there was no disagreement. All of Lessar's projected terms were accepted, with two conditions, suggested by Kuropatkin, which would be presented only if the first group of demands were accepted without complications. It was decided to delay the second phase of the evacuation, in accordance with Kuropatkin's desires, until there were better climatic conditions for the movement of troops. Also, it was decided to make the evacuation of the port of Inkou conditional on the acceptance of the first three Russian terms.[164]

The exact terms, later known as the "Seven Demands," have never been published, although several published versions exist, which agree in general content.[165] The final version as sent to G. A. Planson, Russian chargé d'affaires at Peking, contained the following eight points:

1. The territory evacuated by Russia should not be alienated through cession, lease, or any other form, to any other power.

2. The Chinese Government will not establish any new treaty ports in Manchuria without the consent of Russia.

3. If China should appoint a foreigner to head any administrative organ, the affairs of that part of northern China where Russian interests predominate will be removed from that agency and placed under a special agency headed by a Russian.[166]

These terms were considered essential and were intended to restore the *status quo ante* the Boxer uprising, except for the reservation that on the resignation of Sir Robert Hart, the Director of the Chinese Imperial Maritime Customs, the customs administrations of Manchuria,

Mongolia, and Sinkiang would be headed by a Russian. This was not an unreasonable demand. However, there was a noticeable concession on the first point in that no Russian monopoly in Manchuria was projected. The point specified "powers" and not "subjects of foreign powers."

The second group was of lesser consequence and contained some measures of only a temporary nature:

4. All rights acquired by the Russians during the occupation of Manchuria will be recognized after the evacuation. In addition, Russia is empowered to take sanitary measures along the railroad line.

5. Russia will retain for its military use the Port Arthur–Inkou–Mukden telegraph line as long as the Peking-Inkou line exists.

6. The customs commissar and doctor at Inkou shall be a Russian subject, and the administration and sanitary commission composed of the consuls shall be retained.

7. After the evacuation of the Russian troops the Inkou branch of the Russo-Chinese Bank will continue to function as the agency of the customs.

8. The present form of administration in Mongolia will be retained.

Obviously, some points—the fourth, for example—were purposely left vague. Did that point refer to all concessions acquired from local authorities and yet unratified by Peking? Except as a general sketch of Russian maximum demands obviously scheduled for some reductions in the negotiations, this group of terms and Kuropatkin's two security measures are unimportant.

The Russian government exhibited an unusual dilatoriness in presenting these demands. The conference approved them on February 7, and the Tsar must have approved them almost immediately, for on January 13 he had expressed himself as favoring the suspension of evacuation.[167] The approved project was sent to Planson, and he sent back his revised edition on March 26. Lamsdorf sent him the final approval on April 15. At some point during this interchange, the eighth point, on Mongolia, was dropped, and Planson submitted the "Seven Demands" to Prince Ching on April 18.[168]

The Chinese, on their part, showed unusual celerity. Since it took two days to encode, transmit, and decode a diplomatic message between Peking and St. Petersburg, the Chinese reply to this important matter was dispatched with almost undignified and insulting haste. The Chinese government did not have to wait for the expression of an international reaction toward such proposals. It could count beforehand on the general support of most of the powers in its opposition to any Russian demands. Therefore on April 22, merely four days after the presentation of the "Seven Demands," the Chinese Ambassador at St.

Petersburg presented to Lamsdorf his country's reply—a categorical refusal to discuss any terms until the completion of the evacuation of Manchuria.[169] This was the fourth and most bitter refusal of the Chinese to accept a Russian solution for the Manchurian problem.

The relentless Russian search for a favorable solution of the Manchurian problem had met with an adamant Chinese wall, strongly buttressed by international support. For Russia there remained only two alternatives: (1) to get out of Manchuria according to the terms of the Evacuation Agreement and leave behind a political condition which was obviously hostile to Russia and which perhaps would become even more aggressively hostile because of the Chinese "triumph" in forcing Russia to abide by the Agreement without qualifying terms, or (2) to veer in the direction suggested by Kuropatkin in the Conference of February 7: by suspending the evacuation, wait for a future chance and disregard the international implications of such a measure. The only danger could come from Japan; and a deal might be made with Japan concerning Korea.

At the same time, Russia could allay international hostility by adopting the attitude suggested by point one of the "Seven Demands"—that Manchuria should in reality be administered by the Chinese and should be kept in line with the open-door doctrine. In the meantime, Russian occupation of Manchuria would continue. On April 26, 1903, in another special conference, Witte and Lamsdorf withdrew their objections and agreed to continue the occupation of northern Manchuria.[170] B. A. Romanov in his latest work characterizes this as the "new course" (always in quotation marks).[171] It was not a change from the political pressure applied to China since the occupation of Manchuria in 1900, but it was unquestionably new in that the policy was now accepted by all the ministers without equivocation. Russia would not abide by the Evacuation Agreement, Russia would "wait and see." The main concern now was to avoid friction with Japan.

IX

THE DRIFT TOWARD WAR

In December, 1902, Bezobrazov probably stood higher in the Tsar's favor than at any other time. During the Tsar's customary winter vacation at Livadia, Bezobrazov was present when Witte returned from the Far East with his vague and unsatisfactory report. Favorably impressed by Bezobrazov's sincerity and unequivocal manner of speaking, the Tsar listened to him if only to while away his idle moments. Bezobrazov's honesty was unquestionable; his service as a special agent for the Governor General of Western Siberia for two years had given him the experience necessary for special assignments concerning promotion and investigation of economic enterprises.[1] His interest in the Far East was also well confirmed. It is natural, therefore, that the Tsar regarded Bezobrazov as an "authority," and that he, possibly dissatisfied with Witte's report, decided to send Bezobrazov to the Far East to investigate the conditions there and to report on what measures Russia ought to take to maintain her position, which was advantageous so long it was preserved by occupation.

Before his departure from St. Petersburg, Bezobrazov had a conversation in mid-December with Kuropatkin which graphically reveals some of the characteristics of this "omniscient" bureaucrat. He spoke of his frequent conversations in Livadia, prefacing his statements with the words, "I and the Emperor," "I and Witte and Lamsdorf." In Kuropatkin's words, Bezobrazov's rather pointless conversation could be summed up as "Everything is confused, nobody understands anything, and only he [Bezobrazov] is saving Russian affairs."[2]

The "New Course" of Russian Policy and the Fall of Witte

Bezobrazov must have had an understanding with the Tsar, although the Imperial decision could have been made after the Tsar had received some of Bezobrazov's convincing reports from the Far East. At any rate, on February 1, 1903, Witte received a note from the Tsar with the following instructions: "Order by telegraph the opening to Alexander Mikhailovich Bezobrazov of a credit of two million rubles in the Russo-Chinese Bank at Port Arthur. He probably will not avail himself of the entire amount, but this credit is necessary to give weight and significance to his mission."[3] This was an order which Witte could not refuse, although it was contrary to his wishes and to his policy of

---

[1] For notes to chap. ix see pp. 305–313.

keeping the promotion of Russian interests in the Far East firmly in his own hands through the Russo-Chinese Bank. It was also contrary to his views expressed at a meeting of the Siberian Committee on January 8, 1903, when he urged the greatest possible economy and a retrenchment policy because of the financial crisis in Russia.[4]

From Bezobrazov's actions in the Far East it is possible to determine the true nature of his mission. It was to promote Russian prestige as he saw fit. The variety of interests which Bezobrazov encouraged, either by promises or by funds, and the careful execution of his mission attest to this fact. The details of some of the transactions are not clear, but from the report submitted to the Tsar by Bezobrazov on his return, the following facts are noted: Bezobrazov gave 40,000 rubles for the expansion of the Russian hospital at Mukden; he gave 35,000 rubles to the chauvinistic Russian newspaper *Novyi Krai* of Port Arthur to start a newspaper or journal in English to offset the anti-Russian propaganda of the English journals in the Far East;[5] he formed a project to unify several private Russian collieries and some Chinese collieries at Fushun and thus develop the coal mines so that Russia could export coal from Dalny to other points in the Far East instead of importing Japanese coal. He started projects for the purchase of 250 square versts near Fushun for Russian agricultural settlements. He began negotiations with the Governor General of Mukden for permission to build an electric-power plant in Mukden and to organize an electric tramway service there.[6] He also planned to establish a Russian navigation company for the Liao River and from Port Arthur to the mouth of the Yalu.[7]

These were all to be undertaken simultaneously and to be interwoven with his activity in regard to the Yalu concession. There is no reason to believe that the Yalu concession was Bezobrazov's main concern, but it was the most advanced of the larger projects and the most important historically. Bezobrazov on his arrival found the Tsar's Yalu concession merged, on paper, with the Lvov and Madritov concessions on the Manchurian bank and still unratified. Matiunin and Lvov were then in St. Petersburg and Colonel Madritov was occupied with Army duties; the merger was then under the guidance of Baron G. G. Ginsburg, a Jewish promoter, speculator, and "man of affairs," a director of the Russo-Chinese Bank, and the chief contractor for the Russian Pacific squadron.[8] The group was hardly able to stay together. Matiunin and some private members of the group wanted to sell the concession rights to the Japanese, but Lvov apparently stopped them. Madritov, who had not spent a penny, wanted to sell his part to the English commercial house of Bush and Company of Newchwang, but Lvov, according to his own account, dissuaded Madritov. There were no operations except the annual cutting prescribed by law in order to fulfill the terms of the concession contract. No funds were available, and Ginsburg supposedly spent 70,000 rubles of his own in the month and a half of his nominal control of the merger.[9] There actually was no working company. The only tangible organization was built around the provisional agreement between Lvov and the *daotai* (subgovernor) of Fenghwangcheng, the southeastern division of the Mukden (Fengtien) province. This agreement of December 28, 1902, had been signed by the *daotai*, and in 1903 it was probably resting among the other unratified agreements at the Chinese Ministry of Foreign Affairs in Peking.[10]

When Bezobrazov in the Far East took up the matter of the Yalu concession, he naturally took over Lvov's project, for it was a thoroughly detailed scheme outlining even the salaries and the names of the principal participants and employees. This half-approved project for a Russo-Chinese timber joint-stock company should be examined in some detail, for it not only illustrates a typical organization of a concession in a backward country such as Korea or Manchuria but, with certain changes, it apparently became the backbone of the Yalu enterprise when it was fully launched by Bezobrazov.

Both the Lvov project and the idea which Bezobrazov modeled from the defunct East Asiatic Development Company project planned to finance the company from public shares, reserving a large portion of founders' shares for the owners of the concessions and the founders of the company. The idea of securing patrons and connections in high places was also in the Lvov scheme. Like most concessions in backward areas,[11] the Lvov agreement provided for armed guards and for thinly disguised bribes to local officials and Chinese officials who would help in the formation of the company. All these measures are found in article 27 of the Financial Plan of the projects,[12] which is here summarized from Lvov's text.

FINANCIAL PLAN
(In Rubles)
ANNUAL SALARIES OF THE DIRECTORATE

Chairman: the Governor General of Mukden 24,000
Vice-Chairman: the Military Governor of Mukden 15,000
President: Admiral ABAZA, Assistant to the Director of the Department
    of the Merchant Fleet 30,000
Vice-President: State Counselor MATIUNIN 20,000

General Manager: Lvov	18,000
One Director representing the Russo-Chinese Bank and one Director representing Ginsburg and Company (each 8,000)	16,000

OTHER EXPENDITURES

Manager of the Timber Concession: Skidel'skii......................	9,000
Editor of *Izvestia Vostochnago Kraia*	15,000
Forestry Guards:	
Commander, a Retired Colonel[13]...................................	9,000
Chinese Assistant	3,000
180 Chinese at 15 rubles a month..................................	32,400
60 Russians at 30 rubles a month..................................	21,600
Publication of the newspaper......................................	40,000

The Lvov Agreement went so far as to include in the text the expected income from the founders' shares. It was therefore also a prospectus to encourage ratification. Appended to the financial plan were the initials of persons who were to receive rewards for helping to form the company. A total of 150,000 rubles cash was to go to five Chinese "helpers" and 120,000 rubles to three Russian founders of the company. In the prospectus the Governor General of Mukden was promised 24,000 rubles a year as a salary, 10,000 rubles income from 400 founder shares, and 6,000 rubles from "bonuses." Prospective incomes of other persons were also mentioned.[14]

As soon as Bezobrazov took charge of the enterprise he made some changes. He summarily ousted Ginsburg from control,[15] disregarded Lvov's position in the company and the one-third share promised him by Matiunin,[16] and nominated Colonel Madritov for the post of "Commander of the Forestry Guard."[17] No doubt Bezobrazov envisaged himself as the general manager instead of Lvov. He earmarked 180,000 rubles of his available fund for the construction of a sawmill at the mouth of the Yalu,[18] and he began to make plans for sending the first large expedition to the concession area in the near future. He soon met with opposition.

Actually, Bezobrazov was working under several handicaps and restrictions. Alexeev was at first hostile to his schemes, for he was an advocate of Russian withdrawal from Korea and southern Manchuria. The Director of the Navy Department, Admiral P. P. Tyrtov, was on his deathbed. Admiral Alexeev hoped to succeed him in the department; understandably he was not very much interested in Bezobrazov's promotion schemes.[19] Bezobrazov, through his cousin, A. M. Abaza, in St. Petersburg, reported his actions to the Tsar, and Abaza telegraphed Bezobrazov, about March 16, that he was not to spend more than 300,000 rubles for his enterprises without the specific permission of the Tsar.[20] He must even account for the 300,000 rubles on his return. In the same telegram, Abaza mentioned that the Tsar approved "in principle" of Bezobrazov's plan for the expedition. This was, however, less than decisive support for the essential feature of the plan for the Yalu concession. In addition, no registered company had been formed to handle the business of the enterprise.

In regard to the Manchurian enterprises and even the Yalu project, Bezobrazov's activity may be considered regular, proper, and natural so far as imperialistic enterprises go; however, his personal conduct cannot be considered in the same light. It indicated his main traits of character. Bezobrazov acted in an overweening manner. He gave interviews to newspapers in which he expressed chauvinistic ideas. He talked dogmatically and didactically to all and sundry on grand strategy, naval tactics, Russia's mission in the Far East and the Near East, and whatever else his unquestionably active and agile mind might pounce upon.[21] He traveled around in a special car accompanied by an organized staff, and in every way and at all times encouraged the idea that he was acting with the official backing of the Tsar.[22] In this way he gained the full coöperation of Alexeev toward the end of his stay in the Far East.[23]

Bezobrazov's plan for the first expedition was an ingenious one and was "normal" under the circumstances. Every year the army discharged a large number of soldiers who had served their five-year term. After long separation from their families, these men, with elementary, varied, and semiskilled training acquired during their service, usually constituted a valuable labor force which was available for many jobs in the Russian economy. They made ideal police recruits, forestry guards, and foremen and were particularly good as nonagricultural workers. Including those from the large Russian garrisons in Manchuria and the Kwantung leased territory since 1900, there must have been thousands of soldiers released each year. They were men who, with the prospect of good pay, would be willing to work even under the frontier conditions existing on the Yalu, and who were trained to handle arms if need be. Arms, too, could be made readily available. It was perfectly "normal" for foreigners in the hinterland of China, Korea, and other backward areas of the world to carry arms. Bezobrazov's plan accordingly envisaged the recruitment of these men for his working artels (gangs or units). The men were, to be sure, technically reservists, but that term did not mean that they were in the military service. They were merely discharged soldiers or soldiers awaiting their official discharge and transportation after the expiration of their term of service.

However, in organizing this artel, Bezobrazov was apparently so successful that he telegraphed to Abaza, with his usual frankness, his intention to increase the number from three hundred to six hundred, and Abaza asked Kuropatkin on March 14 to mention his approval of this measure to the Tsar. On this matter there was a misunderstanding, caused either by Abaza's or Bezobrazov's loose terminology in regard to the composition of the *artel*. Kuropatkin had the impression that it would be comprised of men in active service, and stated that he had no idea that even three hundred had been recruited from the lower ranks.[24] In clearing up the matter, it was necessary to communicate with the Tsar, Lamsdorf, Pavlov in Seoul, and Alexeev at Port Arthur. The outcome was that Bezobrazov was permitted to recruit the discharged reservist soldiers of the lower ranks, and Alexeev was ordered to see that no one on active duty be allowed to take part in the undertaking. At the same time, the Tsar and Kuropatkin agreed to permit the issue of rifles from the depots of Port Arthur to the members of the artel for their "personal" use.[25]

The mention of "personal" use[26] possibly referred to Bezobrazov's scheme to utilize the Manchurian *khunhuzes* for his purposes—a scheme he probably mentioned to the Tsar in his reports previous to the first document now available on this subject. In early March the "new course" had not been decided upon. The nearest Russian garrison to the Yalu at Fenghwangcheng was scheduled for withdrawal in compliance with the Evacuation Agreement. Bezobrazov, foreseeing that event, adopted the "normal" imperialistic and concessionary expedient of hiring some of the *khunhuzes* to guard the work of the concession against other *khunhuzes;* this was a common action. The *khunhuzes,* usually former Boxers and former Chinese soldiers, were still active in the three Manchurian provinces;[27] therefore Bezobrazov's plan was a necessary, logical, and practical one. Possibly the mention of the issue of rifles for "personal" use implied that Bezobrazov was not to get arms with which to arm the *khunhuzes* in his pay. The statement by the Tsar during his conversation with Kuropatkin on March 17 that Bezobrazov had been "overzealous" and that he had already decided to call him back[28] gives weight to this theory.

However, the Tsar did not call Bezobrazov back immediately. At St. Petersburg, near the end of March, Kuropatkin learned that

Alexeev had no intention of giving Bezobrazov three hundred reservists but had allowed him a maximum of forty, and that Bezobrazov had refused this number. Abaza informed Kuropatkin that
Bezobrazov could now do without the reservists, since he had hired
khunhuzes to provide protection for the enterprise. It is probable that
the Tsar's decision to recall Bezobrazov was in large part influenced
by the fact that his special envoy continued to cause trouble by his
"overzealous" outbursts. Bezobrazov had sent the Tsar an "Appreciation of the Situation" which was uncalled for and in which Bezobrazov, in his usual manner, expounded his views on the strategical
deployment of troops on the Korean frontier, the lines of communication, operational bases, and the necessity of strategical vanguards.
Although Kuropatkin in his diary labeled the "Appreciation" "arrant
nonsense," such ideas were dangerous when propounded by the irre-
pressible Bezobrazov.[29]

Very soon after the receipt of the "Appreciation," about March
22, the Tsar recalled Bezobrazov. After leaving Port Arthur on April
2, Bezobrazov stopped en route at Harbin and had a conference with
the leading engineers of the C.E.R. in which he once again over-
stepped the bounds of his official capacity.[30] Iugovich reported to
Witte the following summary of Bezobrazov's harangue:

> Bezobrazov finds that Manchuria should belong to us in any case, also that it is
> not worth while to deal with the Chinese in any way. Finding that we command
> in Manchuria a considerably impressive force, Bezobrazov thinks it useless and
> unnecessary to aim at the reconstruction of legal relations based on the correct
> respect of rights. On the contrary, he considers that the only correct system is the
> insistence on demands based on our realization of our armed superiority. With the
> help of the Russian guards, Bezobrazov, according to his own words, hopes to
> establish connections with the leaders of the *khunhuzes* rampant in these parts,
> to take advantage of these connections for action and influence on the local Chinese
> officials if the latter should show opposition to the successful realization of the
> exploitation of the forest products in the valley of Yalu-tsian. On the questionable
> power of the *khunhuzes* Bezobrazov depends for the opposition to the beginnings
> of international commercial enterprises.[31]

Of course such views did not enter into Bezobrazov's official report
to the Tsar, which was a massive conglomeration of sense and nonsense.[32] Apparently it was so long that the Tsar may not have wanted
to read it and ordered Bezobrazov to make a summary of it. But even
in the summary Bezobrazov could not restrain himself from his usual
observations and ramblings on irrelevant and immaterial subjects.
After listing the enterprises he had "started," and discussing his
appointee I. P. Balashev,[33] Bezobrazov expounded his views on the

Turkish straits, the Macedonian question, German policy, British policy, and so forth, all in very general and quite elementary terms. He also discussed at some length, but vaguely, the causes of Russia's lack of success in the Far East, mentioning among the causes the lack of unanimity among the agencies and the lack of correct information and proper evaluation of the situation. The complete report, however, might have contained more substantial and specific information.[34]

Without awaiting Bezobrazov's return—perhaps even to forestall his interference—the matter of the Yalu concessions was brought up for discussion at another special conference on April 8, 1903. This conference was specifically formed to discuss the Yalu concessions and their possible role in Russia's relations with Japan. This conference took place before the Russian "Seven Demands" were submitted to the Chinese government, and consequently before the adoption of the "new course" which envisaged appeasement of Japan in order to avert open opposition to the continued occupation of northern Manchuria. Therefore the decisions of this conference were reached in a period of prospective calm in which no external complications were expected.

The conference was held on the highest level. Ordered by the Tsar to examine the Yalu project, particularly with reference to some of Bezobrazov's schemes, the ministers discussed these schemes as presented in a memorandum specially prepared for the conference by Admiral Abaza. The Grand Duke General-Admiral Alexei Alexandrovich (titular head of the Navy Department), Witte, Kuropatkin, Lamsdorf, and Plehve participated in the conference. Abaza apparently took no part in the discussion, after reading the introductory memorandum.[35]

First of all, the "triumvirate" of Witte, Kuropatkin, and Lamsdorf completely demolished Bezobrazov's plan to have the Yalu concession and its artel of reservists play a strategic defensive part against Japanese economic and military penetration of northern Korea.[36] Kuropatkin stated that even if it were possible to create such a cordon or barrier it would have no strategic significance whatsoever. Kuropatkin did not deny that the concession might have some function. Earlier, in December, 1902, he had expressed his view to Abaza, Bezobrazov, and the Tsar that by keeping the concession and not doing much with it, Russia could have a "neutral zone" in northern Korea where neither the Russians nor the Japanese would penetrate and produce friction. This he labeled at the time a "dog in the manger" policy. The Tsar

expressed his approval of this view in a conversation with Kuropatkin held on December 30, 1902, stating that "by no means should this
business (the Yalu concession) cause us any complications."[37] The
views of the General-Admiral and Plehve on this point are not recorded.[38] It was unanimously decided that the company exploiting the
concession should be purely commercial in character, although it would
require some support from the government.[39]

A more clearly defined Russian policy toward Korea and Manchuria
and the nature of the company's support can be deduced from the
decisions of the conference, reached without any sharp difference of
opinion. It was decided:

1. That the Ministry of Foreign Affairs should examine the legal rights of the
concession and affirm them.

2. That the Ministry of Foreign Affairs should obtain from the Chinese Government similar rights on the Manchurian bank of the Yalu.

3. That both concessions should be united under a Russian enterprise.[40]

These three measures were actually routine. Naturally, the agencies
of the Ministry of Foreign Affairs abroad were at the service of
Russian nationals legitimately interested in points 1 and 2, and point
3 was a routine internal matter.

4. To permit the participation of foreign capital (American, French, and Belgian) in the enterprise.

5. To permit the participation of the Treasury in the enterprise, but only to a
limited extent.

This was in line with the policy Witte had adopted in mid-1902
when he formed the Manchurian Mining Company with a vast number
of concessions and a small indirect government subsidy of 1,000,000
rubles. The failure of private capital to venture into the Manchurian
field had led him to suggest in January and February, 1903, that
Vonliarliarskii undertake the exploitation of some of these concessions
with foreign capital to which Vonliarliarskii supposedly had access.[41]
At the conference Witte readily accepted both points 4 and 5. The next
points were:

6. To limit the activity of the enterprise to the Yalu River basin.

7. To give the Commander of the Kwantung Leased Territory administrative
powers over both [Korean and Manchurian] concessions.[42]

Point 7 was suggested by Kuropatkin and was definitely not to
Witte's liking. However, Witte made no protest. Kuropatkin had
previously disagreed in a friendly fashion with Witte's idea of cen-
tralization;[43] point 7 was accordingly a part of Kuropatkin's decen-

tralization idea and inadvertently fitted into Bezobrazov's plans, which had by then also received the support of Alexeev, the commander mentioned.

The program outlined was quite specific. It was in full agreement with the wishes of the Tsar, who approved it on April 18 with the exception of point 6, which remained unsettled.[44] It was on that day that the Russian "Seven Demands" were presented to Prince Ching and were rejected almost immediately. About that date, the indomitable Bezobrazov returned from the Far East to influence the Tsar once again with his ebullient personality. The situation was then changed, for the Chinese rejection forced Russia to adopt the "new course" and the Manchurian part of the program became unrealizable. Kuropatkin was sent to the Far East to acquaint himself with the situation and was told by the Tsar "to efface the traces of Bezobrazov's activities."[45] In general, however, the program still represented the accepted policy, and Kuropatkin took a copy of the Journal of the Conference of April 8 with him to discuss it with Alexeev in detail.[46]

Kuropatkin left on April 28, and Bezobrazov's eloquence and persuasion again made headway. Nicholas II had a recognized failing of accepting the views of the person who had last talked to him. At that time Witte's influence was already on the wane, partly because of the apparent shortcomings of his economic policies, and partly because, with the passage of years, the Tsar was gaining self-assurance and resented Witte's strong position. Lamsdorf, the reticent member of the "triumvirate," exercised little inflence. Kuropatkin was therefore the strongest member of the responsible ministers, and his absence in the Far East gave Bezobrazov the opportunity to exert his influence on the Tsar.

Two events occurred on May 15 which were of significance in promoting this influence, or which might be considered proof of the influence. The Tsar appointed Bezobrazov to the bureaucratic rank of state secretary.[47] Almost everyone who has studied this period of Russian history has taken this to be a sign of favoritism, the triumph of the "behind the scenes diplomacy," and the acceptance of Bezobrazov's ideas by the Tsar. However, this interpretation is questionable. In the first place, the title state secretary is a designation of bureaucratic rank and not an official post.[48] It was held by many— perhaps dozens—of persons serving various ministries and certain departments within the State Council. What is completely ignored by writers is that sometime before June 13, 1903, Bezobrazov was given an official post in the Chancellery of the State Council as assistant to State Secretary Pokrovskii, the Director of the Department of Industry, Science, and Commerce.[49] The appointment of May 15 therefore was made either to give Bezobrazov a rank commensurate with his post after his appointment to the State Council, or was made before the appointment in order to make him eligible, and equal in rank with his colleagues in that position. In view of Bezobrazov's past services and his sound views on the strictly economic affairs of the Far East, there is no reason to consider him unqualified for the position or rank. The appointment of May 15 must therefore be regarded as a routine matter; it was in no way a spectacular advancement. However, it clearly demonstrated that the Tsar and Bezobrazov were in accord on many matters, and it can be considered a mark of high favor which Bezobrazov enjoyed, but not an expression of favoritism.

The second event was the dispatch of a telegram from the Tsar to Alexeev, which B. A. Romanov claims was sent without the knowledge of the ministers.[50] The telegram was in the form of a directive.[51] It directed Alexeev (1) to "give support to the wide activity of the Russian entrepreneurs in Manchuria . . . especially in those regions which might be considered important in a military and political sense," and (2) "in a minimum time, and without concern over the necessary expenditures, to put our military preparedness in the Far East in equilibrium with our political-economic aims, thus giving an obvious proof to everyone of our decisions to defend our rights to the exclusive influence in Manchuria." Yet these directives were to be followed "in connection with our final decision to comply with the agreement of April 8, 1902"; that is, the Evacuation Agreement. Such a directive must have put Alexeev in a quandary. In fact, the Tsar must have been somewhat confused when he (or Bezobrazov) wrote it, for it indicates a decision to evacuate Manchuria and yet counsels activity foreign to the idea of evacuation. In all probability the intent was to present a bold front to the world, particularly to possible enemies in the Far East, and to take maximum advantage of the presence of Russian troops in Manchuria before the eventful evacuation. Such an interpretation is in line with the "new course" adopted in April and envisaged in the Conference of February 7, 1903.

The confusion in the mind of the Tsar probably had more to do with the next step toward the launching of the Yalu concession scheme than did the importunations of Bezobrazov. On May 20, the Tsar called another special conference on Far Eastern affairs and the Yalu concession enterprise. This was an exceptional meeting in that the Tsar was present, although he said nothing,[52] and no journal was kept. In view of the serious differences of opinions expressed, it was decided that those present should submit their views in writing to Bezobrazov, who in turn would make a summary of them.[53] The story of the conference was therefore presented in the journal of the conference in Bezobrazov's words. This journal was sent to the participants, who made many changes and corrections; Bezobrazov, however, did not incorporate these changes and corrections in the journal but appended them to it in the form of notes.[54] The journal, signed only by Bezobrazov, was then sent to the Tsar.

The history of the conference and the reliability of its documents is therefore disputed. However, it seems to be clear that the conferees decided that it would be "desirable" to include Manchuria in the Russian sphere of political and economic influence but that under the contemporary conditions it would have been impossible to obtain the Manchurian counterpart of the Korean concession. Points 4 and 5 of the decisions of the conference of April 8 were accepted. The Yalu enterprise would not be restricted to timber resources only—a slight extension of point 6—and the role of Alexeev would be expanded to include supervision of other enterprises besides the work in the Yalu basin.[55] In short, this was an official sanction for the restoration of something in the nature of the East Asiatic Development Company.

On June 13 the Russian Timber Company of the Far East was legally formed in St. Petersburg, but as a private, not joint-stock, company, in which shares and profits would be apportioned by private agreement. The aims of the company, as stated in its charter, were "to exploit in the territory of Manchuria, Korea, and the Maritime Province, all types of timber concessions, mineral resources, fisheries, and fur trade enterprises, navigation, trade, and all types of other industrial and commercial enterprises."[56] Consequently it was to be a holding company of the modern "development" type. Some of the registered participants of the company were well known: Count A. P. Ignatiev; General P. P. Hesse, Commander of the Palace; Count V. A. Gendrikov, Master of Ceremonies; Rear Admiral A. M. Abaza; Prince F. F. Iusupov; V. M. Vonliarliarskii; N. G. Matiunin; and Colonel M. A. Serebriakov, Acting Colonel of the Chevalier Guards. The connection with the old East Asiatic Development Company could be clearly perceived. The old company was resurrected. I. P. Balashev was named manager in the Far East, and Abaza and Vonliarliarskii, managers at St. Petersburg. Bezobrazov's name was nowhere mentioned.[57] Nevertheless he continued to act in the interest of the group which formed the company and early in June, 1903, succeeded in persuading Witte to join the interests of the Manchurian Mining Company with those of a group formed by Bezobrazov in March in order to exploit jointly the Fushun collieries.[58]

Bezobrazov served in a capacity similar to that of the present-day "coördinator." He coördinated the interests of the investment group in St. Petersburg with the actual work at the concession in the Far East. Thus, on June 16, he was again sent out to the Far East by order of the Tsar to "coördinate" the Tsar's views with those of Alexeev, Kuropatkin, Vogak, the Russian ministers to the Far Eastern countries, and others.[59] This was the purpose of the so-called Port Arthur conferences, of which there were sixteen sessions, July 1–10, 1903.

Even before Bezobrazov arrived at Port Arthur, Abaza telegraphed him while "en route" the following instructions:

The Emperor orders you to keep in mind that His Majesty had definitely decided to allow the Japanese complete possession of Korea, maybe even to the boundary of our concession on the Tumen in the north and to the boundary of our concession on the Yalu in the west. A more exact delimitation of Japanese Korea is a matter for the future and must depend on Russia. This admission may be communicated to Japan not earlier than after the arrival of troops (two brigades) sent from Russia to the transbaikal region, so as not to bear the appearance of a concession. The Emperor believes that by yielding to Japan on the Korean question we avert the risk of coming into conflict with her.[60]

Bezobrazov was ordered to pass this directive to Alexeev, who in turn was to inform Lessar, Pavlov, and Rosen of its content.[61] However, on his own initiative, Bezobrazov decided not to pass on this directive. The Ministry of Foreign Affairs did not know of its existence until after the outbreak of the Russo-Japanese War.[62] It did not stop Bezobrazov from propagandizing for his favorite views at the various conferences at Port Arthur, nor did it stop him from bombarding the Tsar and Abaza with letters and telegrams stressing the importance of northern Korea for political and strategic purposes, or from expressing such views to newspaper correspondents at Port Arthur.[63]

The history of the Port Arthur conferences illustrates the thoroughness and meticulousness with which Russia was then evolving her Far Eastern policy.[64] Besides the sixteen major conferences there were meetings of committees and subcommittees. Representatives of many interests and Russian agencies were called upon to contribute their views to the discussion. Testimony and opinions were given by Iugovich; S. V. Ignatsius, Assistant to the Chief Engineer of the C.E.R.; D. L. Horvat, Commander of the Railroad Guards; Pokotilov; Balashev; Madritov; and others. The views and discussions were recorded in a series of "journals" and were forwarded to St. Petersburg.

The Port Arthur conferences were not empowered to determine the course of Russian policy, which was a matter reserved for higher levels, but they were free to express their conclusions in the form of suggestions for final approval at St. Petersburg. Bezobrazov, by virtue of his rank, was empowered to relay verbally to the conferences the wishes of the Tsar,[65] but he no doubt was restrained in the execution of this power by the knowledge that the Tsar had been writing freely and frequently to Alexeev, both directly and through Abaza. Alexeev's attitude toward Bezobrazov's personal schemes can therefore be considered the same as that of the Tsar.

In general, the conferences followed the policies established by the St. Petersburg Conference of February 7, 1903, and amplified by later conferences. Kuropatkin submitted a new list of demands of guarantees from China, seventeen in all. They spelled the virtual annexation of northern Manchuria but, as a result of Lessar's and Alexeev's opposition, these terms were considerably reduced in number and severity.[66] The conferences came to the conclusion that the Yalu enterprise should be of a "purely commercial character." Sometime during the sessions, Madritov was ordered to withdraw from the Yalu concession work and return to duty. The whole aggressive intent of Bezobrazov's schemes was completely negated by the decision not to support with government funds any enterprise in Manchuria and to carry out the Evacuation Agreement—though of course with delays—after the acceptance by China of a minimum number of guarantees.[67]

On his return to St. Petersburg, Bezobrazov presented a lengthy memorandum to the Tsar stating his disagreements with the conclusions of the Port Arthur conferences, but the Tsar was now apparently cool to these old views. He might have become tired at last of Bezobrazov's "universal dilettantism,"[68] or he might have been aroused by reports of Bezobrazov's meddling with state affairs, and his intruding into chancelleries. Perhaps he had decided to put an end to the activities of the State Secretary.[69] It might be questioned whether the Tsar had even bothered to read Bezobrazov's report, for on August 6 Kuropatkin submitted a lengthy report on the Russian military situation in the Far East which included in an appendix the "strategic" memorandum which Bezobrazov had presented at the Port Arthur conferences.[70] Kuropatkin presented an annihilating criticism of Bezo-brazov's idea for a strategical barrier or "buffer" in Korea. He stressed his "minority opinion" that without openly abrogating the Evacuation Agreement, Russia should continue to occupy northern Manchuria as a "buffer."[71] The Tsar read and discussed this memorandum with Kuropatkin at some length several times.[72]

With this last effort, Bezobrazov's role as an influential figure in the formulation of Russian policy in the Far East ended. The Tsar no longer sought his counsel, and he was a minor figure even in the affairs of the Russian Timber Company. Of course he was still an official of the government and remained active, apparently—in fact, too active. But his fall from "grace" was certain. On August 14 the Tsar expressed surprise upon hearing from Kuropatkin of some of Bezobrazov's actions at Port Arthur. He gave his permission for Kuropatkin to refuse Bezobrazov access to the files of the Ministry of War.[73]

On September 1, 1903, Kuropatkin had a lengthy conversation with the Tsar on a number of important matters,[74] and in a "heart-to-heart" atmosphere he broached the subject of Bezobrazov. The conversation that followed is of interest both as regards the fate of Bezobrazov and as an illuminating contemporary appraisal of his role. In all probability it is accurate. Kuropatkin's diary states:

I pointed out to the Emperor ... that I do not consider that he [Bezobrazov] was entirely without usefulness. "Yes" added the Emperor, "he awakened us a great deal." The Emperor then added: "Do you think it was pleasant for me to listen two years ago when Bezobrazov told me that we had taken the wrong course in the Far East? But I recognized that he was right. Of course it is not right that he criticizes all the Ministers, and everything, and everyone. It is easy to criticize, especially for a person without responsibility." Then I said that he [Bezobrazov] gets carried away fanatically. Now his usefulness is over. ... Bezobrazov, in the hands of the Tsar, was like a mustard plaster which was put on people and situations. It was necessary to perform a certain cure. The goal is reached. Now we must do with Bezobrazov as we do with mustard plasters which have outlived their usefulness. The Emperor, with a jovial smile, interrupted me: "I know, we must throw him out." "Exactly, Your Highness, it is time to throw Bezobrazov out of the window. After all, Your Highness, if the mustard plaster is kept on too long, then instead of doing good it will cause harm; blisters will appear. In the same way we cannot keep Bezobrazov."[75]

So, without any fuss, Bezobrazov was "thrown out." In August and September he was in St. Petersburg and corresponded with Balashev, who was appealing to him—without avail—for more funds.[76] In October he left to go abroad for more than a year, and although he was still interested in the affairs of the Russian Timber Company, he fulminated against the "triumvirate"[77] and even occasionally wrote to the Tsar. His role in the affairs of the Far East was definitely ended.

The subsequent history of Bezobrazov is not without interest. He returned late in 1904 and was concerned enthusiastically with the promotion of a new type of artillery shell, "which would revolutionize warfare."[78] Apparently nothing came of it. Later, after the Revolution of 1905, he was engaged in several lawsuits and attempted to win election to the Second Duma, but had no further connection with the government.[79] He emigrated after the November Revolution of 1917 and died while in exile in Paris in 1931.[80] Until his death, he apparently believed in the views he had held during his time in ascendancy. In spite of the storm of criticism directed against him and the widespread accusation that he and the "Bezobrazov gang" were responsible for the Russo-Japanese War, he made no effort to defend himself in print. His literary contribution to the historiography of the Russian policy in the Far East consisted of one unilluminating article in *Le Correspondent* (Paris) which consists chiefly of reiteration of his old views.[81]

It must be added, in all fairness, that investigations of his actions, particularly of his financial expenditures, did not incriminate Bezobrazov. Count V. N. Kokovtsev, the Minister of Finance in 1904, made a personal investigation of the funds advanced to Bezobrazov "for purposes known to his Majesty" and found no evidence which might criminally implicate Bezobrazov.[82] It must be remembered that even Bezobrazov's archenemy, Witte, who after 1904 had the opportunity to examine the financial accounts of Bezobrazov's enterprises, also, at the time of the writing of his memoirs (1915), considered Bezobrazov "honest." No doubt had there been incriminating documentation of Bezobrazov's activity in the Russian archives it would have been published by the Soviet Central Archive Commission, which gleaned the collections, publishing such insipid documents about the Bezobrazov group as the ones found in *Krasnyi Arkhiv*.[83]

Thus ended the "Bezobrazov group," which in reality was never Bezobrazov's, nor was it a group or even a cabal. It was, at most, a temporary meeting of minds, a series of incidental personal contacts between Bezobrazov and other members of the so-called "group" and persons of influence, authority, and wealth such as the Tsar, Alexeev, and the Grand Duke Alexander Mikhailovich. Its influence, though persistent and egregious, was only sporadically successful. No sooner had Bezobrazov or some member of his "group" persuaded the Tsar of the advisability of following their projected course than their policy met with defeat. And no sooner had Bezobrazov reached the acme of his power than he was "thrown out of the window." However, his ephemeral influence could have played some part in two later actions of the Tsar, in August, 1903—the establishment of the Viceroyalty of the Far East and the dismissal of Witte.

On August 12, 1903, the day on which the Japanese government opened negotiations with Russia, the Tsar signed an ukase establishing the Viceroyalty of the Far East, which theoretically unified all military, economic, and diplomatic affairs of the Russian possessions in the provinces and territories east of Lake Baikal under Viceroy Alexeev.[84] This was not an unprecedented event. The Viceroyalty of the Caucasus had been established previously and had functioned satisfactorily. However, the establishment of the Viceroyalty of the Far East was untimely. It greatly hindered the negotiations with Japan which followed. The details had not been worked out, and the chain of command and flow of diplomatic and other governmental channels remained confused until the outbreak of the Russo-Japanese War put an end to this partly fictional creation.[85] Along with the Viceroyalty, the Tsar established a Special Committee for Far Eastern Affairs, which was to supervise the activity of the Viceroyalty.[86] This committee was to include the Tsar as president, Plehve as vice-president, and the Ministers of War, Finance, and Foreign Affairs as members. It was to have a permanent secretariat, or chancellery, with A. M. Abaza as the official "reporter" and director of the Secretariat, and N. G. Matiunin as assistant director. Other members were to be appointed if need be. This was only a paper organization, which further complicated matters. As far as it is known, the committee never met.[87] The arrangement made for the routing of affairs was either disregarded or duplicated during the ensuing months. It merely retarded the normal course of events and gained further ill repute for the Bezobrazov "group," of which Abaza and Matiunin were definitely members. Abaza was apparently in a key position, but as it turned out, his personal influence appears to have been negligible.

The new administrative arrangement was not a poor one in theory. The supreme control was still retained in the hands of those who had held that control before—the Tsar and his ministers. It satisfied the requirement of unity of agencies in the Far East, which had been suggested in the Conference of February 7, 1903, and had been hinted to Alexeev in the Tsar's letter of May 15. The arrangement had been discussed privately in some detail between Kuropatkin and Alexeev at Port Arthur in July, 1903.[88] It had finally been worked out in an incomplete but official form by the Tsar, Plehve, and the Grand Duke

Alexei Alexandrovich a few days before its terms were published.[89] Nevertheless, its publication in the *Pravitel'stvennyi Vestnik* on August 13 came as a shock to many of the ministers, particularly Witte, who had been kept in complete ignorance of the scheme, and even Kuropatkin, who did not believe that it would go so far as to remove all military matters concerning the Far East from his jurisdiction.[90] On August 15 the offended Kuropatkin had even hinted that he was ready to resign, but the Tsar placated him. A jurisdictional complication was raised again in Kuropatkin's conversation with the Tsar on September 1. By this time even the Tsar had doubts about the creation of the Viceroyalty. Kuropatkin recorded in his diary:

"The Emperor said ... that he had thought a great deal about it; and that he also occasionally thinks that he might have decided the question of the Viceroyalty incorrectly. But what can be done about it? Now, in one way or another, the question has been decided, and we must all take this into consideration."[91]

The baleful influence of unnecessary delays caused by the new arrangement became apparent almost immediately. On August 14, Witte, Kuropatkin and Lamsdorf met in a joint conference, to which Bezobrazov was invited but from which he elected to absent himself with a dubious excuse.[92] This conference was apparently the second on the subject and met to discuss the conclusions of the Port Arthur conferences. The journal of the conference reaffirmed the decisions of the previous conferences in regard to the eventual withdrawal from even northern Manchuria. It reduced the ten demands on China drafted at the Port Arthur conferences to five. This was the fifth reduction since January, 1901, and it left in the journal merely a shadow of the former demands.[93] Nine days after the conference the Tsar stated that he still had not read the journal.[94] The Tsar was busy, of course, but in all probability he was still undecided what he should do. Should the journal now go to the Viceroy as decreed by the ukase of August 12? Or should it go to the Ministry of Foreign Affairs and then be transmitted to Lessar in Peking? In either case, the ministers present at the conference or the newly appointed Viceroy would be slighted. The decision was thus needlessly delayed, and the demands were finally transmitted to the Chinese government at Peking on September 6;[95] by that time they had been reëdited and further modified.

The terms are immaterial[96] because the Chinese would not accept terms, anyway. As usual, the Chinese revealed them to the other powers[97] and perhaps were ready to give formal notice that they had rejected them. This time, however, they were forestalled by the Russians. On October 3, probably on the suggestion of Alexeev, Lessar was notified to break off negotiations with the Chinese.[98] By this time Russia had definitely decided to make a deal with Japan in order to make a better agreement with China.[99]

Bezobrazov's influence also had much to do with the overthrow of Witte. There were other factors, of course, and it is impossible to determine which one was paramount. A few days after Witte's overthrow, Kuropatkin likened the factors to three mines, neither of which could sink the ship alone, but which conjointly produced the desired effect. The first mine was laid by the Grand Duke Alexander Mikhailovich, who for a long time had considered Witte to have too much power. The second was laid by Bezobrazov, and the third, by Plehve backed by Muraviev and possibly Pobedonostsev.[100] In all probability there were many other contributing factors.

Witte had been aware of his weakened position with the Tsar. It has been mentioned that he was cognizant of this as early as December, 1901. In his memoirs, Witte wrote that the Tsar had been prepared to dismiss him in January, 1903, a date he also had mentioned to Kuropatkin in April and on September 1 of that year.[101] Nevertheless, he felt himself irreplaceable—as indeed he was. Consequently, when the blow fell, it was unexpected. Witte was profoundly shocked by the Tsar's decision, which the Tsar mentioned to him in a private audience on August 28.[102] The dismissal was given to him with a palliative: he was appointed chairman of the Committee of Ministers, an honorable but strictly honorary and inactive position. There was no doubt in anyone's mind that this was a dismissal and that Witte had been promoted to get him out of the way. Nor is there any doubt that the Tsar personally had desired this for some time. In his diary, in the entry for August 28, the date of Witte's dismissal, the Tsar wrote laconically: "Now I rule."[103]

The important effects of this dismissal were manifold. Russia lost the guidance of a truly able man, but what was even worse, the functions of the tremendous system Witte had developed to coördinate Russian interests in the Far East were immediately disrupted. The system had functioned because of the personal contacts and friendships which had been evolved through many years by the Minister of Finance. Now the system was without its central figure. E. D. Pleske, the Assistant Minister of Finance, who was appointed to succeed Witte a few minutes after Witte's dismissal, was an honest, loyal official, but, by his own admission, he could be only a weak imitation of his predecessor.[104] Moreover, he was seriously ill. He earnestly pleaded with the Tsar not to appoint him, because of his ill-health; but the Tsar stated that he did not have anyone else.[105] Pleske loyally took up the task, although by the end of October he was too ill to attend the regular sessions of the State Council.[106] In fact, he was slowly dying, and soon after the outbreak of the Russo-Japanese War he passed away.

Such was the state of affairs in the Russian governmental apparatus at the beginning of negotiations with Japan. The Viceroy did not know exactly over what he ruled; the special committee did not even meet; its secretariat was in the hands of a questionable character;[107] the vast Ministry of Finance and its agencies were without their experienced head. The usually reticent and rather timid Lamsdorf was the only cautious influence at the higher level. One of the prominent ministers was the militaristically inclined, though not unnecessarily aggressive, Kuropatkin. Another was Plehve, who by his own admission was not "competent" to deal with Far Eastern affairs, and who, sometime after the wave of labor troubles and revolutionary manifestations of July and August, 1903, is reputed to have said "to hold back a revolution we need a small and victorious war."[108] Other weaknesses in the apparatus appeared as time went on. The foundations, however, boded ill for proper conduct of diplomatic negotiations at this critical point.

Bezobrazov and his "awakening," which had been mentioned by the Tsar on September 1, contributed indirectly, inadvertently, and unwittingly to the confused situation in the Russian governmental apparatus. If it can be said that the members of the Bezobrazov clique triumphed, they triumphed on the banks of the Neva at St. Petersburg and not on the banks of the Yalu, where their operations were insignificant and their programs were rejected repeatedly. They triumphed by overthrowing Witte and not by elevating Bezobrazov to power. In the new apparatus, Alexeev was not their man; he had opposed and thwarted the aims of the "group" as often as anyone else. It was a hollow and ephemeral triumph. The "group" did not get any more money, nor gain greater prestige, nor exert any great amount of influence on the course of events. The "new course" established by the responsible ministers was maintained, and the ideas upheld by the "triumvirate" remained dominant in Russian policy in the Far East. However, there remained "blisters" after Bezobrazov's role as a "mustard plaster" was over.

The Yalu concession must now be examined in detail in order to determine the part it played in the Russo-Japanese negotiations.

RUSSIAN INTERESTS IN KOREA AND ON THE YALU, 1903

The "new course" adopted in the series of conferences and through discussions in the period from February to August, 1903, had the unmistakable objectives of abandoning the Yalu enterprise, lest it incur the antagonism of Japan and thus prejudice future negotiations regarding Korea as a whole, of retreating from Manchuria gracefully, but as slowly as possible, to the position held before the Boxer rebellion, and of trying to obtain certain guarantees. The five guarantees demanded and finally presented on September 6, 1903, consisted of an article on the nonalienation of Manchurian territory (Art. I) ; one on the right to have military posts along the Sungari, the Manchurian bank of the Amur, and the Tsitsihar-Mergen-Blagoveschensk road (Art. III), or outside the zone of the C.E.R., in which railroad guards could be posted under the terms of the agreements of 1896 and 1898; and three other articles, relatively insignificant, which dealt with the physical protection of the Russo-Chinese Bank and the right to have a Russian sanitary inspector at Inkou.[109]

These demands must again be looked upon as preliminary demands for an opening bid in the negotiations. They were not the final irrefutable program. They represented the fifth attempt of Russia to come to an agreement with China since January, 1901. Each attempt had increasingly milder terms. As an opening bid it must be considered as evidence of Russian intentions to make even further concessions during the negotiations. Even the Japanese Minister of Foreign Affairs, Komura, found these demands "not so drastic as the 'Seven Demands,' " with the possible exception of the first article, which was an "impairment of the territorial integrity of China."[110] To forestall possible criticism of this "impairment," on July 14 the Russian Ministry of Foreign Affairs had circularized the capitals of the United States, Japan, England, France, and Germany with a notice that Russia would have no objection to the opening of new treaty points in Manchuria by China and the establishment of new consulates there, with the exception of Harbin, which was to be regarded as a Russian railroad town in the restricted C.E.R. zone.[111]

In all probability the real reaction to the Russian position in Manchuria did not come from the revelation of the Russian demands but from the fear engendered by the creation of the Viceroyalty and from the realization of the Russian military potential in reference to Manchuria and northern China which had been so clearly manifested in the events of 1900. On September 1, 1903, Edwin Conger, the United

States Minister to Peking, wrote to the Secretary of State: "With Admiral Alexeev as viceroy with almost supreme power, acting through high officers with large military forces in the vicinity of all important provincial officials, the latter will be overawed and the will of Russia carried out as absolutely as when in military control."[112] In this he expressed the common misinterpretation of the role of the Viceroyalty, an understandable error since, at the time, the role was not clearly understood even in St. Petersburg. At the same time, Conger uncovered the crux of the Manchurian problem of 1903. Whether or not there was to be military or administrative control, the influence of Russia through its enlarged potential at Port Arthur, the Russian possessions east of Lake Baikal, and the C.E.R. could be brought to bear not only upon the Chinese officials in Manchuria but also on the higher Chinese circles in Peking.

This influence would continue in Manchuria irrespective of the open-door doctrine which the Russians had agreed to follow in principle. To eliminate that influence, international diplomacy would have to force Russia back to the status quo of pre-Boxer times and to the situation as it existed before the cession of Port Arthur and the railroad penetration of Manchuria in 1896. This was impossible by diplomatic means.

Neither the United States nor England had any intention of solving the Manchurian problem by war. At the most they envisioned an Anglo-American-Japanese entente.[113] Moreover, no action was necessary in view of the repeated promises by Russia to evacuate Manchuria. These promises were to be tested on October 8 by possible clarification of the situation in Manchuria through Russo-Japanese negotiations.

The Russian conferences from February to August, 1903, had definitely ruled out aggression in regard to Korea. They had even ruled out further government financial participation in the Yalu enterprise. To Russian statesmen in St. Petersburg the initial outcries of the press against Russian designs on Korea in May, 1903, were inexplicable. Witte and Lamsdorf were perturbed over these outcries. After an investigation Lamsdorf came to the conclusion that some agency in Japan was trying to create a war scare in order to make a "killing" on the stock market.[114] Until the outbreak of the Russo-Japanese War, these wild rumors of Russian designs on Korea centered around the Yalu basin enterprise and were recurrent in the Far East. Yet the true nature of the Yalu enterprise and the extent of Russian activities in Korea were no doubt well known to those who took the trouble to investigate. Along with the wildest rumors, the Far Eastern press also reported honestly the actual facts concerning the so-called Russian aggression in Korea. These facts, when examined with the documents now published on the Russian policy in Korea, show clearly that Russia in 1903 had not the slightest intention of starting aggressive action in Korea, especially after the elimination of Bezobrazov's influence.

The prominence of Russian activities on the Yalu in the Far Eastern press was due to the fact that they represented the only tangible Russian activities in Korea. On several occasions in 1902 and 1903 the Russian Minister attempted to get Korean consent to the extension of the Russian Maritime Province telegraph line into Korea as far as the treaty port of Gensan. He was refused on all occasions.[115] Several times the ubiquitous Baron Ginsburg, probably on his own initiative, attempted to secure concessions. At one time he negotiated for the handling of the ginseng trade monopoly and was refused. The concession remained in the hands of the Japanese Mitsui firm.[116] At another time he attempted to take over the Seoul-Injou (Wiju) railroad concession held by a French syndicate, which was ready to turn it over to anyone at any price by mid-1903. This paper concession lapsed, and Ginsburg's attempt failed.[117]

These were isolated attempts and appear not to have been supported by the Russian Minister at Seoul. Beset by financial difficulties, the Korean government favored the granting of concessions. Beginning with 1902, concession hunters flocked to Seoul. Americans, Frenchmen, Germans, Englishmen, Japanese, and even Belgians and Italians were more successful than the Russians in getting concessions.[118] Furthermore, most of these concessions were operating concessions, whereas the Russian whaling concession of 1900 was completely unused, and the Yalu concession until the middle of 1903 was maintained only by small annual expeditions meant to confirm the claims of the concession. They were probably made by subcontractors.[119] At Masampo, on the strip of land outside the town leased to the Russians in 1900, there was a Russian settlement of eleven persons, including three women, at the end of 1901. They were distributed among the vice-consulate, a hostelry, and the management office of the coal depot. This was in contrast to 202 Japanese settlers in the town.[120] All the major powers had the right to maintain legation guards in Seoul, but apparently only three did so in 1903. The United States had a handful of marines there, brought into the city in the summer of 1903 to occupy the carbarns of the Seoul tramway during labor troubles;[121] the Russians had a guard of 80 men; the Japanese had an entire battalion. This battalion was replaced by another battalion of 23 officers and 537 men in May, 1903. When the guard was changed there were more than 1,000 Japanese soldiers in Seoul.[122] As usual, the Russian Minister made no protest.

The enormous expansion of Japanese interests in Korea is amply recorded in the contemporary press. Russian activities, as compared with those of the Japanese, were minor. Few of them were reported, because the activities were so insignificant that they went unnoticed. In the three years after 1900 the only Russian church in Korea at Seoul had a staff of two Russians and an attendance of ten Koreans, in comparison with the hundreds of missionaries of other countries and their thousands of converts.[123] If there was any Russian drive to gain influence or to develop interests in Korea, the results by 1904 were pitiful. Because there are no documentary materials which even suggest such a drive, one can safely conclude that no serious effort was made along these lines.

Yet the great Japanese expansion of trade interests, colonization, and concessionary and other activities was not the result of Japanese domination of the Korean government. The government had an American, a Russian, and a Japanese party, and any two could combine against the third to avoid abject submission to its demands. The Japanese also had a series of rebuffs in the period 1900–1904. In 1901, for many months the Japanese protested against the Korean embargo on rice and did not succeed in having the embargo lifted until the rice situation in Korea improved.[124] When in July, 1903, the Seoul-Injou concession was dropped by the French, Japanese interests wanted to acquire it and were refused.[125] In the same month some Japanese interests attempted to get a timber concession on the banks of the Yalu and were told that the previous Russian claim was still valid.[126] Nevertheless, if only through the inactivity of the other powers and their nationals, the Japanese position in Korea grew stronger each year. The Japanese Dai Ichi Bank was the only foreign bank in Korea. The Korean government appealed to it constantly for small sums. Sometimes it was for 500,000 yen to pay for a celebration of the Court, sometimes it was for a paltry 150,000 yen to pay a month's salary for government workers.[127] It was only a matter of course that in 1903 the Dai Ichi Bank became the virtual "Bank of Korea" and its issues of paper yen were made legal tender in all of Korea.[128]

As a matter of routine, the Russian Minister in Seoul occasionally protested some phases of the expansion of Japanese influence. He protested the merger of the Fusan-Seoul railroad concession with the Seoul-Chemulpo concession, but the merger was carried through anyway. He protested the appointment of Kato, a Japanese, as adviser to the Department of Agriculture, Trade, and Industry—a position that would give Japan the strongest influence in the financial councils of the country. This appointment also went through over the Russian protest.[129] Either the protests were not strongly presented or Russia was not sufficiently interested in the matter. She considered Japanese domination of Korea a foregone conclusion. Pavlov, the Russian Minister, was not very much interested in Korea, because he believed that Russia should expand in the direction of China. There was another possible reason for his disinterest. According to the American Minister to Seoul, Pavlov became infatuated and married a teen-age girl in the winter of 1903–1904 and thereafter did not attend to his duties.[130]

A comparison of the scale of Russian activity with that of the Japanese is unnecessary; it was to be expected that Russian trade would be insignificant if Japanese, English, and American goods could outsell Russian products even in northern Manchuria. As in China, Korean trade statistics are unreliable because imports were customarily registered according to the nationality of the firm that sold them or the flag that carried them. A more exact statistical comparison can be made in the number and tonnage of Russian and Japanese ships which entered Korean harbors. The figures given by J. L. Chambers of the Korean customs show that in 1901, of the total of 985,309 tons of ocean-going shipping which entered Korean ports, 807,190 tons was Japanese. Korean shipping was in second place; Russian shipping was in third, with 35,916 tons. A large amount of the Russian tonnage belonged to ships entering Masampo only to pick up bunker coal brought from Japan.[131] A more favorable estimate of the extent of Russian participation in comparison with that of other powers might be deduced from the figures on foreigners in Korean service. Of the 63 foreigners in the Korean governmental service in March, 1903, there were 35 Japanese, 8 Englishmen, 5 Americans, 5 Frenchmen, 4 Russians, 4 Germans, and 2 Danes.[132] It is no wonder that Korea was not stressed in the Russian conferences of 1903, and that the whole history of the Russian policy in the Far East in this period indicates an abandonment of Korea to Japanese domination in one form or another.

Although Russian activities in Korea as a whole were negligible, they may have been greater in northern Korea, for there were some diplomatic disagreements over the control of that area in the Russo-Japanese negotiations from August, 1903, to February, 1904. The available records show no Russian interests in Korea, except the Yalu concession. A detailed account of the treaty port of Chinnampo, the northernmost western open port of Korea, written by A. Tsererin, a student-observer of the Valdivostok Institute in the summer of 1902, contains no evidence of Russian interests there.[133] Since the opening of the port in September, 1897, it had been visited by several hundred foreign ships, including Japanese, English, American, German, and Chinese; but not a single Russian ship entered the port in all that time.[134] The small international settlement, which had business connections with the hinterland of northwestern Korea, was governed by a municipal council in which three members out of five were Japanese, the other two being Korean and Chinese. Of the seventeen policemen in the settlement, fifteen were Japanese and two Chinese. The settlement had a branch of the Dai Ichi Bank, which carried on a brisk business because the port was the entry port feeding a number of foreign concessions. There were several Japanese coal-mining and one gold-mining concession near Pingyang; a large British gold-mining concession—the Gwendoline Mines—seventy miles northeast of Pingyang, and, the most important and lucrative of them all, the Unsan concession of the Oriental Consolidated Mining Company, mainly American-owned, with properties encompassing five hundred square miles of territory, less than twenty miles south of the Yalu River.[135] However, there was not a trace of Russian activity.

The Unsan concession deserves special notice. This American concession lay directly south of the Yalu concession and was therefore on the road of the purported march of Russian imperialism into Korea. It was a going concern obtained in the concessionary grabs of 1896, but in contrast to the Yalu enterprise it quickly developed into a large and profitable concern. A detailed account of its operations, personnel, methods, and other factors serve as an interesting basis of comparison with the Russian "imperialistic" venture on the Yalu.[136] The information on the concession given by Tsererin applied to 1901, but the figures must have been even larger in the next few years, for the concession continued to expand operations and production. Until the Japanese annexation of Korea in 1910, and even under the Japanese from 1910 to 1941, the Unsan concession was the greatest gold producer in Korea.

By 1901 the Unsan concession employed 96 Americans and Englishmen in engineering, clerical, and supervisory capacities. At that time the total Russian population in Korea was 45 persons, exclusive of the legation guards but including the diplomatic corps.[137] In addition, the concession employed 200 Chinese, 200 Japanese, and about 2,000 Koreans. The company had exclusive mining rights in the entire province of Unsan. It had its own local administration and police. It provided escorts of armed Americans for the shipment of its concentrates and bullion. It owned a steamer that made regular runs between Chinnampo and other ports, and it may have had any number of other privileges and local immunities from interference usually enjoyed under such concessions. It was in a frontier country and operated under wild frontier conditions. The concessionaries protested, through the American Minister in Seoul in 1902, that Japanese and Korean interlopers were illegally operating in their territory. The Korean government made no attempt to check them, yet these operations stopped.[138] No doubt the interlopers were dealt with in some "frontier" fashion.

A few miles to the northwest, the Russians, with their 1,800-square-mile concession along the Korean bank of the Yalu, did practically nothing until 1903. In May or early June of that year, after Bezobrazov's first organizing visit to the Far East and shortly before the legal registration of the Russian Timber Company, Colonel Madritov, officially retired from active duty but still flaunting the red-silk lining of his cloak which was the sign of service in the General Staff, arrived on the Yalu with a small cossack escort. He found a very unsatisfactory state of affairs.[139] Chinese and Japanese interlopers and Koreans were cutting down timber on both banks of the Yalu without concern for the rights of others. Timber cutting on a small scale had been going on for years on the Yalu. Since there was no real port at the mouth of the river, because of sandbars, the logs cut were usually towed like rafts, in scattered and unrecorded quantities, from the mouth by seagoing junks.

The situation enraged the energetic Madritov.[140] He apparently reacted in a determined manner. Little is known definitely of his actions except that he was later accused of having struck a Chinese local official of comparatively high rank, and that shortly afterward, in typical frontier fashion, local *khunhuzes* attacked a party of interlopers and killed and wounded some forty of them, including seven Japanese.[141] This affair was never investigated nor was the responsibility ever traced to the proper source. It is now known that Bezobrazov had hired or paid protection money to some of the *khunhuzes* in the region. It is also a fact that when news of such activities on the Yalu reached Alexeev, Madritov was recalled to give testimony at the Port Arthur conferences and was ordered back to active duty.[142] Possibly this was to keep him out of further mischief.

In June the first artel of eighty-nine Russian "reservists," with one officer who had withdrawn from active duty, arrived on the Yalu. There the party broke up into smaller groups, the men acting as supervisors, overseers, and guards on the exploited lots—and the timber rafts floated down the river.[143] Another small party soon afterward made its way by sea to the mouth of the Yalu, where the company had leased some plots of land on the Manchurian shore for a lumber-mill site, obtaining it by using a Chinese as figurehead. Here again, the Russians encountered interloping squatters, fishermen, lumberjacks, Chinese, Koreans, and Japanese living on "their" land. The party proceeded to disperse this settlement and burn it down in frontier fashion—without bloodshed, however.[144] On this "leased" spit of land, the local staff of the enterprise proceeded to claim any and all unescorted rafts and logs as their own, no doubt putting their own mark on the logs that had previously had Chinese brands or marks. This aroused some Chinese and Korean protests, and the company thereafter acted more cautiously. They bought rafts of logs from the Chinese and Koreans, because their own timber-felling operations were not progressing satisfactorily.[145]

In late June or early July the local headquarters of the enterprise was moved to the Korean bank of the river in the town of Yonnampo, where the company, through diplomatic channels at Seoul, attempted to lease a plot of ground near the town for the construction of the projected sawmill and the installation of other facilities. The lease was refused by the Korean government, but the company resorted to the usual expediency of renting the land through a figurehead and began construction of installations.[146] By this time Russian "imperialism" in northern Korea had attracted a good deal of attention. The Yalu basin was visited by several foreigners who left graphic descriptions of the scope of the enterprise. One of the first was a Japanese officer "on leave" who traveled through many districts in Manchuria with the avowed intention of observing the Russians. At the end of his trip he visited the Yalu basin about July, 1903.[147] He reported that in the Russian settlement at Yonnampo at that time there were "four Russians, including women," and that a few miles north of the port there was an outpost of Russian troops, "not more than twenty-four."[148] No doubt the observer missed the scattered encampments of Russian "reservists" on the tributaries of the Yalu where felling operations were in progress. Nevertheless, his account is a far more reliable report of the Russian activity than other contemporary accounts which reported large movements of Russian troops to the Yalu, and particularly one Chinese account, which stated "on excellent authority" that the Russians at Yonnampo were building a fort having walls "twenty meters high, of which fifteen meters had already been raised."[149]

Work at the concession made some progress in August and September. Another visitor, this one apparently an Englishman, reported that a lumber mill was being built at Yonnampo, that stores of coal, brick, and other construction materials were in evidence, that a wharf and a Decauville railroad from it had been built, and that at Sha-he, eleven miles upstream on the Manchuria bank, there was a Russian post for a sotnia (hundred men) of cossacks which had been established in 1900.[150] It is also recorded that in August the Russian Timber Company chartered the steamship *Stanley Dollar* of the Dollar Line of San Francisco to pick up a load of lumber at Yonnampo for Newchwang, and that this steamer was intercepted by a Korean packet boat and turned back because Yonnampo was not a treaty port and was not open for such entrance.[151] Nevertheless, the Timber Company sent off one shipload of lumber. After logging operations on the Yalu ceased, in early November, no more shipments were made, partly because of the unsatisfactory condition of the logs on hand. To satisfy the terms of a previously made contract, the Russian Timber Company had to purchase lumber from the United States.[152]

By this time the Russian Timber Company was fast approaching collapse. On September 19, 1903, Balashev telegraphed Bezobrazov that its operations would be successful only if the company could have a monopoly of the entire timber resources of the Yalu basin. For this, 6,000,000 rubles were needed. On September 29 Balashev telegraphed a statement that money was desperately needed—any amount of money—because only 5,000 rubles remained in the coffers of the company. The enterprise was now completely abandoned by its patrons, and no money could be raised. In October its dissolution began with dismissal of employees. An attempt was made to sell the electric power and tramway concession at Mukden, to any takers. There were none. In November, without production the Russian Timber Company was accumulating debts. Finally on January 1, 1904, the Tsar came to the rescue of the company's good name by ordering a further credit of 200,000 rubles, but only for the liquidation of the company's debts.[153] Actually, the activity of the company ended in October, 1903. In late January, 1904, a series of conferences was held in St. Petersburg to discuss the fate of the enterprise. But these were primarily stockholders' meetings, and in them no decision was reached.[154] The final dissolution of the company came by order of the Tsar in 1904 and 1905 after the beginning of the Russo-Japanese War.[155]

The attitude of the important members of the Russian government toward the enterprise from August, 1903, on, leaves no doubt that the company was deprived of official encouragement. In August, 1903, Alexeev may have vacillated from his previous stand, which was to deny the company any government support,[156] but in October his mind was made up. He recognized the economic importance of the enterprise and refused to take any steps to back it until the Manchurian problem was solved. Furthermore he refused to influence the Russo-Chinese Bank, which was now out of Witte's control, to give aid to the impoverished company.[157] The Tsar's coolness to the whole scheme was expressed on a number of occasions in October and November, 1903.[158] In view of the insignificance of the actual operations at the Yalu concession, and the attitude of the controlling figures of Russian policy in the Far East, especially the Tsar and Alexeev, the real part the concession played in the Russo-Japanese negotiations of 1903–1904 ranged from negligible to nil.

RUSSO-JAPANESE NEGOTIATIONS, AUGUST 12, 1903 TO FEBRUARY 8, 1904

If one accepts Galperin's thesis that the Japanese entered into negotiations with Russia only to acquire a semblance of legality and justification for their attack on Russia,[159] the history of the negotiations is inconsequential. Galperin's argument is convincing, and until Japanese documents on the inner council of the Japanese Empire are made available and the true intent of the Japanese government is revealed, his theory cannot be disproved. Indeed, it may never be disproved, for the higher councils ordinarily do not record their decisions and the Genro of 1903 and 1904 probably carried their secrets with them to their graves. However, the history of the negotiations is still of importance in substantiating the fact that the "new course" of Russian policy was still in force, and that the conduct of the negotiations was never dominated by Alexeev and the Bezobrazov "group."

The decision to open negotiations with Russia was made in Japan at the Throne Conference of June 23, 1903, which was attended by five members of the Genro—Ito, Yamagata, Oyama, Matsukata, and Inouye—and four ministers—Katsura (Premier), Komura (Foreign Affairs), Terauchi (War), and Yamamoto (Navy). The conference unanimously adopted a decision to open negotiations with Russia.[160] The British government was notified at an early date both of the intent and the terms of the opening *démarche*,[161] and on July 28 Komura notified Kurino, the Minister to Russia, to acquaint Lamsdorf with the Japanese intention. Lamsdorf, on behalf of Russia, agreed to the negotiations; this was, after all, exactly what the Russians had been waiting for since the adoption of the "new course."[162] On August 12, Kurino submitted the first Japanese proposals.[163] The proposals were extremely one-sided and must be regarded as an initial position from which many concessions were to be expected. The nature of the proposals leads one to question Galperin's thesis because there was the possibility of a humiliating Russian rejection and the breaking of negotiations then and there. As it turned out, the Japanese had to wait fifty-two days for a counterproposal. If the intention of the Japanese was only to obtain the semblance of a justification for their attack, they should have been prepared for it in August. Yet, according to the reports of Captain Rusin, the Russian naval attaché at Tokyo, there were no unusual preparations of the Japanese fleet for such a contingency, although it was in battle readiness as fleets always are supposed to be.[164]

From the day of Lamsdorf's acceptance of the Japanese *note verbale* (August 5) and the orders to Kurino to transmit the first Japanese proposals (August 7),[165] there ensued a number of delays in the negotiations. Some of them can be explained and some remain inexplicable. Kurino was unable to present Lamsdorf with the text of the proposals until the twelfth, and not until the twenty-third was he able to bring up the proposals again.[166] Lamsdorf gave as reasons for the delay the absence of the Tsar on maneuvers and the necessity of discussing some points with Alexeev.[167] He suggested that the negotiations be transferred to Tokyo. There followed some diplomatic exchanges of views on that point between Russia and Japan, which accounted for further delay. Lamsdorf wanted the negotiations held in Tokyo because he and the Tsar were scheduled to leave for a prolonged trip to Germany and Italy and would be removed from close contact with Kurino.[168] The Japanese government may have felt that this was an attempt to belittle them in the eyes of the world by forcing them to negotiate at Tokyo with Rosen, who was to be under Alexeev according to the statutes of the Viceroyalty. This would have been humiliating. However, Komura signified his willingness to accept the transfer if the Russian government would accept the Japanese proposals as the basis for the agreement at St. Petersburg.[169] To this Lamsdorf made a rather caustic reply to the effect that, "according to his experience of forty years in the Foreign Office, negotiations of an international character had always been conducted on the proposals of one Power with the reply of the other, and it was not usual to accept the proposition of one Power as the sole basis of negotiations."[170] Finally, on September 9, the Japanese agreed to the transfer.[171]

The first Japanese proposals were unacceptable to the Russians. They included some undesirable and some definitely objectionable provisions. The first article read: "Mutual engagement to respect the independence and territorial integrity of the Chinese and Korean Empires and to maintain the principles of equal opportunity for the commerce and industry of all nations in those countries."[172] This article was too binding. Its acceptance would have tied Russia's hands in the future not only with respect to northern Manchuria but for Mongolia and Sinkiang as well. But the main Russian objections were to the wording of other articles. In Article II, Russia was to recognize "Japan's preponderant interests in Korea," whereas Japan was to recognize only the special Russian railway interests in Manchuria. The right of intervention by both nations to protect such interests was recognized. This was hardly a *quid pro quo* arrangement.

Article III, dealing with a reciprocal agreement not to impede economic and industrial activities, contained the following "bombshell": "An additional engagement on the part of Russia to agree not to impede the eventual extension of the Korean railway [i.e., Japanese Seoul-Fusan railway] into Manchuria so as to connect with the East China and Shanhaikwan-Newchwang lines." By this the Japanese would acquire in southern Manchuria equal rights with the Russians, who were to be restricted only to the railway interests. This would have undermined the jealously guarded railway monopoly of the C.E.R. in southern Manchuria by cutting across its route. Article IV defined and limited the rights of intervention of both powers, but Article V would have established Japan's right to intervene in the political affairs of Korea: in fact would have made Korea a virtual protectorate of Japan. It read: "Recognition on the part of Russia of the exclusive right of Japan to give advice and assistance in the interest of good government in Korea, including necessary military assistance."

The sixth and last article was a declaration that this agreement superseded all other Russo-Japanese agreements on Korea.

The Russian government began the discussion of the Japanese terms almost immediately, although the reply was not sent for some time. On August 29 the Tsar personally drew up an answer to the Japanese proposals, but in line with the newly established apparatus of the Viceroyalty the terms were sent to Alexeev for his perusal. Alexeev conscientiously felt that he had to discuss the proposals personally with Rosen and called him to Port Arthur.[173] After this meeting, Alexeev's opinions had to go to Nicholas II, who was in Europe, and Alexeev had to confer with Lamsdorf, who might be separated from Nicholas II, as was possible at one time in September.[174] Then the counterproposals must be sent to Alexeev, who in turn would send them to Rosen. This diplomatic channel was the result of the creation of the Viceroyalty. Because of the encoding and decoding of each message, the transmission of views took an unusually long time. However, in this routing of the negotiations, Lamsdorf and Rosen were never ignored,[175] nor did Alexeev's position dominate the negotiations.[176] If anyone was ignored, it was Abaza, at St. Petersburg, who was furious because the Tsar, during his visit abroad, had completely circumvented him, and because Alexeev had written directly to the Tsar without even sending a copy of his messages to the "secretary general" of the Special Committee for Far Eastern Affairs.[177]

The Tsar's personal text of the counterproposals is important because it illustrates the basic and not merely the bargaining points of the Russian counterproposals as expressed in further negotiations. The essential articles read:

2. Mutual recognition of the existing analogous interests of Japan in Korea and of Russia in Manchuria.

3. Mutual undertaking on the part of Russia and Japan not to impede the development of those industrial and commercial activities which are not inconsistent with the provisions of article 1 of this agreement. [Respect of independence and territorial integrity of Korea and China.]

4. [Art. 4 of the Japanese text accepted.]

5. Recognition by Russia of the right of Japan to give advice and instructions in the interests of reform and good government in Korea.[178]

The first Russian counterproposals delivered to the Japanese government at Tokyo on October 3, 1903, changed the broad terms of the policy set forth in the Tsar's draft into specific terms restricting Japanese aspirations. In this they probably echoed the views of Admiral Alexeev, who had strongly criticized the one-sided nature of the Japanese proposals.[179] The counterproposals omitted the objectionable points of articles 1, 2, and 3 of the Japanese text, modified the rights of Japanese intervention (art. 4) by including the words "with the knowledge of Russia," and then added three articles which were increasingly objectionable to the Japanese.[180]

5. Mutual engagement not to use any part of the territory of Korea for strategical purposes nor to undertake on the coast of Korea any military works capable of menacing the freedom of navigation in Korea Strait.

6. Mutual engagement to consider that part of the territory of Korea lying to the north of the 39th parallel as a neutral zone into which neither of the contracting parties shall introduce troops.

7. Recognition by Japan of Manchuria and its littoral as being in all respects outside her sphere of influence.

The initial position was clear. Japan wanted a free hand in Korea and the restriction of Russian interests in Manchuria to those having to do with the railroad. Russia was willing to grant Japan a free hand in Korea with a few reservations in return—principally a self-imposed Japanese restriction similar to that contained in article 7 of the Russian counterproposal. However, these views were not irreconcilable if the intentions of the negotiating parties were to keep the peace. Apparently they had such intentions, for Japan in discussions with Rosen and with Sir Claude MacDonald in Tokyo[181] indicated her willingness to try to modify, but not expunge, articles 6 and 7 of the Russian counterproposals.

On October 8, 1903, the date of the expiration of the third phase of the Evacuation Agreement, came a slight change; the United States and Japan signed separate commercial treaties with China which carried provisions for the opening of the cities of Mukden and Antung in Manchuria as "treaty ports."[182] This step is often understood to be an attempt to test Russian intentions in Manchuria;[183] but this view can hardly be considered valid, not only because of the repeated Russian declarations in regard to Manchuria, but principally because the July 14 circular had stated beforehand that Russia would have no objections to such a step. This was also possible because the "new course" of policy in regard to Manchuria regarded it impossible and undesirable to keep the commercial interests of other nations out of Manchuria.

The opening of the new treaty ports actually weakened Japan's position. In the usual frank exchange of opinions between Japan and Great Britain, Lansdowne stated that he now found the Russian proposals more or less acceptable because the treaties of October 8 guaranteed commercial rights in Manchuria to Japan on a par with other powers. He suggested that the article 7, which he found objectionable, could be circumvented by including a clause on the new situation.[184] The Japanese position was further weakened by events in Europe. The British government, then engaged in preliminary negotiations which were to lead to the Anglo-French Entente of 1904, was showing some interest in achieving a peaceful solution of the Far Eastern crisis over Manchuria.[185]

On October 30 Komura handed to Rosen in Tokyo the second Japanese proposals. These represented a definite compromise. The Japanese suggested a neutral zone of fifty kilometers on each side of the Korean-Manchurian border (art. 6), and the thorny Manchurian problem was handled in accordance with the British suggestion by the addition of three articles:

7. Recognition by Japan that Manchuria is outside her sphere of special interest, and recognition by Russia that Korea is outside her sphere of special interest.

8. Recognition by Japan of Russia's special interest in Manchuria and of the right of Russia to take such measures as may be necessary for the protection of those interests.

9. Pledge by Japan not to interfere with the commercial and residential rights and immunities belonging to Russia in virtue of her treaty engagements with Korea, and pledge by Russia not to interfere with the commercial and residential rights and immunities belonging to Japan by virtue of her treaty with China.[186]

The railroad provision of the first Japanese proposals was thoroughly modified and was now presented as follows:

10. Mutual agreement not to impede the connection of the Korean railway and the C.E.R. when those railways shall have been extended to the Yalu.

These proposals reached the Tsar at Darmstadt, Germany. The Japanese Minister at St. Petersburg repeatedly tried to elicit some response from Prince Obolenskii, Acting Minister of Foreign Affairs in the absence of Lamsdorf.[187] When Lamsdorf was finally approached directly, on November 12, he remarked that it would be difficult for Russia to accept the Japanese terms relative to Manchuria because the Manchurian issue was a matter between Russia and China. He avoided making any commitment, by stating that the second Russian counterproposals were then in the hands of Alexeev.[188] According to Rosen in Tokyo, however, Alexeev had by November 14 already forwarded his edition of the counterproposals to the Tsar.[189] The delays continued. The Japanese became anxious. In October and November, diplomatic events in western Europe were not in their favor. Lansdowne on October 27 had stated to the French Ambassador to London that the British were also interested in the maintenance of the status quo in Korea; and, what was more dangerous for Japan, the British were discussing with the Russians a wide range of matters on which the two countries had disagreements.[190] If this presaged an Anglo-Russian *rapprochement*, the Japanese would be diplomatically isolated, as Lamsdorf hoped they would be.[191]

Certain events were in Japan's favor if she wanted war during these crucial days of October and November when Russian policy was undecided. Within Russia there was a further disintegration of regular diplomatic channels and ministerial solidarity. In October, Alexeev, fearing that the Japanese might take action and begin landing operations in northern Korea, began to plan countermeasures.[192] The Tsar, after consulting with Lamsdorf, telegraphed Alexeev a stern order with the statement: "I do not want a war between Russia and Japan and will not allow it. Take all measures so that war will not occur."[193] To prevent the possibility of Alexeev's taking rash action, the Tsar, in a conference with Kuropatkin decided to deprive the Viceroyalty of the power to order mobilization.[194] The position of the Viceroyalty became more confused than ever. Having cut short his trip to western Europe, the Tsar in November was on his Polish estate at Skernevitsy with the Tsarina, who was critically ill.[195] The ministers probably did not dare approach the Tsar with such "trifles" as the Far Eastern situation, which the Tsar considered to have already "calmed down."[196]

At the end of October or the beginning of November, Kuropatkin transmitted to the Tsar a long memorandum on Russian aims in the Far East.[197] This memorandum, with a conclusion and summary sent to the Tsar on December 10, could not play a decisive part in the formulation of the second Russian counterproposals handed to the Japanese at Tokyo on December 11, but they may have influenced the Tsar, and through him, Alexeev and Rosen. The memorandum was shown to Witte on November 10 in St. Petersburg and was explained to Plehve on November 20. It received the approval of both.[198] The text of the long memorandum has not been published, except for the conclusions sent on December 10.[199] Kuropatkin's summary of the memorandum, however, has been published several times.[200] The memorandum proposed to solve Russia's strategic and economic problems in the Far East by the following steps:

To give Kwantung back to China with Port Arthur and Dalny; to hand over the southern branch of the Chinese Eastern Railway to China, but in return, to receive all the rights in northern Manchuria, in addition to 250,000,000 rubles in compensation for the Russian expenses incurred in the building of the railroad and Port Arthur.

On December 16 Witte once again expressed his agreement with the Kuropatkin plan and offered to get Lamsdorf's support. He also supported Kuropatkin's idea that the 250,000,000 rubles obtained should be spent in the development of the Far East, where it could produce great results.[201] On December 24 Lamsdorf told Kuropatkin that he had read the proposal with delight and would be glad to support it.[202] The memorandum had no immediate effect on the second Russian counterproposals, however.

These counterproposals[203] were probably the work of Alexeev and Rosen, and they constituted a break in the accord so far reached. Except for the acceptance of the Japanese proposal concerning the junction

of the Chinese and Japanese railroads on the Yalu (art. 10), Manchuria was not even mentioned by implication. The entire text dealt
with Korea, reintroducing the 39th-parallel clause and the mutual
agreement not to use any part of Korean territory for strategical purposes (arts. 5 and 6). Of course these terms were completely unacceptable to the Japanese, because their specific reason for launching the
negotiations had been to limit or at least define the Russian policy in
Manchuria. The Japanese answer to the Russian counterproposal followed on December 23 in a *note verbale,* which expressed regret that
the Russian government did not include "the same territorial extension
as was deemed essential by Japan," and it asked the Russian government "to reconsider its position on the subject."[204] Some changes in the
Russian proposals were also included, but the *note verbale* actually
insisted on the inclusion of Manchuria in the negotiations before all else.

Only after realizing the seriousness of the existing situation do I dare to express,
in all sincerity, my opinion that further concession to Japan will lead us to a more
certain break. I consider it more desirable in every way that the Government of
Tokyo realize its aims toward Korea without the sanction of Russia.[205]

The Tsar called a special conference on December 28, 1903,[206] in order
to discuss whether to discontinue negotiations or continue the negotiations and include an article on Manchuria. Because of the illness of
Pleske, this conference was not on as high a level as some of the previous
conferences. Although he was generally ignored and was now actually
dying, Pleske was Minister of Finance. Plehve was also absent. The
Tsar presided. Kuropatkin, Lamsdorf, the Grand Duke Alexei Alexandrovich, representing the Navy, and Rear Admiral Abaza were present.
Whether this constituted a meeting of the Special Committee for Far
Eastern Affairs cannot be determined from the available documents.[207]
     The conference rejected Alexeev's proposal and came to the conclu-
sion that negotiations should be continued and that Manchuria should
be included in the next Russian counterproposals; but it was not determined how this was to be done. Lamsdorf pointedly remarked that
Russia should first decide what she wanted in Manchuria—a matter that
had not been made definite in all the conferences of 1903. The Grand
Duke agreed with Lamsdorf, remarking: "In the Manchurian question
we are taking the role of the dog in the manger, we are not using Manchuria, and we refuse to let others use it." Kuropatkin considered the
provision of the 39th parallel and the neutralization of the Korean
straits as of the utmost importance and the rest as only secondary matters. He reiterated his position in regard to northern Manchuria, which
was that it was not worth while to risk a war over claims in southern

Manchuria. He also added significantly that the incomplete condition of the C.E.R. would seriously hamper Russian military plans in the event of war, when 300,000 men would have to be routed over it.[208]

Abaza, supposedly a member of the Bezobrazov "group," which reputedly always stood for an aggressive policy in Korea, came forth with some surprising views. He said that Russia should avoid war and that she should allow Japan to occupy Korea because a Japanese protectorate in Korea would not be harmful to Russian interests. He was in favor of Alexeev's suggestion, because any concession to the Japanese would only lead to other demands. His argument was that the Japanese government would have to yield to the demands of the Japanese people and therefore would take Korea. This would be advantageous to Russia because other nations would resent the step. The Japanese would fail to get a strong position in Korea because they are "petty traders, not large merchants." Abaza felt that as soon as the Japanese crossed over to the continent of Asia their power would disappear; hence Russia should protest but not oppose the Japanese occupation of Korea.[209]

In general, the conference agreed with the opinion expressed by the Tsar early in the discussion, that "war is unquestionably undesirable. Time is Russia's best ally. Every year strengthens us."[210] This was quite true. Reinforcements from European Russia and increases in local formations had been planned by Kuropatkin since the summer of 1903. Now with every month Russian strength in the Far East increased by 7,000 more effective units.[211] On the sea, the Pacific squadron was also receiving reinforcements, but under the watchful eyes of the British and Japanese. In December, 1903, a modern battleship and an armored cruiser were added to the squadron. Comparative tables of Russian and Japanese naval strength at the time show the Japanese as slightly superior,[212] but with every new arrival of Russian ships the margin became smaller. Two battleships were being built for Japan in England, but she could not expect to receive them for a year. Russia could reinforce her Pacific squadron with the units of the Baltic Fleet, some of which were in stages of modernization and overhaul. The new battleship *Osliaba* and the first-class cruisers *Avrora* and *Dmitrii Donskoi* were to have been with the squadron which reached Port Arthur in December, but the *Osliaba* had run aground off Italy and had to undergo repairs at Spezzia. The outbreak of the Russo-Japanese War found this squadron in the Red Sea on the way to the Far East. Nevertheless, its arrival had to be reckoned with in estimates of the Russian naval position before the war.[213]

The evaluation of the Russian and Japanese naval potential in the Far East has been frequently discussed, with naval bases, dry docks, coal, armor, gunpowder, personnel, training, and other factors being taken into consideration. Irrespective of the conclusion drawn, there is little doubt that the Japanese margin of superiority was not a comfortable one. It was not an idle gesture that in December, 1903, the Japanese government began to negotiate with Argentina for the purchase of two first-class armoured cruisers that were being completed for Argentina in Italian shipyards.[214]

In accordance with the decision of the conference of December 28, the third Russian counterproposals of January 6, 1904, reintroduced the subject of Manchuria by including an article which read: "Japan recognizes Manchuria and her littoral as being outside her sphere of interests, while Russia, within the limits of that province, will not impede Japan, nor any other powers, in the enjoyment of rights and privileges acquired by them under existing treaties with China, exclusive of the establishment of settlements."[215] However, this provision was made conditional on the acceptance by Japan of the article on the mutual agreement not to use Korea for strategical purposes, which had been tacitly agreed to by Japan in the second Japanese proposals and the clause dealing with the 39th parallel. To allay suspicions concerning the provision in regard to Manchuria, the Russian government on January 8 issued a circular to the major powers announcing that Russia had no intention of preventing other nations from exercising their treaty rights in Manchuria.[216]

Nevertheless, the Japanese were doubtful of Russian sincerity.[217] In late December and early January the Japanese seemed convinced that a break in negotiations was inevitable and directed their diplomacy toward preparation for war. Hayashi in London asked the British government what type of "benevolent neutrality" Japan could expect from the British, and whether the Japanese would be permitted to use British coaling stations. On several occasions he brought up the possibility of raising a loan in London. He was also interested in steps Great Britain would take if the Russians should try to obtain the right of passage of the Turkish straits for their Black Sea fleet.[218] Above all, the Japanese seemed to want to avert mediation on the subject of the outstanding Russo-Japanese points of controversy.[219]

In Tokyo, the Genro and the Cabinet met on January 11. Komura expounded his view that there was no longer reason for negotiating, because the Russians refused to consider the essential point of the Manchurian issue,[220] namely, the recognition of the territorial integrity of China and Manchuria. Nevertheless, on January 13, the fourth and last Japanese proposals were given to Rosen at Tokyo, and on January 14 to Lamsdorf at St. Petersburg. These proposals, contained in another *note verbale,* represented an extreme Japanese view. Furthermore, it was indicated that these were final conditions. A threat was implied in the instructions in a verbal statement that "further delay in the solution of the question will be extremely disadvantageous to the two countries.[221]

The proposals called for the suppression of the article concerning the neutral zone and the elimination from the fifth article of the second Russian counterproposal the clause "not to use any part of Korean territory for strategic purposes." As to Manchuria, the Russian proposal was modified as follows:

a. Recognition by Japan of Manchuria and its littoral as being outside her sphere of interest and an agreement on the part of Russia to respect the territorial integrity of China in Manchuria.

b. Russia within the limits of Manchuria will not impede Japan nor other Powers in the enjoyment of rights and privileges acquired by them under the existing treaties with China.

c. Recognition by Russia of Korea and its littoral as being outside her sphere of influence.

The Japanese therefore clearly rejected those terms deemed by Russia as absolutely prerequisite to discussion of the Manchurian question. By their fourth set of proposals, the Japanese were throwing the negotiations into an impasse and preparing for the breakdown of negotiations which, according to recent Russian works on the causes of the Russo-Japanese War, would provide Japan with justifiable grounds for attacking Russia.[222] The Japanese proposals were an ultimatum in that sense.

Meanwhile, preparations for war were made by Russia and Japan. As early as December 28 the Japanese Cabinet approved certain emergency measures such as censorship and the purchase of the Argentine cruisers. On January 14, 1904, the High Military Council was formed for the direction of military operations, and on January 22, an Imperial Order was published placing certain restrictions on foreign vessels entering Japanese ports and special naval zones.[223] In St. Petersburg Kurino asked Lamsdorf at least twice for an answer to the last Japanese proposal-ultimatum. He stressed the need of haste in making the decision.[224] Perhaps he was hopeful of a satisfactory answer. But in London, Minister Hayashi stressed the finality of the Japanese proposals with words to the effect that nothing would content the Japanese government "but a distinct bilateral agreement on the subject of Manchuria." Of the situation in Japan he said, "there is no peace party now."[225] Hayashi's interview of January 29 left Lansdowne with the impression that "nothing short of a complete acceptance of the Japanese proposals would avert war."[226]

Alexeev was well informed by his agents of many details of Japanese military preparations—of the massing of transports and loading of troops at Moji in the first week of January, 1904.[227] On January 6, he asked permission of the Tsar to mobilize the troops in the Far East and to move detachments to the Yalu River;[228] but the Tsar, after conferring with Kuropatkin, permitted only preparations for mobilization and the movement of troops to the Yalu, although he permitted Alexeev to take special measures in gathering supplies and transport facilities.[229] Alexeev's alarm brought further restrictions of his viceregal powers, as he was informed that he should take no action without notifying the Tsar.[230] On January 27 the Tsar telegraphed him:

> Keep in mind for your own information that in case of a Japanese landing in southern Korea or on the eastern shore at a parallel south of Seoul, Russia will look upon it through her fingers and avert her eyes, and this will not be considered a cause for war. We can allow Japanese occupation up to the mountains forming the watershed of the Yalu and Tumen-ula.[231]

Nevertheless, among the statesmen in Russia there was increased hostility toward the Japanese as a result of the fourth proposal. Kuropatkin wrote a memorandum to the Tsar again insisting on the creation of a neutral zone north of the 39th parallel, while the Tsar considered the Japanese insistence on the inclusion of a "Chinese integrity in Manchuria" clause as an "impertinence."[232]

On January 28, 1904, another conference was held to discuss the Japanese terms and suggest a counterproposal. The Grand Duke Alexei Alexandrovich, Admiral Avelan (Director of the Navy Department), Rear Admiral Abaza, Lamsdorf, and Kuropatkin were in attendance. The conference revealed differences of opinion; but Kuropatkin and Lamsdorf, apparently with the approval of others, decided not to permit a discussion of "Chinese territorial integrity in Manchuria" in the counterproposals. As to the other terms, it was decided to omit all forms of the demand for the neutral zone, to omit the reservation in regard to "settlements" in the clause respecting the rights of other powers in Manchuria, and to retain the article concerning the Japanese obligation not to use Korea for strategical purposes.[233] The counterproposals were therefore in the nature of a compromise and again indicate the amenable attitude of the Russian statesmen toward the negotiations.

The text of the final counterproposals was approved by the Tsar on February 2 and was sent to Port Arthur for transmission to Tokyo on February 3. If only the usual delays in transmission had taken place, the telegram probably should have reached Port Arthur on February 3 or 4 and have reached Tokyo on either February 4 or 5. According to one source, the Japanese purposely delayed transmitting the coded telegram to Rosen until February 7.[234] However, in all probability this would have made no difference in the course of events. On February 3, the Japanese Cabinet and the Privy Council met and decided to wage war against Russia. On February 4, the same group met in a Throne Council and the decision received Imperial sanction.[235] On February 5 Admiral Togo received orders to begin operations, and on February 6 the loaded transports sailed for Chemulpo to begin military operations by landing in Korea.[236] On the same day, Komura telegraphed Kurino orders to break off diplomatic relations with Russia.[237] The orders were carried out the same afternoon.[238] Also on that day, the Japanese fleet began taking offensive action by seizing Russian vessels in Japanese harbors and on the high seas;[239] but news of these seizures was kept from the general public and was not widely known until after the end of the war.

On February 8, the Tsar called another special conference, over which he presided personally. Lamsdorf and Kuropatkin again attended, and so did the Grand Duke Alexei Alexandrovich, Aveland, and Abaza. The conference discussed only strategical considerations involved in permitting the Japanese to land in certain parts of Korea. Kuropatkin's views that any landing north of Chemulpo would give Russia a great advantage in initial deployment were accepted.[240] As a result of the discussion a telegram was dispatched to Alexeev from the Tsar with the following orders:

It is desirable that the Japanese, and not we, begin military actions. Therefore, if they do not begin operations against us, you must not take any measures against their landing in southern Korea, or on the eastern shore [of Korea] up to Gensan, inclusive. But if their fleet, with a landing force or without one, should cross north of the 39th parallel, on the western coast of Korea, then you can attack them without waiting for the first shot. I depend on you. God be with you.[241]

Consequently, on the night of February 8–9, the Japanese torpedo boats launched their deadly attack at the unsuspecting Russian Pacific squadron anchored in the open roadstead of Port Arthur. The orders to the Russian fleet to attack any Japanese war vessel north of the 39th parallel had already been issued and were probably in transmission. It was only a matter of chance who would fire the first shot of the war. The declarations of war on February 10 were mere formalities following the intention and the fact.

NOTES

ABBREVIATIONS

B.D.   *British Documents on the Origins of the War, 1898–1914.* Ed. by George Peabody Gooch and Harold Temperley. London, 1926–1938.

C.E.R.   Chinese Eastern Railway.

D.D.F   *Documents diplomatiques (Français).* Paris, 1871–1931.

G.P.   *Die grosse Politik der europäischen Kabinette, 1871–1914.* Berlin, 1922–1927.

G.S.S.   *Glavny Shtab, Sbornik ... materialov po Azii* (Russian General Staff, Collection of Geographical, Topographical, and Statistical Materials on Asia). Moscow, 1883–1896, 1896–1914.

I.I.R.G.O.   *Izvestiia Imperatorskago Russkago Geograficheskago, obshchestva, 1865–1885* (News of the Imperial Russian Geographical Society ...). St. Petersburg, 1887.

I.V.I.   *Izvestiia Vostochnago Instituta* (News of the Oriental Institute). Vladivostok, 1898–1922.

I.V.I., Chronicle. A supplement of magazine articles in German, French, English, Japanese, and Chinese.

Journal R.U.S.I. Journal of the Royal United Service Institute.

K.A.   *Krasnyi Arkhiv* (Red Archive). Moscow, 1922–1941.

M.I.D.   *Ministerstvo Inostrannykh Del* (Ministry of Foreign Affairs).

S.M.R.   South Manchurian Railway.

Z.I.R.G.O.   *Zapiski Imperatorskago Russkago Geograficheskago Obshchestva* (Records of the Imperial Russian Geographic Society). St. Petersburg, 1867–1916.

NOTES TO CHAPTER I

[1] A. V. Efimov, *Iz istorii russkikh ekspeditsii na Tikhom Okeane* (Moscow, 1948), pp. 49–54.

[2] For representative criticism around 1870, 1880, and 1890, see N. M. Prjevalskii, *Puteshestvie v Ussuriiskom krae, 1866–1869* (St. Petersburg, 1870); [Arkhimandrit] Palladii, "Istoricheskii ocherk Ussuriiskago kraia v sviazi s istoriei Manzhurii," *Z.I.R.G.O.*, VIII (1879), 221–228; S. I. Korzhinskii, *Amurskaia oblast' kak zemledel'cheskaia koloniia* (St. Petersburg, 1892).

[3] Report of Muraviev-Amurskii to the Minister of War, Feb. 27 (March 11), 1857. I. P. Barsukov, *Graf Nikolai Nikolaevich Amurskii* (Moscow, 1891), II, 150–151; T. I. Polner (ed.), *Priamur'e: Fakty, tsifry, nabliudeniia* (Moscow, 1909), pp. 61, 75, cited hereafter as *Priamur'e;* Constantin von Zepelin, *Der Ferne Osten* (Berlin, 1907–1911), II, 66; Great Britain, Naval Intelligence Division, *Handbook of Siberia and Arctic Russia* (London, 1922), pp. 64 ff., cited hereafter as *Handbook of Siberia.*

[4] *Handbook of Siberia*, pp. 204–205; Zepelin, *op. cit.*, II, 51.

[5] *Handbook of Siberia*, p. 205. In 1869 the population consisted of 67 settlements on the Amur with 13,209 inhabitants, 28 settlements on the Ussuri with 5,310 inhabitants, or a total of 95 settlements with 18,519 inhabitants. *Priamur'e*, p. 82.

[6] *Priamur'e*, p. 59.

[7] Zepelin, *op. cit.*, II, 52–53. In 1880 more people left the Amur region than settled there. The Zeya River district was almost entirely depopulated. K. A. Skal'kovskii, *Russkaia torgovlia v Tikhom Okeane* (St. Petersburg, 1883), p. 65.

[8] Palladii, *op. cit.*, VIII, 226.

[9] Nazarov [Colonel], "Materialy dlia voenno-statisticheskago obzora Priamurskago voennago okruga i Manzhurii," *G.S.S.*, XXXI (1888), 249; *Priamur'e*, p. 210.

[10] *Priamur'e*, p. 210.

[11] I. Nadarov, "Severno-Ussuriiskii krai," *Z.I.R.G.O.*, VII (1887), 51.

[12] For example, see the account of the return of Muraviev-Amurskii's expedition of 1855, which had to ascend the river in the autumn and winter of 1856. M. I. Veniukov, "Amur v 1857–1858 godu," *Russkaia Starina*, XXIV (1879), 99–100; *Priamur'e*, pp. 66–68; Barsukov, *op. cit.*, I, 456–465.

[13] See report of Muraviev-Amurskii to the Grand Duke Constantine, chairman of the committee on Siberia, Sept. 20 (Oct. 11), 1858. Barsukov, *op. cit.*, II, 186–189.

[14] An average of 11.5 inches of rain fell during the three summer months, June, July, and August. Holt S. Hallet, "Russian Possessions in the Far East," *Nineteenth Century*, XLI (1902), 489; D. M. Pozdneev (ed.), *Opisanie Manzhurii* (St. Petersburg, 1897), II, App. I, table E.

[15] Hallet, *op. cit.*, p. 489.

[16] Palladii, *op. cit.*, VIII, 224.

[17] "P'ianyi khleb."

[18] A. V. Eliseev, "Otchet o poezdke na Dal'nii Vostok," *I.I.R.G.O.*, XXVI (1890), 337–338. Eliseev was the botanist who solved this problem of grain pathology.

[19] Skal'kovskii, *op. cit.*, pp. 31–33.

[20] Korzhinskii, *op. cit.*, p. 60.

[21] In 1881, 2,400 head of cattle were imported from Manchuria. Skal'kovskii, *op. cit.*, p. 31. See also Pozdneev, *op. cit.*, II, App. VIII, tables 4 and 5; V. L. Komarov, "Usloviia dal'neishei kolonizatsii Amura," *I.I.R.G.O.*, XXXII (1896), 459, 490.

[22] Korzhinskii, *op. cit.*, pp. 59–60. The author recommended the cultivation of soya beans. *Ibid.*, p. 110. It is interesting to note that Soviet Russia has adopted the cultivation of soya beans in the Far East.

[23] Skal'kovskii, *op. cit.*, pp. 78–79.

[24] *Ibid.*, pp. 81–82.

[25] Chiefly from San Francisco. Skal'kovskii, *op. cit.*, p. 82.

[26] *Ibid.*, p. 80. Russian missionaries reported a complete extermination of the natives. But the reports must have been exaggerated; probably the natives migrated elsewhere in search of food.

[27] Zepelin, *op. cit.*, II, 58. Vladivostok was then a small outpost of Novgorodsk.

[28] A. Seich, "Sakhalin kak koloniia," *Russkaia Mysl'*, 1904, No. 7, p. 152. This was the period of the final Russo-Japanese negotiations over Sakhalin, and it would seem that a strong position on the island would have been required.

[29] *Handbook of Siberia*, p. 205; Zepelin, *op. cit.*, II, 62.

[30] I. P. Iuvachev, "Bor'ba s khunhuzami na Manzhurskoi granitse," *Istoricheskii Vestnik*, LXXXII (October, 1900), 177–206 (December, 1900), 538–564.

[31] See chap. ii.

[32] Skal'kovskii, *op. cit.*, pp. 88–92.

[33] *Ibid.*, p. 88.

[34] *Ibid.*, p. 89.

[35] Barsukov, *op. cit.*, I, 387; Skal'kovskii, *op. cit.*, p. 67; Zepelin, *op. cit.*, III, 96–97.

[36] Skal'kovskii, *op. cit.*, p. 409; *Priamur'e*, 210.

[37] Skal'kovskii, *op. cit.*, p. 409. These trips were made more imperative after 1867, when a new Russo-Japanese commercial treaty, signed at Hakodate Dec. 11 (23), forbade the export of such Japanese staple products as rice, rye, wheat, and flour. See art. 11 of the treaty, *ibid.*, p. 511.

[38] Construction of the first dock in Vladivostok was begun in 1883. *Ibid.*, p. 15.

[39] That of Nagasaki, built in 1877, was most frequently used by Russian ships. See V. Rudnev, "Iz vospominanii o plavanii na kreisere 'Africa,'" *Russkaia Starina*, CLII (October, 1912), 208; Skal'kovskii, *op. cit.*, p. 428.

[40] Barsukov, *op. cit.*, pp. 47–48.

[41] *Priamur'e*, pp. 167–168.

[42] Beginning with the Tientsin Conventions of England and France in 1860 and ending with the Trade Convention between China and Austria-Hungary in 1869. Edward Hertslet, *China Treaties* (London, 1908), I, *passim*.

[43] The average number of poods (one pood = 36 American pounds) from 1851 to 1860 was 401,820; in 1860, 453,577; in 1865, 711,504; in 1870, 1,139,070; in 1875, 1,358,734; in 1880, 2,142,237. See annual table in Skal'kovskii, *op. cit.*, p. 188.

[44] V. L., von. "Torgovye zadachi Rossii na Vostoke i v Amerike," *Vestnik Evropy*, VI, No. 2 (February, 1871), 756. Skal'kovskii's figures for 1875 are 14,000,000 pounds (Russian) for Kiakhta and 134,000 pounds for the Amur. In 1879 no tea went by the Amur route. Skal'kovskii, *op. cit.*, p. 310.

[45] V. L., von, *op. cit.*, p. 757.

[46] *Ibid.*

[47] A detailed analysis of freight costs in 1871 is given in V. L., von, *op. cit.*, pp. 758–759; also in Skal'kovskii, *op. cit.*, pp. 307–309; and N. G. Matiunin, "Nashi sosedi na krainem vostoke," *Vestnik Evropy* XXIII, No. 7 (July, 1888), 84.

[48] M. I. Veniukov, "Ocherki krainego Vostoka," *Vestnik Evropy*, VI, No. 8 (August, 1871), 495.

[49] Skal'kovskii, *op. cit.*, p. 313.

[50] *Ibid.*, p. 299.

[51] D. M. Pozdneev, "Materialy po voprosu o peresmotre deistvuiushchikh v kitaiskikh morskikh tamozhniakh...," *I.V.I.*, XIV (1906), 81.

[52] V. L., von, *op. cit.*, p. 756.

[53] With the ships *Nakhimov* and *Chikhachev. Ibid.*, p. 771.

[54] In 1876. Skal'kovskii, *op. cit.*, p. 451.

[55] *Ibid.*, p. 298.

[56] *Ibid.,* p. 298.

[57] *Ibid.,* p. 367.

[58] In the 1860's, 5,000 inhabitants; in the 1870's, 2,500; in 1881, 1,500. *Ibid.,* p. 68.

[59] From 1865 to 1875 Nikolaevsk was visited by an average of 16 vessels annually. 70 per cent were German. In the period 1875–1879, foreigners sent out 1,770,000 rubles through the local bank; Russian merchants only 142,000. Skal'-kovskii, *op. cit.,* pp. 71–72.

[60] *Ibid.,* pp. 16–34.

[61] Zepelin, *op. cit.,* III, 98.

[62] Local Russian merchants bitterly complained against the *porto franco* status and said that they were being "exploited by American and Hamburg firms." Matiunin, "Nashi sosedi . . .," *Vestnik Evropy,* XXXIII, No. 7 (July, 1888), 84. Certain foreign firms—notably Kunst and Albers of Hamburg—eventually became completely Russified.

[63] In the year 1876, imports amounted to 1,154,781 rubles, exports 44,097 rubles; in 1878, imports 2,185,000 rubles, exports 104,521 rubles; in 1880, imports 2,742,200 rubles, exports 260,096 rubles. Skal'kovskii, *op. cit.,* p. 17.

[64] *Ibid.,* p. 29.

[65] *Priamur'e,* p. 164.

[66] For example, the exports of Vladivostok in 1878 included 57,850 rubles worth of *bêche de mer,* and 25,500 rubles worth of "velvet" horns. Therefore, 83,350 out of 104,521 rubles worth of exports was entirely in the hands of the Chinese. Skal'-kovskii, *op. cit.,* p. 17.

[67] *Ibid.,* p. 400.

[68] Prjevalskii, *op. cit.,* p. 111.

[69] Muraviev-Amurskii's report to Nicholas I, Sept. 7, 1848, Barsukov, *op. cit.,* II, 33–34.

[70] Nadarov, *op. cit.,* VII (1887), 100; *Priamur'e,* pp. 545–551.

[71] See letter of Muraviev-Amurskii to the Director of the Siberian Committee, Dec. 15, 1858, Barsukov, *op. cit.,* II, 220–224.

[72] The withdrawal of 1856 left only a few military colonists, and the work had to be begun anew. *Priamur'e,* p. 105.

[73] Zepelin, *op. cit.,* II, 42. *Priamur'e,* pp. 103–105, which gives the date as April 27. V. L. Komarov in "Usloviia dal'neishei kolonizatsii Amura," p. 468, gives it as April 27. By 1890, 25,000 dessiatines had been bought.

[74] Zepelin, *op. cit.,* II, 66–67. This inducement was incorporated in the first regulations for the settlement of the Amur in 1858; it was suggested by Muraviev-Amurskii. Barsukov, *op. cit.,* II, 194.

[75] K. Kochurovskii, "Krest'ianskoe khoziaistvo i pereselenie," *Russkaia Mysl',* 1894, No. 3, p. 25. In the period 1861–1891, 570,000 to 600,000 settled in Asiatic Russia, of which Eastern Siberia took 60,000 to 70,000.

[76] "Whereas in southern Russia the main problem was irrigating the fields, on the Amur it was how to drain them." Komarov, *op. cit.,* p. 459.

[77] Zepelin, *op. cit.,* II, 43.

[78] *Ibid.,* II, 55; *Handbook of Siberia,* p. 204.

[79] *Priamur'e,* p. 81; M. I. Veniukov, "Amur v 1857–1858 godu," *Russkaia Starina.* XXIV (1879), 279–280.

[80] There were eight major floods between 1855 and 1882. Franz Shperk, *Rossiia Dal'nego Vostoka* (St. Petersburg, 1885), pp. 201–203, 389; Komarov, *op. cit.,* p. 470.

[81] The annual average number of volunteer settlers from 1861 to 1869 was 1,044; from 1869 to 1882, only 96. *Priamur'e,* p. 108.

[82] Zepelin, *op. cit.,* II, 37.

[83] See analysis of cossack grants in Komarov, *op. cit.*, pp. 470–471; *Priamur'e*, pp. 75–83. It must be noted that the cossack settlers were not of the best quality. A substitute purchase system was in use in the transbaikal region, and the richer and more energetic cossaks were able to hire drunken and ne'er-do-well substitutes. *Ibid.*, p. 69; Skal'kovskii, *op. cit.*, p. 3.

[84] Komarov, *op. cit.*, pp. 460, 467.

[85] Yet the Siberian squadron was dependent on foreign coal to the extent of 600,000 to 700,000 poods per year. A. Seich, *op. cit.*, pp. 158–159.

[86] *Ibid.*, p. 156. For other minor attempts see A. A. Panov, *Sakhalin kak koloniia* (Moscow, 1905), pp. 22–25.

[87] Seich, *op. cit.*, pp. 158–159.

[88] See p. 13.

[89] Seich, *op. cit.*, pp. 161–162.

[90] In 1904, during the Russo-Japanese War, no attempt was made to defend the island, and the island penal colony was scattered. E. V. Lebedev, *Sovetskii Sakhalin* (Moscow, 1933), p. 18.

[91] Nadarov, *op. cit.*, p. 106.

[92] In 1869, 7,000 Koreans entered Russian territory, Zepelin, *op. cit.*, II, 62–63; *Handbook of Siberia*, pp. 210–211; *Priamur'e*, pp. 151–152.

[93] Nazarov, *op. cit.*, p. 5.

[94] Eliseev, *op. cit.*, p. 340. In the Amur region in 1882 the population consisted of 41,500 Russians and 15,000 Orientals. Nazarov, *op. cit.*, pp. 5–7.

[95] Nadarov, *op. cit.*, p. 103.

[96] Matiunin, *op. cit.*, p. 84.

[97] See p. 24.

[98] A detailed and interesting account of this episode is found in Pozdneev, *Opisanie Manzhurii*, I, 485–504. See also A. Lebedev, "Zheltuginskaia Respublika v Kitae," *Russkoe Bogatstvo*, 1896, No. 9, pp. 144–171.

[99] The preamble of their constitution read: "We, the partners and owners of the independent mines of the California on the Amur..." Pozdneev, *op. cit.*, I, 493. See also periodical bibliography in which "the California of the Amur" is frequently mentioned. Pozdneev, *op. cit.*, II, 21–24.

[100] *Ibid.*, II, 493–494

[101] Lebedev, *op. cit.*, pp. 146–147, 155; Pozdneev, *op. cit.*, pp. 499–501.

[102] Lebedev, *op. cit.*, pp. 157–158.

[103] *Ibid.*, pp. 155–156; Pozdneev, *op. cit.*, p. 502.

[104] Pozdneev, *op. cit.*, pp. 502–506.

[105] E. D. Grimm, *Sbornik dogovorov i drugikh dokumentov po istorii mezhdunarodnykh otnoshenii na Dal'nem Vostoke* (Moscow, 1927), p. 71.

[106] Nadarov, *op. cit.*, pp. 116, 125.

[107] *Ibid.*, p. 127.

[108] *Ibid.*, p. 129; Skal'kovskii, *op. cit.*, p. 9.

[109] M. N. Pokrovskii, "Vostochnyi Vopros" in *Istoriia Rossii v XIX veke* (Moscow, 1913–1914), VI, 63; Skal'kovskii, *op. cit.*, p. 466; Zepelin, *op. cit.*, I, 210.

[110] They were tried on a route from Russia to America but proved unprofitable. Skal'kovskii, *op. cit.*, p. 466.

[111] *Ibid.*, pp. 466–467; Zepelin, *op. cit.*, I, 210–211.

[112] Zepelin, *op. cit.*, I, 210–211.

[113] Skal'kovskii, *op. cit.*, p. 467.

[114] For a detailed account of the cargoes carried between 1879 and 1883, see *ibid.*, pp. 468–472.

[115] Operations in 1882–1886 left a deficit of 240,000 rubles. Zepelin, *op. cit.*, I, 211.

[116] Skal'kovskii, *op. cit.*, p. 22.

[117] N. A. Voloshinov, "Sibirskaia zheleznaia doroga," *I.I.R.G.O.*, XXVII (1891), 14.

[118] *Priamur'e*, pp. 97–105.

[119] Skal'kovskii, *op. cit.*, pp. 31, 68, 69.

[120] In the 1860's there were ten steamers; in 1881, fifty. In the same period the population increased from 10,000 to 40,000. *Ibid.*, p. 65.

[121] R. R. Rosen, *Forty Years of Diplomacy* (New York, 1922), I, 46.

[122] Rosen in his first diplomatic post in Japan served as chargé d'affaires. *Ibid.*, p. 53.

[123] Skal'kovskii, *op. cit.*, p. 352.

[124] For example, Muraviev-Amurskii, Governor General of Eastern Siberia.

[125] Skal'kovskii, *op. cit.*, p. 81.

[126] By Baron Korf in 1886. See A. P. Chekhov, *Na Sakhaline* (St. Petersburg, 1890), p. 120.

[127] *G.S.S.*, XLI (1889), 143, 145.

[128] *Ibid.*, p. 194.

[129] N. M. Prjevalskii, "Ussuriiskii krai," *Vestnik Evropy*, V, No. 5 (May, 1870), 237–238. The author was an eyewitness of such trade.

[130] *Ibid.*, p. 238.

[131] K. N. Pos'iet, "Prekrashchenie ssylki v Sibir'," *Russkaia Starina*, XLIX (1899), No. 7, p. 52.

[132] *Ibid.*, p. 59.

[133] The two famous Russian explorers Prjevalskii and Veniukov never entered Korea; they wrote about it from foreign accounts.

[134] Except for a few short news items, the first publication on Korea was the translation of W. E. Griffis, *Corea, the Hermit Nation*, *G.S.S.*, XIV (1885).

[135] Prince Dadeshkaliani, "Ocherki Korei," *G.S.S.*, XXII (1886), 61–119.

[136] Korean Treaties, 1876–1884. The circumstances of the opening of Korea are briefly and illuminatingly described in T. F. Tsiang, "Sino-Japanese Diplomatic Relations, 1870–1894," *Chinese Social and Political Science Review*, XVII (April, 1933), 1–106.

[137] Text in *G.S.S.*, XLI (1889), App. I. English text in Great Britain, Foreign Office, *British Foreign and State Papers*, LXXV (1883–1884), 510–517.

[138] Art. VIII, sec. 1.

[139] See chap. ii.

[140] G. M. McCune, "Korea's International Debut, 1882–1885" (seminar report), March, 1936, citing exchange of telegrams between Ito and Inouye in November, 1882, from *Inouye Biography*, III, 492, 494–495.

[141] *G.S.S.*, XLI (1889), App. II.

[142] A. Popov, "Pervye shagi russkago imperializma na Dal'nem Vostoke (1888–1903)," *K.A.*, LII (1932), 55–56.

[143] 1885. China and Japan mutually promised to withdraw troops from Korea and to take no action in the future toward Korea without notifying the other signatory. Text in Grimm, *op. cit.*, p. 91.

[144] *K.A.*, LII (1932), 56.

[145] *G.S.S.*, XLI (1889), 195.

[146] Ministry of Finance, *Opisanie Korei* (St. Petersburg, 1900), III, 176–179.

[147] *G.S.S.*, XLI, 215, App. III.

[148] *Ibid.*, p. 206.

[149] Rosen, *op. cit.*, p. 26.

[150] *Ibid.*, p. 53. Skal'kovskii claims that Russia agreed to a treaty revision in 1880 when a proposed tariff was discovered to contain a provision under which duties on Russian fish coming into Japan would be smaller than in the period 1861–1867. Skal'kovskii, *op. cit.*, pp. 372–373.

[151] Skal'kovskii, *Vneshniaia politika Rossii i polozhenie inostrannykh derzhav* (St. Petersburg, 1897), p. 493.

[152] Grimm, *op. cit.*, p. 51.

[153] Report on Manchuria, 1886, Great Britain, Parliamentary Papers, *China No. 2 (1887)*; hereafter cited as *China No. 2 (1887)*, etc. "Dvadtsat' piat' let Pekinskago Dogovora," *Istoricheskii Vestnik*, XXII (1885), 734; Pozdneev, *Opisanie Manzhurii*, I, 34–38.

[154] Pozdneev, *op. cit.*, pp. 34–38.

[155] *Ibid.*, pp. 36–38.

[156] T. Iuzefovich, *Dogovory Rossii s Vostokom* (St. Petersburg, 1869), pp. 269–275.

[157] Art. I.

[158] Especially in a vile Chinese liquor called "hanshin." Nadarov, *op. cit.*, p. 105.

[159] The northern districts had definite frontiers bordering on this "no man's land" beyond which settlers were forbidden to go. *G.S.S.*, XXXVIII (1889), 17.

[160] In 1885 an export of 8,298,000 taels. *G.S.S.* XXXII (1888), 77–78.

[161] Russian cloth in Kirin province, imported through Vladivostok, sold at twice the price of English cloth brought overland from Inkou. *G.S.S.*, XXXVIII (1889), 74.

[162] *Ibid.*

[163] Report on Manchuria, 1886, *China No. 2 (1887)*, pp. 11–12.

[164] During the Mohammedan rebellion in 1865, Kuldja, a town of Eastern Turkestan, was destroyed and its Chinese population exterminated. By agreement with China in 1871 Russia occupied the city and province. By treaty in 1881 Russia withdrew, but retained some of the land as a place "where the rebels could find a refuge." For withdrawing, she received an indemnity of 9,000,000 rubles. *New International Encyclopedia* (New York: Dodd, Mead, 1921), XIII, 385.

NOTES TO CHAPTER II

[1] The history of these negotiations and the role of Li Hung-chang in preserving peace are found in an account based on Chinese sources: A. P. Ludwig, "Li Hung-chang and Chinese Foreign Policy, 1870–1885" (unpublished Ph.D. dissertation, University of California, Berkeley, 1936). A shorter account, also based on recently published Chinese sources, is given by Chu Djang, "War and Diplomacy over Ili," *Chinese Social and Political Science Review*, XX (October, 1936), 369–392.

[2] See text on Imperial Maritime Customs, *Treaties and Conventions Between China and Foreign States*, I, 72 ff.

[3] K. A. Skal'kovskii, *Vneshniaia politika Rossii . . . .*, p. 458.

[4] More than 5,000 men were sent to the Far East in 1879–1880. *G.S.S.*, XII (1884), 166.

[5] Henri Cordier, *Histoire des relations de la Chine avec les Puissances Étrangères* (Paris, 1902), II, 240; also cited in H. B. Morse, *International Relations of the Chinese Empire* (New York, 1918), II, 339.

[6] Chu Djang, *op. cit.*, p. 391.

[7] Cordier, *op. cit.*, II, 166 ff.

[8] It began with a bloody anti-Japanese riot. See T. C. Lin, "Li Hung-chang: His Korean Policies, 1870–1885," *Chinese Social and Political Science Review*, XIX (July, 1935), 227; T. F. Tsiang, "Sino-Japanese Diplomatic Relations, 1870–1894," *Chinese Social and Political Science Review*, XVII (April, 1933), 70–76.

[9] Tsiang, *op. cit.*, p. 76; Lin, *op. cit.*, p. 228.

[10] Ludwig, *op. cit.*, pp. 346, 392–394.

[11] Tsiang, *op. cit.*, p. 78.

[12] Chu Djang, *op. cit.*, p. 380.

[13] *Annual Register*, 1883, p. 371.

[14] This important boundary question was not settled until 1886.

[15] Chu Djang, *op. cit.*, p. 381.

[16] For example, by art. 2 of Treaty of Tientsin, June, 1858, and arts. 8 and 9 of Treaty of Peking of November, 1860, the military governor of the Amur district had the right to communicate directly with the Chinese governor of Heilungkiang. But from 1863 to 1884, all Russian couriers from the Amur district were stopped on the frontier on the ground that the Chinese copies of the treaties which were kept at Aigun did not contain that provision. See Captain Evtiugin, "Poezdka iz Blagoveschenska v Tsitsihar v 1884 godu," *G.S.S.*, XIV (1885), 179–180.

[17] *Ibid.*, p. 218; "Zapiski o Manzhurii polkovnika Barabasha i Matiunina," *G.S.S.*, I (1883), 25 ff.; Prjevalskii, "Soobrazheniia o vozmozhnoi voine s Kitaem," *G.S.S.*, I, 120.

[18] *G.S.S.*, XXII (1886), 130 ff.

[19] *G.S.S.*, XIV (1885), 208, 218.

[20] Lt. Col. Butakov, "Vooruzhennye sily Kitaia i Iaponii," *G.S.S.*, III (1883), 36.

[21] *G.S.S.*, I (1883), 22; XIV, 213–218; XXXVII, 228.

[22] See the sound analysis of the strategic position of the Amur district in Evtiugin, *op. cit.*, XIV, 213–219.

[23] D. A. Davydov, "Kolonizatsiia Manzhurii i severo-vostochnoi Mongolii," *I.V.I.*, XXXVII (1911), 27. Also D. V. Putiata, "Zapreshchenie kitaitsam selitsia na Manzhurskikh zemliakh," *G.S.S.*, XLII (1889), 159–163.

[24] Palladii, "Dorozhnyia zapiski na puti ot Pekina do Blagoveschenska cherez Manzhuriiu v 1870 godu," *Z.I.R.G.O.*, IV (1871), 373, 395, 415, 423–424; Davydov, *op. cit.*, p. 27.

[25] Davydov, *op. cit.*, pp. 27–29.

[26] *Ibid.*, pp. 98–117.

[27] D. V. Putiata, "Otchet o poezdke v Manzhuriiu v 1888 godu," *G.S.S.* XXXVIII (1889), 17.

[28] *Ibid.*, 15.

[29] *Ibid.*, 16.

[30] N. A. Voloshinov, "Sibirskaia zheleznaia doroga," I.I.R.G.O., XXVII (1891), 15.

[31] *G.S.S.*, XXXVIII (1889), 33, 41, 113. Compared with 55,000 men (13,500 of new formations) in 1884. *G.S.S.*, XXXIV (1888), 1–3.

[32] Putiata, "Polozhenie severnoi eskadry," *G.S.S.*, XVI (1885), 126–135.

[33] P. Nadin, "Kvantun i ego proshloe," *Vestnik Evropy*, XXXIX, No. 3 (May-June, 1904), 725.

[34] *Ibid.* Putiata, "Opisanie Port Artura," *G.S.S.*, XXXII (1888), 1–3, gives a valuable strategic analysis of the port's value and defects.

[35] Tsiang, *op. cit.*, p. 79.

[36] The conference of May 8, 1888, contemplated the possibility that Chinese demands for the recognition of Korea as a vassal state might be merely a pretext for the establishment of a firm position in Korea, which would menace the Ussuri region. *K.A.*, LII (1932), 57, 60.

[37] T. F. Tsiang has traced clearly the various machinations of the King of Korea and his advisers to play one country against another and thus establish Korean independence; yet he calls them Russian intrigues. Tsiang, *op. cit.*, pp. 88–94.

[38] See p. 27, below.

[39] Ludwig, *op. cit.*, p. 394; Cordier, *op. cit.*, II, 476 ff.

[40] Skal'kovskii, *op. cit.*, p. 460. Prjevalskii considered that an attack on Russia would soon follow. See Georgievskii, "Prjevalskii," *Vestnik Evropy* XXI, No. 6 (June, 1886), 777, 796.

[41] A. Lebedev, "Zheltuginskaia Respublika v Kitae," *Russkoe Bogatstvo*, 1896, No. 9, pp. 161–164; Pozdneev, Opisanie Manzhurii, I, 503–504; Putiata, "Opisanie Port Artura," *G.S.S.*, XXXII (1888), 137. A confused account of this campaign reached Europe. See *Annual Register*, 1885, pp. 336–337.

[42] Lebedev, *op. cit.*, pp. 164–166; Pozdneev, *op. cit.*, p. 504.

[43] Lebedev, *op. cit.*, p. 167.

[44] Skal'kovskii, *Vneshniaia politika*, p. 461.

[45] Memorandum of May 8, 1888, *K.A.*, LII (1932), 58.

[46] Tsiang, *op. cit.*, p. 79.

[47] In October, 1886. *Annual Register*, 1886, p. 441.

[48] N. G. Matiunin, "Nashi sosedi na krainem Vostoke," *Vestnik Evropy*, XXII, No. 7 (July, 1887), 82.

[49] A. Svechin, *Evoliutsiia voennogo iskusstva* (Moscow, 1928), II, 458. In 1885 there were 18,000 men east of Lake Baikal.

[50] *Ibid.*

[51] *G.S.S.*, XVI (1885), 127.

[52] G. N. Curzon, *Problems of the Far East* (London, 1894), p. 225.

[53] *Priamur'e*, p. 116.

[54] It was actually a ten-year extension of provisions of the law of 1861, but with certain changes. *Priamur'e*, pp. 116–117; Constantin von Zepelin, *Der Ferne Osten*, II, 45; *Handbook of Siberia*, p. 210.

[55] This is in keeping with a general policy of "Russia for the Russians" then advanced by Minister N. Bunge. By 1888, purchase of land by foreigners was prohibited in ten provinces of Poland and eleven provinces of eastern Russia. See B. B. Glinskii, "Period tverdoi vlasti," *Istoricheskii Vestnik*, CXXIX (July, 1912), 275–276.

[56] *Priamur'e*, pp. 116–117; Zepelin, *op. cit.*, II, 45.

[57] *Priamur'e*, p. 95.

[58] Matiunin, *op. cit.*, pp. 64–89, 80.

[59] *Ibid.*, pp. 80–81.

[60] *Ibid.*, p. 80.

[61] "Andrei Nikolaevich Korf," *Russian Encyclopedia* (St. Petersburg, 1895), p. 354.

[62] Zepelin, *op. cit.*, II, 64; *Handbook of Siberia*, p. 211.

[63] *G.S.S.*, XLI (1889), 193.

[64] I. Nadarov, "Severno-Ussuriiskii krai," *Z.I.R.G.O.*, VII (1887), 126.

[65] *G.S.S.*, XLI (1889), 193.

[66] I. P. Iuvachev, "Bor'ba s khunhuzami na Manzhurskoi granitse," *Istoricheskii Vestnik*, LXXXII (October–December, 1900), 183.

[67] A. V. Eliseev, "Po Iuzhno-Ussuriiskomu kraiu," *Istoricheskii Vestnik*, XLIII (February–March, 1891), 448–449.

[68] *Idem*, "Otchet o poezdke na Dal'nii Vostok," *I.I.R.G.O.*, XXVI (1890), 341.

[69] *G.S.S.*, XXXVIII (1889), 41.

[70] N. A. Voloshinov, *op. cit.*, p. 27.

[71] A. N. Kulomzin (ed.), *Sibirskaia zheleznaia doroga* (St. Petersburg, 1903), p. 72.

[72] *Vestnik Evropy* XXXIV, No. 8 (August, 1899), 355–356.

[73] Kulomzin, *op. cit.*, p. 69.

[74] Cited in H. S. Hallet, "Russian Possessions in the Far East," *Nineteenth Century*, XLI (1902), 487.

[75] Tsiang, *op. cit.*, pp. 81–84; Ludwig, *op. cit.*, pp. 380–382.

[76] The Tientsin Agreement was considered a Japanese victory. From that time until 1894 Japanese influence in Korea was augmented mainly through economic penetration, while China strove to exert its influence through cultural and political ties. Tsiang, *op. cit.*, pp. 87, 88–106.

[77] Tsiang, *op. cit.*, p. 88.

[78] W. L. Langer, *The Diplomacy of Imperialism* (New York, 1935), I, 168–169.

[79] See *ibid.*, p. 169.

[80] An excellent contemporary evaluation of Vladivostok is in Matiunin, *op. cit.*, p. 81–82. The author, for many years the border commissioner of the Ussuri region, claimed that "Vladivostok, as a commercial port, is excellent." If an ice-free port were required, Posieta Bay could be developed and made into an impregnable fortress by an expenditure of 15,000,000 rubles; the Pallada anchorage of the bay is free from ice all year round.

[81] Tsiang, *op. cit.*, pp. 61–62.

[82] *Ibid.*, p. 63.

[83] *Ibid.*, pp. 63–64. In 1882 Li Hung-chang "recognized the importance of the place but did not think that Russia was likely in the near future to take positive action." *Ibid.*, p. 79.

[84] *Ibid.*, p. 64. Also, U. S. Congress, Foreign Affairs Committee, *Papers Relating to the Foreign Affairs of the United States;* cited hereafter as *U. S. Foreign Affairs.* See letters and dispatches of Foote and Freylinghausen, 1880.

[85] W. E. Griffis, *Corea, the Hermit Nation* (New York, 1905), pp. 205, 212, 373, 528, 430. The author accepts a Chinese document dealing with a "lust for land" by "Russia, the ravenous." This "aggression" contrasts effectively with the bombardments of Korean coasts by France, Japan, the United States, and England at various times from 1866 to 1876. *Ibid., passim.*

[86] The best account of this crisis, based on extensive use of manuscripts and original dispatches of the British Record Office of London (102 vols.), is in James G. Allen, "Anglo-Russian Rivalry in Central Asia, 1865–1885" (unpublished Ph.D. thesis, University of California, Berkeley, 1936), particularly chaps. 10 and 11.

[87] *Ibid.*, pp. 373 ff. Also William Habberton, *Anglo-Russian Relations Concerning Afghanistan, 1837–1907* (Urbana, 1937), pp. 54–55. It has been suggested that the crisis was not so serious as generally believed, but that gross exaggeration by the press created a war panic. J. F. Baddeley, *Russia in the Eighties* (London, 1921), p. 220.

[88] Also known by its Korean name, Chu Wen. The suggestion came from Lord Northbrook, First Lord of the Admiralty, on March 8, 1885. James Allen, *op. cit.*, p. 378; Philip Guedalla, *The Queen and Mr. Gladstone* (London, 1933). Gladstone to Victoria, April 11, 1885: "The crisis began in Parliament, April 9th." James Allen, *op. cit.*, pp. 372–373.

[89] See description in *Annual Register*, 1885, CXXVI, 339–340.

[90] Granville to Tseng, April 16, 1885, Great Britain, Foreign Office, *British Foreign and State Papers*, 1886–1887, LXXVIII, 143. Cited hereafter as *State Papers.* This volume includes most of the correspondence about Port Hamilton found in *China No. 1 (1885–1886)* and *China No. 1 (1886–1887)* of Great Britain, Parliamentary Papers, "Blue Books."

[91] James Allen, *op. cit.*, p. 375.

[92] Lord Edmond George Fitzmaurice, *The Life of Granville* (London, 1905), II, 440; James Allen, *op. cit.*, p. 377. The decision to occupy Port Hamilton was announced to all British ministers in the Far East on April 17. See Granville to Plunkett, April 17, 1885, *State Papers*, 1886–1887, p. 144. It is also alleged that the ground for the occupation of Port Hamilton had been prepared by Sir Harry Parkes, British Minister to China, before his death on March 22, 1885. See Matiunin, *op. cit.*, p. 79; *Annual Register*, 1886, p. 446.

[93] *K.A.*, LII (1932), 58; Skal'kovskii, *Vneshniaia politika*, pp. 483–484. The exact date of this is not mentioned.

[94] G. N. Curzon, *Problems of the Far East* (London, 1894), pp. 163–164.

[95] The occupation was "discovered" by a vessel of the Volunteer Fleet on May 10, 1885. H. N. G. Bushby, "The Agreement Between Great Britain and Japan," *Nineteenth Century*, LI (March, 1902), 372.

[96] Granville to O'Conor, May 6, 1885, *State Papers*, 1886–1887, p. 147.

[97] Griffis, *op. cit.*, pp. 215, 426.

[98] James Allen, *op. cit.*, p. 392; Habberton, *op. cit.*, p. 55.

[99] Note of the Korean Foreign Office to Acting Consul General Carles, May 20, 1885, *State Papers*, 1886–1887, p. 153.

[100] For their use as a coaling station. Granville to O'Conor, May 29, 1885, *ibid.*, p. 148; James Allen, *op. cit.*, pp. 378–379.

[101] China refused to recognize the legality of the occupation unless England would "guarantee to protect Korea from possible Russian aggression." James Allen, *op. cit.*, p. 379; *State Papers*, 1886–1887, p. 156.

[102] Delivered to Sir William Dowell at Nagasaki, May 19, 1885. *State Papers*, 1886–1887, p. 152. Also Dowell to the Admiralty, May 19, 1885, *ibid.*, pp. 149–150.

[103] Tsiang, *op. cit.*, pp. 90–91.

[104] Having broken off friendly relations with Li Hung-chang, Möllendorf was dismissed in July, 1885. *Ibid.*, pp. 88–89; Griffis, *op. cit.*, p. 470.

[105] Tsiang, *op. cit.*, pp. 90–91; *K.A.*, LII (1932), 61. However, Russia did not encourage this measure, fearing it might be construed as a Russian intrigue. *Ibid.*

[106] Birilev, a journalist of the popular *Russkii Vestnik*, suggested in the January, 1886, issue a comprehensive program of retaliation which included (1) the seizure of Port Lazarev and a strip of Korean territory from the Port to the Tumen River, (2) immediate construction of a trans-Siberian railroad, (3) a demand on China to open the Sungari River for Russian trade, and (4) the right of Russian trade in Manchuria along the Ussuri River beyond the already guaranteed 50-verst strip. See analysis in Matiunin, *op. cit.*, pp. 64–65.

[107] *K.A.*, LII (1932), 57.

[108] Marquis Tseng stated to the British Foreign Office that "the Russian Minister to Peking has on several occasions urged the Chinese Government to obtain the withdrawal of the British force from the islands forming Port Hamilton; he has stated that in the event of the British occupation being continued, Russia would feel obliged to occupy some place in Korea." Rosebury to O'Conor, April 1, 1886, *State Papers*, 1886–1887, p. 160; V. Avarin, *Imperializm v Manzhurii* (Moscow, 1931), p. 18.

[109] Account of the first Russian agent in Korea, Prince Dadeshkaliani, "Ocherk Korei ...," *G.S.S.*, XXII (1886), 71. Actually it is covered by several inches of ice for about two months. See *Sailing Directions for Siberia and Chosen*, 3d ed., *U. S. Hydrographic Office*, No. 122 (Washington, 1932), pp. 732–733.

[110] Shown on English charts as Broughton's Bay; also spelled Djensan, Yuensan, Wensan, and Jinsen.

[111] Opened since May, 1880, and frequently visited by English and Japanese vessels in winter. Griffis, *op. cit.*, p. 426; Dadeshkaliani, *op. cit.*, p. 71. After the Sino-Japanese agreement of Tientsin in April, 1885, the Japanese withdrew a number of their troops from Seoul to this port.

[112] Dadeshkaliani, *op. cit.*, pp. 71–72.

[113] Tsiang, *op. cit.*, p. 93.

[114] *Ibid.*, pp. 93, 96–97.

[115] This plan was deemed acceptable by Germany and England. *Ibid.*, p. 90; Currie to Macartney, April 14, 1886, *State Papers*, 1886–1887, pp. 160–161.

[116] Tyler Dennett, "Early American Policy in Korea, 1883–1887," *Political Science Quarterly*, XXXVIII (1923), 102.

[117] Salisbury to O'Conor, Dec. 12, 1885, *State Papers*, 1886–1887, p. 157.

[118] Currie to Macartney, April 14, 1886, *ibid.*, pp. 160–161.

[119] The Chinese kept a verbatim record of these conversations. Tsiang, *op. cit.*, pp. 97–98, gives an analysis of them based on the Chinese source, *Collected Writings of Li Hung-chang*, ed. by Wu Ju-lin (Nanking, 1908). The main points are con-

firmed by the Russian memorandum of May 8, 1888 in *K.A.*, LII (1932); Walsham to Iddesleigh, Nov. 5, 1886, *State Papers*, 1886–1887, pp. 103-104.

[120] *K.A.*, LII (1932), 58.

[121] *Ibid.* The interpretation by Tsiang, *op. cit.*, p. 99, suggests that the pledge was only on the part of Russia.

[122] Walsham to Iddesleigh, Nov. 5 (received Dec. 27, 1886), *State Papers*, 1886–1887, pp. 103–104.

[123] Walsham to Iddesleigh, Dec. 25, 1886; Iddesleigh to Walsham, Nov. 19, 1886; Walsham to Salisbury, March 2, 1887, *ibid.*, pp. 160, 162, 169.

[124] MacGregor, Secretary of the Admiralty, to Currie, Jan. 21, 1886, *ibid.*, pp. 157–158.

[125] Zepelin, *op. cit.*, III, 97–98.

[126] Skal'kovskii, *Vneshniaia politika Rossii*, p. 485. "On November 15 [1885], at a dinner of the Amur Society, it was proved quite thoroughly that the occupation of Port Hamilton by the English . . . paralyzes the importance of Vladivostok in the Pacific Ocean." *Istoricheskii Vestnik*, XXII (1885), 734.

[127] *K.A.*, LII (1932), 60.

[128] Matiunin, *op. cit.*, p. 82.

[129] P. Chikhachev, "Kaliforniia i Ussuriiskii krai," *Vestnik Evropy* XXV, No. 6 (June, 1890), 562.

[130] Zepelin, *op. cit.*, I, 211; U. S. Office of Naval Intelligence, General Information Series, VI, *Recent Naval Intelligence*, June, 1887 (Washington, 1887), pp. 287–288.

[131] Zepelin, *op. cit.*, I, 212.

[132] Eleven ships, of which only one was an ironclad frigate. *Annual Register*, 1877, p. 302.

[133] E. A. Falk, *Togo and the Rise of Japanese Sea Power* (New York, 1936), p. 98; Count Shigenobu Okuma, *Fifty Years of New Japan* (New York, 1909), p. 226.

[134] Falk, *op. cit.*, p. 98.

[135] Okuma, *op. cit.*, p. 226.

[136] In 1885–1889 the Japanese fortified the anchorage of Tsushima and could convert it into an efficient secondary base for intercepting ships passing through the strait. Report of Colonel K. A. Vogak, *G.S.S.*, LX (1895), 152–153. For a contrary view see Skal'kovskii, *op. cit.*, p. 469.

[137] Chapters on "Naval Progress" in *Lord Brassey's Naval Annual for 1884–1887*.

[138] *G.S.S.*, XVII (1885), 107.

[139] Japan acquired the first destroyer in 1887. Falk, *op. cit.*, p. 127.

[140] Eliseev, *op. cit.*, pp. 372–373.

[141] Entry of March 14, 1899, analyzing a report from Shevich of Jan. 26 (Feb. 7), 1889, V. N. Lamsdorf, *Dnevnik, 1886–1890* (Moscow, 1926), p. 181.

[142] *Ibid.*

[143] *K.A.*, LII, 69.

[144] "Vladimir" [Volpicelli], *Russia on the Pacific and the Siberian Railroad* (London, 1899), p. 268. It has been suggested that the work was written by I. A. Zinoviev, the head of the Asiatic Department of the Ministry of Foreign Affairs.

[145] "The Asiatic Department was considered, from the social point of view, inferior to the Chancellery," but "the Balkan Peninsula and Egypt, as well as the whole American continent belonged to the domain of this department whose very name seemed to indicate, however, that after all Asia was considered or instinctively felt to be the real and most important field for the activity of Russia's foreign policy." R. R. Rosen, *Forty Years of Diplomacy* (New York, 1922), I, 18.

[146] James G. Allen, *op. cit.*, pp. 189 ff.; Habberton, *op. cit.*, pp. 49–52.

[147] James Allen, *op. cit.*, pp. 156–188; Habberton, *op. cit.*, pp. 44–46.

[148] James Allen, *op. cit.*, pp. 156–187.

[149] Habberton, *op. cit.*, pp. 56–57.

[150] *Ibid.*, p. 57; *State Papers*, 1887–1888, pp. 388–389.

[151] J. V. Fuller, *Bismarck's Diplomacy at Its Zenith* (Cambridge, 1922), pp. 69, 71; Staal to Giers, Sept. 20 and 25, 1886, in Baron A. Meyendorff, *Correspondence diplomatique du Baron de Staal, 1884–1900* (Paris, 1929), I, 304–305, 323–325. The first of the two letters reports an almost general European coalition against the Russian candidate.

[152] The pact was in the form of an exchange of notes. Alfred F. Pribram, *The Secret Treaties of Austria-Hungary, 1879–1914* (Cambridge, 1920), I, 55–101, 125–128.

[153] *Ibid.*, II, 45 ff.; text in I, 104; Serge Goriainov, "The End of the Alliance of the Emperors," *American Historical Review*, XXIII (January, 1918), 324–350.

[154] Meyendorff, *op. cit.*, I, 353–354; Adlerberg to Giers, Oct. 12, 1887, *ibid.*, 360; Goriainov, *op. cit.*, p. 338.

[155] Fuller, *op. cit.*, p. 285, citing *Turkey, No. 1*, 1888, p. 169, Morier to Salisbury, Dec. 17, 1887.

[156] Staal to Giers, Dec. 27, 1887, Meyendorff, *op. cit.*, I, 368; Giers to Staal, Jan. 23, 1888, *ibid.*, I, 378.

[157] Gregor Alexinskii, *Modern Russia* (London, 1913), p. 216.

[158] P. P. Migulin, *Russkii gosudarstvennyi kredit, 1769–1899* (Kharkov, 1900), II, 182–186.

[159] *Ibid.*, pp. 76–77.

[160] A. N. Kulomzin (ed.), *Sibirskaia zheleznaia doroga v eia proshlom i nastoia-shchem* (St. Petersburg, 1903), p. 8.

[161] Including the Ministers of Communication, War, Finance, and Naval Affairs, the Government Controller, and the Chief of Staff but not the Minister of Foreign Affairs.

[162] Kulomzin, *op. cit.*, p. 72; B. B. Glinskii, *Prolog* (St. Petersburg, 1916), p. 5.

[163] Glinskii, *op. cit.*, p. 5.

[164] Lamsdorf, *op. cit.*, entry for Jan. 2, 1888, p. 2. A. Popov, "Anglo-russkoe sopernichestvo na putiakh Irana," *Novyi Vostok*, 1926, No. 12, pp. 133–136.

[165] G. N. Curzon, "British and Russian Commercial Competition in Central Asia," *Asiatic Quarterly Review*, VIII (July–October, 1889), 438–457.

[166] Lamsdorf, *op. cit.*, entry for Nov. 16, 1889, p. 221. Giubbinet, the Minister of Communication, favored this project.

[167] *Ibid.*, entry of Dec. 9, 1889, p. 240.

[168] A. Popov, *op. cit.*, p. 134.

[169] Glinskii, *Prolog*, pp. 7–8.

[170] Kulomzin, *op. cit.*, p. 105; Glinskii, *Prolog*, p. 8.

NOTES TO CHAPTER III

[1] For a general account of the Slavophile movement, see L. Levine, *Pan-Slavism and European Politics* (New York, 1914); "Slavianofilstvo," *Bol'shaia Sovetskaia Entsiklopediia;* N. Rubinstein, "Istoricheskaia teoriia slavianofilov i ee klassovye korni," *Russkaia istoricheskaia literatura v klassovom osveshchenii* (Moscow, 1927), I, 51 ff.; Thomas Masaryk, *Pan-Slavism* (London, 1919).

[2] This theory was popularized by the accepted leader of the Slavophiles, N. Ia. Danilevskii, in his *Rossiia i Evropa* (St. Petersburg, 1887). See also P. M. Golova-chev, *Rossiia na Dal'nem Vostoke* (St. Petersburg, 1904), p. 8.

[3] The later Eurasian school *(Evraziitsy)* had the same concept but without the imperialistic implication. The *Vostochniki* may have received their original impulse from German historians and political writers. N.S., "Russkaia i nemetskaia vosto-chnaia politika," *Russkaia Mysl'*, 1882, No. 1, pp. 37–60.

[4] Cited in "General Prejevalskii on Central Asia," *Asiatic Quarterly Review*, VI (October, 1887), 416.

[5] *Ibid.*, pp. 417–423.

[6] *Ibid.*, p. 422.

[7] F. F. Martens, *Rossiia i Kitai* (St. Petersburg, 1881) ; *idem.*, *Russia and England in Central Asia* (London, 1887).

[8] V. P. Vasil'ev, "Sovremennoe polozhenie Azii i Kitaiskii vopros," *Otchet po St. Ptb. Universitetu za 1882 god* (St. Petersburg, 1883), pp. 1–3. See also *G.S.S.*, XVIII (1885), 37. For Vasil'ev's dominant position among Russian orientalists, see A. Pozdneev, "Vasil'ev, V. P.," *Bol'shaia Sovetskaia Entsiklopediia.*

[9] Maxim Kovalevskii, *Russian Political Instructions* (Chicago, 1902), p. 22.

[10] V. Solov'ev, "Kitai i Evropa," *Sobranie Sochinenii* (St. Petersburg, 1913), VI, 84–137.

[11] For additional views see L. I. Duman, "Russkaia i inostrannaia literatura o Dunganskom vostanii 1861–1877 gg. v Kitae," *Bibliografiia Vostoka*, VII (1934), 55–78; A. A. Petrov, "Filosofiia Kitaia v russkom burzhuaznom kitaevedenii," *Bibliografiia Vostoka*, VII, 5–28. A diametrically opposite view decrying Russian advances as "one of the greatest misfortunes of the Russian nation" is expressed by the anarchist Petr Kropotkin in "The Russians in Manchuria," *Forum*, XXXI (May, 1901), 267–274.

[12] The contemporary recognition of Ukhtomskii's importance is attested by the large number of periodical articles on his life and views. A good but brief account is "Prince Ukhtomskii, a Russian of the Russians," *Review of Reviews*, XXX (1904), 72.

[13] Ukhtomskii favored religious toleration and extension of local self-government. *Ibid.;* "Sovremennik" (pseud.), *Nikolai II, Razoblacheniia* (Berlin, 1909), p. 202.

[14] E. E. Ukhtomskii, *Ot Kalmytskoi stepi do Bukhary* (St. Petersburg, 1891) ; review in *Istoricheskii Vestnik*, XLVII (1892), 263–265.

[15] "Sovremennik," *op. cit.*, p. 35.

[16] E. E. Ukhtomskii, *Travels in the East of Nicholas II . . . when Cesarevich, 1890–1892* (London, 1896–1900) ; *Poezdka Naslednika* (St. Petersburg, 1893). Sir Bernard Pares has called this book "practically . . . the textbook of the government expansion eastward." Pares, *My Russian Memoirs* (London, 1931), p. 58.

[17] *K sobytiiam v Kitae* (St. Petersburg, 1900) ; *K vostoku* (St. Petersburg, 1900) ; review in *Russkoe Bogatstvo*, 1900, No. 9, pp. 227–236; *Iz oblasti Lamaizma* (St. Petersburg, 1904) ; "The Genius in China," *Contemporary Review*, LXXXI (1902), 788–804.

[18] *Ibid.*, pp. 789–790.

[19] Quoted in P. S. Reinsch, "Governing the Orient on Western Principles," *Forum*, XXXI (June, 1901), 385-400.

[20] E. E. Ukhtomskii, "Russia Will Crush Japan," *Independent*, LVI (June 23, 1904), 1418–1420; Pares, *op. cit.*, p. 58.

[21] "Sovremennik," *op. cit.*, p. 202; "Kriticheskaia Zametka," *Mir Bozhii*, XIV, No. 3 (March, 1905), 6–13.

[22] S. Iu. Witte, *Vospominaniia* (Berlin, 1922), I, 38; cited hereafter as Witte, *Vospominaniia.*

[23] Geoffrey Drage, *Russian Affairs* (London, 1904), p. 62; J. D. Rees, "The Tsar's Friend," *Fortnightly Review*, LXXV (April, 1901), 612–622.

[24] Noncritical literature on Witte is extensive. For the best accounts see B. B. Glinskii, "Graf Sergei Iul'evich Witte (Materialy dlia biografii)," *Istoricheskii Vestnik*, CXL (1915), 232–279, 573–589, CXL I(1915), 204–233, 521–555, 893–906, CXLII (1915), 592–609, cited hereafter as Glinskii, *Witte;* Nikolai Savitskii, "Serge Witte," *Le Monde Slave*, n.s. III (August, 1932), 161–191, (September, 1932), 321–348; I. I. Korostovets, *Graf Witte* (Berlin, 1929).

[25] As manager of the South-Western Railway Company in 1891 Witte cleared his company of blame in the accident to the Imperial train at Borki and thus attracted the attention of Alexander III. In 1892 Witte married Matilda Nurok, a Jewess. The indignation of the anti-Semitic elements threatened to end his career, but Alexander III retained his faith in Witte, distinguishing "the man from the minister." Witte, *Vospominaniia*, III, 158–163, 236; Korostovets, *op. cit.*, pp. 46, 47; S. R. Tompkins, "Witte as a Finance Minister," *Slavonic Review*, XI (April, 1934), 590–606. Glinskii, *Witte*, CXL, 242.

[26] B. B. Glinskii, "Cherty iz zhizni Grafa S. Iu. Witte," *Istoricheskii Vestnik*, CXL (1915), 220, 225. See also chap. 16, "My Colleagues," in Witte, *Vospominaniia*, III, 282–319.

[27] French Strother, "Witte, the Key to Russia," *World's Work*, XL (October, 1920), 566.

[28] E. de Cyon, *M. Witte et les finances russes* (Paris, 1895), p. ix; Glinskii, *Witte*, CXL, 248–250. After Witte's death, his friend Mechnikov, the renowned scientist, wrote, "He often conducted himself in defiance of the most elementary etiquette." See "Mechnikov's Tribute to Count Witte," *American Review of Reviews*, LIII (June, 1916), 728. Witte's system was even characterized as "state socialism." "Dnevnik Polovtseva," *K.A.*, LXVII (1934), 177.

[29] I. Kh. Ozerov, *Russkii biudzhet* (Moscow, 1907), p. 48.

[30] Table, *ibid.*, p. 15. This surplus was 7 to 12 per cent of the annual revenue.

[31] By 1904 the interest alone on the capital so invested by Witte amounted to 17,500,000 rubles, which in turn could be reinvested by the State Bank, i.e., the Minister of Finance. *Ibid.*, p. 120.

[32] This alone accounts for his participation in all special conferences on Far Eastern affairs from 1894 to 1903. See also opinion of M. I. Tugan-Baranovskii in Glinskii, *Witte*, CXL, 268.

[33] In 1893 Witte overcame the opposition of the Minister of War, Vannovskii, by a direct appeal to the Tsar and established an "Independent Corps of Frontier Guards," with its own staff, artillery, and medical and other auxiliary services, including a reserved park of artillery. Witte, *Vospominaniia*, III, 288–289; Cyon, *op. cit.*, p. xxxviii; A. N. Kuropatkin, *Zapiski . . . o Russko-Iaponskoi Voine* (Berlin, 1909), pp. 140–141, cited hereafter as Kuropatkin, *Zapiski*.

[34] Glinskii, *Witte*, CXL, 274. The total budget rose from 965,000,000 in 1892 to 2,071,000,000 in 1903—an increase of 114.5 per cent. Savitskii, *op. cit.*, p. 175. By the law of 1894 the commercial schools were placed under the direction of the Minister of Finance. In 1894 there were 8; in 1902 there were 147. *Ibid.*, p. 327; Ozerov, *op. cit.*, p. 58; Witte, *Vospominaniia*, I, 448, 451–452.

[35] London *Times*, Nov. 15, 1903; Glinskii, *Witte*, CXL, 580. The charge was not pressed. Witte later admitted the practice of making such expenditures, but only to the amount of fifty to sixty million rubles. Witte, *Vospominaniia*, I, 452. In 1894, Witte, through the aid of Alexander III, revised the Comptroller Law of 1819 so that he could nominate his own comptrollers. Cyon, *op. cit.*, pp. x, 147, 160. For a scathing criticism of Witte's subsequent "bookkeeping," see I. Kh. Ozerov, *Kak raskhoduiutsia v Rossii narodnye den'gi* (Moscow, 1907), p. 23; cited hereafter as Ozerov, *Narodnye den'gi*.

[36] Witte, *Vospominaniia*, I, 223.

[37] *Ibid.*, III, 265; Savitskii, *op. cit.*, p. 176.

[38] Among them, Rothstein, an international banker; Poliakov, the Russian railroad magnate; and such capable lieutenants as Pokotilov, chief engineer of the Chinese Eastern Railway, and Victor von Grot, a former employee of the Imperial Chinese Customs later characterized as "a veritable stalking horse of the Witte government." Witte, *Vospominaniia*, III, 97, 292–319, *passim*; B. L. Simpson, *Manchu and Muscovite* (London, 1904), pp. 130–131; Alexander Ular, *A Russo-Chinese*

Empire (Westminster, 1904), pp. 184–186; "Mechnikov's Tribute to Count Witte," *American Review of Reviews*, LIII (1916), 728.

[33] Friedrich List, *Das Nationale System der politischen Ökonomie* (Berlin, 1841). In 1900–1902 Witte gave a series of lectures to Grand Duke Mikhail Alexandrovich (heir presumptive to the Russian throne in absence of a male heir to Nicholas II); these lectures were published in a pamphlet, *Narodnoe khoziaistvo* (St. Petersburg, 1902). See also A. Finn-Enotaevskii, "Graf Witte kak ekonomist," *Sovremennyi Mir*, 1912, No. 2, pp. 253–267; Glinskii, *Witte*, CXL, 261.

[40] An excellent analysis by Tugan-Baranovskii is in Glinskii, *Witte*, CXL, 269–270. See Ozerov, *Narodnye den'gi*, p. 55. In an unguarded moment Witte said, "A minister cannot practice economy in the administration of a state; money can only be found by spending it lavishly." Princess Catherine Radziwill, *Memories of Forty Years* (London, 1914), p. 69.

[41] Witte was quite proud of the fictional surplus. Witte, *Vospominaniia*, I, 223. Witte also boasted that he "brought" into the country three billion rubles, though this amount appears too large; in 1900 the true figure was about one billion. *Ibid.*, I, 448; Tompkins, *op. cit.*, pp. 593, 594.

[42] In fairness to Witte it must be added that he did try to initiate reforms for the peasants but was blocked by a strong combination of conservatives. Glinskii, *Witte*, CXLI, 521–540; Witte, *Vospominaniia*, I, 467–473; Savitskii, *op. cit.*, pp. 181–182, 188–189.

[43] By 1899 the state was contracting for more than half of Russia's steel and iron production. V. Ia. Avarin, *Imperializm v Manzhurii* (Moscow, 1934), I, 24. See table in M. I. Tugan-Baranovskii, *Russkaia fabrika* (St. Petersburg, 1915), pp. 341, 364; Tompkins, *op. cit.*, p. 593.

[44] B. A. Romanov, *Rossiia v Manzhurii (1892–1906)* (Leningrad, 1928), p. 51, cited hereafter as Romanov, *Rossiia*. He must have had some views on the East through his relationship and acquaintance with Mme. Blavatskii, the theosophist, and his trip in 1890 to examine the railroads of Russian Turkestan. Strother, *op. cit.*, p. 568; Glinskii, *Witte*, CXL, 247.

[45] Glinskii, "Cherty … Witte," *Istoricheskii Vestnik*, CXL, 226. The estimate by Tugan-Baranovskii is in Glinskii, *Witte*, CXL, 270.

[46] *Ibid.*, p. 247.

[47] Romanov, *Rossiia*, pp. 57–60; Glinskii, *Prolog Russko-Iaponskoi Voiny* (Petrograd, 1916), pp. 10–13, cited hereafter as Glinskii, *Prolog*.

[48] Cited in Romanov, *Rossiia*, p. 60. Glinskii, *Prolog* omits this passage.

[49] V. I. Gurko, *Features and Figures of the Past* (Stanford University Press, 1939), p. 257.

[50] Foreign Office Memorandum, Oct. 31, 1905, British Documents, IV, 367; Ozerov, *Russkii biudzhet*, pp. 66–67; Witte, *Vospominaniia*, III, 321–322.

[51] Ular claimed that "Russia does not hope to find in China fresh outlets for the produce of her industry, but, on the contrary, fresh centres of industrial productiveness." Ular, *op. cit.*, p. 18. For Ular's Russophobia see *ibid., passim;* and *Russia from Within* (London, 1905).

[52] The Badmaev plan is presented in a series of documents in V. P. Semennikov, *Za kulisami tsarizma: Arkhiv Tibetskogo vracha Badmaeva* (Leningrad, 1925).

[53] Serguei Markov, *Liudi velikoi tseli* (Moscow, 1944), pp. 56–57; Semennikov, *op. cit.*, p. iv n. 2.

[54] Markov, *loc. cit.;* Romanov, *Rossiia*, pp. 61–62; Semennikov, *op. cit.*, p. xix.

[55] Witte, *Vospominaniia*, I, 39; Semennikov, *op. cit.*, p. iv, n. 2.

[56] Dated Feb. 25, 1893. Semennikov, *op. cit.*, pp. 49–75.

[57] *Ibid.*

[58] Plan drawn up in 1887 by Rear Admiral Kopytov, Glinskii, *Prolog*, pp. 29–30.

[59] Semennikov, *op. cit.*, p. 80; Romanov, *Rossiia*, p. 63.

[60] Romanov, *Rossiia*, pp. 63, 64.

[61] Notation on Badmaev's memorandum, *ibid.*, p. 62, editor's note.

[62] Letters, Badmaev to Witte, July 1, 1893, Sept. 9, 1893, Semennikov, *op. cit.*, pp. 83–85; Romanov, *Rossiia*, p. 64.

[63] Semennikov, *op. cit.*, pp. 87, 106; Romanov, *Rossiia*, p. 64.

[64] Semennikov, *op. cit.*, pp. 87, 106; Romanov, *Rossiia*, p. 64.

[65] Romanov, Rossiia, pp. 64, 108.

[66] A. I. Svechnikov, "Skotovodstvo severo-vostochnoi Mongolii," *I.I.R.G.O.*, XXXVIII (1902), 496.

[67] Witte, *Vospominaniia*, III, 356–357.

[68] *Ibid.*, p. 356.

[69] *Ibid.*, p. 355.

[70] "Dnevnik A. A. Polovtseva," *K.A.*, LXVII (1934), 174. "His chairmanship was purely honorary, and it was common knowledge that he exercised no influence upon the decisions of the committee." Gurko, *op. cit.*, p. 13.

[71] For examples see Nicholas II, *Dnevnik, 1890–1906* (Berlin, 1923); E. J. Bing (ed.), *The Secret Letters of the Last Tsar* (New York, 1938).

[72] Characterizations by Gurko, *op. cit.*, p. 14; E. J. Dillon, *The Eclipse of Russia* (New York, 1918), pp. 113–114, 116. In August, 1903, on the day of Witte's dismissal, the Tsar proudly wrote in his diary, "Now, I rule." Nicholas II, *op. cit.*, p. 21.

[73] Dillon, *op. cit.*, pp. 117, 235; "Sovremennik," *op. cit.*, pp. 158–165.

[74] Erwin Baelz, *Awakening Japan: The Diary of a German Doctor* (New York, 1932), pp. 95–96; Bing, *op. cit.*, p. 51.

[75] Bing, *op. cit.*, p. 53.

[76] Waclaw Gasiorovskii, *Tragic Russia* (London, 1908), p. 243.

[77] E. J. Dillon, "Russia and Europe," *Contemporary Review*, LXXV (November, 1896), 621.

[78] W. L. Langer, *The Diplomacy of Imperialism, 1890–1902* (New York, 1935), I, 3–66.

[79] Baron A. Meyendorff, *Correspondence diplomatique du Baron de Staal* (Paris, 1929), pp. 157–164; V. N. Lamsdorf, *Dnevnik, 1886–1890* (Moscow, 1926), pp. 222–257.

[80] Pourtales to Caprivi, Sept. 15, 1890, *G.P.*, IX, 193–194.

[81] Throughout 1890–1894 Russia awaited and finally accepted English leadership in the Armenian matter. Langer, *op. cit.*, I, 158–164; Werder to Foreign Office, Dec. 8, 1894, *G.P.*, IX, 212.

[82] Ribot to French Foreign Office, Nov. 21, 1891, *D.D.F.*, 2d ser., IX, 111.

[83] Ribot to Washington and Berlin, Sept. 14, 1891, *ibid.*, p. 15.

[84] *Ibid.*, p. 146 n. 2.

[85] Ribot's note of Nov. 21, 1891, *ibid.*, p. 112.

[86] Ribot's circular, Dec. 2, 1891, *ibid.*, p. 134.

[87] Montebello to Ribot, Dec. 7, 1891, *ibid.*, p. 146.

[88] Herbette to Ribot, Dec. 7, 1891, *ibid.*, p. 148.

[89] For details of the project see A. N. Kulomzin (ed.), *Sibirskaia zheleznaia doroga* ... (St. Petersburg, 1903), pp. 1–128.

[90] H. B. Morse, *International Relations of the Chinese Empire* (London and New York, 1918), III, 18 ff.; R. H. Akagi, *Japan's Foreign Relations, 1542–1936* (Tokyo, 1936), p. 137. As the Japanese were foremost in spreading western culture in Korea, they bore the brunt of Tonghak enmity.

[91] Akagi, *loc. cit.* An interesting version is that the Korean government made a "deal" with the Tonghaks. See dispatch, Cassini to Ministry of Foreign Affairs, March 10, 1894, *K.A.*, L–LI (1932), 5.

[92] Dispatch, Khitrovo to Weber (Russian chargé at Seoul), Feb. 21, 1894, *K.A.*,

L–LI, 4–5; report of Colonel Vogak, June 14, 1894, *G.S.S.*, LXI (1895), 30; A. Heard, "China and Japan in Korea," *North American Review*, XLIX (1894), 300–308. Aronin, who took part in the preparation of the rebellion, wrote his memoirs in *Japan Chronicle*, Nov. 16, 1933, April 12, 1934.

[93] Telegram, Cassini to Ministry of Foreign Affairs, June 5, 1894, *K.A.*, L–LI, 7–8; dispatch, Khitrovo to Ministry of Foreign Affairs, June 8, 1894, *ibid.*, pp. 9–13.

[94] Kapnist to Secretary of Legation at Seoul, June 8, 1894, *ibid.*, p. 8. The warship *Koreets* (1,213 tons) was classed also as a third-class cruiser (for colonial service). See distribution of Russian warships in Lord Thomas Brassey, "Naval Progress," *Naval Annual*, 1895, p. 54, and tables 263–269.

[95] Akagi, *op. cit.*, p. 137. Excerpts of documents in Z. Volpicelli ("Vladimir"), *The China-Japan War* (London, 1896), App. B, pp. 338–340.

[96] Note, Komura to Tsungli-Yamen, June 17, 1894, *ibid.*, pp. 342–343.

[97] Dispatch, Khitrovo to Ministry of Foreign Affairs, June 8, 1894, *K.A.*, L–LI, 10–11; telegrams, Kerberg to Ministry of Foreign Affairs, June 11, 15, 18, 22, 1894, *K.A.*, L–LI, 15, 17; Akagi, *op. cit.*, pp. 138–139.

[98] Akagi, *op. cit.*, p. 139; G. M. McCune, "The Korean Problem, 1885–1895" (unpublished doctoral dissertation, University of California, Berkeley, 1937), p. 41, quoting from Mutsu to Wang, June 22, 1894, *Liu-shih-nien ... (Documentary History of Sixty Years of Sino-Japanese Relations)*, (Tientsin, 1932), II, 28–29.

[99] Telegram, Cassini to Ministry of Foreign Affairs, June 24, 1894, *K.A.*, L–LI, 17. This may have been a diplomatic trick to spur on Russian reaction to the Chinese appeal for mediation. See *infra*.

[100] Telegram, Cassini to Ministry of Foreign Affairs, June 22, 1894, *K.A.*, L–LI, 16.

[101] Giers's Memorandum to the Tsar, June 22, 1894, *ibid.*, pp. 15–16.

[102] *Ibid.*, n. 1.

[103] Telegram, Khitrovo to Ministry of Foreign Affairs, June 25, 1894, *ibid.*, pp. 18–19.

[104] Telegram, Kerberg to Ministry of Foreign Affairs, June 25, 1894, *ibid.*

[105] Several conversations are described in *K.A.*, L–LI, 21–52, *passim*, including one between Kapnist and Nishi (St. Petersburg), five between Khitrovo and Mutsu (Tokyo), two between Khitrovo and Hayashi (Tokyo), and at least one each between Khitrovo and Ito (Tokyo) and Kerberg and Otori (Seoul).

[106] The only written communication seems to have been a *note verbale* by Khitrovo, pointing out the great responsibility Japan would incur if she failed to agree with China on the evacuation of Korea. Telegram, Khitrovo to Ministry of Foreign Affairs, July 1, 1894, *ibid.*, p. 23.

[107] Telegram, Khitrovo to Ministry of Foreign Affairs, July 27, 1894, and July 30, 1894, *ibid.*, pp. 50, 52.

[108] Telegram, Cassini to Ministry of Foreign Affairs, July 21, 1894, *ibid.*, pp. 43–44.

[109] Telegram, Cassini to Ministry of Foreign Affairs, July 1, 1894, *ibid.*, p. 22.

[110] Telegram, Giers to Cassini, July 10, 1894; telegram, Cassini to Ministry of Foreign Affairs, July 14, 1894; *ibid.*, pp. 32, 36–37.

[111] Telegram, Khitrovo to Ministry of Foreign Affairs, June 25, 1894, *ibid.*, p. 18.

[112] Telegram, Cassini to Ministry of Foreign Affairs, July 21, 1894, *ibid.*, p. 43.

[113] Telegram, Cassini to Ministry of Foreign Affairs, July 14, 1894, *ibid.*, p. 37.

[114] Memoir of Kapnist, Director of the Asiatic Department, June 30, 1894, *ibid.*, p. 21.

[115] Telegram, Cassini to Ministry of Foreign Affairs, July 3, 1894; memoir of Kapnist, July 5, 1894, *ibid.*, pp. 26–27, 27–28. The double-dealing was revealed by the French Ambassador to Russia.

[116] Telegram, Giers to Cassini, July 7, 1894; telegram, Giers to Cassini, July 23, 1894, *ibid.*, pp. 29, 45.

[117] Letter, Giers to Cassini, Aug. 8, 1894, *ibid.*, pp. 58–59.

[118] *Ibid.*

[119] Telegram, Weber to Ministry of Foreign Affairs, July 18, 1894, *K.A.*, L–LI, 41 and n. 2.

[120] Telegram, Giers to Staal, July 9, 1894; telegram, Staal to Giers, July 11, 1894, *ibid.*, pp. 31, 32.

[121] Note of Lascelles to Giers, July 9, 1894, *ibid.*, p. 37.

[122] Memoir of Giers, July 24, 1894, *ibid.*, p. 47.

[123] Telegram, Charykov to Ministry of Foreign Affairs, July 23, 1894, *ibid.*, pp. 45–46; letter, Staal to Ministry of Foreign Affairs, July 24, 1894, *ibid.*, pp. 47–49.

[124] Giers' Memoir to the Tsar, July 18, 1894, *ibid.*, pp. 39–40.

[125] Telegram, Weber to Ministry of Foreign Affairs, July 4, 1894, *ibid.*, p. 27.

[126] Telegram, Weber to Ministry of Foreign Affairs, July 17, 1894, *ibid.*, p. 39.

[127] Telegram, Khitrovo to Ministry of Foreign Affairs, July 1, 1894, *ibid.*, pp. 22–23.

[128] Memoir of Kapnist, July 19, 1894, *ibid.*, pp. 41–42.

[129] See Witte's views in Journal of Special Conference of April 11, 1895, *K.A.*, LII (1932), 80; Badmaev's memoir to Nicholas II on the Sino-Japanese War and the problems of Russian policy, March 6, 1895, Semennikov, *op. cit.*, p. 89.

[130] Ito Hirobumi, *Hisho-ruisan kaika-kai* (Tokyo, 1934), I, 538–562.

[131] For comparison of Japanese and Chinese naval strength, see Brassey, *op. cit.*, tables, pp. 267–273; H. C. Bywater, *Sea-Power in the Pacific* (London, 1934), p. 135.

[132] A. M. Pooley (ed.), *The Secret Memoirs of Count Tadasu Hayashi* (New York and London, 1915), pp. 40–41, 45–46, cited hereafter as Pooley, *Hayashi Memoirs;* Bywater, *op. cit.*, pp. 54–55. On June 28, 1894, the Japanese Minister to Washington revealed the same view to Walter Q. Gresham, the Secretary of State. See P. J. Treat, *Diplomatic Relations Between the United States and Japan, 1853–1895* (Stanford University Press, 1932), II, 460, 463; Langer, *op. cit.*, I, 173. Contemporary Russians also recognized this view. D. D. Pokotilov, *Koreia i Iapono-Kitaiskoe stolknovenie* (St. Petersburg, 1895), p. 60.

[133] Anonymous, "The Japanese Constitutional Crisis and the War," *Contemporary Review*, LXVIII (1895), 457, 467–476.

[134] Shu-hsi Hsü, *China and Her Political Entity* (New York, 1926); T. F. Tsiang, "Sino-Japanese Diplomatic Relations, 1870–1894," *Chinese Social and Political Science Review*, XVII (1933), 1–107.

[135] Tsiang, *op. cit.*, p. 104; H. N. Allen, *Korea, Fact and Fancy* (Seoul, 1904), p. 173.

[136] *Ibid.*, p. 172; Morse, *op. cit.*, pp. 12-18.

[137] Hau, *op. cit.*, pp. 133–135.

[138] Colonel Vogak's report, June 14, 1894, *G.S.S.*, LXI (1895), 29; Akagi, *op. cit.*, p. 137.

[139] A good account of the Japanese seizure of the Korean government is in Akagi, *op. cit.*, pp. 144–145. See also telegram, Cassini to Ministry of Foreign Affairs, July 23, 1894, *K.A.*, L–LI (1932), 46; Sill to Gresham, July 18, 1894, *U.S. Foreign Affairs*, 1894, App. I, 31. By this time the Japanese had 18,000 troops in the vicinity of Seoul.

[140] Akagi, *op. cit.*, p. 145; telegram, Cassini to Ministry of Foreign Affairs, July 26, 1894, *K.A.*, L–LI, 50.

[141] The foreign representatives at Tokyo were informed of the state of war by the Japanese Minister of Foreign Affairs on July 31. On Aug. 1, declarations were telegraphed to foreign capitals. See note of the Japanese Minister to St. Petersburg, Aug. 1, 1894, *K.A.*, L–LI, 54 and n. 1; *ibid.*, p. 50.

[142] Reports of German advisers to Chinese military forces indicated that Li Hung-chang did not expect war. See letter, Charykov to Ministry of Foreign Affairs, Aug. 8, 1894, *K.A.*, L–LI, 59–60.

[143] Telegram, Cassini to Ministry of Foreign Affairs, Aug. 4, 1894, *ibid.*, p. 57.

[144] Telegram, Cassini to Ministry of Foreign Affairs, Aug. 9, 1894, *ibid.*, p. 61.

[145] Telegram, Morenheim to Ministry of Foreign Affairs, Aug. 10, 1894, *ibid.*, pp. 62–63.

[146] The Journal of the Special Conference is published in full in *K.A.*, LII (1932), 62–67. Giers, Witte, Vannovskii, Chikhachev, Shishkin, and Kapnist attended the conference. *Ibid.*, p. 62 n. 3.

[147] *Ibid.*, pp. 64, 65.

[148] *Ibid.*, p. 65.

[149] *Ibid.*, p. 66.

[150] *Ibid.*

[151] Akagi, *op. cit.*, pp. 146–149; Auguste Gérard, *Ma Mission en Chine (1893–1897)* (Paris, 1918), pp. 1–5.

[152] Langer, *op. cit.*, I, 174–175; Gérard, *op. cit.*, p. 7; Treat, *op. cit.*, pp. 492–495; Malet to the German Foreign Office, Oct. 7, 1894, *G.P.*, IX, 243; Marschall to British Foreign Office, Oct. 9, 1894, *ibid.*, pp. 243–244.

[153] Gérard, *op. cit.*, pp. 10–11; Langer, *op. cit.*, I. 175.

[154] "Sovremennik," *op. cit.*, p. 5.

[155] Most of the documents, published in *K.A.*, L–LI, 3–63, bear evidence that Alexander III read and studied them. Some are annotated. See *passim.*

[156] "Chronique," *Revue Politique et Parlementaire*, II (1894), 566.

[157] *Ibid.*, III, 390.

[158] Akagi, *op. cit.*, pp. 149–151; Gérard, *op. cit.*, pp. 14–15, 17.

[159] *Ibid.*, pp. 18–19; Akagi, *op. cit.*, p. 154.

[160] The journal of this conference is published in *K.A.*, LLI (1932), 67–74. The conference was attended by Vannovskii, Chikhachev, Witte, Shishkin, Obruchev, Kremer (Chief of Naval Staff), and Kapnist; the Grand Duke Alexei Alexandrovich, the General-Admiral of the Russian navy, presided. On his qualifications see "Sovremennik," *op. cit.*, pp. 151–158.

[161] *K.A.*, LII, 69. The logic of this is difficult to understand. The only explanation I can suggest is that an occupation of an island remote from main bases would be regarded as only the first step in a Russian plan to link it with the Ussuri region and thus eventually to seize northeastern Korea.

[162] *K.A.*, LII, 68–69.

[163] *Ibid.*, p. 69.

[164] *Ibid.*, pp. 69–70.

[165] *Ibid.*, p. 71.

[166] *Ibid.*, pp. 73–74.

[167] Raising the strength of the squadron from 16 ships (with 241 guns) to 22 ships (360 guns). See Brassey, *op. cit.*, pp. 52, 54; *Revue Politique et Parlementaire*, IV (April, 1895), 172; *Proceedings of the United States Naval Institute*, XXI (January, 1895), 206. Commanding the Mediterranean squadron was Vice-Admiral Alexeev, soon to become prominent in Far Eastern affairs.

[168] Meyendorff, *op. cit.*, II, 259–264. At the same time, Russia was lulled by assurances of Mutsu to Khitrovo on Feb. 15 that Japan would respect the interests of other powers and would probably demand of China an indemnity and some territorial compensation, probably in Formosa. V. N. Lamsdorf, "Dnevnik," *K.A.*, XLVI (1931), 32.

[169] The British Minister to St. Petersburg confirmed this directly to Prince Lo-

banov. Memoir of Lobanov to Nicholas II, April 6, 1895, *K.A.*, LII (1932), 74; Langer, *op. cit.*, I, 175, quoting *St. James Gazette* of March 18, 1895.

[170] Memoir of Lobanov to Nicholas II, April 6, 1895, *K.A.*, LII, 74.

[171] Akagi, *op. cit.*, p. 158; Gérard, *op. cit.*, p. 34. The terms were made known to the world through the Tsungli Yamen on April 3, though since November, 1894, Japanese newspapers had been projecting demands which closely paralleled those made at Shimonoseki. See Baelz, *op. cit.*, p. 105.

[172] Semennikov, *op. cit.*, p. 89.

[173] *Ibid.*, p. 90.

[174] Letter, Badmaev to Nicholas II, May 11, 1895, *ibid.*, pp. 96–97.

[175] *K.A.*, LII, 72.

[176] *Ibid.*, pp. 75–76.

[177] *Ibid.*, n. 1.

[178] *Ibid.*, n. 2.

[179] *K.A.*, LII, 75–76 and n. 1.

[180] Gérard, *op. cit.*, p. 35. The Japanese did not disguise their intention of making Port Arthur a "Gibraltar of the East." The Japanese Minister to Berlin claimed that without a Japanese wedge the independence of Korea would exist only on paper. Mühlberg's Memorandum, April 2, 1895, *G.P.*, IX, 260–261.

[181] *Ibid.*

[182] Marschall to Hohenlohe, Nov. 17, 1894; Brandt's memorandum, April 8, 1895, *G.P.*, IX, 246–247, 265–266; A. J. Irmer, *Die Erwerbung von Kiatschou, 1894–1898* (Cologne, 1930), pp. 8–12.

[183] Memorandum, Lobanov to Nicholas II, April 14, 1895, *K.A.*, LII, 77.

[184] Marschall to Tschirsky, April 8, 1895, *G.P.*, IX, 265, nos. 2232 ff.

[185] *Ibid.*, Langer, *op. cit.*, I, 182.

[186] Graf Münster to German Foreign Office, April 10, 1895, *G.P.*, IX, 268; Langer, *op. cit.*, p. 182.

[187] Gérard, *op. cit.*, p. 38.

[188] Journal of the Special Conference, published in full in *K.A.*, LII (1932), 78–83. The conference was attended by Lobanov, Vannovski, Witte, Chikhachev, Obruchev, and Shishkin; the Grand Duke Alexei Alexandrovich presided.

[189] *Ibid.*, p. 79. This view was currently popularized in Russia. A. Maximov wrote a pamphlet in 1894 presenting China as the real enemy of Russia. He claimed that China would have attacked Russia had the Sino-Japanese War not taken place, and that Japan "is our only true ally on the shores of the Pacific; her friendship to us is as important as our friendship is to her." *Nashi zadachi na Tikhom Okeane* (St. Petersburg, 1894), pp. 27–28, 39, 69–71. Colonel D. V. Putiata, actively on the General Staff and one of its Far Eastern experts, warned of the menace of China under the tutelage of a foreign power. Putiata, *Ocherki geograficheskago sostoianiia administrativnago i voennago ustroistva Kitaia* (St. Petersburg, 1895), p. 265.

[190] *K.A.*, LII, 79.

[191] *Ibid.*, p. 80.

[192] *Ibid.*, pp. 79–80.

[193] *Ibid.*, pp. 80, 81, 82.

[194] *Ibid.*, p. 81.

[195] *Ibid.*, p. 83.

[196] Lobanov doubted the possibility of success of such negotiation. *Ibid.*

[197] *Ibid.*

[198] Memorandum, Lobanov to Nicholas II, April 14, 1895, *ibid.*, p. 77.

[199] *Ibid.*, n. 1.

[200] In submitting the journal, Lobanov suggested that the Tsar hold a personal conference because the situation required haste. Yet he himself had withheld the journal. *Ibid.*, p. 78 n. 1.

[201] Witte, *Vospominaniia*, I, 35–37; Romanov, *Rossiia*, pp. 75–79.

[202] Witte, *Vospominaniia*, I, 37.

[203] Marschall to Gutschmid, April 17, 1895, *G.P.*, IX, 270; Langer, *op. cit.*, I, 184, 185.

[204] Langer, *op. cit.*, I, 185.

[205] Marschall to Gutschmid, April 17, 1895, *G.P.*, IX, 270.

[206] Telegrams, Wilhelm II to the German Commander of the Pacific Squadron, April 17, 1895, *Perepiska Vil'gel'ma II s Nikolaem II* (Moscow, 1923), p. 6.

[207] Gérard, *op. cit.*, p. 41. For text of the Treaty of Shimonoseki, see J. V. A. MacMurray, *Treaties and Agreements with or Concerning China, 1894–1919* (New York, 1921), I, 52.

[208] Tschirsky to German Foreign Office, April 20, 1895, *G.P.*, IX, 271; Gérard, *op. cit.*, pp. 43–44; Akagi, *op. cit.*, pp. 162–163.

[209] Meyendorff, *op. cit.*, II, 270–272; Akagi, *op. cit.*, pp. 162–164.

[210] Akagi, *op. cit.*, pp. 164–165.

[211] The dubious honor of originating the "Triplice" is also claimed by Germany. Bülow in 1897 wrote, "the Far Eastern Alliance made by Holstein..." Prince von Bülow, *Memoirs* (Boston, 1931), I, 52.

[212] There had been sporadic outbreaks of anti-Russian agitation in 1891 and 1894, Baelz, *op. cit.*, pp. 75, 101.

[213] Japan began an extensive program of armament. See Giichi Ono, *War and Armament Expenditures of Japan* (New York, 1922), pp. 116–142; Russia, Ministry of Foreign Affairs, *Finansy Iaponii posle voiny s Kitaem* (St. Petersburg, 1899), pp. 3, 6, 7, 11.

[214] Vannovskii and Obruchev in Special Conference of April 11, 1895, *K.A.*, LII (1932), 82.

[215] "Chronique," *Revue Politique et Parlementaire*, VII (1896), 656.

[216] *Ibid.*, IV (1895), 172.

NOTES TO CHAPTER IV

[1] For a discussion of the value of the Kuping tael, see J. Soyeda, "The Adoption of Gold Monometallism in Japan," *Political Science Quarterly*, XIII (March, 1898), 76. The first payment was due Oct. 17, 1895, for the amount of £8,225,245; the second, in May, 1896, for the same amount. *Ibid.*, p. 77. The 30,000,000 taels agreed upon for the Retrocession of Liaotung were paid first in one sum.

[2] Art. 4 of the Treaty of Shimonoseki. *Sbornik dogovorov po delam Dal'nego Vostoka, 1895–1905* (St. Petersburg, 1906), p. 4, cited hereafter as *Sbornik Dal'nego Vostoka;* Soyeda, *op. cit.*, p. 76.

[3] R. S. Gundry, "China, England and Russia," *Fortnightly Review*, LXVI (October, 1896), 507.

[4] In 1894 Great Britain had 65 per cent of China's trade, and British ships carried 85 per cent of China's imports and exports. W. L. Langer, *The Diplomacy of Imperialism*, I, 167.

[5] Gundry, *op. cit.*, p. 508.

[6] The only major previous loans were: 1887—5,000,000 gold marks from Germany, at 5½ per cent; 1894—10,000,000 silver taels from Hong Kong and Shanghai Banking Corporation, at 7 per cent; 1895—£3,000,000 gold from Hong Kong and Shanghai Bank, at 6 per cent; 1895—£1,000,000 gold from Charter Bank of India, at 6 per cent. Gundry, *op. cit.*, p. 509; A. G. Coons, *The Foreign Public Debt of China* (Philadelphia, 1930), pp. 1–6.

[7] Romanov, *Rossiia*, pp. 86–87; Langer, *op. cit.*, I, 188.

[8] Telegram, Charykov to Foreign Office, April 26, 1895, Romanov, *Rossiia*, p. 87 n. 1.

[9] Romanov, *op. cit.*, p. 87 n. 2.

[10] In May, 1894, Witte obtained the approval of the Committee for the Siberian Railway of his plan to complete the Trans-Siberian (with the exception of the Lake Baikal sector) by 1901. Romanov, *Rossiia*, p. 65. In 1894–1895, during the Sino-Japanese War, the rate of construction was increased from "587 versts per year to double that amount." *Ibid.*, p. 9.

[11] *Ibid.*, pp. 87–88.

[12] *Ibid.*, p. 88; Langer, *op. cit.*, I, 188.

[13] Romanov, *Rossiia*, p. 89. In the 1890's western European capital eagerly supported Russian industrialization. By 1899 Russian capital supported only 21 per cent of Russian industry; 72 per cent of capitalization was French and Belgian. M. N. Pokrovskii, *Russkaia istoriia v szhatom ocherke* (Moscow, 1925), III, 24; N. Vanag, "Promyshlennost v kontse XIX st.," in M. N. Pokrovskii, *Sbornik 1905 god* (Moscow, 1925), I, 185.

[14] Dispatch, Radolin to Hohenlohe, Aug. 8, 1895, *G.P.*, IX, p. 312, no. 2290.

[15] Romanov, *Rossiia*, p. 87, citing telegram, Rafalovich to Witte, May 17, 1895. At the same time, Franco-Russian coöperation in China was persuading the Chinese government to accept a Franco-Russian loan. Cassini and Gérard, known in Peking diplomatic circles as "les deux inséparables," overcame the opposing influence of Hillier, the manager of the Hong Kong and Shanghai Banking Corporation. W. J. Oudendyk, "Russia and China," *Journal of the Royal Central Asian Society*, XXII (July, 1935), 373–374; Gérard, *op. cit.*, pp. 68–71.

[16] London *Times*, June 21, 1895, p. 3.

[17] Romanov, *Rossiia*, pp. 89–90, 90 n. 1. For text of the contract see *Sbornik Dal'nego Vostoka*, pp. 56–60; J. V. A. MacMurray, *Treaties and Agreements with or Concerning China* (New York, 1921), I, 35–40, cited hereafter as MacMurray, *Treaties*.

[18] MacMurray, *Treaties*, I, 35–40; Langer, *op. cit.*, I, 188; Coons, *op. cit.*, pp. 6–8; *Revue Politique et Parlementaire*, V (July, 1895), 390.

[19] Romanov, *Rossiia*, pp. 90–91.

[20] *Ibid.*

[21] See text in Lucien de Reinach, *Recueil des traités conclus par la France en Extrême Orient, 1684–1902* (Paris, 1902), I, 331–334; *Revue Politique et Parlementaire*, V (July, 1895), 390.

[22] Romanov, *Rossiia*, p. 91, citing letter, Witte to N. N. Muraviev, Jan. 29, 1899.

[23] *Revue Politique et Parlementaire*, V, (July, 1895), 392.

[24] Romanov, *Rossiia*, p. 91 n. 2.

[25] *Ibid.*, p. 92; Langer, *op. cit.*, I, 398; Glinskii, *Prolog*, pp. 28–29.

[26] Glinskii, *Prolog*, p. 27.

[27] Romanov, *Rossiia*, p. 92.

[28] *Ibid.*, pp. 92–93. On this document Nicholas II put his mark of approval, "S" (*Soglasen*—I approve), *ibid.*, n. 1.

[29] Kulomzin (ed.), *Sibirskaia zheleznaia doroga*, pp. 233–235; Glinskii, *Prolog*, pp. 30–33. For map comparing Kopytov's route with the final route, see Langer, *op. cit.*, I, 183.

[30] Romanov, *Rossiia*, pp. 81–92.

[31] Memorandum, Witte to the Tsar, April 12, 1896, *K.A.*, LII, (1932), 92.

[32] V. M. Sergeev, "Issledovaniia bolot po linii Amurskoi zheleznoi dorogi," *I.I.R.G.O.*, XXXIV (1898), 483. See also descriptions of surveys of 1895 on the projected Amur railway, *ibid.*, pp. 318–332.

[33] One of the leading opponents of the Amur River railway was Makeev, Director and General Manager of the Amur Transit and Commercial Company. Romanov, *Rossiia*, p. 83; V. E. Timonov, "O glavneishikh putiakh Priamurskago kraia . . . ," *I.I.R.G.O.*, XXXIV, 332–334.

[34] Romanov, *Rossiia*, p. 83. Map in Langer, *op. cit.*, I, 183.

[35] *K.A.*, LII, 75.

[36] Romanov, *Rossiia*, p. 84.

[37] *Ibid.*, n. 1.

[38] Werth, General Manager of the Shanghai branch, and P. M. Romanov, General Manager of the Tientsin branch, were previously employees of the Ministry of Finance. Romanov, *Rossiia*, p. 91 n. 1.

[39] Contract of March 26, 1896. For text see MacMurray, *Treaties*, I, 55–59. The French vigorously opposed the loan, but Witte was indifferent to it because he wanted to placate Germany after her exclusion from participation in the capitalization of the Russo-Chinese Bank, and because he had committed himself wholeheartedly to the project of a Manchurian railroad. E. J. Dillon, *The Eclipse of Russia* (New York, 1918), p. 245; *Revue Politique et Parlementaire*, VIII (April, 1896), 214; Romanov, *Rossiia*, p. 96.

[40] Letter, William II to Nicholas II, April 26, 1895. I. D. Levine (ed.), *Letters of the Kaiser to the Tsar* (New York, 1920), p. 10.

[41] Telegram, Hatzfeldt to Foreign Office, Oct. 25, 1895, *G.P.*, X, pp. 35–36, no. 2393; dispatch Hatzfeldt to Hohenlohe, Nov. 2, 1895, *ibid.*, pp. 149–151, no. 2493.

[42] Romanov, *Rossiia*, pp. 97–98.

[43] Estimate made in 1894. P. S. Popov, "Dvizhenie naseleniia v Kitae," *I.I.R.G.O.*, XXXII (1896), 226–228.

[44] Published in full in *K.A.*, LII (1932), 83–91.

[45] *Ibid.*, pp. 87–88.

[46] *K.A.*, LII, 90. "The whole of the cattle and grain, required for the consumption of the residents and workmen of the Russian mines and industrial establishments in the Amur region, traversed by the Amur River for over 750 miles; all derived from the Manchu province; they are collected and dispatched from the Manchu city of Aigun." Hallet, *op. cit.*, p. 489.

[47] *K.A.*, LII, 88.

[48] *Ibid.* and n. 1.

[49] Published in full, except for paragraphs paraphrasing Dukhovskoi's memorandum in *K.A.*, LII, 91–102.

[50] *Ibid.*, pp. 96, 97–98.

[51] *Ibid.*, pp. 93–94, 101–102.

[52] *Ibid.*, pp. 94–95.

[53] *Ibid.*, p. 98.

[54] *Ibid.*, p. 92.

[55] *Ibid.*, p. 100.

[56] *Ibid.*, p. 95.

[57] *Ibid.*, pp. 93–94. Romanov, *Rossiia*, p. 95, citing dispatch, Cassini to Foreign Office, Dec. 28, 1895.

[58] The decisions of the special committee are published in Timonov, *op. cit.*, pp. 361–364.

[59] *Ibid.*, pp. 363–364.

[60] Timonov, *op. cit.*, p. 350. The *Silach*, technically speaking, was not an icebreaker. In 1897 a specially built icebreaker, ordered by the Navy Department, kept the port open all year round. *Ibid.*, p. 351. L. N. Liubimov, "Iz zhizni inzhenera putei soobshcheniia," *Russkaia Starina*, CLV (July–September, 1913), 449.

[61] Timonov, *op. cit.*, p. 366.

[62] Glinskii, *Prolog*, p. 33. Romanov claimed that Cassini first broached the question officially on April 18 but does not deny that there might have been unofficial discussions. Romanov, *op. cit.*, p. 105 n. 1.

[63] *Ibid.*, p. 102.

[64] D. C. Boulger, "The New Situation in the Far East," *Contemporary Review*, LXVIII (December, 1895), 823; V. E. Roborovskii, "Ekspeditsiia v Tsentral'nuiu

Aziiu v 1893–1895 gg.," *I.I.R.G.O.*, XXXIV (November, 1898), 48. The plan to attach Chinese officers to the Russian army was not carried out. D. C. Boulger, "Li Hung-chang," *Contemporary Review*, LXX (July, 1896), 27.

[65] Glinskii, *Prolog*, p. 34; Romanov, *Rossiia*, p. 106 n. 1. On March 27, 1896, the *North China Daily News* published an account of a supposed agreement between Cassini and Li Hung-chang. Henri Cordier, *Histoire des relations de la Chine avec les Puissances Étrangères* (Paris, 1902), III, 347.

[66] J. O. P. Bland, *Li Hung-chang* (New York, 1917), pp. 180–181; Langer, *op. cit.*, I, 401.

[67] Romanov, *Rossiia*, p. 101. This railroad had been creeping northward "at a snail's pace" since 1890. The project of 1896 contemplated the construction of about 110 miles in three years. *Ibid.* Map in Langer, *op. cit.*, I, 183. Chinese merchants refused to invest even in such lucrative railroads as the Peking-Tientsin line, which had to be built with government funds, and these were often lacking. Gundry, *op. cit.*, p. 515.

[68] Romanov, *Rossiia*, pp. 102–103.

[69] *Ibid.*, p. 104; Langer, *op. cit.*, I, 401.

[70] Text in MacMurray, *Treaties*, I, 79–81. See also "Alleged Russo-Chinese Convention," *Saturday Review*, Dec. 12, 1896, p. 616; Hallet, *op. cit.*, p. 487.

[71] The analysis of this document in Romanov, *Rossiia*, pp. 135–139; Cordier, *op. cit.*, III, 347–348; P. H. Clyde, *International Rivalries in Manchuria* (Columbus, 1926), pp. 40-41.

[72] Contrary to widely held opinion neither Cassini nor Pokotilov held preliminary negotiations with Li on the trans-Manchurian railroad project. Romanov, *Rossiia*, p. 106 and n. 1.

[73] *Ibid.*, pp. 106–107.

[74] Romanov, *Rossiia*, p. 104; Langer, *op. cit.*, I, 401; Oudenyk, *op. cit.*, p. 375.

[75] Romanov, *Rossiia*, pp. 104–105. Contributing to Cassini's failure were his poor state of health and his failure to prepare his *démarche* by bribery. There is no record that he received or used the 1,000,000 rubles approved by the Tsar for such purpose. *Ibid.*, p. 105 n. 1.

[76] *Ibid.*, pp. 107–109; Langer, *op. cit.*, I, 402. Witte incorrectly claimed the credit for arranging the transfer. Witte, *Vospominaniia*, I, 40; Romanov, *Rossiia*, p. 109 n. 1.

[77] Witte, *Vospominaniia*, I, 42. He was royally "dined and wined." Comte Louis de Turenne, "Journal d'un français à Moscou," *Revue de Paris*, 1896, No. 4, p. 824.

[78] Romanov, *Rossiia*, p. 110. Probably Grot and Rothstein arranged all the preliminaries of subsequent conferences by May 4.

[79] It is not known at what point in the negotiations Li Hung-chang was offered the bribe. The bribery protocol of June 4, 1896, which established the so-called "Li Hung-chang fund" is published in Romanov, *Rossiia*, p. 116 n. 1.

[80] *Ibid.*, pp. 113–114; telegram, Li Hung-chang to Tsungli Yamen, May 14, 1896, quoted in Dillon, *op. cit.*, pp. 262–263; Witte, *Vospominaniia*, I, 44.

[81] For details of these negotiations see Li Hung-chang's telegrams to the Tsungli Yamen, May 3, 9, and 14, quoted in Dillon, *op. cit.*, pp. 260–263; Glinskii, *Prolog*, pp. 35–38; Witte, *Vospominaniia*, I, 41–45. A good compilation is in Tsubai, *Saikin Seiji Gaiko-Shi* (Tokyo, 1936), pp. 18-25.

[82] Romanov, *Rossiia*, p. 114.

[83] The coronation ceremony was scheduled for May 30.

[84] Romanov, *Rossiia*, p. 115; Langer, *op. cit.*, I, 403.

[85] The treaty was kept a secret by Imperial Russia. Li Hung-chang's son, who was present at the St. Petersburg–Moscow negotiations, sold a copy of the French text of the treaty to the London *Daily Telegraph*, which published it on Feb. 15, 1910. This text is reproduced in MacMurray, *Treaties*, I, 81–82. The French text in the

Russian archives was first published by B. A. Romanov in *Bor'ba Klassov*, 1924, nos. 1–2, pp. 101–102, then in *Rossiia*, p. 113 n. 1. An English translation of the French Moscow text has been published in V. A. Yakhontov, *Russia and the Soviet Union in the Far East* (New York, 1931), pp. 365–366.

[86] English translation of French and Russian text in G. B. Rea, *The Case for Manchoukuo* (New York, 1935), pp. 391–393.

[87] Text in Romanov, *Rossiia*, p. 116 n. 1.

[88] *Ibid.*, p. 117 n. 1; Glinskii, *Prolog*, p. 38.

[89] Anonymous, "Secret History of the Russo-Chinese Treaty," *Contemporary Review*, LXXI (February, 1897), 176.

[90] Li made the rounds of the capitals of Europe ostensibly to get approval of the revision of customs duties. He remained two or three weeks in every capital and returned to China on Oct. 19, 1896, via America. *Revue Politique et Parlementaire*, X (November, 1896), 480; "Li Hung-chang's Mission," *Saturday Review*, Aug. 22, 1896, pp. 178–179.

[91] Text in MacMurray, *Treaties*, I, 75–77. The original French and Russian text is published in *Izvestiia Ministerstva Inostrannykh Del*, 1916, Nos. 3 and 4, Special Supplement, pp. 4–13, cited hereafter as *Izvestiia M.I.D.*

[92] The rough estimate of 1896 placed the cost of construction at 114,000,000 rubles. By 1914, with accrued interest, extravagant expenditures, and many financial setbacks, the amount to be redeemed was more than 700,000,000 rubles—an impossible sum for the Chinese government. Witte's plan from the beginning seems to have had this in view. Glinskii, *Prolog*, p. 39; Romanov, *Rossiia*, p. 124 and n. 1.

[93] *Ibid.*, pp. 126–127.

[94] Glinskii, *Prolog*, p. 40. However, since the C.E.R. had the exclusive right of establishing freight rates, it could force the Chinese coal mines to sell their coal to the C.E.R. by establishing prohibitive rates.

[95] Letter, Shu to Russo-Chinese Bank, Sept. 8, 1896. *Izvestiia M.I.D.*, 1916, Nos. 3 and 4, pp. 8–9 (French text), p. 13 (Russian text).

[96] Glinskii, *Prolog*, p. 41; Romanov, *Rossiia*, p. 121.

[97] For the deleted article see *ibid.*, pp. 119–120.

[98] *Ibid.*, p. 121.

[99] Quoted *ibid.*, n. 3.

[100] For financial manipulations see Romanov, *Rossiia*, pp. 121–124; V. Ia. Avarin, *Imperializm v Manzhurii* (Moscow, 1931), I, 31.

[101] Romanov, *Rossiia*, p. 125 n. 2.

[102] V. L. Komarov, "Manzhurskaia ekspeditsiia 1896 g.," *I.I.R.G.O.*, XXXIV (1898), 117–194, 166; Dugald Christie, *Thirty Years in Moukden, 1898–1913* (London, 1914), *passim*.

[103] See *G.S.S.*, Bibliography.

[104] See Bibliographical survey in "Issledovaniia Manzhurii," *Bibliograficheskii Biulleten* of the Central Library of the C.E.R. (Harbin, 1927), I, Nos. 1–6, pp. 5–18 and map, p. 6.

[105] Christie, *op. cit.*, p. 72.

[106] E. E. Ahnert, "Puteshestvie po Manzhurii," *Z.I.R.G.O.*, XXXV (1904); S. I., "Na Kvantune," *Russkaia Mysl'*, 1907, No. 7, p. 136.

[107] Liubimov, *op. cit.*, pp. 669–670.

[108] Komarov, *op. cit.*, pp. 117, 123; Ahnert, *op. cit.*, pp. i–vii. There may have been secret general investigations in 1895. See Romanov, *Rossiia*, p. 129.

[109] Komarov, *op. cit.*, pp. 123, 125. From 1894 on, the *khunhuzes* made attacks on Chinese, Korean, and Gold settlements of workers engaged in the construction of the Ussuri railway. I. P. Iuvachev, "Bor'ba s khunhuzami na Manzhurskoi granitse," *Istoricheskii Vestnik*, LXXXII (October–December, 1900), 185.

[110] *Ibid.*, pp. 186, 541–549. In July, 1896, three battalions were deployed in a pro-

tective cordon on the Manchurian border. With the permission of Chinese authorities, cossacks pursued the *khunhuzes* into Manchuria.

[111] Romanov, *Rossiia*, pp. 129–130; Ahnert, *op. cit.*, p. vii. The Russians were so little known in Manchuria that the members of the first reconnaissance expedition of 1896 were taken for Japanese. S.I., *op. cit.*, p. 158.

[112] Liubimov, *op. cit.*, p. 670.

[113] *Revue Politique et Parlementaire*, IX (September, 1896), 228; *ibid.* X (October, 1896), 455; Ular, *op. cit.*, p. 182; *Saturday Review*, Dec. 12, 1896, p. 616; Romanov, *Rossiia*, p. 174.

[114] Romanov, *Rossiia*, p. 599; Ular, *op. cit.*, pp. 186–187. Ular suggests that the Manchu government purposely granted the concession in order to "embroil" the Russians with the Mongols and Tibetans. *Ibid.*, p. 188.

[115] Romanov, *Rossiia*, pp. 599–600. There were some Russian operations by individual prospectors (*zoloto-promyshlenniki*) in Mongolia. E. I. Baranovskii, "Zolotopromyshlennost' v vostochnoi Sibiri," *Vestnik Evropy* XXXIII, No. 7 (July, 1898), 148–149, 150, 151–156.

[116] Romanov, *Rossiia*, p. 160.

[117] F. H. Harrington, *God, Mammon, and the Japanese* (Madison, 1944), p. 88. In 1884 there was one Protestant missionary.

[118] *Ibid.*, p. 252 n. 1, citing consular dispatch, Heard to Assistant Secretary of State, Dec. 31, 1892.

[119] Russian Ministry of Finance, *Opisanie Korei* (3 vols.; St. Petersburg, 1900), III, App. tables, pp. 176–179. In 1884 Russian-Korean interchange was valued at $14,243, Japanese-Korean at $2,508,000.

[120] Great Britain, Consular, *Report on the Trade of Korea, 1892* (London, 1893), Annex IV. See also p. 3 and Annex I (Shipping in Korea).

[121] Harrington, *op. cit.*, pp. 144, 146, 156, 158.

[122] These demands were made public for the first time by the *North China Herald*, April 19, 1895; Romanov, *Rossiia*, pp. 139–140.

[123] Harrington, *op. cit.*, p. 168. See characterization of Miura in *North China Herald*, Nov. 1, 1895, quoted in "Russia and England in the Far East," *Fortnightly Review*, LXV (June, 1896), 874; Akagi, *op. cit.*, p. 171.

[124] H. B. Hulbert, *The Passing of Korea* (New York, 1906), pp. 129–147; Harrington, *op. cit.*, pp. 266–271. For evidence of Japanese complicity, see quotations of court records of the Hiroshima trials in F. A. McKenzie, *The Tragedy of Korea* (London, 1908), pp. 263–267. See also reports of the Hiroshima trial published in *Japan Daily News* and *North China Herald*, Jan. 31, 1896; *Korean Repository*, II (1895), 432–434. The Japanese-trained and -armed Korean force numbered two battalions of some 800 men each. See report of Captain Sokovnikov of the Russian General Staff, "O sovremennykh koreiskikh voiskakh," *G.S.S.* LXIX (1896), 1–7.

[125] Harrington, *op. cit.*, pp. 271, 275.

[126] *Ibid.*, pp. 272–274, 275; "Russia and England in the Far East," *Fortnightly Review*, LXV (June, 1896), 874.

[127] Harrington, *op. cit.*, p. 275. Weber was possibly influenced by his wife, who was a close friend of the Queen of Korea. H. N. Allen, *A Chronological Index* (Seoul, 1901), p. 32; *North China Herald*, Nov. 8, 1895.

[128] "In the face of the most damning evidence" they were acquitted. *North China Herald*, Jan. 31, 1896. Members of the lower house of the Japanese Diet attacked the judgment of the court, while "the whole Japanese press applauded Miura's villainy," and the *Kokumin no Tomo* excused Miura's actions on the ground that it was a "political crime." *Fortnightly Review*, LXV, 875.

[129] Harrington, *op. cit.*, pp. 277–278.

[130] *Ibid.*, p. 279.

[131] *Ibid.*, pp. 284–285.

[132] Harrington, *op. cit.*, pp. 287–288.

[133] *Ibid.*, p. 288; H. N. Allen, *op. cit.*, p. 32.

[134] Harrington, *op. cit.*, pp. 288–289; H. N. Allen, *op. cit.*, p. 33. The best account of the King's flight is in M. von Brandt, *Drei Jahre ost-asiatischer Politik, 1894–1897* (Stuttgart, 1897), pp. 166–177.

[135] Harrington, *op. cit.*, p. 291; Brandt, *op. cit.*, pp. 169–180.

[136] Harrington, *op. cit.*, pp. 291–292.

[137] *Ibid.*, p. 292.

[138] *Ibid.*, p. 293. Both Weber and Pokotilov welcomed American investments; Weber because they proved that Korea was "independent," Pokotilov because they prevented further encroachments of the Japanese. *Ibid.*, pp. 169, 172–173, 292; Romanov, *Rossiia*, p. 148 n. 2, citing telegram of Pokotilov, April 8, 1896.

[139] Akagi, *op. cit.*, p. 172.

[140] Text in *Sbornik Dal'nego Vostoka*, pp. 146–148; W. W. Rockhill, *Treaties and Conventions with or Concerning China and Korea, 1894–1904* (Washington, 1904), pp. 430, 431; Carnegie Endowment for International Peace, *Korea, Outer Mongolia, Manchuria; Treaties and Agreements* (Washington, D.C.), pp. 21–22, cited hereafter as Carnegie Endowment, *Korea, Treaties;* Romanov, *op. cit.*, pp. 141–142.

[141] *Ibid.*, p. 142.

[142] Langer, *op. cit.*, I, 406; Romanov, *Rossiia*, p. 142.

[143] Romanov, *Rossiia*, pp. 142–143.

[144] *Ibid.*, p. 143, quoting Lamsdorf's memorandum to the Tsar, May 20, 1903. The additional quotation from the memorandum that "the fate of Korea, as a future integral part of the Russian Empire by force of geographical and political conditions, had been previously determined by us," as quoted *ibid.*, and Langer, *op. cit.*, I, 406, may or may not have been applicable in 1896.

[145] Text in *Sbornik Dal'nego Vostoka*, pp. 159–160; Rockhill, *op. cit.*, p. 432; Carnegie Endowment, *Korea, Treaties*, pp. 23–24; Glinskii, *Prolog*, p. 63.

[146] The secret articles are in B. E. Nol'de, *Vneshniaia politika* (Petrograd, 1915), pp. 246–247.

[147] Giichi Ono, *War and Armament Expenditures of Japan* (New York, 1922), pp. 61–68.

[148] Langer, *op. cit.*, I, 405; Glinskii, *Prolog*, p. 63; H. N. Allen, *op. cit.*, p. 33.

[149] The text of the reply, approved by the Tsar, is known from the copy sent to Witte by Lobanov on June 28, 1896. Complete text in Romanov, *Rossiia*, pp. 144–145.

[150] A view popularized by R. R. Rosen, *Forty Years of Diplomacy* (New York, 1922), II, 125; Langer, *op. cit.*, I, 405.

[151] Romanov, *Rossiia*, p. 145.

[152] H. N. Allen, *op. cit.*, p. 34.

[153] *Ibid.*, p. 35; I. L. Bishop, *Korea and Her Neighbors* (London, 1898), pp. 263–290.

[154] B. A. Romanov, "Kontsessiia na Yalu," *Russkoe Proshloe*, I (1923), 97.

[155] Kanichi Asakawa, *The Russo-Japanese Conflict* (Boston, 1904), pp. 262–269.

[156] H. N. Allen, *op. cit.*, p. 35.

[157] Rosen, *op. cit.*, II, p. 151.

[158] H. N. Allen, *op. cit.*, p. 36.

[159] Witte, *Vospominaniia*, I, 59–60.

[160] Romanov, *Rossiia*, p. 149.

[161] *Ibid.*, pp. 149–150.

[162] Pokotilov arrived at Seoul on Aug. 14, but even on July 3 he joined Cassini in warning Witte of negotiations between Korea and the English banks. *Ibid.*, p. 150 n. 1.

[163] *Ibid.*, p. 150.

[164] *Ibid.*, pp. 150–151.

[165] *Ibid.*, p. 151.

[166] *Ibid.*, p. 154 n. 1.

[167] *Ibid.*, p. 153; Harrington, *op. cit.*, pp. 174, 177.

[168] Harrington, *op. cit.*, p. 174; Romanov, *Rossiia*, pp. 151, 152 n. 2.

[169] Romanov, *Rossiia*, p. 153.

[170] *Ibid.*, p. 155. Note of the Korean Minister of Foreign Affairs to the Japanese Minister to Seoul, March 9, 1897, in Carnegie Endowment, *Korea, Treaties*, pp. 22–23.

[171] Romanov, *Rossiia*, p. 155.

[172] *Ibid.*, p. 157.

[173] Quoted *ibid.*, pp. 157–158.

[174] *Ibid.*, p. 158.

[175] *Ibid.*, p. 156.

[176] *Ibid.*

[177] *Ibid.*, p. 159.

NOTES TO CHAPTER V

[1] Romanov, *Rossiia*, pp. 117–118, citing telegram, Ukhtomskii to Witte (at Yalta), Sept. 14, 1896.

[2] *Ibid.*, p. 161.

[3] S. I. Kerbedz (acting chairman), the Vice-President of the C.E.R., and P. M. Romanov, Prince Ukhtomskii, E. K. Tsigler, Ia. G. Alexeev, all members of the Board of Directors, A. I. Iugovich, Chief Engineer, and S. V. Ignatsius, Assistant Engineer. *Ibid.*, p. 162 n. 2.

[4] For the full text of point 2 of the journal of the conference see *ibid.*, pp. 162–168.

[5] Journal of the Conference of Feb. 3, 1897, *ibid.*, pp. 162–163.

[6] *Ibid.*, p. 163.

[7] *Ibid.*, pp. 165–166.

[8] For the eight points of instructions approved by the Tsar, see *ibid.*, pp. 169–170 and 170 n. 1.

[9] *Ibid.*, p. 171, citing telegram from Ukhtomskii, May 15, 1897, and telegram from Pokotilov, June 8, 1897.

[10] *Ibid.*, citing telegram from Ukhtomskii, June 16, 1897.

[11] *Ibid.*, citing telegram from Romanov, June 18, 1897.

[12] *Ibid.*, p. 173; Glinskii, *Prolog*, pp. 79–80.

[13] Romanov, *Rossiia*, pp. 173–176.

[14] *Ibid.*, p. 175.

[15] *Ibid.*, p. 176–177.

[16] W. L. Langer, *The Diplomacy of Imperialism*, II, 449; letter, Marschall to Holl-mann, March 11, 1895, *G.P.*, XIV, 5–7, no. 3645.

[17] Dispatch, Radolin to Hohenlohe, Oct. 29, 1895, *G.P.*, XIV, 18–19, no. 3654.

[18] Dispatch, Schenk to Foreign Office, Oct. 29, 1895, *ibid.*, p. 20; memorandum, Marschall to William II, Feb. 19, 1897, *ibid.*, pp. 49–50, no. 3673.

[19] Langer, *op. cit.*, II, 449–450; A. J. Irmer, *Die Erwerbung von Kiaochow, 1894–1898* (Cologne, 1930), pp. 66–68.

[20] "Only one ship and only for a few days," Memorandum, Muraviev to Nicholas II, Nov. 23, 1897, *K.A.*, LII (1932), 103; cited hereafter as Muraviev Memorandum.

[21] MacMurray, *Treaties*, I, 81.

[22] "Russland habe keinerlei Rechte auf dieser Bucht." Memorandum of Marschall on his conversation with Li Hung-chang, June 19, 1896, *G.P.*, XIV, 31, no. 3663.

[23] Elizabeth von Heyking, *Tagebücher aus vier Weltteilen* (Leipzig, 1926), p. 192.

[24] Dispatch, Radolin to Hohenlohe, July 8, 1897, *G.P.*, XIV, 56–57, no. 3677; Langer, *op. cit.*, II, 450.

[25] Telegram, Heyking to Hohenlohe, Aug. 22, 1897. *G.P.*, XIV, 35–36, no. 3664. But Muraviev in his memorandum of Nov. 23 stated: "it was frankly admitted by

the German Minister to Peking, after his conversation with Count Cassini, who quite clearly established Russian rights on this bay, that the choice of Kiaochow was completely set aside." *K.A.*, LII (1932), 103.

[26] "Iz dnevnika A. A. Polovtseva," *K.A.*, XLVI (1931), 130, entry for Aug. 27, 1900.

[27] Witte, *Vospominaniia*, I, 112.

[28] E. J. Dillon, *The Ecilpse of Russia*, pp. 247–249.

[29] *K.A.*, XLVI (1931), 130.

[30] Letter of Aug. 5, 1897, E. J. Bing (ed.), *The Secret Letters of the Last Tsar* (New York, 1938), pp. 120–121.

[31] Letter, Aug. 1, 1897, *ibid.*, p. 121.

[32] Memorandum, Bülow to Foreign Office, Aug. 11, 1897, *G.P.*, XIV, 58, no. 3679. The contemplated port was Pingyang in western Korea.

[33] Telegram, Heyking to Foreign Office, Oct. 1, 1897, *G.P.*, XIV, 61, no. 3684.

[34] Dispatch, Tschirsky to Hohenlohe, Oct. 14, 1897, *ibid.*, p. 62, no. 3685.

[35] Romanov, *Rossiia*, pp. 182–183; dispatch, Tschirsky to Hohenlohe, Oct. 14, 1897, *G.P.*, XIV, 62, no. 3685.

[36] Irmer, *op. cit.*, pp. 77–84; Langer, *op. cit.*, II, 451–452.

[37] M. N. Pokrovskii, *Perepiska Vil'gel'ma II s Nikolaem II* (Moscow, 1923), p. 21.

[38] *Ibid.*, pp. 21–22.

[39] Dated Nov. 8 and 9. Memorandum, Foreign Office to William II, Nov. 10, 1897, *G.P.*, XIV, 73–74, no. 3693.

[40] The right of first anchorage had been frequently employed by European nations on unsettled or uncivilized coasts: Africa, Borneo, the East Indies. It is doubtful whether it was applicable to China. See A. F. Frangulis (ed.), *Dictionnaire Diplomatique* (Paris, 1933), article "Premier Mouillage."

[41] C. K. von Hohenlohe, *Denkwürdigkeiten der Reichskanzlerzeit* (Stuttgart, 1931), p. 413; Bülow, *op. cit.*, I, 214–215.

[42] R. S. McCordock, *British Far Eastern Policy, 1894–1900* (New York, 1930), pp. 196–198; dispatch, Hohenlohe to Hatzfeldt, Nov. 16, 1897, *G.P.*, XIV, 86, no. 3702; Hatzfeldt to Hohenlohe, Nov. 17, 1897, *ibid.*, p. 92, no. 3708.

[43] Romanov, *Rossiia*, p. 185.

[44] Telegram, Heyking to Foreign Office, Nov. 22, 1897, *G.P.*, XIV, 102, no. 3716.

[45] Romanov, *Rossiia*, p. 185.

[46] Muraviev Memorandum, p. 104.

[47] Muraviev Memorandum, pars. 7, 11; Grand Duke Alexander Mikhailovich, *Kniga Vospominanii* (Paris, 1933), I, 108–109. Even after Russia occupied Port Arthur, the greater part of her Pacific squadron was stationed at Nagasaki during the winter of 1897–98. *North China Herald*, Dec. 31, 1897, p. 1157.

[48] Romanov, *Rossiia*, p. 190.

[49] Quoted in V. Ia. Avarin, *Imperializm v Manzhurii*, I, 35.

[50] Muraviev Memorandum, pars. 8, 9.

[51] *Ibid.*, par. 27.

[52] *Ibid.*, par. 28.

[53] *Ibid.*, par. 24.

[54] *Ibid.*, pars. 14–18.

[55] *Ibid.*, pars. 13, 26.

[56] *Ibid.*, pars. 22, 23.

[57] *Ibid.*, pars. 30, 31.

[58] *K.A.*, LII (1932), 102.

[59] In order to allow a greater freedom of opinion, Nicholas II almost never attended such important conferences. The journal of this conference is paraphrased in Glinskii, *Prolog*, pp. 43–46.

[60] *Ibid.*, p. 44. Port Arthur had been reconnoitered by a naval party in September, 1896. S.I., "Na Kvantune," *Russkaia Mysl'*, 1900, No. 8, pp. 6–7. The port was named for Lt. William Arthur, in command of the gunboat *Algerine* during the naval campaign against China in 1860, who examined the port and recommended its use in preference to Talienwan. Admiral E. H. Seymour, *My Naval Career and Travels* (London, 1911), p. 87.

[61] Glinskii, *Prolog*, pp. 44–46. The day before the conference, Witte expressed the same view to the German Ambassador. Letter, Radolin to Bülow, Nov. 16, 1897, *G.P.*, XIV, 104, n. 3717.

[62] Glinskii, *Prolog*, p. 45.

[63] *Ibid.*, pp. 45–46.

[64] Romanov, *Rossiia*, p. 178.

[65] Witte, *Vospominaniia*, I, 109; Romanov, *Rossiia*, p. 179.

[66] Quoted in Avarin, *op. cit.*, p. 36.

[67] Dispatch, Muraviev to Osten-Sacken, Dec. 14, 1897, *G.P.*, XIV, 122, no. 3734.

[68] *Note-mémoire*, Bülow to Osten-Sacken, Dec. 17, 1897, *ibid.*, p. 122, no. 3734.

[69] Telegram, William II to Nicholas II, Dec. 19, 1897, *ibid.*, p. 129, no. 3739.

[70] Telegram, Osten-Sacken to Russian Foreign Office, Dec. 19, 1897, "Vil'gel'm II o zaniatii Port Artura," *K.A.*, LVIII, 152.

[71] Since the news of the arrival was known in St. Petersburg on Dec. 18 (St. Petersburg time), it appears that the Russian government was anxious to release the information. London *Times*, Dec. 20, 1897, p. 5. But McDonald had already telegraphed Salisbury on Dec. 17 that five Russian warships were at Port Arthur apparently with Chinese permission. A. J. Marder, *The Anatomy of British Sea Power, 1880–1905* (New York, 1940), p. 30.

[72] The cruisers *Immortalité* and *Iphigenia*. "Naval and Military Calendar," *Journal of the Royal United Service Institute*, December, 1897, p. 101, cited hereafter as *Journal R.U.S.I.* On Dec. 19 the cruiser *Daphne* followed the Russian squadron into the harbor against the signaled prohibition of the Chinese port authorities. Glinskii, *Prolog*, p. 48.

[73] Romanov, *Rossiia*, pp. 191–193. Slightly erroneous terms are used in the telegram from McDonald to Salisbury, Dec. 31, 1897, *China No. 1 (1898)*, p. 26.

[74] *Ibid.*, p. 46, no. 30.

[75] Langer, *op. cit.*, II, 463; Glinskii, *Prolog*, pp. 51–52.

[76] Romanov, *Rossiia*, pp. 194–195; Glinskii, *Prolog*, p. 51. Li wanted the branch railroad from the Yalu to the C.E.R. built by China with Russian aid.

[77] Quoted in Romanov, *Rossiia*, p. 196.

[78] *Ibid.*, p. 198.

[79] *Ibid.*

[80] Telegram, Pavlov to Foreign Office, Jan. 20, 1898, "O podkupe kitaiskikh sanovnikov," *K.A.*, II (1923), 287.

[81] Telegram, Witte to Pokotilov, Jan. 21, 1898, *ibid.*, p. 287.

[82] Telegram, Pavlov and Pokotilov to Foreign Office, Jan. 24, 1898, *ibid.*, pp. 288–289.

[83] Romanov, *Rossiia*, p. 200.

[84] Agreement signed on Feb. 23, 1898. MacMurray, *Treaties*, I, 103; A. G. Coons, *The Foreign Public Debt of China* (Philadelphia, 1930), pp. 11–13. Definite negotiations for nonalienation of the Yangtse were started in the last days of January. This term was therefore acceptable to the Chinese before the final refusal of the Russian loan. See telegram, MacDonald to Salisbury, Jan. 29, 1898, *China No. 1 (1898)*, p. 55, no. 66.

[85] Agreement signed on Feb. 25, 1898. MacMurray, *Treaties*, I, 104.

[86] Lease signed March 6, 1898, *ibid.*, I, 112–116.

[87] Witte, *Vospominaniia*, I, 116.

[88] Langer, *op. cit.*, II, 470.

[89] An abstract of this conference is given in Glinskii, *Prolog*, pp. 53–54.

[90] Soon afterward troops were sent from Vladivostok to Port Arthur by sea, but they remained on board their transports for several weeks before the lease of Port Arthur was signed. One day, before the intended official occupation, rioting and looting broke out in Port Arthur and Talienwan. Detachments of Russian troops were then landed to restore order and remained in control of the towns. Hence the confusion of dates for the actual occupation of Port Arthur. S.I., "Na Kvantune," *Russkaia Mysl'*, 1900, no. 8, p. 33; "Military Calendar," *Journal R.U.S.I.*, March, 1898, p. 501.

[91] Romanov, *Rossiia*, p. 203.

[92] Langer, *op. cit.*, II, 471; Romanov, *Rossiia*, p. 204 n. 2; *K.A.*, II, 1923, 287–290; Witte, *Vospominaniia*, I, 127–128.

[93] Telegram, Pokotilov to Witte, March 21, 1898, *K.A.*, II, 290.

[94] *Ibid.; * Langer, *op. cit.*, II, 474.

[95] Telegram, MacDonald to Salisbury, March 24, 1898, *China No. 1 (1898)*, no. 95.

[96] Text in *Sbornik Dal'nego Vostoka*, pp. 331–357; MacMurray, *Treaties*, I, 119–121.

[97] Marder, *op. cit.*, p. 304.

[98] The Japanese fleet was at Tsushima in December, 1898.

[99] Meyendorff, *Correspondence diplomatique du Baron de Staal*, II, 370.

[100] Telegram, Salisbury to MacDonald, Jan. 14, 1898, *China No. 1 (1898)*, no. 67.

[101] *British Documents*, I, no. 5.

[102] Osten-Sacken to Bülow, Jan. 2, 1898, *G.P.*, XIV, 134, no. 3743.

[103] Dispatch, Hatzfeldt to Foreign Office, Jan. 22, 1898, *G.P.*, XIV, 147–148, no. 3751.

[104] *Ibid.*, n. 1.

[105] Dispatch, Hatzfeldt to Foreign Office, Jan. 26, 1898, *ibid.*, pp. 150–151, no. 3753.

[106] Almost all of the British China squadron was concentrated in the Gulf of Pechili; but the secret orders of the Admiralty, telegraphed to the Admiral at Hong Kong on March 26, read: "Collect a force in the Gulf of Pechili superior to the Russian force there. It may become necessary to watch the French ... Object is not to turn the Russians out of Port Arthur and Talienwan, but to support demands made by British minister for lease of Wei-hai-wei when Japanese retire on payment of indemnity in May, and other concessions; Russian opposition being checked by this display of force." Quoted in Marder, *op. cit.*, p. 309.

[107] Telegram, Salisbury to O'Connor, March 26, 1898. *British Documents*, I, no. 41.

[108] Langer, *op. cit.*, II, 474–475.

[109] H. N. Allen, *Korea: Fact and Fancy*, p. 36; F. H. Harrington, *God, Mammon, and the Japanese*, pp. 296, 298–299.

[110] *Ibid.*, p. 299.

[111] *Ibid.*, p. 298.

[112] Romanov, *Rossiia*, p. 177.

[113] Harrington, *op. cit.*, p. 298.

[114] Romanov, *Rossiia*, p. 177; H. N. Allen, *op. cit.*, p. 36.

[115] Asakawa, *The Russo-Japanese Conflict*, p. 269.

[116] McKenzie, *The Tragedy of Korea*, p. 95.

[117] H. N. Allen, *op. cit.*, p. 37.

[118] Romanov, *Rossiia*, pp. 178–179, 179 n. 3.

[119] *Ibid.*, p. 179.

[120] *Ibid.*, citing telegram, Muraviev to Speyer, Dec. 23, 1897.

[121] Marder, *op. cit.*, p. 304 n. 3. The 12 unarmored cruisers included several old and unbattleworthy units of the Chinese fleet surrendered in 1895.

[122] *Revue Politique et Parlementaire,* VI (October, 1895), 189; Langer, *op. cit.,* I, 405. The discrepancy in dates is due to the fact that the "naval program of 1896" was voted for in September, 1895.

[123] Marder, *op. cit.,* p. 308. After the lease of Port Arthur the Russian program was further enlarged to include eight battleships in the Far East by 1904. *Ibid.,* p. 315.

[124] British Naval Intelligence reported in 1906 that the average time for constructing a battleship in the period 1889–1905 was three years and three months for England, five and a half years for Russia. *Ibid.,* p. 184 n. 2; B. M. Allen, *The Right Honorable Sir Ernest Satow* (London, 1933), pp. 110–111.

[125] Langer, *op. cit.,* I, 405.

[126] See Battle Order of the XI Military District (Amur), in "The Defensive Strength of Russia," *Journal R.U.S.I.,* March, 1898, pp. 299–308. *Journal R.U.S.I.,* November, 1897, pp. 1362–1364. The distribution in 1896: 690,000 men in Europe, 112,000 in the Caucasus, 91,000 in Turkestan, western Siberia, and eastern Siberia.

[127] Langer, *op. cit.,* II, 472.

[128] France was then at odds with England over the Egyptian Sudan, Siam, and Madagascar and was eager to avoid precipitating a conflict. "Zagranichnoe puteshestvie M. N. Muravieva," *K.A.,* XLVII–XLVIII (1931), 71–89; Marder, *op. cit.,* p. 304 n. 3.

[129] Romanov, *Rossiia,* p. 206 n. 1.

[130] *Ibid.,* p. 207.

[131] Harrington, *op. cit.,* p. 301.

[132] Rosen, Romanov, and Glinskii entirely omit this phase of negotiations; the only mention of it is in Akagi, *Japan's Foreign Relations,* p. 174.

[133] Harrington, *op. cit.,* p. 301; H. N. Allen, *op. cit.,* p. 38.

[134] H. N. Allen, *loc. cit.;* R. R. Rosen, *Forty Years in Diplomacy,* I, 156; Langer, *op. cit.,* II, 472.

[135] Harrington, *op. cit.,* p. 303; Glinskii, *Prolog,* p. 64.

[136] Text in *Sbornik Dal'nego Vostoka,* pp. 345–348; Carnegie Endowment, *Korea, Treaties,* pp. 24–25.

[137] Rosen, *op. cit.,* I, 159.

[138] See criticism by General Vannovskii in 1900, "Iz dnevnika A.A. Polovtseva," *K.A.,* XLVI (1931), 125.

[139] Memorandum of conversation with Li Hung-chang; Marschall to Foreign Office, June 19, 1896, *G.P.,* XIV, 31, no. 3663.

[140] When Witte demanded an explanation from Muraviev for the change from the decision of the Special Conference of Nov. 26, 1897, Muraviev replied that this step was made without his knowledge. E. J. Dillon, *The Eclipse of Russia,* p. 251.

[141] Romanov, *Rossiia,* p. 167.

[142] Text in MacMurray, *Treaties,* I, 154–156.

[143] Opinion of A. A. Polovtsev in 1900, *K.A.,* XLVI (1931), 120, 122, 127.

[144] Hermann Schumacher, "Eisenbahnbau und Eisenbahnpläne in China," *Archiv für Eisenbahnwesen,* 1899, pp. 901–978, 1194–1226; Langer, *op. cit.,* II, 679–680; Glinskii, *Prolog,* pp. 80–81.

[145] Text of the Additional Protocol of May 7, 1898, in MacMurray, *Treaties,* I, 127.

[146] A preliminary contract with the Chinese government was signed on June 27, 1898. Langer, *op. cit.,* II, 679.

[147] *Ibid.*

[148] *Ibid.*

[149] Langer, *op. cit.,* II, 681.

[150] Glinskii, *Prolog,* p. 97.

[151] A. Popov, "Anglo-russkoe soglashenie o razdele Kitaia (1899)," *K.A.*, XXV (1927), 119–120; Glinskii, *Prolog*, p. 83; Langer, *op. cit.*, II, 680.

[152] *K.A.*, XXV, 119.

[153] *Ibid.*, p. 122; Glinskii, *Prolog*, p. 84.

[154] Romanov, *Rossiia*, p. 215; Langer, *op. cit.*, II, 681–682.

[155] *K.A.*, XXV, 122–123; Romanov, *Rossiia*, pp. 212–215; Glinskii, *Prolog*, p. 84.

[156] In December, 1897, the Shansi railroad loan; in May, 1898, negotiations for a railroad from Tientsin to the Yangtse. Romanov, *Rossiia*, p. 216.

[157] Quoted in Glinskii, *Prolog*, p. 226.

[158] Schumacher, *op. cit.*, pp. 929–930. The terms became known when a subscription for the loan was announced on Feb. 4, 1898. *K.A.*, XXV, 125–126.

[159] Glinskii, *Prolog*, pp. 90–94; Langer, *op. cit.*, II, 688.

[160] For the final phase of these negotiations see *K.A.*, XXV, 126–128; Schumacher, *op. cit.*, pp. 931–932; Glinskii, *Prolog*, pp. 86–87. For the text of the agreement and additional notes see *Sbornik Dal'nego Vostoka*, pp. 358–364; MacMurray, *Treaties*, I, 204–205.

[161] *K.A.*, XXV, 129; Glinskii, *Prolog*, pp. 88–89.

[162] Giers encouraged that line of thought by taking an unexpectedly strong stand in his negotiations with the Tsungli Yamen. *K.A.*, XXV, 128–129.

[163] *Ibid.*, p. 129 n. 1.

[164] Schumacher, *op. cit.*, p. 933.

[165] *Ibid.*, pp. 936–938; London *Times*, June 8, 1899.

[166] U. S. Congress, Foreign Affairs Committee, *Papers Relating to the Foreign Affairs of the United States*, 1899, pp. 132–133; cited hereafter as *U. S. Foreign Affairs*. The open-door doctrine may have originated with the English; they have used that term since February, 1898. A. W. Griswold, *The Far Eastern Policy of the United States* (New York, 1938), pp. 44–51; S. C. Y. Pan, *American Diplomacy Concerning Manchuria* (Boston, 1938), pp. 77–78.

[167] *U. S. Foreign Affairs*, 1899, p. 133.

[168] Romanov, *Rossiia*, p. 243.

[169] *Ibid.*, p. 241.

[170] P. Nadin, "Kvantun i ego proshloe, 1894–1900," *Vestnik Evropy*, XXXIX (May–June, 1904), 742–753.

[171] *Otchet po deloproizvodstvu Gosudarstvennago Soveta za sessiiu 1899–1900 goda* (St. Petersburg, 1900), pp. 623–635.

[172] Romanov, *Rossiia*, p. 243.

[173] Excerpt from the British reply, Salisbury to Choate, Nov. 30, 1899. *U. S. Foreign Affairs*, 1899, p. 136. France replied on Dec. 16, 1899; Japan on Dec. 26, 1899. *Ibid.*, pp. 129, 139.

[174] Italy replied on Jan. 7, 1900; Germany on Feb. 19, 1900. *Ibid.*, pp. 131, 138.

[175] *Ibid.*, p. 142.

[176] *Ibid.*

[177] Romanov, *Rossiia*, p. 245.

[178] V. Ia. Avarin, *Imperializm v Manzhurii*, I, 23; P. Vostokov, "Les chemins de fer russes, d'autrefois et aujourd'hui," *Le Monde Slave*, IV (December, 1935), 465, 473.

[179] Romanov, *Rossiia*, p. 241. In 1898 the Trans-Siberian reported a record-breaking construction speed of 600 kilometers in one year. K. Wiedenfeld, "Die wirtschaftliche Bedeutung der Sibirischen Bahn," *Archiv für Eisenbahnwesen*, 1900, p. 360.

[180] Romanov, *Rossiia*, p. 240. Russian engineers made a disappointing discovery that the industriousness of the average Chinese workman was greatly overrated. In experiments on roadbed construction it was estimated that a hired Russian laborer completed 0.83 cubic *sazhen* of roadbed a day, a Russian soldier 0.33 cubic *sazhen*, a Russian convict 0.27 cubic *sazhen*, and a Chinese hired laborer only 0.12 cubic *sazhen*. Hence, a free Chinese laborer had an efficiency of one-seventh that of

a Russian laborer. S. Iuzhakov, "Chto delat' v Kitae," *Russkoe Bogatstvo*, 1900, No. 8, p. 113.

[181] Glinskii, *Prolog*, pp. 72–73.

[182] *Ibid.*, p. 74.

[183] *Ibid.*, pp. 75–77.

[184] Schumacher, *op. cit.*, p. 920 n. 1; Wiedenfeld, *op. cit.*, p. 384 n. 1. In 1900 the American Car and Foundry Company had orders from the C.E.R. for 3,000 freight cars and 200 passenger cars.

[185] *Izvestiia M.I.D.* 1916, no. 11, Special Supplement, pp. 21–23.

[186] *Ibid.*, pp. 26–28. Both agreements were signed by the Chief Engineer of the C.E.R. and his assistant.

[187] A. Khvostov, "Russkii Kitai, nasha pervaia koloniia na Dal'nem Vostoke," *Vestnik Evropy*, XXXVII (September–October, 1902), 655.

[188] Nadin, *op. cit.*, p. 727; Liubimov, *op. cit.*, pp. 252, 450.

[189] *Ibid.*, Nadin, *op. cit.*, pp. 728, 744–751.

[190] Text in "Tsarskaia diplomatiia o zadachakh Rossii na Vostoke v 1900 g.," *K.A.*, XVIII (1926), 4–18. Approved by the Tsar on Feb. 7, 1900. *Ibid.*, p. 4 n. 1.

[191] *Ibid.*, pp. 6–9.

[192] *Ibid.*, p. 18.

[193] *Ibid.*, pp. 9, 13.

[194] *Ibid.*, p. 16.

[195] *Ibid.*, pp. 17–18.

[196] Text, *ibid.*, pp. 18–21.

[197] *Ibid.*, p. 20.

[198] *Ibid.*, p. 21.

[199] *Ibid.*, pp. 22–25. The reply of General Kuropatkin was brief and added nothing new on the Far Eastern phase of the discussion. *Ibid.*, pp. 21–22.

[200] Undated; probably examined by the Tsar on Mar. 13, 1900. *Ibid.*, p. 25 n. See text, *ibid.*, pp. 25–29.

[201] Text in *Sbornik Dal'nego Vostoka*, pp. 388–392; Langer, *op. cit.*, II, 690–691.

[202] Masampo Protocol, April 12, 1900; text in *Sbornik Dal'nego Vostoka*, pp. 392–395.

[203] Additional agreement of March 30, *ibid.*, pp. 391–392.

[204] Asakawa, *op. cit.*, p. 276; Langer, *op. cit.*, II, 692.

NOTES TO CHAPTER VI

[1] The *I-ho T'uan*, the "Fist of Patriotic Union," and other appellations. See H. B. Morse, *International Relations of the Chinese Empire*, III, 176–178; A. H. Smith, *China in Convulsions* (New York, 1901), I, chap. x. For a standard Russian account of the origins and aims of the movement, see A. V. Rudakov, *Obshchestvo I-kho-tuan i ego znachenie v poslednikh sobytiiakh na Dal'nem Vostoke* (Vladivostok, 1901); D. M. Pozdneev, "Bokserskoe dvizhenie kak etap osvoboditel'noi bor'by v Kitae," *Zvezda*, X (1925), No. 4, pp. 156–172.

[2] G. N. Steiger, *China and the Occident* (New Haven, 1927), pp. 92, 149; Morse, *op. cit.*, III, 180; Paul H. Clements, *The Boxer Rebellion* (New York, 1915), p. 71.

[3] Clements, *op. cit.*, p. 81.

[4] Telegrams, MacDonald to Salisbury, Jan. 4 and 5, 1900, *China No. 3 (1900)*, pp. 1, 3, nos. 1 and 9.

[5] MacDonald to Salisbury, March 10, 1900, *ibid.*, p. 6, no. 11. MacDonald to Tsungli Yamen, Jan. 27, 1900, *ibid.*, p. 13, enclosure in no. 27.

[6] Imperial Edict of Jan. 24, 1900; *British and Foreign State Papers*, XCIV, 1063; Smith, *op. cit.*, I, 230.

[7] Note of Feb. 21, 1900, MacDonald to Salisbury, March 5, 1900, *China No. 3*

(1900), p. 17, no. 32. Joint note of May 21, 1900, accepted by all the foreign representatives in conference of May 20. MacDonald to Salisbury, May 21, 1900, *ibid.*, p. 27, no. 41. For text see Pichon to Delcassé, May 20, 1900, France, Ministère des Affaires Étrangères, *Documents diplomatiques: Chine, 1890–1900* ("Livres Jaunes"), p. 24, enclosure in no. 30; hereafter cited as *Chine, 1899–1900*.

[8] "Memorandum of Interview Between Foreign Representatives and the Yamen, March 1, 1900." *China No. 3 (1900)*, p. 21, enclosure in no. 33.

[9] MacDonald to Salisbury, March 16, 1900, *ibid.*, p. 24, no. 36.

[10] Salisbury to MacDonald, March 25, 1900, *ibid.*, p. 12, no. 24.

[11] MacDonald to Salisbury, May 21, 1900, *ibid.*, p. 27, no. 42.

[12] *Ibid.*, I. I. Korostovets, *Rossiia na Dal'nem Vostoke* (Peking, 1922), pp. 10–11. See also *Pravitel'stvennyi Vestnik*, June 23, 1900, quoted in *Vestnik Evropy*, XXXV (July, 1900), 367.

[13] *K.A.*, XIV (1926), 6–7.

[14] P. S. Popov, "Dva mesiatsa osady v Pekine," *Vestnik Evropy*, XXXVI, No. 2 (February, 1901), 519.

[15] *Statesman's Year Book*, 1902, p. 497.

[16] Korostovets, *op. cit.*, pp. 12–13.

[17] *Ibid.*, p. 12.

[18] A. V. Bogdanovich, *Tri poslednikh samoderzhtsa* (Moscow, 1924), p. 280; "Iz dnevnika A. A. Polovtseva," *K.A.*, XLVI (1931), 122, 127.

[19] Bogdanovich, *op. cit.*, p. 251.

[20] MacDonald to Salisbury, May 27, 1900, *China No. 3 (1900)*, p. 29, no. 49.

[21] *K.A.*, XIV (1926), 12.

[22] MacDonald to Salisbury, May 29, 1900, *China No. 3 (1900)*, p. 30, no. 53; Bülow to Kaiser, May 29, 1900, *G.P.*, XVI, 3, no. 4511.

[23] The number differs with almost every writer. Popov, the diarist, gives 350, including 74 Russians, 75 French, 75 English, 58 Americans, 42 Italians, and 26 Japanese. An interesting account of the Russian detachment is given by its commander, Lt. Baron von Raden, in *Morskoi Sbornik*, 1901, No. 3, translated in *Journal R.U.S.I.*, No. 279 (May 15, 1901), 594–605.

[24] MacDonald to Salisbury, May 29, 1900, *China No. 3 (1900)*, p. 30, no. 56; MacDonald to Salisbury, June 10, 1900, *China No. 4 (1900)*, p. 1, no. 1.

[25] *Ibid.*

[26] Pichon to Delcassé, June 6, 1900, *Chine (1899–1900)*, p. 32, no. 46; Popov, *op. cit.*, p. 518.

[27] *Ibid.*, p. 519.

[28] *Pravitel'stvennyi Vestnik*, June 23, 1900, quoted in *Vestnik Evropy*, XXXV, No. 7 (July, 1900), 367.

[29] Giers to Foreign Office, June 7, 1900, *K.A.*, XIV (1926), 12.

[30] *K.A.*, XIV (1926), 13.

[31] *Ibid.*, p. 13 n.

[32] MacDonald to Salisbury, June 10, 1900, *China No. 4 (1900)*, p. 1, no. 1.

[33] *K.A.*, XIV (1926), 14.

[34] The number and composition differs with different authorities. Morse, *op. cit.*, III, 202; Admiralty to Foreign Office, June 13, 1900, *China No. 3 (1900)*, p. 54, no. 124.

[35] Korostovets, *op. cit.*, pp. 16, 18.

[36] *Pravitel'stvennyi Vestnik*, June 23, 1900, quoted in *Vestnik Evropy*, XXXV, No. 7 (July, 1900), 367.

[37] Romanov, *Rossiia*, p. 248.

[38] Korostovets, *op. cit.*, pp. 18, 19 n.

[39] *K.A.*, XIV, 14–15.

[40] Quoted in Korostovets, *op. cit.*, p. 20 n.

[41] Carles to Salisbury, June 15, 1900, *China No. 3 (1900)*, p. 56, no. 131.

[42] Admirals to Commanders of Taku Forts, June 16, 1900, *China No. 1 (1901)*, p. 83, no. 96.

[43] Commanding Officer of *Endymion* to the Admiralty, June 18, 1900, *China No. 3 (1900)*, p. 63, enclosure no. 154; H. C. Thompson, *China and the Powers* (London, 1902), pp. 32–33. The best account of the Russian participation is in I. P. Iuvachev, "Godovshchina boia pri Taku," *Istoricheskii Vestnik*, LXXXIV (April–May 1901), 1075–1080.

[44] The Russians numbered 1,700 of the 2,500 defenders. Ragsdale to Assistant Secretary of State, July 16, 1900, *U. S. Foreign Affairs*, 1900, p. 270, no. 48.

[45] Several versions of this incident can be found in MacDonald to Salisbury, Sept. 20, 1900, *China No. 4 (1900)*, p. 19, no. 2; B. L. Putnam-Weale, *Indiscreet Letters from Peking* (London, 1904), pp. 44, 50–51; Popov, *op. cit.*, p. 527.

[46] Morse, *op. cit.*, III, 220. Earlier the besieged legations and the outside world had learned of the declaration of war through announcements in Chinese newspapers smuggled through the Boxer lines. See translation in Popov, *op. cit.*, p. 529; *K. A.*, XIV (1926), 14–15.

[47] Bogdanovich, *op. cit.*, p. 252.

[48] Approved as Acting Minister Aug. 7, 1900, *K.A.*, XVIII (1926), 46 n. 7. His appointment as minister was not confirmed until Jan. 7, 1901. *K.A.*, XIV, 17 n.

[49] *K.A.*, XIV (1926), 16–17, 17–19.

[50] *Ibid.*, p. 26.

[51] Salisbury to Scott, July 15, 1900, *B.D.*, II, 3, no. 3. Certain writers give the date as June 13, from the date of the telegram of the British Minister to Japan. Whitehead to Salisbury, June 13, 1900, *China No. 3 (1900)*, p. 54, no. 121.

[52] Scott to Salisbury, June 28, 1900, *ibid.*, p. 81, no. 210; Salisbury to Scott, July 15, 1900, *B.D.*, II, 3, no. 3.

[53] Salisbury to Whitehead, June 25, 1900, *China No. 3 (1900)*, p. 75, no. 190; Hatzfeldt to Foreign Office, June 26, 1900, *G.P.*, XVI, 20–21, no. 4532.

[54] Memorandum of the British Embassy in Berlin, June 27, 1900, *China No. 3 (1900)*, p. 91, no. 236, enclosure 1.

[55] Kaiser to Bülow, June 19, 1900, *G.P.*, XVI, 14, no. 4527.

[56] *Ibid.*

[57] Kaiser to Bülow, June 29, 1900, *ibid.*, p. 26, no. 4537.

[58] Hatzfeldt to Foreign Office, June 26, 1900, *ibid.*, p. 20, no. 4532. The British, anxious to have the coöperation of the Japanese contingent, appealed to the Japanese sense of responsibility and offered financial reimbursement of £1,000,000. See Salisbury to Whitehead, July 6, 1900. *China No. 3 (1900)*, pp. 265–266, no. 162.

[59] Text in Korostovets, *op. cit.*, pp. 28–29.

[60] Whitehead to Salisbury, July 8 and 11, 1900, *China No. 1 (1900)*, p. 8, no. 17; p. 9, no. 23.

[61] Korostovets, *op. cit.*, p. 21.

[62] Thompson, *op. cit.*, pp. 34, 44.

[63] *Ibid.*, pp. 48–49; Ragsdale to Assistant Secretary of State, July 16, 1900, *U. S. Foreign Affairs*, 1900, p. 271, no. 48.

[64] *Ibid.*

[65] *Pravitel'stvennyi Vestnik*, July 12, 1900, quoted in *Vestnik Evropy* XXXV (July, 1900), 370; Thompson, *op. cit.*, pp. 16–17; E. H. Seymour, *My Naval Careers and Travels* (London, 1911), pp. 354–355.

[66] *K.A.*, XIV (1926), 18 and n.

[67] Bülow to Hatzfeldt July 21, 1900, *G.P.*, XVI, 82, no. 4580.

[68] *Ibid.*, p. 82 n.; *K.A.*, XIV, 22.

[69] Kaiser to Bülow, Aug. 6, 1900, *G.P.*, XVI, 83, no. 4602. This provision was

previously suggested by the English. See Hatzfeldt to Foreign Office, July 27, 1900, *ibid.*, p. 74, no. 4590.

[70] Aerenthal to Hatzfeldt, Aug. 7, 1900, *ibid.*, p. 84, no. 4604. William II told the French Ambassador that the idea originated with the Tsar. See memorandum, Lamsdorf to Nicholas II, Aug. 10, 1900, *K.A.*, XIV, 24.

[71] This arrangement was suggested by Alexeev. Korostovets, *op. cit.*, p. 45.

[72] See *supra.*

[73] Romanov, *Rossiia*, pp. 252–253.

[74] Quoted in Lamsdorf's memorandum to Nicholas II, July 13, 1900, *K.A.*, XIV, 18.

[75] Letter, Witte to Sipiagin, July 27, 1900, *K.A.*, XVIII (1926), 33–34.

[76] William II to Nicholas II, Aug. 6, 1900. *K.A.*, XIV (1926), 22; Morse, *op. cit.*, III, 255.

[77] Li Hung-chang was summoned to Peking on June 22. Lofengluh to Salisbury, June 26, 1900, *China No. 3 (1900)*, p. 76, no. 195.

[78] Romanov, *Rossiia*, pp. 250–251.

[79] Salisbury to Scott, June 22, 1900, *China No. 3 (1900)*, p. 69, no. 173.

[80] Salisbury to MacDonald, June 26, 1900, *ibid.*, p. 78, no. 198.

[81] W. H. Carter, *The Life of Lieutenant General Chaffee* (Chicago, 1917), p. 179; Ragsdale to Assistant Secretary of State, July 16, 1900, *U. S. Foreign Affairs*, 1900, p. 272, no. 48; U. S. War Department, *Reports on Military Operations in South Africa and China.* XXXIII (1901), 552–556, cited hereafter as War Dept., *Reports*, XXXIII.

[82] Salisbury to MacDonald, July 22, 1900, *China No. 1 (1901)*, p. 22, no. 51; Delcassé to Pichon, July 20, 1900, *Chine, 1899–1900*, pp. 94–95, no. 173; Noailles to Delcassé, July 21, 1900, *ibid.*, pp. 95–96, no. 174.

[83] *Ibid.*

[84] Announced in *Pravitel'stvennyi Vestnik*, Aug. 2, 1900, quoted in Clements, *op. cit.*, p. 143.

[85] Salisbury to Whitehead, July 10, 1900, *China No. 1 (1901)*, p. 9, no. 22.

[86] Made up of 8,000 Japanese, 4,500 Russians, 3,000 British, 2,500 Americans, 800 French. Clements, *op. cit.*, p. 135; Smith, *op. cit.*, I, 454.

[87] General Frey to Lanessan (Minister of Marine), Aug. 9, 1900, *Chine, 1899–1900*, p. 117, no. 219. The British claim that the initiative came from the British and American commanders. See Treat, *op. cit.*, p. 350; Morse, *op. cit.*, III, 268.

[88] War Dept., *Reports*, XXXIII, 569–575; Carter, *op. cit.*, p. 190.

[89] War Dept., *Reports*, XXXIII, 575–576; Gordon Casserly, *The Land of the Boxers*, pp. 118–119.

[90] War Dept., *Reports*, XXXIII, 576.

[91] Carter, *op. cit.*, p. 191.

[92] War Dept., *Reports*, XXXIII, 499.

[93] *Ibid.*, p. 500.

[94] Bezaare to Delcassé, Aug. 9, 1900, *Chine, 1899–1900*, p. 120, no. 225.

[95] The German government demanded official proof of his appointment. See Boutiron to Delcassé, Aug. 23, 1900, *ibid.*, p. 134, no. 255. The British, with their legation saved and their interests in central China secure, now had no more use for Li Hung-chang. See Salisbury to Scott, July 14, 1900, *China No. 1 (1901)*, p. 15, no. 35.

[96] Admiral Courrejoles to Lanessan, Aug. 26, 1900, *Chine, 1899–1900*, p. 138, no. 259.

[97] All the admirals except the German admiral received orders from their governments to let Li Hung-chang through. Courrejoles to Lanessan, Sept. 12, 1900, *ibid.*, p. 156, no. 296.

[98] Porter (American Ambassador to France) to Delcassé, Aug. 25, 1900, *ibid.*,

p. 134, no. 256; telegram of Adjutant General Corbin to Chaffee, July 19, 1900, quoted in Carter, *op. cit.,* p. 181.

[99] Lascelles to Salisbury, Aug. 24, 1900, *B.D.,* II, 8, no. 8.

[100] *Ibid.*

[101] The original suggestion to this effect was made by Li Hung-chang about Aug. 15, 1900. Clements, *op. cit.,* p. 148.

[102] Lamsdorf to Prince Urusov, Aug. 22, 1900, *Chine, 1899–1900,* p. 133, no. 254.

[103] Lamsdorf's Circular, *K.A.,* XIV (1926), 28–29. With some changes it was published in *Pravitel'stvennyi Vestnik,* Sept. 1, 1900, *ibid.,* p. 28 n.; Montebello to Delacassé, Aug. 26, 1900, *Chine, 1899–1900,* p. 137, no. 258. The Chinese Imperial Court fled from Peking on Aug. 15, 1900. Morse, *op. cit.,* III, 283.

[104] Lamsdorf to Urusov, Sept. 15, 1900, *Chine, 1899–1900,* p. 159, no. 304.

[105] *U. S. Foreign Affairs,* 1900, App. 19.

[106] War Dept., *Reports,* XXXIII, 505. There were then, in and around Peking, 30,000 men of the intervening powers, including 6,200 Russians and 10,000 Japanese. *Ibid.,* p. 508.

[107] Geoffrey to Delcassé, Sept. 10, 1900, *Chine, 1899–1900,* p. 153, no. 289. Not the least probable reason for the refusal was the fact that Li Hung-chang, with a suite of 300 attendants, 30 cooks, and 70 servants, was then safely lodged in a palace of the Russian-controlled part of Tientsin, which he shared with members of Alexeev's staff. Korostovets, *op. cit.,* pp. 95–96.

[108] Glinskii, *Prolog,* p. 110.

[109] Conger to Hay, Sept. 29, 1900, *U. S. Foreign Affairs,* 1900, p. 205.

[110] Pichon to Delcassé, Sept. 29, 1900, *Chine, 1899–1900,* p. 173, no. 325; War Dept., *Reports,* XXXIII, 513. This number was reduced in December to two companies—about 400 men. *Ibid.,* p. 488. France, England, and Germany retained in and around Peking at least a brigade each (3,000–5,000 men) until the end of May, 1901. Beau to Delcassé, May 25 and 31, 1901, *Chine, 1900–1901,* pp. 73–74, nos. 130 and 132.

[111] At Pei-tang and Lutai, Sept. 20 and 21. Courrejoles to Delcassé, Sept. 22, 1900, *Chine, 1899–1900,* p. 167, no. 316.

[112] Morse, *op. cit.,* III, 315; War Dept., *Reports,* XXXIII, 578.

[113] War Dept., *Reports,* 461–476.

[114] Morse, *op. cit.,* III, 317.

[115] Korostovets, *op. cit.,* p. 48.

[116] E. J. Bing (ed.), *The Secret Letters of the Last Tsar* (New York, 1938), p. 138.

[117] Dugald Christie, *Thirty Years in Moukden, 1883–1913* (London, 1914), p. 130.

[118] War Dept., *Reports,* XXXIII, 580.

[119] Christie, *op. cit.,* pp. 131–132.

[120] Romanov, *Rossiia,* pp. 240, 249.

[121] *Ibid.,* pp. 240–241.

[122] *Ibid.,* p. 241.

[123] Witte made three such appeals—on June 15 for an increase of up to 6,000; on July 1, to 7,000; on July 7, to 11,000. Glinskii, *Prolog,* p. 111.

[124] *Ibid.,* pp. 111–112.

[125] Romanov, *Rossiia,* p. 251.

[126] War Dept., *Reports,* XXXIII, 488.

[127] See articles by General N. A. Orlov, one of the commanders of the Russian columns, in *Istoricheskii Vestnik:* "Srazhenie pri Onguni," LXXXIV (April, 1901), 137–162; "Srazhenie pri Iakshi," LXXXIV (May, 1901), 603–627; "Zaniatie Hailara," LXXXVI (October, 1901), 98–139.

[128] *Vestnik Evropy,* XXXV, No. 8 (August, 1900), 826; Romanov, *Rossiia,* p. 252.

[129] Christie, *op. cit.,* p. 142.

[130] *Ibid.*, p. 140.

[131] *Ibid.*, p. 143.

[132] *Ibid.; Vestnik Evropy*, XXXV, No. 8 (August, 1900), 826–827.

[133] Romanov, *Rossiia*, p. 252; Glinskii, *Prolog*, p. 114; War Dept., *Reports*, XXXIII, 590.

[134] War Dept., *Reports*, XXXIII, 581.

[135] Glinskii, *Prolog*, p. 114.

[136] War Dept., *Reports*, XXXIII, 581.

[137] V. Alexandrov, "Argun i Priargun'e," *Vestnik Evropy*, XXXIX, No. 5 (May, 1904), 283.

[138] These are too numerous to warrant special mention. A typical example is the looting of Hailar, where cossacks established a regular tariff of 3 to 5 rubles a wagon for the peasants of the Argun River region who flocked to take a share in the wholesale looting. *Ibid.*, p. 302.

[139] A. V. Vereschagin, "Po Manzhurii," *Vestnik Evropy*, XXXVII, No. 1 (January–February, 1902), 129–146; XXXVII, No. 2 (March–April, 1902), 583, 585.

[140] A detailed account of one small surveying party is given in A. Tsererin, "Rezultaty poezdki po Khulan-chenskomu fudatunstvu," *Izvestiia Vostochnogo Instituta* (Vladivostok), III (1901–1902), 1–2. Cited hereafter as *I.V.I.*

[141] The most nearly complete account of the Blagoveschensk episode in English is in Leo Deutsch, *Sixteen Years in Siberia* (London, 1905), pp. 327–343. Deutsch was at that time a correspondent for one of the newspapers in Blagoveschensk.

[142] Glinskii, *Prolog*, p. 115; Deutsch, *op. cit.*, p. 330.

[143] Deutsch, *op. cit.*, pp. 330–331.

[144] Glinskii, *Prolog*, p. 115.

[145] *Ibid.;* anonymous article "Blagoveschenskaia 'Utopiia,' " *Vestnik Evropy*, XLV, No. 7 (July, 1910), p. 231. Cited hereafter as "Blagoveschenskaia 'Utopiia.' "

[146] Deutsch, *op. cit.*, p. 322. This was in a city of 38,000. *Ibid.*, p. 328.

[147] "Blagoveschenskaia 'Utopiia,' " p. 231.

[148] Paraphrased by Deutsch, who was present when Gribskii made public the information in regard to the Chinese deputation. Deutsch, *op. cit.*, p. 331.

[149] *Ibid.*, pp. 334–335; "Blagoveschenskaia 'Utopiia,' " p. 232.

[150] Deutsch, *op. cit.*, pp. 336–338.

[151] London *Times*, July 29, 1900; *Illustrated London News*, CXVII, Sept. 1, 1900, p. 304. The *News* includes graphic illustrations.

[152] War Dept. *Reports*, XXXIII, 586.

[153] Glinskii, *Prolog*, p. 115.

[154] War Dept., *Reports*, XXXIII, 586. The absence of negotiable roads from Sretensk down the Shilka and the Amur precluded rapid movement of troops. By special order, construction was begun on a permanent pack trail in this period. Vereschagin, *op. cit.*, pp. 108–109.

[155] "Khronika," *Russkoe Bogatstvo*, 1900, No. 9, p. 220.

[156] *Ibid.*, p. 221.

[157] The last group was deported on July 21 without incident. "Blagoveschenskaia 'Utopiia,' " p. 235.

[158] *Ibid.*, p. 239; "Khronika," *Russkoe Bogatstvo*, 1900, No. 9, pp. 218–219.

[159] *Russkoe Bogatstvo*, 1900, No. 9, pp. 218–219, 221.

[160] Announced in *Amurskaia Gazeta*, Aug. 12, 1900. Text in *Russkoe Bogatstvo*, 1900, No. 9, p. 224.

[161] Date uncertain. Glinskii, *Prolog*, pp. 118–119.

[162] "Blagoveschenskaia 'Utopiia,' " pp. 233, 240–241.

[163] Romanov, *Rossiia*, p. 252.

[164] Most of the information on movements of the Russian forces is from War Dept., *Reports*, XXXIII, 579–600. See also Glinskii, *Prolog*, pp. 116–117; and

for a Russian official account, A. Myshliaevskii, *Voennyia deistviia v Kitae, 1900–1901 gg.* (St. Petersburg, 1904–1910), and German translation.

[165] War Dept., *Reports*, XXXIII, 584.

[166] Glinskii, *Prolog*, p. 117.

[167] B. N. Demchinskii, *Rossiia v Manzhurii* (St. Petersburg, 1908), pp. 130–131.

[168] The position of the governors and lieutenant governors at this time is quite confusing; it had been changing constantly since 1898. For simplification these European terms are used. It must be remembered that the governor general of Mukden was *primus inter pares* among the other governors of Manchuria.

[169] Glinskii, *Prolog*, p. 114.

[170] Christie, *op. cit.*, pp. 149–150.

[171] *Ibid.*, pp. 152–153.

[172] *Ibid.*

[173] War Dept., *Reports* XXXIII, 598.

[174] *Ibid.*, p. 599.

[175] Christie, *op. cit.*, p. 154.

[176] Kuropatkin to Lamsdorf, Dec. 16, 1900, *K.A.*, XIV (1926), 42.

[177] Christie, *op. cit.*, p. 161.

[178] Excerpts from *Kölnische Zeitung*, in G. Efimov, "Imperialisticheskaia interventsiia 1900–1901 gg. v Kitae," *Istoricheskii Zhurnal*, 1938, No. 4 (April), pp. 68–69.

[179] For example, a 16-page pamphlet by S. S. Maltsev, *Zheltaia Opasnost'* (Warsaw, 1900).

[180] "Khronika," *Russkoe Bogatstvo*, 1900, No. 9, pp. 215–216.

[181] Letter, Witte to Sipiagin, Oct. 1, 1900, *K.A.*, XVIII (1926), 42.

[182] Witte to Sipiagin, Aug. 26, 1900, *ibid.*, p. 41.

[183] Bing (ed.), *op. cit.*, p. 138.

NOTES TO CHAPTER VII

[1] Radolin to Bülow, Aug. 2, 1900, *G.P.*, XVI, p. 208, no. 4207.

[2] Montebello to Delcassé, July 4, 6, 12, 20, 1900, *Chine, 1899–1900*, pp. 67–68, 73, 78, 91, nos. 116, 127, 139, 167; Urusov to Lamsdorf, Aug. 28, 1900, *K.A.*, XIV (1926), 29–30.

[3] Memorandum, J. A. C. Tilley, Jan. 14, 1904, *B.D.*, II, 1, no. 1.

[4] Article in *New Press* (Shanghai), Aug. 14, 1901, condensed in "Sovremennaia Letopis' Dal'nego Vostoka," *I.V.I.*, II (1901), No. 1, p. 33. Cited hereafter as *I.V.I.*, Chronicle.

[5] I. I. Korostovets, *Rossiia na Dal'nem Vostoke*, pp. 53–55.

[6] Summary of the article in Hong Kong *Telegraph*, March 18, 1902, in *I.V.I.*, III (1901–1902), No. 3, Chronicle, p. 700.

[7] Korostovets, *op. cit.*, p. 55; *I.V.I.*, III, No. 1, Chronicle, p. 34.

[8] "Correspondence Relating to the Russian Occupation of Manchuria and Newchwang," *China No. 2 (1904)*, *passim.*

[9] Korostovets, *op. cit.*, pp. 56–57.

[10] *I.V.I.*, III, No. 1, Chronicle, p. 36.

[11] B. M. Allen, *The Right Honorable Sir Ernest Satow*, pp. 127–128.

[12] *I.V.I*, III, No. 1, Chronicle, p. 36.

[13] Slightly different verbal statements accompanied the circular. *U.S. Foreign Affairs*, 1900, p. 380; Salisbury to Satow, Aug. 28, 1900, *China No. 1 (1901)*, p. 140, no. 256; Lamsdorf to Urusov, Aug. 25, 1900, *Chine, 1899–1900*, p. 138, no. 260. The circular was published in *Pravitel'stvennyi Vestnik* on Oct. 1, 1900. Glinskii, *Prolog*, p. 137.

[14] Glinskii, *Prolog*, p. 120.

[15] H. B. Morse, *International Relations of the Chinese Empire*, III, 323.

[16] *Ibid.*, III, 324. The failure to get satisfaction might have been due to the fact that the Tientsin government at this time had a Russian chairman. *Ibid.* Giers to Lamsdorf, Oct. 11, 1900, *K.A.*, XIV (1926), 37.

[17] Circular of Nov. 6, 1900, *U.S. Foreign Affairs*, 1901, p. 41.

[18] Conger to Giers, Nov. 14, 1900, *ibid.*, p. 45.

[19] Giers to Conger, Nov. 16, 1900, *ibid.*, p. 45.

[20] *Ibid.*, p. 42.

[21] *Ibid.*, pp. 42–43.

[22] Nov. 28, Dec. 1, and Dec. 28, respectively. *Ibid.*, pp. 46–47. The British and the Americans followed suit in March and April, 1901. Morse, *op. cit.*, III, 326.

[23] Hatzfeldt to Foreign Office, Feb. 1, 1901, *G.P.*, XVI, 288, no. 4787.

[24] *Ibid.* Strangely enough, on Aug. 18, the commanders of the intervening contingents suggested that the Russian troops take upon themselves the work of restoring the operation of the entire railroad from Taku to Peking. The Russian commander refused to undertake this work singlehanded. See Chaffee to Adjutant General, Aug. 18, 1900, quoted in W. H. Carter, *The Life of Lieutenant General Chaffee*, pp. 195–196; Korostovets, *op. cit.*, p. 49.

[25] Gordon Casserly, *The Hand of the Boxers*, pp. 32–33; *Vestnik Evropy*, XXXVI, No. 4 (April, 1901), 829–830.

[26] *Ibid.*, p. 831. Waldersee arrived at Peking on Oct. 17, 1900. War Dept., *Reports*, XXXIII, 518.

[27] Lascelles to German Foreign Office, March 17, 1901, *G.P.*, XVI, 300–301, no. 4799.

[28] Morse, *op. cit.*, III, 81, 84; P. H. Kent, *Railway Enterprise in China* (London, 1907), pp. 71–72.

[29] See *infra*, chap. vi. Presumably the recapture of this line was decided by a joint conference of commanders. H. C. Thompson, *China and the Powers*, p. 42.

[30] E. H. Seymour, *My Naval Career and Travels*, pp. 366–367. These detachments, including two companies of Japanese, were still there in November, 1901. See summary from Shanghai *Mercury*, Nov. 12, 1901, *I.V.I.*, III, No. 2, Chronicle, p. 367.

[31] Seymour, *op. cit.*, pp. 366–367. Alexeev also considered the profits from the operation of the railroad to be partial remuneration for Russian expenses incurred. See Alexeev's telegram, Oct. 6, 1900, *K.A.*, XIV (1926), 36–37.

[32] Korostovets, *op. cit.*, p. 118.

[33] Alexeev's telegram, Oct. 6, 1900, *K.A.*, XIV, 36.

[34] Memorandum, Tilley to Foreign Office, Jan. 14, 1905, *B.D.*, II, 22.

[35] *Ibid.*, p. 1.

[36] Prince Ching had been waiting for Li in Peking since Sept. 3; Li arrived on Sept. 20. Kanichi Asakawa, *The Russo-Japanese Conflict* (Boston, 1904), p. 162 n.

[37] Delcassé to Ambassadors to France, Sept. 30, 1900, *Chine, 1899–1900*, p. 174, no. 327; G. N. Steiger, *China and the Occident*, pp. 257–258.

[38] Giers to Russian Foreign Office, Oct. 26, 1900, *K.A.*, XIV (1926), 39–40.

[39] Delcassé to Pichon, Nov. 29, 1900, *Chine, 1900–1901*, p. 14, no. 20; Pierce to Hay, Sept. 27, 1900, *U. S. Foreign Affairs*, 1900, p. 376.

[40] Pichon to Delcassé, Nov. 11, 1900, *Chine, 1900–1901*, pp. 8–9, no. 10.

[41] Quoted from *China No. 2 (1904)*, p. 21; Asakawa, *op. cit.*, p. 164.

[42] Montebello to Delcassé, Feb. 20, 1901, *D.D.F.*, I, 113–114, no. 95; Glinskii, *Prolog*, p. 126.

[43] Conger to Hay, Oct. 28, 1900, *U. S. Foreign Affairs*, 1900, p. 223.

[44] Steiger, *op. cit.*, p. 258.

[45] Delcassé to Beau, Sept. 21, 1901, *D.D.F.*, I, 488–489, no. 407.

[46] Delcassé to Pichon, Nov. 2 and 6, 1900, *Chine, 1900–1901*, pp. 6–7, nos. 7 and 8.

[47] The signature by the minister from the United States was delayed until the following day. See Pichon to Delcassé, Sept. 21, 1900, *Chine, 1900–1901*, p. 17, no. 28, and enclosed note, pp. 17–20; enclosure in Conger to Hay, Dec. 22, 1900, *U. S. Foreign Affairs*, 1901, pp. 244–245; *K.A.*, XIV (1926), 46–49.

[48] Pichon to Delcassé, Dec. 25, 1900, *Chine, 1900–1901*, p. 20, no. 30.

[49] Pichon to Delcassé, Dec. 31, 1900, *ibid.*, p. 22, no. 33.

[50] Lamsdorf to Giers, approved by Nicholas II on Dec. 22, 1900, *K.A.*, XIV, 45–46.

[51] Glinskii, *Prolog*, pp. 125–127.

[52] *Ibid.*, p. 131. Russia was not even represented on the commission for the payment of the Boxer Indemnity, composed of representatives of England, France, Germany, and Japan. *Ibid.*, p. 129.

[53] Text in MacMurray, *Treaties*, I, 278–285.

[54] *Journal R.U.S.I.*, XLV (October, 1901), 1192. This figure is probably too high and included troops in the Shanghai area and Russian troops in Chihli.

[55] War Dept., *Reports*, XXXIII, 598.

[56] R. H. Akagi, *Japan's Foreign Relations*, p. 189.

[57] Steiger, *op. cit.*, App. H, p. 315. The final apportionment of the 450,000,000 tael indemnity was not settled until June 14, 1902.

[58] Romanov, *Rossiia*, p. 262.

[59] Countersigned by Nicholas II at Spala on Sept. 26, 1900 *K.A.*, XIV, 35–36.

[60] "Concerning the second question, it will be possible in the near future to begin completely independent negotiations." *Ibid.*, XIV, 36.

[61] From telegram of Ukhtomskii to Witte, Oct. 1, 1900, cited in Romanov, *Rossiia*, p. 263 and n. 2.

[62] *Ibid.*, p. 264.

[63] *Ibid.*, p. 275.

[64] *Ibid.*

[65] Romanov, *Rossiia*, p. 276.

[66] *Ibid.*, pp. 274–275.

[67] *Ibid.*, p. 276.

[68] *Ibid.*

[69] *Ibid.*, pp. 269–272; Glinskii, *Prolog*, pp. 137–141; Korostovets, *op. cit.*, p. 108.

[70] Many students in the Oriental Institute of Vladivostok were specially mobilized to act as interpreters for Russian commanders in Manchuria. "Otchet deiatel'nosti Dal'nevostochnogo Instituta za 1901–1902 g.," *I.V.I.*, III, No. 3, pp. 1–45. Many of the members received military medals and commendations for their activities. *Ibid.*, IV (1902–1903), xxii–xiii.

[71] Glinskii, *Prolog*, p. 138.

[72] This assertion by Li Hung-chang was later proved to be false. Korostovets, *op. cit.*, pp. 97–98, 120.

[73] *Ibid.*, p. 104.

[74] *Ibid.*, p. 125.

[75] *Ibid.*, p. 126; Romanov, *Rossiia*, p. 266.

[76] Alexeev to Kuropatkin, Oct. 11, 1900, Korostovets, *op. cit.*, p. 126; Romanov, *Rossiia*, p. 267.

[77] Korostovets, *op. cit.*, p. 128.

[78] *Ibid.*, pp. 127–128.

[79] *Ibid.*, p. 128.

[80] *Ibid.*, p. 129.

[81] Text in Romanov, *Rossiia*, pp. 267–269, 269 n.; Korostovets, *op. cit.*, pp. 129–130, 130 n. The version given by Glinskii is a very much condensed version of the document in the Russian archives. Glinskii, *Prolog*, pp. 139–140.

[82] He was later tried and punished but escaped the death penalty. Summary of

the article in Shanghai *Mercury,* Nov. 6, 1901, in *I.V.I.,* III, No. 2, Chronicle, p. 371; and summary from Shanghai *New Press,* July 18, 1901, *ibid.,* III, No. 1, Chronicle, p. 16.

[83] Korostovets, *op. cit.,* pp. 130–131.

[84] Romanov, *Rossiia,* pp. 266–267.

[85] Dated Peking, Dec. 31, 1900. London *Times,* Jan. 3, 1901; MacMurray, *Treaties,* I, 329. One of the angered Chinese envoys at Port Arthur is said to have sent the terms of the agreement to Li Hung-chang, who in turn gave his version of the text to Dr. Morrison and the Japanese. Korostovets, *op. cit.,* p. 131.

[86] *Vestnik Evropy,* XXXV, No. 5 (May, 1900), 376.

[87] *I.V.I.,* III, No. 1, pp. 1–3, *passim.*

[88] Romanov, *Rossiia,* p. 267 n. 2.

[89] Pichon to Delcassé, March 24, 1901, *D.D.F.* I, 152, no. 154.

[90] Paraphrased in letter, Kuropatkin to Lamsdorf, Dec. 16, 1900, *K.A.,* XIV (1926), 40.

[91] Romanov, *Rossiia,* pp. 269–273. A very much garbled version of these instructions appeared in a dispatch from Servan de Bezaure, French Consul General at Shanghai, to Delcassé, Jan. 9, 1901, *D.D.F.* I, pp. 18–19, no. 16.

[92] *K.A.,* XIV, (1926) 41–42. Most of this letter was published in S. Iu. Witte, *Vynuzhdennyia Raz'iasneniia . . .* (Moscow, 1911), p. 63; cited hereafter as Witte, *Raz'iasneniia.*

[93] Romanov, *Rossiia,* pp. 281–282.

[94] In view of Li Hung-chang's domination of the Chinese negotiations at this time, this can be assumed.

[95] Romanov, *Rossiia,* p. 282.

[96] *Ibid.*

[97] Text in Witte, *Raz'iasneniia,* p. 65.

[98] Romanov, *Rossiia,* pp. 284–285. The transfer of negotiations to St. Petersburg had been suggested by Lamsdorf to Giers, Dec. 22, 1900, *K.A.,* XIV, 46. The reason stressed was the delay in the telegraphic communications.

[99] The C.E.R. draft proposal can be deduced from the lengthy discussion in Romanov, *Rossiia,* pp. 285–292.

[100] The complete text was first published in Romanov, *Rossiia,* pp. 296–299; an adequate translation appears in W. L. Langer, *The Diplomacy of Imperialism,* II, 714–716.

[101] In his rendering of the text, Langer errs in considering the passages in italics in Romanov's work to be "those parts which Witte desired to have inserted." Langer, *op. cit.,* II, 714. These passages were not in Witte's drafts of Jan. 22 and 24 but were added during the course of the conferences, probably by Lamsdorf. The explanation given by Romanov (p. 296 n. 2) is rather obscure but is made clearer in the discussion of the terms. Romanov, *Rossiia,* pp. 300–301.

[102] The words "Tarbagatai" and "Kuldja (Ili)" are given in italics by Romanov; i.e., they were not included in Witte's original draft.

[103] Langer, *op. cit.,* II, 712 n. 7; Satow to Lansdowne, March 16, 1901, *B.D.,* II, 38–39.

[104] The text is in Satow to Lansdowne, March 6 and 9, 1901, *China No. 6 (1901),* nos. 158 and 192; Steiger, *op. cit.,* pp. 299–302.

[105] At least the Japanese government had a version by March 14, 1901. Izvolskii to Lamsdorf, March 14, 1901, *K.A.,* LXIII (1934), 17.

[106] Instructions were sent to Izvolskii on Jan. 15, 1901. Izvolskii to Lamsdorf, Jan. 27, 1901, *K.A.,* LXIII (1934), 9–10.

[107] Montebello to Delcassé, Jan. 31, 1901, *D.D.F.* I, 77–80, no. 62.

[108] Text in Langer, *op. cit.,* II, 702. The Russian Ambassador to Berlin, Baron

Osten-Sacken, viewed the agreement with alarm as evidence of an Anglo-German *rapprochement*. Osten-Sacken to Lamsdorf, Dec. 21, 1900, *K.A.*, XIV (1926), 43–44.

[109] Langer, *op. cit.*, II, 703–705.

[110] Lascelles to Lansdowne, Jan. 21, 1901, *B.D.*, II, 22, no. 27.

[111] Quoted from *National Zeitung*, March 15, 1901, *K.A.*, LXIII, (1934) 18 n. 2.

[112] Hatzfeldt to Foreign Office, Jan. 24, 1901, *G.P.*, XVI, 281–282, no. 4781.

[113] *B.D.*, II, 34, nos. 42 and 43.

[114] Hay to Tower, Feb. 1, 1902. *U. S. Foreign Affairs*, 1902, p. 926. The previously reported conversation between Hay and Cassini, the Russian Ambassador, on March 28, 1901, indicated that the United States was not concerned over the fate of Manchuria so long as the open door was retained. Romanov, *Rossiia*, pp. 304–305.

[115] *Ibid.*, pp. 301 n. 2, 302 n. 1.

[116] *Ibid.*, pp. 302–303. A version of the second proposed agreement is the Lamsdorf–Yang Yu convention in MacMurray, *Treaties*, I, 330.

[117] Romanov, *Rossiia*, p. 303.

[118] Full text in *Vestnik Evropy*, XXVI, No. 5 (May, 1901), 369–370.

[119] *Ibid.*, p. 370. This passage formed the essence of a circular note given by Russian representatives to the governments to which they were accredited. Cassini to Hay, April 5, 1901, quoted in A. L. P. Dennis, *Adventures in American Diplomacy, 1896–1906* (New York, 1928), pp. 243–244.

[120] The whole period of Anglo-Russian commercial rivalry is succinctly presented in the British Foreign Office Memorandum of Oct. 31, 1905, *B.D.*, IV, 367, no. 321.

[121] H. J. Whigham, *The Persian Problem* (New York, 1903), p. 324.

[122] M. B. Golman, *Russkii imperializm* (Leningrad, 1926), pp. 126–127. The Volga-Caspian trade was no doubt aided by government subsidies to such leading shipping companies as the "Kavkaz i Merkurii." I. Kh. Ozerov, *Russkii Biudzhet* (Moscow, 1907), p. 66.

[123] Whigham, *op. cit.*, p. 335. The effect of the treaty of November, 1901, can be easily seen in the trade figures of the annual publication of the Russian Department of Customs, *Obzor vneshnei torgovli Rossiia*, 1903, pp. 65–66. See also Earl of Ronaldshay, *On the Outskirts of Empire in Asia* (Edinburgh, 1904), p. 138.

[124] In the English press this trend had been popular ever since publication of Lord G. N. Curzon, *Persia and the Persian Question* (London, 1892).

[125] Great Britain, Parliamentary Papers, *Papers Relating to Tibet* (London, 1904), *passim*.

[126] Harding to Salisbury, Oct. 17, 1900, *ibid.*, p. 113, no. 31; Scott to Lansdowne, June 13, 1901, July 10, 1901, *ibid.*, p. 117, nos. 32 and 36.

[127] Scott to Lansdowne, July 4, 1901, *ibid.*, p. 116, no. 35, and *passim*.

[128] "This assurance has been received with satisfaction and passed on to the Secretary of State for India." Lansdowne to Scott, Aug. 16, 1901, *ibid.*, p. 124, no. 39.

[129] S. Oldenburg, "Noveishaia literatura o Tibete," *Zhurnal Ministerstva Narodnago Prosveshcheniia*, XXXV (1904), Nos. 11–12, pp. 129–168.

[130] M. N. Karataev, *Nikolai Mikhailovich Prjevalskii* (Moscow, 1948), p. 204.

[131] "Protokol zasedaniia Konferentsii 30 Oktiabria 1901 g.," *I.V.I.*, III (1901–1902), No. 3, pp. 119–121; Alexander Ular, *A Russo-Chinese Empire* (Westminster, 1904), pp. 147–151.

[132] *I.V.I.*, III, No. 3, p. 122. Tsybikov's diary kept during his sojourn in Tibet was published later as G. Tsybikov, *Buddist palomnik u sviatyn' Tibeta: Po dnevnikam vedennym v 1899–1902 gg.* (Petrograd, 1918).

[133] *I.V.I.*, III, No. 3, p. 122.

[134] Extracts of interviews in *Novoe Vremia*, July 1 and 3, 1901. Great Britain, Papers Relating to Tibet, pp. 114–115, 116, nos. 34 and 35.

[135] *I.V.I.*, III, No. 3, p. 122.

[136] Extract of letter, Witte to Minister of Education, Sept. 17, 1900, "Protokoly zasedanii Konferentsii Vostochnago Instituta za 1902–1903 akademicheskii god," *I.V.I.*, VI (1903), cvii–cix.

[137] "In case of another Power making use of the complications in China in order to obtain in any form whatever such territorial advantages, the two contracting Parties reserve to themselves the right to come to a preliminary understanding as to the eventual steps to be taken for the protection of their own interests in China." Quoted in Langer, *op. cit.*, II, 702.

[138] V. Nadarov, "Seulo-Fuzanskaia zheleznaia doroga," *I.V.I.*, III, No. 3, pp. 47–56. The ceremonies were held on Aug. 20, 1901, at Seoul, and Sept. 20, 1901, at Fusan. See summary of article in *Japan Weekly Times*, Oct. 19, 1901, in *I.V.I.*, III, No. 2, Chronicle, pp. 339–342.

[139] Giers to Lamsdorf, March 24, 1901, *K.A.*, LXIII (1934), 18.

[140] The group included Hayashi (Minister to Korea), Komura (Minister to Peking), Aoki (Minister of Foreign Affairs, 1898–1900), Marshal Yamagata of the Genro, and others. The Genro as a whole favored the Russo-Japanese alliance. Akagi, *op. cit.*, p. 193; A. Galperin, *Anglo-Iaponskii Soiuz, 1902–1921 g.* (Moscow, 1947), pp. 63–64.

[141] A. M. Pooley (ed.), *The Secret Memoirs of Count Tadasu Hayashi* (New York, 1915), p. 87; cited hereafter as Hayashi, *Secret Memoirs*.

[142] Akagi, *op. cit.*, p. 193; Galperin, *op. cit.*, p. 81.

[143] Witte to Sipiagin, date determined by content and previous letters as *ca.* Oct. 1, 1900, *K.A.*, XVIII (1926), 42.

[144] Izvolskii to Lamsdorf, Feb. 22, 1901, *K.A.*, LXIII (1934), 14.

[145] Izvolskii to Lamsdorf, Jan. 17, 1901, *ibid.*, p. 8. Judging by the published dispatches of Izvolskii, he telegraphed Lamsdorf twice a month at almost regular intervals. The previous dispatch does not mention the subject.

[146] *K.A.*, LXIII (1934), 8–9.

[147] Lamsdorf to Izvolskii, Jan. 20, 1901, *K.A.*, LXIII (1934), 11.

[148] Izvolskii to Lamsdorf, March 14, 1901, *K.A.*, LXIII, 17–18.

[149] Quoted in Romanov, *Rossiia*, p. 303.

[150] Foreign Office Memorandum on the conversation between the Japanese Minister and the Minister of Foreign Affairs, March 25, 1901, *K.A.*, LXIII, 21–22. At this time Lamsdorf had been assured by Bülow's speech of March 15 that the Anglo-German Agreement of Oct. 16, 1900, did not apply to Manchuria. The report of the same speech created a "furor" in Tokyo. Izvolskii to Lamsdorf, March 25, 1900, *K.A.*, LXIII (1934), 18–19.

[151] *Ibid.*, p. 22.

[152] Izvolskii to Lamsdorf, April 5, 1901, *K.A.*, LXIII (1934), 25.

[153] This pamphlet was later confiscated by the police. Summary of the article in *Japan Weekly Times*, Oct. 19, 1901, *I.V.I.*, III, No. 2, Chronicle, p. 336.

[154] Izvolskii to Lamsdorf, April 5, 1901, *K.A.*, LXIII (1934), 25.

[155] *Ibid.*, p. 26.

[156] War Dept., *Reports* XXXIII, 597. This number represented three times the peace strength of Russia east of Lake Baikal in 1900.

[157] The total loss has been given as approximately 1,500 killed. Letter, Nicholas II to Grand Duke Vladimir, Jan. 1, 1900, *K.A.*, XVII (1926), 221.

[158] War Dept., *Reports*, XXXIII, 596; letter, Izvolskii to Lamsdorf, April 5, 1901, *K.A.*, LXIII (1934), 26.

[159] A. J. Marder, *The Anatomy of British Sea Power*, p. 429.

[160] Galperin, *op. cit.*, p. 74; Marder, *op. cit.*, pp. 163, 185–186. Only one battleship was ordered in the United States. *Ibid.*, p. 308.

[161] It is, of course, doubtful whether ships of the Black Sea fleet could get permission to pass through the Turkish straits even in time of peace.

[162] Izvolskii to Lamsdorf, April 5, 1901, *K.A.*, LXIII (1934), 26.

[163] Quoted in Langer, *op. cit.*, II, 723.

[164] On April 16, 1901. Akagi, *op. cit.*, p. 200; Galperin, *op. cit.*, p. 85 n. 2.

[165] Romanov, *Rossiia*, pp. 306–307.

[166] *Ibid.*, p. 307.

[167] *Ibid.*, pp. 312–313.

[168] *Ibid.*, pp. 313–314; Glinskii, *Prolog*, p. 173; Lamsdorf's circular of Aug. 1, 1901, *K.A.*, LXIII, 33.

[169] *K.A.*, LXIII, 32–35; Witte, *Raz'iasneniia*, p. 67. On July 30 Lamsdorf sent a circular to the ministers at Tokyo and Peking to ascertain their views concerning the consequences of a Russian annexation of Manchuria. *K.A.*, LXIII, 32.

[170] This important evidence of Witte's essential policy is omitted by Romanov, who merely mentions Witte's letter answering the query. Romanov, *Rossiia*, p. 316 n. 11. The letter is paraphrased in Glinskii, *Prolog*, pp. 174–175. Neither source gives the date of the answer; it was possibly Aug. 10. A. Popov, "Dal'nevostochnaia politika tsarizma v 1894–1901 gg., " *Istorik Marksist*, LI (1935), 54.

[171] The text of this letter is summarized, with many direct quotations, in Witte, *Raz'iasneniia*, pp. 66–69. Romanov, *Rossiia*, p. 315.

[172] Witte, *Raz'iasneniia*, p. 69.

[173] Romanov, *Rossiia*, p. 317. The Russian government was officially notified only two days later. Giers to Lamsdorf, Aug. 4, 1901, *K.A.*, LXIII (1934), 35–36.

[174] Romanov, *Rossiia*, p. 318, citing telegram, Pozdneev to Witte, Aug. 2, 1901.

[175] Letter, Izvolskii to Lamsdorf, Aug. 7, 1901, *K.A.*, LXVII, 36.

[176] Letter, Lamsdorf to Kuropatkin, July 1, 1901, *K.A.*, LXIII, 29–31.

[177] Romanov, *Rossiia*, pp. 319–320. On Aug. 25 Kuropatkin wrote a strong letter of protest to Lamsdorf, objecting to the evacuation of northern Manchuria. Witte, *Raz'iasneniia*, pp. 71–72.

[178] Romanov, *Rossiia*, pp. 323–329.

[179] *Ibid.*, p. 325 and n. 3, citing Witte to Pozdneev, Sept. 5, 1901.

[180] *Ibid.*, pp. 323, 327. Li Hung-chang's illness since August, 1901, had been a subject of much speculation, but the wily diplomat kept his actual condition secret. See summary of the article in Shanghai *Mercury*, Aug. 15, 1901, in *I.V.I.*, III, No. 1, Chronicle, pp. 24–28.

[181] See summary of the article in *Japan Weekly Times*, Sept. 21, 1901, in *I.V.I.*, III No. 1, Chronicle, p. 192. Langer gives some details of Ito's conversations with other Japanese statesmen before his departure, based on Japanese sources. The purpose of Ito's voyage is still not definitely known. Langer, *op. cit.*, II, 759–760.

[182] Izvolskii to Lamsdorf, Sept. 20, 1901, *K.A.*, LXIII, 37.

[183] Letter, Izvolskii to Lamsdorf, Oct. 19, 1901, *ibid.*, p. 38.

[184] *Ibid.*, pp. 38–40.

[185] *Ibid.*, p. 40.

[186] Memorandum, Lamsdorf to Nicholas II, Nov. 6, 1901, *K.A.*, LXIII, 41.

[187] Lamsdorf to Delcassé, approved by Nicholas II, Nov. 9, 1901, *K.A.*, LXIII, 42–43.

[188] For Ito's activities in St. Petersburg, see Romanov, *Rossiia*, pp. 332–333; Witte, *Vospominaniia*, I, 200; Alvensleben to German Foreign Office, Dec. 4, 1901, *G.P.*, XVII, 144–145; London *Times*, Nov. 26 and 30, 1901; G. N. Trubetskoi, *Russland als Grossmacht* (Stuttgart, 1913), pp. 68–69.

[189] For the record of these conversations kept by Ito, see A. Hiratsuka (ed.), *Ito Hirobumi Hiroku* (Tokyo, 1929), App. pp. 19–23. Some of the conversations are translated in Kengi Hamada, *Prince Ito* (London, 1936), pp. 142–156. Lamsdorf to Izvolskii, Dec. 4, 1901, *K.A.*, LXIII, 47–48.

[190] B. A. Romanov, *Ocherki diplomaticheskoi istorii Russko-Iaponskoi Voiny, 1895–1907* (Moscow, 1947), p. 153; cited hereafter as Romanov, *Ocherki*.

[191] Text in Langer, *op. cit.*, II, 768–769, giving convenient parallel texts; Romanov, *Rossiia*, pp. 335–336; *K.A.*, LXIII, 46, giving parallel texts in Russian.

[192] Memorandum, Lamsdorf to Nicholas II, Dec. 4, 1901, *K.A.*, LXIII, 44–45.

[193] *Ibid.*

[194] Project of a letter, Lamsdorf to Ito, Dec. 13, 1900, *K.A.*, LXIII, 51–52.

[195] Langer, *op. cit.*, II, 770. Ito to Katsura, Dec. 22, 1901, cited in Hiratsuka (ed.), *op. cit.*, App. 47.

[196] Hayashi, *Secret Memoirs*, p. 165; Langer, *op. cit.*, II, 767.

[197] Paul Minrath, *Das English-Japanische Bündniss von 1902* (Stuttgart, 1933); Chung-fu Chang, *The Anglo-Japanese Alliance* (Baltimore, 1931); Langer, *op. cit.*, II, 747–784. A valuable recent Soviet contribution, using Russian archival materials and publishing Japanese materials, is the previously cited Galperin, *Anglo-Iaponskii Soiuz*, especially pp. 65–115.

[198] Langer, *op. cit.*, II, 736–742.

[199] Text of the Alliance in *British and Foreign State Papers*, XCV, 84–86; Russian translations in Romanov, *Ocherki*, pp. 448–449; Russia, Ministry of Foreign Affairs, *Recueil de traités et documents diplomatiques concernant l'Extrême Orient, 1895–1905*, pp. 527–530. For text of a secret naval clause see *B.D.*, II, 119.

[200] Galperin, *op. cit.*, p. 136 and n. 3.

[201] M. N. Pokrovskii, "Iaponskaia Voina," *1905 god*, I, 568.

[202] Romanov, *Rossiia*, p. 346.

[203] Hay to Tower, Feb. 1, 1902, *U. S. Foreign Affairs*, 1902, p. 926; Tyler Dennett, *Roosevelt and the Russo-Japanese War* (New York, 1925), p. 131; E. H. Zabriskie, *American-Russian Rivalry in the Far East, 1895–1914* (Philadelphia, 1946), pp. 78–80; Galperin, *op. cit.*, p. 153.

[204] Montebello to Delcassé, Feb. 19 and 28, 1902, *D.D.F.*, II, 129–130, no. 112.

[205] *Ibid.* See also instructions to Alvensleben in *G.P.*, XVII, 156–157, no. 5049. The decision of the German government not to become entangled in the Far Eastern complications was announced by Chancellor von Bülow at the meeting of the Reichstag on March 3, 1902. See letter of Noailles to Delcassé, March 4, 1902, *D.D.F.*, II, 178.

[206] Text in MacMurray, *Treaties*, I, 325–326; *D.D.F.*, II, 178.

[207] Romanov, *Rossiia*, p. 340.

[208] Text in MacMurray, *Treaties*, I, 326–329; *Recueil de traités*, pp. 535–545; Romanov, *Ocherki*, pp. 451–455.

[209] Text of the transfer agreement in *Recueil de traités*, pp. 546–550.

[210] Excerpts from newspaper reports are given in Geoffrey Drage, *Russian Affairs* (London, 1904), pp. 453–454. The eyewitness account is in W. J. Oudendyk, "Russia and China," *Journal of the Royal Central Asian Society*, XXII (July, 1935), 386.

NOTES TO CHAPTER VIII

[1] Text of the contract in A. I. Gippius, *O prichinakh nashei Voiny s Iaponiei* (St. Petersburg, 1905), App. V, pp. 52–55.

[2] During Speyer's term as minister to Korea attempts were made to secure timber, mineral, railroad, and telegraph concessions, but none of the proposals was ratified. F. H. Harrington, *God, Mammon, and the Japanese*, pp. 298, 300; Tyler Dennett, "The Deer Island Episode," *Korean Repository*, V (1898), 109–113.

[3] Art. II did not specify what "work" must be commenced during that period.

[4] His main interest was an import and export business with Japan and Korea. *Otchet po deloproizvodstvu Gosudarstvennago Soveta, 1902–1903*, pp. 311–312; cited hereafter as *Otchet Gos. Soveta*.

[5] Anonymous article: "Why Russia Went to War with Japan: The Story of the Yalu Concessions," *Fortnightly Review*, XCIII (May, 1910), 821. Undoubtedly written by V. M. Vonliarliarskii, this article was based on documents he was pre-

paring for publication but never published; cited hereafter as Vonliarliarskii, "Yalu Concessions." Romanov, *Rossiia*, p. 385 and n. 2.

[6] Vonliarliarskii, "Yalu Concessions," p. 821; B. A. Romanov, "Kontsessiia na Yalu," *Russkoe Proshloe*, I (1923), 97, cited hereafter as Romanov, "Kontsessiia."

[7] Romanov, *Rossiia*, 385 n. 2. The Chevalier Guards was the most aristocratic of all the Guard regiments; all officers of the regiment, active or retired, had access to the Court.

[8] *Ibid.*, pp. 385–386. For an account of Vonliarliarskii's concession on the Chukchi Peninsula see A. Miagkov, "V poiskakh za zolotom," *Russkoe Bogatstvo*, 1901, No. 8, pp. 102–159.

[9] Vonliarliarskii, "Yalu Concessions," p. 822.

[10] This is no doubt a translation of the Russian adjective *promyshlennaia*, meaning "industrial" but used in a broader sense, with the modern connotation of "a development company."

[11] Vonliarliarskii, "Yalu Concessions," p. 822.

[12] *Ibid.*, p. 823; Romanov, "Kontsessiia," pp. 97–98.

[13] The list of members of the State Council, May 31, 1897, is given in *Otchet Gos. Soveta, 1896–1897*, pp. 596–603. The functions of the State Council are succinctly explained in V. N. Kokovtsev, *Out of My Past: The Memoirs of Count Kokovtsev*, ed. H. H. Fisher (Stanford, 1935), p. 539; cited hereafter as Kokovtsev, *Memoirs*.

[14] This might be just a case of interdepartmental politeness. Vonliarliarskii's office concerned itself with certain matters pertaining to foreign relations, such as the establishment of new consulates and increases in diplomatic staffs abroad. For examples see *Otchet Gos. Soveta, 1896–1897*, pp. 351–355.

[15] Vonliarliarskii, "Yalu Concessions," pp. 822–823; Romanov, *Rossiia*, 385 n. 2.

[16] Vonliarliarskii, "Yalu Concessions," p. 824 and n. 2.

[17] Vonliarliarskii's opinion in Kokovtsev, *Memoirs*, p. 22.

[18] Witte's opinion expressed in Witte, *Vospominaniia*, I, 125, 164–165, 227.

[19] See an impressive portrait of Bezobrazov in *McClure's Magazine*, XXXI (September, 1908), 484.

[20] Vonliarliarskii, "Yalu Concessions," p. 823.

[21] *Ibid.*, p. 824; Romanov, "Kontsessiia," pp. 97–98.

[22] The word *odobriat'* in Russian may also mean "to accept, to assent, to consent."

[23] It was a general policy of the Tsars to give such tests to the grand dukes, partly to keep them occupied and partly to train them in the affairs of state.

[24] Romanov, *Rossiia*, p. 386.

[25] Romanov discusses only the fantastic military angle of the plan, Vonliarliarskii only the constructive features. Cf. Romanov, *Rossiia*, pp. 387–388, and Vonliarliarskii, "Yalu Concessions," p. 825.

[26] Vonliarliarskii, "Yalu Concessions," p. 826.

[27] *Ibid.*, p. 826–827; F. A. Lvov, *Likhodei biurokraticheskago samovlastiia kak neposredstvennye vinovniki pervoi Russko-Iaponskoi Voiny* (St. Petersburg, 1906), p. 20.

[28] Vonliarliarskii, "Yalu Concessions," p. 827; A. A. Lopukhin, *Otryvki iz vospominanii* (Moscow, 1923), p. 64.

[29] Vonliarliarskii, "Yalu Concessions," p. 827.

[30] *Ibid.*, p. 830. The author of this memorandum is not mentioned.

[31] A brief account of topographical and geographical work is given in A. Zvegintsev, "Poezdka v severnuiu Koreiu," *I.I.R.G.O.*, XXXVI (1900), 502–518 and map.

[32] Voniarliarskii, "Yalu Concessions," p. 829; Romanov, "Kontsessiia," p. 99.

[33] Vonliarliarskii, "Yalu Concessions," p. 829; Harrington, *op. cit.*, p. 303.

[34] Vonliarliarskii, "Yalu Concessions," pp. 829–831.

[35] *Ibid.*, pp. 830, 1030.

[36] *Ibid.*, p. 1031; Romanov, *Rossiia*, p. 386 n.

[37] Romanov, *Rossiia*, p. 388; Vonliarliarskii, "Yalu Concessions," p. 1031.

[38] Vonliarliarskii, "Yalu Concessions," pp. 1031–1032; Romanov, "Kontsessiia," pp. 99, 100 n. 2.

[39] Vonliarliarskii, "Yalu Concessions," p. 1032.

[40] *Ibid.*, pp. 1033, 1036; Romanov, *Rossiia*, p. 386 n.

[41] Vonliarliarskii, "Yalu Concessions," pp. 1038–1040.

[42] *Ibid.*, pp. 1034–1035. Matiunin apparently never went to Melbourne. He is not listed in the consular lists in *Statesman's Year Book*, 1900, or in the *Almanach de Gotha*, 1900.

[43] Vonliarliarskii, "Yalu Concessions," p. 1036.

[44] Romanov, *Rossiia*, pp. 388–392.

[45] *Ibid.*, pp. 388–389; Romanov, "Kontsessiia," p. 100 n. 32.

[46] Complete list in Romanov, *Rossiia*, p. 389. Other participants whom I have not identified as possessing great wealth were Count V. A. Gendrikov, I. P. Balashev, Count P. Ia. Dashkov, Prince Shcherbatov, Kristi (Cristi?), Prince Kozlovskii, and M. V. Rodzianko.

[47] Ia. P. Beliaev, of Beliaev and Co., an import and export firm, and N. N. Fedorov, owner of lumber mills at Vyshnii Volochek.

[48] Vonliarliarskii, "Yalu Concessions," p. 1044.

[49] Romanov, *Rossiia*, p. 392.

[50] *Ibid.*, n. 1.

[51] *Ibid.*, Romanov, "Kontsessiia," p. 100.

[52] Romanov, *Rossiia*, p. 392.

[53] *Ibid.*, pp. 392, 394; Romanov, "Kontsessiia," p. 101.

[54] Romanov, *Rossiia*, pp. 394–395.

[55] Japanese lumber and railroad ties competed with American and Canadian lumber and ties on the China coast. *I.V.I.*, III (1901–1902), No. 2, Chronicle, p. 374; K. Dmitriev, "Ekskursiia dlia izucheniia porta In-kou," *I.V.I.*, VII (1903), 93.

[56] Vonliarliarskii, "Yalu Concessions," pp. 1041–1042.

[57] Romanov, *Rossiia*, pp. 396–397, 397 n. 3.

[58] *Ibid.*, pp. 399–400, 399 n.; Romanov, "Kontsessiia," pp. 102–103.

[59] *K.A.*, XVIII (1926), 45–46.

[60] W. C. Ford, "The Economy of Russia," *Political Science Quarterly*, XVII (March, 1902), 122–124; Savitskii, *op. cit.*, pp. 340–341; L. Domeretskii, "Tariff Relations Between Germany and Russia (1890–1914)," U. S. Dept. of Commerce, Bureau of Foreign and Domestic Commerce, *Tariff Series*, No. 38 (1918), pp. 1–23.

[61] From 1894 to 1900, the statutes of 727 Russian and 151 foreign joint-stock companies were ratified by the government. The money invested was estimated at 800,000,000 rubles. E. J. Dillon, "Witte and the Russian Commercial Crisis," *Contemporary Review*, LXXIX (April, 1901), 488–489.

[62] Ford, *op. cit.*, p. 103; Dillon, *op. cit.*, p. 489.

[63] "Nashe zhelezno-dorozhnoe delo i krupnaia promyshlennost'," *Vestnik Evropy*, XXXVIII, No. 8 (August, 1903), pp. 764–791.

[64] More than two-thirds of the railways were state property. In 1900 the State railways bought 86 per cent of all Russian steel rails. Dillon, *op. cit.*, p. 489.

[65] M. B. Golman, *Russkii imperializm* (Leningrad, 1927), pp. 134–136.

[66] See comparative table of quotations of leading shares on April 14, 1899, and Feb. 20, 1901, in Dillon, *op. cit.*, p. 493. The Russo-Chinese Bank shares fell from 268 to 230 rubles. *Ibid.*, p. 486.

[67] In April, 1901, 159,000,000 rubles were obtained from France for private railroads in Russia; in 1902, 182,000,000 rubles from Germany to be repaid with Russia's share of the Boxer indemnity. *Istoricheskii obzor deiatel'nosti Ministerstva Finansov, 1802–1902* (St. Petersburg, 1902), pp. 391–392.

[68] Ford, *op. cit.*, p. 103; Golman, *op. cit.*, p. 137.

[69] Witte, *Raz'iasneniia,* pp. 16, 19, 24–25.

[70] "Dnevnik Kuropatkina," entry for Jan. 12, 1903, *K.A.,* II (1923), 17. Cited hereafter as Kuropatkin's Diary, *K.A.,* II.

[71] Twenty million for payment of interest on bonds, 10,000,000 deficit in operation, and 10,000,000 expenditure on railroad guards. Kuropatkin's Diary, Jan. 18, 1903, *K.A.,* II, 22.

[72] The Special Committee on the Far East demanded this computation after August, 1903. Tables given in Romanov, *Rossiia,* pp. 44–45; Romanov, *Ocherki,* pp. 456–457.

[73] Estimates vary. Most writers give a figure between 400,000,000 and 600,000,000. A careful estimated through 1903 gives the total as 422,000,000 rubles. See M. C. Hsu, *Railway Problems in China* (New York, 1915), p. 55. Included in the total for the C.E.R. are 12,330,409 rubles for the Express Steamship Company of the C.E.R., and 12,952,400 rubles for the port and town construction of Dalny. Romanov, *Rossiia,* p. 45.

[74] Romanov, *Rossiia,* p. 44.

[75] A. V. Bogdanovich, *Tri poslednikh samoderzhtsa* (Moscow, 1924), p. 256.

[76] For direct military expenditures, 100,000,000 rubles; for indemnity for destruction on the C.E.R., 70,000,000 rubles; interest on the two, 14,000,000 rubles. Romanov, *Rossiia,* p. 262 n. 1.

[77] Witte, *Raz'iasneniia,* p. 13.

[78] *Ibid.,* p. 10.

[79] The program also shocked Admiral Tyrtov, Director of the Navy Department. Romanov, *Ocherki,* p. 170; Witte, *Vospominaniia,* I, 184–185; Kuropatkin's Diary, Jan. 7, 1903, *K.A.* II, 15.

[80] Witte, *Raz'iasneniia,* pp. 16, 19–21.

[81] Petr Siviakin, "Geograficheskiia svedeniia o Shandunskoi provintsii i Port Chzhi-fu," *I.V.I.,* III, No. 5, p. 98, tables pp. 120–121.

[82] *Ibid.,* p. 96; Romanov, *Rossiia,* p. 366.

[83] See eyewitness account by Jules Legras, "La Mandchourie Russe," *Revue des Deux Mondes,* 1902, No. 4, p. 124; Romanov, *Rossiia,* p. 367 n.

[84] From Cie de Fives-Lille, Cie Franco-Belge de Valenciennes, and Baldwin Locomotive Works. Jules Legras, *op. cit.,* p. 129.

[85] V. I. Gurko, *Features and Figures of the Past* (Stanford, 1939), p. 275.

[86] The last contract signed by Romanov was for 500,000 tons a year for five years. See summary from *Kobe Weekly Chronicle,* 1901, No. 13, in *I.V.I.,* III, No. 2, Chronicle, p. 392; *ibid.,* III, No. 2, p. 358.

[87] Summary of the article, *ibid.,* III, No. 4, p. 56; summary of report in *Japan Weekly Times,* Oct. 12, 1901, *ibid.,* III, 1, 288; Siviakin, *op. cit.,* pp. 128–129.

[88] Pamphlet by I. S. Levitov, *Zheltaia Rasa* (St. Petersburg, 1900). The author also predicts this future for the western United States.

[89] Summary of the article in *Japan Weekly Times,* Nov. 22, 1902, *I.V.I.,* VI (1902–1903), 218.

[90] P. Nadin, "Kvantun i ego proshloe, 1894–1900," *Vestnik Evropy,* XXXIX, No. 3 (June, 1904), 743.

[91] K. Dmitriev, "Ekskursiia dlia izucheniia porta In-kou," *I.V.I.,* VII (1903), 93.

[92] Constantin von Zepelin, *Der Ferne Osten,* I, 215.

[93] N. Novikov, "Alchukaskoe Fudutunstvo," *I.V.I.,* X (1904), 95, 97–98.

[94] S. Khabarovskii, *Chto takoe Kitaiskaia zheleznaia doroga?* (St. Petersburg, 1908), p. 7. This figure may be erroneous if the amount I have assumed was government freight also included railroad building materials.

[95] Alexander Ular, *A Russo-Chinese Empire,* p. 21.

[96] *Ozsor Vneshnei Torgovli* 1903 (St. Petersburg, 1904), p. 691.

[97] For this and other temporary "deals," see Kuo Ti-chen, "Chinese Tariff Con-

cessions to the C.E.R.," *Chinese Social and Political Science Review*, XIV (October, 1930), 391–392.

[98] M. Kovalevskii, "Porto-franko vo Vladivostoke," *Vestnik Evropy*, XLIV, No. 1 (January, 1909), 426.

[99] MacMurray, *Treaties*, I, 121–122.

[100] H. J. Whigham, *The Persian Problem* (New York, 1903), p. 142.

[101] In 1902–1903 by 30 per cent. *Obzor Vneshnei Torgovli*, 1903, p. 94.

[102] *Ibid.*, p. 96.

[103] P. Nadin, "Piatidesiatiletie Amurskago kraia, 1854–1904," *Vestnik Evropy*, XL, No. 3 (May, 1905), 188.

[104] That is, 48 rubles on the value of 212,212 rubles. The tariff rates were absurdly small on most other staple commodities also.

[105] *Obzor Vneshnei Torgovli*, 1903, pp. 116-117. This was on first-grade teas in leaf form. Brick tea was not a valuable express cargo and carried tariffs as low as two rubles per pood. Most tea of this type was carried by the caravan route, for it ostensibly "improved with age"—it could not get worse.

[106] *Obzor Vneshnei Torgovli*, 1903, p. 36.

[107] Mostly tradesmen and artisans. Summary of the article in *Osaka Mainichi*, May 31, 1902, *I.V.I.*, IV (1902–1903), Chronicle, pp. 828–829; *ibid.*, III, No. 1, Chronicle, p. 204.

[108] Glinskii, *Prolog*, p. 237.

[109] Kovalevskii, *loc. cit.*

[110] *Ibid.*, pp. 425–426.

[111] *Ibid.*, p. 425.

[112] Nadin, "Kvantun i ego proshloe, 1894–1900," *Vestnik Evropy*, XXXIX, No. 3 (June, 1904), 743.

[113] For a detailed history of the financial expenditures in Dalny from 1899 to 1903 see *ibid.*, pp. 744–751; 742 n. 2.

[114] *Ibid.*, p. 752.

[115] The first private bank to enter the Manchurian field was the Iaroslavo-Kostromskoi Bank of Port Arthur. *Ibid.*, p. 736.

[116] Tables of shipping between Chefoo and Port Arthur and Dalny in 1901, Siviakin, *op. cit.*, pp. 120–121.

[117] Nadin, "Kvantun . . . ," p. 752. It did not freeze hard, nor for long. Dalny is technically an ice-free port, but in the winter of 1903–1904 that remained to be proved.

[118] *Ibid.*, p. 740.

[119] Romanov, *Rossiia*, p. 403.

[120] Kuropatkin's Diary, Dec. 11, 1902, *K.A.*, II (1923), 10–11.

[121] The internal story of this struggle is told in Gurko, *op. cit.*, pp. 201–226.

[122] Romanov, *Rossiia*, pp. 369–370.

[123] *Ibid.*, pp. 371–373.

[124] *Ibid.*, pp. 373. The complete text of the new laws is given in *I.V.I.*, IV (1903), Chronicle, pp. 57–59.

[125] The map contains some gross inaccuracies; for example, the locations of Gensan, Port Lazarev, and Shestakov.

[126] See description of the Yentai works in Alexander Spitsyn, "Rabochii vopros na kamenno-ugol'nykh kopiakh Mukdenskoi provintsii," *I.V.I.*, IX (1903), 319–352. Contract for the Fushan colliery with the Russo-Chinese Bank, *ibid.*, X (1904), 243–248.

[127] Novikov, *op. cit.*, in *I.V.I.*, X (1904), 22–23.

[128] Romanov, *Rossiia*, p. 374.

[129] *Ibid.*, pp. 376–377.

[130] *Ibid.*

[131] Spitsyn, *op. cit.*, pp. 325–326. Romanov, *Rossiia*, pp. 380–381.

[132] *Ibid.*, p. 376.

[133] *Ibid.*, p. 375. At the same time, the Russo-Belgian syndicate, "Mongolor," in which the Russo-Chinese Bank and many of Witte's colleagues were financially interested, was forced into retrenchment and eventual bankruptcy through lack of a few hundred thousand rubles. This was the only Russian gold property in Mongolia. Romanov, *Rossiia*, App. II, pp. 599–602. A fantastic account of this is found in Ular, *op. cit.*, pp. 282–287.

[134] Romanov, *Rossiia*, p. 374.

[135] *Ibid.*, p. 402 n.

[136] Lvov, *op. cit.*, p. 21.

[137] *Ibid.*, pp. 5–6.

[138] *Ibid.*, p. 23. On this point, as on many others, Lvov does not appear fully credible, but there are no other authorities on the matter.

[139] *Ibid.*, pp. 21–22.

[140] *Ibid.*, p. 23.

[141] *Ibid.*, pp. 22, 24.

[142] See *infra.*

[143] Glinskii, *Prolog*, p. 190; Romanov, *Rossiia*, p. 379.

[144] Almost the entire report is given in Glinskii, *Prolog*, pp. 190–245. A few passages omitted by Glinskii are discussed in Romanov, *Rossiia*, pp. 412–414. The report was first published in a special appendix of the St. Petersburg *Torgovo-promyshlennaia Gazeta*, 1903, No. 40.

[145] Witte's Report, Glinskii, *Prolog*, pp. 190–193. Witte, *Vospominaniia*, I, 186; Romanov, *Rossiia*, p. 412. This version, however, conflicts with what Witte told Kuropatkin. Kuropatkin's Diary, Feb. 16, 1903, *K.A.* (1923), II, 29.

[146] Witte's Report, Glinskii, *Prolog*, pp. 221–222.

[147] *Ibid.*, pp. 207–211.

[148] *Ibid.*, pp. 213–214.

[149] *Ibid.*, pp. 217–220.

[150] This passage, omitted from the almost complete version of the report in Glinskii's *Prolog*, is included in Romanov, *Rossiia*, p. 414.

[151] Witte's Report, Glinskii, *Prolog*, pp. 216–217.

[152] The only reference to this conference is in Witte, *Raz'iasneniia*, pp. 73–74. Romanov and Glinskii do not even mention it.

[153] Lessar was in St. Petersburg for medical treatment and was in and out of the hospital. This may account for some of his amazing views, such as the one given to Kuropatkin that if Russia should evacuate Manchuria, then Mongolia, Kashgaria, and Kuldja would revolt against Russia. Kuropatkin's Diary, Jan. 18, 1903, *K.A.*, II, 21.

[154] The complete list of guarantees and a discussion of the conference are in Glinskii, *Prolog*, pp. 269–271. References to the conference are given also in the Journal of the Special Conference of Feb. 7, 1903, *K.A.*, LII (1932), 110–111; Romanov, *Rossiia*, p. 416.

[155] Full text of the Journal of the Special Conference of Feb. 7, 1903, *K.A.*, LII, 110–124. Other members of the Conference from the Ministry of Foreign Affairs were Argiropulo, Hartwig, Sementovskii-Kurillo, Neratov, and Savinskii.

[156] The exact date of the Japanese proposals is given in Romanov, *Rossiia*, pp. 417, 420 n.

[157] Journal of Special Conference, Feb. 7, 1903, *K.A.*, LII, 111.

[158] *Ibid.*, pp. 112–114.

[159] *Ibid.*, pp. 115–116. On these points Witte used the arguments he expounded in his report to the Tsar in October, 1902. Cf. Witte's Report, Glinskii, *Prolog*, pp. 221–222.

¹⁶⁰ Journal of Special Conference, Feb. 7, 1903, *K.A.*, LII, 118. It is not clear from the wording of the sentence in the original Russian whether Kuropatkin said "partly" or "part of it"; other statements by Kuropatkin indicate that he meant the latter.

¹⁶¹ Here again the meaning is not clear. Did Kuropatkin contemplate army detachments, or would the military formations of railroad guards suffice? From his conversation with the Tsar on Jan. 13 it seems that the interpretation should be "army." Kuropatkin's Diary, *K.A.*, II (1923), 18.

¹⁶² Journal of Special Conference, Feb. 7, 1903, *K.A.*, LII (1932), 121.

¹⁶³ *Ibid.*, pp. 121–122.

¹⁶⁴ *Ibid.*, p. 122. Summaries of the Journal of the Special Conference of Feb. 7, 1903, are found in Romanov, *Rossiia*, pp. 416–420; Glinskii, *Prolog*, pp. 271–275; Witte, *Raz'iasneniia*, pp. 75–77.

¹⁶⁵ The most nearly complete version of the original, with Kuropatkin's two conditions, is in Glinskii, *Prolog*, pp. 274–275. Romanov, Rossiia, p. 420 n. 3.

¹⁶⁶ These enumerated terms are my abbreviated version of Glinskii's paraphrased version.

¹⁶⁷ Kuropatkin's Diary, Jan. 13, 1903, *K.A.*, II, 18.

¹⁶⁸ Romanov, *Rossiia*, p. 420 n. 3; Clyde, *op. cit.*, pp. 75–76; K. S. Weigh, *Russo-Chinese Diplomacy* (Shanghai, 1928), pp. 109–110.

¹⁶⁹ Romanov, *Rossiia*, p. 421 n. 3.

¹⁷⁰ *Ibid.*, p. 425; Kuropatkin's Diary, April 27, 1903, *K.A.*, II, 43. Nine battalions of infantry would remain in northern Manchuria: 2 in Harbin, 2 in Tsitsihar, 2 in Ninguta, 1 in Hailar, 1 in Hunchun, and 1 along the Sungari and Tsitsihar-Blagoveschensk trace.

¹⁷¹ Romanov, *Ocherki*, pp. 209 ff.

NOTES TO CHAPTER IX

¹ Under A. P. Ignatiev he held the post of *chinovnik osobykh poruchenii* (special agent), similar to the present-day post of official "trouble shooter."

² Kuropatkin's Diary, Dec. 14, 1902, *K.A.*, II (1923), 11–12.

³ Quoted in Pokrovskii, *1905 g.*, I, 578; Romanov, *Rossiia*, p. 404.

⁴ Before this conference Witte asked Kuropatkin not to bring up the poignant subject of the expenditures on the C.E.R. Kuropatkin's Diary, Feb. 1, 1903, *K.A.*, II, 24–25.

⁵ This project had been advocated for several years by the Board of Directors of the Oriental Institute of Vladivostok, who also wanted to establish a propaganda medium in Chinese. See minutes of the Conference of Dec. 12, 1901, *I.V.I.*, III (1901–1902), No. 3, pp. 134–135.

⁶ Not too fantastic an idea. An American electric-power company and tramway had successfully operated in Seoul as a concession since 1899. F. H. Harrington, *God, Mammon, and the Japanese*, pp. 187–189.

⁷ Glinskii, *Prolog*, pp. 254–257; also listed in Bezobrazov's summary of his report to the Tsar, Glinskii, *Prolog*, pp. 260–268. An unfavorable summary is in Romanov, *Rossiia*, p. 405 n.

⁸ Romanov, *Rossiia*, pp. 401, 451; Lvov, *Likhodei biurokraticheskago samovlastiia* . . . , p. 24; see summary of the article in *Ostasiatische Lloyd* in *I.V.I.*, III, No. 3, p. 670.

⁹ Lvov, *op. cit.*, pp. 24–25. Ginsburg later recovered only 12,000 rubles.

¹⁰ Text of the draft of Agreement of Dec. 28, 1902, in Lvov, *op. cit.*, pp. 62–65.

¹¹ The concession obtained from China in Yunnan by French and English promoters in 1901 carried specific provisions for armed guards. *I.V.I.*, IV (1902–1903), 57.

[12] The summary is mine; the full text and full financial plan are given in Lvov, *op. cit.*, pp. 62–69.

[13] Probably the meaning is "not on active duty." Madritov could ask for temporary leave from active duty and thus be eligible.

[14] Financial plan, Lvov, *op. cit.*, pp. 74–75.

[15] No doubt because Bezobrazov's anti-Semitism came into conflict with Ginsburg's racial origin. This, again, was quite "normal" and logical.

[16] In 1905 Lvov sued Ginsburg and later Bezobrazov. Lvov, *op. cit.*, pp. 24–25.

[17] Bezobrazov had to manage this through St. Petersburg. Abaza obtained Kuropatkin's approval first to transfer Madritov from the General Staff to Alexeev's personal staff. Kuropatkin's Diary, Dec. 30, 1902, *K.A.*, II (1923), 14.

[18] Bezobrazov's summary of his report, Glinskii, *Prolog*, p. 261. This is the exact amount Lvov mentioned in November, 1902, as his requirement for starting the operation of the Russo-Chinese Timber Company. Lvov, *op. cit.*, p. 23.

[19] Glinskii, *Prolog*, p. 257.

[20] Quoted by V. L. Burtsev in *Tsar i Vneshniaia politika* (Berlin, 1910), p. 15. The date was arrived at by synchronizing the content with Kuropatkin's Diary.

[21] Glinskii, *Prolog*, p. 254.

[22] *Ibid.*, p. 258.

[23] Alexeev was a strong candidate for the post of head of the Navy Department. After Tyrtov's demise he was passed over; the Tsar possibly wanted to keep him out of the capital. Kuropatkin's Diary, March 18, 1903, *K.A.*, II, 35. The reason for this might be that Alexeev was probably the illegitimate son of Alexander II. Because of this, the Tsar probably felt that he should show him special favor, yet at the same time he understandably might have wanted to keep him away. Article on "Alexeev, E. I.," in *Bol'shaia Sovetskaia Entsiklopediia*. After being turned down, Alexeev naturally wanted to expand the Far Eastern undertaking.

[24] Kuropatkin's Diary, March 16, 1903, *K.A.*, II, 33–34.

[25] *Ibid.*, p. 34.

[26] The Tsar stated that the men of the artel should always carry the rifles with them. *Ibid.*

[27] During this period the governors general of the three Manchurian provinces were asking Peking for more troops, arms, and money to fight the *khunhuzes* and refugee Boxers. See summaries for February and March, 1902, in *I.V.I.*, VII (1903), Chronicle, p. 372; *ibid.*, VIII, Chronicle, p. 417.

[28] Kuropatkin's Diary, March 18, 1903, *K.A.*, II, 34.

[29] Entry of March 28, 1903, *ibid.*, pp. 37–38.

[30] Glinskii, *Prolog*, p. 259.

[31] Quoted in Pokrovskii, *1905 g.*, I, 579.

[32] Glinskii, *Prolog*, p. 260.

[33] Balashev had had some experience as an agent of the Russian Red Cross during the anticholera campaign in Manchuria. Later he told how he had been appointed to the job of manager of the timber concession. When Bezobrazov asked him to take the job, Balashev answered that he knew nothing about the lumber industry. Bezobrazov replied, "Nichevo" (It does not matter). Lvov, *op. cit.*, p. 43.

[34] Almost the full text of Bezobrazov's summary is given in Glinskii, *Prolog*, pp. 260–269.

[35] A detailed summary of the journal of the conference is in Glinskii, *Prolog*, pp. 277–282; for a briefer form see Witte, *Raz'iasneniia*, pp. 85–86. Romanov used the journal in the Russian archives, but his treatment is very sketchy and biased. Romanov, *Rossiia*, pp. 406–407.

[36] Abaza's memorandum stated, on Bezobrazov's evidence, that "thousands" of Japanese were penetrating the Yalu region and cutting down timber in the concession area. Glinskii, *Prolog*, p. 279. In private correspondence Abaza and Bezobrazov

always referred to the three ministers as "the triumvirate" or "the mangy triumvirate." Letters in "Bezobrazovskii kruzhok letom 1904," *K.A.*, XVII (1926), 70–80.

37 Kuropatkin's Diary, Dec. 30, 1902, *K.A.*, II (1923), 14.

38 If any opposite views were expressed and recorded, no doubt Glinskii or Romanov would have mentioned them; the former to further clear Witte, the latter to implicate Plehve.

39 Glinskii, *Prolog*, p. 279; Witte, *Raz'iasneniia*, p. 85. Abaza took part in neither the discussion nor the formulation of the decisions of the ministerial conference; he was merely a "reporter" or "reader" of the memorandum.

40 My summation of the decisions as stated (without quotes) in Glinskii, *prolog*, pp. 281–282; Witte, *Raz'iasneniia*, pp. 85–86.

41 Romanov, *Rossiia*, p. 406. In a conversation with Kuropatkin, Witte designated this measure as Bezobrazov's plan. Kuropatkin's Diary, April 2, 1903, *K.A.*, II, 39.

42 Glinskii, *Prolog*, pp. 279–280; Witte, *Raz'iasneniia*, p. 85.

43 Kuropatkin's Diary, Feb. 1, 1903, *K.A.*, II, 25–26.

44 There is little doubt that room for expansion in Manchuria was desired, judging by Bezobrazov's list of projects.

45 Kuropatkin's Diary, April 23, 1903, *K.A.*, II, 41–42.

46 Witte, *Raz'iasneniia*, p. 86.

47 Romanov, *Rossiia*, pp. 389, 410 n. 1. The date is determined indirectly. *Ibid.*, pp. 410 and 411.

48 For a discussion of the rank and post see A. A. Savinskii, *Recollections of a Russian Diplomat* (London, 1928), p. 43. Article on "Tabel' rangov" in *Entsiklopedicheskii Slovar'* (St. Petersburg, 1901), XXXII, 439–441. Witte was also a state secretary.

49 *Otchet Gos. Soveta, 1902–1903*, p. 459. Bezobrazov's name is also listed for the same post in the *Otchet* for the years 1903–1904 and 1904–1905.

50 This interpretation is subject to doubt. Romanov gives no authority for his statement. Romanov, *Rossiia*, p. 409. Judging by the rather crude wording of the telegram, it is very probable that it was not edited by any minister.

51 Romanov gives the essential part of the telegram in excerpts. Romanov, *op. cit.*, p. 409.

52 This can only be deduced from the title of the journal and the *Otchet* (Report) of the conference. Witte, *Raz'iasneniia*, p. 87. Usually the Tsar did not attend the special conferences, so that the ministers would feel freer to discuss matters.

53 The conference was attended by Witte, Lamsdorf, General Sakharov (Chief of Staff), Plehve, Bezobrazov, Abaza, and Major General Vogak (former military attaché for China and Japan). Witte, *Raz'iasneniia*.

54 *Ibid.*, Glinskii, *Prolog*, pp. 286–287. Witte claimed that he did not see the final draft of the journal until 1909. Romanov does not mention the questionable character of the document he used.

55 The best accounts of the conference are, in order of their completeness: Glinskii, *Prolog*, pp. 282–287; Witte, *Raz'iasneniia*, pp. 86–91; Romanov, *Rossiia*, pp. 410–411. At this conference Plehve reputedly said: "It was not diplomacy that made Russia but bayonets, and with bayonets and not with diplomatic pens we must decide the questions with China and Japan." Pokrovskii, *1905 g.*, I, 583.

56 Full text in Glinskii, *Prolog*, pp. 290–291.

57 *Ibid.*

58 Romanov, *Rossiia*, p. 432.

59 *Ibid.*, p. 431.

60 Abaza to Bezobrazov, June 24, 1903, Burtsev, *op. cit.*, p. 43.

61 *Ibid.*

62 Lamsdorf's memorandum to the Tsar on the publication of the *Malinovaia Kniga*, Burtsev, *op. cit.*, p. 33.

63 Romanov, *Rossiia*, pp. 439, 443 nn. 1 and 2.

64 See "Stats-Sekretar'" in D. N. Ushakov (ed.), *Tolkovyi Slovar' Russkogo Iazyka* (Moscow, 1935–1940), IV, 495.

65 An analysis of the conferences is in Glinskii, *Prolog*, pp. 292–309; a brief summary is in Romanov, *Rossiia*, pp. 437–439. Many excerpts from the journals are in Witte, *Raz'iasneniia*, pp. 93–99; excerpts from the statements of Major General K. A. Vogak are given in A. I. Gippius, *O prichinakh nashei voiny s Iaponiei*, App. III, 48–51.

66 Text in Glinskii, *Prolog*, pp. 306–307.

67 *Ibid.*, p. 308; Romanov, *Rossiia*, pp. 438–439.

68 Character sketch of Bezobrazov in Witte, *Vospominaniia*, I, 164–165.

69 Savinskii, *op. cit.*, p. 50; *K.A.*, XVII (1926), 70.

70 Glinskii, *Prolog*, p. 314; Kuropatkin's Diary, Aug. 6, 1903, *K.A.*, II (1923), 45.

71 The ideas expressed by Kuropatkin have been collated from his *Zapiski generala Kuropatkina o Russko-Iaponskoi Voine* (Berlin, 1908), summarized in Glinskii, *Prolog*, pp. 311–333. Witte and Lamsdorf presented commentaries on the Port Arthur conferences, *ibid.*, pp. 337–340; Romanov, *Rossiia*, pp. 439–440.

72 Kuropatkin's Diary, Aug. 17, and Sept. 1, 1903, *K.A.*, II, 47–48, 57–58.

73 Entry of Aug. 17, 1903, *ibid.*, p. 49.

74 Namely, the establishment of a Viceroyalty of the Far East and his own resignation. See *infra*.

75 *K.A.*, II, 58.

76 Romanov, *Rossiia*, pp. 450–451.

77 *K.A.*, XVII (1926), 70–80, *passim*.

78 Kokovtsev, *Memoirs*, pp. 21–22.

79 Lvov, *op. cit.*, pp. 51–52.

80 Kokovtsev, *Memoirs*, p. 22.

81 A. M. de Bezobrazov, "Les premières causes d'éffondrement de la Russia: Le conflit russo-japonais," *Le Correspondent*, CCXCI (1923), 557–615.

82 Kokovtsev, *Memoirs*, pp. 20–21.

83 Documents edited and prefaced by Romanov, "Bezobrazovskii kruzhok letom 1904 goda," *K.A.*, XVII, 70–80.

84 Romanov, *Rossiia*, p. 443. Text of the Imperial Declaration in MacMurray, *Treaties*, I, 112.

85 The confusion is apparent from the start. Kuropatkin's Diary, Aug. 16, 1903, *K.A.*, II (1923), 46.

86 Text of the ukase to the Senate of Aug. 12, 1903, on the formation of the Special Committee of the Far East in *Russkoe Bogatstvo*, 1903, No. 10, pp. 152–154.

87 Romanov's introduction in *K.A.*, XVII (1926), 70–71.

88 Kuropatkin's Diary, Sept. 1, 1903, *K.A.*, II, 58.

89 Kuropatkin's Diary, Aug. 14, 1903, *ibid.*, p. 45. The Tsar stated that he had first had the idea a year and a half previously. Entry Aug. 17, 1903, *ibid.*, p. 46.

90 Entries of Aug. 14 and 17, 1903, *ibid.*, pp. 45, 46–47.

91 Entries of Aug. 17 and Sept. 1, 1903, *ibid.*, pp. 47, 58.

92 On the ground that he had an appointment with the Tsar. Actually, the appointment was for a time much earlier than the scheduled conference. Bezobrazov probably wanted to avoid a clash with the "triumvirate." Kuropatkin's Diary, Aug. 23, 1903, *ibid.*, pp. 47, 48, 52; Romanov, *Rossiia*, pp. 440–442; Glinskii, *Prolog*, pp. 343–345.

93 The text of the demands is paraphrased in Romanov, *Rossiia*, p. 442 n.; and even more tersely in Glinskii, *Prolog*, pp. 343–345.

94 Kuropatkin's Diary, Aug. 23, 1903, *K.A.*, II, 52.

95 Romanov, *Rossiia*, p. 442 n. 2.

96 Paraphrased text, *ibid.*

[97] Letter, MacDonald to Lansdowne, Sept. 15, 1903, *B.D.*, II, 215.

[98] Romanov, *Rossiia*, p. 447 n.; Alexeev to the Tsar, Sept. 25, 1903; Burtsev, *op. cit.*, p. 48.

[99] The Tsar had approved of the negotiations and by Aug. 29, 1903, had even drafted the first Russian counterproposals. Pokrovskii, *1905 g.* (Moscow, 1925–1927), I, 598–599.

[100] Kuropatkin's Diary, Sept. 1, 1903, *K.A.*, II, 59–60.

[101] Witte, *Vospominaniia*, I, 186; Kuropatkin's Diary, April 2, and Sept. 1, 1903, *K.A.*, II, 39, 59–60.

[102] An interesting account of the actual dismissal is in Kokovtsev, *Memoirs*, pp. 6–7. Witte, *Vospominaniia*, I, 185–186.

[103] *Dnevnik Imperatora Nikolaia II, 1890–1906* (Berlin, 1923), p. 21.

[104] Kuropatkin's Diary, Sept. 1, 1903, *K.A.*, II, 60–61.

[105] Kokovtsev, *Memoirs*, p. 7.

[106] *Ibid.*, pp. 7–8. Pleske repeatedly made efforts to resign.

[107] Abaza was strongly suspected of an attempt to get a huge "bonus" in 1904. He tried to get himself appointed on a commission to purchase South American warships in Paris. *Ibid.*, pp. 46–48.

[108] Witte, *Vospominaniia*, I, 262. A somewhat similar view was attributed to Plehve by Lamsdorf. Kuropatkin's Diary, Dec. 24, 1903, *K.A.*, II, 94.

[109] Romanov, *Rossiia*, pp. 441 n., 442 n. 2.

[110] Letter, MacDonald to Lansdowne, Sept. 15, 1903, *B.D.*, II, 215.

[111] Note, Cassini to Hay, July 14, 1903, *U. S. Foreign Affairs*, 1903, p. 711; A. Ia. Kantorovich, *Amerika v bor'be za Kitai* (Moscow, 1935), p. 151.

[112] Conger to Hay, Sept. 1, 1903, quoted in Zabriskie, *op. cit.*, p. 96.

[113] Kantorovich, *op. cit.*, p. 151, citing Cassini to Lamsdorf, June 18 and 20, 1903.

[114] Scott to Lansdowne, May 14, 1903, *B.D.*, II, 203.

[115] Summary of article in *Korean Review*, 1901, No. 10, in *I.V.I.*, III (1901–1902), No. 1, Chronicle, p. 288.

[116] *I.V.I.*, XI (1904), Chronicle, p. 186.

[117] Romanov, *Rossiia*, p. 451. Summary of the article in *Japan Times*, March 1, 1903, in *I.V.I.*, VII (1903), Chronicle, p. 390. However, Ginsburg apparently did get a mining concession. *Ibid.*, III, No. 3, Chronicle, p. 670.

[118] Harrington, *op. cit.*, pp. 193–194. For a list of all mining concessions in Korea at that time, see article in *Ost Asien*, August, 1901, summary in *I.V.I.*, III (1901–1902), No. 1, p. 169.

[119] Harrington, *op. cit.*, p. 305.

[120] Summary of the article in *Japan Weekly Mail*, Sept. 14, 1901, in *I.V.I.*, III, No. 1, p. 169. When the Russians moved in, they found that the Japanese had preempted the best plots in and around the town. Harrington, *op. cit.*, p. 305.

[121] Caused by the unemployed ricksha boys. *Ibid.*, pp. 190–191. Dr. Horace N. Allen, the American Minister, at that time urged that the United States seize a naval base in Korea as compensation for the claims of American owners.

[122] Summary of article in Shanghai *Mercury*, May 5, 1903, in *I.V.I.*, VIII (1903), Chronicle, pp. 484–485.

[123] Ieromonakh Pavel, "Sovremennoe polozhenie khristianskikh missii v Koree," *I.V.I.*, XII (1904), 253–344, tables pp. 342–344.

[124] Summary of article in Shanghai *Mercury*, Aug. 21, 1901, *I.V.I.*, III (1901–1902), No. 1, p. 78; summary of item in *Japan Weekly Times*, Nov. 2, 1901, *I.V.I.*, III, No. 2, p. 361.

[125] *I.V.I.*, VII (1903), Chronicle, p. 390.

[126] Summary of article in Shanghai *Mercury*, May 5, 1903, in *I.V.I.*, VIII (1903), Chronicle, p. 485.

[127] *I.V.I.*, IV (1902–1903), 129; summary of article in *Japan Weekly Mail*, June

28, 1902, *I.V.I.*, III, No. 5, Chronicle, p. 907. Attempts by the Korean government to get a loan from the Russo-Chinese Bank in November, 1902, failed. Summary of article in *Japan Weekly Times*, Nov. 29, 1902, *I.V.I.*, VI (1903–1904), Chronicle, p. 231.

[128] The Japanese financed the establishment of a Central Korean Bank, with Kato as its "counselor." *I.V.I.*, XI (1904), Chronicle, p. 186.

[129] *I.V.I.*, IV (1902–1903), Chronicle, p. 61.

[130] Harrington, *op. cit.*, p. 320.

[131] *I.V.I.*, VI (1903–1904), Chronicle, pp. 255–256.

[132] *I.V.I.*, VIII (1903), 403. Cf. figures for 1901 in the summary of article in *Japan Weekly Times*, Sept. 21, 1901, in *I.V.I.*, III (1901–1902), No. 1, Chronicle, p. 204.

[133] A. Tsererin, "Chinnampo," *I.V.I.*, IV (1902–1903), 1–48.

[134] Tables in *I.V.I.*, IV, 36–37.

[135] *Ibid.*, pp. 11, 13, 15, 27–33. The American mine nearest the Yalu was 37 miles northwest of Unsan. For the Gwendoline Mine and the German mine see *I.V.I.*, III (1901–1902), No. 2, Chronicle, p. 381

[136] Tsererin gives a profusion of interesting factual details, down to the number of stamps in each stamp mill. *Ibid.*, III, No. 1, pp. 26–33. Entry for June 8, 1903, in Baelz, *Awakening Japan*, p. 207. For the Yalu concession see *infra*.

[137] Tsererin, *op. cit.*, pp. 32–33. Other nationalities: 62 Germans, 80 French, 141 English, 239 Americans. The Japanese numbered between 20,000 and 40,000. *I.V.I.*, III, No. 2, Chronicle, p. 382.

[138] In October, 1902. *I.V.I.*, V (1903), Chronicle, p. 138.

[139] Lvov, *op. cit.*, pp. 31, 47; Glinskii, *Prolog*, pp. 287–288.

[140] He proved himself both an energetic and a courageous officer in the cavalry operations of the Russo-Japanese War and was raised to the rank of brigadier general. Lvov, *op. cit.*, p. 42.

[141] *Ibid.*, pp. 47–48; Glinskii, *Prolog*, pp. 287–288.

[142] *Ibid.*, pp. 304–305; D. G. Ianchevetskii, *Groza s Vostoka* (Revel, 1907), pp. 26–30, 223–224.

[143] Lvov, *op. cit.*, pp. 48–49.

[144] *Ibid.*, p. 50.

[145] *Ibid.*, p. 49.

[146] *Ibid.* Summary of article in *Japan Weekly Mail*, June 13, 1903, in *I.V.I.*, IX (1903), Chronicle, p. 533.

[147] His account was published in several Japanese newspapers and in translation in the *Hong Kong Weekly Press* and the Kobe *Chronicle*, Sept. 12, 1903. Summary with long quotations in *I.V.I.*, X (1904), 89–91. It can be supposed therefore that this version was well known to many.

[148] *Ibid.*, pp. 90–91.

[149] Report circulated in July, *ibid.*, p. 38. On this "authoritative" account the Russian translator could not forbear to comment: "What were they supposed to be building—a Tower of Babel?"

[150] Summary of article in *Celestial Empire* (Peking), Oct. 31, 1903, in *I.V.I*, X (1904), Chronicle, pp. 139–140. Also *I.V.I.*, IX (1903), Chronicle, p. 533.

[151] Summary of article in *Ostasiatische Lloyd*, Sept. 11, 1903, in *I.V.I.*, X (1904), Chronicle, p. 82. The article mentions a Japanese gunboat, which is rather improbable.

[152] Gurko, *op. cit.*, p. 275 n.; Kuropatkin's Diary, Dec. 9, 1903, *K.A.*, II (1923), 86.

[153] Romanov, *Rossiia*, pp. 451–452.

[154] From Jan. 26 to Feb. 23, 1904, *ibid.*, pp. 460–462; also *K.A.*, II, 71.

[155] Kokovtsev, *Memoirs*, p. 23; Romanov, *Kontsessiia*, pp. 105–106.

[156] Romanov, *Rossiia*, p. 447 and n.

[157] *Ibid.*, p. 456.

[158] *Ibid.*, pp. 453–454.

[159] This view is also held in his latest book. Romanov, *Ocherki*, p. 237.

[160] Akagi, *op. cit.*, pp. 223–224; MacDonald to Lansdowne, Oct. 1, 1903, *B.D.*, II, 215–216.

[161] MacDonald to Lansdowne, July 3 and 13, 1903. *B.D.*, II, 206–207, 208–209.

[162] Komura to Kurino, July 28, 1903. Japan, Ministry of Foreign Affairs, *Japanese White Book, Correspondence Regarding the Negotiations Between Japan and Russia, 1903–1904*, presented to the Imperial Diet, March, 1904, pp. 3–5. Known as—and cited hereafter as—*Japanese White Book.*

[163] Text in Komura to Kurino, Aug. 3, 1903, *ibid.*, pp. 7–9.

[164] Romanov, *Ocherki*, pp. 233–234, citing Rusin's dispatches of June 18 and 21 and Sept. 2, 1903. Preparations for war would have involved a large mobilization of transports, which would have been easily noticeable.

[165] Kurino to Komura, Aug. 5, 1903; Komura to Kurino, Aug. 6, 1903, *Japanese White Book*, p. 10.

[166] Kurino to Komura, Aug. 12 and 25, 1903, *ibid.*, p. 11.

[167] Kurino to Komura, Aug. 24, 1903, *ibid.*, p. 12; Kuropatkin's Diary, Sept. 2–12, 1903, *K.A.*, II, 63–74.

[168] Romanov, *Ocherki*, p. 231; *Japanese White Book*, pp. 15–22, nos. 10–15.

[169] Kurino to Komura, Aug. 31, 1903, *Japanese White Book*, pp. 15–17.

[170] Kurino to Komura, Sept. 5, 1903, *ibid.*, pp. 18–20.

[171] Komura to Kurino, Sept. 9, 1903, *ibid.*, p. 21.

[172] Text followed is *ibid.*, pp. 7–9.

[173] He left on Sept. 22 and returned on Oct. 3, Komura to Kurino, Sept. 24, Oct. 5, 1903, *ibid.*, p. 22.

[174] Romanov, *Ocherki*, p. 231.

[175] *Ibid.*, p. 230. Lansdowne to Monson, Nov. 4, 1903, *B.D.*, II, 221–222.

[176] Kuropatkin's Diary, Nov. 10, 1903, *K.A.*, II, 80.

[177] Abaza aired this as a grievance in a St. Petersburg club. Kuropatkin's Diary, Dec. 10, 1903, *ibid.*, p. 86.

[178] Pokrovskii, *1905 g.*, I, 598–599. Of course, Romanov, stressing the imperialistic and intransigent nature of Nicholas II, does not even mention this document.

[179] Alexeev to the Tsar, Sept. 28, 1903, Burtsev, *op. cit.*, pp. 49–50.

[180] Text in Komura to Kurino, Oct. 5, 1903, *Japanese White Book*, pp. 22–24.

[181] Komura to Kurino, Oct. 16, 22, 29, 1903, *ibid.*, pp. 24–27; MacDonald to Lansdowne, Oct. 22, 1903, *B.D.*, II, 217.

[182] Texts of the United States–Chinese Agreement and the Sino-Japanese Commercial Treaty in *Recueil de Traités*, pp. 657–682, 683–709. The immediate effect of the first treaty was lost by the long delay in its ratification. It was ratified by the United States Senate on Dec. 8, 1903, and by China on Jan. 10, 1904, *U. S. Foreign Affairs*, 1903, pp. 91–118. E. H. Zabriskie, *American-Russian Rivalry in the Far East, 1895–1914* (Philadelphia, 1926), pp. 96–100.

[183] K. S. Weigh, *Russo-Chinese Diplomacy* (Shanghai, 1928), pp. 110–111.

[184] Lansdowne to MacDonald, Oct. 26, 1903, *B.D.*, II, 218–219.

[185] Summaries of this trend are in Cambon to Delcassé, Feb. 8 and Oct. 28, 1904, *D.D.F.*, 2d ser., IV, no. 246, no. 398.

[186] Text in Komura to Kurino, Oct. 30, 1903, *Japanese White Book*, pp. 28–29; in abbreviated form it is in MacDonald to Lansdowne, Nov. 2, 1903, *B.D.*, II, 220–221.

[187] Kurino to Komura, Nov. 3, 1903, *Japanese White Book*, pp. 31–32.

[188] Kurino to Komura, Nov. 13, 1903, *ibid.*, pp. 32–34.

[189] Komura to Kurino, Nov. 21, 1903, *ibid.*, pp. 34–35.

[190] Cambon to Delcassé, Oct. 27, 1903, *D.D.F.*, 2d ser., IV, no. 45; Lansdowne to Spring-Rice, Nov. 7, 1903, *B.D.*, II, 222–224. The Japanese wish for hasty conclusion is expressed strongly in Komura's instructions to Kurino: "You will say that the Japanese Government is anxious to proceed with the negotiations, with all possible expedition; you will urge him [Lamsdorf] to exert his influence to secure the early dispatch of instructions to Baron Rosen in order that the negotiations may be resumed and concluded without delay," Nov. 21, 1903. *Japanese White Book*, pp. 34–35.

[191] Romanov, *Ocherki*, p. 253.

[192] Kuropatkin's Diary, Oct. 5, 1903, *K.A.*, II (1923), 77. Alexeev to the Tsar, Sept. 25, 1903, Burtsev, *op. cit.*, p. 48.

[193] Kuropatkin's Diary, Oct. 27, 1903, *K.A.*, II, 77–78.

[194] Kuropatkin's Diary, Nov. 10, 1903, *ibid.*, p. 80.

[195] The Tsarina, after a difficult delivery, gave birth to a girl, who died a few days later. The Tsar and the Tsarina had expected an heir to the throne after having had four daughters. The combination of disappointment and tragic outcome greatly upset the devoted Tsar. Kuropatkin's Diary, Nov. 26, 1903, *K.A.*, II, 84–85; Kurino to Komura, Nov. 22, 1903, *Japanese White Book*, p. 35.

[196] Kuropatkin's Diary, Oct. 27, 1903, *K.A.*, II, 78.

[197] Apparently Kuropatkin sent the memorandum about Oct. 28 and followed it by summaries and additional notes. Kuropatkin's Diary, Dec. 10, 1903, *K.A.*, II, 87–89.

[198] Kuropatkin's Diary, Nov. 10 and 20, 1903, *ibid.*, pp. 79, 83.

[199] *Ibid.*, pp. 87–89.

[200] Kuropatkin's Diary, Dec. 16, 1903, *ibid.*, p. 91; A. N. Kuropatkin, *Zapiski o Russko-Iaponskoi Voine* (Berlin, 1909), pp. 173–174; in English translation as A. N. Kuropatkin, *The Russian Army and the Japanese War* (New York, 1909), I, 188–193.

[201] Kuropatkin's Diary, Dec. 16, 1903, *K.A.*, II, 91.

[202] Entry of Dec. 24, 1903, *ibid.*, p. 94.

[203] Text in Komura to Kurino, Dec. 12, 1903, *Japanese White Book*, pp. 41–42.

[204] Text in Komura to Kurino, Dec. 21, 1903; account of presentation in Kurino to Komura, Dec. 23, 1903, *ibid.*, pp. 42–45.

[205] Alexeev to the Tsar, Dec. 26, 1903, Burtsev, *op. cit.*, p. 55.

[206] Kuropatkin's Diary, Dec. 28, 1903, *K.A.*, II, 95–97; Gurko, *op. cit.*, p. 284. Romanov virtually ignores the conference. Romanov, *Ocherki*, p. 259.

[207] Kuropatkin's Diary, Dec. 28, 1903, *K.A.*, II, 95.

[208] *Ibid.*, pp. 95–96.

[209] *Ibid.*, p. 96. On the following day Abaza submitted to the Tsar a memorandum based on these views. Excerpts in Burtsev, *op. cit.*, pp. 57–60.

[210] Kuropatkin's Diary, Dec. 28, 1903, *K.A.*, II, 85.

[211] Romanov, *Ocherki*, p. 241.

[212] See Great Britain, Committee of Imperial Defense, Historical Section, *Official History of the Russo-Japanese War* (London, 1910), I, App. N and P, pp. 488–489, 502–511; also pp. 36, 39–40. Cited hereafter as *Official History*. See also *Brassey's Naval Annual*, 1903, pp. 62 ff. For brief comparison of the strengths of the major fleets see A. L. Marder, *The Anatomy of British Sea Power, 1880–1905* (New York, 1940), p. 419 n. 7.

[213] *Official History*, I. 35.

[214] *Ibid.*, pp. 35–36.

[215] Text in Komura to Kurino, Jan. 7, 1904, *Japanese White Book*, 46–47. For British attitude toward this article see Lansdowne to MacDonald, Jan. 8, 1904, *B.D.*, II, 231.

[216] Note to France, in *D.D.F.*, IV, no. 163; to Great Britain, in *China No. 2 (1904)*, pp. 229–230; Lansdowne to Scott, Jan. 8, 1904, *B.D.*, II, 231.

[217] Lansdowne to MacDonald, Jan. 11, 1904, *ibid.*, pp. 232–233.

[218] *Ibid.* Lansdowne to MacDonald, Dec. 30, 1903, *ibid.*, pp. 227–228.

[219] Lansdowne to MacDonald, Jan. 5 and 17, 1904, *ibid.*, pp. 229–230, 236; Romanov, *Ocherki*, pp. 260–261.

[220] Akagi, *op. cit.*, p. 231.

[221] Text in Komura to Kurino, Jan. 13, 1904, *Japanese White Book*, pp. 47–49; also as an enclosure in Lansdowne to MacDonald, Jan. 14, 1904, *B.D.*, II, 233–234. The nature of the dispatch was expressed by Lansdowne: "Viscount Hayashi told me that the demands embodied in these instructions were to be regarded as final, and that if an answer was not received in a reasonable time, or if the answer was unsatisfactory, the Japanese Government would have to take steps for the protection of their interests."

[222] Galperin, *op. cit.*, pp. 189 ff.; Romanov, *Ocherki*, p. 292.

[223] Akagi, *op. cit.*, p. 236. Baelz wrote in his diary on Jan. 5, 1904: "An Imperial ordinance has just been issued strictly forbidding the newspapers to publish any kind of military news. This means business." Baelz, *op. cit.*, p. 241.

[224] Kurino to Komura, Jan. 25 and 26, 1904, *Japanese White Book*, pp. 50, 51–52.

[225] Lansdowne to MacDonald, Jan. 29, 1904, *B.D.*, II, 240–241.

[226] *Ibid.*

[227] Alexeev to the Tsar, Jan. 6 and 9, 1904, Burtsev, *op. cit.*, pp. 61–62, 63.

[228] This would involve moving the X and XVII Corps from European Russia to Irkutsk province. Alexeev to the Tsar, Jan. 6, 1904, Burtsev, *op. cit.*, p. 62.

[229] Kuropatkin's Diary, Jan. 13, 1904, *K.A.*, II, 99.

[230] *Ibid.*, p. 100.

[231] Nicholas II to Alexeev, Jan. 27, 1904. Burtsev, *op. cit.*, p. 69. By this time undoubtedly both Russia and Japan were moving supplies or advanced echelons into the zone of expected operations, though both sides officially denied making such moves. Alexeev to the Tsar, Jan. 10, 1904, *ibid.*, p. 65; Komura to Kurino, Jan. 28, 1904, and Kurino to Komura, Jan. 28, 1904, *Japanese White Book*, pp. 52–53.

[232] Kuropatkin's Diary, Jan. 16, 1904, *K.A.*, II, 100–101.

[233] Summary of this conference in Kuropatkin's Diary, Jan. 28, 1904, *K.A.*, II, 103–105; Romanov, *Ocherki*, pp. 275–276.

[234] Romanov, *Ocherki*, p. 277; Kuropatkin's Diary, Feb. 3, 1904, *K.A.*, II, 106. There is mention that the Japanese generally prevented telegraphic communication between Russian agents in Japan on the eve of the war. See Raspopov to Kokovtsev, Aug. 9, 1905, *K.A.*, V (1924), 4–5.

[235] Akagi, *op. cit.*, pp. 236–237.

[236] *Official History*, I, 70.

[237] Komura to Kurino, 2:15 P.M., Feb. 5, 1904, *Japanese White Book*, pp. 56–58, 58–59. At 5:15 P.M., the same day, Tokyo was aware of the fact that the Russian answer was on the way. See Kurino to Komura, Feb. 5, 1904, *ibid.*, p. 40.

[238] Kurino to Komura, Feb. 5, 1904, *ibid.*, p. 61. On Feb. 7 Lamsdorf still hoped that war could be averted. Kuropatkin's Diary, Feb. 7, 1904, *K.A.*, II, 106.

[239] Table of Russian vessels captured, *Official History*, I, 514; also summary of article in *Echo de Chine*, March 13, 1904, in *I.V.I.*, XII (1904), Chronicle, p. 431. In Japan secret mobilization was in full swing. Entry of Feb. 7, 1904, Baelz, *op. cit.*, pp. 244–245.

[240] Kuropatkin's Diary, Feb. 8, 1904, *K.A.*, II, 107–109.

[241] Feb. 8, 1904, Burtsev, *op. cit.*, p. 76.

BIBLIOGRAPHY

BIBLIOGRAPHICAL ESSAY

THERE IS NO complete bibliography in the field of Russian Far Eastern policy, 1881–1904. Such a bibliography would have to encompass events in Bulgaria in the 1880's, financial disturbances in southern Russia about 1900, the political rivalry in St. Petersburg during the crucial years 1902–1903, and innumerable lesser subjects that influenced the course of events in the Far East. A list of bibliographies covering these fields would have to include all bibliographies for Russian history of the period.

On the subject of Russians in the Far East there is, fortunately, the two-volume work edited by Professor Robert J. Kerner, *Northeastern Asia: A Selected Bibliography* (2 vols.; Berkeley, University of California Press, 1939). This work stresses Russian and Far Eastern materials dealing with Russian Far Eastern relations. It supersedes the monumental work of one of the few Russian bibliographers, V. I. Mezhov, noted for his *Bibliographia Asiatica* (St. Petersburg, 1891–1894) and *Sibirskaia Bibliografiia* (1903). Its value is enhanced by its broad scope, covering the area from Alaska to China.

Another Russian bibliographer, P. E. Skachkov, published in 1932 his *Bibliografiia Kitaia ... na russkom iazyke, 1730–1930* (Bibliography of China ... in the Russian Language, 1730–1930); it is in a narrower field. This 840-page work has many useful recent references concerning Russo-Chinese affairs in the period 1881–1904. However, many of the journals and newspapers listed are unavailable in the United States and their titles serve only to tantalize an American or Western European scholar. Whereas Kerner's work emphasizes international relations, Skachkov's includes all fields. This is the weakness and the virtue of Skachkov's bibliography. Kerner includes all languages and deals principally with available material; Skachkov limits himself to works in the Russian language and includes many references to works that are unavailable. The many topics listed in Skachkov's bibliography make it valuable for students other than historians and political scientists. It was reprinted at Ann Arbor, Michigan, in 1948.

In addition to the above works, bibliographies appended to some recent monographs are useful for reference. Unfortunately, the best monographs on the subject of Russian Far Eastern policy in the years before the Russo-Japanese War do not contain bibliographies. (Romanov's works are discussed below.) However, the recently published work by A. Galperin, *Anglo-Iaponskii Soiuz, 1902–1921* (The Anglo-Japanese Alliance, 1902–1921), published in Moscow in 1947, contains a well-edited eleven-page bibliography, adequate for a primary understanding of Russian policy, even as early as 1881.

MONOGRAPHS SHOWING EVOLUTION OF THE HISTORIOGRAPHY OF RUSSIAN FAR EASTERN POLICY

Soon after the outbreak of the Russo-Japanese War, both sides tried to present their cases through historical literature. Ostensibly, Russia was attacked, and therefore only after Russian defeats were manifest was there need for Russian explanations. Then the Russians sought a "scapegoat" for the policy which led to the war. Even this was a secondary consideration, however, because the government was then concerned with the beginnings of the revolution of 1905, which coincided with the last and greatest Russian defeats of Tsushima and Mukden.

Only newspapers and periodicals—principally those published abroad—presented the "scapegoat" interpretation and pounced upon Bezobrazov and the people connected with him.

The Japanese, seeking justification for their acts, produced the first important monograph on the subject. Professor Kanishi Asakawa's *Russo-Japanese Conflict, Its Causes and Issues* was published independently in Boston and London simultaneously toward the end of 1904. Considering the haste with which it must have been written to achieve such early publication, it is a very commendable monograph. The pro-Japanese bias is obvious. Except for a few published declarations, Russian policy had not been explained in documents, and the only documents theretofore available in any language had a pronounced anti-Russian bias—the British *Parliamentary Papers* ("Blue Books"), for example, which provided up-to-date diplomatic material although nothing that was "top secret." In addition, Asakawa used a great deal of periodical literature, mostly Japanese. The Japanese "White Book" was first published by the Japanese Ministry of Foreign Affairs soon after the outbreak of the war. It gave quite faithfully the interchange of Russian and Japanese proposals in 1903–1904.

For the year 1904, Asakawa's work is very commendable. It is still worth reading, with reservations. Its timely publication and wide distribution had helped to popularize what I term "the traditional interpretation of the causes of the Russo-Japanese War." This, in brief, reads as follows: Unbridled Russian imperialism, not content with the illegal seizure of Manchuria, planned to extend itself into Korea in the guise of private enterprise built around the Yalu concessions and headed by the real power behind the Russian throne, Bezobrazov. This was the "scapegoat" idea.

Among the early Russian monographs expounding the "scapegoat" interpretation of the causes of the war is General A. N. Kuropatkin's *Zapiski . . . o Russko-Iaponskoi Voine* (Berlin, 1909), and its abridged counterpart in English, *The Russian Army and the Japanese War* (New York, 1909). Both works were written to justify Kuropatkin's military failures. They also contain some interesting material on the causes of the war and clearly and semiofficially establishes the "scapegoat" interpretation, which, in brief, reads somewhat like this: "I, Kuropatkin, Minister of War, and other responsible ministers wanted a policy of retrenchment and even partial retreat in the Far East, but foreign affairs were then dominated by Bezobrazov's gang, which insisted in pushing forward crazy schemes for secret infiltration of Korea." This can be called "the traditional Russian" interpretation of the causes of the war.

It is not surprising that these two interpretations—the "traditional" and the "traditional Russian"—have persisted to the present time. They were strengthened by later publications. The first comprehensive Russian account of the causes of the Russo-Japanese War emphasized the "traditional Russian" interpretation. This was B. B. Glinskii, *Prolog Russo-Iaponskoi Voiny* (Prologue of the Russo-Japanese War) published in St. Petersburg in 1916. A number of factors helped to distribute this work widely, stimulated an interest in it, and also assured the acceptance of the "traditional Russian" interpretation. Glinskii was regarded as a liberal historian and was well known for his works on the revolutionary movement in Russia in the nineteenth century. In 1915 Witte died abroad, and since Glinskii's volume bore the subtitle *Materialy iz arkhiva Grafa S. Iu. Witte* (Materials from the Archives of Count S. Iu. Witte), the work was timely and the subtitle intriguing. To ensure an even wider distribution for Glinskii's interpretation, the work was also published in that year in installments in *Istoricheskii Vestnik*. This was probably the most popular historical journal published in Russia; in it, besides serious works, were printed historical novels, poems, anecdotes, and other light forms of historical literature.

Glinskii's work is an undisguised apologia for Witte, although why Witte required an apologia at that time cannot be determined. The thesis is the same as that of Kuropatkin. Briefly, it is that Witte always had the right idea, but that the intransigence of some of his colleagues and the influence of Bezobrazov toward imperialistic designs led to war. Glinskii was a historian, however, and did not falsify history. To be sure, his work is faulty in omitting all that was injurious to Witte's memory; but, as has been pointed in the text, Glinskii and Romanov, using the same documents, were both guilty of omissions. Glinskii omitted passages from Witte's report on his trip to the Far East in 1903 which presented Witte in an unfavorable light. Romanov later pounced on these passages and stressed them; yet at the same time he ignored passages which definitely indicated either Witte's perspicacity or his intrinsic moderation. Glinskii is perhaps the less guilty of the two. He did not use the archives of the Ministry of Foreign Affairs but used copies of key documents which Witte apparently had kept for his own private files (not an unusual procedure at that time). Hence Witte's copy of a certain document may have been edited by Witte himself.

The virtues of Glinskii's work are many. It is comprehensive. The history of Russian policy in the Far East is traced from the 1880's. It is honestly written, with perhaps some "sins of omission" but not "sins of commission." Thus Bezobrazov's insidious role is not exaggerated, and there is much material to vindicate Bezobrazov. Finally, Glinskii's work presents valuable documentary material, some of which it would be difficult to find elsewhere. Thus, for example, Witte's report on his trip to the Far East is presented, in part, and comprises twenty pages. As far as I know, the report had never been published elsewhere, except in such publications as the *Pravitel'stvennyi Vestnik* (Government Messenger) and the *Birzhevye Vedomosti* (Stock Market Intelligencer), newspapers which are difficult to find. Even these carried only excerpts of the report. Despite these virtues, however, the work strengthened the "traditional Russian" interpretation.

In 1928 Professor B. A. Romanov of Leningrad University published his monumental work, *Rossiia v Manzhurii, 1892–1906* (Russia in Manchuria, 1892–1906). Romanov, since 1923, had written several articles on phases of Russian policy in the Far East. He had free access to the archives of the Ministry of Foreign Affairs and the Ministry of Finance, and he made full use of them. His work is replete with references to items in those archives. It can be said that he missed nothing, although he admits that the condition of the archives of the Ministry of Finance and the methods under which its chancery was conducted in the period of Witte's control impeded a systematic study. And he was the only Russian historian who studied this period and subject thoroughly in the Russian archives. The Russian historians of the Far East were subjected to increasing restrictions placed on all Russian scientific writers after 1933. Furthermore, after Romanov's exhaustive treatment of the subject, there was almost no need to cover the same ground in the archives.

Romanov proved himself to be a competent, thorough, hard-working historian, but he was by no means perfect. The introduction to his work makes apparent his main aim. He wanted to fix the blame on Witte. The entire work is in the main given over to an exposure of Witte's mistakes, his vanity, chicanery, instability, and all his defamatory actions and characteristics. This, however, detracts little from the value of the work, because Witte was so central a figure in the formulation of Russian policy in the Far East that almost all of the history of that policy can be written as part of Witte's biography. Romanov's attack on Witte can be considered to have a salutary bias, since too much adulation of Witte had been presented by Glinskii and, particularly in the foreign press, by such writers as E. J. Dillon. Romanov's criticism extended to other ministers as well. This scholarly, documented attack completely shattered the "traditional Russian" interpretation; the ministers were now on longer as exempt from criticism as they had been, hiding behind the "scapegoat" Bezobrazov.

Romanov's treatment of the subject may be called "vicious." It seems that he scathingly criticised and ridiculed all Russians connected with Far Eastern affairs at that time. His work was thus basically at fault in that it was frequently guilty of "sins of commission" and that he applied the eclectic method to the selection of documents. Selecting words and expressions from documents, he paraphrased them and presented them as direct quotations. Many interministerial documents are not written judiciously; by the method applied by Romanov, a document, or its writer, could be presented in a very unfavorable light. Thus Romanov's work, although basically valuable because it was drawn from archival materials, must be used with caution. In the long run it does not present a true picture of Russian policy in the Far East—there are too many "sins of omission." Nevertheless, it is the most valuable work on the subject and a "must" for students and scholars of international relations in the Far East during this period. It is certainly worthy of being translated, but a translator would find the task very difficult. There are passages written in so confused a manner that only an expert in the Russian language can translate them, and sometimes the meaning can only be deduced from the text of the pages following the obscure passages.

As a result of the Japanese occupation of Manchuria, Soviet Russian policy toward the printing of documents and the writing of articles and books on Far Eastern history changed radically. The change occurred sometime after 1928; presumably it was soon after 1933 that Romanov fell into disfavor, if not disgrace. Probably his work had revealed too much. Like many of his colleagues who had displeased the Soviet government, Romanov shifted his interest to an innocuous period of the early Middle Ages in Russia. He next appeared as a collaborator in the study of the *Russkaia Pravda* (Russian Truth), the eleventh-century code of laws of Kievan Russia. In the 1940's he once again emerged as a historian of Russian policy in the Far East, writing articles about subjects previously dealt with in his *Russia in Manchuria*.

In 1947 Romanov published a work entitled *Ocherki diplomaticheskoi istorii Russko-Iaponskoi Voiny, 1895–1907* (A Survey of the Diplomatic History of the Russo-Japanese War, 1895–1907). This is a rewriting of his earlier work but with a new and "true" orientation: Romanov now recognized the "true" instigators of Russia's aggressive policy in the Far East. They were, according to this version, the Russian capitalists and *bourgeoisie* who compelled the Imperial Government and the Tsarist ministers to adopt an aggressive policy in order to insure for themselves a profitable market in the Orient in the future. Romanov was still a basically sound historian. After dutifully presenting a few citations from Lenin and Stalin and allotting a certain amount of space to the new and "true" interpretation, he wrote an abbreviated and better-organized version of his *Russia in Manchuria*.

The new version, however, cannot compare with the old as a historical contribution. In it no new archival material is used. Instead of reprinting the valuable references of his first work, Romanov merely cites his own earlier volume. He incorporates some new material from recently published non-Russian documents and monographs, but other than certain editorial improvements, his second work has little or nothing of additional value. The organization is better and simpler. There are two indexes, one of persons and one of topics; a group of key documents, all of which have been published elsewhere; and a table of contents conveniently separated into subsections by topic.

Although Romanov had "recognized" the new and "true" orientation, he soon fell from grace again. He was removed from his field of recent diplomatic history, and in collaboration with other historians he began to work in the field of fifteenth-century Russian history. In 1950 he contributed to a symposium an article on the travels to India of the Russian merchant Afanasii Nikitin in the early fifteenth century. This time, however, even his retirement into the distant past did not save him from criticism. The article was strongly criticized. This was tantamount to an official reprimand. However, regardless of the vagaries of official opinion, his original *Rossiia v Manzhurii* will stand as Romanov's great contribution to the historiography of Russian policy in the Far East.

Professor William L. Langer's *The Diplomacy of Imperialism, 1890–1902* (New York, 1935) should be discussed here, if only as an illustration of the "traditional" interpretation. This two-volume work contains several excellent chapters and parts of chapters illustrating the complexity of international relations in the Far East in which Russia participated. However, Langer does not give a clear picture of Russian policy in the Far East; for he seems to be interested in Russian policy only during periods of embroilment. In periods of turmoil a nation usually tries to take the strongest possible stand, if only for bargaining purposes. Russian policy during such periods appears to have been aggressive at times. Using the same documents published by Soviet Russia that Langer used, I found an entirely different meaning. Langer's selective method led him to ignore such key documents as the Muraviev Memorandum of February, 1900, and the interministerial circular which accompanies it—a group of documents which are important in the determination of Russian policy because they do not deal with any turmoil or coincide with any crisis in which Russia has been embroiled. Langer's work ends with the year 1902; he does not take up the crucial events of 1903, which constitute the direct cause of the crisis which finally led to the Russo-Japanese War. However, his discussion of the background of the war is sufficient to classify him as a proponent of the "traditional" school of interpretation. This is obvious in his treatment of Russian policy in Korea. Here again, I used the same documents as Langer and came to a diametrically opposite conclusion. The reason for this is obvious. Langer, or his assistant translator, mistranslated the key document on Russian policy in Korea in 1888 by constructing a positive from two Russian negatives. According to Langer, Korea had always had great importance to Russia; whereas the true meaning of the sentence on which he bases this statement is that Korea never had any significance for Russia. From that point on, utilizing documents dealing with Korea during periods of conflict, Langer drew a picture of an aggressive Russian policy in Korea. However, as I have illustrated in this work, when one forgets the diplomatic verbiage used with reference to Korea in diplomatic documents and examines the actual Russian activities in that country one sees an entirely different picture. Furthermore, though Langer used Romanov's work, he refuses to accept his interpretation of the insignificance of the Korean issue in the Far Eastern crisis from 1898 to 1904. In short, though Langer's accounts of Russia's role in the international disputes in the Far East are valuable, his interpretation of Russian policy in the Far East is as biased and as erroneous as that of Kanichi Asakawa, who preceded him by thirty years. By disregarding Romanov's valuable findings, Langer sets back the historiography of the subject almost to the original version of the "traditional" school of interpretation.

A similar reversion to the "traditional Russian" interpretation is found in David J. Dallin's *The Rise of Russia in Asia*, published in 1949, of which sixty pages deal with the period 1881–1904. The scholarly value of this work can be judged by one short paragraph: in introducing the Bezobrazov group (whose coming into power Dallin erroneously ascribes to 1900), Dallin makes several glaring mistakes in reporting the four names. He writes of the "Grand Duke Nicholas Alexandrovich" as a member of this group. There was no such person; the only Nicholas Alexandrovich in the Imperial family was the Tsar himself (see the *Almanach de Gotha*). Dallin writes of "General" Alexeev, whereas Alexeev was an active admiral and was never a member of the Bezobrazov group, though this is open to argument. Finally, he writes of "Ivan" Bezobrazov, thus mortally insulting the shades of Alexander Mikhailovich Bezobrazov. One can only suppose that Dallin, pressed for time, sat down and wrote this paragraph from memory alone, trusting that the "traditional Russian" interpretation, which he had learned many years ago, was the "gospel truth"; but his memory failed him in details.

If this was Dallin's method of writing, how can he be trusted in other statements? Although he used the same key documents as I, and although he cites B. A. Romanov frequently, he disregards the findings of Romanov in general. I disagree with almost every page of Dallin's work. His method of infrequent references makes it almost impossible to check his notes. For two pages of material he has only one reference, citing a whole book or a whole group of documents; which part of the book or the group of documents refers to what part of the text in the two pages, the reader must find out for himself. Indubitably there are parts of Dallin's presentation which are correct and which are certainly more modern than Glinskii's work, but Dallin's work is unreliable because of his method of writing. Glinskii's work thus stands out as a far greater and sounder contribution.

It must be noted that the criticism presented above is not meant to be a wholesale condemnation of Dallin's book. It concerns only sixty pages. It is reasonable to assume that when the author dealt with topics of a more recent date, his memory was less likely to play him false than when he wrote the pathetic paragraph mentioned. It is likely also that Dallin has made a thorough study of at least some of the topics covered in the remaining two hundred pages of the book. He has written some commendable books on the foreign policy of Soviet Russia. Perhaps if he had given more time to the preparation of this book—his average rate of production is often one book a year—the inadequate sixty pages would have read differently. However, the net result of this latest "authoritative" publication is that it has set back the historiography of the subject thirty-five to forty years; that is, at least to the time of Glinskii's work.

Thus the cycle of the historiography of the Russian policy in the Far East in the period 1881–1904 is completed. The first writers on the causes of the Russo-Japanese War may seem biased and frequently erroneous, but considering the lack of documentation of the subject in their time and the fact that they were under certain compulsion to take a certain stand, their faults are understandable. Asakawa's and Glinskii's works, although they created or strengthened the "traditional" and the "traditional Russian" interpretations, must be considered very good histories in the final analysis. The apogee of the historiography of the subject came in 1928 with B. A. Romanov's work; this is also biased, but through faithful archival research it completely shatters the "traditional" and the "traditional Russian" interpretation. Romanov was under no patriotic compulsion, because the year 1928 in Soviet Russia was still a liberal year as far as scholars were concerned. The decline came with W. L. Langer and D. J. Dallin, both presumably unbiased and under no compulsion whatsoever, who returned to these discredited "traditional" interpretations. The final result of the cycle seems to be the creation of a need for another monograph which would erase the fallacies of the later writers. With full acknowledgment of Romanov's research, the monograph should shed his biases, rectify his 1947 explanation, and present Russian policy in the Far East before the Russo-Japanese War in its true aspect for the first time.

COLLECTIONS OF TREATIES

The best single collection of treaties is the two-volume work by J. V. A. MacMurray, *Treaties and Agreements with or Concerning China* (New York, 1921). The Russian treaties included in it are well translated, but the collection does not have the correct version of the secret Russo-Chinese Treaty of Alliance of 1896. For that and the Russian-Japanese treaties and agreements, see E. D. Grimm, *Sbornik dogovorov ... 1842–1925* (Collection of Treaties ... 1842–1925), published in 1927. Useful and handy are three publications by the Carnegie Endowment for International Peace, all published in 1921—*Manchuria, Korea,* and *Outer Mongolia*—each with the subtitle *Treaties and Agreements.* A few additional minor agreements, such as territorial adjustments, are to be found in the volume published by the Russian Ministry of Foreign Affairs, *Sbornik dogovorov ...* (1906). This is a bilingual publication with a Russian version on one side and a French translation on the other. The full French title is *Recueil de traités et documents diplomatiques concernant l'Extrême Orient, 1895–1905.* A greater linguistic hodgepodge is found in the collection issued by the Japanese Ministry of Foreign Affairs in 1936: *Recueil de traités et conventions entre le Japon et les puissances étrangères.* Here the Japanese text is paralleled by English, French, and Russian texts. The title of this two-volume collection is a misnomer. The first volume contains many treaties and agreements to which Japan was not a party, as for example, the secret Russo-Chinese Treaty of Alliance as well as the contracts of the Chinese Eastern Railway. I counted in the first volume twelve agreements between China and Russia in which Japan did not participate.

All published documents dealing with Russian policy and not necessarily with the stated Russian position in regard to a particular question should be used with caution. In general, it can be said that no document of foreign origin can be considered representative of Russian policy until it has passed the test of being a Russian document. For instance, the famous "Willy-Nicky Correspondence," as it has been pointed out, presents an erroneous picture; the Tsar, instead of being completely taken in by William II, was actually heartily sick of the Emperor's un-welcome friendship.

To write of Russian policy without recourse to Russian documents would be an extremely dangerous procedure. The four great series of non-Russian publications— *Die Grosse Politik* . . . , *British Documents on the Origins of the War*, *Documents diplomatiques français*, and *Papers Relating to the Foreign Affairs of the United States*—are essential to a study of the Far Eastern events in this period and for the establishment of the Russian position in various crises, embroilments, and en-tanglements. Yet as a source of information about Russian policy they must be used with caution. Fundamentally, every document on Russian policy of non-Russian origin reflects what the author or the authorizing body thought Russian policy was, and every document of Russian origin can be suspected of being a presentation of what the Russians would like to have the recipient believe Russia's policy was. Besides, the statement might be a *ballon d'essai*, a bargaining point, or simply an unauthorized statement.

Fortunately for students of Russian policy, soon after the end of the 1921 civil war in Russia, the Soviets established an organization called *Tsentral'nyi Arkhiv* (Central Archives), which proceeded to publish new and important documents and to edit the *Krasnyi Arkhiv* (Red Archives), which became the recipient of those fragmentary documents which could not be conveniently published in book form. The *Krasnyi Arkhiv*, coming out irregularly, in issues of irregular size (averaging about 200 pages), became rather a hodgepodge of documents. Documents dealing with the West were conveniently placed in separate volumes, and documents con-cerning the Far East were given a good deal of attention and space. It is the docu-ments in the *Krasnyi Arkhiv* which really establish the true nature of Russian policy in the Far East as far as this can be done.

Although probably one of the reasons for the publication of these documents was to discredit the Tsarist regime, the effect is directly to the contrary. Anyone study-ing the documents dealing with the Special Conferences on Far Eastern Affairs can-not but be impressed by the thoroughness, moderation, and common sense which governed these conferences. It is perhaps for these reasons that the three most im-portant groups of documents, each ending with the statement "To be continued," were never continued, and that every subsequent group had a new "responsible edi-tor." Apparently, as B. A. Romanov learned in his career as a historian, what was first found acceptable and publishable was later discovered to be incorrect. Perhaps the documents revealed too much, or perhaps they revealed the wrong thing—the soundness, or at least the validity, of the Imperial Russian policy in the Far East. At any rate, soon after it became apparent to the world (probably in 1933) that the Japanese in Manchuria were there to stay, the authorities of the Tsentral'nyi Arkhiv discontinued publishing documents on Russian policy in the Far East. After the last group was published (in 1934) the *Krasnyi Arkhiv* printed not one item that could be connected remotely with Russian policy in the Far East in the period 1881–1904.

Of the three groups of documents found in *Krasnyi Arkhiv*, Vol. XIV (1926) contains Russian diplomatic correspondence on the Boxer rebellion; Vol. LII (1932) contains Journals of Special Conferences on Far Eastern Affairs from 1888–1903; and Vol. LXIII (1934) contains journals of special conferences of 1902 and 1903. The last two groups are a prime source for determining the Russian attitude and policy in regard to Far Eastern affairs. The journals contain succinct paraphrases of views expressed by the various ministers during the special conferences and frequently contain references to other secret conferences, dispatches, and memoranda of which we have no other knowledge. Almost every journal ends with recommendations, some unanimously approved by the ministers and some not. The journals were approved by the attending ministers and were sent to the Tsar for his approval. His decisions about most of them are recorded. We can thus consider that such documents represent the real Russian policy or attitude toward a given problem. Because not all groups of documents were continued, there are gaps which cannot be filled. Fortunately, Romanov in his thorough research covered many additional conferences and thus presents a more connected study of the evolution of Russian policy in the Far East. The published journals, however, report the most important conferences and thus provide definite keys to Russian policy. The last two groups in *Krasnyi Arkhiv*, in addition to the journals, contain some essential memoranda. All three groups, it should be remembered, contain documents which are strictly Russian and were presumably destined only for Russian eyes. Hence it is unlikely that they are intentionally deceptive.

This can be said also of Kuropatkin's Diary in Vol. II (1923). Kuropatkin kept this terse and pithy diary purely for his own purposes. The notebooks published in Vol. II deal with the year and a half that preceded the Russo-Japanese War. The diary is remarkable for its candor and the writer's ability to recognize important events. Its outlook is unemotional. When Kuropatkin felt excited about some subject he usually postponed writing about it until a subsequent entry was to be made. It is not a day-to-day diary, but the entries succeed one another closely enough to permit certain events to be followed. The General's close connection with the Tsar, his friendship with Witte, which was later impaired, and his presence in all the important conferences on the Far East make the diary particularly valuable. Furthermore, it is the best source available on the role of Bezobrazov in the affairs of state.

Krasnyi Arkhiv contains many other valuable items. In the first sixty-three issues there are at least fourteen items that can be used in the study of Russian policy in the Far East. There are letters of Witte to his closest friend among Russian statesmen, Minister of the Interior Sipiagin. There are important letters from the Tsar to his mother and to some of the grand dukes, expressing the Tsar's real and sincere attitude toward events in the Far East. It is curious that, with the exception of some correspondence between Bezobrazov and Abaza in 1904–1905 (Vol. XVII), all the items show the Russian officials in a favorable light rather than the reverse. The most valuable source for tracing actual events in the Far East, including many Russian activities, is the series of British Parliamentary Papers known as "Blue Books" and designated, for example, *China No. 1 (1900): Further Correspondence Respecting the Affairs in China.* There are many of these "Blue Books"—five for 1900, seven for 1901, six for 1902, and so on. These are on China only, although there are other "Blue Books" pertinent to the Far East. They contain reports of consuls, special agents, and attachés, newspaper excerpts, and other valuable material; but they must be used with extreme caution. The consuls frequently suffered from an excess of zeal; no doubt they had been told to watch and scrutinize the Russians "like hawks"—and they did. They had been instructed to report every detail in regard to the Russian activities—which they did. It is well known that the British diplomatic corps in the Far East before 1904 was not composed of first-class men. Consequently, some of the reports are rather exasperating for their "sins of commission" and "sins of omission." Critically used, however, the "Blue Books" provide

326   *Bibliography*

some excellent material and a mass of detail which is brought together conveniently. The volumes are well edited. A very useful guide to these "Blue Books" is the work of Harold Temperley and Lilian Penson, *A Century of Diplomatic Blue Books, 1814–1914* (Cambridge, 1938).

The French counterpart of the above series is the series of *Documents diplomatiques français* (known as "Livres Jaunes"), published by the Ministry of Foreign Affairs and designated *Chine, 1900–1901*, etc. For China—particularly events in northern China—the documentation is sketchy. The "Livres Jaunes" can therefore be considered of secondary value.

A particularly valuable source for the history of Russian activities in the 1880's is the series, marked "Secret," which was issued by the Russian General Staff, *Sbornik ... materialov po Azii* (Collection of Geographical, Topographical, and Statistical Materials on Asia), published in Moscow and St. Petersburg, 1883–1896. This presents valuable material on a variety of subjects. Although the emphasis of the publication is not on foreign affairs, even that subject has important documentation; for example, the report of Colonel Vogak, the Russian military attaché to Japan and China, on the Tientsin negotiations leading to the Treaty of Shimonoseki of 1895 (issues LX and LXI, both of 1895). There is also the report of the Russian Consul General to Korea, N. G. Matiunin, on the relations of Korea with foreign powers (issue LVIII, 1894). The bulk of the material consists of geographical studies, but these are not without their relation to Russian policy. A description of Ports Lazarev and Shestakov on the eastern coast of Korea, which are frequently mentioned, is worth reading in order that the diplomatic verbiage about them may be evaluated (issue LVIII). What the Russian military thought of the capacities of the Japanese army may be gathered from accounts such as the description of the Japanese maneuvers of 1892 reported in issue LV. Accounts of geographical expeditions are numerous. In addition, the series reproduces, in Russian translation, articles from British consular reports and from Japanese and Chinese newspapers containing information on military or political matters. Of great interest and perhaps decisive importance are several accounts of Chinese settlement of northern Manchuria, and of the infiltration of Chinese settlers to the left (Russian) bank of the Amur River (issue LVIII).

Besides being rich in material on its various subjects, the series has a special value in that its authors unquestionably were honest; they had no intention of deceiving the reader. In the period preceding 1896 there were no factions among the eastern government officials or the military for or against the role of Russia in the Far East. The Russian army followed the example set by the British services and granted special furloughs to promising junior officers with the provision that they would spent a good part of the time "hunting" in strategic places, while dressed in civilian clothes. As a result, in the 1880's and early 1890's the series received a flood of reports on various topics from the geographical area extending from Armenia to Korea. Although the reports published were the best from the mass presented by promising junior officers, their authors were inexperienced. The series must be used with caution. However, it represents the best collection of materials on Chinese Turkestan in a European language.

Another valuable and little-known series is the *Izvestiia Vostochnago Instituta* of Vladivostok, which was begun in 1898 and appeared irregularly. This series is extremely difficult to use: there is no index and often no table of contents for individual issues, and there is no discernible system of numbering either the volumes or the pages. Nevertheless, the series can be of great value to the student of Russian activities in the Far East. If only because of the great variety of topics dealt with in the various reports, translations, and notes contained in this publication, there is always the possibility of discovering something of value and the certainty of obtaining many significant details. As mentioned in the text, the chief document on Russo-Tibetan relations was found in an obscure Protocol of the Conference of the Directors of the Institute (Vol. III, No. 3, 1901–1902). The series was not intended for the publication of documents; yet significant documents, as well as others of varying degrees of importance, are included in some of the articles. The published contracts between the Fushun collieries and the Russo-Chinese Bank (Vols. IX and X, 1904), for instance, richly amplify our knowledge of the nature of Russian exploitation of Manchuria.

In the *Izvestiia Vostochnago Instituta*, pages of Japanese and Chinese are inserted merely as reading texts for the senior students in Oriental languages. There are syllabuses of courses and all sorts of other things. The bulk of valuable material is to be found in the reports of students based on their "field work." The Institute, heavily subsidized by the War Department, accepted an arrangement by which it took four, six, and finally eight new officers every semester for training in Oriental languages. In return, the army or the consular service took four to eight students from the Institute for "field work." The students visited a large number of strategic locations, and upon their return to the Institute they wrote reports, of which the best were published in *Izvestiia;* these indicate that they did a very thorough job. The account of the Russian trade with Chefoo is a scholarly discovery (Vol. III, Nos. 3–5), and the article on Chinnampo makes clear the absurdity of the accusations hurled against the Yalu concessions held by Russia (Vol. IV, 1902–1903). Many accounts have tables and other appendixes copied from information in the Russian consulates, which the students used as their headquarters and to which they were accredited.

The value of these accounts and other information contained in the series again lies in the honesty of the authors. They did their best to be as accurate and thorough as possible. Unlike the inexperienced authors of the General Staff publication, most of these "students" were mature young men who had received training before their field work which fitted them for their roles as observers. They did their field work practically under the eyes of a Russian agent or consul. On their return their reports were scrutinized by the directors, and finally, by the head director of the Institute, Professor A. M. Pozdneev, a very able man.

Soon after publication of the first four issues, the *Izvestiia Vostochnago Instituta* began to issue a supplement entitled "A Chronicle of Magazine Articles." The digest of Far Eastern publications in German, French, English, Chinese, and Japanese grew in importance with every issue. Apparently more and more newspapers and journals subscribed to the "Chronicle," and the translating and editing improved with experience. In a matter of months this section became a very useful source, and the editors selected topics which would be of interest to Russian readers. Among these were the attitude of the foreign press toward Russian activities and factual information contained in the foreign press on Russian activities. The result of this work was the collection of some very useful material. To be sure, the use of such a digest is not the best method of historical research, but since many publications examined by the Institute are unavailable in the United States, and some — particularly those in the Oriental languages — are too difficult to be handled by an

Occidental, there is some excuse for relying on the "Chronicle." It must be remembered that the *Izvestiia* was a technical and an academic publication, honestly and competently edited. There was no reason for anyone to falsify translations, for there was no public or general reader to deceive or propagandize.

Another series that is less useful but important, especially because it is almost entirely ignored by writers of history, is the *Izvestiia Imperatorskago Russkago Geograficheskago Obshchestva* (News of the Imperial Russian Geographical Society). In its pages can be found material on the condition of the early Russian settlers along the Amur, on the first Russian explorations in Manchuria in the 1860's, and on the surreptitious trade relations with the Chinese in Manchuria in the nineteenth century, and many other items of a factual nature dealing with Russian activities in the Far East. This source too is scrupulously honest and thoroughly reliable, because the authors of the accounts were for the most part eminently qualified and experienced.

An invaluable source for information concerning trade relations with the Far East is the series published by the Russian Department of Customs, *Obzor vneshnei torgovli Rossii po Evropeiskoi i Aziatskoi granitsam za 1895 god* (Survey of the Foreign Trade of Russia on the European and Asiatic Frontier for 1895), published in St. Petersburg, 1895–1907. The series consists of annual volumes, each on the trade of the previous year, published from 1895 through 1907, when the series was discontinued.

This well-edited publication contains a wealth of information on imports, exports, tariff regulations, customs receipts, and so forth. In it can be found statistical information classified by nation, commodity, or the port of entry of imports. It is a reliable source, although it has one flaw: certain figures are incorrect because in this period Russia had several places with *porto franco* status, among them Batum in the Caucasus, Vladivostok, Nikolaevsk on the Amur, and Petropavlovsk in Kamchatka. Thus a great many imports were not recorded. Furthermore, by the provisions of the Russo-Chinese Treaty of 1881 the nationals of the two signatory powers had the right of free retail trade for fifty versts on each side of the common frontier. Frontier guards and customs officials kept records on retail goods, since they had to examine caravans to make sure that their future trade would be retail. In 1900 the *porto franco* status of Vladivostok and Nikolaevsk came to an end, but that of Petropavlovsk continued until the Russo-Japanese War.

The *Otchet po deloproizvodstvu Gosudarstvennago Soveta* (Report on Activities of the State Council), in annual volumes, is more useful as a general reference work than for its documentary material. This series contains information on various appointments, including consular appointments, and on changes in the status of foreign diplomatic posts and other miscellaneous subjects. From it I obtained important data on the official positions held by members of the Bezobrazov group.

In using documents found in separate volumes, one should be especially cautious. The volume should be closely examined for duplicates and for translations of documents from another language appearing under a new title. Several years ago I spent a great deal of time and effort translating the title, table of contents, and some headings of documents in Otake Hakukichi's *Gaike hiroku Manshu to Nichi-Ro Senso* (Secret Diplomatic Documents, Manchuria and the Russo-Japanese War), published in Tokyo in 1934, only to find that they were translations of documents published in *Krasnyi Arkhiv*. A similar effort on one of the volumes of *Gaiko Jiho* was cut short when I found that "Burru Bukku" is only the *katakana* way of spelling "Blue Book."

Russko-Iaponskaia Voina: Materialy (Russo-Japanese War: Materials), published by Tsentral'nyi Arkhiv in 1925, contains the six diary notebooks of Kuropatkin, published in *Krasnyi Arkhiv* (issues II, V, and VIII), and the diaries of General Linevich, which begin with the war and have no value for the study of its causes. Other duplications will be noted.

The most important single volume of documents is the *Japanese White Book* issued by the Japanese Ministry of Foreign Affairs. This contains some forty-two documents covering the period June, 1903—February, 1904, which trace the course of the Russo-Japanese negotiations through the series of four proposals and counterproposals. The official title of the pamphlet is *Correspondence Regarding the Negotiations Between Japan and Russia, 1903–1904*. This pamphlet has numerous editions and translations. No doubt there are several Japanese editions; it was published in Tokyo in English by the Ministry of Foreign Affairs and by the *Japanese Times*. Another edition was issued in Washington, D.C., and still another, in London. All these editions appeared in 1904. There are others, possibly—German and French editions certainly—although I made no attempt to ascertain this.

The Russian edition did not appear until June, 1905. Its intriguing title makes the 50-page pamphlet appear to be something entirely new; translated it reads, "Documents on the Negotiations with Japan, 1903–1904, Kept in the Chancellery of the Special Committee on the Far East." From the second part of the title one might infer that these documents present something new, since the *Japanese White Book* had been in wide circulation for more than a year. Why was it designated "kept in the Chancellery"? Was it because it was secret? An examination of the "mysterious documents" shows that they are nothing but the documents of the *White Book* translated from English into Russian. A London firm seized upon this "find," labeled it the Russian "Red Book," translating the documents from Russian back into English, and issued them as a new set of documents, thus adding to the confusion. I deeply regret not having had the opportunity to see this Russian "Red Book."

The *Japanese White Book* also was issued in Russian translation in what has the appearance of being a brand new set of documents: A. I. Gippius, *O prichinakh nashei voiny s Iaponiei: Dokumenty* (On the Causes of Our War with Japan: Documents), St. Petersburg, 1905. In addition to the Russian translation a French translation of the *Japanese White Book* is given in this work. Why there is a French translation—which must have been taken from the English, which is itself a translation of the Russian—only Mr. Gippius can answer. The bulk of this volume, about 166 pages, consists of the translation of the Parliamentary Papers ("Blue Book"), *China No. 2 (1904): Correspondence Respecting the Russian Occupation of Manchuria and Newchwang* (issued February 2, 1904). Gippius has taken brief documents and some short excerpts of documents of Russian origin, which are of some importance. For example, his Appendix V consists of the text of the original Briner concession for timber rights on the Yalu (1896).

In 1904 the Special Committee for the Far East issued a bulky pamphlet with another new title, *Materialy po dal'nemu Vostoku* (Materials on the Far East). Since it emanated from the inner sanctum of the Special Committee, I expected it to be a treasure chest of new documents; but it is only a translation of part of the "Blue Book" *China No. 2 (1904)* mentioned above.

The Russian counterpart of the *Japanese White Book* was to have been published in 1904 under the title "Blue Book," but the documents selected by Lamsdorf were not approved by the Tsar, and the project was held in abeyance until all interest in it was lost. However, the Special Committee for Far Eastern Affairs, having nothing to do, decided to issue a limited number of copies of a collection of key documents on the final phase of Russo-Japanese relations. This pamphlet of about two hundred pages is known as *Malinovaia Kniga*. In translation its title is the same as the one later adopted for the translation of the *Japanese White Book: Documents on the Negotiations with Japan 1903–1904, Kept in the Chancellery of the Special Committee on the Far East*. This collection was to have had a limited circulation. Only four hundred copies were printed and these were to have been distributed among the leading statesmen, diplomats, and other influential and responsible persons. However, before the distribution was carried out, the publication was impounded by the secret police and destroyed, probably by order of Plehve. How many copies escaped destruction is not known; the pamphlet is so rare that it is doubtful whether a copy exists in the United States. The Library of Congress has none. The pamphlet must contain valuable material. One enterprising person made copies of parts of some documents and smuggled the copies to Germany, where they found their way into the hands of V. L. Burtsev, a liberal historian then in self-imposed exile. In 1910 Burtsev published these excerpts under the title *Tsar i vneshniaia politika ... Zapiska Grafa Lamsdorfa i Malinovaia Kniga ...* (The Tsar and Foreign Policy ... Memorandum of Count Lamsdorf and the Malinovaia Kniga, the Instigators of the Russo-Japanese War, from Secret Documents: The Memorandum of Count Lamsdorf and the "Crimson Book"). This sixty-page booklet was published in Berlin in 1910. Its pages are small, the margins wide. The little that the booklet contains is important and it clears up some of the bibliographical confusion mentioned above. The *Malinovaia Kniga* very likely contains the documents which ordered the Russian Navy to attack the Japanese should they try to land or even send their fleet north of the 39th parallel; it thus incurred the disapproval of the Tsar and the Minister of Foreign Affairs—in fact the whole hierarchy of the government—and hence had to be destroyed. I surmise that since the official title of the book was known to many, and some people expected such a book, the Special Committee, to satisfy the public, published a translation of the *Japanese White Book* and gave it the title *Malinovaia Kniga*.

The next group of separate volumes consists of monographs which contain so much documentary material that the works can be classified as documents. In fact, I used them primarily as such. I. I. Korostovets, *Rossiia na Dal'nem Vostoke* (Russia in the Far East), published in Peking in 1922, is the most important and reliable of the three. Under this modest title lies a splendid, well-documented account of Korostovets' diplomatic activity in Manchuria which led to the signing of the famous Alexeev–Tseng-Chitchze Convention (1901). This convention set the pattern for Russian control of Manchuria. This book is an absolute "must" for the understanding of the Russian position in Manchuria between 1900 and 1904.

The second book is Witte's *Vynuzhdennye raz'iasneniia ...* (Compulsory Clarifications Concerning the Account of General Kuropatkin on the War with Japan), published in Moscow in 1911. It is a polemic. By this time Witte had broken off his friendship with Kuropatkin completely. Kuropatkin had published statements to the effect that if his advice had been followed there would not have been a war. Since this implied that others were at fault, Witte felt compelled to issue some explanation concerning Kuropatkin's stand. The result was a lengthy pamphlet containing many documents and long excerpts from documents. The third book is another polemic, by F. A. Lvov, *Likhodei biurokraticheskago samovlastiia ...* (The Criminals of Bureaucratic Willfulness as the Direct Instigators of the Russo-Japanese War), published in St. Petersburg in 1906. This book contains documentary material concerning the scheme for the Yalu concession, as well as a bit of comedy—a clear case of "the pot calling the kettle black."

The volumes of H. V. Bernstein, *The Willy-Nicky Correspondence* (New York, 1918), and I. D. Levine, *Letters of the Kaiser to the Tsar* (New York, 1920), are too well known to warrant any comment. They should be supplemented by their Russian counterpart, which is in part the translation of Levine, the edition by M. N. Pokrovskii of *Perepiska Vil'gel'ma II s Nikolaem II* (Correspondence Between William II and Nicholas II), published in Moscow in 1923. They should be compared with the diary of Nicholas II, *Dnevnik Imperatora Nikolaia II, 1890–1906* (Berlin, 1923), although it is generally worthless. Finally, they should be compared with some fragmentary correspondence of Nicholas II to his mother and to some of the grand dukes which is scattered through many volumes of the *Krasnyi Arkhiv.* My view is that Nicholas II was a person who felt that the first requirement of a gentleman is that he should never say "no." This would explain the discrepancies between the Willy-Nicky correspondence and the Tsar's personal correspondence with the members of his family.

Certain other publications deserve notice. V. P. Semennikov, *Za kulisami tsarizma: Arkhiv Tibetskago vracha Badmaeva* (Behind the Curtain of Tsarism: The Archive of the Tibetan Doctor Badmaev), published in Leningrad in 1925, has some valuable material illustrating the growth of an aggressive ideology based on a fantastic idea of a "White Tsar," who would represent the Buddhists of Asia. The *Dnevnik Lamsdorfa* (Diary of Lamsdorf), published in 1934, is of value chiefly because little documentation for Russian policy in the decade of the 1880's was published before 1893. The publication by the Ministry of Foreign Affairs since 1895 (St. Petersburg, 1906) contains some documents but is for the most part an official historical essay. It can be considered propagandistic and biased, and it should be used with caution. The best impartial treatment of Russian military activities in the Far East during the Boxer rebellion is in the United States War Department, Military Intelligence Division, *Notes on China, 1900* (1901), which contains reports of American military attachés and agents.

In conclusion, it should be mentioned that occasional documents are to be found in various Russian periodicals, such as *Byloe* (The Past), *Russkoe Bogatstvo* (Russian Treasures), *Vestnik Evropy* (European Messenger), *Russkii Arkhiv* (Russian Archive), *Russkaia Mysl'* (Russian Thought), *Russkaia Starina* (Russian Old Times), *Istoricheskii Vestnik* (Historical Messenger), *Russkoe Proshloe* (The Russian Past), and *Novyi Vostok* (The New East). Many of them reprint long passages from the *Pravitel'stvennyi Vestnik* (Government Messenger) and also letters from the Far East. Although most of such material is of little value, occasionally there are interesting documents, such as General Grodekov's proclamation announcing the annexation of the right bank of the Amur in 1900 and the letters dealing with the Blagoveschensk massacre of 1900.

I have not examined Russian newspapers for the period discussed, because they are not available.

BIBLIOGRAPHY

OFFICIAL AND SEMIOFFICIAL PUBLICATIONS

Burtsev, F. L., *Tsar i vneshniaia politika . . . Zapiski Grafa Lamsdorfa i Malinovaia Kniga* (The Tsar and the Foreign Policy . . . Memorandum of Count Lamsdorf and the Malinovaia Kniga . . . the Crimson Book). Berlin, 1910.

Carnegie Endowment for International Peace. *Korea: Treaties and Agreements.* Washington, D.C., 1921.

———. *Outer Mongolia: Treaties and Agreements.* Washington, D.C., 1921.

———. *Manchuria: Treaties and Agreements.* Washington, D.C., 1921.

China, Maritime Customs. *Treaties, Conventions, etc., Between China and Foreign States.* Shanghai, 1905. 2 vols.

France, Ministère des Affaires Etrangères. *Documents diplomatiques: Chine, 1899–1900* ("Livres Jaunes"). Paris, 1900.

———. *Documents diplomatiques: Chine, 1900–1901* ("Livres Jaunes"). Paris, 1901.

———. *Documents diplomatiques français.* 2d ser., Paris, 1931. 4 vols.

Galperin, A. *Anglo-Iaponskii Soiuz, 1902–1921* (Anglo-Japanese Alliance . . .) Moscow, 1947.

Germany, Auswärtiger Amt. (Foreign Office). *Das Staatsarchiv.* Leipzig, 1861–1914. 84 vols.

———. *Die grosse Politik der europäischen Kabinette, 1871–1914.* Berlin, 1922–1927. 40 vols. in 54. Vols. IX, XIV, XVI, and XVII.

Gippius, A. I. *O prichinakh nashei Voiny s Iaponiei: Dokumenty* (The Causes of Our War with Japan: Documents). St. Petersburg, 1905.

Glinskii, B. B. *Prolog Russko-Iaponskoi Voiny: Materialy iz arkhiva Grafa S. Iu. Witte* (Prologue of the Russo-Japanese War: Materials from the Archives of Count Witte). Petrograd, 1916.

Gooch, George Peabody, and Harold Temperley, eds. *British Documents on the Origins of the World War, 1898–1914.* London, 1926–1938. 11 vols. Vols. I and II deal with the period preceding the Russo-Japanese War.

Great Britain. *Consular Report on the Trade of Korea, 1892.* London, 1893. Annex IV; Annex I (Shipping in Korea).

Great Britain, Committee of Imperial Defense, Historical Section. *Official History of the Russo-Japanese War.* London, 1910. 3 vols.

Great Britain, Foreign Office. *British and Foreign State Papers.* London, 1841–1914. 107 vols. Vol. XCIV.

Great Britain, Parliamentary Papers, "Blue Books."

   China No. 1 (1900): Further Correspondence Respecting the Affairs in China.

   China No. 2 (1900): Correspondence with the United States Government Respecting Foreign Trade in China.

   China No. 3 (1900): Correspondence Respecting the Insurrectionary Movement in China. Includes Memorandum of the Interview Between Foreign Representatives and the Tsungli Yamen, March 1, 1900 (enclosure in no. 33, p. 21), and Memorandum of the British Embassy in Berlin, June 27, 1900 (enclosure no. 1, p. 91).

   China No. 4 (1900): Reports from Her Majesty's Minister in China Respecting Events in Peking.

China No. 5 (1900): Correspondence Respecting the Anglo-German Agreement of October 16, 1900, Relating to China.

China No. 1 (1901): Correspondence Respecting the Disturbances in China.

China No. 2 (1901): Despatch from His Majesty's Ambassador at St. Petersburg Respecting the Russo-Chinese Agreement as to Manchuria. Report on Manchuria, 1886.

China No. 3 (1901): Further Correspondence Respecting Events at Peking.

China No. 4 (1901): Further Correspondence Respecting Events at Peking.

China No. 5 (1901): Further Correspondence Respecting the Disturbances in China.

China No. 6 (1901): Further Correspondence Respecting the Disturbances in China.

China No. 7 (1901): Correspondence Respecting the Imperial Railway of North China.

China No. 1 (1902): Correspondence Respecting the Affairs of China.

Great Britain, Parliamentary Papers. *Papers Relating to Tibet.* London, 1904.

Grimm, Ervin Davydovich. *Sbornik dogovorov i drugikh dokumentov po istorii mezhdunarodnykh otnoshenii na Dal'nem Vostoke, 1842–1925* (Collections of Treaties and Other Documents on the History of International Relations in the Far East). Moscow, 1927.

Hertslet, Edward. *Hertslet's China Treaties.* . . . London: H. M. Stationery Office, 1908. 2 vols.

Iarovoi, P. F. *Russko-Iaponskaia Voina: Sbornik materialov* (The Russo-Japanese War: Collection of Materials). Leningrad, 1933.

Ito Hirobumi. *Hisho-ruisan kaika-kai* (Secret Diplomatic Papers While in Office). Tokyo, 1934. 3 vols.

Iuzefovich, T. *Dogovory Rossii s Vostokom* (Russian Treaties with the East). St. Petersburg, 1869.

Izvestiia Imperatorgskago Russkago Geograficheskago Obshchestva, 1865–1885. (News of the Imperial Russian Geographical Society). St. Petersburg, 1887. 87 vols.

Izvestiia Vostochnago Instituta s prilozheniem *Letopisi* (News of the Oriental Institute with a Supplement of the Chronicle). (Magazine articles in German, French, English, Japanese, and Chinese.) Vladivostok, 1898–1922. 47 vols.

Japan, Ministry of Foreign Affairs. *Correspondence Regarding the Negotiations Between Japan and Russia, 1903–1904. Japanese White Book.* Tokyo, London, and Washington, D.C., 1904.

Journal of Special Conference of February 7, 1903, *K.A.*, LII, 1932.

Korostovets, Ivan Iakovlevich. *Rossiia na Dal'nem Vostoke* (Russia in the Far East). Peking, 1922.

Langer, William L. *The Diplomacy of Imperialism, 1890–1902.* New York and London: Knopf, 1935. 2 vols.

Leonov, R. *Documents secrets de la politique russe en Orient, 1881–1890.* Berlin, 1893.

Liu-shi-nien. . . . *Documentary History of Sixty Years of Sino-Japanese Relations.* Tientsin, 1932. 4 vols.

Lobanov-Rostovskii, A. B., Memoir to Nicholas II, April 6, 1895, *K.A.*, LII (1932).

MacMurray, John V. A., *Treaties and Agreements with or Concerning China, 1894–1919.* New York, 1921. 2 vols.

Meyendorff, Baron A. *Correspondence diplomatique du Baron de Staal.* Paris, 1929. 2 vols.

Muraviev, N. V. Memorandum to the Tsar November 23, 1897, *K.A.,* LII.

Pribram, Alfred F. *The Secret Treaties of Austria-Hungary, 1879–1914.* Cambridge, 1920–1921. 2 vols.

Reinach, Lucien de. *Recueil des traités conclus par la France en Extrême Orient, 1684–1902.* Paris: E. Leroux, 1902–1907. 2 vols. (*Revue Politique et Parlementaire,* V, July, 1895.)

Rockhill, William W. *Treaties and Conventions with or Concerning China and Korea, 1894–1904.* Washington, D.C., 1904.

Romanov, B. A., *Ocherki diplomaticheskoi istorii Russko-Iaponskoi Voiny, 1895–1907* (A Survey of the Diplomatic History of the Russo-Japanese War). Moscow, 1947. 2d ed. Moscow, 1955.

——. *Rossiia v Manzhurii, 1892–1906.* Leningrad: Leningrad Oriental Institute, 1928. Translated into English as *Russia in Manchuria, 1892–1906.* Ann Arbor: University of Michigan Press, 1952.

Russia, Department of Customs. *Obzor vneshnei torgovli Rossii po Evropeiskoi i Aziatskoi granitsam za 1895 god* (Survey of the Foreign Trade of Russia on the European and Asiatic Frontier for 1895, etc.) Annual vols. St. Petersburg, 1895–1907.

Russia, General Staff. *Sbornik geograficheskikh, topograficheskikh i statisticheskikh materialov po Azii* (Collection of Geographical, Topographical, and Statistical Materials on Asia). Moscow and St. Petersburg, 1883–1896. 64 issues. 1896–1914. 17 issues.

Russia, Ministerstvo Inostrannykh Del (Ministry of Foreign Affairs). *Recueil de traités et documents diplomatiques concernant l'Extrême Orient, 1895–1905.* St. Petersburg, 1906.

Russia, Osobyi Komitet Dal'nego Vostoka (Special Committee for the Far East). *Dokumenty po peregovoram s Iaponiei, 1903–1904.* St. Petersburg, 1905. Issue 1: *Malinovaia Kniga;* issue 2: *Japanese White Book.*

Russia, *Otchet po deloproizvodstvu Gosudarstvennago Soveta za sessiiu 1899–1900* (Report on Activities of the State Council During the Sessions of 1899–1900). St. Petersburg, 1900. Annual reports in 1902, 1903, etc.

Semennikov, Vladimir P. *Za kulisami tsarisma: Arkhiv Tibetskago vracha Badmaeva* (Behind the Curtains of Tsarism: The Archive of the Tibetan Doctor Badmaev). Leningrad, 1925.

Temperley, Harold W. V., and Lilian M. Penson, eds., *A Century of Diplomatic Blue Books, 1814–1914.* Cambridge [England]: University Press, 1938.

Tilley, J. A., Memorandum, January 14, 1904, *B.D.,* XI No. 1, p. 1.

Treat, Payson J. *Diplomatic Relations Between the United States and Japan, 1853–1895.* Stanford: Stanford University Press, 1932. 2 vols.

Union of Soviet Socialist Republics, Tsentral'nyi Arkhiv (Central Archive). *Krasnyi Arkhiv* (Red Archive). Moscow, 1922–1941. 116 issues in 73 vols.

United States Congress, Foreign Affairs Committee. *Papers Relating to the Foreign Affairs of the United States.* Washington, D.C., 1868–1910. Annual vols. Vols for 1900 and 1901.

United States War Department, U. S. Adjutant-General's Office, Military Information Division. *Notes on China, 1900.* Publication XXXIII. Washington, 1901.

Witte, Sergei Iu. *La guerre avec Japon . . .* Paris, 1911.

———. Memorandum to the Tsar, April 12, 1896, K.A., LII.

———. *Vynuzhdennye raz'iasneniia po povodu otcheta Gen.-Ad. Kuropatkina o voine s Iaponiei* (Compulsory Clarifications Concerning the Account of General Kuropatkin on the War with Japan). Moscow, 1911. *Erzwungene Aufklä-rungen* ... Vienna, 1911.

———. *La guerre avec Japon* ... Paris, 1911.

Zapiski Imperatorskago Russkago Geograficheskago Obshchestva (Records of the Imperial Russian Geographic Society). St. Petersburg, 1867–1916. 44 vols.

MEMOIRS, DIARIES, LETTERS, TRAVEL ACCOUNTS

Alexander Mikhailovich (Grand Duke). *Kniga vospominanii* (Reminiscences). Paris, 1933. 2 vols.

Aronin. "Memoirs," *Japan Chronicle*, Nov. 16, 1933; April 12, 1934.

Baelz, Erwin. *Awakening Japan: The Diary of a German Doctor*. Edited by Toku Baelz. New York: Viking, 1932.

Bing, E. J., ed. *The Secret Letters of the Last Tsar*. New York: Longmans, Green, 1938.

Bülow, Bernhard H. M. K. von. *Memoirs of Prince von Bülow*. Boston: Little, Brown, 1931. 2 vols.

Christie, Dugald. *Thirty Years in Moukden, 1883–1913*. London: Constable, 1914.

Deutsch, Leo. *Sixteen Years in Siberia*. London: J. Murray, 1903.

Efimov, A. V. *Iz istorii russkikh ekspeditsii na Tikhom Okeane* (From the History of Russian Expeditions on the Pacific). Moscow, 1948.

Great Britain, Naval Intelligence Division. *Handbook of Siberia and Arctic Russia*. London, 1922.

Gurko, Vladimir I. *Features and Figures of the Past*. Stanford University Press, 1939.

Heyking, Elizabeth von. *Tagebücher aus vier Weltteilen*. Leipzig, 1926.

Hohenlohe, Chlodwig Karl Victor von. *Denkwürdigkeiten der Reichskanzlerzeit*. Stuttgart, 1931.

Izvolskii, Alexander. *The Memoirs of Alexander Iswolsky*. Ed. and tr. by Charles Louis Seeger. London: Hutchinson, 1920.

Kokovtsev, V. N. (Count). *Out of My Past: The Memoirs of Count Kokovtsev*. Edited by H. H. Fisher. Stanford University Press, 1935.

Kozlov, P. K. *Tibet i Dalai Lama*. Petrograd, 1920.

Kruzenstern, Adam Iohan von. *Puteshestvie vokrug sveta v 1803–1806 gg.* (A Voyage Round the World in 1803–1806). St. Petersburg, 1809–1812.

Kuropatkin, A. N. "Dnevnik" (Kuropatkin's Diary), *K.A.* II (1923), V (1924), VIII (1925).

———. *Zapiski generala Kuropatkina o Russko-Iaponskoi Voine* (Notes of General Kuropatkin on the Russo-Japanese War). Berlin, 1909. 3 vols. An English translation: *The Russian Army and the Japanese War* ... Tr. by A. B. Lindsay. New York: Dutton, 1909. 2 vols.

Lamsdorf, V. N. "Dnevnik [Diary of] V. N. Lamsdorfa," *K.A.*, XLVI (1931).

———. *Dnevnik, 1886–1890*. Moscow, 1926.

Levine, Isaac Don [Iosif Davydovich]. *Letters of the Kaiser to the Tsar*. New York: Stokes, 1920.

Lopukhin, A. A. *Otryvki iz vospominanii* (Extracts from Reminiscences). Moscow, 1923.

Nicholas II. *Dnevnik [Diary of] Imperatora Nikolaia II, 1890–1906.* Berlin, 1923.

Pares, Bernard. *My Russian Memoirs.* London: J. Cape, 1931.

Pokrovskii, M. N., ed. *Perepiska Vil'gel'ma II s Nikolaem II* (Correspondence Between William II and Nicholas II). Moscow, 1923

Polovtseff, P. A. *Glory and Downfall: Reminiscences of a Russian General Staff Officer.* London: G. Bell, 1935.

Polovtsev, A. A. "Iz dnevnika A. A. Polovtseva" (From A. A. Polovtsev's Diary), *K.A.,* LXVII (1934), 168–186.

Pooley, A. M., ed. *The Secret Memoirs of Count Tadasu Hayashi.* New York and London: Putnam, 1915.

Popov, P. S. "Dva mesiatsa osady v Pekine . . ." (A Diary of Two Months in Peking During the Siege, May 18 to July, 1900), *Vestnik Evropy,* XXXVI, No. 2 February, 1901), 517–537, No. 3 (March), 5–37.

Pozdneev, D. M. *Materialy po istorii severnoi Japonii* (Historical Materials on Northern Japan). Yokohama: J. Gluk, 1909.

———. ed. *Opisanie Manzhurii* (A Description of Manchuria). St. Petersburg, 1897. 2 vols.

Prjevalskii, N. M. *Puteshestvie v Ussuriiskom krae, 1867–1869* (Travel in the Ussuri District). St. Petersburg, 1870.

Radzivill, Princess Catherine. *Memories of Forty Years.* London: Funk & Wagnalls, 1914.

Romanov, B. A. "Pis'ma S. Iu. Witte k D. S. Sipiaginu (1900–1901)" (Letters to Sipiagin from Witte . . .), *K.A.,* XVIII (1926).

Rosen, R. R. *Forty Years of Diplomacy.* New York: Knopf, 1922. 2 vols.

Savinskii, Alexander A. *Recollections of a Russian Diplomat.* London: Hutchinson, 1927.

Seymour, E. H. (Admiral). *My Naval Career and Travels.* London: Smith and Elder, 1911.

[Simpson, Bertram Lenox], ed. *Indiscreet Letters from Peking.* Ed. by B. L. Putnam Weale. London: Hurst and Blackett, 1904.

Tsybikov, G. T. *Buddist palomnik u sviatyn' Tibeta: Po dnevnikam vedennym v 1899–1902 gg.* (A Buddhist Pilgrim in Tibet: A Diary of 1899–1902). Petrograd, 1918.

Ukhtomskii, E. E. (Prince). *Ot Kalmytskoi stepi do Bukhary* (From Kalmyk Steppes to Bukhara). St. Petersburg, 1891.

[Ukhtomskii, E. E.] *Poezdka Naslednika . . .* (Travels in the East of Nicholas II . . . when Tsarevitch in 1890–1892). St. Petersburg, 1893. An English translation: *Travels in the East of Nicholas II, Emperor of Russia, when Cesarewitch,* 1890–1891. Tr. by R. Goodlet, ed. by Sir G. Birdwood. 2 vols.

Witte, S. Iu. *Vospominaniia* (Reminiscences). Berlin, 1922. 3 vols.

SECONDARY WORKS

Akagi, R. H. *Japan's Foreign Relations, 1542–1936.* Tokyo: Hokuseido Press, 1936.

Aksakov, I. S. *Slavianskii Vopros, 1860–1886.* Moscow, 1886.

Alexinskii, Gregor. *Modern Russia.* London: Unwin, 1913.

Allen, Bernard M. *The Right Honorable Sir Ernest Satow.* London: Kegan Paul, Trench, Trubner, 1933.

Allen, Horace N. *A Chronological Index.* Seoul, 1901.

————. *Korea, Fact and Fancy.* Seoul, 1904.

Allen, James G. "Anglo-Russian Rivalry in Central Asia, 1865–1885." Unpublished Ph.D. dissertation. University of California, Berkeley, 1936.

Asakawa, Kanichi. *The Russo-Japanese Conflict.* Boston: Houghton Mifflin, 1904.

Avarin, V. Ia. *Imperializm v Manzhurii.* Moscow, 1934. 2 vols.

Baddeley, J. F. *Russia in the Eighties.* London: Longmans, Green, 1921.

————. *Russia, Mongolia, China . . .* London and New York: Macmillan, 1919.

Bakhrushin, S. V. *Kazaki na Amure.* London, 1925.

Barsukov, I. P. *Graf Nikolai Nikolaevich Amurskii.* Moscow, 1891. 2 vols.

Bishop, Isabella Lucy. *Korea and Her Neighbors.* London, 1898. 2 vols.

Bland, J. O. P. *Li Hung-chang.* New York: Holt, 1917.

Bogdanovich, A. V. *Tri poslednikh samoderzhtsa* (Three Last Autocrats). Moscow, 1924.

Bogolepov, M. I., and M. N. Sobolev. *Ocherki Russko-Mongol'skoi torgovli* (Essays on the Russian-Mongolian Trade). Tomsk, 1911.

Brandt, M. von. *Drei Jahre ost-asiatischer Politik, 1894–1897.* Stuttgart, 1897.

Bywater, H. C. *Sea-Power in the Pacific . . .* London: Constable, 1934.

Carter, W. H. *The Life of Lieutenant General Chaffee.* Chicago: University of Chicago Press, 1917.

Casserly, Gordon. *The Land of the Boxers; or, China Under the Allies.* London: Longmans, Green, 1903.

Chang, Chung-fu. *The Anglo-Japanese Alliance.* Baltimore: Johns Hopkins Press, 1931.

Chekhov, Anton P. *Na Sakhaline.* St. Petersburg, 1890.

Clements, Paul H. *The Boxer Rebellion.* New York: Columbia University, 1915.

Clyde, P. H. *International Rivalries in Manchuria.* Columbus: Ohio State University Press, 1926.

Coons, A. G. *The Foreign Public Debt of China.* Philadelphia: University of Pennsylvania Press, 1930.

Cordier, Henri. *Histoire des relations de la Chine avec les Puissances occidentales.* Paris: F. Alcan, 1902. 3 vols.

Curzon, G. N. (Lord). *Persia and the Persian Question.* London, 1892.

————. *Problems of the Far East.* London, 1894.

Cyon, E. de *M. Witte et les finances russes.* Paris, 1895.

Dallin, David Iu. *The Rise of Russia in Asia.* New Haven: Yale University Press, 1949.

Danilevskii, N. Ia. *Rossiia i Evropa.* St. Petersburg, 1887.

Demchinskii, Boris N. *Rossiia v Manzhurii.* St. Petersburg, 1908.

Dennett, Tyler. *Americans in Eastern Asia.* New York: Macmillan, 1922.

————. *Roosevelt and the Russo-Japanese War.* New York: Doubleday, Page, 1925.

Dennis, A. L. P. *Adventures in American Diplomacy.* New York: Dutton, 1928.

Dillon, E. J. *The Eclipse of Russia.* New York: G. H. Doran, 1918.

Drage, Geoffrey. *Russian Affairs.* London: J. Murray, 1904.

Falk, E. A. *Togo and the Rise of Japanese Sea-Power.* New York: Longmans, Green, 1936.

Fisher, Raymond H. *The Russian Fur Trade, 1550–1700.* University of California Publications in History, Vol. XXXI (1943).

Fitzmaurice, Lord Edmond George. *The Life of Granville.* London: Longmans, Green, 1905. 2 vols.

Fuller, Joseph V. *Bismarck's Diplomacy at Its Zenith.* Cambridge: Harvard University Press, 1922.

Gasiorovskii, Waclaw. *Tragic Russia.* London: Cassel, 1908.

Gérard, Auguste. *Ma Mission en Chine (1893–1897).* Paris: Plon-Nourrit, 1918.

Golder, F. A. *Russian Expansion on the Pacific, 1641–1850.* Cleveland: Arthur H. Clark, 1914.

Golman, M. B. *Russkii imperializm.* Leningrad, 1926.

Golovachev, P. M. *Rossiia na Dal'nem Vostoke* (Russia in the Far East). St. Petersburg, 1904.

Griffis, W. E. *Corea, the Hermit Nation.* New York: Scribner, Harper, 1907. Russian translation in *G.S.S.*, XIV (1885).

Griswold, Alfred Whitney. *The Far Eastern Policy of the United States.* New York: Harcourt, Brace, 1938.

Guedalla, Philip, ed. *The Queen and Mr. Gladstone.* London: Hodder and Stoughton, 1933. 2 vols.

Habberton, William. *Anglo-Russian Relations Concerning Afghanistan, 1837–1907.* Urbana: University of Illinois, 1937. Illinois Studies in the Social Sciences, Vol. XXI, No. 4.

Hamada, Kengi. *Prince Ito.* London: Allen & Unwin, 1936.

Harrington, Fred Harvey. *God, Mammon, and the Japanese.* Madison: University of Wisconsin Press, 1944.

Hiratsuka, A., ed. *Ito Hirobumi Hiroku.* Tokyo, 1929.

Hsu, M. C. *Railway Problems in China.* New York: Columbia University, 1915.

Hsü, Shu-hsi. *China and Her Political Entity.* New York and London: Oxford University Press, 1926.

Hulbert, Homer B. *The Passing of Korea.* New York: Doubleday, Page, 1906.

Iadrintsev, N. M. *Sibir' kak koloniia.* St. Petersburg, 1882.

Ianchevetskii, Dmitrii G. *Groza s Vostoka.* Revel, 1907.

Irmer, Arthur J. *Die Erwerbung von Kiatchou [Kiaochow], 1894–1898.* Cologne, 1930; Bonn, 1930.

Iz Oblasti Lamaizma. St. Petersburg, 1904.

Kantorovich, Anatolii Ia. *Amerika v bor'be za Kitai* (America in the Struggle for China). Moscow, 1935.

Karataev, M. M. *Nikolai Mikhailovich Prjevalskii.* Moscow, 1948.

Kent, Percy Horace. *Railway Enterprise in China.* London: E. Arnold, 1907.

Kerner, Robert J. *The Urge to the Sea: The Course of Russian History.* Berkeley and Los Angeles: University of California Press, 1942.

Khabarovskii, S. *Chto takoe Kitaiskaia zheleznaia doroga?* (What Is the Chinese Railroad?). St. Petersburg, 1908.

Kliuchevskii, V. O. *Kurs Russkoi istorii.* Moscow, 1921–1923. 5 vols.

Korostovets, Ivan Ia. *Graf Witte.* Berlin, 1929.

Korzhinskii, S. I. *Amurskaia oblast' kak zemledel'cheskaia koloniia* (The Amur Region as an Agricultural Colony). St. Petersburg, 1892.

Kostomarov, I. N. *Iz nashego Proshlogo: Sibirskie zemleiskateli* (From Our Past: Siberian Pioneers). Berlin, 1922.

Kovalevskii Maxim. *Russian Political Institutions.* Chicago: University of Chicago Press, 1902.

Kulomzin, Anatolii N., ed. *Sibirskaia zheleznaia doroga v eia proshlom i nastoiashchem* (The Siberian Railway, Its Past and Present). St. Petersburg, 1903.

Lantzeff, George V. *Siberia in the Seventeenth Century.* University of California Publications in History, Vol. XXX, 1943.

Lebedev, E. V. *Sovetskii Sakhalin* (Soviet Sakhalin). Moscow, 1933.

Levine, L. *Pan-Slavism and European Politics.* New York: 1914.

Levitov, I. S. *Zheltaia rasa* (The Yellow Race). St. Petersburg, 1900.

Li Hung-chang. *Collected Writings.* Edited by Wu Ju-lin. Nanking, 1908. 100 vols.

List, Friedrich. *Das Nazionale System der Politischen Oekonomie.* Berlin, 1841. Published in Russia as *Natsional'naia ekonomiia i Frants List.* Kiev, 1889.

Ludvig, A. P. "Li Hung-chang and Chinese Foreign Policy, 1870–1885." Unpublished Ph.D. dissertation, University of California, Berkeley, May, 1936.

Lvov, F. A. *Likhodei biurokraticheskago samovlastiia kak neposredstvennye vinovniki pervoi Russko-Iaponskoi Voiny* (The Criminals of Bureaucratic Willfulness as the Direct Instigators of the Russo-Japanese War). St. Petersburg, 1906.

McCordock, R. Stanley. *British Far Eastern Policy, 1894–1900.* New York: Columbia University Press, 1930.

McCune, G. M. "The Korean Problem, 1885–1895." Unpublished Ph.D. dissertation, University of California, Berkeley, 1937.

———. "Korea's International Debut, 1882–1885." Unpublished seminar report, University of California, Berkeley, March, 1936.

McKenzie, F. A. *The Tragedy of Korea.* London: Hodder and Stoughton, 1908.

Maltsev, S. S. *Zheltaia opasnost'* (The Yellow Danger). Warsaw, 1900.

Marder, Arthur J. *The Anatomy of British Sea Power . . . 1880–1905.* New York: Knopf, 1940.

Markov, Sergei. *Liudi velikoi tseli* (Men of Great Goals). Moscow, 1944.

Martens, F. F. *Rossiia i Kitai.* St. Petersburg, 1881.

———. *Russia and England in Central Asia.* London, 1887.

Masaryk, Thomas G. *Pan-Slavism: The Spirit of Russia.* London: Allen & Unwin, 1919.

Maximov, A. *Nashi zadachi na Tikhom Okeane* (Our Tasks on the Pacific). St. Petersburg, 1894.

Migulin, P. P. *Russkii gosudarstvennyi kredit, 1769–1899* (Russian State Loans, 1769–1899). Kharkov, 1900. 2 vols.

Minrath, Paul. *Das Englisch-Japanische Bündniss von 1902.* Stuttgart, 1933.

Morse, H. B. *International Relations of the Chinese Empire.* London and New York: Longmans, Green, 1918. 3 vols.

Myshliaevskii, A. *Voennyia deistviia v Kitae, 1900–1901* (Military Operations in China, 1900–1901). St. Petersburg, 1904–1910. 3 vols. A shorter official account was translated into German as *Die Kämpfe der russischen Truppen in der Mandschurei im Jahre 1900.* Leipzig, 1900.

Nol'de, Boris E. *Vneshniaia politika* (Foreign Policy). Petrograd, 1915.

Okuma, Shigenobu, comp. *Fifty Years of New Japan.* New York: Dutton, 1909.

Okun', Semen B. *Ocherki po istorii kolonial'noi politiki tsarizma v Kamchatskom krae* (Essays on the History of the Colonial Policy of Tsarism in the Kamchatka Region). Leningrad, 1935.

Ono, Giichi. *War and Armament Expenditures of Japan.* New York: Oxford University Press, 1922.

Ozerov, Ivan Kh. *Kak raskhoduiutsia v Rossii narodnye den'gi* (How Russian People's Money is Spent). Moscow, 1907.

340 *Bibliography*

Ozerov, Ivan Kh. *Russkii biudzhet* (The Russian Budget), Moscow, 1907.
Pan, S. C. Y. *American Diplomacy Concerning Manchuria.* Washington: Catholic University of America, 1938.
Panov, A. A. *Sakhalin kak koloniia.* Moscow, 1905.
Pavlovich, M. *Vneshniaia politika i Russko-Iaponskaia Voina* (Foreign Policy and the Russo-Japanese War). St. Petersburg, 1909. 2 vols.
Pokotilov, D. D. *Koreia i Iapono-Kitaiskoe stolknovenie* (Korea and the Sino-Japanese Conflict). St. Petersburg, 1895.
Pokrovskii, M. N. *Russkaia istoriia s drevneishikh vremen* (Russian History from the Earliest Times). Moscow, 1913–1914. 5 vols.
———. *Russkaia istoriia v szhatom ocherke* (Russian History in a Concise Essay). Moscow, 1925.
Polner, Tikhon I., ed. *Priamur'e: Fakty, tsifry, nabliudeniia* (Priamur'e: Facts, Figures, Observations). Moscow, 1909.
Potemkin, V. P., ed. *Istoriia diplomatii i diplomatiia v novoe vremia* (A History of Diplomacy and Diplomacy in Modern Times). Moscow, 1945.
Putiata, D. V. *Ocherki geograficheskago sostoianiia administrativnago i voennago ustroistva Kitaia* (Essays on the Geographical Situation and Administrative and Military Organization of China). St. Petersburg, 1895.
Rea, G. B. *The Case for Manchoukuo.* New York: Appleton-Century, 1935.
Ronaldshay, L. T. (Earl). *On the Outskirts of Empire in Asia.* Edinburgh and London. W. Blackwood, 1904.
Rubenstein, N. L. "Istoricheskaia teoriia slavianofilov i ee klassovye korni" (The Historical Theory of the Slavophiles and Their Class Roots), in *Russkaia Istoricheskaia Literatura v klassovom osveshchenii.* Moscow, 1927. 2 vols.
Rudakov, A. V. *Obshchestvo I-khe-tuan i ego znachenie v poslednikh sobytiiakh na Dal'nem Vostoke* (The I-khe-tuan Society and Its Significance in Recent Events in the Far East). Vladivostok, 1931.
Shoemaker, M. M. *The Great Siberian Railway from St. Petersburg to Peking.* New York and London: Putnam, 1903.
Shperk, Franz. *Rossiia Dal'nego Vostoka.* St. Petersburg, 1885.
Simpson, B. L. *Manchu and Moscovite.* London and New York: Macmillan, 1904.
Skal'kovskii, Konstantin A. *Russkaia torgovlia v Tikhom Okeane* (Russian Trade in the Pacific). St. Petersburg, 1883.
———. *Vneshniaia politika Rossii i polozhenie inostrannykh derzhav* (Russia's Foreign Policy and the Position of the Foreign Powers). St. Petersburg, 1897.
Smith, Arthur H. *China in Convulsion.* New York: Revell, 1901.
Solov'ev, S. M. *Istoriia Rossii s drevneishikh vremen* (History of Russia from the Most Ancient Times). St. Petersburg, 1894–1895. 29 vols. in 7.
Solov'ev, Vladimir. "Kitai i Evropa," *Sobranie Sochinenii.* St. Petersburg, 1913. 10 vols. Vol. VI, pp. 84–137.
"Sovremennik" (pseud.). *Nikolai II, Razoblacheniia* (Nicholas II, an Exposure). Berlin, 1909.
Steiger, G. N. *China and the Occident.* New Haven: Yale University Press, 1927.
Svatikov, S. G. *Rossiia i Sibir'.* Prague, 1909.
Svechin, A. *Evoliutsiia voennogo iskusstva* (The Evolution of Military Art). Moscow, 1928. 2 vols.
Thompson, H. C. *China and the Powers.* London, 1902.
Trubetskoi, G. N. *Russland als Grossmacht.* Stuttgart, 1913.

Tsubai. *Saikin Seiji Gaiko-Shi* (Recent Political and Diplomatic History). Tokyo, 1936.

Tugan-Baranovskii, M. I. *Russkaia fabrika*. St. Petersburg, 1915.

Ular, Alexander. *A Russo-Chinese Empire*. Westminister: Constable, 1904.

———. *Russia from Within*. London: Heinemann, 1905.

United States Hydrographic Office. *Sailing Directions for Siberia and Chosen* ... Washington, D.C., 1932. Publication No. 122.

Vernadskii, G. V. *Nachertanie Russkoi istorii*. Prague, 1927. Vol. I.

"Vladimir" [Z. Volpicelli]. *The China-Japan War*. London, 1896.

———. *Russia on the Pacific and the Siberian Railroad*. London, 1899.

Weigh, K. S. *Russo-Chinese Diplomacy*. Shanghai, 1928.

Whigham, H. J. *The Persian Problem*. New York: Scribner, 1903.

Witte, S. Iu. *Narodnoe khoziaistvo* (The People's Economics). [Witte's lectures on economics to Grand Duke Mikhail Alexandrovich]. St. Petersburg, 1902.

Yakhontov, V. A. *Russia and the Soviet Union in the Far East* ... New York: Coward-McCann, 1931.

Zabriskie, Edward H. *American-Russian Rivalry in the Far East* ... *1895–1914*. Philadelphia: University of Pennsylvania Press, 1946.

Zepelin, Constantin von. *Der Ferne Osten*. Berlin, 1907–1911. 3 vols.

ARTICLES AND ESSAYS

Ahnert, E. E. "Puteshestvie po Manzhurii" (Travel in Manchuria), *Z.I.R.G.O.*, XXXV (1904), 1–525.

Alexandrov, V. "Argun i Priargun'e," *Vestnik Evropy*, XXXIX, No. 5 (September, 1904), 281–310.

"Alleged Russo-Chinese Convention," *Saturday Review*, December 12, 1896.

Baranov, Alexander E. "Na reke Amure v 1854–1855" (On the Amur River in 1854–1855), *Russkaia Starina*, LXXI (August, 1891), 327–354.

Baranovskii, E. I. "Zolotopromyshlennost' v vostochnoi Sibiri" (Gold-Field Mines in Eastern Siberia), *Vestnik Evropy*, XXXIII, No. 7 (July, 1898), 142–181.

Besabrassow [Bezobrazov], Alexander M. "Les premières causes de l'effondrement de la Russie: Le Conflit Russo-Japonais," *Le Correspondent* (Paris), CCXLI (May, 1923), 557–615.

Boulger, D. C. "Li Hung-chang," *Contemporary Review*, LXX (July, 1896), 18–29.

———. "The New Situation in the Far East," *Contemporary Review*, LXVIII (December, 1895), 815–824.

Brassey, Thomas. "Naval Progress," *Naval Annual* (London) for 1884–1887, tables 263–269.

Bushby, H. N. G. "The Agreement Between Great Britain and Japan," *Nineteenth Century*, LI (March, 1902), 369–382.

Butakov (Lt. Col.). "Vooruzhennye sily Kitaia i Iaponii" (The Armed Forces of China and Japan), *G.S.S.*, III (1883), 1–184.

Chikhachev, P. "Kaliforniia i Ussuriiskii krai" (California and the Ussuri Region), *Vestnik Evropy*, XXV, No. 6 (June, 1890), 545–568.

Chu Djang. "War and Diplomacy over Ili," *Chinese Social and Political Science Review*, XX (October, 1936), 369–392.

Curzon, G. N. (Lord). "British and Russian Commercial Competition in Central Asia," *Asiatic Quarterly Review*, VIII, (July–October, 1889), 438–457.

Dadeshkaliani, K. N. (Prince). "Ocherki Korei" (Survey of Korea), *G.S.S.*, XXII–XXIV (1886), 61–119.

Davydov, D. A. "Kolonizatsiia Manzhurii i severo-vostochnoi Mongolii" (Colonization of Manchuria and of Northeastern Mongolia), *I.V.I.*, XXXVII (1911).

Dennett, Tyler. "The Deer Island Episode," *Korean Repository*, V (March, 1898), 109–113.

———. "Early American Policy in Korea, 1883–7," *Political Science Quarterly*, XXXVIII (September, 1923), 82–103.

Dillon, E. J. "M. Witte and the Russian Commercial Crisis," *Contemporary Review*, LXXIX (April, 1901), 472–501.

———. "Russia and Europe," *Contemporary Review*, LXX (November, 1896), 609–622.

Dmitriev, K. "Ekskursiia dlia izucheniia porta In-kou" (Excursion for the Study of the Port of Inkou), *I.V.I.*, VII (1902–1903), 115–270.

Domeratsky [Domeretskii], L. "Tariff Relations Between Germany and Russia 1890–1914," U. S. Department of Commerce, Bureau of Foreign and Domestic Commerce, *Tariff Series* No. 38. Washington, D.C., 1918, pp. 1–23.

Duman, L. I. "Russkaia i inostrannaia literatura o Dunganskom vosstanii 1861–1877 v Kitae gg." (Russian and Foreign Literature About the Dungan Rebellion in China, 1861–1877), *Bibliografiia Vostoka*, VII, 1934, No. 7, pp. 55–78.

"Dvadsat' piat' let Pekinskago Dogovora," *Istoricheskii Vestnik*, XXII (December, 1885), 733–734.

Efimov, G. "Imperialisticheskaia interventsiia 1900–1901 v Kitae i bokserskoe vosstanie" (Imperialist Intervention in China 1900–1901 and the Boxer Rebellion), *Istoricheskii Zhurnal*, 1938, No. 4 (April), 63–75.

Eliseev, A. V. "Otchet o poezdke na Dal'nii Vostok" (Account of a Trip to the Far East), *I.I.R.G.O.*, XXVI (1890), 336–379.

———. "Po Iuzhno-Ussuriiskomu kraiu" (In the South-Ussuri Region), *Istoricheskii Vestnik*, XLIII (February–March, 1891), 435–556.

Evtiugin (Captain), "Poezdka iz Blagoveschenska v Tsitsihar v 1884 godu" (A Journey from Blagoveschensk to Tsitsihar in 1884), *G.S.S.*, XIV (1885), 213–219.

Finn-Enotaevskii, A. "Graf Witte kak ekonomist" (Count Witte as an Economist), *Sovremennyi Mir*, 1912, No. 2, pp. 253–267.

Ford, W. C. "The Economy of Russia," *Political Science Quarterly*, XVII (March, 1902), 99–124.

Frangulis, A. F., ed. "Premier Mouillage," *Dictionnaire Diplomatique*. Paris, 1933.

Gapanovich, J. J. "Russian Expansion on the Amur," *China Journal* XV, No. 4 (October, 1931).

———. "Sino-Russian Relations in Manchuria, 1892–1906," *Chinese Social and Political Science Review*, XVII (July, 1933), 283–306, 457–479.

Georgievskii. "Prjevalskii," *Vestnik Evropy*, XXI, No. 6 (June, 1886), 777–796.

Glinskii, B. B. "Cherty iz zhizni Grafa S. Iu. Witte" (Some Traits of Character of Count Witte," *Istoricheskii Vestnik*, CXL (1915), 220–231.

———. "Graf Sergei Iul'evich Witte (Materialy dlia biografii)" (Count Witte: Biographical Materials), *Istoricheskii Vestnik*, CXL (1915), 232–279; CXLI (1915), 204–233, 521–555, 893–906; CXLII (1915), 592–609.

———. "Period tverdoi vlasti" (The Period of Firm Power), *Istoricheskii Vestnik*, CXXIX (July, 1912), 271–304, (September), 659–693.

Goriainov, Serge. "The End of the Alliance of the Emperors," *American Historical Review*, XXIII (January, 1918), 324–349.

Gundry, R. S. "China, England and Russia," *Fortnightly Review*, LXVI (October, 1896), 506–520.

Hallet, Holt S. "France and Russia in China," *Nineteenth Century*, XLI (March, 1897), 487–502.

Hauptman, H. T. "Russland auf dem Wege zur Vorherrschaft in Ostasien: nach dem Bericht des Finanz Minister Witte über seine Reise nach dem Fernen Osten," *Asien*, VI (1903).

Heard, A. "China and Japan in Korea," *North American Review*, XLIX (1894), 300–308.

"Hiroshima Trial," *Japan Daily News* and *North China Herald*, January 31, 1896.

"Issledovaniia Manzhurii" (Studies of Manchuria), *Bibliograficheskii Biulleten'* of the Central Library of the C.E.R., Nos. 1–6. Harbin, 1927.

Iuvachev, I. P. "Bor'ba s khunhuzami na Manzhurskoi granitse" (Fights with *Khunhuzes* on the Manchurian Border), *Istoricheskii Vestnik*, LXXXII (October–December, 1900), 177–206, 538–564.

————. "Godovshchina boia pri Taku" (Anniversary of the Taku Battle), *Istoricheskii Vestnik*, LXXXIV (April–May, 1901), 1075–1080.

Iuzhakov, S. "Chto delat' v Kitae? (What Is to Be Done in China?), *Russkoe Bogatstvo*, 1900, No. 8 (August), 111–122.

"Japanese Constitutional Crisis and the War, The," *Contemporary Review*, LXVIII (October, 1895), 457–476.

Kaufman, A. A. "Kolonizatsia Sibiri v eia nastoiashchem i budushchem" (Colonization in Siberia Today and Tomorrow), *Sibirskie Voprosy* (1905), No. 1 pp. 171–201.

Khvostov, A. "Russkii Kitai, nasha pervaia koloniia na Dal'nem Vostoke" (Russian China, Our First Colony in the Far East), *Vestnik Evropy*, XXXVII, No. 5 (September–October, 1902), 653–696.

Kochurovskii, K. "Krest'ianskoe khozaistvo i pereselenie" (Peasant Farming and Resettlement), *Russkaia Mysl'*, 1894, No. 3, pp. 18–38.

Komarov, V. L. "Manzhurskaia ekspeditsiia 1896 g.," *I.I.R.G.O.*, XXXIV (1898), 117–194.

————. "Usloviia dal'neishei kolonozatsii Amura" (Conditions of Further Colonization on the Amur), *I.I.R.G.O.*, XXXII (1896), 457–509.

Kovalevskii, Maxim. "Porto franko vo Vladivostoke," *Vestnik Evropy*, XLIV, No. 1 (January, 1909), 423–437.

Kropotkin, Petr. "The Russians in Manchuria," *The Forum*, XXXI (May, 1901), 267–274.

Kuo Ti-chen, "Chinese Tariff Concessions to the C.E.R.," *Chinese Social and Political Science Review*, XIV (October, 1930), 391–402.

Lebedev, A. "Zheltuginskaia Respublika v Kitae" (The Zheltuga Republic in China), *Russkoe Bogatstvo*, 1896, No. 9 (September), pp. 143–171.

Legras, Jules. "La Mandchourie russe," *Revue des Deux Mondes*, 1902, No. 4.

"Li Hung-chang's Mission," *Saturday Review*, August 22, 1896.

Lin, T. C. "The Amur Frontier Question Between China and Russia, 1850–1860," *Pacific Historical Review*, III (1934), 1–27.

————. "Li Hung-chang: His Korean Policies, 1870–1885," *Chinese Social and Political Science Review*, XIX (July, 1935), 202–233.

Liubimov, L. N. "Iz zhizni inzhenera putei soobshcheniia" (From the Life of a Civil Engineer), *Russkaia Starina*, CLV (July–September, 1913), 215–253, 448–463.

Matiunin, N. G. "Nashi sosedi na krainem Vostoke" (Our Neighbors in the Far East), *Vestnik Evropy*, XXII, No. 7 (July, 1887), 64–88.

———. "Zapiska o kitaitsakh i manzhurakh na levom beregu Amura" (An Account of the Chinese and Manchus on the Left Bank of the Amur), *G.S.S.*, LVIII (1894), 33–39.

"Metchnikoff's [Mechnikov's] Tribute to Count Witte," *American Review of Reviews*, LIII (June, 1916), 728–729

Miagkov, A. "V poiskakh za zolotom" (In Search of Gold), *Russkoe Bogatstvo*, 1901, No. 8 (August), 102–159.

"Military Calendar," *Journal R.U.S.I.*, March, 1898.

N.S. "Russkaia i nemetskaia vostochnaia politika" (Russian and German Policy in the East), *Russkaia Mysl'*, 1882, No. 1, pp. 37–60.

Nadarov, I. P. "Severno-Ussuriiskii Krai" (The Northern Ussuri Region), *Z.I.R.-G.O.*, XVII (1887).

Nadarov, V. "Seulo-Fuzanskaia zheleznaia doroga" (Seoul-Fusan Railroad), *I.V.I.*, III (1901–1902), No. 3, pp. 47–56.

Nadin, P. "Kvantun i ego proshloe, 1894–1900 (po lichnym vospominaniiam)" (Kwangtung and Its Past . . .), *Vestnik Evropy*, XXXIX, No. 3 (June, 1904), 723–753.

———. "Piatidesiatiletie Amurskago kraia, 1854–1904" (Fifty Years of the Amur Region, 1854–1904), *Vestnik Evropy*, XL, No. 3 (May, 1905), 166–197.

Nazarov (Colonel). "Materialy dlia voenno-statisticheskago obzora Priamurskago voennago okruga v Manzhurii" (Materials for a Military-Statistical Survey of the Priamur Military District), *G.S.S.*, XXXI (1888), 1–250.

Novikov, N. "Alchukaskoe Fudutunstvo," *I.V.I.*, X (1904), 95–98.

Oldenburg, S. "Noveishaia literatura o Tibete" (The Most Recent Literature on Tibet), *Zhurnal Ministerstva Narodnago Prosveshcheniia*, CCCLVI (1904), Nos. 11 and 12, pp. 129–168.

Orlov, N. A. "Srazhenie pri Iakshi" (The Battle near Iakshi), *Istoricheskii Vestnik*, LXXXIV (May, 1901), 603–627.

———. "Srazhenie pri Onguni" (The Battle on the Onguni), *Istoricheskii Vestnik*, LXXXIV (April, 1901), 137–162.

———. "Zaniatie Hailara v 1900 g." (The Occupation of Hailar), *Istoricheskii Vestnik*, LXXXV (October, 1901), 98–139.

Oudendyk, W. J. "Russia and China," *Journal of the Royal Central Asian Society*, XXII, No. 3 (July, 1935).

Palladii, (Arkhimandrit). "Dorozhnyia zapiski na puti ot Pekina do Blagoveschenska cherez Manzhuriiu v 1870 g." (Travel Notes en route from Peking to Blagoveschensk . . .) *Z.I.R.G.O.*, IV (1871), 329–458.

———. "Istoricheskii ocherk Ussuriiskago kraia v sviazi s istoriei Manzhurii" (A Historical Essay on the Ussuri Region in Connection with the History of Manchuria), *Z.I.R.G.O.*, VIII (1879), 221–228.

Pavel, (Ieromonakh). "Sovremennoe polozhenie khristianskikh missii v Koree" (The Present Position of Christian Missions in Korea), *I.V.I.*, XII (1904), 253–344, tables 342–344.

Petrov, A. A. "Filosofiia Kitaia v russkom burzhuaznom kitaevedenii" (Chinese

Philosophy in Russian Bourgeois Sinology), *Bibliografiia Vostoka*, VII (1934), 5–28.

Popov, A. "Anglo-russkoe soglashenie o razdele Kitaia (1899)" (The Anglo-Russian Agreement Concerning the Partition of China), *K.A.*, XXV (1927), 111–134.

———. "Anglo-russkoe sopernichestvo na putiakh Irana" (Anglo-Russian Rivalry in Iran), *Novyi Vostok*, 1926, No. 12, pp. 133–136.

———. "Dal'nevostochnaia politika tsarizma v 1894–1901 gg." (The Far Eastern Policy of Tsarism in 1894–1901), *Istorik-Marksist*, LI, 1935, No. 11, pp. 38–57.

———. "Pervye shagi russkago imperializma na Dal'nem Vostoke (1888–1903)" (The First Steps of Russian Imperialism in the Far East), *K.A.*, LII (1932), 55–56.

Popov, P. S. "Dvizhenie naseleniia v Kitae" (The Movement of Population in China), *I.I.R.G.O.*, XXXII (1896), 226–228.

Pos'iet, K. N. "Prekrashchenie ssylki v Sibir' " (The End of Russian Exile to Siberia), *Russkaia Starina*, XLIX, No. 7 (July, 1899), 51–59.

Pozdneev, D. M. "Bokserskoe dvizhenie kak etap osvoboditel'noi bor'by v Kitae" (The Boxer Movement as a Stage in the Chinese Liberation Movement), *Zvezda*, X (1925), No. 4, pp. 156–172.

———. "Materialy po voprosu o peresmotre deistvuiushchikh v kitaiskikh morskikh tamozhniakh . . ." (Materials on the Revision of the Chinese Maritime Customs), *I.V.I.*, XIV (1906), 1–114.

"Prince Ukhtomsky, a Russian of the Russians," *Review of Reviews*, XXX (July, 1904), 72.

Prjeval'skii, N. M. "Ussuriiskii krai" (The Ussuri Region), *Vestnik Evropy*, V, No. 5 (May, 1870), 236–267.

———. "Soobrazheniia o vozmozhnoi voine s Kitaem" (On the Possibility of War with China), *G.S.S.*, I (1883).

Putiata, D. V. "Opisanie Port Artura" (The Description of Port Arthur), *G.S.S.*, XXXII (1888), 1–32.

———. "Otchet o poezdke v Manzhuriiu v 1888 godu" (An Account of the Trip to Manchuria in 1888), *G.S.S.*, XXXVIII (1889).

———. "Zapreshchenie kitaitsam selitsia na Manzhurskikh zemliakh" (The Prohibition of Chinese Settlement in Manchuria), *G.S.S.*, XLII (1889), 159–163.

Rees, J. D. "The Tsar's Friend," *Fortnightly Review*, LXXV (April, 1901), 612–622.

Reinsch, P. S. "Governing the Orient on Western Principles," *The Forum*, XXXI (June, 1901), 385–400.

Roborovskii, V. I. "Ekspeditsiia v Tsentral'nuiu Aziiu v 1893–1895 gg." (The Expedition to Central Asia in 1893–1895), *I.I.R.G.O.*, XXXIV (November, 1898), 1–59.

Romanov, B. A. "Konsessiia na Ialu," *Russkoe Proshloe* (Moscow), I (1923).

———. "Portsmut" (Portsmouth), *K.A.*, V (1924), 3–47; VI (1924), 3–31.

———. "Proiskhozhdenie Anglo-Iaponskago Dogovora 1902 g." (The Origin of the Anglo-Japanese Treaty of 1902), *Istoricheskie Zapiski*, X (1941), No. 10, pp. 41–65.

———. "Witte i Konsessiia na reke Ialu," *Sbornik statei po Russkoi istorii* (Leningrad, 1922), pp. 425–459.

———. "Witte kak diplomat, 1895–1903 gg." (Witte as a Diplomat in 1895–1903), *Vestnik Leningradskogo Universiteta*, 1946, Nos. 4–5, pp. 150–172.

Rudnev, V. "Iz vospominanii o plavanii na kreisere 'Afrika' " (Reminiscences of a

Voyage on the Cruiser *Afrika*), *Russkaia Starina*, CXXXVI, No. 4 (October–December, 1908) 415–428.

Savicky [Savitskii], Nikolai. "Serge Witte," *Le Monde Slave*, n.s., III (August, 1932), 161–191; (September, 1932), 321–348.

Schumacher, Hermann. "Eisenbahnbau und Eisenbahnpläne in China," *Archiv für Eisenbahnwesen* (Berlin), 1899, pp. 901–978, 1194–1226; 1900, pp. 341–401, 693–756, 895–943, 1095–1124.

S. I. "Na Kvantune," *Russkaia Mysl'*, 1900, No. 7, pp. 136–162; No. 8, pp. 1–42.

"Secret History of the Russo-Chinese Treaty," *Contemporary Review*, LXXI (February, 1897), 172–183.

Seich, A. "Sakhalin kak koloniia" (Sakhalin as a Colony), *Russkaia Mysl',* 1904, No. 7, pp. 150–171.

Sergeev, V. M. "Issledovaniia bolot po linii Amurskoi zheleznoi dorogi" (The Investigation of Swamps on the Line of the Amur Railroad), *I.I.R.G.O.*, XXXIV (1898), 318–332.

Siviakin, P. "Geograficheskiia svedeniia o Shadunskoi provintsii i Port Chzhi-fu" (Geographical Information About the Province of Shantung and Port Chefoo), *I.V.I.*, III (1901–1902), No. 5, tables on pp. 120–121.

Sokovnikov (Captain). "O sovremennykh koreiskikh voiskakh" (About Contemporary Korean Armies), *G.S.S.*, LXIX (1896), 1–7.

Soyeda, J. "The Adoption of Gold Monometallism in Japan," *Political Science Quarterly*, XIII (March, 1898), 60–90.

Spitsyn, Alexander. "Rabochii vopros na kamenno-ugol'nykh kopiakh Mukdenskoi provintsii" (The Labor Question in the Coal Mines of Mukden Province), *I.V.I.*, IX (1903), 319–382.

Strother, French. "Witte, the Key to Russia," *World's Work*, XL (October, 1920), 560–577.

Svechnikov, A. I. "Skotovodstvo severo-vostochnoi Mongolii" (Cattle-Breeding in Northeastern Mongolia), *I.I.R.G.O.*, XXXVIII (1902), 467–502.

"Tabel' o rangakh." *Entsiklopedicheskii Slovar'*. St. Petersburg, 1901. Vol. XXXII.

Tarle, E. "S. Iu. Witte, frantsuskaia pechat' i russkie zaimy" (S. Iu Witte, the French Press, and the Russian Loans), *K.A.*, X (1925), 36–40.

Terent'ev, N. "Proiskhozhdenie amerikanskoi doktriny otkrytykh dverei v Kitae" (The Origin of the American Open-Door Doctrine in China), *Tikhii Okean*, 1934, No. 2, pp. 75–101.

Timonov, V. E. "O glavneishikh putiakh Priamurskago kraia" (The Main Roads in the Priamur Region), *I.I.R.G.O.*, XXXIV (1898), 321–334.

Tompkins, S. R. "Witte as a Finance Minister, 1892–1903," *Slavonic Review* (London), XI (April, 1934), 590–606.

"Tsarskaia diplomatiia o zadachakh Rossii na Vostoke v 1900 g." (Tsarist Diplomacy on the Problems of Russia in the Far East in 1900), *K.A.*, XVIII (1926).

Tsiang, T. F. "Sino-Japanese Diplomatic Relations, 1870–1894," *Chinese Social and Political Science Review*, XVII (April, 1933), 1–106.

Turenne, Louis de. "Journal d'un Français à Moscou," *Revue de Paris*, 1896, No. 4 (July–August), 793–834.

Ukhtomskii, E. E. "Russia Will Crush Japan," *Independent*, LVI (June, 1904), 1418–1420.

V. L., von. "Torgovye zadachi Rossii na Vostoke i v Amerike" (Russian Trade

Problems in the Far East and in America), *Vestnik Evropy*, XXVII, No. 2 (February, 1871), 753–777.

Veniukov, M. I. "Amur v 1857–1858 godu," *Russkaia Starina*, XXIV (January, 1879), 81–112, 267–304.

Vereschagin, A. V. "Po Manzhurii" (In Manchuria), *Vestnik Evropy*, XXXVII, No. 1 (January–February, 1902), 129–146; XXXVII, No. 2 (March–April, 1902), 583–585.

Voloshinov, N. A. (Colonel of General Staff). "Sibirskaia zheleznaia doroga" (The Siberian Railroad), *I.I.R.G.O.*, XXVII (1891), 11–40.

[Vonliarliarskii, V. M.] "Why Russia Went to War with Japan: the Story of the Yalu Concessions," *Fortnightly Review*, XCIII (May, 1910), 816–831, 1030–1044.

Vostokov, P. "Les chemins de fer russes d'autrefois et aujourd'hui," *Le Monde Slave*, IV (December, 1935), 448–483; V (May, 1936), 280–309.

"Zagranichnoe puteshestvie M. N. Muravieva" (M. N. Muraviev's Trip Abroad), *K.A.*, XLVII–XLVIII (1931), Nos. 4–5, pp. 71–89.

"Zapiski o Manzhurii Polkovnika Barabasha i Matiunina" (Notes on Manchuria by Colonel Barabash and Matiunin), *G.S.S.*, I (1883).

Zavalishin, D. "Les rapports de la Chine a l'égard de la Russie," *Istoricheskii Vestnik*, 1880, No. 9 (September), 110–119.

Zvegintsev, A. "Poezdka v severnuiu Koreiu" (A Trip to Northern Korea), *I.I.R.G.O.*, XXXVI (1900), 502–518.

ACKNOWLEDGMENTS

I AM DEEPLY INDEBTED to the University of California Press, particularly to Mr. August Frugé, its Director, who showed interest in the doctoral dissertation of my late son, Andrew Malozemoff, and gave me encouragement when I first submitted it for publication. I am also grateful to Miss Dorothy Huggins of the Editorial Department for her splendid work in preparing the manuscript for publication: no one could have been more thorough and conscientious. Miss Huggins' indefatigable efforts have resulted in bringing my son's work—to which he devoted ten years of his short life (1910–1952)—into the form which, had he lived, his own corrections would have brought it. I have, myself, read and reread the manuscript; if I have overlooked occasional errors and failed to correct them, the blame is mine.

ELIZABETH MALOZEMOFF

INDEX

INDEX